Lecture Notes in Computer Science 14660

Founding Editors

Gerhard Goos
Juris Hartmanis

Editorial Board Members

The series Lecture Notes in Computer Science (LNCS), including its subseries Lecture Notes in Artificial Intelligence (LNAI) and Lecture Notes in Bioinformatics (LNBI), has established itself as a medium for the publication of new developments in computer science and information technology research, teaching, and education.

LNCS enjoys close cooperation with the computer science R & D community, the series counts many renowned academics among its volume editors and paper authors, and collaborates with prestigious societies. Its mission is to serve this international community by providing an invaluable service, mainly focused on the publication of conference and workshop proceedings and postproceedings. LNCS commenced publication in 1973.

Stefan Kiefer · Jan Křetínský · Antonín Kučera
Editors

Taming the Infinities of Concurrency

Essays Dedicated to Javier Esparza
on the Occasion of His 60th Birthday

 Springer

Editors
Stefan Kiefer
University of Oxford
Oxford, UK

Jan Křetínský
Masaryk University
Brno, Czech Republic

Antonín Kučera
Masaryk University
Brno, Czech Republic

ISSN 0302-9743 ISSN 1611-3349 (electronic)
Lecture Notes in Computer Science
ISBN 978-3-031-56221-1 ISBN 978-3-031-56222-8 (eBook)
https://doi.org/10.1007/978-3-031-56222-8

This Springer imprint is published by the registered company Springer Nature Switzerland AG
The registered company address is: Gewerbestrasse 11, 6330 Cham, Switzerland

Paper in this product is recyclable.

Preface

Javier Esparza is originally from Spain. He received his first degree in theoretical physics at the University of Zaragoza, and in 1990 he earned a PhD in computer science from the same institution. After finishing his doctorate, Javier became assistant professor at the University of Hildesheim, and then research assistant at the University of Edinburgh. In 1994 he accepted a position as associate professor at the Technical University of Munich. In 2001 he returned to Edinburgh to become a professor of theoretical computer science, a prestigious position that had been held before him by, for example, Robin Milner, winner of the ACM Turing Award – which is generally regarded as a Nobel Prize in the field of informatics and computer science. In 2003 Javier moved to the University of Stuttgart. Finally, in 2007 he returned to the Technical University of Munich, where he currently holds the Chair of Foundations of Software Reliability and Theoretical Computer Science as successor of Wilfried Brauer.

Javier is a leading researcher in concurrency theory, distributed and probabilistic systems, Petri nets, analysis of infinite-state models, and, more generally, in formal methods for the verification of computer systems. He has authored or co-authored over 200 publications, many of which have been highly influential and even pioneering. At the beginning of his career, Javier devoted his attention to Petri net theory, and in particular to the class of free-choice nets. In close cooperation with Jörg Desel he published a series of papers that finally led to the monograph *Free Choice Petri Nets* published by Cambridge University Press. In the following years, Javier developed the theory of net unfoldings, a symbolic method for the algorithmic analysis of Petri nets. This research led again to a monograph, *Unfoldings – a Partial Order Approach to Model Checking*, coauthored with Keijo Heljanko and published by Springer. Javier then started to study the theory of infinite-state systems, and pioneered with his co-authors the development of symbolic methods for model-checking systems with unbounded recursion. These results were implemented in the experimental tools Moped and jMoped, which in turn influenced the design of commercial products like SDV, the Static Driver Verifier developed by Microsoft. Since 2004 Javier has worked on the algorithmic analysis of stochastic systems and on the principles of program analysis. His results on infinite-state stochastic systems and on the applicability of Newton's approximation method to non-linear equational systems have been highly appreciated by the scientific community and are marking the way for new research directions. Around 2015, Javier started a new research strand on the design and analysis of population protocols, building on his expertise with infinite-state models of distributed systems. This has led to a prestigious ERC advanced grant.

Javier's most recent book, *Automata Theory – An Algorithmic Approach*, coauthored with Michael Blondin, was recently published with MIT Press, taking a fresh look at automata as system models and at the same time as data structures to be used in algorithms. It is one example of Javier's many activities as a teacher. He has also supervised more than 20 PhD students, taught at more than 20 summer schools, and won many awards for his university teaching.

Javier is a member of the IFIP working group 2.2 *Formal Description of Programming Concepts* and a former member of the EATCS council. For many years, he was on the editorial board of important journals in our community. In 2021, he became a founding editor-in-chief of *TheoretiCS*, an open-access journal that publishes TCS articles of the highest quality. Javier is regularly invited to deliver plenary talks at prestigious computer science conferences and to participate in their Program Committee.

This Festschrift celebrates Javier's contributions on the occasion of his 60th birthday. The articles are written by some of his many friends and colleagues, reflecting the breadth and depth of Javier's activities: Petri nets, concurrency in general, distributed and probabilistic systems, games, formal languages, logic, program analysis, verification and synthesis. This book was presented to Javier at an ETAPS 2024 satellite workshop celebrating his birthday.

We would like to thank all authors for their excellent articles in this volume and for their constructive reviewing, as well as Springer for their support.

Many congratulations on your birthday, Javier! We hope you will enjoy this book. We wish you all the best and look forward to many beautiful papers that *you* will still write!

February 2024

Stefan Kiefer
Jan Křetínský
Antonín Kučera

Organization

Program Committee

Parosh Abdulla	Uppsala University
Eike Best	Universitaet Oldenburg
Tomáš Brázdil	Masaryk University
Pierre Ganty	IMDEA Software Institute
Markus Holzer	Universität Giessen
Petr Jančar	Palacký University Olomouc
Stefan Kiefer	University of Oxford
Jan Křetínský	Masaryk University
	Technical University of Munich
Antonín Kučera	Masaryk University
Orna Kupferman	The Hebrew University
Barbara König	University of Duisburg-Essen
Jérôme Leroux	CNRS
Michael Luttenberger	Technical University of Munich
Richard Mayr	The University of Edinburgh
Anca Muscholl	LaBRI
Jean-François Raskin	Université libre de Bruxelles
Peter Rossmanith	RWTH Aachen University
Helmut Seidl	Technical University of Munich
Tomáš Vojnar	Brno University of Technology

Additional Reviewers

Romain Delpy
Raymond Devillers
Lukáš Holík
Adam Rogalewicz
Chana Weil-Kennedy

Contents

Fairness and Liveness Under Weak Consistency 1
Parosh Aziz Abdulla, Mohamed Faouzi Atig, Adwait Godbole,
Krishna Shankaranarayanan, and Mihir Vahanwala

Restricted Flow Games 22
Ravid Alon and Orna Kupferman

SYNTHLEARN: A Tool for Guided Reactive Synthesis 51
Mrudula Balachander, Emmanuel Filiot, and Jean-François Raskin

On Regular Expression Proof Complexity of Salomaa's Axiom System F_1 72
Simon Beier and Markus Holzer

Hidden Markov Models with Unobservable Transitions 101
Rebecca Bernemann, Barbara König, Matthias Schaffeld,
and Torben Weis

Coverability in Well-Formed Free-Choice Petri Nets 122
Eike Best and Raymond Devillers

On Verifying Concurrent Programs Under Weak Consistency Models:
Decidability and Complexity 133
Ahmed Bouajjani

A Summary and Personal Perspective on Recent Advances in Privacy Risk
Assessment in Digital Pathology Through Formal Methods 148
Tomáš Brázdil

A Uniform Framework for Language Inclusion Problems 155
Kyveli Doveri, Pierre Ganty, and Chana Weil-Kennedy

On the Home-Space Problem for Petri Nets 172
Petr Jančar and Jérôme Leroux

Newton's Method – There and Back Again 181
Michael Luttenberger and Maximilian Schlund

Template-Based Verification of Array-Manipulating Programs 206
Viktor Malík, Peter Schrammel, and Tomáš Vojnar

Memoryless Strategies in Stochastic Reachability Games 225
  Stefan Kiefer, Richard Mayr, Mahsa Shirmohammadi, and Patrick Totzke

Region Quadtrees Verified 243
  Tobias Nipkow

Computing *pre** for General Context Free Grammars 255
  Peter Rossmanith

2-Pointer Logic 281
  Helmut Seidl, Julian Erhard, Michael Schwarz, and Sarah Tilscher

Author Index 309

Fairness and Liveness Under Weak Consistency

Parosh Aziz Abdulla[1][(✉)], Mohamed Faouzi Atig[1], Adwait Godbole[2],
Krishna Shankaranarayanan[3], and Mihir Vahanwala[4]

[1] Uppsala University, Uppsala, Sweden
{parosh,mohamed_faouzi.atig}@it.uu.se
[2] University of California Berkeley, Berkeley, USA
adwait@berkeley.edu
[3] IIT Bombay, Mumbai, India
krishnas@cse.iitb.ac.in
[4] Max Planck Institute for Software Systems, Saarland Informatics Campus,
Saarbrücken, Germany
mvahanwa@mpi-sws.org

Abstract. We consider the verification of concurrent programs running on weakly consistent platforms, i.e., weaker semantics than the classical Sequential Consistency (SC) semantics. We describe a framework for the verification of liveness properties for such programs. To that end, we introduce a notion of fairness that combines the classical transition fairness condition with an additional condition that forbids demonic behaviors of the memory system. We illustrate the framework by instantiating it for the classical Total Store Order (TSO) memory model. The presentation is tutorial-like and based on our previous works [3,4].

1 Introduction

The ubiquity of parallel systems has resulted in an extensive research effort to increase their efficiency, security, and reliability. While designing concurrent systems has always been a difficult challenge, developing correct concurrent systems has become even more challenging in recent years. The main reason is that computing platforms do not provide the fundamental guarantee of *Sequential Consistency* (SC) anymore. The SC semantics interleaves the parallel executions of different processes while preserving the order of actions performed by a single process [19]. The SC model is easy to understand since all components are strongly synchronized so that they all have a *uniform view* of the global state of the system. The SC semantics is so intuitive that programmers of concurrent applications often assume that it is guaranteed by the platforms on which they run their applications. On the flip side, SC is too expensive to maintain since it requires continuous synchronization of all system components. At the hardware level, SC requires strong coherence; at the distributed system level, SC requires that updates by a given site are immediately conveyed to all other sites. Such strong consistency requirements are impossible to achieve with reasonable

S. Kiefer et al. (Eds.): *Taming the Infinities of Concurrency*, LNCS 14660, pp. 1–21, 2024.
https://doi.org/10.1007/978-3-031-56222-8_1

efficiency and energy consumption. Therefore, modern platforms implement optimizations that lead to the relaxation of the inter-component synchronization, offering only *weak* semantic guarantees. The problem is that program behaviors may differ considerably from their behaviors under the SC semantics when run on such platforms. Even standard textbook programs may exhibit faulty behaviors when run under weakly consistent semantics. This paper will describe the classical Dekker mutual exclusion protocol as a case in point. The discrepancy in program behaviors gives rise to new challenges to maintaining the reliability and security of concurrent applications. Extensive research has been undertaken to answer the challenges of modeling, testing, and verifying applications running according to such semantics.

Historically, two classes of specifications have been prominent in program verification, namely safety and liveness properties. Roughly speaking, a safety property states that "nothing bad will happen during the execution of the program" and a liveness property states that "something good will happen during the execution of the program." [16,20]. Despite these properties being complementary, verification frameworks for liveness are usually more complicated. First, checking safety properties, in many cases, can be reduced to the (simple) reachability problem, while checking liveness properties usually amounts to checking repeated reachability of states [22]. Second, concurrency comes with an inherent *scheduling non-determinism*, i.e., at each step, the scheduler may non-deterministically select the following process to run. Therefore, liveness properties must be accompanied by appropriate fairness conditions on the scheduling policies to prohibit trivial blocking behaviors [20]. In the example of two processes trying to acquire a lock, demonic non-determinism [15] may always favor one process over the other, leading to starvation.

The verification of liveness properties (and also safety properties) has attracted much research in the context of programs running under the classical Sequential Consistency (SC) [19]. There is a clear gap in weakly consistent semantics: most existing works concentrate on safety properties, and only recently have works started to appear on verifying liveness properties.

This paper describes a framework introduced in [4] for verifying liveness properties under weak memory models. In Sect. 2, we will recall general concepts related to verification, concurrency, and weak memory models, and then describe their instantiation to the SC case in Sect. 3. We illustrate the challenges that arise in the case of weak memory through the TSO semantics. We recall the model in Sect. 4 and then study fairness and liveness properties for TSO in Sect. 5. In particular, we show the equivalence of memory fairness and probabilistic fairness. In Sect. 6, we consider the verification of Markov chains induced by the probabilistic model of TSO. In Sect. 7, we give some conclusions and directions for future work.

2   Concurrency, Shared Memory, and Verification

A concurrent program consists of multiple processes, or threads, whose executions depend on their scheduling, and communication via shared memory.

Processes are defined by the instructions they must execute; they have access to local variables, or registers, in order to do so. The control state refers to the position of the instruction pointers and the contents of the registers of each of the processes. The shared memory consists of global variables, or locations, that can be addressed by all processes.

For the sake of intuition, it might be helpful to anthropomorphize the processes and think of the shared memory as a messaging service that operates according to the protocol governed by the memory model. Processes interface with the shared memory through write and read operations: these respectively correspond to sending and fetching messages.

The verification problem for a fixed memory model asks, does the control state satisfy the given specification along the run of the concurrent program? For instance, when there is a critical shared resource, it is natural to ask whether it will never be accessed simultaneously by two processes (mutual exclusion, an example of safety) and whether each process is guaranteed to access it often enough (an example of liveness). The answer to such synchronization decision problems crucially depends on the underlying communication protocol, i.e. the memory model.

As mentioned in the Introduction, safety properties specify that "bad things never happen". In the above example, in order to verify safety, the intuitive idea is to prove (by the absence of a counterexample) that there is never a fatal miscommunication. On the other hand, liveness, which specifies that "good things are guaranteed to eventually happen," is harder to meaningfully verify because it often requires that the pivotal message delivery (and scheduling) be *consistently* good: a requirement that is seldom built into the protocols we consider. Therefore, we use judicious *fairness conditions* to rule out behaviors that the protocol technically permits but are practically unreasonable in the long term.

In this paper, we shall consider control state reachability as our canonical safety problem, and termination and repeated state reachability as our canonical liveness problems.

We shall now give an intuitive overview of the key aspects of some fundamental (weak) memory models, and motivate our notions of fairness. As we shall see later, it turns out that under these fairness conditions, our liveness problems reduce to safety queries. We will rely on the intuition of anthropomorphic processes using the shared memory as a messaging service (writes and reads respectively correspond to sending and fetching messages) in the following subsection.

2.1 Memory Models: Intuition

Processes, as users of the messaging system, can only send or request messages through an interface that is common for all protocols. We visualize each process to have a separate mailbox for messages pertaining to each shared variable. To send a message (i.e. write value v to variable x), a process submits it to the messaging service, which then assumes the responsibility of annotating the message with relevant metadata and delivering it to the other processes' x-mailboxes. At the other end, to fetch a message (i.e. to read from variable x), a process requests a message from its x-mailbox, and the service grants one as per the messaging protocol. We assume that on a given day, the service handles at most one write or read.

Sequential Consistency (SC). This is the simplest protocol to reason about. Whenever a process sends a message (writes value v to variable x), the service broadcasts and delivers it *immediately* to all processes' x-mailboxes. When a process requests to fetch a message (read from variable x), the service gives it the most recent message from the mailbox. In this protocol, one can see that the service can discard all but the most recent messages to every variable.

TSO and PSO. As one would expect, it is costly and demanding to implement the high degree of synchronization described above. A popular paradigm is that of *multi-copy atomicity*, exemplified by Total Store Order (TSO) and Partial Store Order (PSO) [21, Section 8 and Appendix D] (see also [14]) - it provides performance by weakening SC's consistency guarantees, while also keeping the protocol centralized enough for its analysis to be manageable.

Total Store Order (TSO). This protocol is not as prompt as SC, but similar in most aspects. The service maintains a buffer, or a FIFO queue, for the outgoing messages of each process. When a process p sends a message (writes value v to variable x), it is added to p's mailbox immediately, but the broadcast is delayed: the service adds it to the queue. To perform its broadcasting duties, the service picks a queue, takes the message at the front, and delivers it to the appropriate mailboxes of all the other processes. When a process p requests to fetch a message (read from variable x), the service first checks p's queue for an x-message and returns the most recent one. If there aren't any, the service returns the most recent message from the mailbox.

Partial Store Order (PSO). PSO differs from TSO by allowing writes to race, i.e. for each process, the service maintains a separate queue for every variable. All other aspects of the protocol are the same. Once again, we observe that the service need only keep track of the messages in the queues and most recently broadcast messages of each variable.

SRA and WRA. As parallel systems get more distributed, the simplicity of multi-copy atomicity no longer offsets the cost of simultaneous broadcasting. In these settings, causal consistency, exemplified by Strong Release Acquire (SRA) and Weak Release Acquire (WRA) [18, Sects. 3 and 4] is the paradigm of choice. The idea is that reading messages creates causal dependencies which must be respected: let Alice write two messages to x, and Bob write a message to y after reading them. Then, if Eve reads Bob's message, the service is forbidden from giving Eve Alice's first message should she wish to read from x - in a certain sense, this is causally far before the events Eve is already aware of, and too stale an update.

Strong Release Acquire (SRA). The messaging service maintains a clock for each variable, and a vector of timestamps for each process, with an entry corresponding to each clock. The clocks are used to totally order all writes to the same variable, the timestamps determine what messages have not been rendered redundant to a process by causal dependencies. When process p sends a message (writes value v to variable x): (i) The x-clock is incremented by 1; (ii) The x-clock entry in p's timestamp vector is updated to the current value; and (iii) The message is annotated with p's new timestamp vector. This message is delivered immediately to p's mailbox, but to other processes, the service can deliver it asynchronously and at leisure.

On the other hand, when p requests a message (reads from x), (i) the service selects a message from p's mailbox whose x-timestamp annotation is at least as large as the x-clock entry in p's vector of timestamps; (ii) the service hands this message, which is guaranteed by construction to not be redundant, over; and (iii) finally, to enforce new dependencies that are created by this read, for each clock, the service updates the corresponding entry in p's vector of timestamps to be the maximum (a) of the old value and (b) the timestamp in the annotation of the message.

Weak Release Acquire (WRA). The protocol is the same with respect to the propagation of messages and updates of timestamps and clocks. The key difference that makes this model significantly weaker than SRA is that the service maintains a clock for every (variable, process) pair. Hence, timestamp vectors also have entries corresponding to each (variable, process) pair.

In these protocols too, the service can safely discard messages which it cannot give to any process for reading: these are messages whose timestamps are smaller than the timestamps of every process.

Remark: Other Models. In the multi-copy atomic models we considered, reads had *acquire* semantics: they were not allowed to race. Relaxed Memory Ordering (RMO) [21, Sect. 8 and Appendix D] is a multi-copy atomic model that weakens PSO by allowing reads to race if they are sufficiently independent of each other, and/or the writes they overtake. In such a protocol, the service would be allowed to buffer read requests too, instead of being obliged to address them immediately.

FIFO consistency [13] is a memory model that is neither multi-copy atomic nor causally consistent. Like TSO, the messaging service maintains for each process, a queue of its writes. However, unlike TSO, these writes are propagated to other processes asynchronously, rather in the style of SRA. Unlike SRA though, causal dependencies are not tracked. When a process wishes to read variable x, the service hands it the most recent x-message that was delivered to it.

2.2 Memory Fairness: Intuition

A common observation for all weak memory models is that the messaging service, i.e., memory, needs to store only those messages that are under propagation and/or have not been rendered redundant by the protocol yet. If the service is an *efficient* medium of communication, the number of such messages will be minimal. In the extreme case, consider SC: it is the most efficient protocol, and at any point, it only needs to store one message per variable.

We refer to the number of messages the service is keeping track of (in models like RMO, this also includes buffered reads) as the *size* of the memory configuration. Configurations with minimal size (one message per variable, no pending reads) are called *plain*.

Recall the requirements for liveness properties we had outlined earlier: consistently good communication between processes, facilitated by consistently efficient message delivery. The latter is what we intended to capture with fairness conditions. The notion of configuration size allows us to accurately quantify the efficiency of messaging, which is inversely related to the extent of weak behavior. Hence, our plan will be to devise formal definitions of fairness that imply, for example, that the configuration size is bounded, or that plain configurations are visited infinitely often: such are the hallmarks of a well-functioning messaging system.

In the following sections, we consider SC and TSO and use running examples to examine the above concepts of shared memory, verification, and fairness notions in more detail. We remark that one can indeed use the intuition of shared memory as a medium of communication and notion of configuration size based fairness described in this section to adapt the following technical discussion to other memory models.

3   Sequential Consistency (SC)

We will first recall the SC semantics and describe the verification of safety properties. Then, we consider liveness properties and describe different fairness conditions needed to verify such properties.

3.1   Model

To illustrate our framework, we consider a simple model for concurrent programs, consisting of processes that communicate by performing read (load) and write (store) operations on a set of shared (global) variables. Figure 1 depicts such a program with two processes p_1 and p_2 sharing two shared variables x and y. In this section, we consider the SC semantics for such programs where process operations are atomic. When the process p_1 performs the write operation, assigning the value 3 to the variable x, we simultaneously update the value of x in the memory and, hence, the new value of x will be immediately readable by p_2. When p_2 reads the value of x in the second transition, it sees the latest value written to x, namely 3.

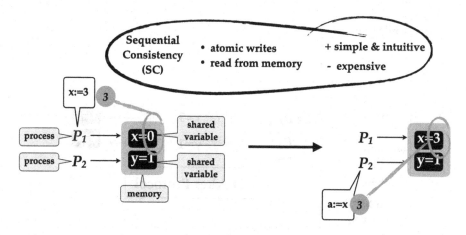

Fig. 1. The SC semantics.

3.2 Safety Properties

The classical interpretation of a safety property is that "nothing bad will happen during the program's execution" [16, 20]. This means that we can reduce checking safety properties to the reachability of a set of *bad* configurations that violate a given requirement of the program. A typical example is *mutual exclusion* where concurrent processes contend a shared resource. The bad configurations are those in which multiple processes access the shared resource. We depict the classical Dekker mutual exclusion protocol in Fig. 2. The program contains two processes p_1 and p_2 sharing two variables x and y. The processes have a local variable each, namely a resp. b. The goal of the protocol is to guarantee *mutual exclusion*, i.e., to prevent the processes from entering their critical section, CS_1 and CS_2, simultaneously. Before moving to its critical section, the process p_1 declares its intention by setting the shared variable x to 1, and then reads y's value, storing it in its local variable a. It halts its progress to its critical section if the value of a is equal to one, i.e., if p_2 is about to enter, or it is inside its critical section. The process p_2 uses the same scenario to synchronize with p_1. Under the SC semantics, the above scenario succeeds, and the program will satisfy mutual exclusion. To see this, assume, without loss of generality, p_1 executes the first instruction. Since the transition assigns 1 to x, process p_2 assigns the value 1 to its local variable b when it executes its read instruction, and hence it will not be able to cross to its critical section.

3.3 Fairness and Liveness

A liveness property states that "something *good* will eventually happen" during the program's execution. For the Dekker protocol, a typical liveness property is that each process infinitely often enters its critical section during any program

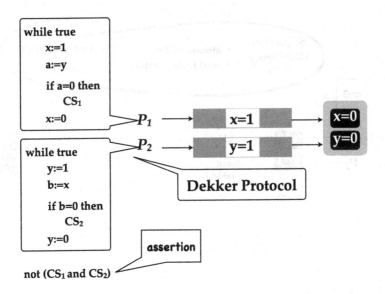

Fig. 2. The Dekker Protocol

run. Liveness properties can be trivially violated without some *fairness condition* that provide certain guarantees concerning the process scheduling. In the case of Dekker, a run that never schedules p_2 to run will trivially violate the above liveness condition since p_2 will never reach its critical section. The literature contains many fairness conditions for verifying liveness properties (see, e.g., [16,20].). The classical *strong fairness* condition states that we must schedule each process infinitely often along each program run. In the Dekker example, we schedule both p_1 and p_2 infinitely often. While strong fairness ensures that p_2 is scheduled infinitely often, it still fails to guarantee that p_2 reaches its critical section infinitely often (or even once). This can happen if p_2 is always scheduled to run when $x = 1$. Although p_2 will perform infinitely many iterations of its loop, it will always fail the if-statement guarding the critical section. A more robust and helpful notion of fairness is *transition fairness* (called strong transition fairness in the comprehensive [17, Sects. 4 and 5]): if a transition t in a process is enabled infinitely often, then t will be taken infinitely often. Transition fairness prevents the above demonic behavior and guarantees that both p_1 and p_2 in the Dekker protocol visit their critical sections infinitely often.

As another example, consider the simple program of Fig. 3. We want to verify that process p_2 always terminates. Strong fairness is not enough to prove p_2's termination. The following strongly fair but demonic scheduling policy prevents p_2 from ever terminating:

- p_1 assigns 1 to the shared variable x.
- p_2 assigns 2 to the shared variable x.
- p_2 reads the value 2 of x and stores it in its local variable a.

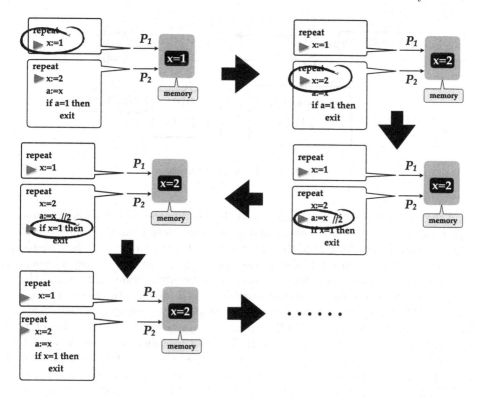

Fig. 3. Simple Program.

– p_2 fails the condition of the if-statement and re-starts the while-loop.
– p_1 assigns 1 to the shared variable x, and we repeat the above sequence.

However, p_2 is guaranteed to terminate under transition fairness since p_1 is guaranteed to be scheduled after p_2 has executed the instruction $x := 2$. Hence, the value of a will be one when p_2 reaches its if-statement.

4   Total Store Order (TSO)

We consider one of the most fundamental weak memory models: the Total Store Order (TSO) semantics. We depict the semantics in Fig. 4 for the case where we have two processes p_1 and p_2 sharing two variables x and y. The operational semantics of TSO make write instructions non-atomic by inserting an unbounded FIFO buffer between each process and the globally visible memory. Technically, the memory comprises both the process buffers and the globally visible component. However, in the context of TSO, we will refer to the latter as "main memory" or simply "memory" for convenience. We refer to the buffers as the *store buffer*, or the *pending buffer* of p_1 resp. p_2. Figure 5 illustrates a typical program run, starting from a configuration γ_0 where the store buffers are empty,

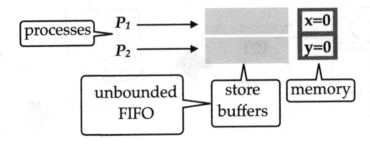

Fig. 4. The TSO architecture.

and the memory state is $x = 0$ and $y = 0$. To simplify the presentation, we omit the local states of the processes p_1 and p_2 and only depict the store buffers and the memory. In the first step, the process p_1 writes the value 1 to the variable x. Instead of immediately updating the memory, p_1 appends a *write message* $x = 1$ to the end of its store buffer, obtaining the configuration γ_1. From γ_1, the process p_1 writes the value 2 to the variable x, so it appends the message $x = 2$ to the store buffer. In γ_2, the store buffer of p_1 in γ_2 contains two messages, while the store buffer of p_2 is still empty. Next, p_1 tries to read the value of x. To that end, it checks its store buffer. If the buffer contains a message on x, then p_1 fetches the value of the latest such a value (2, in the case of γ_2). We say that p_1 performs a *read-own-write* operation since it reads a write instruction it has issued. In γ_3, the process p_1 reads the value of the variable y. Since there are no pending write messages on y in the buffer of p_1 in γ_3, it fetches the value 0 of y from the memory. We all this a *read-from-memory* operation. We observe that read operations do not change the states of the pending buffers or the memory. In a similar manner, p_2 reads the value of y in γ_4. Although p_1 has already performed the write operations on x, their effects are invisible to p_2 since the corresponding message has still not reached the memory. From γ_5, the program performs an *update* operation, where it takes the message $x = 1$ at the *head* of the buffer of p_1 and uses it to update the value of x in the memory. This value will now be visible to p_2 in γ_6. In a nutshell, the TSO semantics is defined by: (i) writing-to-store-buffer, (ii) reading-own-writes. (iii) reading-from-memory. (iv) updating the memory.

The TSO semantics is weaker than the SC semantics. In particular, TSO can mimic any SC run by performing an update after each write instruction. On the other hand, TSO allows more behaviors, introducing bugs in programs that are correct under SC. The Dekker protocol of Sect. 3.1 is a case in point. We will use the run of Fig. 6 to explain why the Dekker protocol does not satisfy mutual exclusion under the TSO semantics. Recall that, before entering its critical section, a process performs a write operation that prevents the other process from moving towards its critical section. Since write operations are not

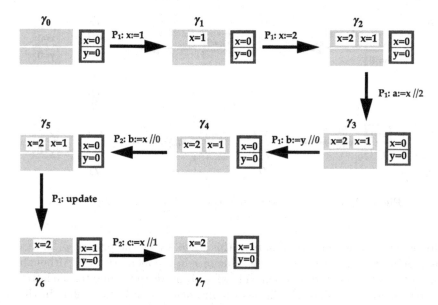

Fig. 5. A run according to the TSO semantics

atomic in the case of TSO, the above scenario will fail, and both processes can move to their critical sections simultaneously. Concretely, the processes p_1 and p_2 perform their write operations appending the corresponding messages to their buffers (the configurations γ_2 and γ_3). When p_1 performs its read operation from γ_3, it does not find pending write messages on y in its buffer, and hence it fetches the value of y from the memory. Since the message on y in process p_2's buffer has not reached the memory, it is not visible to p_1, and p_1 will read the value $y = 0$. Analogously, p_2 reads the value $x = 0$; hence, both processes can enter their critical sections.

5 Fairness and Liveness Under TSO

5.1 Transition Fairness

While transition fairness allows the verification of liveness properties for a wide range of concurrent programs under SC, it is too weak in the case of TSO. In Fig. 7, we re-consider the program of Fig. 3 and run it under TSO. We show that, in contrast to SC, there is now a transition-fair run in which P_2 does not terminate. Roughly speaking, transition fairness implies, among other things, that memory updates occur infinitely often, but it allows updates to occur less frequently than write instructions. This means that we will have program executions in which the process buffers always contain messages and never see the other processes' write operations. We start from the configuration γ_0 where both buffers are empty. The processes p_1 and p_2 execute their write instructions, and we obtain γ_2. In γ_2, the process p_2 reads the value of x. It sees the value of 2

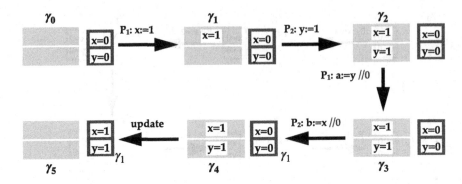

Fig. 6. A run of the Dekker Protocol under TSO semantics

from its buffer, so it will not terminate at this stage. In γ_3, the process p_1 moves the message in its buffer to update the value of x in the memory to 1. Although the value of x in the memory is 1, which is what p_2 needs to terminate, the latter fails to terminate in γ_4 since it still has the message $x = 2$ in its buffer. In the rest of the configurations, this scenario is repeated. Although transition fairness means that the value of x will be equal to 1 infinitely often. The messages from the buffer of p_2 are transferred to the memory infinitely often, p_2's buffer will never become empty. Hence, p_2 will never see $x = 1$ in the memory, meaning it will not terminate.

5.2 Memory-Boundedness Transition (MBT) Fairness

As we observed in the previous sub-section, the problem with transition fairness is that it allows runs in which the store buffers never become empty. The non-empty buffers confine the processes to only reading their own writes, effectively preventing inter-process communication through the shared memory. Therefore, we introduce a new notion of fairness, called *Memory-Boundedness (MB) fairness* that we will use together with transition fairness to strengthen the latter. MB-fairness means that we assume the existence of an (unknown) upper bound on the number of messages that can reside inside the store buffers at any point during the program runs. It is essential to notice that the upper bound is not given and can be arbitrarily large; MB-fairness assumes its mere existence. We use *MBT-fairness* to refer to the conjunction of MB-fairness and transition fairness. MBT-fairness enjoys two properties that make it attractive in the verification of liveness properties under weak memory models, namely (i) *modeling*: it eliminates the demonic behaviors that arise due to bad scheduling and buffer clogging; (ii) it allows algorithmic verification. We will consider the modeling aspect in the rest of this section and discuss the verification aspect in Sect. 6.

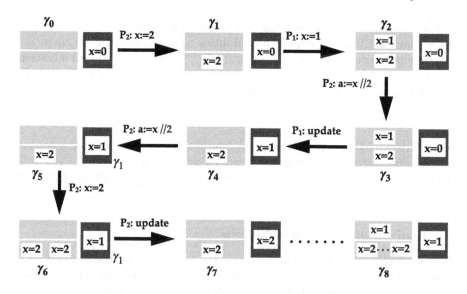

Fig. 7. A transition-fair run under the TSO semantics

Let us study the behavior of the program of Fig. 3 under TSO and MBT-fairness. Assume that the bound on the buffer size is (an unknown value) b. Consider an (infinite) run ρ of the program. By MBT-fairness, all the configurations have buffers of size at most b. Since the update operations are always enabled, it follows by transition fairness that there are infinitely many configurations along ρ of size at most $b - 1$. By repeating the reasoning, there are infinitely many configurations along ρ with empty buffers. For such configurations, the program essentially behaves like in the case of SC. Using the same reasoning as in Sect. 3.3, we conclude the p_2 will terminate.

5.3 Probabilistic Memory Fairness

The notion of MBT-Fairness is arguably dependent on specific aspects of our formalism of the memory. However, as observed in the previous paragraph, it has a crucial consequence that can be expressed in terms of more universal notions, viz. that plain configurations are necessarily visited infinitely often. This property will be the backbone of the verification techniques we adopt.

In this subsection, we illustrate a natural alternative way of ensuring the above property, namely, by viewing the underlying transition system from a stochastic perspective. Interpreting transition systems as Markov Chains yields not only insights on the phenomena being modeled but also a rich body of algorithms to *quantitatively* understand their properties. Thus, we reinforce the benefits of our fairness notions on both the modeling and algorithmic fronts.

The transition system modeling our concurrent program can be converted into a Markov Chain by adding probabilities to the transitions: if there is a transition from configuration γ to configuration γ', then it is assigned a nonzero probability. Probabilities of transitions originating at γ must sum up to 1. By construction, an infinite run of a Markov Chain is transition fair with probability 1.

Probabilistic Memory Fairness. A Markov Chain representing a concurrent program satisfies Probabilistic Memory Fairness if an infinite run visits the set of plain configurations (i.e. those with empty buffers) infinitely often with probability 1.

5.4   Equivalence of Fairness Notions

We conclude this section by demonstrating the sense in which the two notions of memory fairness we introduced are equivalent. This will help us appreciate and leverage the algorithmic techniques presented in the next section.

Recall that our canonical liveness problems are repeated control state reachability and termination. In this subsection, we will consider the former: it is straightforward to adapt the arguments to the latter.

Equivalence Property. There exists N such that for all $n \geq N$, all transition fair runs with configuration size bounded by n visit control state c infinitely often if and only if c is visited infinitely often with probability 1 under probabilistic memory fairness.

Justification. We will demonstrate the equivalence by showing a canonical procedure that decides both repeated reachability queries. Consider a (colored) graph $G(n)$ parametrized by n. The vertices are the finitely many plain configurations (there are finitely many variables, and we assume that they can take finitely many values; in the case of TSO, these are configurations with empty buffers). We draw an edge from γ to γ' if and only if γ' is reachable from γ via configurations of size at most n. Furthermore, nodes are colored green or black. A node γ is colored green if and only if control state c is reachable from γ via configurations of size at most n.

By construction, it is clear that for all n, strongly connected components (SCCs) of the graph $G(n)$ will be uniformly colored. Moreover, this is a finite graph, and by construction, as n increases, edges can only be added, and vertices can only go from black to green. Thus, the graph will saturate at some $n = N$, and be the same thereafter. Let this saturated graph be G, and consider $n \geq N$.

Note that for G, the vertices are plain configurations, the edges and colors indicate reachability *without* restrictions on the size of intermediate configurations. A crucial remark is that G can be computed with conventional reachability queries. This G will serve as our canonical construct.

Recall that any transition fair run with configuration size bounded by n necessarily visits plain configurations infinitely often. Further, by transition fairness, it is guaranteed to eventually sink into a bottom SCC of $G(n) = G$. By similar reasoning, one can also argue that under probabilistic memory fairness, a run eventually sinks into a bottom SCC and visits plain configurations infinitely often with probability 1.

We are now ready to argue that the following three statements are equivalent: (i) all transition fair runs with configuration size bounded by n visit c infinitely often, and (ii) a run under probabilistic memory fairness visits c infinitely often with probability 1, and (iii) all reachable bottom SCC's (SCC's with no outgoing edges) of G are colored green.

The existence of a black reachable bottom SCC indicates a path where, after a finite prefix of nonzero probability, c can never be visited again.

For the converse, recall that if a transition fair run visits a state γ infinitely often, then it necessarily also visits each state γ' reachable from γ infinitely often. Similarly, if a run under probabilistic fairness visits a state γ infinitely often, then under probabilistic memory fairness, each state γ' reachable from γ is also visited infinitely often with probability 1. We apply these observations to the finite set of green nodes which is visited infinitely often, and from which c is reachable, and we are done.

The Centrality of Reachability. As a corollary of the above justification, we note that the core subroutines driving the algorithm deciding repeated reachability (liveness) under our fairness conditions are *simple* reachability (safety) queries. The construction of the canonical graph $G(N) = G$ and indeed, the computation of N reduces to safety queries. Established techniques to resolve them, along with standard algorithms to study the special class of Markov Chains we use, yield a solution to the problem of liveness verification.

6   Verification of Markov Chains

Having studied declarative formulations of fairness notions from the modeling and stochastic perspectives, we now complete the picture by discussing the *algorithmic* perspective. In particular, we consider the stochastic setting (the concurrent program induces a Markov Chain), where fairness is imposed through conditions on the probabilities assigned to the transitions. We will take the TSO memory model as a concrete example: one can use the intuition in Sect. 2 to adapt the observations to other memory models too.

We have already observed how deciding the reachability of a given set F plays a central role in verification. In the context of safety, F is a set of fatal configurations: safety is disproven by showing a (necessarily finite) path to F; it is typically proven by giving an *invariant*, i.e. a subset G of the set of configurations $\widetilde{F}$ from which F is not reachable. We will assume that for any configuration γ, we can decide whether $\gamma \in F$, and whether $\gamma \in \widetilde{F}$.

In the context of liveness, on the other hand, reaching F constitutes desirable behavior that one would want to guarantee or, in the setting of Markov Chains, quantify. More specifically, a decision problem could ask whether F is reached with probability $p \pm \varepsilon$, i.e. whether $|Prob_{\gamma_0}[\Diamond F] - p| < \varepsilon$.

The Algorithm. Given that we can detect both when a configuration γ is in F, and when it is in $\widetilde{F}$, the following approach might immediately spring to mind: maintain an under-approximation α_- (initialized to 0) and an over-approximation α_+ (initialized to 1) of $Prob_{\gamma_0}[\Diamond F]$. Starting from the initial configuration, generate all runs through the transition system in a breadth-first manner, and compute their probabilities up to the current step while doing so. If a path reaches $\gamma \in F$, add its probability to α_-; if a path reaches $\gamma \in \widetilde{F}$, subtract its probability from α_+.

6.1 Necessity of Decisiveness

The under and over-approximations are clearly sound, but do they converge? Observe that we keep track of paths until they reach either F or $\widetilde{F}$, and account for their probabilities in the approximations only after they do. It is indeed possible that the approximations do not converge because of infinite runs that are "indecisive" with respect to F: they visit neither F nor $\widetilde{F}$.

It is precisely this indecision that we seek to tackle with fairness. A Markov Chain is *decisive* [6,11] with respect to a set of configurations F if for any configuration γ, a run starting from it is indecisive with respect to F with probability 0. Formally, for each configuration γ, it is the case that $Prob_\gamma\left(\Diamond F \lor \Diamond \widetilde{F}\right) = 1$. Put differently, if F is always reachable along a run ρ then ρ will almost certainly eventually reach F, i.e., $Prob_\gamma(\Diamond F \mid \Box \exists \Diamond F) = 1$.

Decisiveness ensures that the approximations converge and the algorithm terminates because, by definition, the problematic indecisive paths collectively have probability 0. We now turn to the enforcement of this property through fairness. In fact, we will enforce a stronger condition: that the Markov Chain itself be decisive, i.e. the property of decisiveness holds with respect to *any* set F of configurations.

6.2 Attractors

We enforce decisiveness by asserting the existence of a *finite attractor* [10]. An *attractor* A is a set of configurations, such that each run of the system will almost certainly eventually reach A. Figure 8(a) illustrates an attractor. Formally, for each configuration γ of the system, we have $Prob_\gamma(\Diamond A) = 1$, i.e., we reach the set A from γ with probability one.

Attractors satisfy an even stronger condition, namely any run of the system will almost certainly visit A, not only once, but *infinitely often*. The reason (illustrated in Fig. 8(b)) is the following. Let us consider a run ρ of the system. By definition of an attractor, ρ will almost certainly eventually reach a configuration

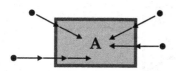
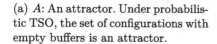
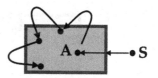

(a) A: An attractor. Under probabilistic TSO, the set of configurations with empty buffers is an attractor.

(b) Repeated reachability of attractors.

Fig. 8. Attractors.

$\gamma_1 \in A$. We apply the definition of an attractor to the continuation of ρ from γ_1. This continuation will almost certainly eventually reach a configuration $\gamma_2 \in A$. The reasoning can be repeated infinitely thus obtaining an infinite sequence $\gamma_1, \gamma_2, \ldots$ of configurations inside A that will be visited. This means that A will be visited infinitely often with probability 1.

By an identical line of reasoning, we can conclude that the property of decisiveness implies that $Prob_\gamma(\Box\Diamond F \mid \Box\exists\Diamond F) = 1$, i.e. if F is always reachable along a path, then the path almost certainly visits F not just once, but infinitely often.

Recall the description of Probabilistic Memory Fairness in Sect. 5.3. We declared that the set of plain configurations (for TSO, those with empty buffers) be visited infinitely often with probability 1. This precisely asserts that the set of plain configurations is an *attractor*. Moreover, when we assume that the processes have finitely many control states and that shared variables can take finitely many values, we get that the set of plain configurations is a *finite* attractor.

6.3 Sufficiency of Finite Attractors

Let us now motivate why our declaration of the existence of finite attractor suffices to enforce decisiveness (Fig. 9). We partition A into two sets: $A_0 := A \cap \widetilde{F}$ and $A_1 := A \cap \neg\widetilde{F}$. In other words, the configurations in A_0 cannot reach F (in the underlying transition system), while from each configuration in A_1 there is a path to F. Consider a run ρ. We need to show that ρ will almost certainly eventually either reach $\widetilde{F}$ or reach F. We know that ρ will almost certainly visit A infinitely often. By construction, exactly one of A_0 or A_1 is visited infinitely often. If A_0 is visited infinitely often, we are done, because $A_0 \subseteq \widetilde{F}$. Otherwise, ρ will visit A_1 infinitely often with probability 1. Since A_1 is a finite set, with probability 1, there is a particular configuration $\gamma \in A_1$ that will be visited infinitely often by ρ. By definition, we know that F is reachable from γ, i.e., there is a path (say of length k) from γ to F. Let β be the probability that this path is taken during the next k steps of the run. This means that each time ρ visits γ, it will reach F during the next k steps with probability at least β, which

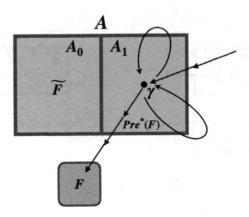

Fig. 9. Attractors and decisiveness.

implies that ρ cannot avoid F forever. Thus ρ will almost certainly eventually reach F.

The above observations allow us to use the framework of Sect. 5.4 and the breadth-first exploration procedure described at the beginning of this section to approximate $Prob_{\gamma_0}[\Box\Diamond F] = 1 - Prob_{\gamma_0}[\Diamond\widetilde{F}] = 1 - Prob_{\gamma_0}[\Diamond A_0]$ too. The first equality follows from decisiveness, the second from the attractor property. Here, we decrement the over-approximation when a path reaches A_0, and increment the under-approximation when a path reaches a configuration in A_1 from which A_0 is unreachable.

Notice how these queries crucially rely on the finite graph we described in Sect. 5.4, as well as on the probabilistic fairness properties discussed in this section for correctness.

6.4 Getting Desired Finite Attractors

In this section, we outlined a simple procedure to verify or quantify the satisfaction of liveness specifications. We identified the notion of decisiveness, a property of Markov Chains essential to the algorithm, and defined the concept of a finite attractor as a means of ensuring decisiveness. This coincided with the fairness notions we obtained from the modeling perspective. To reconcile the declarations of the modeling with the requirements of the algorithm, we now briefly discuss the assignment of transition probabilities to get the finite attractor we desire (Fig. 10).

Recall that we consider systems that consist of finite sets of finite-state processes, communicating through shared variables according to the TSO semantics. Note that TSO uses unbounded store buffers to model message propagation: the underlying transition system is therefore infinite-state. To induce a Markov Chain, choices between different enabled transitions are resolved probabilistically, i.e. the scheduler uses a stochastic policy to pick an enabled process to execute. Furthermore, after each process step, the program probabilistically

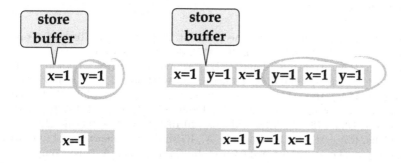

Fig. 10. Probabilistic Fairness under TSO semantics: half the buffers are flushed in expectation

performs memory updates as follows: from each process' store buffer, it picks a prefix whose length is chosen uniformly at random. Messages from the chosen prefixes are randomly interleaved to generate the order in which they are flushed to the main memory.

In this model, at every step, the length of each buffer is halved in expectation. Intuitively, the run almost certainly "gravitates" toward configurations with small buffers. The limit of this tendency, of course, is to (repeatedly) visit the set of configurations with *empty* buffers. In formal terms, the transition probabilities are chosen in such a way that a set of configurations with empty buffers is an *attractor*. There are only finitely many such configurations: consequently, the induced Markov chain is decisive.

7   Conclusions and Future Work

We have presented a framework for verifying liveness properties for concurrent programs running under weak memory models. To that end, we have defined a new notion of fairness corresponding to a natural restriction on program behavior and equivalent to probabilistic fairness. In particular, the latter allows reducing checking liveness properties to checking safety properties for programs running under weak memory models.

There are several directions for future work:

– Applying automata inclusion techniques, such as the one in [7], to check liveness properties efficiently.
– Designing abstraction algorithms for verifying parameterized systems, i.e., systems consisting of arbitrary many processes [1,8,9].
– Developing partial-order reduction technique for more scalable verification [2,5,12].

Disclosure of Interests. The authors have no competing interests to declare that are relevant to the content of this article.

References

1. Abdulla, P.A.: Regular model checking. Int. J. Softw. Tools Technol. Transf. **14**, 109–118 (2012). https://doi.org/10.1007/s10009-011-0216-8
2. Abdulla, P.A., Aronis, S., Jonsson, B., Sagonas, K.: Source sets: a foundation for optimal dynamic partial order reduction. J. ACM **64**(4), 25:1–25:49 (2017)
3. Abdulla, P.A., Atig, M.F., Agarwal, R.A., Godbole, A., Krishna, S.: Probabilistic total store ordering. In: Sergey, I. (ed.) ESOP 2022. LNCS, vol. 13240, pp. 317–345. Springer, Cham (2022). https://doi.org/10.1007/978-3-030-99336-8_12
4. Abdulla, P.A., Atig, M.F., Godbole, A., Krishna, S., Vahanwala, M.: Overcoming memory weakness with unified fairness. In: Enea, C., Lal, A. (eds) Computer Aided Verification, CAV 2023, Part I. LNCS, vol. 13964, pp. 184–205. Springer, Cham (2023). https://doi.org/10.1007/978-3-031-37706-8_10
5. Abdulla, P.A., Atig, M.F., Jonsson, B., Lång, M., Ngo, T.P., Sagonas, K.: Optimal stateless model checking for reads-from equivalence under sequential consistency. PACMPL **3**(OOPSLA), 1–29 (2019)
6. Abdulla, P.A., Bertrand, N., Rabinovich, A.M., Schnoebelen, P.: Verification of probabilistic systems with faulty communication. Inf. Comput. **202**(2), 141–165 (2005)
7. Abdulla, P.A., et al.: Advanced Ramsey-based Büchi automata inclusion testing. In: Katoen, J.-P., König, B. (eds.) CONCUR 2011. LNCS, vol. 6901, pp. 187–202. Springer, Heidelberg (2011). https://doi.org/10.1007/978-3-642-23217-6_13
8. Abdulla, P., Haziza, F., Holík, L.: Parameterized verification through view abstraction. Int. J. Softw. Tools Technol. Transf. **18**(5), 495–516 (2015). https://doi.org/10.1007/s10009-015-0406-x
9. Abdulla, P.A., Ben Henda, N., Delzanno, G., Rezine, A.: Handling parameterized systems with non-atomic global conditions. In: Logozzo, F., Peled, D.A., Zuck, L.D. (eds.) VMCAI 2008. LNCS, vol. 4905, pp. 22–36. Springer, Heidelberg (2008). https://doi.org/10.1007/978-3-540-78163-9_7
10. Abdulla, P.A., Henda, N.B., Mayr, R.: Verifying infinite Markov chains with a finite attractor or the global coarseness property. In: Proceedings of the 20th IEEE Symposium on Logic in Computer Science, LICS 2005, 26–29 June 2005, Chicago, IL, USA, pp. 127–136. IEEE Computer Society (2005)
11. Abdulla, P.A., Ben Henda, N., Mayr, R.: Decisive Markov chains. LMCS **3**(4), 1–32 (2007)
12. Abdulla, P.A., Jonsson, B., Kindahl, M., Peled, D.: A general approach to partial order reductions in symbolic verification. In: Hu, A.J., Vardi, M.Y. (eds.) CAV 1998. LNCS, vol. 1427, pp. 379–390. Springer, Heidelberg (1998). https://doi.org/10.1007/BFb0028760
13. Ahamad, M., Neiger, G., Burns, J.E., Kohli, P., Hutto, P.W.: Causal memory: Definitions, implementation, and programming. Distrib. Comput. **9**(1), 37–49 (1995)
14. Atig, M.F., Bouajjani, A., Burckhardt, S., Musuvathi, M.: On the verification problem for weak memory models. In: Proceedings of the 37th Annual ACM SIGPLAN-SIGACT Symposium on Principles of Programming Languages, POPL 2010, pp. 7–18, New York, NY, USA. Association for Computing Machinery (2010)
15. Broy, M., Wirsing, M.: On the algebraic specification of nondeterministic programming languages. In: CAAP (1981)
16. Chang, E., Manna, Z., Pnueli, A.: Characterization of temporal property classes. In: Kuich, W. (ed.) ICALP 1992. LNCS, vol. 623, pp. 474–486. Springer, Heidelberg (1992). https://doi.org/10.1007/3-540-55719-9_97

17. Glabbeek, R., Höfner, P.: Progress, justness, and fairness. ACM Comput. Surv. **52**, 1–38 (2019)
18. Lahav, O., Boker, U.: What's decidable about causally consistent shared memory? ACM Trans. Program. Lang. Syst. **44**(2), 1–55 (2022)
19. Lamport, L.: How to make a multiprocessor that correctly executes multiprocess programs. IEEE Trans. Comput. **C–28**, 690–691 (1979)
20. Manna, Z., Pnueli, A.: The Temporal Logic of Reactive and Concurrent Systems - Specification. Springer, New York (1992). https://doi.org/10.1007/978-1-4612-0931-7
21. Corporate SPARC International, Inc.: The SPARC Architecture Manual (Version 9). Prentice-Hall Inc., USA (1994)
22. Wolper, P.: Expressing interesting properties of programs in propositional temporal logic. In: POPL, pp. 184–193. ACM Press (1986)

Restricted Flow Games

Ravid Alon[ID] and Orna Kupferman[✉][ID]

School of Computer Science and Engineering, The Hebrew University,
Jerusalem, Israel
ravidalon@gmail.com, orna@cs.huji.ac.il

Abstract. Classical *graph problems* are defined with respect to plain
graphs, namely vertices connected by possibly weighted edges. On the
other hand, *model checking* studies rich graph structure and semantics,
in particular *labeled graphs* and *game graphs*, which model involved realistic settings. Extending classical graph problems to graphs with a rich
semantics offers an interesting and fresh perspective for classical graph
algorithms. In addition, it extends the applicability of graph algorithms
to rich settings.

In the classical *maximum-flow* problem, the goal is to find the maximal amount of flow that can be transferred through a network, by directing the flow in each vertex into outgoing edges. The problem has been
recently extended to labeled graphs and game graphs. We introduce and
study *restricted flow games*, an extension of the maximum flow-problem
to graphs that are both labeled and game graphs. In these games, the
edges of the network are labeled by letters over some alphabet, and the
vertices are partitioned between two players, the authority and the environment. Each player directs the flow entering her vertices to outgoing
edges. The goal of the authority is to maximize the amount of flow that
reaches the target along routes that satisfy a given specification – a language over the alphabet of labels. We study several aspects of restricted
flow game as well as the complexity of decision problems on them.

1 Introduction

Graphs are used to model many types of relations and processes in physical, biological, social, and information systems. Many practical problems can be reduced
to problems about graphs, making graph theory a preeminent research area in
theoretical computer science [10,12]. Different settings call for different types of
graphs. For example, the edges of the graph may be *directed* or *weighted*, say for
modeling lengths or costs. In many applications, the edges of the graph carry
further information. For example, an edge may be associated with an action
(e.g., in planning or in VLSI design), a query (e.g., in databases), properties like
its provider or its security level (e.g., in a network of channels), and many more.
For such applications, we need *labeled graphs*, in which each vertex or edge is
labeled by a letter from some alphabet. Further, in some applications, vertices
and edges may be controlled by different entities (e.g., in the modeling of reactive or multi-agent systems, where transitions depend on actions taken by the
underlying entities), giving rise to *game graphs*.

© The Author(s), under exclusive license to Springer Nature Switzerland AG 2024
S. Kiefer et al. (Eds.): *Taming the Infinities of Concurrency*, LNCS 14660, pp. 22–50, 2024.
https://doi.org/10.1007/978-3-031-56222-8_2

Labeled graphs and game graphs have been extensively researched in the context of *model checking* [8]. A model-checking algorithm gets as input a model of the system, where vertices correspond to the configurations of the system and edges correspond to transitions between configurations. Given a specification for the system, the algorithm decides whether the model satisfies the specification. The graph algorithms that model checking uses are fairly basic, and evolve around reachability [33] or partitioning to strongly connected components [7,32]. They are applied, however, to graphs with a rich structure and semantics. In comparison, graph algorithms solve rich problems on basic graphs. A recent research direction is a study of extensions of classical graph algorithms to labeled graphs and game graphs [23].

An example to an extension of a classical graph-theory problem to labeled graphs are *regular path queries*, where we find all pairs of vertices connected by a path such that the word read along the path satisfies a specification [6,28]. Then, rather than finding any *shortest* path between two given vertices in a graph [10], it is sometimes desirable, say in transportation planning [5], web searching [1], or network routing, to restrict attention to paths that satisfy some constraint [4]. As a more elaborated example, the *constrained Eulerian path* problem is the problem of deciding whether a labeled graph has an Eulerian path that satisfies a given specification [25].

As for game graphs, for the basic problem of reachability, the two-player setting gives rise to *alternating graph reachability* [9]. As a more complex example, consider the general setting in which two players alternately claim edges of a graph G while making sure the graph they build together satisfies some monotone decreasing property. The *Turán numbers* and *Saturation numbers* refer to the number of edges that can be claimed while the property is maintained [15,20]. Then, *spanning-tree games* are an extension of the spanning-tree problem [21]. In spanning-tree games, two players alternate turns constructing a spanning tree of a given connected weighted graph. In each turn, a player chooses an edge that does not close a circle. The game ends when the chosen edges form a spanning tree. The goal of the *min player* is to minimize the total weight of edges in the obtained spanning tree, while the goal of the *max player* is to maximize it.

The extensions of graph algorithms to rich settings typically have a computational cost. For example, reachability is in NLOGSPACE, while regular path queries are only known to be in P [28], and alternating reachability is P-complete; the classic Eulerian path problem can be solved in polynomial time, while the constrained variant is NP-complete [25]; finding a max spanning-tree can be done in polynomial time, whereas even evaluating a given strategy for the max player in a spanning-tree game is NP-hard [21].

A classical problem to which both the label-graph and game-graph extensions have been applied is the *maximum-flow problem* [10,17]. A *flow network* is a directed graph where each edge has a capacity. The capacity is a bound on the amount of flow that can go through each edge. The amount of flow entering a vertex must be the same as the amount of flow leaving the vertex, except for the *source* vertex, which only has outgoing flow, and the *target* vertex, which only has incoming flow. The maximum-flow problem is, given a flow network with source and target vertices, to determine the maximum flow that can go from the source to the target. The maximum-flow problem was first studied in the 1950s [13,14], and has been researched extensively since then [2,11,18], with applications in routing, scheduling, and more.

Flow networks on labeled graphs were introduced by means of *capacitated automata* with a *utilization semantics* [3,24]. Capacitated automata are finite word automata in which each transition has a capacity. In the utilization semantics of capacitated automata, the automata are viewed as accepting multiple words simultaneously, while respecting the capacity of each transition. Thus, an automaton mutually accepts a *multiset* of words if there is a multiset of accepting runs on these words, such that the number of times each transition is traversed by the runs is at most its capacity. The set of multisets mutually accepted by a capacitated automaton is its *multi-language*. The *maximum restricted-utilization* problem gets as input a capacitated automaton and a specification, and searches for the biggest multiset of words in the multi-language that contains only words that satisfy the specification. This problem is equivalent to an extension of the maximum-flow problem to labeled graphs. Indeed, capacitated automata are equivalent to labeled graphs, with states as vertices and capacitated transitions as labeled edges. In addition, each unit of flow in the network corresponds to a word, and so a flow in the network corresponds to a multiset of words. Thus, maximizing the number of words that are mutually accepted is the same as maximizing the flow that reaches the target along paths that satisfy the specification. It is shown in [24] that the maximum restricted-utilization problem is APX-complete. Thus, it is NP-complete, and there exists a constant c such that it is already NP-hard to approximate it within a multiplicative factor of c. When the specification contains only words of length at most 2, the problem can be solved in polynomial time.

Flow networks in a game setting were introduced and studied in [19,27]. In *flow games*, the vertices of a flow network are partitioned between two players. Each player controls the flow through her vertices, by directing flow entering her vertices to outgoing edges. The goal of Player 0, the authority, is to maximize the total flow that reaches the target source, while Player 1, the environment, tries to minimize the flow. A *policy* for a vertex maps incoming flow to a function describing how the incoming flow is partitioned between the edges leaving that vertex. A policy for the source vertex assigns a flow to each outgoing edge, bounded by the edge's capacity. A strategy for a player consists of policies for all of her vertices. We consider *acyclic* flow networks. Then, given strategies for both players, calculating the flow in the game can be done in polynomial time. Finding the maximal flow in the game, as well as the optimal strategy for Player 0, is Σ_2^P-complete, and it is already Σ_2^P-hard to approximate. In the *unfortunate-flow problem* [26], the edges leaving the source are saturated, and all vertices besides the source are controlled by Player 1. The problem of finding the maximum flow in this case is co-NP-hard. Thus, the setting corresponds to evacuation scenarios, where we want to analyze the amount of flow that is guaranteed to reach the target when the most unfortunate routing decisions are made. In the multi-player variant [19] of flow games, the vertices are partitioned between multiple players. Each player has a target vertex, and she tries to maximize the flow entering her own target. A *Nash Equilibrium* in a multi-player flow game is a set of strategies, one for each player, such that for every player, changing her own strategy does not increase the flow entering her target vertex. There exist multi-player flow games with no Nash Equilibrium, and the problem of deciding whether there exists a Nash Equilibrium in a given multi-player flow game is Σ_2^P-complete.

Example 1. Consider the labeled flow network N in the figure below. We represent vertices of Player 0 by circles and vertices of Player 1 by squares. Sinks are represented by filled circles. The labels are defined over the alphabet $\Sigma = \{a, b, c\}$. In the classical max-flow problem, the max flow in the network is 4. Indeed, 3 units of flow can travel via u, and 1 unit of flow can travel via v.

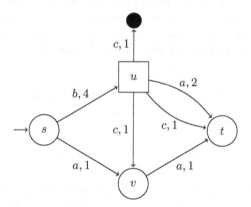

Consider the capacitated automaton obtained from N if we ignore the partition of the vertices between the players and the sink. Its language consists of the multisets $\{aa, ba, ba, bc\}$ and $\{bca, ba, ba, bc\}$. Consider a specification $(a + b)^*$. In the maximum restricted-utilization problem with this specification, the network needs to process only words that contain only a's and b's, and can thus process the multiset $\{aa, ba, ba\}$, inducing a flow of 3 units. For the specification $\Sigma^* \cdot c \cdot \Sigma^*$, where only words that contain c are needed, the network can process only 2 units of flow, induced by the multiset $\{bca, bc\}$.

Now, if we ignore the labels and analyze N as a flow game, a strategy for Player 0 saturates all edges leaving the source, so 5 units of flow leave s. An optimal strategy for Player 1 then direct one unit of flow entering u to a sink, one unit to v, and two units to t. The incoming flow to v is 2, while its outgoing capacity is 1. Thus, one unit of flow is lost, and one is directed to t. The flow in this case is 3, and it is the maximal flow Player 0 can ensure.   □

We introduce and study *restricted flow games* (RFGs), an extension of flow games to graphs that are both labeled and game graph. As in flow games, the vertices in an RFG are partitioned between two players, and each player directs the flow entering the vertices in her control. The input in RFGs includes a specification. The goal of Player 0, the authority, is to maximize the number of units of flow that reach the target vertex via paths that induce words that satisfy the specification. Player 1 corresponds to the environment, and tries to minimize the number of such units of flow, either by directing them into sinks (namely, vertices that have no outgoing edges), into vertices whose incoming flow is greater than their outgoing capacity, or through paths that do not satisfy the specification.

The strategies of the players in RFGs are the same as in flow games. Thus, they consist of policies for the vertices. Consequently, strategies are independent of the "history" of the units of flow entering their vertices, i.e., the path each unit of flow has traversed before reaching the vertex. While this enables a compact representation of strategies, it creates ambiguity in the path each unit of flow traverses. Indeed, given the incoming flow to some vertex, the player controlling this vertex can direct the flow into different outgoing edges, but we cannot determine which unit of flow goes to which outgoing edge. For example, consider the RFG below, and assume the edges leaving s are saturated.

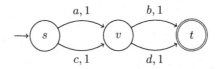

Since the incoming flow to v is 2, the strategy for Player 0 saturates both outgoing edges. However, the strategy does not determine whether the flow traversing the a-labeled edge is directed to the b-labeled edge or the d-labeled edge, and so, its path might correspond to either ab or ad. Respectively, the path starting in the c-labeled edge might be labeled by either cd or cb.

In order to address this, we define two variants of RFGs: the maximal variant, which considers the "best-case scenario" for Player 0, and the minimal variant, which considers the "worst-case scenario" for Player 0. Formally, given a flow in the network $f : E \rightarrow \mathbb{N}$, a *decomposition* of the flow is a multiset of paths P from the source to the target in the network, such that the number of times each edge is traversed by paths in P is at most the flow through the edge. A decomposition P is *complete* if for every edge entering the target vertex, the number of times the edge is traversed in P is equal to the flow through the edge. Each decomposition of f is a possible outcome of the players directing the flow. Given a decomposition P, we consider the multiset of words $\ell(P)$ corresponding to the paths in P. Thus, in the example above, there are two complete decompositions P_1 and P_2, with $\ell(P_1) = \{ab, cd\}$ and $\ell(P_2) = \{ad, cb\}$. In the max variant, the outcome is the decomposition that maximizes the number of words in the specification. In the min variant, the outcome is the complete decomposition that minimizes this number.

Example 2. Consider an RFG played on the flow network shown in Example 1 with the specification $(a + b)^*$. If Player 0 and Player 1 play as described in Example 1, then Player 1 needs to decide through which edge from u to t to direct the flow. An optimal strategy for Player 1 directs one unit of flow through each outgoing edge. Thus, one unit of flow traverses the c-labeled edge, and does not satisfy the specification. The other unit of flow entering u is directed to the a-labeled edge, and corresponds to the word ba, which satisfies the specification.

The incoming flow to v is 2, and so one unit of flow is lost and one is directed to t. Since Player 0 does not know the history of the flow entering v, we do not know which of the two units is lost and which is directed to t. In the maximal variant, the best case for Player 0 is considered, and so the unit of flow entering v from s is directed to t, and corresponds to the word aa, which satisfies the specification. Thus, the flow in the maximal variant is 2. Alternatively, in the minimal variant, the flow reaching v from s is lost, while the unit of flow reaching v from u is directed to t, but corresponds to a word not satisfying the specification. Thus, the flow in the minimal variant is 1. □

Analyzing the complexity of RFGs, we consider specifications given by automata and distinguish between different branching modes of the automaton: deterministic (DFA, which has a single run on every input word), nondeterministic (NFA, which may have several runs, and one of them has to be accepting), or universal (UFA, which may have several runs, all have to be accepting).

We start by studying the complexity of calculating the outcome of an RFG. That is, given strategies for both players, we calculate the number of words that satisfy the specification in the maximal and minimal decompositions. For this problem, as well as all subsequent problems we study, we consider the corresponding decision problem, parameterized by a threshold.

As mentioned above, calculating the flow in the game can be done in polynomial time. However, finding the maximal and minimal decompositions requires an additional computation. We show that for all types of automata, calculating the outcome is NP-complete for the maximal variant, and is co-NP-complete for the minimal variant. We proceed to consider the problem of determining the *positivity* of the outcome, namely whether the maximal or minimal outcome is positive or is 0. This is the special case of the general problem when the threshold is 1, and is of interest in settings where we do not care about loss of flow as long as at least one unit of flow is guaranteed to reach the target. We show that in the maximal variant, determining whether the outcome is positive is NP-complete when the specification is given by a UFA, but becomes NLOGSPACE-complete when it is given by a DFA or an NFA. In the minimal variant, determining the positivity is co-NP-complete for all types of automata.

We continue and study the complexity of the main problem in the context of RFG, namely finding the value of a given game in the maximal and minimal variants, as well as an optimal strategy for Player 0. That is, given an RFG, we find the strategy for Player 0 that ensures the best outcome against Player 1's best response, and the outcome in that case. The differences in the complexity of calculating the outcome and its positivity carry over to this problem:

NP-completeness translates to an additional quantifier alternation and a "step up" in the polynomial hierarchy, compared to the Σ_2^P-completeness in flow games, whereas co-NP-completeness does not. Thus, finding the flow is Σ_3^P-complete in the maximal variant, and is Σ_2^P-complete in the minimal variant. Similarly, when considering the problem of determining the positivity of the value, the maximal universal variant is Σ_3^P-complete, while all other variants are Σ_2^P-complete.

Our results, as well as directions for future research, are summarized in Sect. 5.

2   Preliminaries

2.1   Automata

An *automaton* is $\mathcal{A} = \langle \Sigma, Q, Q_0, \Delta, F \rangle$, where Σ is a finite alphabet, Q is a finite set of states, $Q_0 \subseteq Q$ is a set of initial states, $\Delta \subseteq Q \times \Sigma \times Q$ is a transition relation, and $F \subseteq Q$ is a set of final states. If $|Q_0| = 1$, and for all $q \in Q$ and $\sigma \in \Sigma$, there is at most one $q' \in Q$ such that $\langle q, \sigma, q' \rangle \in \Delta$, then we say that $\mathcal{A}$ is deterministic, or a DFA, for short. The size of $\mathcal{A}$ is given by $|Q|$.

A *run* of $\mathcal{A}$ on a word $w = w_1 \cdots w_n \in \Sigma^*$ is $r = q_0, q_1, \ldots, q_n$, such that $q_0 \in Q_0$ and for all $0 \le i < n$, we have that $\langle q_i, w_{i+1}, q_{i+1} \rangle \in \Delta$. We say that r is *accepting* if $q_n \in F$. Let $w \in \Sigma^*$. Note that if $\mathcal{A}$ is deterministic, then there is a unique run of $\mathcal{A}$ on w. In this case, we say that w is accepted by $\mathcal{A}$ if the unique run of $\mathcal{A}$ on w is accepting. Alternatively, $\mathcal{A}$ may be *nondeterministic* or *universal*, denoted NFA and UFA, respectively. If $\mathcal{A}$ is nondeterministic, we say that w is accepted by $\mathcal{A}$ if there *exists* an accepting run of $\mathcal{A}$ on w. If $\mathcal{A}$ is universal, we say that w is accepted by $\mathcal{A}$ if *every* run of $\mathcal{A}$ on w is accepting. The language of $\mathcal{A}$, denoted $L(\mathcal{A})$, is the set of words in Σ^* that are accepted by $\mathcal{A}$.

2.2   Flow Games

A *flow network* is a tuple $N = \langle V, E, c, s, t \rangle$, where V is a set of vertices, $E \subseteq V \times V$ is a set of directed edges, $c : E \to \mathbb{N}$ is a capacity function, and $s, t \in V$ are source and target vertices. We assume that t is reachable from s and that the capacities are given in unary. A *flow game* [27] is $\mathcal{G} = \langle V_0, V_1, E, c, s, t \rangle$, such that $\langle V_0 \cup V_1, E, c, s, t \rangle$ is an acyclic flow network whose vertices are partitioned between two players, denoted Player 0 and Player 1. Each player controls the vertices in its vertex set. Player 0 tries to maximize the flow in the network and Player 1 tries to minimize the flow.

For a vertex $u \in V$, let E^u and E_u be the sets of incoming and outgoing edges to and from u, respectively. That is, $E^u = (V \times \{u\}) \cap E$ and $E_u = (\{u\} \times V) \cap E$. A *policy* for a vertex $u \in V$, for $u \ne s$, is a function that partitions an incoming flow between the outgoing edges. Formally, a policy for u is a function $f_u : \mathbb{N} \to \mathbb{N}^{E_u}$ such that for every flow $x \in \mathbb{N}$ and edge $e \in E_u$, we have $f_u(x)(e) \le c(e)$ and $\sum_{e \in E_u} f_u(x)(e) = \min\{x, \sum_{e \in E_u} c(e)\}$. Thus, $f_u(x)$ assigns to each edge outgoing from u a flow that is bounded by its capacity. Also, when the incoming flow is larger than the capacity of the outgoing edges (which bounds the outgoing flow), then flow is *lost* and the outgoing flow is lower than the incoming flow. In practice, loss of flow may correspond to leaks – fluid in a pipe system that is lost when the system is overflowed, to traffic that gets stuck – in jammed road systems, or to packets that are thrown by routers all whose outgoing channels are filled. Note that this is different from the traditional definition of flow in a network, which corresponds to the case all vertices belong to Player 0, and in which the "flow conservation" property is respected. Note also that $f_u(0)(e) = 0$ for every e. For the source vertex s, a policy is a function $f_s \in \mathbb{N}^{E_s}$ such that for every edge $e \in E_s$, we have $f_s(e) \leq c(e)$.

A *flow* in a flow game is a function $f \in \mathbb{N}^E$ that assigns to each edge the flow that travels in it. We require that for every edge $e \in E_u$, we have $f(e) \leq c(e)$, and for every vertex $u \in V$, except for s and t, we have $\sum_{e \in E_u} f(e) = \min\{\sum_{e \in E^u} f(e), \sum_{e \in E_u} c(e)\}$. That is, the flow in each edge is bounded by its capacity, and the flow that leaves each vertex is the minimum between the flow that enters the vertex and the sum of the capacities of edges outgoing from it. We focus on the case where the graph $\langle V, E \rangle$ is acyclic. Then, given policies f_u for all vertices in $u \in V$, we can calculate the flow in the game as follows. First, we order the vertices in a topological ordering. Then, we start from the vertex s (we ignore every vertex preceding s), and use f_s to assign a flow to each edge in E_s. Now, we continue to the next vertex in the topological ordering. Whenever we reach a vertex u, the incoming flow to u, denoted x, has already been calculated. We then use $f_u(x)$ to assign a flow for each edge in E_u, and continue along the topological ordering until we reach t. Since the flow that enters a vertex u depends only on the sub-game that reaches u, it is easy to see that the calculation above is independent of the topological ordering. Indeed, if u_1 and u_2 are not ordered, then flow that leaves u_1 does not reach u_2, and vice versa.

A strategy for Player i is a collection of policies, one for each vertex in V_i. Let F_0 and F_1 be the sets of all possible strategies of Player 0 and Player 1 respectively. Given strategies $\alpha \in F_0$ and $\beta \in F_1$, the flow in the game, denoted $f^{\alpha,\beta}$, can be calculated in polynomial time as described above.

2.3   Restricted Flow Games

A *restricted flow game*, RFG for short, is $\mathcal{G} = \langle \Sigma, V_0, V_1, E, c, s, t, L \rangle$, and it extends a flow game by a finite alphabet Σ and a regular language $L \subseteq \Sigma^*$, which we call the *specification*. In addition, the transition relation is $E \subseteq V \times \Sigma \times V$, thus each edge is labeled by a letter in Σ. Now, the goal of Player 0 is to maximize the number of units of flow that reach t, while traversing a path labeled by a word in L. That is, every unit of flow that reaches t is associated with the labels of the edges it traversed on its path from s to t. These labels are concatenated and form a word in Σ^*. Player 0 tries to maximize the number of such words that are in L.

We define the size of the graph of $\mathcal{G}$ as $\sum_{e \in E} c(e)$. Note that our definition corresponds to a representation of the graph with capacities given in unary. The specification L is given by an automaton $\mathcal{A}$ over the alphabet Σ, thus $L = L(\mathcal{A})$. The size of the specification is defined to be the size of $\mathcal{A}$, and the size of $\mathcal{G}$ is the sum of the sizes of its graph and its specification. We indicate the type of $\mathcal{A}$ with the letter $\lambda \in \{D, N, U\}$, indicating whether it is a DFA, NFA, or UFA.

The definitions of policies, strategies, and their outcome are similar to their definitions in unrestricted flow games, except that now, $E^u = E \cap (V \times \Sigma \times \{u\})$ and $E_u = E \cap (\{u\} \times \Sigma \times V)$. Note that possibly $\langle v, \sigma_1, u \rangle, \langle v, \sigma_2, u \rangle \in E$ for $\sigma_1 \neq \sigma_2$, and the function c assigns capacity to labeled edges.

Note that policies determine the outgoing flow based on the incoming flow alone. The *history* of the flow, namely, the path traversed by each unit of flow, is unknown. A representation of policies that do depend on the history of the incoming flow is more complex (see discussion in Sect. 5.1). Our setting, where we give up dependency in the history result in simpler strategies but creates ambiguity in determining the outcome of the game, which we discuss below.

Given an edge $e = (v_1, \sigma, v_2) \in E$, we denote by $\ell(e) = \sigma$ the label of the edge. We expand ℓ to paths. Thus, given a path $\rho = e_1, \ldots, e_m$ such that for every $1 \leq i \leq m$, we have $e_i \in E$, we define $\ell(\rho) = \ell(e_1) \cdot \ell(e_2) \cdots \ell(e_m)$. We then expend ℓ to multisets of paths. A *multiset* is a generalization of a set in which each element may appear more than once. We use multisets, as paths may have a flow greater than 1 flowing through them. Given a multiset of paths $P = \{\rho_1 \ldots, \rho_m\}$, we define $\ell(P) = \{\ell(\rho_1), \ldots, \ell(\rho_m)\}$. Note that $\ell(P)$ is a multiset of words in Σ^*.

Let $P = \{\rho_1, \ldots, \rho_m\}$ be a multiset of paths in $\langle E, V \rangle$, such that for every $1 \leq i \leq m$, we have that $\rho_i = e_1^i, \ldots, e_{k_i}^i$ is a path in $\langle E, V \rangle$ with $e_1^i \in E_s$ and $e_{k_i}^i \in E^t$. Let $f \in \mathbb{N}^E$ be a flow function. We say that P is a *decomposition* of f if for every $e \in E$ it holds that $|\{(i, j) : 1 \leq i \leq m, 1 \leq j \leq k_i \text{ and } e_j^i = e\}| \leq f(e)$. That is, the number of times every edge $e \in E$ is traversed in paths in P is at most the flow through e. We say that P is *complete* if, additionally, it contains all paths reaching t. That is, for every $e \in E^t$ it holds that $|\{(i, j) : 1 \leq i \leq m, 1 \leq j \leq k_i \text{ and } e_j^i = e\}| = f(e)$. Since flow can get lost in the game, we do not require equality for all edges.

For a multiset M of words in Σ^*, we denote by M_L the restriction of M to words from L. That is, $M_L = \{w \in M : w \in L\}$. Then, for a decomposition P of f, the goal of Player 0 is to maximize the number of words in $\ell(P)$ that are also in L, namely, $|\ell(P)_L|$.

As Example 3 below demonstrates, a given the flow in the game may have several decompositions.

Example 3. See for example the RFG below.

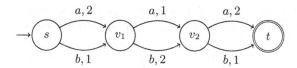

Let f be a flow function described in the numbers labeling the edges (that is, the numbers labeling the edges in this example represent flow, rather than capacity). Let $L = a^* + b^*$ be the specification.

Let $\rho_1 = (s, a, v_1), (v_1, b, v_2), (v_2, a, t)$ and $\rho_2 = (s, b, v_1), (v_1, a, v_2), (v_2, b, t)$ be paths in the game. It is easy to verify that the multiset $P = \{\rho_1, \rho_1, \rho_2\}$ is a decomposition of the flow function f and that $\ell(P) = \{aba, aba, bab\}$. Thus, $\ell(P)_L = \emptyset$. Alternatively, let $\rho_3 = (s, a, v_1), (v_1, a, v_2), (v_2, a, t)$ and $\rho_4 = (s, b, v_1), (v_1, b, v_2), (v_2, b, t)$ be paths in the game. The multiset $P' = \{\rho_1, \rho_3, \rho_4\}$ is also a decomposition of f, with $\ell(P') = \{aba, aaa, bbb\}$. Thus, $\ell(P')_L = \{aaa, bbb\}$. In particular, we get that $|\ell(P)_L| \neq |\ell(P')_L|$. $\qquad\square$

We define two variants of restricted flow games. One where we consider the most beneficial decomposition to Player 0, and one where we consider the least beneficial decomposition to Player 0. In both settings, Player 0 plays first and determines the policies for all her vertices. This models the fact that we want the setting to capture the most hostile environment when we refer to the flow itself.

In the first variant, which we call the maximal variant, the outcome of the game is given by

$$outcome\_max(\alpha, \beta) = \max\{|\ell(P)_L| : P \text{ is a decomposition of } f^{\alpha, \beta}\}.$$

We refer to a decomposition that achieves the maximum value as a maximal decomposition, and denote it (one of them, in case of multiplicity) by P_{max}. The maximal value of an RFG is then given by

$$rval\_max(\mathcal{G}) = \max_{\alpha \in F_0} \min_{\beta \in F_1} outcome\_max(\alpha, \beta).$$

That is, given strategies for both player, we take the decomposition that maximizes the number of words in the specification. This corresponds to a setting in which Player 0 plays first and determines the policies for all her vertices, then Player 1 responds by determining the policies for all her vertices, and finally, Player 0 chooses a decomposition that benefits her the most.

In the second variant, which we call the minimal variant, the outcome of the game is given by

$$outcome\_min(\alpha, \beta) = \min\{|\ell(P)_L| : P \text{ is a complete decomposition of } f^{\alpha, \beta}\}.$$

Since we are taking the minimal outcome, we require P to be a complete decomposition. Otherwise, we would have that for $P = \emptyset$, the outcome is always 0. We refer to a complete decomposition that achieves the minimal value as a minimal decomposition, and denote it by P_{min}. The minimal value of an RFG is then given by

$$rval\_min(\mathcal{G}) = \max_{\alpha \in F_0} \min_{\beta \in F_1} outcome\_min(\alpha, \beta).$$

This corresponds to a setting in which Player 0 plays first and determines the policies for all her vertices, and then Player 1 responds by determining the policies for all her vertices, and choosing a complete decomposition of the obtained flow in a way that benefits Player 0 the least.

3 Calculating the Outcome in Restricted Flow Games

In this section we study the complexity of calculating the outcome in RFGs. Recall that in the unrestricted settings, calculating the outcome of the game, given strategies for both players, can be done in polynomial time [27]. We show that in restricted flow games, calculating the maximal and minimal outcomes is NP-complete and co-NP-complete, respectively, and is independent of the branching mode of the specification automaton. On the other hand, determining whether the maximal outcome is positive depends on the representation of the specification, is NP-complete for specifications given by a UFA, and is NLOGSPACE-complete for ones given by a n NFA or DFA.

We consider the corresponding decision problems, which are parameterized by a threshold. Formally, for $\lambda \in \{U, N, D\}$, the input to a λ-*maximal outcome* problem, denoted λ-OUTCOME-MAX, is an RFG $\mathcal{G}$ with a specification given by a λ-auotmaton, a flow $f : E \rightarrow \mathbb{N}$ in $\mathcal{G}$, and a threshold $\gamma \in \mathbb{N}$. The goal is to decide whether there exists a decomposition P of f such that $|\ell(P)_L| \geq \gamma$. The input to a λ-*minimal outcome* problem (denoted λ-OUTCOME-MIN) is the same, but the goal is to decide whether for all complete decompositions of f it holds that $|\ell(P)_L| \geq \gamma$. Then, the input to the λ-*positive maximal outcome* and λ-*positive minimal outcome* problems, denoted λ-OUTCOME-MAX+ and λ-OUTCOME-MIN+, respectively, is similar, except that γ is not given, as it is fixed to 1. Thus, the goal in the max variant is to decide whether there exists a decomposition P of f such that $|\ell(P)_L| > 0$, and in the min variant to decide whether for all complete decompositions P of f, it holds that $|\ell(P)_L| > 0$.

3.1 Solving the Maximal and Minimal Outcome Problems

We start with the λ-maximal and λ-minimal outcome problems. For the lower bounds, we use reductions from the maximum 3-bounded 3-dimensional matching problem (3DM-3 problem, for short), shown to be APX-hard in [22]. That is, there exists a constant c such that it is NP-hard to find an approximation algorithm with approximation ratio better than c. In particular, it is NP-hard to solve the problem exactly. A similar reduction was shown in [24], from the 3DM-3 problem to the maximum restricted utilization problem of capacitated automata. In fact, we can show a simple reduction from the maximum restricted utilization problem to the D-maximal outcome problem, but we reduce directly from the 3DM-3 problem for completeness.

The input to the 3DM-3 problem is a set of triples $T \subseteq X \times Y \times Z$, where $|X| = |Y| = |Z| = n$. The number of occurrences of every element of $X \cup Y \cup Z$ in T is at most 3. The number of triples is $|T| \geq n$. The desired output is a 3-dimensional matching in T of maximal cardinality; i.e., a subset $T' \subseteq T$, such that every element of $X \cup Y \cup Z$ appears at most once in T', and $|T'|$ is maximal. The equivalent decision problem is parameterized by a threshold.

Theorem 1. *The λ-OUTCOME-MAX problem is NP-complete, for $\lambda \in \{U, N, D\}$.*

Proof. First, for every $\gamma \geq 1$, if $outcome\_max(\alpha, \beta) \geq \gamma$ then there is a decomposition P of f such that $|\ell(P)_L| \geq \gamma$. The decomposition P is a polynomial witness. Indeed, we can verify that P is a decomposition of f by counting the number of traversals of each edge in the graph. Calculating $\ell(P)$ requires one iteration over the edges in each path. We then count the number of words in $\ell(P)$ that are also in L. This can also be done in polynomial time for universal, nondeterministic and deterministic automata. Finally, the number of edges traversed in P is bounded by the total capacity of the game. Since capacities are given in unary, the total capacity is polynomial in the input, and so is the length of P.

We show the lower bound for the most restricted case, namely $\lambda = D$, by reducing from the 3DM-3 problem.

Given sets X, Y and Z with $|X| = |Y| = |Z| = n$, and a set of triples $T \subseteq X \times Y \times Z$, we construct an RFG $\mathcal{G} = \langle \Sigma, V_0, V_1, E, c, s, t, L \rangle$, as shown in Fig. 1. First, $\Sigma = X \cup Y \cup Z$, $V_0 = \{v_0, v_1, v_2, v_3\}$, $V_1 = \emptyset$, $s = v_0$ and $t = v_3$. As for edges and capacities, there are n edges from each vertex to the next one, all with capacity 1. The edges from v_0 to v_1 correspond to elements in X, the edges from v_1 to v_2 correspond to elements in Y, and the edges from v_2 to v_3 correspond to elements in Z. Formally, $E = (\{v_0\} \times X \times \{v_1\}) \cup (\{v_1\} \times Y \times \{v_2\}) \cup (\{v_2\} \times Z \times \{v_3\})$, and $c \equiv 1$. We then define the flow in $\mathcal{G}$ to be $f \equiv 1$. That is, we have a flow of 1 in all edges.

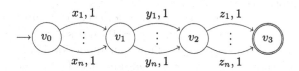

Fig. 1. The flow network in $\mathcal{G}$

To complete the reduction, let $L = \{x \cdot y \cdot z : (x, y, z) \in T\}$. Note that since the 3DM instance is 3-bounded, we have that $|L| = O(n)$. Thus, we can describe L by a DFA with $O(n)$ states.

We claim that for every $\gamma \geq 1$, the maximal matching T_{max} satisfies $|T_{max}| \geq \gamma$ iff the maximal decomposition P_{max} of f satisfies $|\ell(P_{max})_L| \geq \gamma$.

Every matching $T' \subseteq T$ corresponds to a set P of paths in $\mathcal{G}$. Since every element of $X \cup Y \cup Z$ appears at most once in a matching, every edge in the set of paths is traversed at most once. Thus, P is a decomposition of f. In addition, since $T' \subseteq T$, we have that for every $w \in \ell(P)$, it holds that $w \in L$. It follows that $|\ell(P)_L| = |P| = |T'|$.

Conversely, for decomposition P of f, denote by $P' \subseteq P$ the multiset of paths in P that corresponds to words in L. That is, $\ell(P)_L = \ell(P')_L = \ell(P')$. Let $T' \subseteq T$ be the subset of T corresponding to the paths in P'. Since P is a decomposition of f, we know that every edge appears at most once in P, and in particular, in P'. Thus, T' is a matching such that $|T'| = |P'| = |\ell(P)_L|$.

Hence, $|T_{max}| \geq \gamma$ iff $|\ell(P_{max})_L| \geq \gamma$, and we are done. $\square$

Theorem 2. *The λ-OUTCOME-MIN problem is co-NP-complete, for $\lambda \in \{U, N, D\}$.*

Proof. First, for every $\gamma \geq 1$, if $outcome\_min(\alpha, \beta) < \gamma$, then there is a decomposition P of f such that $|\ell(P)_L| < \gamma$. The decomposition P is a polynomial witness. As we have shown in the proof of Theorem 1, the size of P is polynomial in the input and we can verify it in polynomial time.

We show the lower bound for the most restricted case, namely $\lambda = D$. We modify the reduction from the 3DM-3 problem shown in Theorem 1, such that a maximal matching would induce a minimal complete decomposition. Thus, we reduce from the complement of the 3DM-3 problem.

Given an instance of the 3DM-3 problem, we construct a game $\mathcal{G}$ and flow f as in the proof of Theorem 1. We then define the specification to be $L' = \{x \cdot y \cdot z : (x, y, z) \notin T\}$. That is, the set of words corresponding to triples that are not in T. Recall the specification L described in the proof of Theorem 1, and consider $\bar{L}$, namely, the set of words that are not in L. We have that $L' = \bar{L} \cap (X \cdot Y \cdot Z)$. We can describe $\bar{L}$ by a DFA with $O(n)$ states, and $X \cdot Y \cdot Z$ by a DFA with $O(1)$ states. Thus, we can describe their intersection L' by a DFA with $O(n)$ states. Finally, we set $\gamma' = \max\{0, n - \gamma + 1\}$.

We claim that the maximal matching T_{max} satisfies $|T_{max}| < \gamma$ iff the minimal decomposition satisfies $\ell(P_{min})_{L'} \geq \gamma'$.

First, in case $\gamma > n$, we know that $|T| < \gamma$ for every matching T, in particular T_{max}. In addition, $\gamma > n$ implies that $\gamma' = 0$, and so $\ell(P)_{L'} \geq \gamma'$ for every decomposition P, in particular P_{min}. Thus, our reduction holds.

Assume now that $|T_{max}| < \gamma \leq n$, and let P be the corresponding decomposition of f. Namely, for every $(x, y, z) \in T_{max}$, P contains the path $(v_0, x, v_1), (v_1, y, v_2), (v_2, z, v_3)$. We note that P is not a complete decomposition, since its size is less than n. Consider some choice of paths P' such that $P \cup P'$ is a complete decomposition of f. There must exist such a choice, since the incoming and outgoing flow of all vertices is n. In addition, since T_{max} is a maximal matching, the paths in P' must correspond to triples that are not in T. Denote $P'' = P \cup P'$. Since T_{max} is maximal, we get that P'' is minimal. Finally,

$|\ell(P'')_{L'}| = |\ell(P)_{L'}| + |\ell(P')_{L'}| = 0 + (n - |T_{max}|) > n - \gamma = \gamma' - 1$, and thus $|\ell(P'')_{L'}| \geq \gamma'$.

Conversely, assume that there is matching $T' \subseteq T$ such that $|T'| \geq \gamma$. Let P be the decomposition induced by T', and let P' be an expansion of P as above. Denote $P'' = P \cup P'$. We get that $|\ell(P'')_{L'}| = n - |T'| \leq n - \gamma < \gamma'$. Thus, $|\ell(P_{min})_{L'}| \leq |\ell(P'')_{L'}| < \gamma'$.

Hence, $|T_{max}| < \gamma$ iff $|\ell(P_{min})_{L'}| \geq \gamma'$, and we are done. $\square$

3.2   Solving the Positive Maximal and Minimal Outcome Problems

We now consider the problem of determining whether the maximal and minimal outcomes are positive, thus deciding the λ-positive maximal and minimal outcome problems. We show that in some cases, depending on λ, solving the λ-OUTCOME-MAX$^+$ problem is easier than the general case. However, solving the λ-OUTCOME-MIN$^+$ problem is as hard as the general problem for all $\lambda \in \{U, N, D\}$.

Note that since every algorithm that approximates the solution of a problem within a multiplicative factor can determine whether the solution is positive or is 0, a lower bound for the complexity of solving the positivity problems is also a lower bound for all approximation algorithms.

We start with some simple constructions that we later use in our reductions.

Let $X = \{x_1, \ldots, x_n\}$ be a set of variables. We encode an assignment to X as a word $w \in \{T, F\}^n$ in the expected way. Thus, if $w = w_1 \cdots w_n$, then for every $1 \leq i \leq n$, the value of x_i is w_i. Consider a Boolean formula ψ over X. Let $L_\psi \subseteq \{T, F\}^n$ be the set of encodings of assignments to X that satisfy ψ. We say that ψ is in *conjunctive normal form*, CNF for short, if it is a conjunction of clauses, where a clause is a disjunction of literals. Alternatively, we say that ψ is in *disjunctive normal form*, DNF for short, if it is a disjunction of clauses, where a clause is a conjunction of literals. We show that when ψ is given in CNF or DNF, we can recognize L_ψ with a UFA or an NFA, respectively, whose number of states is polynomial in the size of ψ. We note that we prove this for a simple encoding over $\{T, F\}$. In further proofs, we might use an encoding over $\{T, F, \$\}$, where $\$$ is used as a delimiter. Modifying the proof to accommodate for the different encodings is simple.

Lemma 1. *Let ψ be a Boolean formula over $X = \{x_1, \ldots, x_n\}$. Let L_ψ be the set of encodings of assignments that satisfy ψ. Then*

1. *If ψ is given in DNF, there is an NFA of size $O(|\psi|)$ that recognizes L_ψ.*
2. *If ψ is given in CNF, there is a UFA of size $O(|\psi|)$ that recognizes L_ψ.*

Proof. First, assume that ψ is in DNF. Thus, there are clauses $c_1, \ldots, c_k$ such that $\psi = \bigvee_{i=1}^{k} c_i$, and each clause is a conjunction of literals.

We claim that we can recognize L_ψ with an NFA $\mathcal{A}_\psi$ with $k \cdot (n+1)$ states. The NFA $\mathcal{A}_\psi$ is the union of k DFAs, one for each clause in ψ. For every clause c_i, we construct a DFA with states $q_0, \ldots, q_n$, where q_0 is the initial state and

q_n is the accepting state. For every $1 \leq j \leq n$, the state q_{j-1} corresponds to the variable x_j, and is connected to q_j. If x_j appears in c_i, there is a transition from q_{j-1} to q_j when reading T. If $\bar{x}_j$ appears in c_i, there is a transition from q_{j-1} to q_j when reading F. If neither appear, there is a transition from q_{j-1} to q_j when reading either T or F. The NFA $\mathcal{A}_\psi$ is the union of the DFAs, obtained by putting them side-by-side. Indeed, a word in their union encodes an assignment to X, such that at least in one of the clauses, all of the literals have positive value.

We assume now that ψ is in CNF. Thus, $\neg\psi$ is in DNF, and there is an NFA $\mathcal{A}$ of size $O(|\psi|)$ with $L(\mathcal{A}) = L_{\neg\psi}$. Let $\mathcal{A}'$ be the UFA obtained from $\mathcal{A}$ by setting $F' = Q \setminus F$. It is easy to verify that $L(\mathcal{A}') = \overline{L_{\neg\psi}}$. In addition, we know that $L_\psi = \{T, F\}^n \cap \overline{L_{\neg\psi}}$. We can recognize $\{T, F\}^n$ with a DFA of size $O(n)$. It follows that we can recognize the intersection $\{T, F\}^n \cap \overline{L_{\neg\psi}}$ by putting $\mathcal{A}'$ and the DFA side-by-side. The obtained UFA is of size $O(|\psi|)$, and recognizes L_ψ. $\square$

We now use this construction to prove NP-hardness of the U-OUTCOME-MAX$^+$ problem.

Theorem 3. *The U-OUTCOME-MAX$^+$ problem is NP-complete.*

Proof. Membership in NP follows from Theorem 1.

For the lower bound, we reduce from SAT. Let $X = \{x_1, \ldots, x_n\}$ be a set of variables, and ψ be a Boolean formula over X given in CNF. We encode an assignment to X as described above. We construct a game $\mathcal{G}$ as follows. First, $\Sigma = \{T, F\}$, $V_0 = \{v_i : 1 \leq i \leq n\} \cup \{t\}$, $V_1 = \emptyset$, and $s = v_1$. That is, we have $n + 1$ vertices, one for each variable in X, and a target vertex. For each v_i, we have two outgoing edges, one labeled with T and one with F. The last variable vertex, v_n, is connected to the target vertex t. Formally,

$$E = \{(v_i, T, v_{i+1}), (v_i, F, v_{i+1}) : 1 \leq i \leq n-1\} \cup \{(v_n, T, t), (v_n, F, t)\}.$$

We define the capacity c and the flow f to be 1 in all edges. Finally, we define the specification L_ψ to be the set of all encodings of assignments to X that satisfy ψ. By Lemma 1, we can recognize L_ψ with a UFA of size $O(|\psi|)$.

We claim that there exists a decomposition P of f with $|\ell(P)_{L_\psi}| > 0$ iff ψ is satisfiable.

We identify a path in $\mathcal{G}$ with an assignment to X. Indeed, every path ρ_1 from v_0 to t must have $\ell(\rho_1) \in \{T, F\}^n$. If $|\ell(P)_{L_\psi}| > 0$, then there is a path $\rho_1 \in P$ such that $\ell(\rho_1) \in L_\psi$. Thus, the path ρ_1 encodes an assignment to X that satisfies ψ, and it is satisfiable.

Conversely, if ψ is satisfiable, then there is an assignment π to X that satisfies ψ. Let ρ_π be the path in $\mathcal{G}$ that corresponds to π. Hence, we have that $\ell(\rho_\pi) \in L_\psi$, and $|\ell(\{\rho_\pi\})_{L_\psi}| > 0$. $\square$

On the other hand, for the cases $\lambda = N$ and $\lambda = D$, we can solve the positivity problem more efficiently.

Theorem 4. *The λ-OUTCOME-MAX$^+$ problem is NLOGSPACE-complete, for $\lambda \in \{N, D\}$.*

Proof. Let $\mathcal{G} = \langle \Sigma, V_0, V_1, E, c, s, t, L \rangle$ be an RFG, f be a flow, and $\mathcal{A}$ be the DFA or NFA for which $L = L(\mathcal{A})$. The maximal decomposition P of f satisfies $|\ell(P)_L| > 0$ iff there is a path from s to t traversing edges with positive flow in f, such that there is an accepting run of $\mathcal{A}$ on the word labeling the path. Indeed, if there is such a path ρ, then $P' = \{\rho\}$ is a decomposition of f with $|\ell(P')_L| = 1$. On the other hand, if $|\ell(P)_L| > 0$, then there is a path $\rho \in P$ such that $\ell(\rho) \in L(\mathcal{A})$, and so there is an accepting run of $\mathcal{A}$ on $\ell(\rho)$. Thus, we can guess a path from s in $\mathcal{G}$ and a run of $\mathcal{A}$, one transition at a time on the fly, such that at each step, the edge guessed in $\mathcal{G}$ and the transition guessed in $\mathcal{A}$ are labeled with the same letter. In addition, we make sure every edge guessed in $\mathcal{G}$ has a positive flow through it. Hence, the problem can be solved in NLOGSPACE.

For the lower bound, we reduce from the reachability problem, known to be NLOGSPACE-hard [29]. Given a DAG $G = \langle V, E \rangle$ and vertices $s, t \in V$, we let Player 0 control all vertices, label all edges with some letter a, let the capacity and flow in all edges be 1, and set the specification to be $L = a^*$. If there is a path from s to t, then it must be labeled with a word in L. Thus, the multiset P containing this path is a decomposition of the flow with $|\ell(P)|_L > 0$. Conversely, if there is such a decomposition, there must be a path from s to t, and t is reachable from s. □

In the minimal variant, solving the positivity problem remains as hard as the general problem for all types of specifications.

Theorem 5. *The λ-OUTCOME-MIN$^+$ problem is co-NP-complete, for $\lambda \in \{U, N, D\}$.*

Proof. The upper bound follows from Theorem 2.

For the lower bound, consider the reduction shown in the proof of Theorem 2. The case where $\gamma = n$ is the *perfect* variant. That is, the problem of determining whether there is a matching that matches all elements in $X \cup Y \cup Z$. This was shown to be NP-complete in the bounded variant of 3-dimensional matching in [30]. In addition, when $\gamma = n$, we get that $\gamma' = 1$. Thus, we get that the reduction is from the complement of the perfect variant to the positivity variant, and achieves the desired lower bound. □

4 Calculating the Value in Restricted Flow Games

In this section we study the problem of finding the maximal and minimal values of RFGs. We show that the difference in the complexity of calculating the maximal and minimal outcomes translates to a difference in the complexity of calculating the value. Thus, the maximal version has one more quantifier alternation, which results in a "step up" in the polynomial hierarchy. The polynomial hierarchy is a hierarchy of complexity classes that use oracles. The lowest level is defined $\Sigma_0^P = \Pi_0^P = P$. Then, we define $\Sigma_{i+1}^P = \text{NP}^{\Sigma_i^P}$ and $\Pi_{i+1}^P = \text{co-NP}^{\Pi_i^P}$, where A^B is the set of decision problems that can be solved in A using an oracle to some problem complete in class B. Thus, Σ_2^P is the set of problems that can be solved using a polynomial time nondeterministic Turing Machine with an oracle to some NP-complete problem.

We consider the decision problems, which are parameterized by a threshold. Formally, the input to a *maximum λ-restricted flow game problem*, λ-RFG-MAX problem, for short, is an RFG $\mathcal{G}$ and a threshold $\gamma \in \mathbb{N}$. The goal is to decide whether $rval\_max(\mathcal{G}) \geq \gamma$. The input to the *minimum λ-restricted flow game problem*, λ-RFG-MIN problem, for short, is the same, and the goal is to decide whether $rval\_min(\mathcal{G}) \geq \gamma$. As in the problem of calculating the maximal and minimal outcomes, we also study the special case with $\gamma = 1$, namely the positivity problems. Formally, the input to the *positive maximum* and *positive minimum λ-restricted flow game problems* (λ-RFG-MAX$^+$ and λ-RFG-MIN$^+$, for short) is an RFG $\mathcal{G}$, and the goal is to decide whether $rval\_max(\mathcal{G}) > 0$ and whether $rval\_min(\mathcal{G}) > 0$, respectively.

4.1   Solving the Maximum and Minimum Restricted Flow Problems

Recall that in the unrestricted case, the FG problem is in Σ_2^P. Since calculating the maximal outcome is in NP, we can "step up" in the hierarchy by using an oracle.

Theorem 6. *The λ-RFG-MAX problem is in Σ_3^P, for $\lambda \in \{U, N, D\}$.*

Proof. Consider an RFG and a threshold $\gamma \in \mathbb{N}$. Given a strategy α for Player 0, deciding whether there is a strategy β for Player 1 such that $outcome\_max(\alpha, \beta) < \gamma$ can be done by guessing β in NP, and using a co-NP oracle for deciding whether $outcome\_max(\alpha, \beta) < \gamma$ (as we have shown in Theorem 1). Thus, it is in Σ_2^P. Consequently, deciding whether there is a strategy α for Player 0 such that $outcome\_max(\alpha, \beta) \geq \gamma$ for every $\beta \in F_1$ can be done in NP with a Σ_2^P oracle, by guessing α and checking it as above. It follows that the λ-RFG-MAX problem is in Σ_3^P.   □

We now show that this "step up" in the polynomial hierarchy is necessary by proving a matching lower bound. To show that, we use a reduction from QBF$_3$.

For $k \geq 1$, the problem QBF$_k$ is the satisfiability problem of quantified Boolean formulas with $k-1$ alternations of quantifiers, where the most external quantifier is "exists". By [31], the problem QBF$_k$ is Σ_k^P-complete when k is odd and the formula is given in CNF, and when k is even and the formula is given in DNF.

For the QBF$_3$ problem, let $X = \{x_1, \ldots, x_n\}$, $Y = \{y_1, \ldots, y_m\}$, and $Z = \{z_1, \ldots, z_k\}$ be sets of variables. We denote by $\bar{X}, \bar{Y}$ and $\bar{Z}$ the sets of negative literals. We also denote $W = X \cup Y \cup Z$ and $\bar{W} = \bar{X} \cup \bar{Y} \cup \bar{Z}$. Let ψ be a Boolean propositional formula over the variables in W, and let $\theta = \exists x_1 \ldots \exists x_n \forall y_1 \ldots \forall y_m \exists z_1 \ldots \exists z_k \psi$.

We assume that ψ is given in CNF. Thus, $\psi = \bigwedge_{i=1}^r c_i$ for clauses $c_1, \ldots, c_r$.

Let π be an assignment to $W' \subseteq W$. We denote by $\psi|_\pi$ the Boolean formula obtained from ψ by substituting all literals from $W' \cup \bar{W}'$ with their value in π.

The obtained formula $\psi|_\pi$ is a Boolean formula over $W \setminus W'$. We then denote by $\theta|_\pi$ the quantified Boolean formula obtained from θ by replacing ψ with $\psi|_\pi$ and deleting the variables in W' from the prefix of quantifiers in θ. The obtained formula $\theta|_\pi$ is a quantified Boolean formula over $W \setminus W'$. For example, if $W' = X$, we get that $\theta|_\pi = \forall y_1 \ldots \forall y_m \exists z_1 \ldots \exists z_k \psi|_\pi$.

We say that π satisfies θ if $\theta|_\pi$ holds. Thus, we get that θ holds iff there exists an assignment π to X such that π satisfies θ. Equivalently, $\theta|_\pi$ holds iff for all assignments π' to Y we have that π' satisfies $\theta|_\pi$.

Theorem 7. *The U-RFG-MAX problem is Σ_3^P-hard.*

Proof. We show that the U-RFG-MAX problem is Σ_3^P-hard using a reduction from QBF$_3$. Given a formula θ as above, we construct an RFG $\mathcal{G}_\theta$ such that $rval\_max(\mathcal{G}_\theta) \geq 1$ iff θ holds. Thus, we set $\gamma = 1$.

First, we encode an assignment to the variables in W as a word $w = w_z \cdot \$ \cdot w_x \cdot w_y \in \{T, F, \$\}^*$, where $w_x, w_y, w_z \in \{T, F\}^*$ encode assignments to X, Y, and Z, respectively, as we described in Lemma 1.

We define the game $\mathcal{G}_\theta$ so that the choices of Player 0 induce w_x, the choices of Player 1 induce w_y, and w_z is chosen when determining the outcome.

As can be seen in Fig. 2, the game consists of a single vertex for every variable in W, as well as a vertex for reading $\$$, and a target vertex t. We refer to vertices by the variable associated with them.

The source vertex is z_1. Every vertex is then connected to the vertex of the next variable with two edges, one labeled T and one labeled F, both with capacity 1. We connect z_n to the $\$$ vertex, and then connect it to x_1 with a $\$$-labeled edge with capacity 1. Finally, x_n is connected to y_1, and y_m is connected to the target vertex.

We let Player 0 control the vertices associated with variables in X and Z, and Player 1 control the vertices associated with variables in Y. Since the vertex associated with $\$$ has a single outgoing edge, we arbitrarily let Player 0 control it.

The $\$$-labeled edge is a minimum cut of the graph, assuring that only a single unit of flow reaches the X and Y vertices. Thus, a strategy for Player 1 is equivalent to choosing either T or F for each variable in Y. Similarly, a strategy for Player 0 induces an assignment for variables in X. Player 0 can also determine the flow leaving the source vertex. However, saturating the two edges leaving the source vertex is a dominant strategy for Player 0, and so we can consider only the case where the outgoing edges of Z vertices are saturated.

Finally, we define the specification L_ψ to be the set of assignments that satisfy ψ. The specification can be recognized by a UFA of size $O(|\psi|)$, as described in Lemma 1.

We claim that θ holds iff $rval\_max(\mathcal{G}_\theta) \geq 1$.

First, assume that θ holds, and let π_X be an assignment to X that satisfies it. Let $\alpha_\pi \in F_0$ be the strategy that corresponds to π_X. That is, for each $1 \leq i \leq n$, the strategy α_π directs the single unit of flow entering the x_i vertex to the T-labeled edge if $\pi_X(x_i) = 1$, and directs it to the F-labeled edge if $\pi_X(x_i) = 0$.

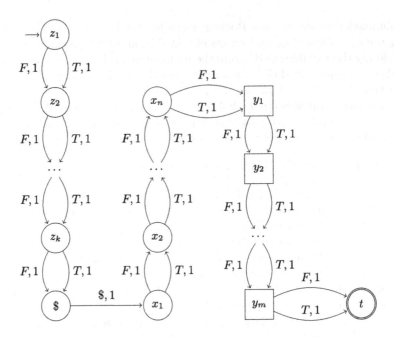

Fig. 2. The flow network in $\mathcal{G}_\theta$

In order to show that α_π ensures that the outcome of the game is 1, consider a strategy $\beta \in F_1$ for Player 1. Let π_β be the assignment to Y that corresponds to β. That is, for every $1 \leq j \leq m$, we have $\pi_\beta(y_j) = 1$ iff β directs the single unit of flow entering y_j to the T-labeled edge. We know that $\theta|_{\pi_X}$ holds. Thus, every assignment π' to Y satisfies $\theta|_{\pi_X}$. In particular, $\theta|_{\pi_X,\pi_\beta}$ holds. It follows that there exists an assignment π_Z to Z that satisfies $\psi|_{\pi_X,\pi_\beta}$.

Let $w = w_z \cdot \$ \cdot w_x \cdot w_y$ be the word that encodes the assignment π_X, π_β and π_Z. It follows that $w \in L_\psi$. In addition, the flow in the game can be decomposed such that the path that corresponds to w is in the decomposition. Thus, we get that $outcome\_max(\alpha_\pi, \beta) = 1$, as desired.

Assume now that $rval\_max(\mathcal{G}_\theta) \geq 1$. Thus, there is a strategy $\alpha \in F_0$ for Player 0 such that for every strategy $\beta \in F_1$, it holds that $outcome\_max(\alpha, \beta) \geq 1$. Let π_α be the assignment to X that corresponds to α. That is, for every $1 \leq i \leq n$, we have that $\pi_\alpha(x_i) = 1$ iff α directs the flow entering x_i to the T-labeled edge. We claim that π_α satisfies θ. Let π_Y be some assignment to variables in Y, and $\beta_\pi \in F_1$ be the strategy that corresponds to π_Y. That is, for all $1 \leq j \leq m$, the strategy β_π directs the flow entering y_j to the T-labeled edge iff $\pi_Y(y_j) = 1$. It follows that $outcome\_max(\alpha, \beta_\pi) \geq 1$. Thus, there is a decomposition P of f^{α,β_π} such that $|\ell(P)_{L_\psi}| \geq 1$. In particular, there is a path in the decomposition that encodes an assignment that satisfies ψ. This assignment must agree with π_α and π_Y. Thus, there must be an assignment to Z that satisfies $\psi|_{\pi_\alpha,\pi_Y}$, and θ holds. $\qquad\square$

Note that the specification L_ψ used in the proof of Theorem 7 cannot be recognized by a deterministic automaton with a polynomial number of states. The richness of the universal model allowed us to simply let the players induce an assignment, and check if it gives a true value to θ when calculating the outcome. In the deterministic case, we need a more complex game that "helps" in checking the truth value of θ.

Theorem 8. *The λ-RFG-MAX problem is Σ_3^P-hard, for $\lambda \in \{N, D\}$.*

Proof. We show the lower bound for the more restricted case, $\lambda = D$, by reducing from QBF_3.

Let θ and ψ be as above. We assume that there is $d \geq 1$ such that every literal in $W \cup \bar{W}$ appears in ψ exactly d times. It is easy to see that every formula in CNF can be converted with at most a quadratic blow-up to an equivalent formula that satisfies this condition.

We construct an RFG $\mathcal{G}_\theta$ such that the maximal flow in the game is $(k+1) \cdot r$, and that it can be decomposed into $(k+1) \cdot r$ words in L iff θ holds. Thus, we set $\gamma = (k+1) \cdot r$, and so $rval\_max(\mathcal{G}_\theta) \geq \gamma$ iff θ holds.

The construction is a combination of three constructions: the reduction from 3SAT to the 3-dimensional matching problem, shown in [16, Theorem 3.2], the reduction from QBF_2 to the flow game problem, shown in [27, Theorem 2], and the reduction shown here in Theorem 1.

The graph includes three parts: one for determining the values of variables in X and Y, one for ensuring that all clauses are satisfied, and one for ensuring that variables in Z have legal values. In addition, the specification L ensures that all clauses are satisfied legally and that the values of variables in Z are consistent.

First, we construct *variable vertices* for variables in $X \cup Y$, as shown in Fig. 3. Vertices associated with variables in X are in V_0, and the vertices associated with variables in Y are in V_1. There is an edge from the source $s \in V_0$ to each variable vertex, with capacity $2d$ and labeled with x or y, respectively.

Each variable vertex is then connected to two *literal vertices*, each associated with choosing a positive or a negative value to this variable. The edges have capacity $2d$ and are labeled with $*$. Literal vertices associated with literals in $X \cup \bar{X}$ are in V_1, and have an outgoing edge to a sink, with capacity d. Literal vertices associated with literals in $Y \cup \bar{Y}$ are in V_0.

We now define a layer of *clause vertices*. Each clause c_j, for $1 \leq j \leq r$, has a single vertex v_{c_j}, controlled by Player 0. Each clause vertex is connected to the target t with a single edge with capacity 1, labeled with c_j. In addition, each literal vertex is connected to each vertex associated with a clause that contains the literal. Each edge has capacity 1 and is labeled with $*$.

Finally, we define two vertices v_z and v_t for handling variables in Z, as shown in Fig. 4. Both vertices are in V_0. The vertex v_z is used to choose the value of the variables in Z. There are $2kr$ edges from the source s to v_z, one for each literal and clause pair. That is, for every $1 \leq i \leq k$ and $1 \leq j \leq r$, we have the edges $(s, z_{i,j}, v_z)$ and $(s, \bar{z}_{i,j}, v_z)$. Each edge has capacity 1. Then, we have an edge from v_z to each clause vertex. Thus, for $1 \leq j \leq r$, we add an edge (v_z, c_j, v_{c_j}) with capacity 1.

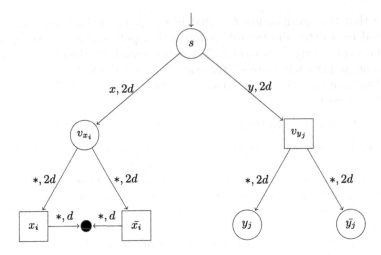

Fig. 3. The variable and literal vertices in $\mathcal{G}_\theta$, where $1 \leq i \leq n$ and $1 \leq j \leq m$.

The vertex v_t is then used to ensure the "truthfulness" of the values chosen for variables in Z. We connect v_z to v_t and v_t to the target t, in such a way that we could find a flow of words from the specification L iff the values given to variables in Z are consistent. We connect v_z to v_t with an edge for each variable in Z and each clause with capacity 1. That is, for every $1 \leq i \leq k$ and $1 \leq j \leq r$ we have the edges $(v_z, a_{i,j}, v_t)$ and $(v_t, b_{i,j}, t)$, both with capacity 1.

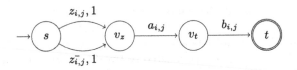

Fig. 4. The vertices v_z and v_t, where $1 \leq i \leq k$ and $1 \leq j \leq r$.

It is easy to verify that the size of the graph and the total capacity are polynomial in the size of ψ.

We now need to define the specification. Note that the alphabet we used is $\Sigma = \{*, x, y\} \cup \{c_j\}_{1 \leq j \leq r} \cup \{z_{i,j}, \bar{z}_{i,j}, a_{i,j}, b_{i,j}\}_{1 \leq i \leq k, 1 \leq j \leq r}$. This is also polynomial in the size of the input.

First, flow coming from a clause vertex into t originates in a literal that appears in that clause. For variables in $X \cup Y$, this follows from the construction. Thus, we allow all flow that goes through these variable vertices, and define $L_{x,y} = x\Sigma^* \cup y\Sigma^*$.

In Z, every literal induces an edge from s to v_z. A flow from v_z to a clause vertex is legal iff it came from a literal that appears in that clause. Thus, we define $L_{z,c} = \{z_{i,j}c_jc_j\}_{z_i \in c_j} \cup \{\bar{z}_{i,j}c_jc_j\}_{\bar{z}_i \in c_j}$.

Flow coming from v_t to t is then used to ensure the consistency of the values chosen for variables in Z. Consider a variable $z_i \in Z$. There are r incoming edges to t that are associated with z_i, one for each clause. We direct flow through these edges that comes from the edge associated with the value of z_i that was not chosen. Thus, if z_i is true, the flow goes through edges labeled with $z_{i,j}^-$. We ensure that only one value can be given to z_i by "intertwining" the legal flows for true and false values. Thus, we define $L_{z,t} = \{z_{i,j}a_{i,j}b_{i,j}, z_{i,j}^-a_{i,j+1}b_{i,j}\}_{1 \leq i \leq k, 1 \leq j \leq r}$, where $j + 1$ is calculated modulo r.

Finally, we define $L = L_{x,y} \cup L_{z,c} \cup L_{z,t}$. It is easy to verify that L can be recognized by a DFA of size polynomial in $|\theta|$.

First, we note that the only vertices where the strategies affect the flow are the variable vertices. Indeed, the incoming flow to every other vertex in the graph is greater than its outgoing capacity. Since saturating all outgoing edges from s is a dominant strategy for Player 0, it follows that all edges, besides those between variable and literal vertices, are saturated, regardless of the strategies. Thus, Player 0 and Player 1 have control over directing $2d$ units of flow to the positive or negative literal vertices associated with each variable in V_0 or V_1, respectively. We also note that for both players, directing all $2d$ units of flow to the same literal vertex is a dominant strategy, and so we can consider just these strategies.

We now prove the correctness of the reduction, thus that $rval\_max(\mathcal{G}_\theta) \geq \gamma$ iff θ holds.

Assume θ holds. Let π_x be an assignment to X that satisfies θ. Let $\alpha_\pi \in F_0$ be the strategy that directs the incoming flow in each variable vertex in V_0 according to π. That is, if $\pi_x(x_i) = 1$, the strategy α_π directs $2d$ units of flow to the positive literal vertex of x_i, and if $\pi_x(x_i) = 0$, it directs $2d$ units of flow to the negative literal vertex of x_i. We show that for every $\beta \in F_1$, it holds that $outcome\_max(\alpha, \beta) = (k + 1) \cdot r$. Directing flow to both literal vertices is a dominated strategy for Player 1. Thus, it is enough to show that Player 0 can guarantee an outcome of $(k+1) \cdot r$ against a strategy $\beta \in F_1$, such that it directs all incoming flow to a variable vertex in V_1 to only one literal vertex.

Denote by π_β the assignment to Y that assigns values according to β. That is, $\pi_\beta(y_i) = 1$ iff the strategy β directs $2d$ units of flow to the positive literal vertex. Since π_X satisfies θ, there exists an assignment π_Z to Z such that it satisfies $\psi|_{\pi_X, \pi_\beta}$. Denote by π the assignment to W that agrees with π_X, π_β and π_Z. We know that π satisfies ψ.

We construct a decomposition P of $f^{\alpha_\pi, \beta}$, such that $|\ell(P)_L| = (k + 1) \cdot r$. Thus, $outcome\_max(\alpha_\pi, \beta) \geq (k + 1) \cdot r$.

For every clause c_j, for $1 \leq j \leq r$, there is a literal φ_j that is assigned a positive value in π. Assume $\varphi_j = x_i$ for some $1 \leq i \leq n$. Denote by ρ_{c_j} the path $(s, x, v_{x_i}), (v_{x_i}, *, x_i), (x_i, *, c_j), (c_j, c_j, t)$. That is, the path that traverses the variable vertex, literal vertex and clause vertex that correspond to x_i and c_j. The edge $(x_i, *, c_j)$ exists because c_j contains x_i. Note that $\ell(\rho_{c_j}) = x * *c_j \in L_{x,y}$. When φ_j is in $\bar{X} \cup Y \cup \bar{Y}$, we define ρ_{c_j} in a similar way. Now, assume $\varphi_j = z_i$ for some $1 \leq i \leq k$. In this case, we define ρ_{c_j} to be the path

$(s, z_{i,j}, v_z), (v_z, c_j, c_j), (c_j, c_j, t)$. We have that $\ell(\rho_{c_j}) = z_{i,j}c_jc_j$. Since z_i appears in c_j, we have that $\ell(\rho_{c_j}) \in L_{z,c}$. When $\varphi_j \in \bar{Z}$, we define ρ_{c_j} in a similar way. Let $P_c = \{\rho_{c_j}\}_{1 \le j \le r}$.

Consider indices $1 \le i \le k$ and $1 \le j \le r$. If $\pi(z_i) = 1$, let $\rho_{i,j}$ be the path $(s, z_{i,j}^-, v_z), (v_z, a_{i,j+1}, v_t), (v_t, b_{i,j}, t)$ (with $j + 1$ being calculated modulo r). If $\pi(z_i) = 0$, let $\rho_{i,j} = (s, z_{i,j}, v_z), (v_z, a_{i,j}, v_t), (v_t, b_{i,j}, t)$. In both cases, it is easy to verify that $\ell(\rho_{i,j}) \in L_{z,t}$. Let $P_z = \{\rho_{i,j}\}_{1 \le i \le k, 1 \le j \le r}$. Finally, let $P = P_c \cup P_z$. As noted above, all paths in P correspond to words in L, and so $|\ell(P)_L| = |P| = (k+1) \cdot r$. In addition, it is easy to verify that P is a decomposition of $f^{\alpha_\pi, \beta}$. Thus, $outcome\_max(\alpha_\pi, \beta) = (k+1) \cdot r$. That is, the strategy α_π for Player 0 ensures an outcome of at least γ, and so $rval\_max(\mathcal{G}_\theta) \ge \gamma$.

For the other direction, assume that $rval\_max(\mathcal{G}_\theta) \ge \gamma$. Let $\alpha \in F_0$ be a strategy for Player 0 that ensures an outcome of at least γ. Strategies that direct all incoming flow to a variables vertex to only one literal vertex are dominant strategies for Player 0, and so we can assume α is such a strategy. Denote by π_α the assignment to X that assigns values according to how α directs flow entering variable vertices. That is, $\pi_\alpha(x_i) = 1$ if the strategy α directs the $2d$ units of flow entering the variable vertex of x_i to the positive literal vertex, and $\pi_\alpha(x_i) = 0$ if α directs the flow to the negative literal vertex.

We claim that π_α satisfies θ. To show that, let π_Y be an assignment to Y. We need to show that there is an assignment to Z that satisfies $\psi|_{\pi_\alpha, \pi_Y}$.

Let $\beta_\pi \in F_1$ be the strategy that directs flow entering variable vertices according to π_Y. That is, if $\pi_Y(y_i) = 1$, the strategy β_π directs $2d$ units of flow to the positive literal vertex of y_i, and if $\pi_Y(y_i) = 0$, it directs $2d$ units of flow to the negative literal vertex of y_i. By the way we chose α, we know that $outcome\_max(\alpha, \beta_\pi) \ge (k+1) \cdot r$. Thus, there is a decomposition P of f^{α, β_π} such that $|\ell(P)_L| \ge (k+1) \cdot r$. Since the incoming capacity of t is exactly $(k+1) \cdot r$, we know that $|P| = |\ell(P)_L| = (k+1) \cdot r$. In particular, we know that there are $k \cdot r$ paths in P that traverse the edges between v_t and t.

Consider $1 \le i \le k$. For all $1 \le j \le r$, denote by $\rho_j^i \in P$ the path that traverses the edge $(v_t, b_{i,j}, t)$. Since $\ell(\rho_j^i) \in L$, we must have $\ell(\rho_j^i) = z_{i,j}a_{i,j}b_{i,j}$ or $\ell(\rho_j^i) = z_{i,j}^- a_{i+1,j}b_{i,j}$. We claim that either $\ell(\rho_j^i) = z_{i,j}a_{i,j}b_{i,j}$ holds for all j, or $\ell(\rho_j^i) = z_{i,j}^- a_{i,j+1}b_{i,j}$ holds for all j. Indeed, if $\ell(\rho_1^i) = z_{i,1}^- a_{i,2}b_{i,1}$, then it cannot be that $\ell(\rho_2^i) = z_{i,2}a_{i,2}b_{i,2}$, because the edge $(v_z, a_{i,2}, v_t)$ has capacity 1. Thus, $\ell(\rho_2^i) = z_{i,2}^- a_{i,2}b_{i,2}$. Inductively, we get that all ρ_j^i must traverse $(s, z_{i,j}^-, v_z)$. On the other hand, if $\ell(\rho_1^i) = z_{i,1}a_{i,1}b_{i,1}$, then it cannot be that $\ell(\rho_r^i) = z_{i,r}^- a_{i,1}b_{i,r}$. Thus, $\ell(\rho_r^i) = z_{i,r}a_{i,r}b_{i,r}$. We continue similarly to get that all ρ_j^i must traverse $(s, z_{i,j}, v_z)$. We let π_P be the assignment to Z that chooses the negation of ρ_j^i. That is, if all ρ_j^i traverse $(s, z_{i,j}^-, v_z)$ then $\pi_P(z_i) = 1$. If all ρ_j^i traverse $(s, z_{i,j}, v_z)$, then $\pi_P(z_i) = 0$.

We claim that π_P satisfies $\psi|_{\pi_\alpha, \pi_Y}$. To show this, we consider the r units of flow that reach t from the clause vertices. Let $1 \le j \le r$, and let $\rho_j \in P$ be the path that traverses the edge (v_{c_j}, c_j, t). By the structure of the game, we know that ρ_j goes through a literal vertex or through v_z. Assume that ρ_j goes through the literal vertex x_i. Then, $\rho_j = (s, x, v_{x_i}), (v_{x_i}, *, x_i), (x_i, *, v_{c_j}), (v_{c_j}, c_j, t)$. It follows that α directs the flow entering v_{x_i} to x_i, and thus, $\pi_\alpha(x_i) = 1$. In addition, since the edge $(x_i, *, c_j)$ exists in the graph, we know that x_i appears in c_j. So c_j has a positive value in $\psi|_{\pi_\alpha, \pi_Y}$. We use similar reasoning in the case ρ_j goes through a literal vertex in $\bar{X} \cup Y \cup \bar{Y}$. Now, assume ρ_j goes through v_z. Thus, ρ_j traverses the vertices s, v_z, v_{c_j} and t. Since $\ell(\rho_j) \in L$, we know that $\ell(\rho_j) = z_{i,j} c_j c_j$ and z_i appears in c_j, or $\ell(\rho_j) = \bar{z}_{i,j} c_j c_j$ and $\bar{z}_i$ appears in c_j. We assume w.l.o.g that the first case is true. Thus, ρ_j traverses the edge $e = (s, z_{i,j}, v_z)$. Since the capacity of e is 1, it follows that ρ_j^i does not traverse e. Hence, it traverses $(s, \bar{z}_{i,j}, v_z)$, and $\pi_P(z_i) = 1$. Since z_i appears in c_j and has a positive value, we get that c_j is satisfied by π_P. Thus, all clauses are satisfied by π_α, π_Y and π_P, and π_P satisfies $\psi|_{\pi_\alpha, \pi_Y}$. It follows that π_α satisfies θ, and θ holds. □

We can now conclude with the tight complexity for the problem:

Theorem 9. *The λ-RFG-MAX problem is Σ_3^P-complete, for $\lambda \in \{U, N, D\}$.*

We continue to minimal variant. We can view this variant as the problem of deciding whether the exists a strategy α for Player 0, such that for every strategy β for Player 1 and *every* complete decomposition P of $f^{\alpha,\beta}$, we have that $|\ell(P)_L| \geq \gamma$. In this case, there is only one quantifier alternation. Thus, there is no increase in the number of alternation with respect to the unrestricted settings, and we remain in the same level of the polynomial hierarchy.

We start by showing a simple construction that we use in several proofs.

Lemma 2. *Given an unrestricted flow game $\mathcal{G}$, there is an RFG $\mathcal{G}'$ such that $value(\mathcal{G}) = rval\_max(\mathcal{G}') = rval\_min(\mathcal{G}')$.*

Proof. Given an unrestricted flow game $\mathcal{G}$, we obtain $\mathcal{G}'$ by labeling all edges with some letter a, and then defining $L = a^*$. The specification L can be recognized by a single state DFA. Since all paths in the game correspond to words in L, the maximal and minimal decompositions of a flow f coincide, and the size of their restriction to L must be equal to the value of f. Thus, trying to maximize the flow in $\mathcal{G}$ coincides with trying to maximize the maximal and minimal outcomes of $\mathcal{G}'$. □

Theorem 10. *The λ-RFG-MIN problem is Σ_2^P-complete, for $\lambda \in \{U, N, D\}$.*

Proof. Consider an RFG $\mathcal{G}$ and a threshold $\gamma \in \mathbb{N}$. Given a strategy α for Player 0, deciding whether there exists a strategy β for Player 1 such that $outcome\_min(\alpha, \beta) < \gamma$ can be done in NP, by guessing β and a complete decomposition P of $f^{\alpha,\beta}$ such that $|\ell(P)_L| < \gamma$. Calculating $f^{\alpha,\beta}$, verifying that P is a complete decomposition of $f^{\alpha,\beta}$ and computing $\ell(P)$ can all be done in polynomial time. Calculating $|\ell(P)_L|$ requires checking the membership of words in L, which can be done in polynomial time for all λ. Consequently, deciding whether there is a strategy α for Player 0 such that $outcome\_min(\alpha, \beta) \geq \gamma$ can be done in NP with a co-NP oracle, by guessing α and checking it as above. Thus, we have shown membership in Σ_2^P.

For the lower bound, we reduce from the unrestricted flow game problem, shown to be Σ_2^P-hard in [27]. Given an unrestricted flow game $\mathcal{G}$, the reduction outputs $\mathcal{G}'$ as described in Lemma 2. Correctness is immediate.   □

4.2 Solving the Positive Maximum and Minimum Restricted Flow Problems

We continue to the positivity problems and show that their complexity is strongly related to the complexity of calculating the maximal and minimal outcomes: In the cases where the problem of determining whether the maximal outcome is positive is easier than the general problem, determining whether the maximal value is positive is also easier than the general problem. In other cases, the complexity of determining whether the maximal and minimal values are positive coincides with the complexity of the general problem.

Theorem 11. *The U-RFG-MAX$^+$ problem is Σ_3^P-complete.*

Proof. The reduction used for proving the Σ_3^P lower bound in the proof of Theorem 7 is such that the maximal value of the RFG is 1 if θ holds and is 0 otherwise. Hence, the reduction works for the positivity problem as well. Thus, both the upper and lower bounds follow from Theorem 7.   □

Theorem 12. *The N-RFG-MAX$^+$ and D-RFG-MAX$^+$ problems are Σ_2^P-complete.*

Proof. For the upper bound, let $\alpha \in F_0$ and $\beta \in F_1$ be strategies for Player 0 and Player 1, respectively. We can calculate the flow in the game $f^{\alpha,\beta}$ in polynomial time. Checking if there is a decomposition P of $f^{\alpha,\beta}$ such that $\ell(P)_L > 0$ can be done in NLOGSPACE, as shown in Theorem 4. It follows that given $\alpha \in F_0$, the problem of checking if there is a $\beta \in F_1$ such that $outcome\_max(\alpha, \beta) = 0$ is in NP, by guessing β. Consequently, deciding whether there is $\alpha \in F_0$ such that for every $\beta \in F_1$ we have $outcome\_max(\alpha, \beta) > 0$, can be done by a nondeterministic polynomial-time Turing machine with an NP oracle.

For the lower bound, we reduce from the problem of approximating the value of an unrestricted flow game within any multiplicative factor, shown to be Σ_2^P-hard in [27]. Given an unrestricted flow game $\mathcal{G}$, the reduction outputs $\mathcal{G}'$ as described Lemma 2. Since every approximation algorithm can determine whether the outcome is positive, the correctness is immediate.   □

Theorem 13. *The λ-RFG-MIN$^+$ problem is Σ_2^P-complete, for $\lambda \in \{U, N, D\}$.*

Proof. The upper bound follows from Theorem 10. The lower bound follows from Lemma 2, in the same way as in the proof of Theorem 12.   □

5   Discussion

We introduced and studied restricted flow games – an extension of the classical max-flow problem to graphs that are both labeled and game graphs. We studied different variants of these games. Each variant is parameterized by two parameters: (1) the outcome of the game, namely, whether it is the maximal or minimal decomposition, and (2) the branching mode of the specification automaton, namely, whether it is a UFA, NFA, or DFA. For each variant, we considered four decision problems: calculating the outcome of given strategies, calculating the value of the game, and deciding the positivity of the two measures. Our results are summarized in Fig. 5. Below we discuss two directions for future research: memoryful strategies, and no-tolerance to flow loss and waste.

Outcome	$\lambda = U$	$\lambda \in \{N, D\}$
MAX		NP-complete
MAX$^+$		NLOGSPACE-complete
MIN		co-NP-complete
MIN$^+$		

Value	$\lambda = U$	$\lambda \in \{N, D\}$
MAX		Σ_3^P-complete
MAX$^+$		
MIN		Σ_2^P-complete
MIN$^+$		

Fig. 5. The complexity of calculating the outcome and the value.

5.1   Memoryful Strategies

A major challenge in our research arises from the ambiguity in determining the outcome, caused by the strategies being memoryless. We addressed this by considering two possible outcomes: maximal and minimal. Further research could examine a variant in which strategies do depend in the history of the flow. Below we discuss such a variant. Consider a setting in which the specification is given by a DFA, the history of a unit of flow can be abstracted by a single state in the DFA, namely, the state reached by the run of the DFA on the word corresponding to the history of the unit. Indeed, all histories that reach the same state are right-congruent. Then, a policy for a vertex v gets not just the number of units that enter v, but the history of each of the units. Note that a representation of such a strategy requires exponential space, which makes the approach infeasible. We can, however, consider policies for vertices in which the players do not specify how they direct the flow for every possible input. Instead, the policies give "symbolic instructions" on how to direct the flow. For example, a policy can prioritize the states in the DFA, that is, determine which unit of flow should be handled first, based on its history. Then, for each state in the DFA, the policy prioritizes the outgoing edges. Thus, given the incoming flow as a multiset of states in the DFA, the policy handles the most important units first, and tries to direct them to the highest priority edge that is not saturated. While this limits the control the players have in their vertices, the outcome of a game with such policies is determined, and can be calculated in polynomial time.

Alternatively, we could consider different settings, where the game is played *sequentially*, rather than in parallel. Thus, the game is played in rounds, and in each round, a single unit of flow traverses the network until it reaches a sink or the target vertex. The players have a different policy for each vertex for each round, which maps the history of the current unit (given by a state in a DFA, as above) to an outgoing edge. In these settings, we can find the path traversed by each unit of flow, round-by-round, and check if it corresponds to a word that satisfies the specification, in polynomial time. Thus, we do not need the maximal and minimal variants, as the paths traversed by the units of flow are determined. Finally, one could consider a probabilistic setting, where policies specify a distribution on the outgoing edges, and the goal of Player 0 is to maximize the expected value of the outcome.

5.2   No Tolerance to Loss and Waste

Recall that "flow conservation", which holds in all vertices in the traditional definition of flow, does not hold in the game setting. Indeed, flow gets lost in vertices (in particular, sinks) whose incoming flow is greater than the total capacity of their outgoing edges. In restricted flow games, there is an additional notion of loss, which we term *waste*: A unit of flow is wasted if it reaches the target vertex, but does so along a route that does not satisfy the specification. In some cases, loss or waste cannot be tolerated, and the authority prefers to reduce the flow in order to avoid them. For example, when leaks are hazardous or reveal sensitive information, or when flow that reaches the target while violating the specification contaminates the rest of the flow or conflicts with the privacy requirements of the network.

In order to cope with such settings, it is interesting to study a *no-loss* and *no-waste* variants of restricted flow games, where the authority is limited to strategies that ensure no loss and/or no waste of flow.

References

1. Abiteboul, S., Vianu, V.: Regular path queries with constraints. J. Comput. Syst. Sci. **58**(3), 428–452 (1999)
2. Ahuja, R.K., Magnanti, T.L., Orlin, J.B.: Network Flows: Theory, Algorithms, and Applications. Prentice Hall Englewood Cliffs (1993)
3. Alon, R., Kupferman, O.: Mutually accepting capacitated automata. In: Jirásková, G., Pighizzini, G. (eds.) DCFS 2020. LNCS, vol. 12442, pp. 1–12. Springer, Cham (2020). https://doi.org/10.1007/978-3-030-62536-8_1
4. Barrett, C., Jacob, R., Marathe, M.: Formal-language-constrained path problems. SIAM J. Comput. **30**(3), 809–837 (2000)

5. Blue, V., Adler, J., List, G.: Real-time multiple-objective path search for in-vehicle route guidance systems. J. Transp. Res. Board **1588**, 10–17 (1997)

6. Calvanese, D., de Giacomo, G., Lenzerini, M., Vardi, M.Y.: Reasoning on regular path queries. SIGMOD Rec. **32**(4), 83–92 (2003)

7. Clarke, E.M., Emerson, E.A.: Design and synthesis of synchronization skeletons using branching time temporal logic. In: Kozen, D. (ed.) Logic of Programs 1981. LNCS, vol. 131, pp. 52–71. Springer, Heidelberg (1982). https://doi.org/10.1007/BFb0025774

8. Clarke, E.M., Grumberg, O., Peled, D.: Model Checking. MIT Press (1999)

9. Cook, S.A.: Path systems and language recognition. In: Proceedings of the 2nd ACM Symposium on Theory of Computing, pp. 70–72 (1970)

10. Cormen, T.H., Leiserson, C.E., Rivest, R.L.: Introduction to Algorithms. MIT Press and McGraw-Hill (1990)

11. Dinic, E.A.: Algorithm for solution of a problem of maximum flow in a network with power estimation. Soviet Math. Doklady **11**(5), 1277–1280 (1970). English translation by RF. Rinehart

12. Even, S.: Graph Algorithms, 2nd edn. Cambridge University Press (2011)

13. Ford, L.R., Fulkerson, D.R.: Maximal flow through a network. Can. J. Math. **8**(3), 399–404 (1956)

14. Ford, L.R., Fulkerson, D.R.: Flows in Networks. Princeton University Press, Princeton (1962)

15. Füredi, Z., Reimer, D., Seress, A.: Triangle-free game and extremal graph problems. Congr. Numer. **82**, 123–128 (1991)

16. Garey, M., Johnson, D.S.: Computers and Intractability: A Guide to the Theory of NP-Completeness. W. H. Freeman and Company (1979)

17. Goldberg, A.V., Tardos, É., Tarjan, R.E.: Network flow algorithms. Technical report, DTIC Document (1989)

18. Goldberg, A.V., Tarjan, R.E.: A new approach to the maximum-flow problem. J. ACM **35**(4), 921–940 (1988)

19. Guha, S., Kupferman, O., Vardi, G.: Multi-player flow games. In: Proceedings of the 17th International Conference on Autonomous Agents and Multiagent Systems, pp. 104–112 (2018)

20. Hefetz, D., Krivelevich, M., Naor, A., Stojaković, M.: On saturation games. Eur. J. Comb. **41**, 315–335 (2016)

21. Hefetz, D., Kupferman, O., Lellouche, A., Vardi, G.: Spanning-tree games. In: 43rd International Symposium on Mathematical Foundations of Computer Science, volume 117 of LIPIcs, pp. 35:1–35:16. Schloss Dagstuhl - Leibniz-Zentrum fuer Informatik (2018)

22. Kann, V.: Maximum bounded 3-dimensional matching is MAX-SNP-complete. Inf. Process. Lett. **37**(1), 27–35 (1991)

23. Kupferman, O.: Examining classical graph-theory problems from the viewpoint of formal-verification methods. In: Proceedings of the 49th ACM Symposium on Theory of Computing, p. 6 (2017)

24. Kupferman, O., Tamir, T.: Properties and utilization of capacitated automata. In: Proceedings of the 34th Conference on Foundations of Software Technology and Theoretical Computer Science, volume 29 of LIPIcs, pp. 33–44. Schloss Dagstuhl - Leibniz-Zentrum fuer Informatik, Germany (2014)

25. Kupferman, O., Vardi, G.: Eulerian paths with regular constraints. In: 41st International Symposium on Mathematical Foundations of Computer Science, volume 58 of Leibniz International Proceedings in Informatics (LIPIcs), p. 62:1 (2016)

26. Kupferman, O., Vardi, G.: The unfortunate-flow problem. In: Proceedings of the 45th International Colloquium on Automata, Languages, and Programming, volume 107 of LIPIcs, pp. 157:1–157:14. Schloss Dagstuhl - Leibniz-Zentrum fuer Informatik (2018)

27. Kupferman, O., Vardi, G., Vardi, M.Y.: Flow games. In: Proceedings of the 37th Conference on Foundations of Software Technology and Theoretical Computer Science, volume 93 of Leibniz International Proceedings in Informatics (LIPIcs), pp. 38:38–38:16 (2017)

28. Mendelzon, A.O., Wood, P.T.: Finding regular simple paths in graph databases. SIAM J. Comput. 24(6), 1235–1258 (1995)

29. Papadimitriou, C.H.: Computational Complexity, 2nd edn. Addison-Wesley (1994)

30. Petrank, E.: The hardness of approximation: gap location. In: The 2nd Israel Symposium on Theory and Computing Systems, pp. 275–284 (1993)

31. Stockmeyer, L.J.: The polynomial-time hierarchy. Theoret. Comput. Sci. 3, 1–22 (1977)

32. Tarjan, R.E.: Depth first search and linear graph algorithms. SIAM J. Comput. 1(2), 146–160 (1972)

33. Vardi, M.Y., Wolper, P.: Reasoning about infinite computations. Inf. Comput. 115(1), 1–37 (1994)

SynthLearn: A Tool for Guided Reactive Synthesis

Mrudula Balachander$^{(\boxtimes)}$, Emmanuel Filiot , and Jean-François Raskin

Université libre de Bruxelles, Brussels, Belgium
mrudu.balachander@gmail.com

Abstract. In this paper, we introduce the SynthLearn tool. It implements an algorithm for reactive synthesis using LTL specifications, supplemented with examples of desired execution prefixes. Using automata learning techniques and zero-sum two player games, the synthesis procedure produces a Mealy machine that realizes the LTL specification and matches the given examples, whenever possible. By providing desired execution prefixes, users can guide the synthesis towards interesting solutions without having to specify low-level properties in LTL. We demonstrate the tool's ability to produce effective solutions with a series of examples. Our tool can be accessed through a user-friendly web interface.

To infinity and beyond...!

$-Woody,\ Toy\ story,\ 1995^a$

^{a}This document serves as a modest tribute to Javier Esparza, a cinephile and a distinguished theoretical computer scientist. While he began his career with significant work in verifying infinite state systems, his scholarly contributions have extended well beyond this initial area of research.

1 Introduction

From the early days of computer science, researchers have sought to provide abstraction mechanisms that allow programmers to write high-level code [4], independent of the specific machine on which the code will be executed. Such abstractions have materialized as programming language constructs or styles,

----

This work is partially supported by the two PDR projects Subgame perfection in graph games and Rational (F.R.S.-FNRS), the EOS project Verifying Learning Artificial Intelligence Systems (F.R.S.-FNRS and FWO), and the COST Action 16228 GAMENET (European Cooperation in Science and Technology).
Mrudula Balachander is an "Aspirant FNRS".
Emmanuel Filiot: Emmanuel Filiot is an F.R.S.-FNRS Senior Research Associate.
Jean-François Raskin is supported by the "Fondation ULB".

S. Kiefer et al. (Eds.): *Taming the Infinities of Concurrency*, LNCS 14660, pp. 51–71, 2024.
https://doi.org/10.1007/978-3-031-56222-8_3

including object-oriented, logic, and functional programming. These programming languages enable programmers to express algorithmic solutions at a high level of abstraction. However, high-level programming languages were just a first step. Pioneering efforts by scientists, notably Dijkstra and Hoare, utilized formal methods supported by logic to synthesise programs directly from high-level specifications [25], potentially rendering traditional programming redundant. The primary advantage of this synthesis approach is the production of programs that are "correct by construction" from logical descriptions. These descriptions focus on the *what* (the specification) and reduce or eliminate the need to dwell on the *how* (the detailed operational solution), addressing the inherent challenges and errors associated with manual programming.

From the mid 1980 s, the model-checking community focused on automating the verification of temporal properties for reactive systems, see [11] for a recent extensive survey. Unlike traditional sequential programs, reactive systems [23] constantly interact with their surrounding environment, which is only partially controllable. Designing these systems is especially complex for several reasons: the limited controllability of the environment, the intricate temporal properties characterizing the ongoing interactions between the system and its environment (an interaction that, importantly, lacks a definitive endpoint), and the stark contrast of these specifications to the conventional "pre-and-post" specifications of sequential programming. Given these challenges, it is unsurprising that designing and programming reactive systems prove even more error-prone than standard sequential programming. As a natural progression, researchers began to investigate the application of the synthesis approach to these reactive systems.

Research in this domain began with the foundational contributions of Pnueli and Rosner [31], and of Abadi, Lamport and Wolper [1]. They devised algorithms that, starting from linear temporal logic (LTL) specifications (or omega-regular languages articulated as infinite word automata), automatically construct finite state machines with inputs and outputs to realize the given specification. This approach set the stage for the automatic design of reactive systems that satisfied their specifications —the *what*— without delving into the complexities of manual implementation —the *how*. Though their methods were elegant, they also introduced intricate automata constructions, like Safra determinisation of infinite word automata [34], complicating the practical implementation of these techniques. More recent advancements have led to the development of more streamlined automata constructions, such as the Safraless algorithms (see e.g. [17,22,28,35]), which have been incorporated into tools like ACACIA [8], ACACIA-BONSAI [10], BOSY [21], and STRIX [29]. These tools are able to automatically handle intricate LTL specifications. However, the industrial adoption of automatic synthesis for reactive systems remains notably limited. The remaining challenges are multiple: formulating precise LTL specifications for reactive systems is challenging, and while partial specifications are enough for verification purposes (with model-checking being widely utilized in industry), synthesis demands thorough system specifications. Moreover, simply detailing the *what* often falls short of producing practically relevant synthesized outcomes. This latter issue, closely connected to the previous, is the primary motivation for the tool that we introduce in this paper. We further explore these challenges in our recent paper [5], summarized in the following paragraphs.

LTL Synthesis with a Few Hints. To illustrate the issue at hand, let us consider the classical problem of mutual exclusion. The high-level specification of a "mutex" protocol is provided by the LTL formula below. Here, atomic propositions r_1 and r_2 (controlled by the environment) represent requests from two processes to access their respective critical sections. The propositions g_1 and g_2 (controlled by the reactive system) govern the arbitration of mutual exclusive access to these sections:

$$\varphi_{CORE}^{ME} \equiv \Box(\neg g_1 \lor \neg g_2) \land \Box(r_1 \to \Diamond g_1) \land \Box(r_2 \to \Diamond g_2).$$

This formula expresses the core correctness properties that we would want to verify on *any* solution to mutual exclusion problem, e.g. Peterson, Dedekker, Bakery algorithms, namely: mutual exclusion (no simultaneous grants) and fairness (every request is eventually served). However, employing this formula φ_{CORE}^{ME} within LTL synthesis tools, such as ACACIA [8], ACACIA-BONSAI [10], BoSY [21], or STRIX [29], results in the solution shown in Fig. 1-(left) (uniformly returned by all tools). Although this solution correctly realizes the specification, it fails to account for environmental input and simply allocates access to critical sections in a cyclical order. It is clearly *not* optimal, or even practical, for the mutual exclusion problem, highlighting the limitations of the synthesis algorithm when provided solely with the core correctness specification, i.e. the *what*. It is important to note at this point that the blame should not be put on the synthesis tools, or algorithms, as the solution that they propose is perfectly correct with regard to the high-level specification they are provided with.

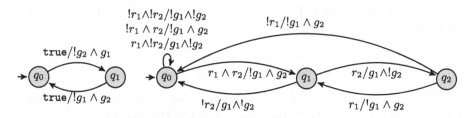

Fig. 1. (Left) The solution of Strix to the mutual exclusion problem for high-level specification φ_{CORE}^{ME}. Edge labels are of the form φ/ψ where φ: Boolean formula on input atomic propositions (Boolean variables controlled by environment) and ψ: maximally consistent conjunction of literals over set of output propositions (Boolean variables controlled by system). (Right) A natural solution that could be drawn by hand, and is automatically produced by our learning/synthesis algorithm for the same specification plus two simple examples.

So, it should be clear that, to produce solutions as the natural solution shown in Fig. 1-(right), automatic synthesis tools should be provided with additional information. Yet, to preserve the essence and advantages of the synthesis approach, we must not be burdened with detailing the *how* extensively. Ideally, we would limit the reliance on low-level property specifications to a minimum. Rather than expressing these low-level properties using LTL—which is arguably suboptimal—our proposed method, detailed in [5] and summarised in this tool paper, is an innovative solution: guiding synthesis through *illustrative behavior examples*. So, alongside the core specification φ_{CORE}^{ME}, our approach supplies the synthesis algorithm with examples of execution sequences expected in the solution. Our new synthesis algorithm then performs two tasks: first, it generalizes (i.e. learns) from these examples while making sure that the generalization is compatible with a solution for the core specification. This first phase ends with a partial solution, called a preMealy machine, that generalizes the examples while maintaining the possibility to obtain a full solution for the core LTL specification φ_{CORE}^{ME}. Then in a second phase, our algorithm transforms the partial solution obtained during the learning phase into a complete Mealy machine that realises the specification and is compatible with the examples. By constraining the synthesis algorithm to focus on solutions that adhere to and expand upon the user-provided examples, we leverage the recognized efficacy of execution scenarios (a term synonymous with'examples' in requirements engineering), mitigating the need for complex low-level system specifications. When it comes to reactive system design, these scenarios or examples are *invariably easier* to formulate than comprehensive, or even semi-detailed, low level specifications. This simplicity stems from the user's ability, during example formulation, to control *both* the inputs (from the environment) and the outputs (of the system), effectively sidestepping the primary difficulty at the core of reactive system design: accommodating *all* potential environmental inputs.

To better understand the concept of using execution examples to achieve a desired solution, as the one depicted on the right side of Fig. 1, let us keep φ_{CORE}^{ME} as our *core* LTL specification for mutex, but additionally, consider the following two execution prefixes that demonstrate the desired behavior of solutions to the mutex problem:

(1) $(\neg r_1 \wedge \neg r_2).(\neg g_1 \wedge \neg g_2)\#(r_1 \wedge \neg r_2).(g_1 \wedge \neg g_2)\#(\neg r_1 \wedge r_2).(\neg g_1 \wedge g_2)$
(2) $(r_1 \wedge r_2).(g_1 \wedge \neg g_2)\#(\neg r_1 \wedge \neg r_2).(\neg g_1 \wedge g_2)$

These trace prefixes define specific responses to *predetermined finite input sequences*, making them straightforward to express. For example:

– In prefix (1): Initially, when no requests are made, no access is provided. We can immediately observe that this straightforward example effectively eliminates the round robin solution that previously issued unsolicited grants. Then, if process 1 makes the initial request, it gains access to its critical section. Following this, if process 2 submits a request, it then gains access to its critical section.
– In prefix (2): When both processes place a request at the same time, process 1 is granted access first, followed by process 2.

By adding these two simple prefixes of trace to φ_{CORE}^{ME}, our algorithm produces the solution depicted in Fig. 1-(right). Further variations of this mutex example will be explored in subsequent sections of the paper. It is crucial to emphasize that these prefixes are adequate for obtaining the desired machine because they are generalized by the learning phase of our new algorithm. When these prefixes are encoded into LTL formulas (which can always be done, see end of Sect. 2 below), and submitted to the conventional synthesis algorithm, the solutions offered by the aforementioned tools align with the prefixes. However, they revert to the round robin solution after these prefix sequences. This can be attributed to the inability of the classical reactive synthesis algorithm to generalize the provided examples. If instead the user inputs an LTL-encoded generalization of the examples, such as, e.g. $\Box((\neg r_i \wedge \bigcirc(\neg r_i)) \rightarrow (\neg g_i))$, then classical tools such as STRIX outputs the expected machine. However, the learning phase of our SYNTHLEARN algorithm precisely allow the user to avoid this step, as it automatically does the generalization from a few examples.

Related Works. In this section on related work, we take the opportunity to highlight the contributions of Javier and his collaborators on topics pertinent to this paper. Javier has played a pivotal role in the advancement of algorithms for transforming LTL specifications into ω-word automata, pivotal for synthesis applications [16–19,27,36]. This research has significantly influenced reactive synthesis for LTL and has been substantially integrated into the STRIX synthesis tool [29]. Additionally, Javier has recently resolved a long-standing open question regarding the normalization of LTL formulas [20], a contribution that could influence our approach to LTL synthesis in the future.

Let us now turn to more specific related works on reactive synthesis and our approach that uses examples in addition to the core LTL specification. A more complete discussion is provided in [5], and we refer the interested reader to this paper for more details. Execution scenarios are promoted in requirements engineering for specification elicitation, as shown in [12,13]. In [32], learning techniques transform examples into LTL formulas. Such methods complement our work, helping derive the high-level specification φ_{CORE}. In non-vacuous synthesis [7], examples are auto-generated from LTL specifications. Our approach offers more flexibility, allowing user-specified examples and leaning on learning algorithms, unlike the constraint-solving technique in [7]. The syntax-guided synthesis framework, or SyGuS [2], integrates user-given information with formal specification. SyGuS and our method differ in that the former does not use user-provided examples and relies heavily on SAT/SMT solvers. The work in [3] uses formal specifications and scenarios for distributed protocols synthesis. They do not use learning techniques for generalization or address adversarial environments as we do. Alternative methods to enhance synthesis solution quality include extending formal specifications with quantitative aspects, as seen in [6,9]. The first phase of our algorithm draws inspiration from automata learning methods like RPNI [24]. Modifying such algorithms is essential to generate partial solutions that maintain the realizability of φ_{CORE}.

Contribution and Structure of the Paper. This paper introduces our tool, SYNTHLEARN, which implements the novel synthesis algorithm that we presented in [5]. To allow users to gain a comprehensive understanding of how our tool works, we begin by providing an overview of the underlying algorithms that combine learning and reactive synthesis techniques. The reader interested in correctness proofs for the algorithms is referred to [5]. Subsequently, we illustrate our methodology for deriving high quality solutions from high-level LTL specifications and examples, illustrated in-depth on two families examples. We encourage the interested readers to use SYNTHLEARN through a web-interface here.

The structure of the paper is as follows: Sect. 2 introduces the essential preliminaries and provides a formal definition of the example-guided reactive synthesis problem addressed by our tool. Section 3 summarizes the core algorithmic concepts behind our tool. In Sect. 4, we delve into two case studies, which illustrate the functionalities of our tool and outline the methodology that should be employed to automatically generate relevant reactive systems from LTL specifications and examples.

2   Preliminaries

Words. An *alphabet* is a finite set of symbols. A *word* u over an alphabet Σ is a finite sequence of symbols from Σ. The set of finite words over alphabet Σ is denoted by Σ^* (resp. Σ^ω). We denote the length of a finite word u by $|u| \in \mathbb{N}$, with ϵ representing the empty word of length 0. Correspondingly, we define an *infinite word* w as an infinite sequence of symbols from Σ, with the set of infinite words denoted by Σ^ω. We use $u[i : j]$ to denote the *infix* of word u from position i to position j (both inclusive), and $u[i]$ to denote the letter $u[i : i]$. We say that u is a *prefix* of v (denoted by $u \preceq v$) if $v = u.w$, for some $w \in \Sigma^*$. The set of prefixes of v are denoted by $\mathsf{Prefs}(v)$.

Throughout this text, we assume the existence of two alphabets $\mathcal{I}$ and $\mathcal{O}$ of elements called *input* and *output* respectively. Every word $u \in (\mathcal{IO})^\omega$ is an infinite word of the form $u = i_0 o_0 i_1 o_1 \ldots$, where $i_n \in \mathcal{I}$ and $o_n \in \mathcal{O}$. We let $\mathsf{in}(u) = i_0 i_1 \ldots$ (resp. $\mathsf{out}(u) = o_0 o_1 \ldots$) be the projections of u on $\mathcal{I}$ (resp. on $\mathcal{O}$) and we naturally extend these functions to languages.

Automata Over ω-Words. A *universal coBüchi* automaton over alphabet Σ is a tuple $\mathcal{A} \equiv \langle Q, Q_0, \Delta, F \rangle$, where Q is the finite set of states, $Q_0 \subseteq Q$ the set of initial states, $\Delta \subseteq Q \times \Sigma \times Q$ the transition relation, and $F \subseteq Q$. Often, we represent the transition relation $\Delta \subseteq Q \times \Sigma \times Q$ as a function $\delta : Q \times \Sigma \to 2^Q$. A *run* on $\mathcal{A}$ over an ω-word $w = w_0 w_1 w_2 \ldots$ is an infinite sequence of states $r = q_0 q_1 q_2 \ldots$, where $q_0 \in Q_0$ and $\forall i \in \mathbb{N}, q_{i+1} \in \delta(q_i, w_i)$. Let $\mathsf{Inf}_{\mathcal{A}}(r) \subseteq Q$ be the set of states visited infinitely often by the run r. We say that r is *accepting* for the coBüchi condition if $\mathsf{Inf}_{\mathcal{A}}(r) \cap F = \varnothing$. The *language* of $\mathcal{A}$ is the set of words on which all runs satisfy the coBüchi condition. We also define a stronger accepting condition called *K-co-Büchi*, which requires that, a run r is accepting if it visits any state from F at most K times. We denote by $L_K(\mathcal{A})$ the language of words on which all the runs are accepting for the K-co-Büchi condition.

(Pre)Mealy Machines. Given a (partial) function $f : X \to Y$, we denote by $\mathrm{dom}(f)$ its *domain*, i.e. the set of elements $x \in X$ such that $f(x)$ is defined. A *preMealy machine* M on $\mathcal{I}, \mathcal{O}$ is a tuple $(S, s_0, \delta, \lambda)$ such that S is a non-empty finite set (of states), $s_0 \in S$ is the initial state, $\delta : S \times \mathcal{I} \to S$ and $\lambda : S \times \mathcal{I} \to \mathcal{O}$ are partial functions, called *transition* and *output* functions respectively, such that $\mathrm{dom}(\delta) = \mathrm{dom}(\lambda)$. Intuitively, when the machine M reads a sequence of inputs, it is in some state q according to the transition function δ, and produces some output according to λ. Accordingly, the semantics of M is defined as a language of words alternating between inputs and outputs. Formally, we first extend those functions to partial functions $\delta^* : \mathcal{I}^* \to S$ and $\lambda^* : \mathcal{I}^+ \to \mathcal{O}$: $\delta^*(\epsilon) = s_0$ and $\delta^*(ui) = \delta(\delta^*(u), i)$ (if defined) and $\lambda^*(ui) = \lambda(\delta^*(u), i)$ (if defined). The language $L(M) \subseteq (\mathcal{I}\mathcal{O})^*$ of M is defined as

$$L(M) = \{i_0 \lambda^*(i_0) i_1 \lambda^*(i_0 i_1) \ldots i_n \lambda^*(i_0 \ldots i_n) \mid \forall 0 \le k \le n : i_0 i_1 \ldots i_k \in \mathrm{dom}(\lambda^*)\}$$

We also let $L_\omega(M) \subseteq (\mathcal{I}\mathcal{O})^\omega$ be the topological extension of $L(M)$ to infinite words, i.e. $L_\omega(M) = \{w \in (\mathcal{I}\mathcal{O})^\omega \mid \mathrm{Prefs}(w) \cap (\mathcal{I}\mathcal{O})^* \subseteq L(M)\}$.

A *hole* in M is a pair $(s, i) \in S \times \mathcal{I}$ such that $(s, i) \notin \mathrm{dom}(\delta)$. A preMealy machine M such that both δ and λ are total functions, i.e., $\mathrm{dom}(\delta) = \mathrm{dom}(\lambda) = S \times \mathcal{I}$, is called a *Mealy machine*. Note that for a Mealy machine M, both δ^* and λ^* are total functions, and $\mathrm{in}(L_\omega(M)) = \mathcal{I}^\omega$.

The Reactive Synthesis Problem. A *specification* is a language $S \subseteq (\mathcal{I}\mathcal{O})^\omega$. The *reactive synthesis problem* (synthesis problem in short) is the problem of constructing, given a specification S, a Mealy machine M such that $L_\omega(M) \subseteq S$ if it exists (written $M \models S$). A specification S is *realizable* if there exists M such that $M \models S$. The induced decision problem is called the *realizability problem*.

In this paper, we consider specifications given in *Linear Temporal Logic* (LTL), a popular logic in verification and synthesis [11]. We only give the syntax of LTL formulas, to fix notations, and refer the reader for instance to [11] for the semantics. Given a finite set P whose elements are called *propositions*, the syntax of LTL formulas is defined as:

$$\varphi := \mathsf{True} \mid \mathsf{False} \mid p \mid \neg p \mid \varphi_1 \wedge \varphi_2 \mid \varphi_1 \vee \varphi_2 \mid (\bigcirc \varphi) \mid (\varphi_1 \mathcal{U} \varphi_2)$$

where $p \in P$, and $\bigcirc$ (Next) and $\mathcal{U}$ (Until) are temporal connectives. We use the abbreviations $\Diamond \varphi \equiv \mathsf{True} \, \mathcal{U} \varphi$ (Eventually φ) and $\Box \varphi \equiv \neg \Diamond \neg \varphi$ (Always φ), and $\varphi_1 \mathcal{W} \varphi_2 \equiv \varphi_1 \mathcal{U} \varphi_2 \vee \Box \varphi_1$ (Weak Until). The semantics of an LTL formula φ is a set of ω-words over alphabet 2^P, denoted $[\varphi]$, and we write $w \models \varphi$ to denote $w \in [\varphi]$. In the context of reactive synthesis, P is partitioned into propositions controlled by the environment (P_{in}) and propositions controlled by the system (P_{out}), and we let $\mathcal{I} = 2^{P_{\mathsf{in}}}$ and $\mathcal{O} = 2^{P_{\mathsf{out}}}$. The specification defined by an LTL formula φ is defined as $S_\varphi = \{i_0 o_0 i_1 o_1 \cdots \in (\mathcal{I}\mathcal{O})^\omega \mid (i_0 \cup o_0)(i_1 \cup o_1) \ldots \models \varphi\}$. It is well-known that for LTL specifications, the realizability problem is 2ExpTime-c [31].

P-Realizability. Given two preMealy machines P_1, P_2, we say that P_2 *extends* P_1, written $P_1 < P_2$, if there is an *injective homomorphism* from P_1 to P_2 (i.e. an injective function from the states of P_1 to the states of P_2 which preserves the initial states, the transitions and the outputs). A specification S is P-*realizable*, for a preMealy machine P, if there exists a Mealy machine M which extends P and realizes S. For LTL specifications, the P-realizability problem, is not harder than plain LTL realizability, it is 2EXPTIME-C [5].

Example-Guided Reactive Synthesis. The *example-guided reactive synthesis* problem (or just guided synthesis problem for short) is the problem of constructing, given a specification $S \subseteq (\mathcal{IO})^\omega$ and a finite set $E \subseteq (\mathcal{IO})^*$ (of elements called *examples*), a Mealy machine M such that $L_\omega(M) \subseteq S$ and $E \subseteq L(M)$ if it exists (denoted by $M \models_{\text{guided}} S, E$). A pair (S, E) is *realizable* if there exists M such that $M \models_{\text{guided}} S, E$. The induced decision problem is called the guided-realizability problem. When S is given by an LTL formula, it is worth mentioning that the guided-realizability problem is 2EXPTIME-C: decidability is for instance obtained by hard-coding the examples from E as an LTL formula φ_E and testing the realizability of $\varphi \wedge \varphi_E$. Briefly, to encode one example $e = i_0 o_0 \ldots i_n o_n$, we let $\varphi_e = \bigwedge_{0 \leq n' \leq n}(\bigwedge_{0 \leq j \leq n'} \bigcirc^j i_j) \rightarrow \bigcirc^{n'} o_{n'}$, where i_j here stands for $\bigwedge_{p \in i_j} p \wedge \bigwedge_{p \notin i_j} \neg p$, and we let $\varphi_E = \bigwedge_{e \in E} \varphi_e$. However, the cost is doubly exponential in the size of the examples, while the method we present in this paper is only polynomial in the size of the examples. Moreover, our method tries to generalize as much as possible the given set of examples, while maintaining the realizability of the specification. This will be formalized in Theorem 4 in [5].

A finite set of examples $E \subseteq (\mathcal{IO})^*$ is said to be *consistent* if $\forall e.i \in$ Prefs$(E) \cap (\mathcal{IO})^* \mathcal{I}$, there exists a unique element denoted $o_E(e.i) \in \mathcal{O}$ such that $e.i.o_E(e.i) \in$ Prefs(E). For the rest of this paper, for the **example-guided reactive synthesis problem**, we always assume that the given set E of examples is consistent.

3   SynthLearn Algorithm

Our approach to solving *example-guided synthesis* is to combine passive learning algorithms with reactive synthesis techniques. We split the algorithm in two phases: the *generalization* phase and the *completion* phase. The generalization phase starts from a preMealy machine that accepts exactly the examples (and nothing else), and generalize the examples by trying to merge its states (in the same spirit as the RPNI algorithm [26]), with the invariant that the constructed preMealy machines can always be extended to a Mealy machine realizing the specification. Therefore, the generalization phase produces a machine with potential *holes* (missing transitions). The completion phase fills these holes by adding missing transitions, to existing states or new states, while maintaining specification-realizability. To ensure termination of the completion phase, as well as to exploit the examples as much as possible, the algorithm first tries to add missing transitions towards existing states that were created during the generalization phase.

Both phases intensively use P-realizability testing, for the preMealy machines P constructed during the algorithm: after merging two states, or after completing

---

Algorithm 1: SynthLearn - Overview

Input: A specification $\varphi \subseteq (I.O)^\omega$ given in LTL, a consistent finite set of
examples $E \subseteq (\mathcal{I}.\mathcal{O})^*$

Output: A Mealy machine $M \models \varphi$ such that $E \subseteq L(M)$ if it exists, otherwise
UNREAL

1 $\varphi_E \leftarrow$ LTL encoding of E;   // $[\varphi_E] = E(\mathcal{I}\mathcal{O})^\omega$
2 **if** $\varphi \wedge \varphi_E$ *is unrealizable;*   // call to ACACIA-BONSAI
3 **then**
4 │   **return** UNREAL
5 **else**
6 │ $\mathcal{A} \leftarrow$ universal coBüchi aut. equivalent to φ// Computed by SPOT [14]
7 │   **foreach** $k = 0, \ldots, +\infty$ **do**
8 │   │   antichain $\leftarrow$ ACACIA-BONSAI$(\mathcal{A}, k)$;   // call to ACACIA-BONSAI on
   │   │   the safety specification $L_k(\mathcal{A})$, returns an antichain repr.
   │   │   of the winning region
9 │   │   **if** $L_k(\mathcal{A})$ *is* PTA(E)*-realizable* **then**
10 │   │   │ $M \leftarrow$ Generalize$(E,$ antichain$)$;
11 │   │   │ $M \leftarrow$ Complete$(M,$ antichain$)$;
12 │   │   │   **return** M;

---

a transition. Although the problem is 2EXPTIME-C, the algorithm precomputes a compact data structure (an antichain) such that each of those tests can be performed in polynomial time (in the size of the antichain). This structure is computed by ACACIA-BONSAI [10].

More precisely, the algorithm, whose pseudo-code is given in Algorithm 1, works as follows. First, it tests whether both the specification and the examples are realizable (line 2) using ACACIA-BONSAI. If that is the case, it constructs a universal coBüchi automaton $\mathcal{A}$ equivalent to the LTL specification φ, and then strengthens the specification to a safety specification $L_k(\mathcal{A})$ for increasing values of k (it is known that for a large enough k – which is small in practice–, $L_k(\mathcal{A})$ is realizable, if $L(\mathcal{A})$ is so [22]). ACACIA-BONSAI is then called to compute a compact antichain representation of the most permissive strategy in the safety game induced by the safety spec $L_k(\mathcal{A})$ (line 8). Then, it tests whether the *prefix-tree acceptor* PTA(E) obtained from the examples, i.e., a tree-structured preMealy machine such that $L(\text{PTA}(E)) = E$, can be extended into a full Mealy machine which realizes the safety specification $L_k(\mathcal{A})$ (line 9). This test can be done in polynomial time in the size of the antichain and the size of the examples, as explained in Sect. 3.1. If the test is positive, then the two phases, generalization and completion, which are the core of SynthLearn, are started, and take as a parameter the antichain data structure to efficiently test for P-realizability of the specification $L_k(\mathcal{A})$. The call to ACACIA-BONSAI on Line 8, is worst-case exponential in the size of the automaton $\mathcal{A}$, but is done only as many times as the smallest k needed (which is in our case studies very small, typically less than 4). The generalization and completion phase run in polynomial time in the number of examples and the size of the antichain. Those phases are incremental with respect to adding examples: for a fixed safety specification $L_k(\mathcal{A})$, adding more examples induce only an extra polynomial cost in the size of the antichain data structure and the examples, as the structure only depends on $\mathcal{A}$ and k (and not on the examples).

The efficient P-realizability testing is described in Sect. 3.1, the generalization phase in Sect. 3.2 and the completion phase in Sect. 3.3.

3.1   Testing P-Realizability of Safety Specifications Efficiently

Given an LTL specification φ, SYNTHLEARN first transforms it into an equivalent universal co-Büchi automaton $\mathcal{A}$ [28]. Let $k \in \mathbb{N}$ and consider now the safety language $L_k(\mathcal{A})$, defined by strenghtening the acceptance condition of $\mathcal{A}$ to K-co-Büchi. The language $L_k(\mathcal{A})$ defines a safety specification. We now briefly explain the results of [22] which allow to compute an antichain data structure that is used in SYNTHLEARN to check for P-realizability, for any preMealy machine P, in polynomial time in the size of this structure and the size of P.

Let $\mathcal{A} = (Q, Q_0, \delta, F)$. Given k, we first explain how to construct a deterministic safety automaton $D_{\mathcal{A},k} = (Q^D, q_0^D, \delta^D, \mathsf{Safe})$ such that $L(D_{\mathcal{A},k}) = L_k(\mathcal{A})$. Its set of states is a set of *counting functions*, which are functions $f : Q \to \{-1, 0, 1, \ldots, k, k+1\}$. We denote by $CF(\mathcal{A}, k)$ the set of counting functions. For a state $q \in Q$, the value $f(q)$ represents the maximal number of times any run reaching q visits states from F (the value $k+1$ indicates that it has exceeded k strictly, and the value -1 indicates that no run has reached state q). This information can be easily updated when reading a symbol from the alphabet (see [22]), to define the transition function δ^D. The initial state q_0^D is defined as the initial counting function f_0, mapping any state of $Q_0 \cap F$ to 1, any state of $Q_0 \setminus F$ to 0, and the other states to -1. The automaton $D_{\mathcal{A},k}$ accepts a word if its run only visits states of $\mathsf{Safe} = \{f \mid \forall q \in Q : f(q) \le k\}$.

Note that $CF(\mathcal{A}, k)$ forms a complete lattice for the partial order $\preceq$ defined by $f_1 \preceq f_2$ if $f_1(q) \le f_2(q)$ for all $q \in Q$. We denote by $f_1 \bigsqcup f_2$ the least upper-bound of any two functions f_1, f_2. Let $W_{\mathcal{A},k}$ be the set of counting functions f (called winning counting functions) such that $L_f := L((Q^D, f, \delta^D, \mathsf{Safe}))$ is realizable. We recall some important properties of $W_{\mathcal{A},k}$ [22]: (*i*) it is downward-closed for $\preceq$, (*ii*) $f_0 \in W_{\mathcal{A},k}$ iff $L_k(\mathcal{A})$ is realizable, (*iii*) for all $f \in W_{\mathcal{A},k}$, all $i \subseteq P_{\mathsf{in}}$, there exists $o \subseteq P_{\mathsf{out}}$ such that $\delta^D(f, i \cup o) \in W_{\mathcal{A},k}$. While (*ii*) and (*iii*) are properties that allow to synthesize a machine when one exists, from (*i*), we obtain that $W_{\mathcal{A},k}$ can be represented by the antichain $\lceil W_{\mathcal{A},k} \rceil$ of its $\preceq$-maximal elements as it is a downward-closed set. SYNTHLEARN uses ACACIA-BONSAI to compute this antichain.

Given a preMealy machine $P = (S, s_0, \delta_P, \lambda)$ and $W_{\mathcal{A},k}$, we define the *annotation* of P as a function $\mathcal{F}^* : S \to CF(\mathcal{A}, k)$, obtained as the limit of the sequence $(\mathsf{Update}^n(\mathcal{F}_0))_{n \ge 0}$, where $\mathcal{F}_0$ maps s_0 to f_0 and any other state to the constant counting function $q \mapsto -1$, and Update is defined for any annotation $\mathcal{F} : S \to CF(\mathcal{A}, k)$ by

$$\mathsf{Update}(\mathcal{F}) : s \in S \mapsto \mathcal{F}(s) \sqcup (\bigsqcup_{s = \delta_P(s', \sigma)} \delta^D(\mathcal{F}(s'), \sigma \cup \lambda(s', \sigma)))$$

The sequence converges in at most $(k+1).|S|.|Q|$ steps because the counting functions which annotate the states of P can only increase with respect to $\preceq$. Intuitively, for any state $s \in S$ and any state $q \in Q$, if $\mathcal{F}^*(s)(q) = x$, then there exists a word u of $L(P)$ such that P reaches state s on u, and there exists a run of $\mathcal{A}$ on u which visits x states from F.

Lemma 1. *[5] $L_k(\mathcal{A})$ is P-realizable iff $\mathcal{F}^*(s) \in W_{\mathcal{A},k}$ for all $s \in S$.*

We have seen that $\mathcal{F}^*$ can be computed in polynomial time, and the tests $\mathcal{F}^*(s) \in W_{\mathcal{A},k}$ can also be done in polynomial time in the size of the antichain representing $W_{\mathcal{A},k}$. To summarize:

Lemma 2. *[5] Given a preMealy machine P, deciding whether the safety specification $L_k(\mathcal{A})$ is P-realizable can be done in polynomial time in the size of P and in the size of $\lceil W_{\mathcal{A},k} \rceil$.*

Let us note that the antichain $W_{\mathcal{A},k}$ can be doubly-exponential in the size of the LTL specification in the worst-case [22]. Nevertheless, this antichain is usually small in practical cases, and is always computed by Acacia-Bonsai for the plain LTL part of the specification, in order to decide if it is realizable. So, our algorithm being polynomial in this structure, which is nonetheless computed, is beneficial.

3.2 Generalization Phase

The generalization phase (Algorithm 2) is a realizability-guided variant of the state-merging based learning algorithm RPNI [26], in which state merges are acceptable only if they lead to a preMealy machine which can be extended to a Mealy machine realizing the specification.

It starts from a consistent set of examples E and computes an equivalence relation $\sim \subseteq (\mathsf{Prefs}(E) \times \mathsf{Prefs}(E)) \cap (\mathcal{IO})^* \times (\mathcal{IO})^*$, initially set to be the finest (the diagonal). Such an equivalence relation is called a *Mealy congruence* if for all $e \sim e'$, all $i \in \mathcal{I}$, if $ei, e'i \in \mathsf{Prefs}(E)$, then (a) $o_E(e.i) = o_E(e'.i)$ and (b) $e.i.o_E(e.i) \sim e'.i.o_E(e'.i)$. From a Mealy congruence $\sim$, one can define the preMealy machine $M_\sim = (E/{\sim}, [\epsilon]_\sim, \delta_\sim, \lambda_\sim)$ where $\delta_\sim([e]_\sim, i) = [e.i.o_E(e.i)]_\sim$ and $\lambda_\sim([e]_\sim, i) = o_E(e.i)$, for all $e.i \in \mathsf{Prefs}(E)$.

Starting intially from the finest equivalence relation, the algorithm attempts to merge classes. This is done by the procedure $\mathsf{Merge}(\sim, \mathsf{e}, \mathsf{e}')$ which attempts to merge $[e]_\sim$ and $[e']_\sim$ (and inductively its successor classes, preserving condition (b) of the definition of Mealy congruence). The resulting equivalence might not be a Mealy congruence, when condition (a) is not satisfied, in which case the merge is not possible. If the merge succeeds, then, using the antichain structure, following the algorithm of Sect. 3.1, Algorithm 2 tests whether the resulting pre-Mealy machine can be extended to a Mealy machine realizing the specification

$L_k(\mathcal{A})$. If it does not, then the merge it discarded, otherwise the Mealy congruence is updated. The merges are done in a specific order to ensure a completeness result: for any preMealy machine P realizing the specification, there exists a set of examples E_P of polynomial size such that $\mathsf{Generalize}(E_P, \text{antichain})$ returns a machine equivalent to P [5].

Algorithm 2: $\mathsf{Generalize}(E, \text{antichain})$: Generalization Algorithm

---

Input: A consistent finite set $E \subseteq (\mathcal{I}.\mathcal{O})^*$ and an antichain representing $W_{\mathcal{A},k}$
Output: A preMealy machine M such that φ is M-realizable and $E \subseteq L(M)$

1 $E \leftarrow \mathsf{Prefs}(E) \cap (\mathcal{I}\mathcal{O})^*$;
2 $\sim\ \leftarrow \{(e,e) \mid e \in E\}$;
3 **for** $e \in E$ *in length-lexicographic order* $\preceq_{ll}$ **do**
4 | **if** $\exists e' \in E : e' \preceq_{ll} e \wedge \mathsf{Merge}(\sim, \mathsf{e}, \mathsf{e}') \neq \mathsf{fail} \wedge \varphi$ *is* $M_{\mathsf{Merge}(\sim,\mathsf{e},\mathsf{e}')}$-*realizable*
   | **then**
5 | | $\sim\ \leftarrow \mathsf{Merge}(\sim, \mathsf{e}, \mathsf{e}')$;
6 **return** $M_\sim$;

Merging Strategy. In Line 4 of Algorithm 2, we may define a strategy to choose e' that can be *merged* with e, if there are multiple candidates. The current implementation of SYNTHLEARN chooses the smallest candidate e' (for length-lexicographic order) which satisfies the condition of the **if**.

3.3   Completion Phase

The completion phase takes as input a preMealy machine and completes its holes by connecting missing transitions to existing states whenever possible, and if not possible, by creating new states. It does so while maintaining the invariant that the machines M computed along its execution can be extended to Mealy

---

Algorithm 3: $\mathsf{Complete}(M, \text{antichain})$: Completion Algorithm

---

Input: A preMealy machine $M = (S, s_0, \delta, \lambda)$ which can be extended to a Mealy
machine realizing $L_k(\mathcal{A})$, and an antichain representing $\lceil W_{\mathcal{A},k} \rceil$
Output: A Mealy machine realizing $L_k(\mathcal{A})$

1 **while** M *has some hole* $\langle s,i \rangle$ **do**
2 | **if** $\exists s' \in S, o \in \mathcal{O}$ *such that* $L_k(\mathcal{A})$ *is* $M_{s,i,o,s'}$-*realizable* **then**
3 | | $M \leftarrow M_{s,i,o,s'}$;   // $M_{s,i,o,s'}$ extends M with $\delta(s,i) = s'$, $\lambda(s,i) = o$.
4 | **else**
5 | | $s' \leftarrow$ fresh new state;
6 | | $M \leftarrow M_{s,i,o,s'}$ for some $o \in \mathcal{O}$ such that $L_k(\mathcal{A})$ is $M_{s,i,o,s'}$-realizable ;
   | | // such an o necessarily exists
7 **return** M

---

machines satisfying the specification $L_k(\mathcal{A})$. This is ensured at line 2 and tested in polynomial time in the size of M and the antichain $\lceil W_{\mathcal{A},k} \rceil$ (as explained in Sect. 3.1).

Completion Strategy. In Line 2 of Algorithm 3, we may define a strategy to choose s' if there are multiple candidates. The current implementation of SYNTHLEARN prioritises the states of M generated at the end of Algorithm 2 to reuse states that were created during the generalization of the examples. If any of those states cannot be reused to complete a missing transition, then the algorithm tries to reuse states created during the completion so far. Otherwise, it creates a new state. This is crucial to ensure termination of the completion [5].

4 Case Studies

The algorithm presented in the previous section has been implemented in a tool called SYNTHLEARN, written in Python and published on github: https://github.com/mrudu/synth-learn. An online demo can be found here which also provides a visual interface for the tool Strix [29]. This tool depends on other existing libraries such as Spot [15] and AALpy [30] for automata/mealy machine manipulation.

In this section, we present two case studies that illustrate a possible methodology supported by SYNTHLEARN, by interacting with it. First, the user inputs an LTL specification φ_{CORE}, and possibly some initial examples, and runs the tool to get a Mealy machine realizing the specification and compatible with the initial examples (or a negative answer if unrealizable). If the user is not satisfied by this first Mealy machine, she can supplement the specification with (additional) examples of execution traces that are desired but not part of the returned solution. The tool is run again, and this iterative process can go on until the user is satisfied (or the tool returns that the specification and the examples are not realizable). By providing sufficiently many examples, the user is always able to get any machine realizing the specification, up to language equivalence; see Theorem 4 in [5] (a polynomial number of examples in the size of the minimal machine suffices).

Input Format. The user specifies the set of input and output Boolean propositions P_{in} and P_{out}, as well as the LTL specification (the syntax is standard). Traces in $(2^{P_{\mathsf{in}}} 2^{P_{\mathsf{out}}})^*$ have the following format: $i_0.o_0 \# i_1.o_1 \# i_2.o_2 \# \ldots i_k.o_k$ where the i_j, o_j are conjunctions of literals over P_{in} and P_{out} respectively. While the conjunctions i_j are not necessarily complete (some symbols of P_{in} do not necessarily appear in i_j), the conjunctions o_j must always be complete, so that traces have a deterministic output-behaviour. Traces with non-complete inputs are called *symbolic*, and are expanded into a set of input-complete traces automatically by the tool. For example, if $P_{\mathsf{in}} = \{a, b\}$ and $P_{\mathsf{out}} = \{c\}$, then the symbolic trace $a.c \# \neg a. \neg c$ imposes the synthesized machine to have the four following behaviours: $(a \wedge b).c \# (\neg a \wedge b). \neg c$, $(a \wedge \neg b).c \# (\neg a \wedge b). \neg c$, $(a \wedge b).c \# (\neg a \wedge \neg b). \neg c$, $(a \wedge \neg b).c \# (\neg a \wedge \neg b). \neg c$.

4.1 Variations on Mutual Exclusion Arbiters

We recall here the classical problem of *mutual exclusion* introduced in Sect. 1: design an arbiter that controls access to a critical section. The arbiter receives *requests* from two processes and *grants* access to the critical section. We model this as $I_{env} = \{r_1, r_2\}$ and $O_{sys} = \{g_1, g_2\}$ with the core LTL specification $\varphi_{\text{MUTEX}}^{\text{CORE}} \equiv \Box(\neg g_1 \vee \neg g_2) \wedge \Box(r_1 \Rightarrow \Diamond g_1) \wedge \Box(r_2 \Rightarrow \Diamond g_2)$. We have already seen in Sect. 1 how a natural solution (that could be obtained manually) would look like for this specification, and it is automatically produced by SYNTHLEARN for the same specification supplemented with two simple examples. Now, we will consider other variations that our tool and methodology can easily handle.

Mutex with Delay. To demonstrate the generalization capabilities of SYNTH-LEARN, let us consider the mutex example with the following additional property: "every time there is no pending request, the arbiter cannot grant access to the critical section directly after the next request" (for instance because the resource needs to wake up to be used again). Identifying the absence of pending requests is hard to express in LTL as noticed in [5]. Let us show that, on the contrary, it is easy to express examples illustrating this property, and show that our algorithm is able to generalize those examples and provide us with an adequate solution automatically.

First, the following symbolic example that expresses that at timestep 0, no grants to the critical section should be given: $E_1 = \{true.\neg g_1 \wedge \neg g_2\}$, as there are no pending requests.

Providing as input $\varphi_{\text{MUTEX}}^{\text{CORE}}$ and examples E_1, we obtain the machine of Fig. 2(a). We can observe that this machine is not the best solution: there are some traces with unsolicited grants. We can improve upon this machine by adding more examples such as $E_2 =$

1. True.$\neg g_1 \wedge \neg g_2$,
2. $r_1 \wedge \neg r_2.\neg g_1 \wedge \neg g_2 \# \neg r_2.$ $g_1 \wedge \neg g_2 \#$True.$\neg g_1 \wedge \neg g_2$,
3. $\neg r_1 \wedge r_2.\neg g_1 \wedge \neg g_2 \# \neg r_1.\neg g_1 \wedge g_2 \#$True.$\neg g_1 \wedge \neg g_2$,
4. $r_1 \wedge r_2.\neg g_1 \wedge \neg g_2 \# \neg r_2.$ $g_1 \wedge \neg g_2 \# \neg r_1.\neg g_1 \wedge g_2 \#$True.$\neg g_1 \wedge \neg g_2$

Providing as input $\varphi_{\text{MUTEX}}^{\text{CORE}}$ and examples E_2, we obtain the solution in Fig. 2(b). The machine is now satisfactory as it enforces the mutex with delay. For instance, in state q_0, there are never pending requests. As a consequence, when the machine receives request r_1 from q_0, it moves to q_1, where it awaits for one time step before granting access as expected.

Mutex with Alternating Grants. Let us now consider another variation. In this one, we want to synthesize an arbiter with the following additional priority rule: at concurrent requests, it first serves the process that was not the last served. For example, if the last access was granted to process 1, at the next concurrent requests, process 2 is granted first.

We again start from $\varphi_{\text{MUTEX}}^{\text{CORE}}$. Instead of trying to encode the priority rule directly in LTL, we instead provide a few examples to guide SYNTHLEARN. To represent the traces in a more readable format, we shall use the following abbreviations (they are supported by our tool):

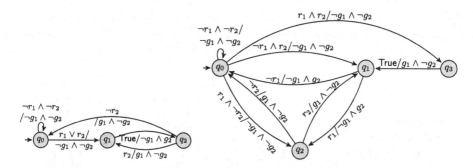

Fig. 2. (Left) The machine obtained from $\varphi_{\mathsf{MUTEX}}^{\mathsf{CORE}}$ and examples E_1. (Right) the machine obtained from $\varphi_{\mathsf{MUTEX}}^{\mathsf{CORE}}$ and examples E_2.

1. $\mathsf{pr}_1 = (r_1 \wedge r_2).(g_1 \wedge \neg g_2)$ and $\mathsf{pr}_2 = (r_1 \wedge r_2).(\neg g_1 \wedge g_2)$ represent that for simultaneous requests, priority is given to process 1 and process 2 resp.
2. $\mathsf{noreqgrant} = (\neg r_1 \wedge \neg r_2).(\neg g_1 \wedge \neg g_2)$ represents no unsolicited grants.
3. $\mathsf{grant}_1 = (g_1 \wedge \neg g_2)$ and $\mathsf{grant}_2 = (\neg g_1 \wedge g_2)$ represent grant access given to process 1 and process 2 respectively.

We define the set of examples E_1 as follows:

1. $\mathsf{noreqgrant}$
2. $(r_1 \wedge \neg r_2).\mathsf{grant}_1 \# \mathsf{pr}_2$
3. $(\neg r_1 \wedge r_2).\mathsf{grant}_2 \# \mathsf{pr}_1$.

The first example is straightforward and expresses that the system must not provide unsolicited grants at the first step. The second and third examples cover two situations which enforce grant alternations: when there is a concurrent request, we make the choice based on the last grant.

Providing the tool with $\varphi_{\mathsf{MUTEX}}^{\mathsf{CORE}}$ and examples E_1, we obtain the machine represented in Fig. 3(Left). Although this is already a nice solution, we can see that some traces that are not optimal. For instance, consider the trace $(r_1 \wedge \neg r_2).\mathsf{grant}_1$ which reaches state q_1. We now have *no pending requests*, but however we observe an unsolicited grant from q_1 via the trace $(r_1 \wedge \neg r_2).\mathsf{grant}_1 \#(\neg r_1 \wedge \neg r_2).\mathsf{grant}_2$.

To obtain a better machine, we add a set of examples that correct the incorrect executions highlighted above and additional examples obtained by two additional interactions with the tool. The final set of examples is defined as follows $E_2 = \{$

1. $\mathsf{noreqgrant}$,
2. $(r_1 \wedge \neg r_2).\mathsf{grant}_1 \# \mathsf{pr}_2 \#(\neg r_2).\mathsf{grant}_1 \# \mathsf{pr}_2$,
3. $(\neg r_1 \wedge r_2).\mathsf{grant}_2 \# \mathsf{pr}_1 \# (\neg r_1).\mathsf{grant}_2 \# \mathsf{pr}_1$,
4. $(\neg r_1 \wedge r_2).\mathsf{grant}_2 \#(\neg r_1 \wedge r_2).\mathsf{grant}_2 \# \mathsf{pr}_1$,
5. $(\neg r_1 \wedge r_2).\mathsf{grant}_2 \#(\neg r_1 \wedge r_2).\mathsf{grant}_2 \# \mathsf{noreqgrant}$,
6. $(\neg r_1 \wedge r_2).\mathsf{grant}_2 \# \mathsf{noreqgrant}$,
7. $(\neg r_1 \wedge r_2).\mathsf{grant}_2 \# \mathsf{pr}_1 \#(\neg r_1).\mathsf{grant}_2 \# \mathsf{pr}_1$,
8. $(\neg r_1 \wedge r_2).\mathsf{grant}_2 \# \mathsf{pr}_1 \#(\neg r_1).\mathsf{grant}_2 \# \mathsf{noreqgrant}\}$

Providing the tool with $\varphi_{\text{MUTEX}}^{\text{CORE}}$ and examples E_2, we obtain the solution in Fig. 3(Right). This machine correctly enforces $\varphi_{\text{MUTEX}}^{\text{CORE}}$ and the alternating property, additionally it does not output unsolicited grants.

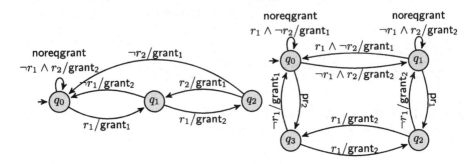

Fig. 3. (Left) the machine obtained from $\varphi_{\text{MUTEX}}^{\text{CORE}}$ and examples E_1. (Right) the machine obtained from $\varphi_{\text{MUTEX}}^{\text{CORE}}$ and examples E_2.

4.2   Arbiter for a Three-Way Intersection

Here, we consider a three-way intersection as shown in Fig. 4a. There are 6 routes $\{1 \rightarrow 2, 2 \rightarrow 1, 2 \rightarrow 3, 3 \rightarrow 2, 3 \rightarrow 1, 1 \rightarrow 3\}$. We aim to design an arbiter which grants access to these routes safely, for instance route $1 \rightarrow 3$ should not be allowed together with route $2 \rightarrow 1$ to avoid a potential car collision. Additionally, an *urgency* signal can be emitted to block all the routes with the intention to allow emergency vehicles to operate safely. We model this using the following atomic propositions $I_{env} = \{u\}$ and $O_{sys} = \{g_{ij} \mid i, j \in \{1, 2, 3\}, i \neq j\}$, where g_{ij} represents access to route $i \rightarrow j$.

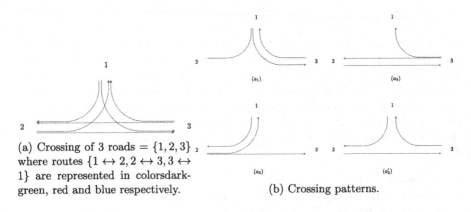

(a) Crossing of 3 roads $= \{1, 2, 3\}$ where routes $\{1 \leftrightarrow 2, 2 \leftrightarrow 3, 3 \leftrightarrow 1\}$ are represented in colorsdark-green, red and blue respectively.

(b) Crossing patterns.

Fig. 4. Representation of 3 cross roads and crossing patterns.

Our requirements (guarantees) $\varphi_{\text{CROSS}}^{G}$ can be modelled as a conjunction of the following formulas expressing guarantees that must be enforced:

1. $\Box(u \rightarrow (\neg g_{12} \wedge \neg g_{21} \wedge \neg g_{13} \wedge \neg g_{31} \wedge \neg g_{23} \wedge \neg g_{32}))$ to represent that if the arbiter receives an urgency request, then it must close all directions of traffic to prioritize the crossing of *emergency services*.
2. $\Box\Diamond g_{ij}$ for all $i,j \in 1,2,3, i \neq j$ represents that every direction of traffic must be granted access infinitely often (*liveness*).
3. Additionally, we add the following requirements avoid potential collisions:
   (a) $\Box(g_{23} \rightarrow \neg g_{13})$
   (b) $\Box(g_{32} \rightarrow (\neg g_{12} \wedge \neg g_{21}))$
   (c) $\Box(g_{21} \rightarrow \neg g_{31})$
   (d) $\Box(g_{21} \rightarrow \neg g_{13})$
   (e) $\Box(g_{13} \rightarrow \neg g_{32})$

We also make a realistic assumption $\varphi^A_{\text{CROSS}} := \Box\Diamond\neg u$, which denotes that the traffic will not be blocked by *emergency services*. Thus, our *core* LTL specification is $\varphi^{\text{CORE}}_{\text{CROSS}} \equiv \varphi^A_{\text{CROSS}} \implies \varphi^G_{\text{CROSS}}$. Providing this as input to the tool SYNTHLEARN, we obtain the machine in Fig. 5(Left), where, for better readability, we use the following abbreviations:

1. $a_1 = (\quad g_{12} \wedge \quad g_{13} \wedge \neg g_{23} \wedge \neg g_{32} \wedge \quad g_{31} \wedge \neg g_{21})$
2. $a_2 = (\quad g_{21} \wedge \quad g_{23} \wedge \quad g_{12} \wedge \neg g_{32} \wedge \neg g_{31} \wedge \neg g_{13})$
3. $a_3 = (\quad g_{23} \wedge \quad g_{31} \wedge \quad g_{32} \wedge \neg g_{13} \wedge \neg g_{21} \wedge \neg g_{12})$
4. $none = \neg g_{23} \wedge \neg g_{31} \wedge \neg g_{32} \wedge \neg g_{13} \wedge \neg g_{21} \wedge \neg g_{12}$.

Those decisions a_1, a_2, and a_3 are depicted pictorially in Fig. 4b.

We observe that this is already an interesting machine. But now, assume that the routes $2 \rightarrow 3$ and $3 \rightarrow 2$ are the principal routes and we would like to give them some priority. Those roads are both enabled under a_3. To obtain a new machine where those roads have higher priority, we simply add the following example: $e_1 = \neg u.a_3 \# \neg u.a_3 \# \neg u.a_1 \# \neg u.a_2\}$, so that the frequency of a_3 is twice the frequency of the other.

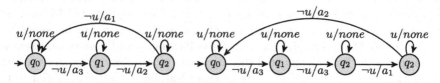

Fig. 5. (Left) the machine obtained from φ_{CROSS} and no examples. (Right) the machine obtained from $\varphi^{\text{CORE}}_{\text{CROSS}}$ and example e_1.

Cross Section with Sensors. Let us consider another variation. In this one, we introduce a sensor on route $2 \rightarrow 1$ which will emit a signal e_{21} if the route is empty. So the input atomic propositions are $I_{env} = \{u, e_{21}\}$ and we keep the same output propositions as before. Our requirements (guarantees) $\varphi^G_{\text{CROSS}-\text{SENSOR}}$ are the same as before (φ^G_{CROSS}), with the exception that we replace $\Box\Diamond g_{21}$ with $\Box(\neg e_{21} \rightarrow \Diamond g_{21})$. The assumptions are the same as before plus some extra: $\varphi^A_{\text{CROSS}-\text{SENSOR}} = \varphi^A_{\text{CROSS}} \wedge \Box(\neg e_{21} \rightarrow (\neg e_{21} W g_{21}))$. The additional assumption states that the sensor e_{21} will remain activated until the access to route $2 \to 1$ is granted. We let $\varphi_{\text{CROSS-SENSOR}}^{\text{CORE}} := \varphi_{\text{CROSS-SENSOR}}^{A} \implies \varphi_{\text{CROSS-SENSOR}}^{G}$.

Providing the tool with $\varphi_{\text{CROSS-SENSOR}}^{\text{CORE}}$ and no examples, we obtain the already interesting solution in Fig. 6 (Left). Again, let us assume that we prioritise a_3. When e_{21} is true, there is no need to enable route $2 \to 1$ and hence a_2 is replaced by $a_2' = (\neg g_{21} \wedge g_{23} \wedge g_{12} \wedge \neg g_{32} \wedge g_{31} \wedge \neg g_{13})$ which instead enables route $3 \to 1$ (see Fig. 4b). Now, we add the following two examples which discrimate between two situations depending on whether e_{21} is true or not, both are prioritising a_3: $E_3 =$

1. $(\neg u \wedge \neg e_{21}).a_3 \# (\neg u \wedge \neg e_{21}).a_3 \# (\neg u \wedge \neg e_{21}).a_2 \# (\neg u \wedge \neg e_{21}).a_1,$
2. $(\neg u \wedge \ e_{21}).a_3 \# (\neg u \wedge \ e_{21}).a_3 \# (\neg u \wedge \ e_{21}).a_2' \# (\neg u \wedge \ e_{21}).a_1$

The tool then returns the solution in Fig. 6(Right): it has inferred that for decisions a_3 and a_1, whether e_{21} is true or not does not matter.

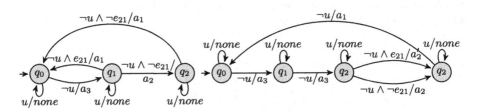

Fig. 6. (Left) the machine obtained from $\varphi_{\text{CROSS-SENSOR}}^{\text{CORE}}$ and no examples. (Right) the machine obtained from $\varphi_{\text{CROSS-SENSOR}}^{\text{CORE}}$ and example E_3. In both figures, in contrast to the output provided by SYNTHLEARN, one edge that was not complying with the assumption has been omitted for the sake of readability.

5   Conclusion

We have developed a synthesis method that leverages user-provided examples of executions, addressing the issue of unnatural solutions generated by existing tools with only high-level specifications. Our algorithm, proven to be complete, can derive any Mealy machine M from a specification φ and a set of representative examples E. We implemented this algorithm in a prototype tool, enhancing Acacia-Bonzai with specialized state-merging learning algorithms. Initial tests show that few examples are needed to produce high-quality machines from LTL specifications.

Future work will focus on improving the user interface for specifying (counter-)examples interactively and concisely. We plan to explore parametric examples (like an elevator with a variable number of floors), necessitating a concise syntax and an efficient synthesis algorithm for such scenarios. Additionally, we aim to integrate negative examples into the tool. We have already explored how to integrate negative example in our framework in [33] and plan to integrate them in the tool. Nevertheless, the way we treat negative examples for the moment is naive as we do not try to generalize them. This will require more work in the future.

References

1. Abadi, M., Lamport, L., Wolper, P.: Realizable and unrealizable specifications of reactive systems. In: Ausiello, G., Dezani-Ciancaglini, M., Della Rocca, S.R. (eds.) ICALP 1989. LNCS, vol. 372, pp. 1–17. Springer, Heidelberg (1989). https://doi.org/10.1007/BFb0035748
2. Alur, R., Fisman, D., Singh, R., Solar-Lezama, A.: Results and analysis of syguscomp'15. In: Cerný, P., Kuncak, V., Madhusudan, P. (eds.) Proceedings Fourth Workshop on Synthesis, SYNT 2015, San Francisco, CA, USA, 18th July 2015. EPTCS, vol. 202, pp. 3–26 (2015). https://doi.org/10.4204/EPTCS.202.3
3. Alur, R., Martin, M., Raghothaman, M., Stergiou, C., Tripakis, S., Udupa, A.: Synthesizing finite-state protocols from scenarios and requirements. In: Yahav, E. (ed.) HVC 2014. LNCS, vol. 8855, pp. 75–91. Springer, Cham (2014). https://doi.org/10.1007/978-3-319-13338-6_7
4. Backus, J.W., et al.: Revised report on the algorithmic language ALGOL 60. Comput. J. 5(4), 349–367 (1963). https://doi.org/10.1093/comjnl/5.4.349
5. Balachander, M., Filiot, E., Raskin, J.: LTL reactive synthesis with a few hints. In: Sankaranarayanan, S., Sharygina, N. (eds.) Tools and Algorithms for the Construction and Analysis of Systems - 29th International Conference, TACAS 2023, Held as Part of the European Joint Conferences on Theory and Practice of Software, ETAPS 2022, Paris, France, 22–27 April 2023, Proceedings, Part II. LNCS, vol. 13994, pp. 309–328. Springer (2023). https://doi.org/10.1007/978-3-031-30820-8_20
6. Bloem, R., Chatterjee, K., Henzinger, T.A., Jobstmann, B.: Better quality in synthesis through quantitative objectives. In: Bouajjani, A., Maler, O. (eds.) CAV 2009. LNCS, vol. 5643, pp. 140–156. Springer, Heidelberg (2009). https://doi.org/10.1007/978-3-642-02658-4_14
7. Bloem, R., Chockler, H., Ebrahimi, M., Strichman, O.: Synthesizing non-vacuous systems. In: Bouajjani, A., Monniaux, D. (eds.) VMCAI 2017. LNCS, vol. 10145, pp. 55–72. Springer, Cham (2017). https://doi.org/10.1007/978-3-319-52234-0_4
8. Bohy, A., Bruyère, V., Filiot, E., Jin, N., Raskin, J.: Acacia+, a tool for LTL synthesis. In: Madhusudan, P., Seshia, S.A. (eds.) Computer Aided Verification - 24th International Conference, CAV 2012, Berkeley, CA, USA, 7–13 July 2012 Proceedings. LNCS, vol. 7358, pp. 652–657. Springer (2012). https://doi.org/10.1007/978-3-642-31424-7_45
9. Bruyère, V., Filiot, E., Randour, M., Raskin, J.: Meet your expectations with guarantees: beyond worst-case synthesis in quantitative games. Inf. Comput. 254, 259–295 (2017). https://doi.org/10.1016/j.ic.2016.10.011
10. Cadilhac, M., Pérez, G.A.: Acacia-bonsai: A modern implementation of downset-based ltl realizability (2022)
11. Clarke, E.M., Henzinger, T.A., Veith, H., Bloem, R. (eds.): Handbook of Model Checking. Springer (2018). https://doi.org/10.1007/978-3-319-10575-8
12. Damas, C., Lambeau, B., van Lamsweerde, A.: Scenarios, goals, and state machines: a win-win partnership for model synthesis. In: Young, M., Devanbu, P.T. (eds.) Proceedings of the 14th ACM SIGSOFT International Symposium on Foundations of Software Engineering, FSE 2006, Portland, Oregon, USA, 5–11 November 2006, pp. 197–207. ACM (2006). https://doi.org/10.1145/1181775.1181800
13. Dupont, P., Lambeau, B., Damas, C., van Lamsweerde, A.: The QSM algorithm and its application to software behavior model induction. Appl. Artif. Intell. 22(1&2), 77–115 (2008). https://doi.org/10.1080/08839510701853200

14. Duret-Lutz, A., et al.: From spot 2.0 to spot 2.10: what's new? In: Shoham, S., Vizel, Y. (eds.) Computer Aided Verification - 34th International Conference, CAV 2022, Haifa, Israel, 7–10 August 2022, Proceedings, Part II. LNCS, vol. 13372, pp. 174–187. Springer (2022). https://doi.org/10.1007/978-3-031-13188-2_9

15. Duret-Lutz, A., et al.: From Spot 2.0 to Spot 2.10: What's new? In: Proceedings of the 34th International Conference on Computer Aided Verification (CAV 2022). LNCS, vol. 13372, pp. 174–187. Springer (2022). https://doi.org/10.1007/978-3-031-13188-2_9

16. Esparza, J., Křetínský, J.: From LTL to deterministic automata: a safraless compositional approach. In: Biere, A., Bloem, R. (eds.) CAV 2014. LNCS, vol. 8559, pp. 192–208. Springer, Cham (2014). https://doi.org/10.1007/978-3-319-08867-9_13

17. Esparza, J., Křetínský, J., Raskin, J.-F., Sickert, S.: From LTL and limit-deterministic büchi automata to deterministic parity automata. In: Legay, A., Margaria, T. (eds.) TACAS 2017. LNCS, vol. 10205, pp. 426–442. Springer, Heidelberg (2017). https://doi.org/10.1007/978-3-662-54577-5_25

18. Esparza, J., Kretínský, J., Sickert, S.: One theorem to rule them all: A unified translation of LTL into ω-automata. In: Dawar, A., Grädel, E. (eds.) Proceedings of the 33rd Annual ACM/IEEE Symposium on Logic in Computer Science, LICS 2018, Oxford, UK, 09–12 July 2018, pp. 384–393. ACM (2018). https://doi.org/10.1145/3209108.3209161

19. Esparza, J., Kretínský, J., Sickert, S.: A unified translation of linear temporal logic to ω-automata. J. ACM **67**(6), 33:1–33:61 (2020). https://doi.org/10.1145/3417995

20. Esparza, J., Rubio, R., Sickert, S.: A simple rewrite system for the normalization of linear temporal logic (2023). https://doi.org/10.48550/ARXIV.2304.08872, CoRR abs/arXiv: 2304.08872

21. Faymonville, P., Finkbeiner, B., Tentrup, L.: Bosy: An experimentation framework for bounded synthesis (2018)

22. Filiot, E., Jin, N., Raskin, J.-F.: An antichain algorithm for LTL realizability. In: Bouajjani, A., Maler, O. (eds.) CAV 2009. LNCS, vol. 5643, pp. 263–277. Springer, Heidelberg (2009). https://doi.org/10.1007/978-3-642-02658-4_22

23. Harel, D., Pnueli, A.: On the development of reactive systems. In: Apt, K.R. (ed.) Logics and Models of Concurrent Systems - Conference proceedings, Colle-sur-Loup (near Nice), France, 8–19 October 1984. NATO ASI Series, vol. 13, pp. 477–498. Springer (1984). https://doi.org/10.1007/978-3-642-82453-1_17

24. Heinz, J., de la Higuera, C., van Zaanen, M.: Grammatical Inference for Computational Linguistics. Synthesis Lectures on Human Language Technologies, Morgan & Claypool Publishers (2015). https://doi.org/10.2200/S00643ED1V01Y201504HLT028

25. Hoare, C.A.R.: An overview of some formal methods for program design. Computer **20**(9), 85–91 (1987). https://doi.org/10.1109/MC.1987.1663697

26. Oncina, J., Garcia, P.: Inferring regular languages in polynomial updated time. Pattern Recogn. Image Anal., 49–61 (1992)

27. Křetínský, J., Esparza, J.: Deterministic automata for the (F,G)-fragment of LTL. In: Madhusudan, P., Seshia, S.A. (eds.) CAV 2012. LNCS, vol. 7358, pp. 7–22. Springer, Heidelberg (2012). https://doi.org/10.1007/978-3-642-31424-7_7

28. Kupferman, O., Vardi, M.Y.: Safraless decision procedures. In: 46th Annual IEEE Symposium on Foundations of Computer Science (FOCS 2005), 23–25 October 2005, Pittsburgh, PA, USA, Proceedings, pp. 531–542. IEEE Computer Society (2005). https://doi.org/10.1109/SFCS.2005.66

29. Meyer, P.J., Sickert, S., Luttenberger, M.: Strix: explicit reactive synthesis strikes back! In: Chockler, H., Weissenbacher, G. (eds.) CAV 2018. LNCS, vol. 10981, pp. 578–586. Springer, Cham (2018). https://doi.org/10.1007/978-3-319-96145-3_31
30. Muškardin, E., Aichernig, B.K., Pill, I., Pferscher, A., Tappler, M.: AALpy: an active automata learning library. In: Hou, Z., Ganesh, V. (eds.) ATVA 2021. LNCS, vol. 12971, pp. 67–73. Springer, Cham (2021). https://doi.org/10.1007/978-3-030-88885-5_5
31. Pnueli, A., Rosner, R.: On the synthesis of an asynchronous reactive module. In: Ausiello, G., Dezani-Ciancaglini, M., Della Rocca, S.R. (eds.) ICALP 1989. LNCS, vol. 372, pp. 652–671. Springer, Heidelberg (1989). https://doi.org/10.1007/BFb0035790
32. Raha, R., Roy, R., Fijalkow, N., Neider, D.: Scalable anytime algorithms for learning fragments of linear temporal logic. In: TACAS 2022. LNCS, vol. 13243, pp. 263–280. Springer, Cham (2022). https://doi.org/10.1007/978-3-030-99524-9_14
33. Ren, Z.: LTL synthesis problem with examples (Master Thesis). Master's thesis, Université libre de Bruxelles (2023)
34. Safra, S.: On the complexity of omega-automata. In: 29th Annual Symposium on Foundations of Computer Science, White Plains, New York, USA, 24–26 October 1988, pp. 319–327. IEEE Computer Society (1988). https://doi.org/10.1109/SFCS.1988.21948
35. Schewe, S., Finkbeiner, B.: Bounded synthesis. In: Namjoshi, K.S., Yoneda, T., Higashino, T., Okamura, Y. (eds.) ATVA 2007. LNCS, vol. 4762, pp. 474–488. Springer, Heidelberg (2007). https://doi.org/10.1007/978-3-540-75596-8_33
36. Sickert, S., Esparza, J., Jaax, S., Křetínský, J.: Limit-Deterministic Büchi automata for linear temporal logic. In: Chaudhuri, S., Farzan, A. (eds.) CAV 2016. LNCS, vol. 9780, pp. 312–332. Springer, Cham (2016). https://doi.org/10.1007/978-3-319-41540-6_17

On Regular Expression Proof Complexity of Salomaa's Axiom System F_1

Simon Beier and Markus Holzer[(✉)]

Institut für Informatik, Universität Giessen, Arndtstr. 2, 35392 Giessen, Germany
holzer@informatik.uni-giessen.de

Abstract. We investigate the proof complexity of Salomaa's axiom system F_1 for regular expression equivalence. We show that for two regular expression E and F over the alphabet Σ with $L(E) = L(F)$ an equivalence proof of length at most $O\left(|\Sigma|^4 \cdot \text{TOWER}(\max\{h(E), h(F)\} + 4)\right)$ can be derived within F_1, where $h(E)$ ($h(F)$, respectively) refers to the height of E (F, respectively) and the tower function is defined as $\text{TOWER}(1) = 2$ and $\text{TOWER}(k + 1) = 2^{\text{TOWER}(k)}$, for $k \geq 1$. In other words

$$\text{TOWER}(k) = 2^{2^{2^{\cdot^{\cdot^{\cdot^2}}}}} \Big\} k.$$

It is well known that regular expression equivalence admits exponential proof length if *not* restricted to the axiom system F_1. From the theoretical point of view the exponential proof length seems to be best possible, because we show that regular expression equivalence admits a polynomial bounded proof if and only if NP = PSPACE.

1 Introduction

Regular expressions were introduced in the seminal paper of Kleene [6] on nerve nets and finite automata. They allow a beautiful set-theoretic characterization of languages accepted by finite automata. Early results concerning regular expressions can be found in [1,7]. These papers were very influential in shaping automata theory. Compared to automata, regular expressions are better suited for human users and therefore are often used as interfaces to specify certain patterns or languages. On the other hand, automata are regularly used for its manipulation, since the methods developed during the years turned out to be usually more efficient compared to those for regular expressions. For instance, if one wants to check regular expressions for equivalence, they are converted to equivalent nondeterministic finite automata, followed by determinizing these devices to equivalent deterministic finite state devices, which are finally minimized and checked for equivalence up to isomorphism. It is worth mentioning

This paper is a completely revised and expanded version of the paper "On Regular Expression Proof Complexity" presented at the 21st International Conference Developments in Language Theory (DLT) held in Liège, Belgium, August 7–11, 2017.

S. Kiefer et al. (Eds.): *Taming the Infinities of Concurrency*, LNCS 14660, pp. 72–100, 2024.
https://doi.org/10.1007/978-3-031-56222-8_4

that a relatively simple decision procedure for the equivalence of regular expressions was given in [3]. In general the equivalence of regular expression is a costly task, because it was classified to be PSPACE-complete in [9]—see also [5].

A completely different method for regular expression equivalence, which is entirely based on regular expressions, is to give a proof in the complete and sound axiom system F_1 for regular expression equivalence developed in [8]. It is clear that with this approach one cannot overcome the PSPACE barrier, but to our knowledge the proof length complexity of regular expressions and problems related to this question is not studied in the relevant literature up to now. In general proof complexity asks the question how difficult it is to prove a theorem—here we view regular expression equivalence as a "theorem" to prove. One natural measure on the complexity of a theorem is its proof length within a certain proof system. Thus, the question on the proof length complexity of Salomaa's axiom system F_1 arises. By a careful analysis of Salomaa's proof on the completeness of the axiom system F_1 we obtain an upper bound on the proof length complexity of regular expression equivalence for expressions E and F over the alphabet Σ, if $L(E) = L(F)$, which is enormous, namely bounded by

$$O(|\Sigma|^4 \cdot \text{TOWER}(\max\{h(E), h(F)\} + 4)),$$

where $h(E)$ ($h(F)$, respectively) refers to the height of expression E (F, respectively) and the tower function is defined as

$$\text{TOWER}(1) = 2 \quad \text{and} \quad \text{TOWER}(k+1) = 2^{\text{TOWER}(k)}, \quad \text{for } k \geq 1.$$

In other words

$$\text{TOWER}(k) = 2^{2^{2^{\cdot^{\cdot^{\cdot^2}}}}} \Big\} k.$$

Whether this bound is best possible (at least asymptotically) or can be improved is left open. Up to our knowledge no lower bound for regular expression equivalence using Salomaa's axiom system F_1 is known. On the other hand, what happens, if we do not restrict ourselves to regular expression equivalence proofs in the axiom system F_1? This immediately leads us to proof complexity in general as developed in [2]. The following result is well known in propositional proof complexity: NP=coNP if and only if the set TAUT of all propositional tautologies admits a polynomial bounded proof system. The ultimate goal of propositional proof complexity is to show that there is no propositional proof system allowing for efficient proofs of tautology. But what is the relation of the aforementioned result to regular expression equivalence? We show that within the proof system of [2] that NP=PSPACE if and only if the set

$$\text{EQUIV} = \{\, (E, F) \mid E \text{ and } F \text{ are regular expressions with } L(E) = L(F) \,\}$$

gives rise to a polynomial bounded proof. This is in perfect line with the PSPACE-completeness of EQUIV of [9]. This already shows that we cannot hope for "short" proofs on regular expression equivalence because this is equivalent to a quite unrealistic assumption NP=PSPACE from a computational complexity perspective.

The paper is organized as follows: in the next section we introduce the necessary notations on regular expressions and the axiom system F_1. Then in Sect. 3 we analyze Salomaa's completeness proof of the axiom system F_1 for regular expression equivalence from [8]. This section is the main part of this paper, because first we have to show how to obtain an equational characterization of the involved regular expressions only using the power of the axiom system F_1. Then this characterization is used to develop a proof on equivalence, if both given expressions E and F describe the same set, that is $L(E) = L(F)$. Finally, in Sect. 4, we study the proof complexity of regular expression equivalence in general.

2   Preliminaries

We assume the reader to be familiar with the notations in automata and formal language theory as contained in [4]. Let Σ be an alphabet and Σ^* be the set of all words over the alphabet Σ, including the empty word λ. A set $L \subseteq \Sigma^*$ is called a *language*. Operations on languages we are interested in are union, concatenation, and Kleene star.

The *regular expressions* over an alphabet Σ and the languages that they denote are inductively defined as follows:[1] 0 and every letter a with $a \in \Sigma$ is a regular expression, and when E and F are regular expressions, then $E + F$, $E \cdot F$, and E^* are also regular expressions. The language defined by a regular expression is defined as follows: $L(0) = \emptyset$, $L(a) = \{a\}$, $L(E + F) = L(E) \cup L(F)$, $L(E \cdot F) = L(E) \cdot L(F)$, and $L(E^*) = L(E)^*$. Observe that the empty word must be represented by 0^*, since we have not introduced an extra regular expression denoting λ. We write $E \equiv F$, if the regular expressions E and F are syntactically the same. Of course $E \equiv F$ implies $L(E) = L(F)$, but not the other way around. For convenience, parentheses are sometimes omitted and the concatenation is simply written as juxtaposition. The priority of operators is specified in the usual fashion: concatenation is performed before union, and star before both product and union. We further assume that bracketing of expressions $E_1 + E_2 + \cdots + E_n$ is done from left-to-right, that is $((\ldots ((E_1 + E_2) + E_3) + \ldots) + E_{n-1}) + E_n$. We use the same convention for concatenation.

In [8] a sound and complete axiom system, called F_1, for regular expression equivalence was given. The axioms of F_1 are

(A_1) $E + (F + G) = (E + F) + G$ (A_7) $0^* \cdot E = E$

(A_2) $E \cdot (F \cdot G) = (E \cdot F) \cdot G$ (A_8) $0 \cdot E = 0$

(A_3) $E + F = F + E$ (A_9) $E + 0 = E$

(A_4) $(E + F) \cdot G = E \cdot G + F \cdot G$ (A_{10}) $E^* = 0^* + E^* \cdot E$

(A_5) $E \cdot (F + G) = E \cdot F + E \cdot G$ (A_{11}) $E^* = (0^* + E)^*$,

(A_6) $E + E = E$

---

[1] For convenience, parentheses in regular expressions are sometimes omitted and the concatenation is simply written as juxtaposition. The priority of operators is specified in the usual fashion: concatenation is performed before union, and star before both product and union.

where E, F, and G are regular expressions. The inference rules of F_1 are substitution (R_1)

$$\frac{E = F \qquad C[E] = G}{C[F] = C[E], \quad C[F] = G}$$

and solution of equations (R_2)

$$\frac{E = E \cdot F + G}{E = G \cdot F^*} \text{ if } o(F) = 0$$

where again E, F, and G are regular expressions and $C[E]$ refers to a regular expression C that contains E as a subexpression. Here

$$o(F) = \begin{cases} 1 & F \text{ possesses e.w.p.} \\ 0 & \text{otherwise,} \end{cases}$$

where e.w.p. is an abbreviation for empty word property. A regular expression E possesses e.w.p. if $\lambda \in L(E)$. This property can be inductively verified as follows:

$$o(0) = o(a) = 0,$$

$$o(E + F) = \begin{cases} 1 & \text{if } o(E) = 1 \text{ or } o(F) = 1 \\ 0 & \text{otherwise,} \end{cases}$$

$$o(E \cdot F) = \begin{cases} 1 & \text{if } o(E) = 1 \text{ and } o(F) = 1 \\ 0 & \text{otherwise,} \end{cases}$$

and

$$o(E^*) = 1.$$

A proof in the axiom system F_1 is a finite sequence of applications of the rules R_1 and R_2 where each equation at the top of the rules is an axiom or appears at the bottom of an earlier rule in the sentence. An equation $E = F$ is derivable within the system F_1 if there is a proof where the equation $E = F$ stands at the bottom of the last rule. A set of equations T is derivable from a finite set of equations S if there is a finite sequence of applications of the rules R_1 and R_2 where each equation at the top of the rules is an axiom or an equation out of S or appears at the bottom of an earlier rule in the sentence and all of the equations of T are contained somewhere in the sequence.

We give a small example of a derivation in the axiom system F_1. A more elaborated one can be found in the Appendix.

Example 1. Obviously $L(0 \cdot a) = L(0)$ and $L(a \cdot 0) = L(0)$, too. While the first equation $0 \cdot a = 0$ is an axiom in the system F_1, the latter equation $a \cdot 0 = 0$ has to be proven explicitly. The axiom A_2 gives us $a \cdot (0 \cdot 0) = (a \cdot 0) \cdot 0$ and A_8 gives us $0 \cdot 0 = 0$. With R_1 we get

$$\frac{0 \cdot 0 = 0 \qquad a \cdot (0 \cdot 0) = (a \cdot 0) \cdot 0}{a \cdot 0 = a \cdot (0 \cdot 0), \, a \cdot 0 = (a \cdot 0) \cdot 0}$$

One use of R_1 tells us $a \cdot 0 + 0 = a \cdot 0 + 0$—compare with Lemma 2—and using R_1 again gives

$$\frac{a \cdot 0 = (a \cdot 0) \cdot 0 \qquad a \cdot 0 + 0 = a \cdot 0 + 0}{(a \cdot 0) \cdot 0 + 0 = a \cdot 0 + 0, \ (a \cdot 0) \cdot 0 + 0 = a \cdot 0 + 0}$$

With R_1 we get $a \cdot 0 + 0 = (a \cdot 0) \cdot 0 + 0$ and Axiom A_9 implies $a \cdot 0 + 0 = a \cdot 0$. Another use of R_1 tells us

$$\frac{a \cdot 0 + 0 = a \cdot 0 \qquad a \cdot 0 + 0 = (a \cdot 0) \cdot 0 + 0}{a \cdot 0 = a \cdot 0 + 0, \ a \cdot 0 = (a \cdot 0) \cdot 0 + 0}$$

Now we use R_2:

$$\frac{a \cdot 0 = (a \cdot 0) \cdot 0 + 0}{a \cdot 0 = 0 \cdot 0^*}$$

The rule R_1 gives $0 \cdot 0^* = a \cdot 0$ and Axiom A_8 leads us to $0 \cdot 0^* = 0$. We use R_1 one last time and obtain

$$\frac{0 \cdot 0^* = a \cdot 0 \qquad 0 \cdot 0^* = 0}{a \cdot 0 = 0 \cdot 0^*, \ a \cdot 0 = 0}$$

So we have found a proof for $a \cdot 0 = 0$ using R_1 seven times and R_2 once. □

Next we define some descriptional complexity measures for regular expressions. For a regular expression E, we define $|E|.$ and $|E|_*$ to be the numbers of appearances of the symbols "$\cdot$" and "$*$" in E. For a regular expression E over the alphabet Σ the *height* is inductively defined by

$$h(E) = \begin{cases} 0 & \text{if } E \equiv 0 \text{ or } E \equiv a, \text{ for } a \in \Sigma \\ 1 + \max\{h(F), h(G)\} & \text{if } E \equiv F + G \text{ or } E \equiv F \cdot G \\ 1 + h(F) & \text{if } E \equiv F^*. \end{cases}$$

Finally, we introduce equational characterizations of regular expressions, see, e.g., [8]. Assume $\Sigma = \{a_1, a_2, \ldots, a_r\}$. Then for a regular expression E over the alphabet Σ an *equational characterization* is a system of equations

$$E_i = \sum_{j=1}^{r} E_{i,j} a_j + \delta_i, \quad \text{for } i = 1, 2, \ldots, n,$$

for some $n \geq 1$ and regular expressions $E_1, E_2, \ldots, E_n$ over Σ with $E_1 \equiv E$. Furthermore, for every i we have $\delta_i \equiv 0$ or $\delta_i \equiv 0^*$. For each i and j there is a $k \in \{1, 2, \ldots, n\}$ such that $E_{i,j} \equiv E_k$. From [8, Lemma 4] we know that for every regular expression there exists a derivable equational characterization in the axiom system F_1.

3 Regular Expression Proof Complexity Within Salomaa's Axiom System F_1

Our goal is, for regular expressions E and F with $L(E) = L(F)$, to give an upper bound for a proof of the equation $E = F$ in the axiom system F_1. It suffices to determine how often the inference rules R_1 and R_2 are applied. From this one can deduce a trivial upper bound on the proof length. To do this, (i) we will proof some equations that hold for every regular expression and are often needed in the following (ii) Then, we will give an upper bound for the number of equations in a derivable equational characterization for a regular expression and for the proof of the equational characterization. (iii) Finally, we will show how to derive the equation $E = F$ from the equational characterizations for E and F. We start with the observation that $=$ is an equivalence relation:

Lemma 2. *Let E, F, and G be regular expressions. The equation $E = E$ is derivable with one use of R_1 and no uses of R_2. The equation $F = E$ is derivable from $E = F$ with one use of R_1 and no uses of R_2. The equation $E = G$ is derivable from $E = F$ and $F = G$ with two uses of R_1 and no uses of R_2.*

Proof. The axiom A_6 tells us $E + E = E$. We use R_1:

$$\frac{E + E = E \qquad E + E = E}{E = E + E,\ E = E}$$

Also with R_1 we get

$$\frac{E = F \qquad E = F}{F = E,\ F = F}$$

Another use of R_1 gives us

$$\frac{F = E \qquad F = G}{E = F,\ E = G}$$

$\square$

Next we give upper bounds for the proofs of $E \cdot 0 = 0$ and $E \cdot 0^* = E$.

Lemma 3. *For a regular expression E the equation $E \cdot 0 = 0$ is derivable with seven uses of R_1 and one use of R_2. From the equation $E \cdot 0 = 0$ the equation $E \cdot 0^* = E$ is derivable with four uses of R_1 and one use of R_2.*

Proof. The axiom A_2 gives us $E \cdot (0 \cdot 0) = (E \cdot 0) \cdot 0$ and A_8 gives us $0 \cdot 0 = 0$. With R_1 we get

$$\frac{0 \cdot 0 = 0 \qquad E \cdot (0 \cdot 0) = (E \cdot 0) \cdot 0}{E \cdot 0 = E \cdot (0 \cdot 0),\ E \cdot 0 = (E \cdot 0) \cdot 0}$$

One use of R_1 tells us $E \cdot 0 + 0 = E \cdot 0 + 0$ and using R_1 again gives

$$\frac{E \cdot 0 = (E \cdot 0) \cdot 0 \qquad E \cdot 0 + 0 = E \cdot 0 + 0}{(E \cdot 0) \cdot 0 + 0 = E \cdot 0 + 0,\ (E \cdot 0) \cdot 0 + 0 = E \cdot 0 + 0}$$

With R_1 we get $E \cdot 0 + 0 = (E \cdot 0) \cdot 0 + 0$ and Axiom A_9 implies $E \cdot 0 + 0 = E \cdot 0$. Another use of R_1 tells us

$$\frac{E \cdot 0 + 0 = E \cdot 0 \qquad E \cdot 0 + 0 = (E \cdot 0) \cdot 0 + 0}{E \cdot 0 = E \cdot 0 + 0,\ E \cdot 0 = (E \cdot 0) \cdot 0 + 0}$$

Now we use R_2:

$$\frac{E \cdot 0 = (E \cdot 0) \cdot 0 + 0}{E \cdot 0 = 0 \cdot 0^*}$$

The rule R_1 gives $0 \cdot 0^* = E \cdot 0$ and Axiom A_8 gives $0 \cdot 0^* = 0$. We use R_1 one last time and get

$$\frac{0 \cdot 0^* = E \cdot 0 \qquad 0 \cdot 0^* = 0}{E \cdot 0 = 0 \cdot 0^*,\ E \cdot 0 = 0}$$

So, we have found a proof for $E \cdot 0 = 0$ using R_1 seven times and R_2 once.

From $E \cdot 0 = 0$ we get $0 = E \cdot 0$ with one use of R_1. Axiom A_9 gives the equation $E + 0 = E$. Now we use R_1:

$$\frac{0 = E \cdot 0 \qquad E + 0 = E}{E + E \cdot 0 = E + 0,\ E + E \cdot 0 = E}$$

Because of A_3 we have $E + E \cdot 0 = E \cdot 0 + E$. With R_1 we get

$$\frac{E + E \cdot 0 = E \qquad E + E \cdot 0 = E \cdot 0 + E}{E = E + E \cdot 0,\ E = E \cdot 0 + E}$$

The rule R_2 tells us

$$\frac{E = E \cdot 0 + E}{E = E \cdot 0^*}$$

With R_1 we finally get $E \cdot 0^* = E$. We used R_1 four more times and R_2 one more time. This proves the lemma.   □

3.1   Equational Characterizations for Regular Expressions

We analyze the proof of [8, Lemma 4], which uses the inductive definition of regular expressions, to give an upper bound for the number of equations in a derivable equational characterization for a regular expression and for the proof of the equational characterization. Our results are summarized in Table 1. All our regular expressions will be over the alphabet $\{a_1, a_2, \ldots, a_r\}$. We first establish the bounds from Table 1 for the regular expressions 0, 0^*, and a_i, for $i = 1, 2, \ldots, r$.

Lemma 4. *For the regular expression 0 an equational characterization with one equation is derivable with $O(r)$ uses of R_1 and no use of R_2.*

Proof. Axiom A_9 gives us $0 + 0 = 0$. With R_1 we get $0 = 0 + 0$ and use R_1 again:

$$\frac{0 = 0 + 0 \qquad 0 + 0 = 0}{0 + 0 + 0 = 0 + 0,\ 0 + 0 + 0 = 0}$$

Table 1. Equational characterizations of regular expressions over the alphabet Σ of size r. Here the number of equations derivable with the use of the inference rules R_1 and R_2 in the axiom system F_1 are given. It is assumed that E (F, respectively) has an equational characterization with n (m, respectively) equations.

Regular expression	Axiom system F_1		
	Equational characterization	No. of inference rules used	
	No. of equations	R_1	R_2
0	1	$O(r)$	0
0^*	2	$O(r)$	0
a, for $a \in \Sigma$	3	$O(r)$	0
$E + F$	$n \cdot m$	$O(r^4 nm)$	0
$E \cdot F$	$m \cdot 2^n$	$O((r \cdot n)^4 m \cdot 2^n)$	2
E^*	2^n	$O((r \cdot n)^4 \cdot 2^n)$	2

Iterating this we get that the equation $\sum_{j=1}^{r} 0+0 = 0$ is derivable with $O(r)$ uses of R_1. For $j \in \{1, 2, \ldots, r\}$ Axiom A_8 tells us $0a_j = 0$ and R_1 gives $0 = 0a_j$. Again with R_1 we can replace an occurrence of 0 in the left-hand side of an equation by $0a_j$. So $\sum_{j=1}^{r} 0a_j + 0 = 0$ is derivable with $O(r)$ uses of R_1. One last use of R_1 leads to $0 = \sum_{j=1}^{r} 0a_j + 0$. This equation is an equational characterization for the regular expression 0.   □

Next we consider the regular expression 0^*.

Lemma 5. *For the regular expression 0^* an equational characterization with two equations is derivable with $O(r)$ uses of R_1 and no use of R_2.*

Proof. From Axiom A_9 we get $0^* + 0 = 0^*$ and from A_3 we get $0^* + 0 = 0 + 0^*$. We use R_1:

$$\frac{0^* + 0 = 0 + 0^* \qquad 0^* + 0 = 0^*}{0 + 0^* = 0^* + 0, \ 0 + 0^* = 0^*}$$

In $0 + 0^* = 0^*$ we can replace the first occurrence of 0 by $\sum_{j=1}^{r} 0a_j$ with $O(r)$ uses of R_1 as in the proof of Lemma 4. This gives $\sum_{j=1}^{r} 0a_j + 0^* = 0^*$ and with R_1 we get $0^* = \sum_{j=1}^{r} 0a_j + 0^*$. This equation together with $0 = \sum_{j=1}^{r} 0a_j + 0$ (see proof of Lemma 4) is an equational characterization for the regular expression 0^*.   □

The final base case is the regular expression a in Σ. There we find the following situation.

Lemma 6. *Let $i \in \{1, 2, \ldots, r\}$. For the regular expression a_i an equational characterization with three equations is derivable with $O(r)$ uses of R_1 and no use of R_2.*

Proof. We consider an arbitrary a_i from Σ. Axiom A_9 tells us $a_i + 0 = a_i$ and A_3 gives $a_i + 0 = 0 + a_i$. The rule R_1 implies

$$\frac{a_i + 0 = 0 + a_i \qquad a_i + 0 = a_i}{0 + a_i = a_i + 0,\, 0 + a_i = a_i}$$

From axiom A_7 we get $0^* \cdot a_i = a_i$ and with R_1 we have $a_i = 0^* \cdot a_i$. Another use of R_1 leads to

$$\frac{a_i = 0^* \cdot a_i \qquad 0 + a_i = a_i}{0 + 0^* \cdot a_i = 0 + a_i,\, 0 + 0^* \cdot a_i = a_i}$$

In $0 + 0^* \cdot a_i = a_i$ we can replace the first occurrence of 0 by $\sum_{j=1}^{i-1} 0a_j$ with $O(r)$ uses of R_1 as in the proof of Lemma 4. This gives us $\sum_{j=1}^{i} \epsilon_{i,j} a_j = a_i$. Here, for $i, j \in \{1, 2, \ldots, r\}$, we define $\epsilon_{i,i} := 0^*$ and $\epsilon_{i,j} := 0$, if $i \neq j$. Now axiom A_9 tells us $\sum_{j=1}^{i} \epsilon_{i,j} a_j + 0 = \sum_{j=1}^{i} \epsilon_{i,j} a_j$ and by R_1 we get $\sum_{j=1}^{i} \epsilon_{i,j} a_j = \sum_{j=1}^{i} \epsilon_{i,j} a_j + 0$. We use R_1 again

$$\frac{\sum_{j=1}^{i} \epsilon_{i,j} a_j = \sum_{j=1}^{i} \epsilon_{i,j} a_j + 0 \qquad \sum_{j=1}^{i} \epsilon_{i,j} a_j = a_i}{\sum_{j=1}^{i} \epsilon_{i,j} a_j + 0 = \sum_{j=1}^{i} \epsilon_{i,j} a_j,\, \sum_{j=1}^{i} \epsilon_{i,j} a_j + 0 = a_i}$$

Iterating this and replacing appropriate occurrences of the expressions 0 by $0a_j$ for $j \in \{i+1, i+2, \ldots, r\}$ as in the proof of Lemma 4 we get that the equation $\sum_{j=1}^{r} \epsilon_{i,j} a_j + 0 = a_i$ is derivable with $O(r)$ uses of R_1. Another use of R_1 gives $a_i = \sum_{j=1}^{r} \epsilon_{i,j} a_j + 0$. This equation together with $0^* = \sum_{j=1}^{r} 0a_j + 0^*$ (see proof of Lemma 5) and $0 = \sum_{j=1}^{r} 0a_j + 0$ (see proof of Lemma 4) is an equational characterization for the regular expression a_i. $\qquad\square$

Before we investigate the inductive cases $E + F$, $E \cdot F$, and E^* we have to prove a result on large sums and products. We need to look into how often we have to use associativity if we want to change the positions of parentheses in large sums or products.

Let us consider an easy example first. Axiom A_1 allows us to replace an occurrence of an expression of the form $E + (F + G)$, where E, F, and G are regular expressions, by the expression $(E + F) + G$ in the left-hand side of an equation. To do this we need to use the rule R_1 once. To do the replacement the other way around we use R_1 to get $(E+F)+G = E+(F+G)$ from A_1. Then we can replace $(E+F)+G$ by $E+(F+G)$ in the left-hand side of an equation with another use of R_1. So we use R_1 twice in this case. This idea obviously generalizes to larger sums. To this end we define sum-trees, since there is an obvious one-to-one correspondence between sums of regular expressions and strict non-empty binary trees where every inner node is labelled by the symbol + and every leave is a regular expression. We call such trees *sum-trees*, in the forthcoming. Further notations on sum-trees follow: the *leaves of a sum-tree* are referred to as LEAVES$(T) = (E_1, E_2, \ldots, E_n)$, where $E_1, E_2, \ldots, E_n$ are the regular expressions in the leaves of T ordered by their appearance in T from the left to the right. Moreover, we assume an edge in a sum-tree to point downwards (from the parent node to the child node). Then every edge points either to the left (called *left edge*) or to the right (*right edge*). Let T be a sum-tree and p be an inner node of T. We define $\text{RIGHT}_T(p)$ to be the number of right edges that you pass when you walk from the root of T to p. Furthermore we set

$$\text{RIGHT}(T) = \sum_{p \text{ is an inner node of } T} \text{RIGHT}_T(p).$$

Our aforementioned small example is applied to sum-trees—see Fig. 1. Then in a sum-tree we can replace the subtree drawn in the left of Fig. 1 by the subtree on the right with one use of R_1. Replacing the subtrees the other way around takes two uses of R_1. Moreover, we apply the definition of RIGHT to the trees T and T' drawn in Fig. 1. For every inner node p in the subtrees T_1 and T_2 we have $\text{RIGHT}_T(p) = \text{RIGHT}_{T'}(p)$. For every inner node q in the subtree T_3 we get $\text{RIGHT}_{T'}(q) = \text{RIGHT}_T(q) - 1$. Let s_1 (s_2, respectively) be the inner node of T (T', respectively) that is not the root of the tree and does not belong to any of the subtrees T_1, T_2, and T_3. We have $\text{RIGHT}_{T'}(s_2) = 0 = \text{RIGHT}_T(s_1) - 1$. This implies $\text{RIGHT}(T') < \text{RIGHT}(T)$.

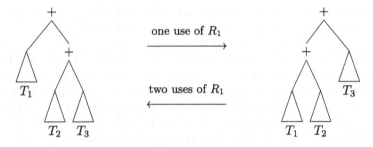

Fig. 1. Two sum-trees T (left) and T' (right) build from the same sum-trees T_1, T_2, and T_3 by different bracketing. It holds $\text{RIGHT}(T') < \text{RIGHT}(T)$.

Now we are ready for a claim, which gives an upper bound for the number of uses of R_1 necessary to get from a given sum-tree T to an arbitrary sum-tree with the same leaves.

Claim. Let T and T' be two sum-trees with the same n leaves (also in order of appearance). Then we can get from T to T' with $O(n^2)$ uses of R_1.

Proof. Let $\text{LEAVES}(T) = \text{LEAVES}(T') = (E_1, E_2, \dots, E_n)$. Observe that there is exactly one sum-tree T_L with

$$\text{LEAVES}(T_L) = \text{LEAVES}(T) \quad \text{and} \quad \text{RIGHT}(T_L) = 0.$$

This tree can be constructed in the following way. In case $n = 1$, the sum-tree T_L is just the node E_1. For $i = 2, 3, \dots, n$ the sum tree T_L looks as shown in Fig. 2.

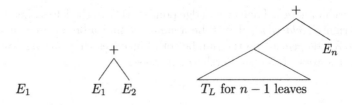

Fig. 2. The sum-trees T_L with LEAVES(T_L) = $(E_1, E_2, \ldots, E_n)$ for different n. Case $n = 1$ is drawn left, case $n = 2$ is shown in the middle, and the general case $n \geq 3$ is depicted right. These sum-trees satisfy RIGHT(T_L) = 0.

We can get from T to T_L with at most RIGHT(T) uses of R_1. This is shown by induction on RIGHT(T). For RIGHT(T) = 0 we have $T = T_L$. For RIGHT(T) > 0 the tree T has a subtree as shown on the left of Fig. 1. We can replace this subtree in T by a subtree drawn on the right of Fig. 1, where T_1, T_2, and T_3 are not changed, with one use of R_1. For the resulting tree T'' we have LEAVES(T'') = LEAVES(T) and RIGHT(T'') < RIGHT(T) because the substitution of the subtrees has decreased the right value accordingly. From T'' we can get to T_L with at most RIGHT(T) − 1 uses of R_1 by induction. That means we can get from T to T_L with at most RIGHT(T) uses of R_1.

The same way we can get from T' to T_L with at most RIGHT(T') uses of R_1. Doing all the replacements backwards we can get from T_L to T' with at most $2 \cdot$ RIGHT(T') uses of R_1, because replacing the subtree shown on the right of Fig. 1 by the subtree on the left in this figure takes two uses of R_1. So we can get from T to T' with at most RIGHT(T)+2·RIGHT(T') uses of R_1. Both sum-trees T and T' have n leaves each, so they have $n − 1$ inner nodes each. For every inner node the path length is at most $n − 2$, so we have RIGHT(T) $\leq (n − 1)(n − 2)$ and also RIGHT(T') $\leq (n − 1)(n − 2)$. This proves the claim.

We can directly apply the claim above to sums of regular expressions to get an upper bound for the number of uses of R_1 necessary to change the positions of parentheses.

Lemma 7. *Let $n \geq 1$ and $E_1, E_2, \ldots, E_n$ be regular expressions. Let F_1 be the same expression as E_1 and F_i be the expression $F_{i-1}+E_i$, where the symbols F_{i-1} and E_i are replaced by the expressions they stand for without adding parentheses, for $i = 2, 3, \ldots, n$. Let G and H be regular expressions that both can be obtained from the expression F_n by adding parentheses to give the $+$ symbols that were added to the E_i a priority. Then we can replace an occurrence of G by H in the left-hand side of an equation with $O(n^2)$ uses of R_1 and no use of R_2. Obviously we can deal with $\cdot$ instead of $+$ analogously.*

Now we are ready to give an upper bound for the number of equations in a derivable equational characterization for a regular expression of the form $E + F$ and for the proof of the equational characterization.

Lemma 8. *Let E be a regular expression with an equational characterization with n equations and F be a regular expression with an equational characterization with m equations. Then from these two equational characterizations an equational characterization for the regular expression $E + F$ with $n \cdot m$ equations is derivable with $O(r^4 nm)$ uses of R_1 and no use of R_2.*

Proof. Let $E_i = \sum_{j=1}^r E_{i,j} a_j + \delta_i$, for $i = 1, 2, \ldots, n$, be an equational characterization for E and $F_k = \sum_{j=1}^r F_{k,j} a_j + \gamma_k$, for $k = 1, 2, \ldots, m$, be an equational characterization for F. For $(i, k) \in \{1, 2, \ldots, n\} \times \{1, 2, \ldots, m\}$, we get $E_i + F_k = E_i + F_k$ with one use of R_1. Two more uses of R_1 give

$$\sum_{j=1}^r E_{i,j} a_j + \delta_i + \left(\sum_{j=1}^r F_{k,j} a_j + \gamma_k \right) = E_i + F_k.$$

There are $2r + 2$ summands on the left-hand side. Because of axiom A_3 we can switch positions of two adjacent summands. However it may be necessary to change the positions of parentheses first. So we can switch two adjacent summands with $O(r^2)$ uses of R_1 due to Lemma 7. With switching adjacent summands $O(r^2)$ times we can get the summands in any order we like. Thus we get $\sum_{j=1}^r (E_{i,j} a_j + F_{k,j} a_j) + (\delta_i + \gamma_k) = E_i + F_k$ with $O(r^4)$ uses of R_1. Because of Axiom A_4 we get $\sum_{j=1}^r ((E_{i,j} + F_{k,j}) a_j) + (\delta_i + \gamma_k) = E_i + F_k$ with $2r$ uses of R_1. Let $\epsilon_{i,k}$ be the regular expression 0 if $\delta_i \equiv \gamma_k \equiv 0$, and 0^* otherwise. Axioms A_3, A_6, and A_9 give us $\sum_{j=1}^r ((E_{i,j} + F_{k,j}) a_j) + \epsilon_{i,k} = E_i + F_k$ with at most two uses of R_1. Another use of R_1 leads to $E_i + F_k = \sum_{j=1}^r ((E_{i,j} + F_{k,j}) a_j) + \epsilon_{i,k}$. These equations, for $(i, k) \in \{1, 2, \ldots, n\} \times \{1, 2, \ldots, m\}$, are an equational characterization for the regular expression $E + F$. □

Next we deal with regular expressions of the form $E \cdot F$.

Lemma 9. *Let E be a regular expression with an equational characterization with n equations and F be a regular expression with an equational characterization with m equations. Then from these two equational characterizations an equational characterization for the regular expression $E \cdot F$ with $m \cdot 2^n$ equations is derivable with $O((rn)^4 m \cdot 2^n)$ uses of R_1 and two uses of R_2.*

Proof. Let

$$E_i = \sum_{j=1}^r E_{i,j} a_j + \delta_i, \quad \text{for } i = 1, 2, \ldots, n,$$

be an equational characterization for E and

$$F_k = \sum_{j=1}^r F_{k,j} a_j + \gamma_k, \quad \text{for } k = 1, 2, \ldots, m,$$

be an equational characterization for F. For $k \in \{1, 2, \ldots, m\}$ and $I = \{i_1, i_2, \ldots, i_h\}$ with $h \in \{0, 1, \ldots, n\}$ and $1 \leq i_1 < i_2 < \cdots < i_h \leq n$, we get

$$EF_k + \sum_{g=1}^{h} E_{i_g} = EF_k + \sum_{g=1}^{h} E_{i_g}$$

with one use of R_1. Now $h+1$ more uses of R_1 give us

$$E \cdot \left(\sum_{j=1}^{r} F_{k,j} a_j + \gamma_k \right) + \sum_{g=1}^{h} \left(\sum_{j=1}^{r} E_{i_g,j} a_j + \delta_{i_g} \right) = EF_k + \sum_{g=1}^{h} E_{i_g}.$$

Axiom A_5 and r uses of R_1 lead to

$$\sum_{j=1}^{r} EF_{k,j} a_j + E \cdot \gamma_k + \sum_{g=1}^{h} \left(\sum_{j=1}^{r} E_{i_g,j} a_j + \delta_{i_g} \right) = EF_k + \sum_{g=1}^{h} E_{i_g}.$$

As in the proof of Lemma 8 we can change the order of the summands with $O((rn)^4)$ uses of R_1 and get

$$\sum_{j=1}^{r} \left(EF_{k,j} a_j + \sum_{g=1}^{h} E_{i_g,j} a_j \right) + \sum_{g=1}^{h} \delta_{i_g} + E \cdot \gamma_k = EF_k + \sum_{g=1}^{h} E_{i_g}.$$

Axiom A_4 and $2rh$ uses of R_1 give us

$$\sum_{j=1}^{r} \left(EF_{k,j} + \sum_{g=1}^{h} E_{i_g,j} \right) a_j + \sum_{g=1}^{h} \delta_{i_g} + E \cdot \gamma_k = EF_k + \sum_{g=1}^{h} E_{i_g}. \qquad (1)$$

Let $\epsilon_{k,I}$ be the regular expression 0 if $L\left(\sum_{g=1}^{h} \delta_{i_g} + \delta_1 \cdot \gamma_k \right) = \emptyset$, and 0* otherwise. We first consider the case $\gamma_k \equiv 0$. Then, because of Lemma 3 and Axiom A_9, with nine uses of R_1 and one use of R_2 we get

$$\sum_{j=1}^{r} \left(EF_{k,j} + \sum_{g=1}^{h} E_{i_g,j} \right) a_j + \sum_{g=1}^{h} \delta_{i_g} = EF_k + \sum_{g=1}^{h} E_{i_g}.$$

Axioms A_3, A_6, and A_9 give us

$$\sum_{j=1}^{r} \left(EF_{k,j} + \sum_{g=1}^{h} E_{i_g,j} \right) a_j + \epsilon_{k,I} = EF_k + \sum_{g=1}^{h} E_{i_g}$$

with at most h uses of R_1. We change the order of the summands in $\sum_{g=1}^{h} E_{i_g,j}$ and use Axiom A_6. This leads, for each $j \in \{1, 2, \ldots, r\}$, to a set $J_{I,j} = \{i_{I,j,1}, i_{I,j,2}, \ldots, i_{I,j,h_{I,j}}\}$ with $h_{I,j} \in \{0, 1, \ldots, n\}$ and $1 \le i_{I,j,1} < i_{I,j,2} < \cdots < i_{I,j,h_{I,j}} \le n$ such that we get

$$\sum_{j=1}^{r} \left(EF_{k,j} + \sum_{g=1}^{h_{I,j}} E_{i_{I,j,g}} \right) a_j + \epsilon_{k,I} = EF_k + \sum_{g=1}^{h} E_{i_g}$$

with $O(rn^4)$ uses of R_1. One more use of R_1 gives us

$$EF_k + \sum_{g=1}^{h} E_{i_g} = \sum_{j=1}^{r} \left(EF_{k,j} + \sum_{g=1}^{h_{I,j}} E_{i_{I,j,g}} \right) a_j + \epsilon_{k,I}. \tag{2}$$

Now we consider the case $\gamma_k \equiv 0^*$. Then, because of Lemma 3, from Eq. (1) we get

$$\sum_{j=1}^{r} \left(EF_{k,j} + \sum_{g=1}^{h} E_{i_g,j} \right) a_j + \sum_{g=1}^{h} \delta_{i_g} + E = EF_k + \sum_{g=1}^{h} E_{i_g}$$

with twelve uses of R_1 and two uses of R_2. One more use of R_1 leads to

$$\sum_{j=1}^{r} \left(EF_{k,j} + \sum_{g=1}^{h} E_{i_g,j} \right) a_j + \sum_{g=1}^{h} \delta_{i_g} + \left(\sum_{j=1}^{r} E_{1,j} a_j + \delta_1 \right) = EF_k + \sum_{g=1}^{h} E_{i_g}.$$

With $O(r^4)$ uses of R_1 we get

$$\sum_{j=1}^{r} \left(EF_{k,j} + E_{1,j} + \sum_{g=1}^{h} E_{i_g,j} \right) a_j + \left(\delta_1 + \sum_{g=1}^{h} \delta_{i_g} \right) = EF_k + \sum_{g=1}^{h} E_{i_g}.$$

Axioms A_3, A_6, and A_9 give us

$$\sum_{j=1}^{r} \left(EF_{k,j} + E_{1,j} + \sum_{g=1}^{h} E_{i_g,j} \right) a_j + \epsilon_{k,I} = EF_k + \sum_{g=1}^{h} E_{i_g}$$

with at most $h + 1$ uses of R_1. We change the order of the summands in $E_{1,j} + \sum_{g=1}^{h} E_{i_g,j}$ and use Axiom A_6. This leads, for each $j \in \{1, 2, \ldots, r\}$, to a set $J'_{I,j} = \{i'_{I,j,1}, i'_{I,j,2}, \ldots, i'_{I,j,h'_{I,j}}\}$ with $h'_{I,j} \in \{1, 2, \ldots, n\}$ and $1 \leq i'_{I,j,1} < i'_{I,j,2} < \cdots < i'_{I,j,h'_{I,j}} \leq n$ such that we get

$$\sum_{j=1}^{r} \left(EF_{k,j} + \sum_{g=1}^{h'_{I,j}} E_{i'_{I,j,g}} \right) a_j + \epsilon_{k,I} = EF_k + \sum_{g=1}^{h} E_{i_g}$$

with $O(rn^4)$ uses of R_1. One more use of R_1 gives us

$$EF_k + \sum_{g=1}^{h} E_{i_g} = \sum_{j=1}^{r} \left(EF_{k,j} + \sum_{g=1}^{h'_{I,j}} E_{i'_{I,j,g}} \right) a_j + \epsilon_{k,I}. \tag{3}$$

So for each $(k, I) \in \{1, 2, \ldots, m\} \times 2^{\{1,2,\ldots,n\}}$ we derive an equation of the form (2) or (3) from the equational characterizations for E and F with $O((rn)^4)$ uses of R_1 and two uses of R_2. To derive all these equations, two uses of R_2 are sufficient: One use to show $E \cdot 0 = 0$ and another use to show $E \cdot 0^* = E$. The derived equations are an equational characterization for the regular expression $E \cdot F$. The statement of the lemma follows with $\left| \{1, 2, \ldots, m\} \times 2^{\{1,2,\ldots,n\}} \right| = m \cdot 2^n$. $\square$

We finally consider regular expressions of the form E^*.

Lemma 10. *Let E be a regular expression with an equational characterization with n equations. Then from this equational characterization an equational characterization for the regular expression E^* with 2^n equations is derivable with $O((rn)^4 \cdot 2^n)$ uses of R_1 and two uses of R_2.*

Proof. Let

$$E_i = \sum_{j=1}^{r} E_{i,j} a_j + \delta_i, \quad \text{for } i = 1, 2, \ldots, n,$$

be an equational characterization for E. With one use of R_1 we get $E^* = E^*$ and another use of R_1 leads to

$$\left(\sum_{j=1}^{r} E_{1,j} a_j + \delta_1 \right)^* = E^*.$$

Axioms A_3, A_9, and A_{11} give us

$$\left(\sum_{j=1}^{r} E_{1,j} a_j \right)^* = E^*$$

with at most three uses of R_1. Now A_{10} and one use of R_1 implies

$$0^* + \left(\sum_{j=1}^{r} E_{1,j} a_j \right)^* \cdot \sum_{j=1}^{r} E_{1,j} a_j = E^*.$$

With one more use of R_1 we have

$$0^* + E^* \cdot \sum_{j=1}^{r} E_{1,j} a_j = E^*.$$

Axioms A_2, A_3, and A_5 give us

$$\sum_{j=1}^{r} E^* E_{1,j} a_j + 0^* = E^*$$

with $2r$ uses of R_1. One more use of R_1 leads to

$$E^* = \sum_{j=1}^{r} E^* E_{1,j} a_j + 0^*. \tag{4}$$

For $I = \{i_1, i_2, \ldots, i_h\}$ with $h \in \{1, 2, \ldots, n\}$ and $1 \le i_1 < i_2 < \cdots < i_h \le n$, we get

$$E^* \cdot \sum_{g=1}^{h} E_{i_g} = E^* \cdot \sum_{g=1}^{h} E_{i_g}$$

with one use of R_1. Another h uses of R_1 give

$$E^* \cdot \sum_{g=1}^{h} \left(\sum_{j=1}^{r} E_{i_g,j} a_j + \delta_{i_g} \right) = E^* \cdot \sum_{g=1}^{h} E_{i_g}.$$

As in the proof of Lemma 8 we can change the order of the summands with $O((rn)^4)$ uses of R_1 and get

$$E^* \cdot \left(\sum_{j=1}^{r} \sum_{g=1}^{h} E_{i_g,j} a_j + \sum_{g=1}^{h} \delta_{i_g} \right) = E^* \cdot \sum_{g=1}^{h} E_{i_g}.$$

Axiom A_5 and r uses of R_1 lead to

$$\sum_{j=1}^{r} E^* \cdot \sum_{g=1}^{h} E_{i_g,j} a_j + E^* \cdot \sum_{g=1}^{h} \delta_{i_g} = E^* \cdot \sum_{g=1}^{h} E_{i_g}.$$

Because of Axiom A_4 we have

$$\sum_{j=1}^{r} E^* \cdot \left(\left(\sum_{g=1}^{h} E_{i_g,j} \right) \cdot a_j \right) + E^* \cdot \sum_{g=1}^{h} \delta_{i_g} = E^* \cdot \sum_{g=1}^{h} E_{i_g}$$

with $2r(h-1)$ uses of R_1. Now Axiom A_2 and r uses of R_1 give us

$$\sum_{j=1}^{r} E^* \cdot \left(\sum_{g=1}^{h} E_{i_g,j} \right) \cdot a_j + E^* \cdot \sum_{g=1}^{h} \delta_{i_g} = E^* \cdot \sum_{g=1}^{h} E_{i_g}. \tag{5}$$

We first consider the case that $\delta_{i_g} \equiv 0$ for all $g \in \{1, 2, \ldots, h\}$. Axiom A_9 and Lemma 3 implies

$$\sum_{j=1}^{r} E^* \cdot \left(\sum_{g=1}^{h} E_{i_g,j} \right) \cdot a_j + 0 = E^* \cdot \sum_{g=1}^{h} E_{i_g}$$

with $h+7$ uses of R_1 and one use of R_2. We change the order of the summands in $\sum_{g=1}^{h} E_{i_g,j}$ and use Axiom A_6. This leads, for each $j \in \{1, 2, \ldots; r\}$, to a set $J_{I,j} = \{i_{I,j,1}, i_{I,j,2}, \ldots, i_{I,j,h_{I,j}}\}$ with $h_{I,j} \in \{1, 2, \ldots, n\}$ and $1 \le i_{I,j,1} < i_{I,j,2} < \cdots < i_{I,j,h_{I,j}} \le n$ such that we get

$$\sum_{j=1}^{r} E^* \cdot \left(\sum_{g=1}^{h_{I,j}} E_{i_{I,j,g}} \right) \cdot a_j + 0 = E^* \cdot \sum_{g=1}^{h} E_{i_g}$$

with $O(rn^4)$ uses of R_1. Another use of R_1 leads to

$$E^* \cdot \sum_{g=1}^{h} E_{i_g} = \sum_{j=1}^{r} E^* \cdot \left(\sum_{g=1}^{h_{I,j}} E_{i_{I,j,g}} \right) \cdot a_j + 0. \tag{6}$$

Now we consider the case that there is a $g \in \{1, 2, \ldots, h\}$ with $\delta_{i_g} \equiv 0^*$. Then, because of Axioms A_3, A_6, and A_9, we get

$$\sum_{j=1}^{r} E^* \cdot \left(\sum_{g=1}^{h} E_{i_g,j}\right) \cdot a_j + E^* \cdot 0^* = E^* \cdot \sum_{g=1}^{h} E_{i_g}$$

from Eq. (5) with at most h uses of R_1. Lemma 3 implies

$$\sum_{j=1}^{r} E^* \cdot \left(\sum_{g=1}^{h} E_{i_g,j}\right) \cdot a_j + E^* = E^* \cdot \sum_{g=1}^{h} E_{i_g}$$

with twelve uses of R_1 and two uses of R_2. Equation eq$_\emptyset$ and one use of R_1 gives us

$$\sum_{j=1}^{r} E^* \cdot \left(\sum_{g=1}^{h} E_{i_g,j}\right) \cdot a_j + \left(\sum_{j=1}^{r} E^* E_{1,j} a_j + 0^*\right) = E^* \cdot \sum_{g=1}^{h} E_{i_g}.$$

With $O(r^4)$ uses of R_1 we get

$$\sum_{j=1}^{r} E^* \cdot \left(E_{1,j} + \sum_{g=1}^{h} E_{i_g,j}\right) \cdot a_j + 0^* = E^* \cdot \sum_{g=1}^{h} E_{i_g}.$$

We change the order of the summands in $E_{1,j} + \sum_{g=1}^{h} E_{i_g,j}$ and use Axiom A_6. This leads, for each $j \in \{1, 2, \ldots, r\}$, to a set $J_{I,j} = \{i_{I,j,1}, i_{I,j,2}, \ldots, i_{I,j,h_{I,j}}\}$ with $h_{I,j} \in \{1, 2, \ldots, n\}$ and $1 \le i_{I,j,1} < i_{I,j,2} < \cdots < i_{I,j,h_{I,j}} \le n$ such that we get

$$\sum_{j=1}^{r} E^* \cdot \left(\sum_{g=1}^{h_{I,j}} E_{i_{I,j,g}}\right) \cdot a_j + 0^* = E^* \cdot \sum_{g=1}^{h} E_{i_g}$$

with $O(rn^4)$ uses of R_1. With one more use of R_1 we have

$$E^* \cdot \sum_{g=1}^{h} E_{i_g} = \sum_{j=1}^{r} E^* \cdot \left(\sum_{g=1}^{h_{I,j}} E_{i_{I,j,g}}\right) \cdot a_j + 0^*. \tag{7}$$

So for each $I \in 2^{\{1,2,\ldots,n\}}$ we can derive an equation of the form (4), (6) or (7) from the equational characterization for E with $O((rn)^4)$ uses of R_1 and two uses of R_2. To derive all these equations two uses of R_2 are sufficient: one use to show $E^* \cdot 0 = 0$ and another use to show $E^* \cdot 0^* = E^*$. The derived equations are an equational characterization for the regular expression E^*. The statement of the lemma follows with $|2^{\{1,2,\ldots,n\}}| = 2^n$.   □

Having the results from Table 1, we are almost ready, given a regular expression, to give an explicit formula for an upper bound for the number of equations in a derivable equational characterization and for the proof of the equational characterization. To this end we define the *tower function* Tow by

$$\text{Tow}(b_1) = 2^{b_1}$$

and

$$\text{Tow}(b_1, b_2, \ldots, b_k) = 2^{b_1 \cdot \text{Tow}(b_2, \ldots, b_k)},$$

for $b_1, b_2, \ldots, b_k > 0$. For $k \geq 0$, the convention $b^{\otimes k} = (b, b, \ldots, b)$, where there are k values b, is used. Then, we define $\text{TOWER}(k) = \text{Tow}\left(1^{\otimes k}\right)$, for $k > 0$. Thus, $\text{TOWER}(k)$ is an exponential tower of height k which has just the number 2 on each level, that is,

$$\text{TOWER}(k) = 2^{2^{2^{\cdot^{\cdot^{\cdot^2}}}}} \Big\} k$$

We need some properties of the Tow function, which can easily be seen:

Lemma 11. *For $k > 0$ and $b_1, b_2, \ldots, b_k > 0$, we have:*

1. $\text{Tow}(1, b_1, b_2, \ldots, b_k) = 2^{\text{Tow}(b_1, b_2, \ldots, b_k)}$.
2. $(\text{Tow}(b_1, b_2, \ldots, b_k))^a = \text{Tow}(ab_1, b_2, b_3, \ldots, b_k)$, for $a > 0$.
3. $\text{Tow}(b_1, b_2, \ldots, b_k) = \text{Tow}(b_1, b_2, \ldots, b_{i-1}, b_i \cdot \text{Tow}(b_{i+1}, b_{i+2}, \ldots, b_k))$, for $0 < i < k$.
4. $\text{Tow}(b_{i+1}, b_{i+2}, \ldots, b_k) < \text{Tow}(b_1, b_2, \ldots, b_i, b_{i+1}, \ldots, b_k)$, for $0 < i < k$. □

To get our upper bound for an equational characterization we use the following estimation.

Lemma 12. *For $k \geq 0$, we have*

$$4 \cdot \text{Tow}\left(2^{\otimes k}, 1, 1\right) \leq \left(\text{Tow}\left(2^{\otimes k}, 1, 1\right)\right)^2 \leq \text{TOWER}(k + 3).$$

Proof. We have

$$4 \cdot \text{Tow}\left(2^{\otimes k}, 1, 1\right) = \text{Tow}(1, 1) \cdot \text{Tow}\left(2^{\otimes k}, 1, 1\right) \leq \left(\text{Tow}\left(2^{\otimes k}, 1, 1\right)\right)^2.$$

By induction on k, we show that $\left(\text{Tow}\left(2^{\otimes k}, 1, 1\right)\right)^2 \leq \text{TOWER}(k+3)$. For $k = 0$, we have

$$(\text{Tow}(1, 1))^2 = \left(2^2\right)^2 = 16 = 2^{2^2} = \text{TOWER}(3).$$

Now let $k > 0$. We get

$$\left(\text{Tow}\left(2^{\otimes k}, 1, 1\right)\right)^2 = \text{Tow}\left(4, 2^{\otimes(k-1)}, 1, 1\right)$$

$$= \text{Tow}\left(4 \cdot \text{Tow}\left(2^{\otimes(k-1)}, 1, 1\right)\right)$$

$$\leq \text{Tow}\left(\left(\text{Tow}\left(2^{\otimes(k-1)}, 1, 1\right)\right)^2\right)$$

which by the induction hypothesis results in

$$\text{Tow}\left(\left(\text{Tow}\left(2^{\otimes(k-1)},1,1\right)\right)^2\right) \leq \text{Tow}(\text{Tower}(k+2))$$

$$= 2^{\text{Tower}(k+2)} = \text{Tower}(k+3),$$

and proves the stated claim.   □

Now we are ready to give an upper bound formula for an equational characterization for a regular expression:

Theorem 13. *For a regular expression E an equational characterization with at most $\text{Tower}(h(E)+3)/4$ equations is derivable with $O(r^4 \cdot \text{Tower}(h(E)+3))$ uses of R_1 and $2 \cdot (|E| + |E|_*)$ uses of R_2.*

Proof. In the results presented in Table 1 the bound for the number of R_1 uses is given in O-notation. Thus, there is a constant $c > 0$ such that in each of the above mentioned lemmata the number of uses of R_1 is at most c times the bound given inside of O-notation. Now we show by induction on the structure of E that for every regular expression E an equational characterization with at most $\text{Tow}\left(2^{\otimes h(E)},1,1\right)$ equations is derivable with $c \cdot r^4 \cdot \left(\text{Tow}\left(2^{\otimes h(E)},1,1\right)\right)^2$ uses of R_1 and $2 \cdot (|E| + |E|_*)$ uses of R_2. Then, the result follows by Lemma 12.

It remains to prove the above statement by induction. For the base case let $E \equiv 0$ or $E \equiv a_i$, for $i \in \{1,2,\ldots,r\}$. Then $h(E) = 0$ and, by the bounds stated in Table 1 an equational characterization for E with at most $4 = \text{Tow}(1,1)$ equations is derivable with $c \cdot r$ uses of R_1 and no use of R_2. Now, for the inductive step let $E \equiv F + G$, or $E \equiv F \cdot G$, or $E = F^*$, for regular expressions F and G of height at most $h(E) - 1$, where we set $G \equiv 0$ in the last case. Then, by the induction hypothesis equational characterizations for F and G, both with at most $\text{Tow}\left(2^{\otimes(h(E)-1)},1,1\right)$ equations, are derivable with $2c \cdot r^4 \cdot \left(\text{Tow}\left(2^{\otimes(h(E)-1)},1,1\right)\right)^2$ uses of R_1 and $2 \cdot (|F+G| + |F+G|_*)$ uses of R_2. By the results stated in Table 1 an equational characterization for E with at most

$$\left(2^{\text{Tow}\left(2^{\otimes(h(E)-1)},1,1\right)}\right)^2 = \left(\text{Tow}\left(1,2^{\otimes(h(E)-1)},1,1\right)\right)^2 = \text{Tow}\left(2^{\otimes h(E)},1,1\right)$$

equations is derivable with

$$2c \cdot r^4 \cdot \left(\text{Tow}\left(2^{\otimes(h(E)-1)},1,1\right)\right)^2$$

$$+ c \cdot r^4 \left(\text{Tow}\left(2^{\otimes(h(E)-1)},1,1\right)\right)^5 \cdot 2^{\text{Tow}\left(2^{\otimes(h(E)-1)},1,1\right)} \quad (8)$$

uses of R_1 and $2 \cdot (|E| + |E|_*)$ uses of R_2. Simplifying Expression (8) using the fact that $2n^2 + n^5 2^n < 2^{4n}$, for $n \geq 0$, which can easily be seen *via* induction, we obtain an upper bound of

$$c \cdot r^4 \cdot 2^{4 \cdot \text{Tow}\left(2^{\otimes(h(E)-1)},1,1\right)} = c \cdot r^4 \cdot \text{Tow}\left(4, 2^{\otimes(h(E)-1)},1,1\right)$$

$$= c \cdot r^4 \cdot \left(\text{Tow}\left(2^{\otimes h(E)},1,1\right)\right)^2$$

for the uses of R_1, which proves the stated result.   □

3.2 From Equational Characterizations to the Equality of Regular Expressions

Given regular expressions E and F with $L(E) = L(F)$, we will now show how to derive the equation $E = F$ from their equational characterizations. First, we give [8, Lemma 4], which shows that the coefficients in equations of the form $E = \sum_{i=1}^{r} E_i a_i + \delta$ are in some sense determined by $L(E)$.

Lemma 14. *Let E and F be regular expressions with $L(E) = L(F)$. Furthermore let $E_1, E_2, \ldots, E_r$ and $F_1, F_2, \ldots, F_r$ be regular expressions and $\delta, \gamma \in \{0, 0^*\}$ such that $E = \sum_{i=1}^{r} E_i a_i + \delta$ and $F = \sum_{i=1}^{r} F_i a_i + \gamma$. Then $\delta \equiv \gamma$ and $L(E_i) = L(F_i)$, for all $i \in \{1, 2, \ldots, r\}$.*

Proof. We have $\lambda \in L(E)$ if and only if $\delta \equiv 0^*$. The sets $L(E_i a_i)$ are pairwise disjoint. Together with the analogous statements for F, this proves the lemma. $\qquad\square$

In the proof of [8, Theorem 2] it is shown how equational characterizations for regular expressions E and F with $L(E) = L(F)$ can be transformed into a special kind of system of equations, which is later used to derive a proof for the equation $E = F$. We analyze how often the rules R_1 and R_2 are used along the way:

Lemma 15. *Let E be a regular expression with an equational characterization with n equations and F be a regular expression with an equational characterization with m equations and $L(E) = L(F)$. Then, there exists $1 \leq k \leq mn$, for each $i \in \{1, 2, \ldots, k\}$ a pair of regular expressions[2] (G_i, H_i) with $(G_1, H_1) \equiv (E, F)$, regular expressions ϵ_i, and for each $(i, h) \in \{1, 2, \ldots, k\}^2$ a regular expression $D_{i,h}$ with $\lambda \notin L(D_{i,h})$ such that the system of equations*

$$(G_i, H_i) = \sum_{h=1}^{k} (G_h, H_h) \cdot D_{i,h} + (\epsilon_i, \epsilon_i), \quad for \ i = 1, 2, \ldots, k,$$

is derivable from the two given equational characterizations with $O((mn+r^4)mn)$ uses of R_1 and $m + n$ uses of R_2.

Proof. Let

$$E_p = \sum_{j=1}^{r} E_{p,j} a_j + \delta_p, \quad for \ p = 1, 2, \ldots, n,$$

---

[2] The notation $(E_1, E_2) \equiv (F_1, F_2)$, for regular expressions E_1, E_2, F_1, F_2, stands for $E_1 \equiv F_1$ and $E_2 \equiv F_2$. The equation $(E_1, E_2) = (F_1, F_2)$ is a shorthand notation for the system of the two equations $E_1 = F_1$ and $E_2 = F_2$. Furthermore, the expressions $(E_1, E_2) + (F_1, F_2)$ and $(E_1, E_2) \cdot F_1$ define $(E_1 + F_1, E_2 + F_2)$ and $(E_1 \cdot F_1, E_2 \cdot F_1)$, respectively.

be an equational characterization for E such that the E_p are pairwise different regular expressions and

$$F_q = \sum_{j=1}^{r} F_{q,j} a_j + \gamma_q, \quad \text{for } q = 1, 2, \ldots, m,$$

be an equational characterization for F such that the F_q are pairwise different regular expressions. We define $P = \{(G_1, H_1), (G_2, H_2), \ldots, (G_k, H_k)\}$ to be the set

$$\{ (E_p, F_q) \mid (p, q) \in \{1, 2, \ldots, n\} \times \{1, 2, \ldots, m\} \text{ with } L(E_p) = L(F_q) \}$$

ordered by the indices (p, q). Thus we have $(G_1, H_1) \equiv (E, F)$. By Lemma 14 we have $\delta_1 \equiv \gamma_1$ and $L(E_{1,j}) = L(F_{1,j})$, for all $j \in \{1, 2, \ldots, r\}$. Then by repeatedly applying Lemma 14 we get a system of equations

$$(G_i, H_i) = \sum_{j=1}^{r} (G_{i,j}, H_{i,j}) a_j + (\epsilon_i, \epsilon_i), \quad \text{for } i = 1, 2, \ldots, k, \tag{9}$$

out of the given equational characterizations, where all ϵ_i are in $\{0, 0^*\}$ and all $(G_{i,j}, H_{i,j})$ are in P. For each $(i, h) \in \{1, 2, \ldots, k\}^2$ let $I_{i,h}$ be the ordered set

$$I_{i,h} = \{ j \in \{1, 2, \ldots, r\} \mid (G_{i,j}, H_{i,j}) \equiv (G_h, H_h) \}$$

and $D_{i,h}$ be the regular expression $\sum_{j \in I_{i,h}} a_j$. From the system of Eq. (9) we can derive

$$(G_i, H_i) = \sum_{h=1}^{k} (G_h, H_h) \cdot D_{i,h} + (\epsilon_i, \epsilon_i), \quad \text{for } i = 1, 2, \ldots, k. \tag{10}$$

We do this the following way: for every $p \in \{1, 2, \ldots, n\}$ and $q \in \{1, 2, \ldots, m\}$ we get $E_p \cdot 0 = 0$ and $F_q \cdot 0 = 0$ with Lemma 3. For this we use R_1 $O(m + n)$ times and R_2 $m + n$ times. For each $i \in 1, 2, \ldots, k$ we have given a pair of equations in the system of Eq. (9). In such a pair we change the order of the summands $(G_{i,j}, H_{i,j}) a_j$ and use Axiom A_5 at most $2(r - 1)$ times. This can be done with $O(r^4)$ uses of R_1. Then, in the sum, we insert at most k times the regular expression 0 with Axioms A_3 and A_9 and replace it by an expression of the form $(G_h, H_h) \cdot 0$. For this we use R_1 $O(mn)$ times. That way we derive the pair of equations given for our i in the system of Eq. (10). Because of $i \in \{1, 2, \ldots, k\}$ and $k \leq mn$ the lemma is proved. $\qquad\square$

Next, we analyze the proof of [8, Lemma 2]. There it is shown how one can get from the system of equations that we derived in the previous lemma to the equation $E = F$. First we make the system of equations smaller by reducing the parameter k:

Lemma 16. *For $k \geq 2$, let (G_i, H_i) be a pair of regular expressions and ϵ_i be a regular expression for each $i \in \{1, 2, \ldots, k\}$ and let $D_{i,h}$ be a regular expression with $\lambda \notin L(D_{i,h})$ for each $(i, h) \in \{1, 2, \ldots, k\}^2$. Then, from the system of equations*

$$(G_i, H_i) = \sum_{h=1}^{k}(G_h, H_h) \cdot D_{i,h} + (\epsilon_i, \epsilon_i), \quad for \ i = 1, 2, \ldots, k,$$

we can derive a system of equations of the form

$$(G_i, H_i) = \sum_{h=1}^{k-1}(G_h, H_h) \cdot D'_{i,h} + (\epsilon'_i, \epsilon'_i), \quad for \ i = 1, 2, \ldots, k-1,$$

where all the ϵ'_i and $D'_{i,h}$ are regular expressions with $\lambda \notin L(D'_{i,h})$, with $O(k^5)$ uses of R_1 and two uses of R_2.

Proof. We have

$$(G_k, H_k) = \sum_{h=1}^{k-1}(G_h, H_h) \cdot D_{k,h} + (G_k, H_k) \cdot D_{k,k} + (\epsilon_k, \epsilon_k).$$

Axioms A_1 and A_3 imply

$$(G_k, H_k) = (G_k, H_k) \cdot D_{k,k} + \left(\sum_{h=1}^{k-1}(G_h, H_h) \cdot D_{k,h} + (\epsilon_k, \epsilon_k)\right)$$

with $O(1)$ uses of R_1. Now two uses of R_2 give us

$$(G_k, H_k) = \left(\sum_{h=1}^{k-1}(G_h, H_h) \cdot D_{k,h} + (\epsilon_k, \epsilon_k)\right) \cdot (D_{k,k})^*.$$

From the system of equations

$$(G_i, H_i) = \sum_{h=1}^{k}(G_h, H_h) \cdot D_{i,h} + (\epsilon_i, \epsilon_i), \quad for \ i = 1, 2, \ldots, k-1,$$

we get

$$(G_i, H_i) = \sum_{h=1}^{k-1}(G_h, H_h) \cdot D_{i,h}$$
$$+ \left(\sum_{h=1}^{k-1}(G_h, H_h) \cdot D_{k,h} + (\epsilon_k, \epsilon_k)\right) \cdot (D_{k,k})^* \cdot D_{i,k} + (\epsilon_i, \epsilon_i),$$

for $i = 1, 2, \ldots, k-1$, with $O(k)$ uses of R_1. Axioms A_1 and A_4 and another $O(k)$ uses of R_1 lead to

$$(G_i, H_i) = \sum_{h=1}^{k-1}(G_h, H_h) \cdot D_{i,h} + \left(\sum_{h=1}^{k-1}(G_h, H_h) \cdot D_{k,h}\right) \cdot (D_{k,k})^* \cdot D_{i,k} + (\epsilon'_i, \epsilon'_i),$$

with $\epsilon'_i \equiv \epsilon_k \cdot (D_{k,k})^* \cdot D_{i,k} + \epsilon_i$, for $i = 1, 2, \ldots, k - 1$. Because of A_2 and A_4 with $O(k^2)$ more uses of R_1 we have

$$(G_i, H_i) = \sum_{h=1}^{k-1}(G_h, H_h) \cdot D_{i,h} + \sum_{h=1}^{k-1}(G_h, H_h) \cdot \hat{D}_{i,h} + (\epsilon'_i, \epsilon'_i), \quad \text{for } i = 1, 2, \ldots, k-1,$$

where $\hat{D}_{i,h} \equiv D_{k,h} \cdot (D_{k,k})^* \cdot D_{i,k}$, for $(i, h) \in \{1, 2, \ldots, k - 1\}^2$. Now we change the order of the summands with $O(k^5)$ uses of R_1 and get

$$(G_i, H_i) = \sum_{h=1}^{k-1}\left((G_h, H_h) \cdot D_{i,h} + (G_h, H_h) \cdot \hat{D}_{i,h}\right) + (\epsilon'_i, \epsilon'_i), \quad \text{for } i = 1, 2, \ldots, k - 1.$$

For $(i, h) \in \{1, 2, \ldots, k - 1\}^2$, we let $D'_{i,h}$ be the regular expression $D_{i,h} + \hat{D}_{i,h}$. Because of $\lambda \notin L(D_{i,h})$ and $\lambda \notin L\left(\hat{D}_{i,h}\right)$ we have $\lambda \notin L(D'_{i,h})$. Axiom A_5 implies

$$(G_i, H_i) = \sum_{h=1}^{k-1}(G_h, H_h) \cdot D'_{i,h} + (\epsilon'_i, \epsilon'_i), \quad \text{for } i = 1, 2, \ldots, k - 1,$$

with $O(k^2)$ uses of R_1. This proves the lemma. $\square$

We can reduce k repeatedly with the previous lemma until $k = 1$. Then, we can show the equation $G_1 = H_1$ with the help of rule R_2:

Corollary 17. *For $k \geq 1$, let (G_i, H_i) be a pair of regular expressions and ϵ_i be a regular expression for each $i \in \{1, 2, \ldots, k\}$ and let $D_{i,h}$ be a regular expression with $\lambda \notin L(D_{i,h})$ for each $(i, h) \in \{1, 2, \ldots, k\}^2$. Then, from the system of equations*

$$(G_i, H_i) = \sum_{h=1}^{k}(G_h, H_h) \cdot D_{i,h} + (\epsilon_i, \epsilon_i), \quad for \ i = 1, 2, \ldots, k,$$

one can derive the equation $G_1 = H_1$ with $O(k^6)$ uses of R_1 and $2k$ uses of R_2.

Proof. Due to Lemma 16 there is a constant $c \geq 3$ such that, for $k \geq 2$, from the system of equations

$$(G_i, H_i) = \sum_{h=1}^{k}(G_h, H_h) \cdot D_{i,h} + (\epsilon_i, \epsilon_i), \quad \text{for } i = 1, 2, \ldots, k, \qquad (11)$$

we can derive a system of equations of the form

$$(G_i, H_i) = \sum_{h=1}^{k-1}(G_h, H_h) \cdot D'_{i,h} + (\epsilon'_i, \epsilon'_i), \quad \text{for } i = 1, 2, \ldots, k-1, \qquad (12)$$

where all the ϵ'_i and $D'_{i,h}$ are regular expressions with $\lambda \notin L(D'_{i,h})$, with ck^5 uses of R_1 and two uses of R_2.

Now, we will prove by induction on k that, for $k \geq 1$, from the system of Eq. (11) we can derive the equation $G_1 = H_1$ with ck^6 uses of R_1 and $2k$ uses of R_2. For $k = 1$ we have

$$(G_1, H_1) = (G_1, H_1) \cdot D_{1,1} + (\epsilon_1, \epsilon_1).$$

With two uses of R_2 we get $(G_1, H_1) = (\epsilon_1, \epsilon_1) \cdot (D_{1,1})^*$. This implies $(\epsilon_1, \epsilon_1) \cdot (D_{1,1})^* = (G_1, H_1)$ with two uses of R_1. Another use of R_1 gives $G_1 = H_1$. So we used R_1 at most $3 \leq c$ times.

Let now $k \geq 2$. Then, from the system of Eq. (11) we can derive the system of Eq. (12) with ck^5 uses of R_1 and two uses of R_2. From that system of equations we can derive the equation $G_1 = H_1$ with $c(k-1)^6$ uses of R_1 and $2(k-1)$ uses of R_2, by induction. So we used R_1

$$ck^5 + c(k-1)^6 < ck^5 \cdot (1 + (k-1)) = ck^6$$

times and R_2 at most $2k$ times.   □

Lemma 15 and Corollary 17 show us how to derive the equation $E = F$ from the equational characterizations of E and F:

Corollary 18. *Let E be a regular expression with an equational characterization with n equations and F be a regular expression with an equational characterization with m equations and $L(E) = L(F)$. Then, the equation $E = F$ is derivable from the two given equational characterizations with $O((mn)^6 + r^4mn)$ uses of R_1 and $2mn + m + n$ uses of R_2.*   □

With Theorem 13 and Corollary 18 we can derive the equation $E = F$, for regular expressions E and F with $L(E) = L(F)$:

Theorem 19. *Let E and F be regular expressions with $L(E) = L(F)$. Then, the equation $E = F$ is derivable with $O(r^4 \cdot \text{TOWER}(h + 4))$ uses of R_1 and $\text{TOWER}(h + 4)/1024$ uses of R_2, where $h = \max\{h(E), h(F)\}$.*

Proof. By Theorem 13 equational characterizations for E and F, both with at most $\text{TOWER}(h + 3)/4$ equations, are derivable with $O(r^4 \cdot \text{TOWER}(h + 3))$ uses of R_1 and

$$2 \cdot (|E + F| \cdot + |E + F|_*) < 2 \cdot 2^{h(E+F)} = 2^{h+2}$$

uses of R_2. By Corollary 18 the equation $E = F$ is derivable with

$$O\left(r^4 \cdot (\text{TOWER}(h + 3))^{12}\right) \subseteq O\left(r^4 \cdot \text{TOWER}(h + 4)\right)$$

uses of R_1 and

$$2^{h+2} + (\text{TOWER}(h+3))^2/8 + \text{TOWER}(h+3)/2 \tag{13}$$

uses of R_2. The term in (13) is bounded from above by

$$(\text{TOWER}(h+3))^2/8 + \text{TOWER}(h+3) < 2^{\text{TOWER}(h+3)-10}$$
$$= \text{TOWER}(h+4) \cdot 2^{-10},$$

where we have used $n^2/8 + n < 2^{n-10}$, for $n \geq 16$. □

4   Proof Complexity of Regular Expressions in General

The study of the efficiency of propositional proof systems dates back to the seminal paper of Cook and Reckhow [2]. There the notion of a proof system in general was introduced, which reads as follows—we literally take the definition from there: if $L \subseteq \Sigma^*$, a *proof system* for L is a deterministic polynomial time computable function $f : \Sigma^* \to L$ such that f is onto. A proof system is *polynomially bounded* if there is a polynomial p such that for all $y \in L$ there is an $x \in \Sigma^*$ such that $y = f(x)$ and $|x| \leq p(|y|)$, where $|z|$ denotes the length of z. If $y = f(x)$, then we will say that x is a proof of y, and x is a *short* proof of y if in addition $|x| \leq p(|y|)$. The ultimate goal of propositional proof complexity is to show that there is no propositional proof system allowing for efficient proofs of tautology.

Up to our knowledge the relation between proof complexity and regular expression equivalence is not investigated so far. In the line of the proof of the statement NP=coNP if and only if the set TAUT of all propositional tautologies admits a polynomial bounded proof system [2], we show a similar relation for the set

$$\text{EQUIV} = \{ (E, F) \mid E \text{ and } F \text{ are regular expressions with } L(E) = L(F) \}$$

and the complexity classes NP and PSPACE—we assume the reader to be familiar with the basics in complexity theory as contained in [4]. Note that it is well known that EQUIV is PSPACE-complete [9].

Theorem 20. NP = PSPACE *if and only if* EQUIV *admits a polynomial bounded proof system.*

Proof. Observe that EQUIV is in PSPACE. If NP = PSPACE, then EQUIV belongs to NP. Since a language L is in NP if and only if $L = \emptyset$ or L has a polynomially bounded proof system as shown in [2] it follows that the set EQUIV obeys a polynomially bounded proof system as well. Conversely we argue as follows: assume that EQUIV has a polynomially bounded proof system. Then by the aforementioned statement of [2] it implies that the PSPACE-complete set EQUIV is in NP, which in turn gives us PSPACE $\subseteq$ NP due to the closure of both complexity classes under deterministic polynomial many-one reductions. Hence NP = PSPACE. □

Can we say more on the connection between regular expression and proof systems? One possibility is to restrict the equivalence problem for regular expressions. If we consider expressions that use union and concatenation only, the complexity of the equivalence problem drops to coNP-completeness [5]. This is a dramatic change in complexity compared to the general regular expression equivalence problem. In similar veins as in the proof above, we can show the next result, where $\text{EQUIV}_{\text{fin}}$ refers to the equivalence problem of regular expressions with the operations union and concatenation only—the subscript "fin" refers to the fact that the involved expressions can only describe finite languages. The proof is straight forward and thus left to the reader.

Theorem 21. $\text{NP} = \text{coNP}$ *if and only if* $\text{EQUIV}_{\text{fin}}$ *admits a polynomial bounded proof system.*   □

Let us turn back to the equivalence of regular expressions in general. The most efficient proof that we can come up for EQUIV is simply to convert both expressions into equivalent nondeterministic finite automata, then to determinize these automata in order to obtain equivalent deterministic finite state devices, followed by a minimization, and finally check for isomorphism in order to verify the equivalence. This strategy leads to a proof system f that is in fact deterministic polynomial time computable on the size of the *whole* proof x, which is of exponential length, because the conversion of a regular expression into an equivalent deterministic finite automaton increases its size at most exponential. This is far from a polynomially bounded proof system, but it is the best possible we can come up with at the moment.

Acknowledgement. Thanks to Christian Rauch for reading a preliminary version of this paper and for his useful comments.

Appendix

Here we give a more elaborated example of a derivation in the axiom system F_1.

Example 22. We have $L(a^*) = \{a\}^* = L(a^{**})$. To illustrate the previous definitions we show that the equation $a^* = a^{**}$ is derivable in F_1. Axiom A_6 gives us $a^{**} + a^{**} = a^{**}$. With rule R_1 we get

$$\frac{a^{**} + a^{**} = a^{**} \qquad a^{**} + a^{**} = a^{**}}{a^{**} = a^{**} + a^{**}, \quad a^{**} = a^{**}.}$$

Axiom A_{10} gives us $a^* = 0^* + a^*a$ and R_1 leads to

$$\frac{a^* = 0^* + a^*a \qquad a^{**} = a^{**}}{(0^* + a^*a)^* = a^{**}, \quad (0^* + a^*a)^* = a^{**}.}$$

Because of Axiom A_{11} we have $(a^*a)^* = (0^* + a^*a)^*$. So with R_1 we get

$$\frac{(a^*a)^* = (0^* + a^*a)^* \qquad (a^*a)^* = (0^* + a^*a)^*}{(0^* + a^*a)^* = (a^*a)^*, \quad (0^* + a^*a)^* = (0^* + a^*a)^*.}$$

Another use of R_1 gives us

$$\frac{(0^* + a^*a)^* = (a^*a)^* \qquad (0^* + a^*a)^* = a^{**}}{(a^*a)^* = (0^* + a^*a)^*, \quad (a^*a)^* = a^{**}.}$$

Axiom A_{10} leads to $(a^*a)^* = 0^* + (a^*a)^*(a^*a)$ and R_1 implies

$$\frac{(a^*a)^* = 0^* + (a^*a)^*(a^*a) \qquad (a^*a)^* = a^{**}}{0^* + (a^*a)^*(a^*a) = (a^*a)^*, \quad 0^* + (a^*a)^*(a^*a) = a^{**}.}$$

With one more use of R_1 we have

$$\frac{(a^*a)^* = a^{**} \qquad 0^* + (a^*a)^*(a^*a) = a^{**}}{0^* + a^{**}(a^*a) = 0^* + (a^*a)^*(a^*a), \quad 0^* + a^{**}(a^*a) = a^{**}.} \tag{14}$$

Axiom A_2 gives us $a^{**}(a^*a) = (a^{**}a^*)a$. With R_1 we get

$$\frac{a^{**}(a^*a) = (a^{**}a^*)a \qquad 0^* + a^{**}(a^*a) = a^{**}}{0^* + (a^{**}a^*)a = 0^* + a^{**}(a^*a), \quad 0^* + (a^{**}a^*)a = a^{**}.} \tag{15}$$

We use A_6 and R_1 again:

$$\frac{a^{**}a^* + a^{**}a^* = a^{**}a^* \qquad a^{**}a^* + a^{**}a^* = a^{**}a^*}{a^{**}a^* = a^{**}a^* + a^{**}a^*, \quad a^{**}a^* = a^{**}a^*.}$$

Because of Axiom A_{10} we have $a^* = 0^* + a^*a$. Now R_1 leads to

$$\frac{a^* = 0^* + a^*a \qquad a^{**}a^* = a^{**}a^*}{a^{**}(0^* + a^*a) = a^{**}a^*, \quad a^{**}(0^* + a^*a) = a^{**}a^*.}$$

Axiom A_5 tells us $a^{**}(0^* + a^*a) = a^{**} \cdot 0^* + a^{**}(a^*a)$. So with R_1 we get

$$\frac{a^{**}(0^* + a^*a) = a^{**} \cdot 0^* + a^{**}(a^*a) \qquad a^{**}(0^* + a^*a) = a^{**}a^*}{a^{**} \cdot 0^* + a^{**}(a^*a) = a^{**}(0^* + a^*a), \quad a^{**} \cdot 0^* + a^{**}(a^*a) = a^{**}a^*.}$$

We will show in Lemma 3 that the equation $a^{**} \cdot 0^* = a^{**}$ is derivable with eleven uses of R_1 and two uses of R_2. Having this equation, rule R_1 shows

$$\frac{a^{**} \cdot 0^* = a^{**} \qquad a^{**} \cdot 0^* + a^{**}(a^*a) = a^{**}a^*}{a^{**} + a^{**}(a^*a) = a^{**} \cdot 0^* + a^{**}(a^*a), \quad a^{**} + a^{**}(a^*a) = a^{**}a^*.}$$

From (14) we have $0^* + a^{**}(a^*a) = a^{**}$. Rule R_1 gives

$$\frac{0^* + a^{**}(a^*a) = a^{**} \qquad 0^* + a^{**}(a^*a) = a^{**}}{a^{**} = 0^* + a^{**}(a^*a), \quad a^{**} = a^{**}.}$$

Another use of R_1 leads to

$$(0^* + a^{**}(a^*a)) + a^{**}(a^*a) = a^{**}a^*,$$

as before. Because of Axiom A_1 we get

$$0^* + (a^{**}(a^*a) + a^{**}(a^*a)) = (0^* + a^{**}(a^*a)) + a^{**}(a^*a).$$

One use of R_1 gives

$$(0^* + a^{**}(a^*a)) + a^{**}(a^*a) = 0^* + (a^{**}(a^*a) + a^{**}(a^*a)).$$

Using R_1 again implies

$$0^* + (a^{**}(a^*a) + a^{**}(a^*a)) = a^{**}a^*.$$

With A_6 we have

$$\frac{a^{**}(a^*a) + a^{**}(a^*a) = a^{**}(a^*a) \qquad 0^* + (a^{**}(a^*a) + a^{**}(a^*a)) = a^{**}a^*}{0^* + a^{**}(a^*a) = 0^* + (a^{**}(a^*a) + a^{**}(a^*a)), \quad 0^* + a^{**}(a^*a) = a^{**}a^*.}$$

Axiom A_3 and R_1 lead to $a^{**}(a^*a) + 0^* = a^{**}a^*$. Then, A_2 and R_1 give $(a^{**}a^*)a + 0^* = a^{**}a^*$. With one more use of R_1 we get $a^{**}a^* = (a^{**}a^*)a + 0^*$. Now, because $o(a) = 0$, we can use R_2:

$$\frac{a^{**}a^* = (a^{**}a^*)a + 0^*}{a^{**}a^* = 0^* \cdot a^*.}$$

Rule R_1 gives us $0^* \cdot a^* = a^{**}a^*$. With A_7 and R_1 we have $a^* = a^{**}a^*$. Rule R_1 again leads to $a^{**}a^* = a^*$. From (15) we get $0^* + (a^{**}a^*)a = a^{**}$. Then, R_1 gives $0^* + a^*a = a^{**}$. Axiom A_{10} tells us $a^* = 0^* + a^*a$ and R_1 implies $0^* + a^*a = a^*$. With one last use of R_1 we have

$$\frac{0^* + a^*a = a^* \qquad 0^* + a^*a = a^{**}}{a^* = 0^* + a^*a, \quad a^* = a^{**}.}$$

So, we have proven the equation $a^* = a^{**}$ in the axiom system F_1. $\square$

References

1. Brzozowski, J.A.: Canonical regular expressions and minimal state graphs for definite events. In: Mathematical Theory of Automata. MRI Symposia Series, vol. 12, pp. 529–561. Polytechnic Press, New York (1962)
2. Cook, S.A., Reckhow, R.A.: The relative efficiency of propositional proof systems. J. Symbol. Logic **44**(1), 36–50 (1979)
3. Ginzburg, A.: A procedure of checking equality of regular expressions. J. ACM **14**(2), 355–362 (1967)
4. Hopcroft, J.E., Ullman, J.D.: Introduction to Automata Theory, Languages and Computation. Addison-Wesley (1979)
5. Hunt, H.B., III., Rosenkrantz, D.J., Szymanski, T.G.: On the equivalence, containment, and covering problems for the regular and context-free languages. J. Comput. System Sci. **12**, 222–268 (1976)

6. Kleene, S.C.: Representation of events in nerve nets and finite automata. In: Shannon, C.E., McCarthy, J. (eds.) Automata Studies. Annals of Mathematics Studies, vol. 34, pp. 2–42. Princeton University Press (1956)
7. McNaughton, R., Yamada, H.: Regular expressions and state graphs for automata. IRE Trans. Electron. Comput. **EC-9**(1), 39–47 (1960)
8. Salomaa, A.: Two complete axiom systems for the algebra of regular events. J. ACM **13**(1), 158–169 (1966)
9. Stockmeyer, L.J., Meyer, A.R.: Word problems requiring exponential time. In: Proceedings of the 5th Symposium on Theory of Computing, pp. 1–9 (1973)

Hidden Markov Models
with Unobservable Transitions

Rebecca Bernemann$^{(\boxtimes)}$, Barbara König, Matthias Schaffeld, and Torben Weis

Universität Duisburg-Essen, Duisburg, Germany
{rebecca.bernemann,barbara_koenig,matthias.schaffeld,
torben.weis}@uni-due.de

Abstract. We consider Hidden Markov Models (HMMs) that admit unobservable ε-transitions (also called null transitions), allowing state changes of which the observer is unaware. Due to the presence of ε-loops this additional feature complicates the theory and requires to carefully set up the corresponding probability space and random variables. In particular we present an algorithm for determining the most probable explanation given an observation (a generalization of the Viterbi algorithm for HMMs) and a method for parameter learning that adapts the probabilities of a given model based on an observation (a generalization of the Baum-Welch algorithm). The latter algorithm guarantees that the given observation has a higher (or equal) probability after adjustment of the parameters and its correctness can be derived directly from the so-called EM algorithm. We also provide runtime results in order to evaluate the efficiency of the proposed algorithms.

This paper is dedicated to Javier Esparza on the occasion of his 60th birthday. Javier Esparza made several seminal contributions to the verification and analysis of probabilistic systems: he published ground-breaking work on probabilistic pushdown automata, programs and abstractions, systems of polynomials, workflow nets and population protocols. Studying stochastic systems is a recurring thread in his work. In this line we here present a contribution to analyzing and learning probabilistic systems that are only partially observable: Hidden Markov Models.

1 Introduction

There are many practical applications that involve the observation of a probabilistic system with hidden state, where the aim is to infer properties about the state of the system only from the observations that are available. That is, we want to explain what happened in a software or real-world system that is only partially observable.

In particular we are motivated by the following scenario in which we want to determine the most probable cause of a given observation: imagine a building equipped with sensors that are triggered when a person walks past. However, these sensors might produce both false positives (nobody walked past, but the sensor sends a signal) and false negatives (somebody was present, but did not

S. Kiefer et al. (Eds.): *Taming the Infinities of Concurrency*, LNCS 14660, pp. 101–121, 2024.
https://doi.org/10.1007/978-3-031-56222-8_5

trigger the sensor). This can be modelled by a probabilistic transition system which has both observable symbols and ε-transitions (also referred to as null transitions), corresponding to false negatives. Now assume that there are three rooms, the bedroom (B), the corridor (C) and the kitchen (K), all of them connected through C and equipped with sensors. Sensors B, K trigger, but not C. However, in order to reach the kitchen from the bedroom, the person should have passed the corridor! Hence our analysis should tell us that the most likely explanation for the observation is indeed the sequence B, C, K.

While here this reasoning is straightforward, finding the most probable explanation may become increasingly more complex with additional missing sensor data and multiple possible paths.

In order to make matters more concrete, consider the following system depicting our motivational example. The start state is s_0 and from each state we label the transitions with symbols and probabilities. For instance, from s_0 there is a 0.1 probability of going to C with an unobservable ε-transition.

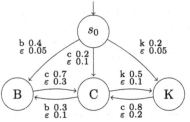

Now we detect the observation sequence: b, k. What happened? In fact there are several possible paths, the most probable being s_0, B, C, K (first transition b, second one ε and the third k) whose probability is

$$\delta(s_0)(b, B) \cdot \delta(B)(\varepsilon, C) \cdot \delta(C)(k, K) = 0.4 \cdot 0.3 \cdot 0.5 = 0.06$$

The question is how to efficiently determine the most likely path and its probability.

A second issue is how to learn the probabilities that label the transitions. Assume the basic structure of the system is known, in particular the number of states, but the parameters, i.e., the probabilities are not. Now we observe the system and want to estimate its parameters.

Of course, such systems have been extensively studied under the name of Hidden Markov Models (HMMs) [21,25]. Markov models are useful for modelling systems for which we want to find the most likely explanation for a given observation sequence.

Unobservable transitions, also known as null transitions or ε-transitions, i.e. HMMs that may change state without the observer being aware of it, have been proposed in the literature, especially in the context of speech recognition [3,15]. However, to the best of our knowledge, there is no theory of systems that allows for ε-loops. Related work only treats specific HMMs, where either loops cannot appear altogether (so-called left-to-right HMMs) [19] or ε-loops are forbidden [3,5]. Also [15] does not allow ε-loops in the context of learning. It does describe an algorithm to eliminate ε-transitions, which can increase the size of the model and alters the system such that probabilities of ε-transitions cannot be learned directly.

On the other hand ε-loops can occur naturally in applications, e.g., in the application described above that we have in mind, and there are no easy work-arounds. We can only speculate why the generalization has not been made, but observe that for systems with ε-loops the theory is substantially more complex.

Adapting the Viterbi algorithm calls for computing the probability of reaching a target state from a source state, using only ε-transitions, which corresponds to determining the termination probability of a probabilistic transition system [4].

Complications also arise when adapting the techniques for learning the model parameters, a fundamental task, since the transition probabilities are usually not known, but can only be derived via learning. The well-known Baum-Welch algorithm for parameter learning has to be fundamentally adapted to deal with the presence of ε-loops. In particular the usual forward-backward algorithm [21] for parameter estimation can not be used directly, but has to be generalized.

Given an observation, we propose to compute the conditional expectation of passing each transition (remember that the state and so the transitions are hidden) and this is turned into a probability function (by normalizing), which is the new parameter estimate. The guarantee provided by this estimate is that the observation sequence becomes more probable given the new parameters. This result can be derived from the so-called expectation-maximization (EM) algorithm [9] that gives us a general framework for such results.

Our contributions are:

- We rephrase the theory behind HMMs with ε-transitions, in terms of the used probability space and random variables.
- We extend the theory to systems with ε-transitions, a very natural extension for such systems and indispensable for some applications – such as the motivational example – which complicates the formalization and the algorithms. In particular, we have to handle ε-loops which we deal with by setting up fixpoint equations.
- We spell out explicitly why parameter learning based on the EM algorithm works in this setting.
- We provide runtime results for both algorithms presented in this paper. Since these are strictly more general and work for a more general class of systems than the standard algorithms, it is no surprise to see that they perform less efficiently than the original algorithms. But we show that they are feasible for case studies of a non-trivial size.

While HMMs have been known for some time, we feel that, due to the renewed interest in learning approaches (e.g., machine learning or the L^* algorithm [2]), it makes sense to revive the theory and close existing gaps in the literature.

Furthermore HMMs provide us with valuable methods for offering explanations in a probabilistic setting and figuring out the most likely cause of an observation in a system with hidden states, which integrates well with the current quest for more explainability in algorithms and software systems.

2   Preliminaries

Probability Theory. We recapitulate the basics of discrete probability theory.

A *probability space* (Ω, P) consists of a (countable) *sample space* Ω and a probability function $P\colon \Omega \to [0,1]$ such that $\sum_{\omega \in \Omega} P(\omega) = 1$. Given a set Ω we denote by $\mathcal{D}(\Omega)$ the set of all *probability functions* on Ω.

A *random variable* for a probability space (Ω, P) is a function $X\colon \Omega \to V$. We assume a special random variable $Z\colon \Omega \to \Omega$, which is the identity. For $v \in V$ we denote by $P(X = v) = \sum_{X(\omega)=v} P(\omega)$ the probability that X has value v. Given two random variables $X_i\colon \Omega \to V_i$, $i = 1, 2$, the conditional probability that X_1 takes value v_1, under the condition that X_2 takes value v_2, is

$$P(X_1 = v_1 \mid X_2 = v_2) = \frac{P(X_1 = v_1 \wedge X_2 = v_2)}{P(X_2 = v_2)},$$

provided that $P(X_2 = v_2) > 0$.

For a random variable $X\colon \Omega \to \mathbb{R}$, we define its *expectation* as $E[X] = \sum_{\omega \in \Omega} X(\omega) \cdot P(\omega)$. Given another random variable $Y\colon \Omega \to V$, conditional expectation is defined, for $v \in V$, as

$$E[X \mid Y = v] = \sum_{\omega \in \Omega} X(\omega) \cdot P(X = \omega \mid Y = v).$$

Hidden Markov Models. We are working with HMMs with ε-transitions (also called null transitions in the literature [3,15]). In particular we put observations on the transitions, rather than on the states [21]. This is a standard variant of HMMs and is for instance done in [3,10,15]. Since we use ε-transitions, we need not assume an initial probability function, but instead later fix a start state s_0.

Definition 2.1 (HMM with ε-Transitions). *An HMM with ε-transitions is a three-tuple (S, Σ, δ), consisting of a finite state space S, an alphabet Σ and a transition function $\delta\colon S \to \mathcal{D}((\Sigma \cup \{\varepsilon\}) \times S)$. The set of transitions is defined as $T_\delta = \{(s, a, s') \mid s, s' \in S, a \in \Sigma \cup \{\varepsilon\}, \delta(s)(a, s') > 0\}$. In addition $T_\delta^s = T_\delta \cap (\{s\} \times (\Sigma \cup \{\varepsilon\}) \times S)$ is the set of transitions originating at state s.*

3   Probability Space and Random Variables

We introduce the probability space of observation sequences that contains alternating sequences of states and observation symbols (or ε) and is dependent on n, denoting the number of observable symbols (from Σ). We fix a start state $s_0 \in S$ and restrict the possible sequences to those where the second to last element is contained in Σ and is hence observable. This makes sure that the probabilities in fact sum up to 1.

$$\Omega_{s_0}^n = s_0((\varepsilon S)^* \Sigma S)^n$$

The probability for an element from the probability space $\tilde{z} \in \Omega_{s_0}^n$ can be calculated by multiplying the corresponding transition probabilities. Whenever $\tilde{z} = s_0 a_1 s_1 a_2 \ldots a_m s_m \in \Omega_{s_0}^n$ where $s_i \in S$ and $a_i \in \Sigma \cup \{\varepsilon\}$ we define: $P_{s_0}^n(\tilde{z}) = \prod_{i=1}^m \delta(s_{i-1})(a_i, s_i)$. Furthermore $P_{s_0}^0(s_0) = 1$.

Note that due to the presence of ε-transitions we have to take care to set up a probability space where the probabilities add up to 1. An alternative could be to use the solution of [15] and to distinguish a final state, which is however inconvenient for some applications.

We continue by showing that the probability space is well-defined under some mild condition, namely that for each state there is an outgoing path of non-zero probability that reaches a symbol different from ε. This is equivalent to requiring that states are transient wrt. ε-transitions in the sense of [13,14], that is the probability of returning to a state is less than one. This condition has the additional benefit that the fixpoint equations are power contractions (i.e., they become contractive after a number of iterations) and hence have unique solutions (for more details see Sect. 6).

Proposition 3.1. *Assume that for each state $s \in S$ there is an outgoing path of non-zero probability that contains a symbol in Σ. Then the probability space $(\Omega_{s_0}^n, P_{s_0}^n)$ is well-defined, in particular $\sum_{\tilde{z} \in \Omega_{s_0}^n} P_{s_0}^n(\tilde{z}) = 1$.*

Proof. Given a sequence $\tilde{z} = s_0 a_1 s_1 a_2 \ldots a_m s_m = s_0 a_1 \tilde{z}_1$ we observe that

$$P_{s_0}^n(\tilde{z}) = \delta(s_0)(a_1, s_1) \cdot P_{s_1}^n(\tilde{z}_1) \qquad \text{if } a_1 = \varepsilon$$
$$P_{s_0}^n(\tilde{z}) = \delta(s_0)(a_1, s_1) \cdot P_{s_1}^{n-1}(\tilde{z}_1) \qquad \text{if } a_1 \in \Sigma$$

We abbreviate $S_{s_0}^n = \sum_{\tilde{z} \in \Omega_{s_0}^n} P_{s_0}^n(\tilde{z})$. Since $\Omega_{s_0}^0 = \{s_0\}$, it is easy to see that $S_{s_0}^0 = 1$ and if $n \geq 1$:

$$S_{s_0}^n = \sum_{\tilde{z} \in \Omega_{s_0}^n} P_{s_0}^n(\tilde{z})$$
$$= \sum_{s_1 \in S} \sum_{\tilde{z}_1 \in \Omega_{s_1}^n} \delta(s_0)(\varepsilon, s_1) \cdot P_{s_1}^n(\tilde{z}_1) + \sum_{a_1 \in \Sigma, s_1 \in S} \sum_{\tilde{z}_1 \in \Omega_{s_1}^{n-1}} \delta(s_0)(a_1, s_1) \cdot P_{s_1}^{n-1}(\tilde{z}_1)$$
$$= \sum_{s_1 \in S} \delta(s_0)(\varepsilon, s_1) \cdot \sum_{\tilde{z}_1 \in \Omega_{s_1}^n} P_{s_1}^n(\tilde{z}_1) + \sum_{a_1 \in \Sigma, s_1 \in S} \delta(s_0)(a_1, s_1) \cdot \sum_{\tilde{z}_1 \in \Omega_{s_1}^{n-1}} P_{s_1}^{n-1}(\tilde{z}_1)$$
$$= \sum_{s_1 \in S} \delta(s_0)(\varepsilon, s_1) \cdot S_{s_1}^n + \sum_{a_1 \in \Sigma, s_1 \in S} \delta(s_0)(a_1, s_1) \cdot S_{s_1}^{n-1}$$

Since the probabilities of all outgoing transitions of a state sum up to 1, we observe that $S_s^n = 1$ for all $n, s \in S$ is a solution to this system of fixpoint equations. Since we assume that each state will eventually reach an observation symbol in Σ with non-zero probability, the corresponding fixpoint function is a power contraction (becomes contractive after some iterations), since the probability to stay with index n is strictly less than 1 after at most $|S|$ steps (for more details see Sect. 6).

This implies that the fixpoint is unique and hence the statement of the proposition follows. □

The above result could also have been achieved by contracting ε-transitions, given that the states are transient. This solution can however not be employed in later states of the paper where explanation finding and learning techniques should be applied to the original model.

We will in the following assume that the requirement of Proposition 3.1 holds. Otherwise there might be states that can never reach an observation symbol, for which the probability of all outgoing paths is 0.

Given this probability space, we define some required random variables.

Random Variables	
$Z : \Omega_{s_0}^n \to \Omega_{s_0}^n$	Identity on $\Omega_{s_0}^n$
$Y : \Omega_{s_0}^n \to \Sigma^n$	Projection to observable symbols (removal of ε's and states)
$L : \Omega_{s_0}^n \to S$	Last state of a given observation sequence
$X_t : \Omega_{s_0}^n \to \mathbb{N}_0$	Number of times a transition $t = (s, a, s')$ occurs in a sequence

We omit the indices n, s_0 if they are clear from the context: if we write $P(\widetilde{z})$ or $P(Z = \widetilde{z})$ we work in the probability space $\Omega_{s_0}^n$ and mean the probability function $P_{s_0}^n$, where $n = |Y(\widetilde{z})|$ and s_0 is the first element of $\widetilde{z}$. And if we write $P_{s_0}(Y = \widetilde{y})$, the value n is understood to be $|\widetilde{y}|$. We do the same for expectations.

4   Finding the Best Explanation for an Observation

As a warmup we will describe a method for finding the best explanation, given an observation sequence. More concretely, an observation sequence $\widetilde{y} \in \Sigma^*$ is given and it is our aim to compute the most probable sequence of states and its probability. For standard HMMs there is a well-known algorithm for this task: the Viterbi algorithm [16,21,24]. Instead of enumerating all paths and checking which one is most probable, it uses dynamic programming with intermediate results, by computing step-by-step the most probable path ending at a given state s, for each prefix of the observation sequence $\widetilde{y}$.

We adapt the Viterbi algorithm, taking ε-transitions into account. While in the standard case it is straightforward to obtain the likeliest path in the case of a single observation symbol, in our case the path might have taken an arbitrary number of ε-transitions in between. Remember that the probability space is set up in such a way that the last transition in every sequence that we consider is always observable, which is no restriction, since there is always some explanation with maximal probability that satisfies this condition.

Proposition 4.1 (Maximal Probability for One Observation). *Let (S, Σ, δ) be an HMM and $a \in \Sigma$ be an observation. By $\mathcal{E}_{s_0,s}^a$, for $s_0, s \in S$ we denote the probability for the most likely path in $\Omega_{s_0}^1$, starting in state s_0 and ending in state s, where a is the observation, that is:*

$$\mathcal{E}_{s_0,s}^a := \max_{\substack{\widetilde{z} \in \Omega_{s_0}^1 \\ L(\widetilde{z})=s}} P(Z = \widetilde{z} \wedge Y = a)$$

Then we have:

$$\mathcal{E}^a_{s_0,s} = \max\left(\delta(s_0)(a,s), \max_{s'\in S}\delta(s_0)(\varepsilon,s') \cdot \mathcal{E}^a_{s',s}\right)$$

Proof.

$$\mathcal{E}^a_{s_0,s} = \max_{\substack{\widetilde{z}\in\Omega^1_{s_0} \\ L(\widetilde{z})=s}} P^1(Z = \widetilde{z} \wedge Y = a) = \max_{\substack{\widetilde{z}\in \\ s_0(\varepsilon S)^* as}} P^1(Z = \widetilde{z} \wedge Y = a)$$

$$= \max\left(\underbrace{P^1(Z = s_0 a s \wedge Y = a)}_{\delta(s_0)(a,s)}, \max_{\substack{\widetilde{z}_1\in \\ S(\varepsilon S)^* as}} P^1(Z = s_0\varepsilon\widetilde{z}_1 \wedge Y = a)\right)$$

$$= \max\left(\delta(s_0)(a,s), \max_{s'\in S}\max_{\substack{\widetilde{z}_1\in \\ s'(\varepsilon S)^* as}} \delta(s_0)(\varepsilon,s') \cdot P^1(Z = \widetilde{z}_1 \wedge Y = a)\right)$$

$$= \max\left(\delta(s_0)(a,s), \max_{s'\in S}\delta(s_0)(\varepsilon,s') \cdot \underbrace{\max_{\substack{\widetilde{z}_1\in \\ s'(\varepsilon S)^* as}} P^1(Z = \widetilde{z}_1 \wedge Y = a)}_{\mathcal{E}^a_{s',s}}\right)$$

$$= \max\left(\delta(s_0)(a,s), \max_{s'\in S}\delta(s_0)(\varepsilon,s') \cdot \mathcal{E}^a_{s',s}\right)$$

$\square$

The equation of Proposition 4.1 has a unique fixpoint (for more details see Sect. 6) due to the requirement that from every state there is a path of non-zero probability that contains an observation. In order to compute $\mathcal{E}^a_{s_0,s}$ one could hence perform fixpoint iteration or use an external solver. In fact, the computation is simplified in this case since among the paths with the highest probability there is always one that does not contain duplicate states (apart from the final state s). By equipping the computation with an extra parameter $S_0 \subseteq S$ (the set of states that can still be visited), we can easily ensure termination, even in the presence of ε-loops, and the equation becomes the following, where $\mathcal{E}^a_{s_0,s} = \mathcal{E}^a_{s_0,s}(S)$.

$$\mathcal{E}^a_{s_0,s}(S_0) = \max\left(\delta(s_0)(a,s), \max_{s'\in S_0\backslash\{s_0\}}\delta(s_0)(\varepsilon,s') \cdot \mathcal{E}^a_{s',s}(S_0\backslash\{s_0\})\right)$$

Note that in order to efficiently implement this approach in practice, it is useful to simply introduce a matrix storing the probability of the most probable ε-path between each two states. This step has to be done only once per HMM provided that its transition probabilities do not change. We can now address the task of computing the maximal probability for a longer sequence of observations. For this purpose, we extend the established Viterbi algorithm [24]. Here, the probability for the likeliest path that results in a given observation is computed inductively and is based on Proposition 4.1.

Proposition 4.2 (Maximal Probability for Observation Sequence). *Let (S, Σ, δ) be an HMM and let $\widetilde{y} = a_1 \ldots a_n = \widetilde{y}_1 a_n$ be an observation sequence.*

We define $V^{\tilde{y}}_{s_0,s}$ as the maximum probability of observing $\tilde{y}$ and ending in state s, more formally

$$V^{\tilde{y}}_{s_0,s} := \max_{\substack{\tilde{z} \in \Omega^n_{s_0} \\ L(\tilde{z})=s}} P(Z = \tilde{z} \wedge Y = \tilde{y})$$

Then for $n = 0$ it holds that $V^{\varepsilon}_{s_0,s} = 1$ if $s = s_0$ and 0 otherwise. For $n > 0$:

$$V^{\tilde{y}}_{s_0,s} = \max_{s' \in S} V^{\tilde{y}_1}_{s_0,s'} \cdot \mathcal{E}^{a_n}_{s',s}$$

Proof.

$$V^{\tilde{y}}_{s_0,s} = V^{a_1 \ldots a_n}_{s_0,s} = \max_{\substack{\tilde{z} \in \Omega^n_{s_0} \\ L(\tilde{z})=s}} P(Z = \tilde{z} \wedge Y = a_1 \ldots a_n)$$

$$= \max_{s' \in S} \max_{\substack{\tilde{z}_1 \in \Omega^{n-1}_{s_0} \\ L(\tilde{z}_1)=s'}} \max_{\substack{\tilde{z}_2 \in \Omega^1_{s'} \\ L(\tilde{z}_2)=s}} P(Z = \tilde{z}_1 \wedge Y = a_1 \ldots a_{n-1}) \cdot P(Z = \tilde{z}_2 \wedge Y = a_n)$$

$$= \max_{s' \in S} \underbrace{\max_{\substack{\tilde{z}_1 \in \Omega^{n-1}_{s_0} \\ L(\tilde{z}_1)=s'}} P(Z = \tilde{z}_1 \wedge Y = a_1 \ldots a_{n-1})}_{V^{a_1 \ldots a_{n-1}}_{s_0,s'}} \cdot \underbrace{\max_{\substack{\tilde{z}_2 \in \Omega^1_{s'} \\ L(\tilde{z}_2)=s}} P(Z = \tilde{z}_2 \wedge Y = a_n)}_{\mathcal{E}^{a_n}_{s',s}}$$

$$= \max_{s' \in S} V^{a_1 \ldots a_{n-1}}_{s_0,s'} \cdot \mathcal{E}^{a_n}_{s',s} = \max_{s' \in S} V^{\tilde{y}_1}_{s_0,s'} \cdot \mathcal{E}^{a_n}_{s',s}$$

$\square$

In order to obtain the best explanation starting at s_0, regardless of its final state, we have to take the maximum $\max_{s \in S} V^{\tilde{y}}_{s_0,s}$. If we are instead interested in the conditional probability, i.e., $\max_{\tilde{z} \in \Omega^n_{s_0}} P(Z = \tilde{z} \mid Y = \tilde{y})$, it can be obtained from this maximum by dividing by $P_{s_0}(Y = \tilde{y})$.

Obtaining the probability alone is not sufficient for our purposes, as we are also interested in how this probability emerged. For that reason we make use of the calculated highest probabilities. We do not only expect a sequence of states as explanation, but also the intermediate symbols or ε's used when transitioning from state to state. This is necessary because a possible ε-transition can implicitly occur in an observation, creating an ambiguity problem when working out which exact transitions were taken at what time in the state sequence.

By unravelling the fixpoint equation of Proposition 4.1, we obtain the following construction, where $\mathcal{E}Path^a_{s_0,s} \in \Omega^1_{s_0}$ denotes the likeliest state sequence for a path starting in state s_0 and ending in state s that produces the observation a in its last transition. This is feasible whenever $\mathcal{E}^a_{s_0,s} > 0$.

$$\mathcal{E}Path^a_{s_0,s} = \begin{cases} s_0 a s & \text{if } \mathcal{E}^a_{s_0,s} = \delta(s_0)(a,s) \\ s_0 \varepsilon \mathcal{E}Path^a_{s',s} & \text{otherwise, with } s' = \arg\max_{s' \in S} \delta(s_0)(\varepsilon, s') \cdot \mathcal{E}^a_{s',s} \end{cases}$$

Note that in the following the operator $\circ$ denotes concatenation and the tail function T removes the first element of a given input sequence and returns the rest.

Proposition 4.3 (Likeliest State Sequence for Observation Sequence).
Let an HMM (S, Σ, δ) and an observation sequence $\widetilde{y} = a_1 \ldots a_n$ be given. Whenever $V_{s_0,s}^{\widetilde{y}} > 0$, we let the term $\psi_{s_0,s}^{\widetilde{y}}$ denote the likeliest state sequence starting in state s_0, ending in s, that explains $\widetilde{y}$, i.e., we define

$$\psi_{s_0,s}^{\widetilde{y}} := \underset{\substack{\widetilde{z} \in \Omega_{s_0}^n \\ L(\widetilde{z})=s}}{\arg\max} \, P(Z = \widetilde{z} \wedge Y = \widetilde{y}).$$

Then it holds that $\psi_{s_0,s_0}^{\varepsilon} = s_0$. Furthermore, whenever $\widetilde{y} = \widetilde{y}_1 a_n$:

$$\psi_{s_0,s}^{\widetilde{y}} = \psi_{s_0,s'}^{\widetilde{y}_1} \circ T(\mathcal{E}Path_{s',s}^{a_n}),$$

where $s' = \arg\max_{s' \in S} V_{s_0,s'}^{\widetilde{y}_1} \cdot \mathcal{E}_{s',s}^{a_n}$.

Proof.

$$\psi_{s_0,s}^{\widetilde{y}} = \psi_{s_0,s}^{a_1 \ldots a_n}$$

$$= \underset{\widetilde{z} \in \Omega_{s_0}^n \, L(\widetilde{z})=s}{\arg\max} \, P(Z = \widetilde{z} \wedge Y = a_1 \ldots a_n)$$

$$= \underbrace{\underset{\substack{\widetilde{z}_1 \in \Omega_{s_0}^{n-1} \\ L(\widetilde{z}_1)=s'}}{\arg\max} P(Z = \widetilde{z}_1 \wedge Y = a_1 \ldots a_{n-1})}_{\psi_{s_0,s'}^{a_1 \ldots a_{n-1}}} \circ T(\underbrace{\underset{\substack{\widetilde{z}_2 \in \Omega_{s'}^1 \\ L(\widetilde{z}_2)=s}}{\arg\max} P(Z = \widetilde{z}_2 \wedge Y = a_n)}_{\mathcal{E}Path_{s',s}^{a_n}})$$

$$= \psi_{s_0,s'}^{a_1 \ldots a_{n-1}} \circ T(\mathcal{E}Path_{s',s}^{a_n})$$

$$= \psi_{s_0,s'}^{\widetilde{y}_1} \circ T(\mathcal{E}Path_{s',s}^{a_n})$$

where $s' = \arg\max_{s' \in S} V_{s_0,s'}^{a_1 \ldots a_{n-1}} \cdot \mathcal{E}_{s',s}^{a_n}$ is the state where the maximum is reached. □

Example 4.4. *Take the HMM from the introduction (Sect. 1) and consider the proposed observation sequence b, k. In order to find the best explanation for this observation, the dynamic programming approach determines for each state of the HMM the probability of finishing there after observing the sequence and then takes the maximum probability over all states, namely $\max_{s \in S} V_{s_0,s}^{bk}$. This term is then unravelled inductively, shaving off one symbol at a time.*

$$\max_{s \in S} V_{s_0,s}^{bk} = \max_{s \in S} \left(\max_{s' \in S} V_{s_0,s'}^b \cdot \mathcal{E}_{s',s}^k \right)$$

$$= \max_{s \in S} \left(\max_{s' \in S} \left(\max_{s'' \in S} V_{s_0,s''}^{\varepsilon} \cdot \mathcal{E}_{s'',s'}^b \right) \cdot \mathcal{E}_{s',s}^k \right)$$

$$= \max_{s',s \in S} \mathcal{E}_{s_0,s'}^b \cdot \mathcal{E}_{s',s}^k$$

The last equality is due to Proposition 4.2 requiring $s'' = s_0$ for a non-zero probability. Both $\mathcal{E}$ variables in the resulting equation represent the observation of one visible symbol (b and k respectively), possibly preceded by multiple null observations. This calculation will result in the probability for the likeliest path, the state sequence itself can be found by determining $\max_{s \in S} \psi_{s_0,s}^{bk}$.

5   Parameter Learning

We now discuss a method for determining the system parameters. We assume that the structure of the system and initial estimated probabilities are given, and those probabilities have to be adjusted through observing output sequences. The traversed states can not be observed directly. This core problem for HMMs is traditionally solved by the Baum-Welch algorithm [5], which is based on the forward-backward algorithm, but because of ε-transitions and in particular ε-loops, it is necessary to develop a different approach.

5.1   Conditional Expectation of the Number of Transition Traversals

To adjust the probabilities, we have to solve the following subtask: Given an HMM with initial state s_0, an observation sequence $\tilde{y}$ and a transition t, determine the expected value of the number of traversals of t, when observing sequence $\tilde{y}$, starting from s_0. For each state, we determine these values for all outgoing transitions and normalize them to obtain probabilities. This gives us new parameters and we later discuss the guarantees that this approach provides.

If there are no ε-loops, it is sufficient to compute the probability of crossing a given transition t while reading the i-th symbol of the observation sequence and to sum up over all i. This is done with the forward-backward algorithm, determining the probability of reaching the source state of t, multiplied with the probability of t and the probability of reading the remaining observation sequence from the target state. In the present setup, this has to be adapted, since t can be an ε-transition and we may cross it several times while reading the i-th symbol.

We want to determine $E_{s_0}[X_t \mid Y = \tilde{y}]$ or, equivalently, $E_{s_0}[X_t \mid Y = \tilde{y}] \cdot P_{s_0}(Y = \tilde{y})$. This is defined if $P_{s_0}(Y = \tilde{y}) > 0$, which we assume since the sequence $\tilde{y}$ has actually been observed. Note that due to the nature of our probability space, ε-transitions that might be traversed after the last observation do not count. We compute the conditional expectation by setting up a suitable fixpoint equation, similar to the Bellman equations specifying the expected reward for a Markov decision process [6].

Proposition 5.1. *We fix an HMM and an observation sequence* $\tilde{y} = a_1 \ldots a_n = a_1 \tilde{y}_1$. *Let* $t = (s, a, s')$ *and we define*

$$C_{s_0,t}^{\tilde{y}} := E_{s_0}[X_t \mid Y = \tilde{y}] \cdot P_{s_0}(Y = \tilde{y}).$$

Then $C_{s_0,t}^{\varepsilon} = 0$ *and the following fixpoint equation holds: whenever* $a \in \Sigma$

$$C_{s_0,t}^{\tilde{y}} = \sum_{s_1 \in S} \delta(s_0)(a_1, s_1) \cdot C_{s_1,t}^{\tilde{y}_1} + \sum_{s_1 \in S} \delta(s_0)(\varepsilon, s_1) \cdot C_{s_1,t}^{\tilde{y}} +$$
$$[s_0 = s \wedge a_1 = a] \cdot \delta(s)(a, s') \cdot P_{s'}(Y = \tilde{y}_1)$$

and whenever $a = \varepsilon$ *the last summand has to be replaced by* $[s_0 = s] \cdot \delta(s)(\varepsilon, s') \cdot P_{s'}(Y = \tilde{y})$. *We use the notation* $[b]$ *where* $[b] = 1$ *if* b *holds and* $[b] = 0$ *otherwise.*

Proof. Note that by assumption $P_{s_0}(Y = \tilde{y}) > 0$. We compute

$$
\begin{aligned}
C_{s_0,\mathsf{t}}^{\tilde{y}} &= E_{s_0}[X_\mathsf{t} \mid Y = \tilde{y}] \cdot P_{s_0}(Y = \tilde{y}) \\
&= \sum_{\tilde{z} \in \Omega_{s_0}^n} X_\mathsf{t}(\tilde{z}) \cdot P(Z = \tilde{z} \mid Y = \tilde{y}) \cdot P_{s_0}(Y = \tilde{y}) \\
&= \sum_{\tilde{z} \in \Omega_{s_0}^n} X_\mathsf{t}(\tilde{z}) \cdot P(Z = \tilde{z} \wedge Y = \tilde{y}) \\
&= \sum_{\substack{\tilde{z} \in \Omega_{s_0}^n \\ Y(\tilde{z}) = \tilde{y}}} X_\mathsf{t}(\tilde{z}) \cdot P(Z = \tilde{z}) \\
&= \sum_{s_1 \in S} \sum_{\substack{\tilde{z}_1 \in \Omega_{s_1}^{n-1} \\ Y(s_0 a_1 \tilde{z}_1) = \tilde{y}}} X_\mathsf{t}(s_0 a_1 \tilde{z}_1) \cdot P(Z = s_0 a_1 \tilde{z}_1) + \\
&\qquad \sum_{s_1 \in S} \sum_{\substack{\tilde{z}_1 \in \Omega_{s_1}^n \\ Y(s_0 \varepsilon \tilde{z}_1) = \tilde{y}}} X_\mathsf{t}(s_0 \varepsilon \tilde{z}_1) \cdot P(Z = s_0 \varepsilon \tilde{z}_1) \\
&= \sum_{s_1 \in S} \sum_{\substack{\tilde{z}_1 \in \Omega_{s_1}^{n-1} \\ Y(\tilde{z}_1) = \tilde{y}_1}} (X_\mathsf{t}(\tilde{z}_1) + [s_0 = s \wedge a_1 = a \wedge s_1 = s']) \cdot \delta(s_0)(a_1, s_1) \cdot \\
&\qquad P(Z = \tilde{z}_1) + \sum_{s_1 \in S} \sum_{\substack{\tilde{z}_1 \in \Omega_{s_1}^n \\ Y(\tilde{z}_1) = \tilde{y}}} X_\mathsf{t}(\tilde{z}_1) \cdot \delta(s_0)(\varepsilon, s_1) \cdot P(Z = \tilde{z}_1) \\
&= \sum_{s_1 \in S} \delta(s_0)(a_1, s_1) \cdot \sum_{\substack{\tilde{z}_1 \in \Omega_{s_1}^{n-1} \\ Y(\tilde{z}_1) = \tilde{y}_1}} X_\mathsf{t}(\tilde{z}_1) \cdot P(Z = \tilde{z}_1) + \\
&\qquad \sum_{s_1 \in S} \delta(s_0)(\varepsilon, s_1) \cdot \sum_{\substack{\tilde{z}_1 \in \Omega_{s_1}^n \\ Y(\tilde{z}_1) = \tilde{y}}} X_\mathsf{t}(\tilde{z}_1) \cdot P(Z = \tilde{z}_1) + \\
&\qquad \sum_{s_1 \in S} [s_0 = s \wedge a_1 = a \wedge s_1 = s'] \cdot \delta(s_0)(a_1, s_1) \cdot \sum_{\substack{\tilde{z}_1 \in \Omega_{s_1}^{n-1} \\ Y(\tilde{z}_1) = \tilde{y}_1}} P(Z = \tilde{z}_1) \\
&= \sum_{s_1 \in S} \delta(s_0)(a_1, s_1) \cdot C_{s_1,\mathsf{t}}^{\tilde{y}_1} + \sum_{s_1 \in S} \delta(s_0)(\varepsilon, s_1) \cdot C_{s_1,\mathsf{t}}^{\tilde{y}} + \\
&\qquad [s_0 = s \wedge a = a_1] \cdot \delta(s)(a, s') \cdot P_{s'}(Y = \tilde{y}_1)
\end{aligned}
$$

$\square$

Example 5.2. *Given the HMM in Fig. 1 where the states and transitions are known, but the probabilities have to be adjusted by observing the system. Assume that the observation sequence is $\tilde{y} = \alpha$ (one single observation for simplicity) and the transition labels are $\mathsf{t}_1 = (s_0, \varepsilon, s_0)$, $\mathsf{t}_2 = (s_0, \alpha, s_1)$ and $\mathsf{t}_2 = (s_0, \beta, s_2)$. Then, using our notation, we obtain:*

$$C_{t_1,\widetilde{y}}^{s_0} = \underbrace{\delta(s_0)(\alpha,s_1)}_{1/4} \cdot C_{t_1,\varepsilon}^{s_2} + \underbrace{\delta(s_0)(\varepsilon,s_0)}_{0} \cdot C_{t_1,\widetilde{y}}^{s_0} + 1 \cdot \underbrace{\delta(s_0)(\varepsilon,s_0)}_{1/2} \cdot \underbrace{P_{s_0}(Y=\widetilde{y})}_{1/4+1/2 \cdot P_{s_0}(Y=\widetilde{y})}$$

$$= 1/2 \cdot C_{t_1,\widetilde{y}}^{s_0} + 1/4$$

This implies that $C_{t_1,\widetilde{y}}^{s_0} = 1/2 = E_{s_0}[X_{t_1} \mid Y=\widetilde{y}] \cdot \underbrace{P_{s_0}(Y=\widetilde{y})}_{1/2}$, *which gives us*

$E_{s_0}[X_{t_1} \mid Y=\widetilde{y}] = 1$.
Furthermore:

$$C_{t_2,\widetilde{y}}^{s_0} = \underbrace{\delta(s_0)(\alpha,s_1)}_{1/4} \cdot C_{t_1,\varepsilon}^{s_2} + \underbrace{\delta(s_0)(\varepsilon,s_0)}_{0} \cdot C_{t_1,\widetilde{y}}^{s_0} + 1 \cdot \underbrace{\delta(s_0)(\alpha,s_1)}_{1/4} \cdot \underbrace{P_{s_1}(Y=\varepsilon)}_{1},$$

which implies that $C_{t_2,\widetilde{y}}^{s_0} = 1/2 = E_{s_0}[X_{t_2} \mid Y=\widetilde{y}] \cdot \underbrace{P_{s_0}(Y=\widetilde{y})}_{1/2}$ *and hence*

$E_{s_0}[X_{t_2} \mid Y=\widetilde{y}] = 1$.
Similarly we derive $E_{s_0}[X_{t_3} \mid Y=\widetilde{y}] = 0$.
After computing the conditional expectation values for t_1, t_2 *and* t_3 *on the basis of observing* $\widetilde{y} = \alpha$, *the adjusted probability parameters now are:*

$$\delta(s_0)(\varepsilon,s_0) = \frac{1}{1+1} = \frac{1}{2} \qquad \delta(s_0)(\alpha,s_1) = \frac{1}{1+1} = \frac{1}{2} \qquad \delta(s_0)(\beta,s_2) = \frac{0}{1+1} = 0$$

In a more practical example, there will be multiple observations before adjusting the parameters. In that case, the individual conditional expectation values for a transition t_i *will be summed up:* $\sum_j E_{s_0}[X_{t_i} \mid Y=\widetilde{y}_j]$ *and normalized as usual. Because* s_1 *and* s_2 *have only one outgoing transition respectively, the probability attached will always be 1, no matter the observation.*

Since the equations are power contractive (cf. Sect. 6), they have a unique fixpoint, which can be approximated by (Kleene) iteration or computed via a solver (for more details see Sect. 7). For this we have to be able to determine $P_{s_0}(Y=\widetilde{y})$ for $\widetilde{y} = a_1\widetilde{y}_1$, which can be done with a similar fix-point equation (adapt the proof of Proposition 5.1 to the case where X_t is the constant 1-function): $P_{s_0}(Y=\varepsilon) = 1$ and otherwise:

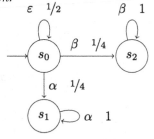

Fig. 1. Example HMM

$$P_{s_0}(Y=\widetilde{y}) = \sum_{s_1 \in S} \delta(s_0)(a_1,s_1) \cdot P_{s_1}(Y=\widetilde{y}_1) + \sum_{s_1 \in S} \delta(s_0)(\varepsilon,s_1) \cdot P_{s_1}(Y=\widetilde{y}).$$

5.2 Using the EM Algorithm

We will now introduce the so-called Expectation Maximization (EM) Algorithm [9], which is commonly used to derive the Baum-Welch algorithm [7,21] for parameter estimation. It explains how to suitably adjust (probabilistic) parameters of a system in such a way that the likelihood of observing the given output of the system increases. We assume that the higher the probability for observed sequences, the closer the parameters are to their actual values. This procedure is divided into two phases: the Expectation and Maximization phase.

Fix an HMM with known (graph) structure and unknown parameters (transition probabilities). The unknown parameters, denoted by θ, can be learned by observing the system. We will use θ in conditional probabilities or expectations to clarify the parameter dependency. E.g., $\delta(t \mid \theta)$ with $t = (s, a, s')$ stands for $\delta(s)(a, s')$ under the parameter setting θ.

The algorithm works iteratively in two phases. The parameter θ^t always denotes our current best guess of the probabilistic parameters, while θ denotes the new parameters that we wish to learn and improve iteratively given an observation sequence $\widetilde{y}$. In the first phase we calculate $Q(\theta \mid \theta^t)$ denoting the expected value of the log likelihood function for θ with respect to the current conditional probability of Z given an observation and the current estimates of the parameter θ^t. More concretely:

$$Q(\theta \mid \theta^t) = E_{Z|Y,\theta^t}[\log P(Y, Z \mid \theta)],$$

which denotes the expectation of the random variable $\widetilde{z} \mapsto \log P(Y = \widetilde{y}, Z = \widetilde{z} \mid \theta)$ in an updated probability space where the probability function is $P'(\widetilde{z}) = P(Z = \widetilde{z} \mid Y = \widetilde{y}, \theta^t)$. Here it is understood that $\log 0 = -\infty$ and $0 \cdot (-\infty) = 0$ (we enrich the real numbers with $-\infty$).

After the first phase follows the Maximization phase, where θ^{t+1} is determined as $\arg\max_\theta Q(\theta \mid \theta^t)$ and the algorithm subsequently starts again with phase one. This happens iteratively until $\theta^{t+1} = \theta^t$ or the improvements are below some threshold. In general we will converge to a local optimum, finding the global optimum is typically infeasible. The guarantee of the EM algorithm is that $P(Y = \widetilde{y} \mid \theta) > P(Y = \widetilde{y} \mid \theta^t)$ whenever $Q(\theta \mid \theta^t) > Q(\theta^t \mid \theta^t)$.

Theorem 5.3. *In our setting it holds that*

$$Q(\theta \mid \theta^t) = \sum_{s \in S} \sum_{t=(s,a,s') \in T_\delta} \log \delta(t \mid \theta) \cdot E_{s_0}[X_t \mid Y = \widetilde{y}, \theta^t].$$

The value $Q(\theta \mid \theta^t)$ is maximal when the parameters θ are as follows: for every transition t we set $\delta(t \mid \theta)$ proportional to $E_{s_0}[X_t \mid Y = \widetilde{y}, \theta^t]$. This means that the resulting values are normalized and therefore form a valid probability space.

Proof. In this proof we write $t_i(\widetilde{z})$ for the i-th transition of $\widetilde{z}$, i.e., if $\widetilde{z} = s_0 a_1 s_1 a_2 \ldots a_m s_m$, then $t_i(\widetilde{z}) = (s_{i-1}, a_i, s_i)$. Note that $1 \leq i \leq (|\widetilde{z}|-1)/2$. Hence $P(Z = \widetilde{z} \mid \theta) = \prod_{i=1}^{(|\widetilde{z}|-1)/2} \delta(t_i(\widetilde{z}) \mid \theta)$.

Furthermore:

$$Q(\theta \mid \theta^t) = E_{Z\mid Y,\theta^t}[\log P(Y, Z \mid \theta)]$$

$$= \sum_{\substack{\tilde{z}\in\Omega_{s_0}^n}} \log P(Y = \tilde{y}, Z = \tilde{z} \mid \theta) \cdot P(Z = \tilde{z} \mid Y = \tilde{y}, \theta^t)$$

$$= \sum_{\substack{\tilde{z}\in\Omega_{s_0}^n \\ Y(\tilde{z})=\tilde{y}}} \log P(Z = \tilde{z} \mid \theta) \cdot P(Z = \tilde{z} \mid Y = \tilde{y}, \theta^t)$$

$$= \sum_{\substack{\tilde{z}\in\Omega_{s_0}^n \\ Y(\tilde{z})=\tilde{y}}} \log \prod_{i=1}^{(|\tilde{z}|-1)/2} \delta(\mathsf{t}_i(\tilde{z}) \mid \theta) \cdot P(Z = \tilde{z} \mid Y = \tilde{y}, \theta^t)$$

$$= \sum_{\substack{\tilde{z}\in\Omega_{s_0}^n \\ Y(\tilde{z})=\tilde{y}}} \sum_{i=1}^{(|\tilde{z}|-1)/2} \log \delta(\mathsf{t}_i(\tilde{z}) \mid \theta) \cdot P(Z = \tilde{z} \mid Y = \tilde{y}, \theta^t)$$

$$= \sum_{\mathsf{t}\in T_\delta} \sum_{\substack{\tilde{z}\in\Omega_{s_0}^n \\ Y(\tilde{z})=\tilde{y}}} X_{\mathsf{t}}(\tilde{z}) \cdot \log \delta(\mathsf{t} \mid \theta) \cdot P(Z = \tilde{z} \mid Y = \tilde{y}, \theta^t)$$

$$= \sum_{\mathsf{t}\in T_\delta} \log \delta(\mathsf{t} \mid \theta) \cdot \underbrace{\sum_{\substack{\tilde{z}\in\Omega_{s_0}^n \\ Y(\tilde{z})=\tilde{y}}} X_{\mathsf{t}}(\tilde{z}) \cdot P(Z = \tilde{z} \mid Y = \tilde{y}, \theta^t)}_{E_{s_0}[X_{\mathsf{t}}\mid Y=\tilde{y},\theta^t]}$$

$$= \sum_{s\in S} \sum_{\mathsf{t}\in T_\delta^s} \log \delta(\mathsf{t} \mid \theta) \cdot E_{s_0}[X_{\mathsf{t}} \mid Y = \tilde{y}, \theta^t]$$

The third-last equality is given by the following computation, where $A \subseteq B^*$ and a_i denotes the i-th symbol of $a \in B^*$. In this case nested sums can be rewritten as follows, where $\#_b(a)$ stands for the number of occurrences of b in a:

$$\sum_{a\in A}\sum_{i=1}^{|a|} T_{a_i}\cdot S_a = \sum_{a\in A} S_a\cdot\sum_{i=1}^{|a|} T_{a_i} = \sum_{a\in A} S_a\cdot\sum_{b\in B}\overbrace{\sum_{\substack{1\le i\le|a| \\ a_i=b}} T_{a_i}}^{T_b} = \sum_{b\in B}\sum_{a\in A}\underbrace{\#_b(a)\cdot T_b\cdot S_a}_{\#_b(a)\cdot T_b}$$

The last value in the computation above can be maximized for each $s \in S$ independently and we obtain:

$$\sum_{\mathsf{t}\in T_\delta^s} \underbrace{\log \delta(\mathsf{t} \mid \theta)}_{p_i} \cdot \underbrace{E_{s_0}[X_{\mathsf{t}} \mid Y = \tilde{y}, \theta^t]}_{a_i} = \sum_{i} (\log p_i) \cdot a_i$$

This value is maximal if $p_i = \frac{a_i}{\sum_i a_i}$, which concludes the proof. This is a consequence of Gibbs' inequality, which says that, given a probability function

$p\colon I \to [0,1]$ with I finite, then for every other probability function $q\colon I \to [0,1]$, we have that

$$\sum_{i \in I} p_i \log p_i \geq \sum_{i \in I} p_i \log q_i.$$

It is also related to the fact that Kullback-Leibler divergence is always non-negative. Since the result is easy to derive we prove it in Lemma 5.4.   □

Lemma 5.4. *Let $a_i \geq 0$, $i \in \{1, \ldots, m\}$, be fixed. Let $p_i \in [0,1]$ be unknown values such that $\sum_{i \in 1}^{m} p_i = 1$. Then*

$$\sum_{i=1}^{m} a_i \cdot \log p_i$$

is maximal if $p_i = \frac{a_i}{\sum_{i=1}^{m} a_i}$.

Proof. We can assume that log denotes the natural logarithm, since logarithms differ only by a constant factor. Furthermore we can see that in order to achieve the maximal value, p_i must be strictly larger than 0 whenever $a_i > 0$ and $p_i = 0$ otherwise. (Remember the convention that $0 \cdot \log 0 = 0 \cdot (-\infty) = 0$.) Hence we can assume without loss of generality that $a_i > 0$ for all i.

Since $\sum_{i=1}^{m} p_i = 1$ we can replace p_m by $1 - \sum_{i=1}^{m-1} p_i$ and obtain

$$\sum_{i=1}^{m-1} a_i \cdot \ln p_i + a_m \cdot \ln \left(1 - \sum_{i=1}^{m-1} p_i\right)$$

Remembering that $\frac{d}{dx} \ln x = \frac{1}{x}$, we now compute the partial derivates with respect to p_j where $j \neq m$.

$$\frac{\partial}{\partial p_j} \left(\sum_{i=1}^{m-1} a_i \cdot \ln p_i + a_m \cdot \ln \left(1 - \sum_{i=1}^{m-1} p_i\right) \right) = \frac{a_j}{p_j} + a_m \cdot \frac{1}{1 - \sum_{i=1}^{m-1} p_i} \cdot (-1)$$

$$= \frac{a_j}{p_j} - \frac{a_m}{p_m} = \frac{a_j \cdot p_m - p_j \cdot a_m}{p_j \cdot p_m}$$

This equals 0 if $a_j \cdot p_m - p_j \cdot a_m = 0$. We sum up over all indices j and get

$$0 = \sum_{j=1}^{m} (a_j \cdot p_m - p_j \cdot a_m) = p_m \cdot \sum_{j=1}^{m} a_j - a_m \cdot \sum_{j=1}^{m} p_j = p_m \cdot \sum_{j=1}^{m} a_j - a_m$$

This implies

$$p_m = \frac{a_m}{\sum_j a_j}$$

and by substitution, we obtain an analogous formula for all p_j. We can check that all conditions $a_j \cdot p_m - p_j \cdot a_m = 0$ are satisfied.

The maximum must be reached in the point where all derivatives are zero, from which the statement follows.   □

Note that there might be states where all outgoing transitions have conditional expectation zero, i.e., such a state cannot be reached via the observation sequence. In this case we keep the previous parameters. If we adhere to this, we can always guarantee that the requirement of Lemma 3.1 is maintained, since if an outgoing transition of a state has conditional expectation greater than zero, there must be a path of non-zero probability to an observation.

6   Contractivity

The claims on contractivity made in the paper deserve further elaboration. We first define the notion of a contractive function.

Definition 6.1 (Contractive Function). *Let $\mathbb{R}^W$ be the set of all functions from a set W to $\mathbb{R}$. We use the supremum (or maximum) distance and define $d_{\sup}(g_1, g_2) = \|g_1 - g_2\|_\infty := \sup_{w \in W} |g_1(w) - g_2(w)|$ for $g_1, g_2 \colon W \to \mathbb{R}$.*

A function $F \colon \mathbb{R}^W \to \mathbb{R}^W$ is contractive whenever for all $g_1, g_2 \in \mathbb{R}^W$ it holds that $d_{\sup}(F(g_1), F(g_2)) \leq q \cdot d_{\sup}(g_1, g_2)$ for some $0 \leq q < 1$.

We say that F is is power contraction if there is an index k such that F^k is contractive.

It is well-known from the Banach fixpoint theorem that contractive functions over complete metric spaces have unique fixpoints and $\mathbb{R}^W$ with the sup-metric is complete. Furthermore any sequence $(g_i)_{i \in \mathbb{N}}$ with $g_{i+1} = F(g_i)$ converges to this fixpoint. Now, every fixpoint of F is a fixpoint of F^k and vice versa. The latter direction holds, since a fixpoint x of F^k satisfies $F(x) = F(F^k(x)) = F^k(F(x))$, so $F(x)$ is also a fixpoint of F^k and by uniqueness $F(x) = x$. Hence a power contraction F also has a unique fixpoint and enjoys the same convergence property (although with a potentially slower convergence rate).

We now argue why the fixpoint functions that we consider are power contractive.

The fixpoint equation systems set up in Sect. 3 (proof of Proposition 3.1) and Sect. 5.1 are over a set W of variables of the form $w_s^{\tilde{y}}$, where $s \in S$ and $\tilde{y} \in \Sigma^*$ is the suffix of a given word $\bar{y} \in \Sigma^*$ with $n = |\bar{y}|$. (Or alternatively the variables are of the form S_s^n, see the proof of Proposition 3.1, leading to an analogous argument.) We define $o(w_s^{\tilde{y}}) = \tilde{y}$. Note that W is finite, since the state space S is finite.

The corresponding fixpoint function is a monotone function $F \colon \mathbb{R}^W \to \mathbb{R}^W$ where, for $g \colon W \to \mathbb{R}$:

$$F(g)(w) = \sum_{w' \in W} p_{w,w'} \cdot g(w') + D_w, \tag{1}$$

where $p_{w,w'} \in [0,1]$ such that for each $w \in W$ we have $\sum_{w' \in W} p_{w,w'} \leq 1$ and D_w is a non-negative constant. Furthermore $p_{w,w'} > 0$ implies $|o(w)| \geq |o(w')|$. In addition we can assume that $o(w) = \varepsilon$ implies $p_{w,w'} = 0$ (and hence $F(g)(w) = D_w$ is a constant).

Such functions are clearly non-expansive (which means that the contractivity requirement holds for $q = 1$) but not necessarily contractive.

However, we know that the probabilities $p_{w,w'}$ are transition probabilities and the length of the observed sequence decreases if one takes a transition that is labelled with an observable symbol. Due to the requirement of Proposition 3.1 we know that each state has a path of non-zero probability that contains such an observation. For each state $s \in S$ we consider the minimum length of such a path and we take the maximum over all these minimums and obtain k. Then we know that the fixpoint equation associated with F^k is of the same form as for F above (see (1)) and additionally for each $w \in W$

- there exists $\overline{w} \in W$ with $p_{w,\overline{w}} > 0$ and $|o(w)| > |o(\overline{w})|$ (if we take a transition with the next label to observe, reducing the length of the observation sequence) *or*
- $\sum_{w' \in W} p_{w,w'} < 1$ (if a state has an outgoing transition with a label that does not match the next observation).

This means that either the second condition holds after at most $m = n \cdot k$ iterations or we reach the last observation of $\bar{y}$ on a path of non-zero probability of length at most $n \cdot k$. The latter means that the term for $F^{n \cdot k}(g)(w)$ contains – multiplied with a non-zero probability – a variable $\overline{w}$ with $o(\overline{w}) = \varepsilon$, for which $F(g)(\overline{w})$ is constant. That is, after $m + 1$ iterations the corresponding fixpoint Eq. (1) satisfies $q_w := \sum_{w' \in W} p_{w,w'} < 1$ for each $w \in W$. Then we have, given $g_1, g_2 \colon W \to \mathbb{R}$:

$$
\begin{aligned}
&d_{\mathrm{sup}}(F^{m+1}(g_1), F^{m+1}(g_2)) \\
&= \max_{w \in W} \left| \left(\sum_{w' \in W} p_{w,w'} \cdot g_1(w') + D_w \right) - \left(\sum_{w' \in W} p_{w,w'} \cdot g_2(w') + D_w \right) \right| \\
&\leq \max_{w \in W} \sum_{w' \in W} p_{w,w'} \cdot |g_1(w') - g_2(w')| \\
&\leq \max_{w \in W} \underbrace{\left(\sum_{w' \in W} p_{w,w'} \right)}_{q_w} \cdot \max_{w' \in W} |g_1(w') - g_2(w')| \\
&\leq \underbrace{(\max_{w \in W} q_w)}_{q} \cdot \max_{w' \in W} |g_1(w') - g_2(w')| = q \cdot d_{\mathrm{sup}}(g_1, g_2)
\end{aligned}
$$

The first inequality uses the fact that $|\sum_{i \in I} a_i| \leq \sum_{i \in I} |a_i|$, while the second inequality holds since $\sum_{i \in I} p_i \cdot a_i \leq (\sum_{i \in I} p_i) \cdot \max_{i \in I} a_i$.

Since $q = \max_{w \in W} q_w < 1$ we have contractivity after $m + 1$ iterations.

In fact, the arguments are similar to the setting of absorbing Markov chains [13,14], where the absorption property and the fact that non-absorbing states are transient is used to guarantee unique solutions.

7   Runtime Results

In order to evaluate the performance of the proposed (fixpoint-based) algorithms and check whether the approach is feasible in practice, we implemented both algorithms for finding the best explanation and parameter learning. We also implemented the two standard algorithms solving both tasks: the Viterbi and the Baum-Welch algorithm. For the implementation we used the *ndarray-linalg* crate in Rust and its module *solve* for solving systems of linear equations. As discussed in Sect. 6, the solution to any linear equation systems obtained in the parameter learning algorithm is always unique, which enables us to use a linear equation system solver.

When comparing the results, i.e., computed probabilities, of our approaches with the established algorithms on standard HMMs we obtained equal results, which confirms the formal proofs given in the paper. Hence we can dismiss any examination of efficacy and only examine and compare the runtimes.

Runtime results were obtained by considering two HMMs with four states each: one HMM allowing for ε-transitions (depicted on the right-hand side) and one without ε-transitions, that is, a standard HMM (very similar to the one on the right). Based on those HMMs, random observation sequences with varying lengths were generated in order to be used in either the explanation or parameter learning algorithms.

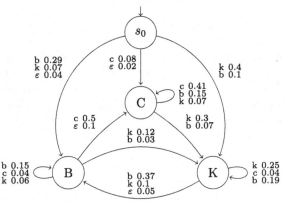

For both algorithms we expect the runtime of our approach to be worse when compared directly to the established algorithms. The new algorithms are more general, being able to handle ε-transitions as well.

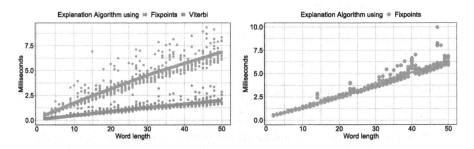

Fig. 2. Averaged runtime results for the explanation algorithm. The underlying HMM on the left side does not allow for ε emission, the one on the right does.

The plot on the left of Fig. 2 compares the Viterbi algorithm to our algorithm from Sect. 4 and reveals a linear runtime for both approaches. The right-hand side diagram in Fig. 2 shows that our approach works efficiently even with HMMs including ε-emissions. This is due to the efficient implementation in which we introduced a matrix storing the most probable ε-path between each two states, a computation that has to be done only once for every HMM. The new variant of the explanation algorithm has some overhead compared to the original Viterbi algorithm, since it has to query for the presence of ε-transitions, but still has linear runtime.

The performance results comparing both algorithms for parameter learning are depicted on the left of Fig. 3. For both approaches we start with an emission sequence of varying length up to 20 and an HMM with uniformly distributed parameters. Then we perform five iterations of the parameter learning algorithm, subsequently adjusting the parameters of the HMM. We opted for repeating the adjustment of one HMM a fixed number of times instead of letting the parameters converge towards a local optimum, in order to retain better comparability of the runtimes. This restriction is set solely for the purpose of sensibly comparing runtimes with different word lengths as both algorithms would converge with the same amount of iterations.

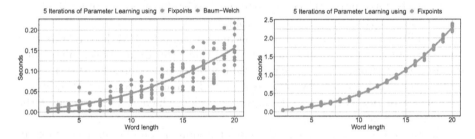

Fig. 3. Averaged runtime results performing five iterations of a Parameter Learning Algorithm. The underlying HMM on the left side does not allow for ε emission, the one on the right does.

On the right-hand side of Fig. 3 we investigated whether our approach is feasible for HMMs with empty emissions. Although the runtime is clearly not linear in the length of the observation sequence, we still consider our approach practical. Note that it has clearly more functionality as the original Baum-Welch algorithm since it can handle more general HMMs. Note that the runtime is dependent on the runtime of the solver that was used in the calculations and that is not controlled by us.

8 Conclusion

In this paper, we considered HMMs that admit unobservable ε-transitions. We presented algorithms for determining the most probable explanation (i.e. a sequence of hidden states) given an observation and a method for parameter learning. For this, we generalized the Viterbi and the Baum-Welch algorithm to consider ε-transitions (including ε-loops) and provided the respective proofs of their soundness. By allowing state changes of which the observer is unaware we can model false negatives, i.e. actions that have taken place but have not been observed by a sensor. This extends the applicability of HMMs as a modeling technique to the domain of sensor-based systems, which always have to consider the probability of sensor errors. For example, we now have the methods to compare observations made by sensors with the computed most likely explanation. When these two drift further apart over time, we can conclude that the real-world system is subject to parameter drift or degrading sensor quality. Furthermore, we plan to use the HMMs to clean data sets by replacing observations with their most probable explanation. Parameter learning will be needed to learn and adapt the model parameters based on recorded observations. Potential applications are described in [22] in more detail.

One direction for future work is to find suitable methods to measure the distance between a learned HMM and the original model. Distance measures for HMMs have for instance been studied in [17]. One sensible option could be to consider HMMs as probabilistic automata [10] and check – given two probabilistic automata – whether the difference for weights for all words is below some threshold. Unfortunately the corresponding threshold problem is undecidable for such automata [20], requiring a workaround.

In addition to the adaptation of classical algorithms for HMMs to HMMs with unobservable transitions, such as the Viterbi and the Baum-Welch algorithm, we also plan to work on the generalization of other procedures for HMMs, such as the sequential probability ratio test (SPRT) that – given two HMMs and a sequence of observations – attempts to decide which model generated the sequence [8,18,23].

HMMs can be seen as stochastic regular grammars and an analogous extension of context-free grammars is known as probabilistic or stochastic context-free grammar [1,11]. The question is now whether the parameter learning techniques can be generalized to this recursive setting.

Another avenue of future research is to integrate methods for black-box testing (of liveness properties) as studied by Esparza et al. in [12] with procedures designed for HMMs.

Acknowledgements. We would like to thank Michael Luttenberger and the anonymous reviewers of the paper for their valuable remarks and suggestions.

References

1. Abney, S.P., McAllester, D.A., Pereira, F.: Relating probabilistic grammars and automata. In: Proceedings of ACL 1999 (Annual Meeting of the Association for Computational Linguistics), pp. 542–549. ACL (1999)
2. Angluin, D.: Learning regular sets from queries and counter-examples. Inf. Control **75**(2), 87–106 (1987)

3. Bahl, L.R., Jelinek, F., Mercer, R.L.: A maximum likelihood approach to continuous speech recognition. IEEE Trans. Pattern Anal. Mach. Intell. **5**(2), 179–190 (1983)
4. Baier, C., Katoen, J.-P.: Principles of Model Checking. MIT Press (2008)
5. Baum, L.E., Petrie, T., Soules, G., Weiss, N.: A maximization technique occurring in the statistical analysis of probabilistic functions of Markov chains. Ann. Math. Stat. **41**(1), 164–171 (1970)
6. Bellman, R.: A markovian decision process. J. Math. Mech. **6**(5), 679–684 (1957)
7. Bilmes, J.: A gentle tutorial of the EM algorithm and its application to parameter estimation for Gaussian mixture and Hidden Markov Models. Technical Report TR-97-021, International Computer Science Institute (1997)
8. Darwin, O., Kiefer, S.: On the sequential probability ratio test in hidden Markov models. In: Proceedings of CONCUR 2022. LIPIcs, vol. 243, pp. 9:1–9:16. Schloss Dagstuhl - Leibniz-Zentrum für Informatik (2022)
9. Dempster, A.P., Laird, N.M., Rubin, D.B.: Maximum likelihood from incomplete data via the EM algorithm. J. Roy. Stat. Soc. **39**(1), 1–38 (1977)
10. Dupont, P., Denis, F., Esposito, Y.: Links between probabilistic automata and Hidden Markov Models: probability distributions, learning models and induction algorithms. Pattern Recognit. **38**(9), 1349–1371 (2005)
11. Esparza, J., Gaiser, A., Kiefer, S.: A strongly polynomial algorithm for criticality of branching processes and consistency of stochastic context-free grammars. Inf. Process. Lett. **113**(10–11), 381–385 (2013)
12. Esparza, J., Grande, V.P.: Black-box testing liveness properties of partially observable stochastic systems. In: Proceedings of ICALP 2023. LIPIcs, vol. 261, pp. 126:1–126:17. Schloss Dagstuhl - Leibniz-Zentrum für Informatik (2023)
13. Filar, J., Vrieze, K.: Competitive Markov Decision Processes. Springer, New York (1996). https://doi.org/10.1007/978-1-4612-4054-9
14. Grinstead, C., Laurie Snell, J.: Introduction to Probability. American Mathematical Society (1997)
15. Jelinek, F.: Statistical Methods for Speech Recognition. MIT Press (1998)
16. David Forney, Jr., G.: The Viterbi algorithm. Proc. IEEE **61**(3), 268–278 (1973)
17. Juang, B.-H., Rabiner, L.R.: A probabilistic distance measure for hidden Markov models. AT&T Tech. J. **64**(2), 391–408 (1985)
18. Kiefer, S., Sistla, A.P.: Distinguishing hidden Markov chains. In: Proceedings of LICS 2016, pp. 66–75. ACM (2016)
19. Orr, J., Tadepalli, P., Doppa, J., Fern, X., Dietterich, T.: Learning scripts as hidden Markov models. Proc. AAAI Conf. Artif. Intell. **28**(1) (2018)
20. Paz, A.: Introduction to Probabilistic Automata. Academic Press, New York (1971)
21. Rabiner, L.R.: A tutorial on hidden Markov models and selected applications in speech recognition. Proc. IEEE **77**(2), 257–286 (1989)
22. Schaffeld, M., Bernemann, R., Weis, T., König, B., Matkovic, V.: Lifecycle-based view on cyber-physical system models using extended hidden Markov models (work-in-progress paper). In: Proceedings of MEMOCODE 2022. IEEE (2022)
23. Akshay, E.F.S., Bazille, H., Genest, B.: Classification among hidden Markov models. In: Proceedings of FSTTCS 1919. LIPIcs, vol. 150, pp. 29:1–29:14. Schloss Dagstuhl - Leibniz-Zentrum für Informatik (2019)
24. Viterbi, A.: Error bounds for convolutional codes and an asymptotically optimum decoding algorithm. IEEE Trans. Inf. Theory **13**(2), 260–269 (1967)
25. Westhead, D.R., Vijayabaskar, M.S. (eds.): Hidden Markov Models: Methods and Protocols. Springer, New York (2017)

Coverability in Well-Formed Free-Choice Petri Nets

Eike Best[1][(✉)] and Raymond Devillers[2]

[1] Department of Computing Science, Carl von Ossietzky Universität Oldenburg, D-26111 Oldenburg, Germany
eike.best@posteo.de
[2] Département d'Informatique, Université Libre de Bruxelles, B-1050 Brussels, Belgium
raymond.devillers@ulb.be

Abstract. This paper recalls Hack's two coverability theorems for free-choice Petri nets as well as the history of some of their proofs. It also describes two relatively short, symmetric, and partly novel, proofs.

Keywords: Petri nets · free-choice nets · liveness · boundedness · liveness criterion · coverability theorems

1 Motivation

About 50 years ago, Michel Hack and Frederic Commoner[1] discovered that the class of *Free-Choice Petri Nets* has a very elegant structural theory. In a seminal piece of work [Hac74], Hack put forward the following three theorems:

- The *liveness theorem* (attributed to Commoner): An initially marked free-choice Petri net is live if, and only if, its initial marking satisfies certain structurally checkable conditions.
- Two *covering theorems*: A well-formed free-choice Petri net[2] is covered both by strongly connected S-components and by strongly connected T-components. Such components are structurally defined subnets that are, in a certain sense, duals of each other.

The beginning of Javier Esparza's career was marked by his PhD Thesis on Free-Choice Petri Nets (supervised by Manuel Silva, submitted to the University of Zaragoza, and accepted there in 1990 with the best possible mark). This thesis gave rise to no less than four publications [ES89a, ES89b, ES90, Esp90], sparking a spate of research and eventually culminating in a monograph on free-choice nets, co-authored by Jörg Desel and Javier Esparza [DE95]. Until now, this nicely written book is the standard reference for free-choice Petri net theory.

Hack's two covering theorems are symmetric duals of each other, although they can definitely not be derived from each other. Hack's two proofs also embody a

---

[1] Son of the environmentalist, Barry Commoner, who devised the *Four Laws of Ecology*.
[2] Where a net is well-formed if it has a live and bounded marking.

© The Author(s), under exclusive license to Springer Nature Switzerland AG 2024
S. Kiefer et al. (Eds.): *Taming the Infinities of Concurrency*, LNCS 14660, pp. 122–132, 2024.
https://doi.org/10.1007/978-3-031-56222-8_6

certain symmetry. The book [DE95] contains two further proofs which may be interpreted as "tightening" (and shortening) some of the arguments of [Hac74]. However, they are no longer symmetric. Indeed, as the authors write on page 101:

> The proof of (... the T-coverability Theorem ...) *is very different from that of the S-coverability Theorem.*

The present authors started to wonder whether this is a necessary state of affairs, or whether it is possible to devise a pair of rigorous proofs that are both concise and still reflect the symmetry embodied in the pair of theorems. This paper is the result of this research.

2   Some Context

This section describes some standard definitions and a running example.

A (place/transition) *Petri net* is a triple $N = (S, T, F)$, where S is a finite set of *places*, T is a finite set of *transitions* disjoint from S, and $F \colon (S \times T) \cup (T \times S) \to \mathbb{N}$ is a weight function on the *arcs* from S to T and from T to S. It is *plain* if $\mathbb{N}$ is replaced by its subset $\{0, 1\}$. For any node $x \in S \cup T$, its *preset* is ${}^\bullet x = \{y \in T \cup S | F(y, x) > 0\}$ and its *postset* is $x^\bullet = \{y \in T \cup S | F(x, y) > 0\}$; this may be extended to sets of nodes: if $X \subseteq S \cup T$, ${}^\bullet X = \bigcup_{x \in X} {}^\bullet x$ and $X^\bullet = \bigcup_{x \in X} x^\bullet$. Moreover, for any transition $t \in T$, F induces two integer functions on S defined, for any $s \in S$, by $F(t, .)(s) = F(t, s)$ and $F(., t)(s) = F(s, t)$.

A *marking* M is a function $M \colon S \to \mathbb{N}$. A *marked net* is a tuple (N, M) where N is a net and M is a marking of N. If $X \subseteq S$, one defines $M(X) = \sum_{x \in X} M(x)$, and X is *marked* if $M(X) > 0$. A transition t is *enabled* at a marking M, denoted by $M \xrightarrow{t}$, if $M \geq F(., t)$. An enabled transition may be *fired at* M and then *leads to* a marking $M' = M - F(., t) + F(t, .)$, denoted $M \xrightarrow{t} M'$. This may be extended to *firing sequences* $\sigma \in T^*$, by defining $M \xrightarrow{\varepsilon} M$ and $M \xrightarrow{t\sigma} M''$ if $M \xrightarrow{t} M'$ and $M' \xrightarrow{\sigma} M''$. The *reachability set* $[M\rangle$ of a marking M is defined as $[M\rangle = \{M' \mid \exists \sigma \in T^* : M \xrightarrow{\sigma} M'\}$. A transition t is *live* at a marking M if $\forall M' \in [M\rangle \, \exists M'' \in [M'\rangle \colon M'' \xrightarrow{t}$, and *dead* at a marking M if $\forall M' \in [M\rangle \colon \neg(M' \xrightarrow{t})$. A marking M is *live* if every transition is live at M. A marking M is *bounded* if $[M\rangle$ is finite. A net is *well-formed* if it has a marking that is both live and bounded.

A plain net is a *T-net* if $\forall s \in S \colon |{}^\bullet s| \leq 1 \wedge |s^\bullet| \leq 1$, and an *S-net* if $\forall t \in T \colon |{}^\bullet t| \leq 1 \wedge |t^\bullet| \leq 1$. A net is *free-choice* if it is plain and $\forall t_1, t_2 \in T \colon {}^\bullet t_1 \cap {}^\bullet t_2 \neq \emptyset \Rightarrow {}^\bullet t_1 = {}^\bullet t_2$. A net is *choice-free* if $\forall s \in S \colon |s^\bullet| \leq 1$, and *join-free* if $\forall t \in T \colon |{}^\bullet t| \leq 1$. Clearly, plain choice-free and plain join-free Petri nets are also free-choice, and T-nets are choice-free while S-nets are join-free.

Figure 1 shows an example. Places and transitions are drawn as circles and squares, respectively. The weight function is represented by arcs, where "no arc" means weight zero and "no weight" means weight 1. A marking is represented by small tokens inside places (in this example, some tokens are drawn as hollow gray

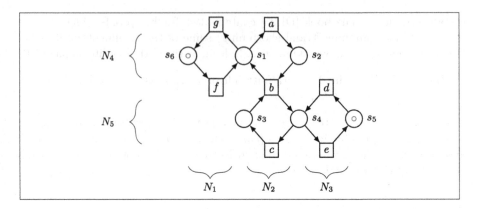

Fig. 1. A well-formed free-choice Petri net. A live and bounded marking is indicated by hollow gray circles. This net is covered by three T-components N_1, N_2, N_3 and two S-components N_4, N_5. There are two non-singleton transition clusters, $\{a, g\}(Color figure online)$ and $\{c, e\}$. The other transition clusters, $\{b\}$, $\{d\}$, and $\{f\}$, are singletons. There is one non-singleton place cluster, $\{s_2, s_3\}$. The other place clusters, $\{s_1\}$, $\{s_4\}$, $\{s_5\}$, and $\{s_6\}$, are singletons. Clusters are defined and explained later in the text.

circles). The T-components and S-components shown in the figure are special T-(sub)-nets and S-(sub)-nets, as defined next.

Let $S' \subseteq S$ and $T' \subseteq T$ in a net $N = (S, T, F)$. The *subnet* induced by S' and T' is the net $N(S', T') = (S', T', F|_{(S' \times T') \cup (T' \times S')})$. If N is provided with a marking M, the subnet will be provided with the restricted marking $M|_{S'}$. A *T-component* of N is a subnet $N(S_1, T_1)$ which is a T-net and where $S_1 = T_1^\bullet \cup {}^\bullet T_1$, and an *S-component* of N is a subnet $N(S_1, T_1)$ which is an S-net and where $T_1 = S_1^\bullet \cup {}^\bullet S_1$ (in both cases, presets and postsets are taken in N).

Since a Petri net – neglecting arcs with a null weight and abstracting from markings and arc weights > 1 – is a bipartite graph, all the usual graph-theoretical concepts are applicable, in particular those concerning (directed) paths, (simple, directed) cycles, and (strongly) connected components. It may be observed that any connected component of a net is a subnet of it. A net may consist of several separated components; for instance, there may be isolated places and/or isolated transitions. A strongly connected component is a subgraph which contains a directed path from any node to any other node. We shall be encountering nets that consist of several disjoint strongly connected components, where isolated elements are counted as strongly connected. The following is a general (and well-known) property linking liveness, boundedness, and strong connectedness:

Proposition 1. Strong connectedness
A connected well-formed Petri net $N = (S, T, F)$ is strongly connected.

Proof: (Sketch.) Suppose $(x, y) \in F$ and $(y, x) \notin F^*$. If x is a place and y is a transition, the net cannot have a live marking that is bounded. If x is a transition and y is a place, no live marking can be bounded. The claim follows with connectedness.   ∎

3   T-Coverability

A net is covered by T-components if every transition belongs to a subnet which is a T-component. Hack's T-coverability theorem is formalised as follows:

Theorem 2. T-COVERABILITY
A well-formed free-choice Petri net is covered by strongly connected T-components.

The proof will be given algorithmically, by reducing the existence of certain Petri net structures called transition clusters, which are of particular relevance in free-choice nets. Compare Fig. 1 for some examples.

A *transition cluster* is defined as a maximal set of transitions $\{t_1, \ldots, t_n\}$ whose presets agree, i.e., ${}^\bullet t_1 = \ldots = {}^\bullet t_n$. In a free-choice net, two transitions belong to the same transition cluster if their presets are non-disjoint. In a marking enabling one of these transitions, all others are enabled as well (and could be chosen to be fired instead of the first one). For easy reference, the transitions of a transition cluster will be called "rivals".

The following proposition is tailored towards the T-coverability algorithm:

Proposition 3. CHOICE-FREE NETS AND T-NETS
A well-formed, plain, choice-free Petri net is a T-net.

Proof: Let $N = (S, T, F)$ be a well-formed, plain, choice-free net. Its arcs are covered by directed cycles, by Proposition 1. Suppose there is a place $s \in S$ with two distinct input transitions $t_1, t_2 \in {}^\bullet s$. Pick any directed cycle through t_1 and s. In any live marking, t_2 can put ever more tokens on the places of this cycle, but none of these tokens can be taken away from the cycle by plainness and choice-freeness. Hence no live marking can be bounded, contradicting well-formedness. This contradiction shows that no such place exists, and the net is, in fact, a T-net.   ∎
Proof: (of Theorem 2.)
Let N be a well-formed free-choice net, with an initial live and bounded marking M_0. Let us pick and fix u to be any transition of N. We want to show that there is a T-component covering u. The property is trivial if u is isolated. From Proposition 1, we may also restrict our attention to the strongly connected component containing u.

If all transitions of N are singleton clusters (i.e., there is no proper rivalry), then we are already done since N is then also choice-free and a T-net, from Proposition 3, and because N is plain and well-formed.

Otherwise, let t be a transition with rivals such that there is no rivalry strictly between t and u (we allow $t = u$): from strong connectedness and the existence of rivalries, it is always possible to choose such a t.[3] We thus have a path

$$s \rightarrow t = u_0 \rightarrow s_1 \rightarrow u_1 \rightarrow s_2 \rightarrow u_2 \ \ldots \ s_n \rightarrow u_n = u$$

where for all $i \in \{1, \ldots, n-1\}$: $|s_i^\bullet| = 1$, $s^\bullet = \{t, t_1, \ldots, t_k\}$ with $k > 0$ (i.e., the $\{t_1, \ldots, t_k\}$ are the rivals of t, and there is at least one such rival).

The idea is to see what happens if we consider the net N' which is just like N, except that all transitions in $\{t_1, \ldots, t_k\}$ and all their surrounding arcs are deleted. Then N' is again free-choice and all firing sequences of (N', M_0) are also firing sequences of (N, M_0), so that the set of reachable markings of (N', M_0) is a subset of the set of reachable markings of (N, M_0) and M_0 is again a bounded marking of N'. However, some transitions may no longer be live.

We claim, first of all, that not all transitions are non-live in (N', M_0); in fact, t is amongst the live transitions of (N', M_0). To see this, consider any marking M reachable in (N', M_0). Then M is also reachable in (N, M_0), and since t is live in (N, M_0), there is some sequence τ such that $M \xrightarrow{\tau} M'$ and M' enables t in (N, M_0). If τ does not contain any of the $\{t_1, \ldots, t_k\}$, it is also firable from M in (N', M_0), enabling t there as well. But if some t_i is contained in τ, say $\tau = \tau_1 t_i \tau_2$, then τ_1 already enables t from M (by the free-choice property, since t is in the same cluster as t_i). In both cases, t can be enabled after M in (N', M_0); hence, t is live in (N', M_0).

But all the transitions in the selected path between t and u are also live from M_0. Indeed, if u_j is live while u_{j+1} is not, let us consider a marking reachable from M_0 where u_{j+1} is dead; then, by activating u_j, s_{j+1} may receive as many tokens as we want while they may not be absorbed (due to the choice of t), contradicting the boundedness assumption. Hence, in particular, u remains live.

Let T_d denote the set of transitions which are not live in (N', M_0) and let M_1 be a marking reached in (N', M_0) in which all transitions in T_d are dead (i.e., cannot be fired after any firing sequence). (Of course, M_1 can also be reached in (N, M_0).) Now take all transitions in T_d, and all of their surrounding arcs, out of N', keep the strongly connected component of N' containing u (suppressing T_d will in general disconnect the previously connected net under consideration) and call the new net N_1. By construction, (N_1, M_1) is a live and bounded (hence strongly connected) free-choice net with less rivalry. And u is in N_1 (as well as the whole chain from t to u).

Continuing the construction, we shall eventually construct a bounded and live (i.e., well-formed), strongly connected choice-free net containing u. From Proposition 3 it is also a T-net, and since it was built by dropping transitions and keeping connected components, it is a T-component of the original net, which completes the proof since u was chosen arbitrarily. ∎

Figure 2 illustrates this algorithm, using the running example. (1) $u = b$ is picked. It has no proper rivals. (2) We may find a transition with proper rivals (close to b) by backtracking from b. This could be either a or c; we choose a. (3) We delete transition g because it is a rival of a. Now f is non-live and should be

---

[3] We may, for instance, start from any transition with rivals, go forward to u, and keep the last visited transition with rivals.

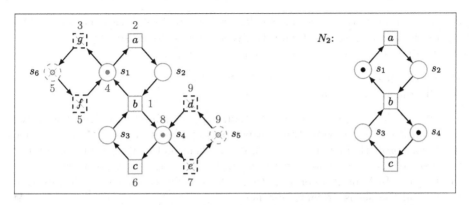

Fig. 2. Finding a T-component covering transition b. The various steps are exhibited in blue on the left-hand side. An initial, live and bounded, marking M_0 is shown (hollow gray tokens on s_5 and s_6). These tokens are moved during the construction of new live markings to places s_4 and s_1, respectively (gray tokens on these places). The end result is shown on the right-hand side. The live and bounded marking constructed during the proof is also shown (tokens on s_1 and s_4). (Color figure online)

deleted next. (4) However, before doing so, a new live marking has to be found in which f is dead. In this case, f is fired once and a token is moved from s_6 to s_1. (5) Transition f is now dead and can be deleted. Place s_6 no longer belongs to the strongly connected component containing b and is deleted (or neglected) as well. (6) The search for transitions with proper rivals continues, and we find c by backtracking from a transition without rivals (in this case, b). (7) Transition e is now eliminated since it is a proper rival of c. (8) Now d is non-live. A new marking has to be found in which d is dead (in this case, by moving a token from s_5 to s_4). (9) Transition d is deleted, and so is s_5. No further rivalry exists. By Proposition 3, the result is a T-net, and it is a T-component of the original net.

4 S-Coverability

A net is covered by S-components if every place belongs to a subnet which is an S-component. Hack's S-coverability theorem is formalised as follows:

Theorem 4. S-COVERABILITY
A well-formed free-choice Petri net is covered by strongly connected S-components.

The proof will be given algorithmically, as before, but instead of reducing rivalry, we shall now reduce place clusters, which are symmetric to transition clusters.

A *place cluster* is defined as a maximal set of places $\{s_1, \ldots, s_n\}$ with $s_1^\bullet = \ldots = s_n^\bullet$. In a free-choice net, two places belong to the same place cluster if their postsets are non-disjoint. Before one of the output transitions of a place cluster can be fired, all of the places in the cluster need to have at least one token. The places of a place cluster will figuratively be referred to as "siblings".

We shall also need a symmetric version of Proposition 3.

Proposition 5. JOIN-FREE NETS AND S-NETS
A well-formed, plain, join-free Petri net is an S-net.

Proof: Let $N = (S, T, F)$ be a well-formed, plain, join-free net. Suppose there is a transition $t \in T$ with two distinct output places $s_1, s_2 \in t^\bullet$. In any live marking, t properly increases the number of tokens on the net, with no possibility to decrease it, due to plainness, well-formedness and join-freeness. Hence no live marking can be bounded, contradicting well-formedness. Thus no such transition exists, and the net is, in fact, an S-net. ∎

We shall need an argument to ensure that dropping siblings does not lead to the unboundedness of the surviving place (just like, before, dropping rivals did not lead to the non-liveness of the surviving transition). For this purpose, we shall borrow some results from [Hac74, DE95], whose proofs do not, however, depend on the S-covering property. A subset $D \subseteq S$ of places is called a *siphon* if $^\bullet D \subseteq D^\bullet$, and a subset $Q \subseteq S$ is called a *trap* if $Q^\bullet \subseteq {}^\bullet Q$. A siphon is called *proper* if it is nonempty, and *minimal* if none of its proper subsets is a siphon.

Theorem 6. COMMONER'S LIVENESS THEOREM (PROOFS IN [Hac74, DE95])
A free-choice Petri net N without isolated places is live under some initial marking M_0 if, and only if, every proper siphon D contains a trap $Q \subseteq D$ with $M_0(Q) > 0$.

For every proper siphon to contain a marked trap, it already suffices that every minimal proper siphon contains a marked trap. With a view to the proof of Theorem 4, we need to know that every place s of a well-formed free-choice net is inside some minimal proper siphon.

Lemma 7. PROPOSITION 5.4(1) AND LEMMA 5.5 OF [DE95]
Let N be a well-formed free-choice net and let s be a place of N. Then there is a minimal proper siphon D containing s. Moreover, D is also a trap.

Lemma 8. REDUCING SIBLINGS
Let N be a well-formed free-choice net with a live and bounded marking M_0 and let $\{s, s_1, \ldots, s_k\}$ be a place cluster with $k > 0$. Define N' as N, except that the places $\{s_1, \ldots, s_k\}$ are dropped (i.e., all siblings of s, but s, are removed). Then the net N' with the marking inherited from M_0 is still live and s is bounded in it.

Proof: Let D be a minimal proper siphon containing s; such a siphon exists by Lemma 7, and it is also a minimal proper siphon and a trap in N'. Let $M_1 \xrightarrow{t} M_2$ be a transition firing in N'. We prove $M_1(D) = M_2(D)$ by case distinction over t.

Case 1: $t \notin {}^\bullet D \cup D^\bullet$.
Then t neither removes tokens from D nor adds tokens to D, i.e., $M_1(D) = M_2(D)$.

Case 2: $t \in D^\bullet \setminus {}^\bullet D$.

This is not possible since D is also a trap.

Case 3: $t \in {}^\bullet D$.

(3a): $|D \cap t^\bullet| \geq |D \cap {}^\bullet t|$, since otherwise, D is not minimal (one of the places of $D \cap {}^\bullet t$ can be taken away without destroying the siphon property).

(3b): $|D \cap t^\bullet| \leq |D \cap {}^\bullet t|$, for suppose $|D \cap t^\bullet| > |D \cap {}^\bullet t|$. Together with (3a) and the fact that D is a trap, this would lead to any live marking being unbounded, contradicting well-formedness. Combining (3a) and (3b), $M_1(D) = M_2(D)$.

Thus, such a minimal proper siphon D provides a structural bound for the number of tokens on s: s can never receive more tokens than D had initially.

Now suppose that we remove the places $\{s_1, \ldots, s_k\}$ from the net. This does not destroy any minimal siphon through s, by the fact that every minimal siphon contains at most one place from each place cluster (Case (3a) above), so that any minimal siphon containing s does not contain any of the places $s_1, \ldots, s_k$. This is also due to the fact that, since we only drop places (and no transition), the presets and postsets of places and place sets are left unchanged, so that for instance siphons in the original net which survive the modification remain siphons in the new net. Thus, after removing $\{s_1, \ldots, s_k\}$, the obtained net with any marking inherited from a live marking of N remains live, the structural bound for s still exists, and s remains bounded.   ∎

Proof: (of Theorem 4.)

From the previous lemmata, there is a short proof, given in [DE95]; however, instead of repeating this, we shall present a constructive proof which is more symmetrical to the one given for the T-covering theorem 2.

Let N be a free-choice Petri net and M_0 a live and bounded marking.

Let us pick and fix x to be any place of N. We want to show that there is an S-component covering x. As before, the property is trivial if x is isolated, and from Proposition 1, we may also restrict our attention to the strongly connected component containing x. If there is no kinship in the net, the latter is join-free, and from Proposition 5, it is an S-net (containing x).

Let us thus assume there are non-singleton siblings and let us choose a path

$$x = x_0 \; \rightarrow \; u_0 \rightarrow \; x_1 \; \rightarrow \; u_1 \; \rightarrow \; x_2 \; \rightarrow \; u_2 \ldots x_{n-1} \; \rightarrow \; u_{n-1} \; \rightarrow \; x_n = s \; \rightarrow \; u_n$$

such that s has proper kinship but there is no proper kinship strictly between x and s (we allow $s = x$); from strong connectedness and the existence of kinships, this is always possible.[4] We thus have that for all $i \in \{0, \ldots, n-1\}$: ${}^\bullet u_i = \{x_i\}$, ${}^\bullet u_n = \{s, s_1, \ldots, s_k\}$ with $k > 0$ (i.e., the $\{s_1, \ldots, s_k\}$ are the siblings of s, and there is at least one of them.)

A main point is that, from the previous lemmata, any minimal siphon D containing s also contains x. This is obvious if $s = x$. Otherwise, $u_{n-1} \in {}^\bullet x_n \subseteq {}^\bullet D \subseteq D^\bullet$ so that x_{n-1} must belong to D and we may continue (retro-)progressing to x.

---

[4] We may, for instance, start from any place with proper kinship, go back to x, and keep the last visited place with proper kinship.

Now, let us remove all siblings of s (but not s). After that, the net remains live and s is still bounded by Lemma 8, and the latter is also true for all places in any minimal siphon containing s, including x. However, this may render some other places unbounded. Then, as long as there are unbounded places, we throw them away. This may not cause the places in the minimal siphons containing s and x to become unbounded. The result is still free-choice (we only dropped places). It is also live because any siphon in the result is also a siphon in the original net (still because we only dropped places) and contains a marked trap from the liveness criterion (Theorem 6) for free-choice nets, both in the original net and the new one (still for the same reason).

The result is thus a well-formed free-choice net containing x. We may restrict ourselves to the strongly connected component containing x and continue the construction until there is no longer any proper kinship. The result is an S-net, and since we only dropped places and connected components, it is an S-component of the original net containing x, as requested.   ∎

Figure 3 illustrates this algorithm on the net shown in Fig. 1. Suppose we wish to construct a strongly connected S-component covering s_4 (1). Since it is its only sibling, we search forward, rather than backward, finding s_3 with sibling s_2 (2). After dropping place s_2 (3), places s_1 and s_6 are unbounded. After dropping them (4), no place has proper siblings. Transitions a, f, g are also dropped (5) since they do not belong to the strongly connected component containing s_4. The S-component N_5 shown in Fig. 1 remains. The token stays put, since no firing takes place during the construction.

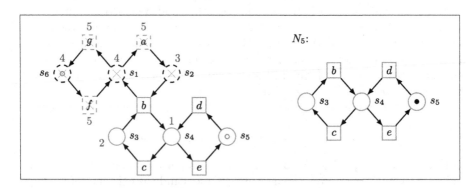

Fig. 3. Finding an S-component covering place s_4. The various steps are exhibited in blue on the left-hand side. The end result (N_5 of Figure 1 (Color figure online)), with a live and bounded marking, is shown on the right-hand side.

5   Concluding Remarks

A pleasant outcome of this research has been the somewhat surprising discovery of a concise, stand-alone proof of Theorem 2 described in Sect. 3, for which some novelty can be claimed. All other proofs of Theorem 2 we know of (including, besides [Hac74, DE95], also [Bes86, BD90]) are substantially longer, and the proof in [DE95] uses quite a different method.[5]

Less novelty and less independence can be claimed for the S-coverability proof (Sect. 4). It uses Commoner's liveness theorem, but so do all other proofs we know of (including [Hac74, DE95, BD24]). With Lemma 7, we have used another substantial part of the proof in [DE95]. The main new ideas in Sect. 4 are to appreciate the relevance of Proposition 5 and Lemma 8 in order to cast the existing proof into an algorithm which is symmetric to the algorithm presented in Sect. 3.

In describing algorithms to reduce nets, our proofs are similar in spirit to those in [Hac74]. But whereas [Hac74] defines reduction rules in a purely structural way and justifies them behaviourally afterwards, in our approach, structural reductions are motivated and justified step by step on behavioural grounds.

As far as duality is concerned, the algorithms proposed in Sects. 3 and 4 are symmetric. The role played by a chain of transitions in the T-coverability proof is taken over by a minimal proper siphon in the S-coverability proof. The S-coverability proof in [BD24] (Theorem 5.34(1)) is altogether different, and it is actually the shortest of the four; but it is non-constructive and has no symmetric counterpart, as it works by exhaustive examination of minimal siphons, using Theorem 6 many times over. Combining this with the concise, one-page, proof of Theorem 6 presented by Petr Jancar in [Jan24], we also obtain a short proof for Theorem 4.

Acknowledgement. The authors would like to extend their thanks to three reviewers for reading this paper and suggesting improvements for its presentation.

References

[BD24] Best, E., Devillers, R.: Petri Net Primer - a Compendium on Core Model, Analysis, and Synthesis. Computer Science Foundations and Applied Logic. Birkhäuser, Springer Nature, 2024. https://doi.org/10.1007/978-3-031-48278-6

[BD90] Best, E., Desel, J.: "Partial Order Behaviour and Structure of Petri Nets". In: Formal Aspects Comput. 2.2 (1990), pp. 123-138. https://doi.org/10.1007/BF01888220. URL: https://doi.org/10.1007/BF01888220

[Bes86] Best, E.: Structure theory of Petri nets: the free choice hiatus. In: Brauer, W., Reisig, W., Rozenberg, G. (eds.) ACPN 1986. LNCS, vol. 254, pp. 168–205. Springer, Heidelberg (1987). https://doi.org/10.1007/978-3-540-47919-2_8

[DE95] Desel, J., Esparza, J.: Free Choice Petri Nets. Vol. 40. Cambridge Tracts in Theoret. Comput. Sci. Cambridge University Press, 1995

[ES89a] Esparza, J., Silva, M.: Circuits, handles, bridges and nets. In: Rozenberg, G. (ed.) ICATPN 1989. LNCS, vol. 483, pp. 210–242. Springer, Heidelberg (1991). https://doi.org/10.1007/3-540-53863-1_27

---

[5] Essentially, this proof considers an infinite firing sequence and separates transitions by means of an exchange lemma, in order to filter out the firings of a single T-component containing the given transition. It does not appear to have a symmetric counterpart.

[ES89b] Esparza, J., Silva, M.: On the analysis and synthesis of free choice systems. In: Rozenberg, G. (ed.) ICATPN 1989. LNCS, vol. 483, pp. 243–286. Springer, Heidelberg (1991). https://doi.org/10.1007/3-540-53863-1_28

[ES90] Esparza, J., Silva, M.: Top-down synthesis of live and bounded free choice nets. In: Rozenberg, G. (ed.) ICATPN 1990. LNCS, vol. 524, pp. 118–139. Springer, Heidelberg (1991). https://doi.org/10.1007/BFb0019972

[Esp90] Esparza, J.: Synthesis rules for Petri nets, and how they lead to new results. In: Baeten, J.C.M., Klop, J.W. (eds.) CONCUR 1990. LNCS, vol. 458, pp. 182–198. Springer, Heidelberg (1990). https://doi.org/10.1007/BFb0039060

[Hac74] Hack, M.H.T.: Analysis of Production Schemata by Petri Nets. Tech. rep. Massachussetts Inst. Tech., MAC TR-94, 1974 (based on his MSc thesis, 1972)

[Jan24] Jancar, P.: A concise proof of Commoner's theorem. 2024. arXiv: 2401. 12067 [cs.LO]

On Verifying Concurrent Programs Under Weak Consistency Models: Decidability and Complexity

Ahmed Bouajjani[✉]

IRIF, Université Paris Cité, Paris, France
abou@irif.fr

Abstract. We present an overview of existing results about the decidability and the complexity of verifying concurrent programs under weak memory consistency models. We show that this problem can be undecidable for some models, and decidable for others but highly complex. Then, we presents approaches that allow to overcome undecidability and high complexity, allowing to prove either reachability or non-reachability by solving reachability queries under strong consistency. (This overview is based on a series of joint work with students and collaborators: Parosh Aziz Abdulla, Mohamed Faouzi Atig, Sidi Mohamed Beillahi, Sebastian Burckhardt, Constantin Enea, Egor Derevenetc, Roland Meyer, Madanlal Musuvathi, Tuan Phong Ngo, and Gennaro Parlato. Many thanks to them)

1 Introduction

The semantics of shared memory concurrent programs is determined by the considered memory consistency model. The latter defines when and in which order memory updates become visible to the different processes of the program. The highest level of consistency, where updates are considered to be visible immediately to all processes, corresponds to the Sequential Consistency model (SC) [29]. However, only weaker consistency levels can be ensured by memory systems for performance reasons. Examples of weak memory consistency models are Total Store Order (TSO) [33] that is adopted for the x86 architectures, and Power [21,32]. In weakly memory models different processes may have different sets of visible states along computations. For instance, in the TSO model, write operations are not necessarily visible to other processes immediately as in SC, so there is some delay between the time they are issued by some process and the time they are committed to the memory and becoming visible to other processes. In this interval, reads by the process that issued delayed writes can overtake them in order to fetch potentially old values from the memory since there might be freshly issued values by other processes that are still not visible in the memory.

Reordering between operations as allowed by weak memory models makes the semantics of programs running over these models particularly complex. The verification of such programs is challenging since it requires reasoning about all

S. Kiefer et al. (Eds.): *Taming the Infinities of Concurrency*, LNCS 14660, pp. 133–147, 2024.
https://doi.org/10.1007/978-3-031-56222-8_7

possible reorderings of operations allowed by the weakly consistent semantics. To model formally such reorderings one needs typically to use unbounded queues, which threaten the decidability of verification problems.

This paper presents an overview on the work we have been doing in the last fifteen years, together with many students and collaborators, on the verification of concurrent programs under weak consistency models. We address in this paper solving the reachability problem and investigate its decidability and its complexity, and how to overcome undecidability and high complexity. We present only a sample of the existing results, illustrating the main approaches and techniques that we have adopted.

We show that while the reachability problem is undecidable for memory models such as Power [3], it is actually decidable for some models such as TSO [11,12]. We show that this holds both when the number of parallel processes is fixed, and the case when this number is a parameter that can be arbitrarily large [5]. However, we show that the complexity of the problem is non-primitive recursive.

To overcome undecidability and high complexity, we consider two sound but not complete approaches, one for proving non-reachability (safety satisfaction) and the other one for proving reachability (safety violation).

The first approach is based on the concept of robustness. A program is robust for a model M_1 against a weaker model M_2 if the sets of observable behaviors of that program under M_1 and under M_2 are the same. We consider as observable behaviors the computation traces that capture the essence of computations under SC by keeping the information about how data flow from write to reads, in which order are executed writes, and the order between operations in the code of the program. We show that trace-robustness for SC against TSO of a given program can be reduced polynomially to verifying reachability under SC in an instrumented version of that program, which is a PSPACE-complete when the number of processes is fixed, and EXPSPACE-complete in the parametric case. Since trace-robustness implies preserving the set of reachable states (the converse does not hold in general), by establishing trace-robustness and by verifying that some state is not reachable under SC, one can deduce that the state is not reachable under TSO either. This provide a method allowing to prove safety correctness that consists in solving reachability problems in SC, which is a spectacular saving in the complexity w.r.t. the exact approach that is non-primitive recursive. Trace-robustness has been investigated for many other models, in particular it has been shown that checking robustness against Power is decidable with also a PSPACE-complete complexity in the case of a fixed number of processes [19]. This shows that the approach based on checking robustness can be applicable in cases where there is no exact approach (since reachability under Power is undecidable as mentioned earlier).

The second approach is based on adapting the concept of context-bounding [31] to the case of weakly consistent semantics. This approach is useful for finding efficiently bugs. We show that context-bounded analysis of a program under TSO can be reduced polynomially to the context-bounded analysis under SC of an instrumented version of that program [13]. We have applied this approach in the case of the Power model too [4], providing a bug detection approach in this case while the reachability problem for this model is undecidable.

2   Program Semantics

We consider programs with a finite number of variables, let X be the set of these variables, ranging over a finite data domain D. Programs are composed of a number of parallel processes accessing concurrently to the variables in X using write operations $w(x, v)$ (that writes a value $v \in D$ on a variable $x \in X$) and read operations $r(x, v)$ (that reads the value $v \in D$ from the variable $x \in X$). A computation of a program is a sequence of such operations. We associate with each computation ρ the following three relations between its operations:

- The *read-from* relation, denoted rf, relates a write operation $w(x, v)$ with an operation $r(x, v)$, meaning that the source of the value read by the operation $r(x, v)$ is the write operation $w(x, v)$.
- The *program order* relation, denoted po is the order in which operations of ρ appear in the program. The projection of po on each process is a total order, and operations of different processes are not related by po.
- The *store order* relation, denoted so, is a total order between all write operations in ρ defining the order in which these writes are executed.

The three relations above define an abstraction of the computation ρ: The *trace* of the computation ρ, denoted $trace(\rho)$, is the structure defined by the set of operations in ρ related by rf $\cup$ po $\cup$ so.

Given a program, the set of possible executions is determined by the consistency model ensured by the storage system (memory) used by the program. The consistency model depends on how (when, and in which order) memory updates become visible to each of the processes of the program. The highest level of consistency, called strong consistency, is obtained when every update is immediately visible to all processes. However, most storage systems ensure weaker levels of consistency for performance reasons. In the next section, we define two consistency models, one is *sequential consistency* that ensures strong consistency, and *total store order* that is weaker as it allows the following behaviors: Write operations issued by a process can be committed to the memory (and made visible to all processes) after some delay that is not bounded a priori. Then, a read operation on a variable x of that process fetches the last value of the delayed write operations on x issued by the process, if it exists. Otherwise, the read operation fetches the value of x in the memory, overtaking all the on other variables that are still pending.

2.1   Sequential Consistency

Sequential Consistency (SC) is the model where each computation corresponds to an interleaving of the sequences of operations issued by the different processes, taken in the order they appear in the program. The operational semantics of programs running under SC is therefore obtained by associating to the program the asynchronous product of the state machines corresponding to each of its parallel processes. We omit the details of this definition here as it is standard.

However, we give hereafter an alternative definition of SC following the axiomatic style. Let ρ be a computation of a program. In addition to the relations rf, po, and so introduced earlier, we consider the *conflict* relation, denoted cf that is derived from the relations rf and so as follows: Let $r(x,v)$ be a read operation from x of some value v, and let $w(x,v)$ such that $w(x,v) \xrightarrow{\text{rf}} r(x,v)$. Then, for every other write operation $w(x,u)$ on x, we have $r(x,v) \xrightarrow{\text{cf}} w(x,u)$ whenever $w(x,v) \xrightarrow{\text{so}} w(x,u)$. In other words, $r(x,v)$ must be executed before that $w(x,u)$ changes the value of x from v to u.

The *happen-before* relation hb is the union of the four relations defined above, i.e., hb $=$ rf$\cup$po$\cup$so$\cup$cf. Then, a computation is said to be *sequentially consistent* if its happen-before relation is *acyclic*. It can be seen that a computation is sequentially consistent if and only if it is trace-equivalent to a computation that is an interleaving of sequences of operations issued by the parallel processes of the program (i.e., as produced by the operational model mentioned earlier).

2.2   Total Store Order

A very common relaxation of the strong consistency semantics consists in allowing that read operations overtake write operations (issued by the same process) on different variables. Consider for instance the program in Fig. 1.

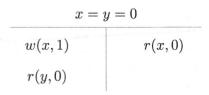

Fig. 1. Program where a read can safely overtake a write.

In the SC model, the only possible computation is $\rho = r(x,0)w(x,1)r(y,0)$. Starting from the state $(x = 0, y = 0)$, the execution of ρ leads to the state $(x = 1, y = 0)$. However, one can observe that the two operations issued by process p_1 concern two different variables. By swapping these two operations, it would be possible to execute the operations of the program in the following order $\rho' = r(x,0)r(y,0)w(x,1)$ which will also lead to the state $(x = 1, y = 0)$ when executed starting from $(x = 0, y = 0)$. Considering this order allows to execute first the two read operations (which can be executed in parallel), and then execute the write operation. As writes take in general more time to be executed than reads, this relaxation of the semantics avoids making reads wait for writes when this is not needed. However, this relaxation may lead in some situations to undesirable behaviors as we will see later. In that case, one needs to impose that reads wait for the writes that have been already issued.

Formally, the operational semantics of programs running under TSO is defined by adding unbounded FIFO store buffers, one per process, to model the possibility of delaying writes. The operational semantics is defined as follows:

- a write issued by a process is stored in the buffer associated with that process. Write operations pending in the store buffer of a process are not visible to other processes.
- at any time a write can be taken from any store buffer (while respecting the FIFO order in the buffers) to be committed to the memory and made visible to all processes.
- a process executing a read operation on a variable x starts by checking if there is a write operation on x that is still pending in its buffer. In this case, the read operation takes that value (this is called a read own write operation), otherwise it takes the value of x that is present in the memory.
- in addition to reads and writes, it is possible to uses *atomic read-write* operations (combining a read and a write, executed without interference from other processes). Such an operation requires that the store buffer (of the process issuing it) is empty to be executed. It is also possible to use a *fence* operation which again requires that the store buffer is empty to be executed. Fences are needed in situations where it is necessary to ensure that all issued writes at some point of the computation have been made visible to all processes.

Consider the program in Fig. 2.

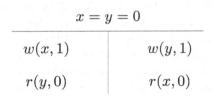

Fig. 2. Dekker program.

The three states that are reachable under SC by maximal computations are $(x = 0, y = 1)$, $(x = 1, y = 0)$, and $(x = 1, y = 1)$. However, under TSO, it is also possible to reach the state $(x = 0, y = 0)$ since the write operations can be delayed, making possible that both processes read the old values 0 of the two variables. To forbid reaching the state $(x = 0, y = 0)$ under TSO, it is necessary to insert two fences right after the two write operations in the program. Adding theses fences ensures that the writes are committed before the value of the variables are fetched by the read operations.

3   Solving the State Reachability Problem

The state of a program is composed of the the control locations of each of the processes and the memory valuation (values associated with each variable). The state reachability problem consists in checking whether, given a set of initial states I and set of target states T, there is an execution of the program starting from a state in I and reaching a state in T. Typically the set T represents the set of *unsafe* states, and solving the state reachability problem allows to verify if the program has a computation that violates some desired safety property stating that all reachable states are in some specified set of safe states. We will consider two versions of the state reachability problem. The first one assumes that the number of processes in the program is fixed and is finite. The second one is the parametric state reachability problem which consists in verifying if there is a number of identical processes for which the program defined as their parallel composition can reach T from I. So, in the parametric version of problem, the reachability question is addressed for a family of programs with an arbitrarily large number of identical processes. When we mention the state reachability problem without further precision we always mean the first version of the problem where the number of processes is fixed.

The state reachability problem under SC is known to be PSPACE-complete, while the parametric state reachability problem under SC is EXSPACE-complete. However, for relaxed consistency models the decidability of these problems are nontrivial due to the potentially unbounded reordering of operations along computations.

In fact, the state reachability problem has been proved to be undecidable in the case of several weak memory models. However, for other ones such as TSO and some of its relaxations, this problem can be shown to be decidable.

The decidability of the state reachability problem for program under TSO is established by a reduction to the state reachability problem of well-structured systems that are a type of lossy channel systems. The reduction is not straightforward. Clearly, turning store buffers to lossy FIFO queues is not correct since ignoring some write operations can add new behaviors to the program. For instance, assume that a program has two variables x and y and two processes p_1 and p_2. Then, starting from the memory state $(x = 0, y = 0)$, if after issuing $w(x, 1)$ the process p_1 issues $w(y, 1)$, then after performing $r(y, 1)$ the process p_2 cannot perform $r(x, 0)$ since when the value of y in the memory is 1, the value of x in the memory is necessarily 1 too. But obviously, if the operation $w(x, 1)$ is lost, the old value of x in the memory, which is 0, can still be read by p_2.

Then, the idea is instead of storing the issued write operations, to store the memory states (i.e. valuations $m : X \rightarrow D$ of all the program variables) obtained from the application of the issued write operations to the last reachable memory state. So, in the example above, the queue associated with p_1 will receive successively the states $(x = 1, y = 0)$ and then $(x = 1, y = 1)$, and the memory can be correctly updated by these states in the same order. This way, the fact that when $y = 1$ we also have $x = 1$ is guaranteed.

3.1   Reachability in Programs with a Fixed Number of Processes

Given a program with n processes, we construct a lossy channel system with n channels that simulates precisely the program. We start by building for each process p_i a lossy channel machine M_i with one channel c_i which simulates the process p_i. It maintains in its control state the last memory state that has been sent to the channel c_i, in addition to the control location of the process, and to the valuation of the main memory. Then, the machine simulates performs the following actions:

- given a write operation $w(x, v)$ of p_i, the machine M_i (1) sends to c_i at tuple $(m', w(x, v), i)$ formed of the memory state $m' = m[x \leftarrow v]$ where m is the memory state stored in the control state of M_i, the write operation $w(x, v)$, and the process identity i of process p_i, and (2) moves to a state where m has been updated by $m[x \leftarrow v]$. This transition of the machine M_i is labelled by the pair $w(x, v)$ and i.
- in addition, to take into account updates made by the other processes, the machine M_i can guess at any point that some process p_j updates the memory state by issuing a write operation. Then, the effect of this write operation is computed on the last state stored in the machine and sent to the channel c_i, together with the operation and the process identity j of the process that issued the operation. This transition of M_i is labelled by the write operation that has been executed and the identity of the process that has issued it.
- at any point, the machine can chose to withdraw the first element (m, op, pid) of the channel commit c_i and use it to update the main memory component of the state of M_i by the memory state m.
- reads are simulated straightforwardly: either from c_i or from the main memory as before. To be able to read its own writes from c_i, we need to mark for each variable the last elements in c_i which corresponds to an update of that variable by p_i.

Finally, the machine that simulates the whole program is the parallel composition of the machines M_i's associated with all the processes, synchronized on the labelled transitions. This ensures that all the machines M_i agree on the sequence of memory states that is sent to all of their channels (representing the sequence of reachable states that the memory will successively have). Now, it can be observed that elements of the channels can be lost without affecting the semantics. Indeed, skipping a state in the channel corresponds to a memory update. There is a detail however. In each channel c_i, a state corresponding to the last operation on a variable done by the process p_i cannot be lost in order to perform correctly the read-own-write operations. The number of such states is bounded since the number of variables is finite. This allows to define a variant of lossy channel systems where all symbols in the channels can be lost except a finite number of special symbols, that are well-structured.

The approach used for establishing the decidability of the reachability problem under TSO can be applied for a variety of other weak memory models, including for instance TSO with persistent memory, and a variant of the release-acquire model. For each of these models a reduction of the reachability problem to verifying reachability in a class of well-structured systems must be defined, which is in general a nontrivial task. Concerning complexity, the state reachability problem under TSO can be shown to be non-primitive recursive by a reduction of the reachability problem for lossy channel systems. This lower bound holds also for the other weaker models for which the reachability problem has been shown to be decidable.

3.2   The Parametric Reachability Problem

While the construction given in the previous section provides a decidability proof for the reachability problem under TSO, the fact that it is based on storing memory states limits its potential use in practice. In addition, the construction refers to the identities of the processes, which makes it depends crucially on the fact that the number of processes is finite and known. To overcome these issues, the idea is to change our way of modeling the fact that writes can be delayed. In the formal model we presented earlier, writes are sent to store buffers before becoming visible to all processes, while reads can overtake them for fetching values in the memory that are potentially old since recent writes may still be pending in the buffers of other processes (and visible only the their issuers) without being visible to them. This type of behavior can also be modeled by reversing the buffering mechanism: writes can be committed immediately to the main memory upon their issue, and the memory is in charge of sending nondeterministically to the processes, using load buffers, the values they need to read. This way, a process can read from values issued by other processes and that have been sent earlier by the main memory to its buffer. More precisely:

- when a process p executes an operation $w(x, v)$, the value of x in the main memory is updated by v, and the read operation $r(x, v)$ is sent to the buffer of the process p with a mark indicating that this value comes from one of its own writes. If a marked value exists already in the buffer, it loses its mark. The mark allows p to recognize the last value it has written on variable x.
- nondeterministically, the memory can send an operation $r(x, v)$ where v is the value of x in the memory, to any load buffer.
- nondeterministically, non-marked operations $r(x, v)$ in load buffer can be deleted.
- when a process executes a read operation, it starts by checking if there is a marked operation $r(x, v)$ in its buffer, and if yes, it executes that operation. Otherwise, it executes the first read operation on x in the buffer. In both cases, all operations in the buffer that are before the operation that will be executed are deleted.

It can be shown that as far as reachability is concerned, this load buffer-based model is equivalent to the store buffer-based model. The advantages of the new model are the following. First, the load buffers are by definition lossy in the sense that read operations in these buffers can be lost at any time, except those that are marked, but there is only a finite number of them (the number of variables which is finite and fixed) per buffer. This allows to prove directly that these models are well-structured systems without the need of considering channels storing whole memory states, which is not practical. Second, this construction does not refer to process identities. This makes it suitable for solving the parametric state reachability problem.

So, the load buffer semantics for TSO allows to obtain a simple decision procedure for the state reachability problem (compared with the one based on the store buffer semantics), and moreover it allows also to solve the parametric version of that problem.

4 Overcoming Undecidability and High Complexity

We have seen in the previous section that the state reachability problem is undecidable for models such as Power, and decidable for other models such as TSO, but highly complex. This imposes adopting approximate methods for checking reachability that can be used in practice with lower complexity. In this respect one can consider as usual two types of methods, either methods for proving reachability (in the context of finding safety bugs), or for proving non-reachability (in the context of establishing safety). We present hereafter an approach of the second type, based on the notion or robustness. We mention shortly afterwards an approach of the first type, based on the concept of context-bounding. For both approaches, we show that verifying state reachability/non-reachability can be reduced to verifying state reachability under SC, i.e., without manipulating explicitly unbounded store/load buffer, although these approaches do not restrict the size of buffers in the semantics. This leads to important savings in the complexity, from non-primitive recursive to PSPACE, or EXSPACE for the parametric case.

4.1 Verifying Program Robustness

We introduce a sound algorithmic approach for proving non-reachability efficiently. This approach is based on checking robustness that we define in the following.

Given a program P and two memory models M_1 and M_2, M_1 being stronger than M_2, and let $P[M_i]$ denote the set of computations of P executed under the model M_i for $i \in \{1, 2\}$. Then, we say that P is trace-robust for M_1 against M_2 if $traces(P[M_1]) = traces(P[M_2])$.

It can be seen that if a program P is trace-robust for M_1 against M_2, then the set of reachable of states of P under M_1 is equal to its set of reachable states under M_2 (the converse is not true in general). This implies that : Given a set of states S of P, if (1) S is non-reachable in P under M_1, and (2) $traces(P[M_1]) = traces(P[M_2])$, then S is non-reachable in M_2, which means that robustness allows to preserve the property of non-reachability.

Let us consider that M_1 is SC, and M_2 is TSO in the following. Then, by establishing that $traces(P[\text{SC}]) = traces(P[\text{TSO}])$, it becomes sufficient to verify non-reachability under SC to deduce that non-reachability also holds under TSO. This is interesting if the verification of robustness is less complex than verifying reachability under TSO. We prove that this is indeed the case [17]. More precisely, it is possible to prove that verifying trace-robustness for SC against TSO can be reduced (polynomially) to the state reachability problem under SC. The reduction is valid for both the case where the number of processes is fixed, and the parametric case. This leads to the fact that verifying trace-robustness is PSPACE-complete for a fixed number of processes, and EXPSPACE-complete in the parametric case. This is particularly useful since it allows to obtain a method for verifying non-reachability under TSO that does not explore explicitly the program behaviors under the complex TSO model, but rather explores its behaviors under SC while checking that TSO reorderings cannot create robustness violations, i.e., computations under TSO for which the happen-before relation as defined in Sect. 2.1 is cyclic.

The reduction of trace-robustness against TSO to state reachability under SC is based on showing that is it sufficient to track a particular class of violations in oder to decide if TSO can create robustness violations. These violations are computations where all processes behave under the SC semantics, except one. To illustrate this, consider again the Dekker program in Fig. 2. This program is clearly not trace-robust. A robustness violation witness for this program where only one process reorders its operations is given in Fig. 3.

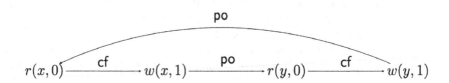

Fig. 3. Trace-robustness violation.

This example shows actually the pattern that is satisfied by the special violations we consider: It contains a write and a read operations that have been swapped, $w(y,1)$ and $r(y,0)$ in this example, in order to let the read operation $r(y,0)$ to be executed right before a conflicting write operation $w(x,1)$. The delayed operation is then executed right after the execution of conflicting reads, $r(y,0)$ in this example, while the whole sequence of operations between $r(x,0)$ and $w(y,1)$ constitutes a happen-before path. This leads to a cycle in the happen-before relation since the delayed write $w(y,1)$ is related with the read operation $r(x,0)$ in the program order.

Now, given a program P, it is possible to build a program P' that is an instrumentation of P such that, P under TSO has a trace-robustness violation if and only if some specific state s of P' is reachable in that program when it runs under SC.

First, we guess the process that is going to reorder its operations, and we guess also the pair of write and read operations in the code of the program that are going to be swapped (since a sequence of reads can overtake a sequence of writes, we actually guess the last read of the moved reads, and the first write of the delayed writes) and that will be the first and the last operation of the computation segment that has a cyclic happen-before relation. Then, the goal of the instrumentation of P is to check the correctness of the guess. At a write operation, the program chooses nondeterministically if it will delay that write and proceed to the next operations while checking that a cycle witnessing robustness violation can be constructed starting from that point. On the example of Fig. 3, at the write operation $w(y, 1)$ the program can choose to delay it, and proceed to the read operation $r(x, 0)$. Then, the program will schedule the other process in order to execute $w(x, 1)$ followed by $r(y, 0)$ in their program order, while checking that all of these operations are related by the happen-before relation, which can be done along the computation by considering progressively each pair of successive operations. After the $r(y, 0)$ operation, it checks that it can execute the pending write operation $w(y, 1)$ in order to close the happen-before cycle, and then jumps to a special termination state s. The state s is reachable under SC if and only if the program is not trace-robust against TSO.

By adopting the same principle (characterizing a finite set of patterns to track to decide the existence of robustness violations, and instrumenting the program to detect these patterns while running under SC), it has been proved that verifying robustness against Power is actually decidable [19] and PSPACE-complete (for a fixed number of processes), while verifying state reachability under this model is undecidable [3].

4.2 Context-Bounded Verification for Weak Memory Models

Context-bounding has been used successfully in the context of bug finding in concurrent programs [30,31]. The idea is to split a computation in computation phases where only one process in running (and accessing memory) while all the others are idle, and allow each process to run for a fixed number of rounds. The motivation is that concurrency bugs typically show up after a rather small number of context switches between processes. One of the main interests of context-bounding is the fact that it allows reducing the verification of state reachability in concurrent programs to checking state reachability in a sequential program [28,34,35]. This is due to a compositional reasoning about the computation rounds of the processes. Basically each process receives at the beginning of each of its computation rounds the state in the memory, and sends a memory state at the end of each of its computation rounds. Then, after running successively each of the processes until completion, the input/ouput interfaces of the processes are compared to check that they match, which validates the guesses and ensure that their composition is possible. Symbolic methods can be used to make these operations efficient [28,35].

Originally context-bounding has been defined and developed assuming strong consistency. In [13], we have extended the definition of context-bounding to computation under weak memory models such as TSO. We have also shown that interestingly, a compositional method can again be defined for reasoning about computation in this case, using only bounded interfaces. For TSO, one needs basically to add K copies of the variables, where K is the number of rounds per process, representing the last values written on each variable at each round. This approach has been also applied to the case of Power in [4], although verifying the general state reachability problem for Power is undecidable [3].

5   Conclusion

We have presented a high-level overview of existing results about verifying state reachability in concurrent programs running under weak memory models. We highlight some of the main approaches and techniques used in this context. First, we have shown that while the considered problem is undecidable for models like for instance Power, it can be proved to be decidable for other models such as TSO is using reductions to the state reachability problem in well-structured systems, but the problem is intrinsically highly complex.

To overcome undecidability and high complexity, we have shown that it is possible to adopt sound but non-complete methods, either for proving safety correctness by solving a stronger non-reachability problem based on checking trace-robustness, or for finding safety violations by performing an under-approximate reachability analysis based on the concept of context-bounding. The approaches we have presented for this purpose are therefore complementary. Importantly, the application of both approaches requires only solving reachability problems under the SC semantics. This allows to reduce drastically the complexity and leads to practical methods that avoid manipulating explicitly unbounded buffers for modeling operation reorderings.

There are still many open problems concerning the three problems:

1. solving the precise reachability problem under weak consistency. Indeed, weak consistency concerns several levels, hardware architectures (such as x86, Power, ARM, etc.) considered in this paper, and also programming languages (such as C, Java) and distributed storage systems and data bases where various weak consistency/isolation concepts are considered (such as causal consistency, snapshot isolation) [2,25,26].
2. defining efficient procedures for exploring the space of computations under weak consistency. One of the issue is what are relevant concepts to guide the search and prioritizing classes of behaviors in order to speed up the search and find quickly bugs if they exist. We have mentioned some work on the use of the concept of context-bounding under weak consistency, but still other strategies should to be investigated. Stateless-model checking and partial-order techniques have been also defined in the context of weak consistency/isolation [1,6–9,18,22,24].
3. verifying robustness against weak models w.r.t. stronger ones, for relevant concepts of observable behaviors. As we have seen, using robustness for checking state reachability is an interesting approach that is based on the idea of

separating two issues: correctness of the program with the strong semantics, and invariability of the program semantics under the loss of some consistency guarantees. Beyond the cases we mentioned in the paper, this approach has been investigated for many other consistency models such as the release-acquire model [27], and consistency/isolation models used in distributed systems [14–16].

Finally, an interesting challenge is to design generic frameworks allowing to formally specify consistency models, and to derive systematically solutions for the three problems mentioned above. Interesting work on this line of research has been done in [10, 20, 23].

References

1. Abdulla, P.A., Aronis, S., Atig, M.F., Jonsson, B., Leonardsson, C., Sagonas, K.: Stateless model checking for TSO and PSO. In: Baier, C., Tinelli, C. (eds.) TACAS 2015. LNCS, vol. 9035, pp. 353–367. Springer, Heidelberg (2015). https://doi.org/10.1007/978-3-662-46681-0_28
2. Abdulla, P.A., Arora, J., Atig, M.F., Krishna, S.N.: Verification of programs under the release-acquire semantics. In: McKinley, K.S., Fisher, K. (eds.) Proceedings of the 40th ACM SIGPLAN Conference on Programming Language Design and Implementation, PLDI 2019, Phoenix, AZ, USA, 22–26 June 2019, pp. 1117–1132. ACM (2019). https://doi.org/10.1145/3314221.3314649
3. Abdulla, P.A., Atig, M.F., Bouajjani, A., Derevenetc, E., Leonardsson, C., Meyer, R.: On the state reachability problem for concurrent programs under power. In: Georgiou, C., Majumdar, R. (eds.) NETYS 2020. LNCS, vol. 12129, pp. 47–59. Springer, Cham (2021). https://doi.org/10.1007/978-3-030-67087-0_4
4. Abdulla, P.A., Atig, M.F., Bouajjani, A., Ngo, T.P.: Context-bounded analysis for POWER. In: TACAS, pp. 56–74 (2017)
5. Abdulla, P.A., Atig, M.F., Bouajjani, A., Ngo, T.P.: A load-buffer semantics for total store ordering. Logical Methods Comput. Sci. **14**(1) (2018). https://doi.org/10.23638/LMCS-14(1:9)2018
6. Abdulla, P.A., Atig, M.F., Jonsson, B., Leonardsson, C.: Stateless model checking for power. In: Chaudhuri, S., Farzan, A. (eds.) CAV 2016. LNCS, vol. 9780, pp. 134–156. Springer, Cham (2016). https://doi.org/10.1007/978-3-319-41540-6_8
7. Abdulla, P.A., Atig, M.F., Jonsson, B., Ngo, T.P.: Optimal stateless model checking under the release-acquire semantics. PACMPL **2**(OOPSLA), 135:1–135:29 (2018). https://doi.org/10.1145/3276505
8. Abdulla, P.A., Atig, M.F., Jonsson, B., Ngo, T.P.: Dynamic partial order reduction under the release-acquire semantics (tutorial). In: Atig, M.F., Schwarzmann, A.A. (eds.) NETYS 2019. LNCS, vol. 11704, pp. 3–18. Springer, Cham (2019). https://doi.org/10.1007/978-3-030-31277-0_1
9. Abdulla, P.A., Atig, M.F., Krishna, S., Gupta, A., Tuppe, O.: Optimal stateless model checking for causal consistency. In: Sankaranarayanan, S., Sharygina, N. (eds.) Tools and Algorithms for the Construction and Analysis of Systems - 29th International Conference, TACAS 2023, Held as Part of the European Joint Conferences on Theory and Practice of Software, ETAPS 2022, Paris, France, 22–27 April 2023, Proceedings, Part I. LNCS, vol. 13993, pp. 105–125. Springer (2023). https://doi.org/10.1007/978-3-031-30823-9_6

10. Alglave, J., Maranget, L., Tautschnig, M.: Herding cats: modelling, simulation, testing, and data mining for weak memory. ACM Trans. Program. Lang. Syst. **36**(2), 7:1–7:74 (2014). https://doi.org/10.1145/2627752

11. Atig, M.F., Bouajjani, A., Burckhardt, S., Musuvathi, M.: On the verification problem for weak memory models. In: Hermenegildo, M.V., Palsberg, J. (eds.) Proceedings of the 37th ACM SIGPLAN-SIGACT Symposium on Principles of Programming Languages, POPL 2010, Madrid, Spain,17–23 January 2010. pp. 7–18. ACM (2010). https://doi.org/10.1145/1706299.1706303

12. Atig, M.F., Bouajjani, A., Burckhardt, S., Musuvathi, M.: What's decidable about weak memory models? In: Seidl, H. (ed.) ESOP 2012. LNCS, vol. 7211, pp. 26–46. Springer, Heidelberg (2012). https://doi.org/10.1007/978-3-642-28869-2_2

13. Atig, M.F., Bouajjani, A., Parlato, G.: Getting rid of store-buffers in TSO analysis. In: Gopalakrishnan, G., Qadeer, S. (eds.) CAV 2011. LNCS, vol. 6806, pp. 99–115. Springer, Heidelberg (2011). https://doi.org/10.1007/978-3-642-22110-1_9

14. Beillahi, S.M., Bouajjani, A., Enea, C.: Checking robustness against snapshot isolation. In: Dillig, I., Tasiran, S. (eds.) CAV 2019. LNCS, vol. 11562, pp. 286–304. Springer, Cham (2019). https://doi.org/10.1007/978-3-030-25543-5_17

15. Beillahi, S.M., Bouajjani, A., Enea, C.: Checking robustness between weak transactional consistency models. In: ESOP 2021. LNCS, vol. 12648, pp. 87–117. Springer, Cham (2021). https://doi.org/10.1007/978-3-030-72019-3_4

16. Beillahi, S.M., Bouajjani, A., Enea, C.: Robustness against transactional causal consistency. Log. Methods Comput. Sci. **17**(1) (2021). https://lmcs.episciences.org/7149

17. Bouajjani, A., Derevenetc, E., Meyer, R.: Checking and enforcing robustness against TSO. In: Felleisen, M., Gardner, P. (eds.) ESOP 2013. LNCS, vol. 7792, pp. 533–553. Springer, Heidelberg (2013). https://doi.org/10.1007/978-3-642-37036-6_29

18. Bouajjani, A., Enea, C., Román-Calvo, E.: Dynamic partial order reduction for checking correctness against transaction isolation levels. Proc. ACM Program. Lang. **7**(PLDI), 565–590 (2023). https://doi.org/10.1145/3591243

19. Derevenetc, E., Meyer, R.: Robustness against power is PSpace-complete. In: Esparza, J., Fraigniaud, P., Husfeldt, T., Koutsoupias, E. (eds.) ICALP 2014. LNCS, vol. 8573, pp. 158–170. Springer, Heidelberg (2014). https://doi.org/10.1007/978-3-662-43951-7_14

20. Haas, T., Meyer, R., de León, H.P.: CAAT: consistency as a theory. Proc. ACM Program. Lang. **6**(OOPSLA2), 114–144 (2022). https://doi.org/10.1145/3563292

21. IBM: Power ISA, Version 2.07 (2013)

22. Kokologiannakis, M., Lahav, O., Sagonas, K., Vafeiadis, V.: Effective stateless model checking for C/C++ concurrency. PACMPL **2**, 17:1–17:32 (2018)

23. Kokologiannakis, M., Lahav, O., Vafeiadis, V.: Kater: automating weak memory model metatheory and consistency checking. Proc. ACM Program. Lang. **7**(POPL), 544–572 (2023). https://doi.org/10.1145/3571212

24. Kokologiannakis, M., Marmanis, I., Gladstein, V., Vafeiadis, V.: Truly stateless, optimal dynamic partial order reduction. Proc. ACM Program. Lang. **6**(POPL), 1–28 (2022). https://doi.org/10.1145/3498711

25. Lahav, O., Boker, U.: Decidable verification under a causally consistent shared memory. In: Donaldson, A.F., Torlak, E. (eds.) Proceedings of the 41st ACM SIGPLAN International Conference on Programming Language Design and Implementation, PLDI 2020, London, UK, 15–20 June 2020, pp. 211–226. ACM (2020). https://doi.org/10.1145/3385412.3385966

26. Lahav, O., Boker, U.: What's decidable about causally consistent shared memory? ACM Trans. Program. Lang. Syst. **44**(2), 8:1–8:55 (2022). https://doi.org/10.1145/3505273

27. Lahav, O., Margalit, R.: Robustness against release/acquire semantics. In: McKinley, K.S., Fisher, K. (eds.) Proceedings of the 40th ACM SIGPLAN Conference on Programming Language Design and Implementation, PLDI 2019, Phoenix, AZ, USA, 22–26 June 2019, pp. 126–141. ACM (2019). https://doi.org/10.1145/3314221.3314604

28. Lal, A., Reps, T.W.: Reducing concurrent analysis under a context bound to sequential analysis. Formal Methods Syst. Des. **35**(1), 73–97 (2009). https://doi.org/10.1007/S10703-009-0078-9

29. Lamport, L.: How to make a multiprocessor that correctly executes multiprocess programs. IEEE Trans. Comput. **C-28**, 690–691 (1979)

30. Musuvathi, M., Qadeer, S.: Iterative context bounding for systematic testing of multithreaded programs. In: PLDI. ACM (2007)

31. Qadeer, S., Rehof, J.: Context-bounded model checking of concurrent software. In: Halbwachs, N., Zuck, L.D. (eds.) TACAS 2005. LNCS, vol. 3440, pp. 93–107. Springer, Heidelberg (2005). https://doi.org/10.1007/978-3-540-31980-1_7

32. Sarkar, S., Sewell, P., Alglave, J., Maranget, L., Williams, D.: Understanding POWER multiprocessors. In: Hall, M.W., Padua, D.A. (eds.) Proceedings of the 32nd ACM SIGPLAN Conference on Programming Language Design and Implementation, PLDI 2011, San Jose, CA, USA, 4–8 June 2011, pp. 175–186. ACM (2011)

33. Sewell, P., Sarkar, S., Owens, S., Nardelli, F.Z., Myreen, M.O.: x86-tso: a rigorous and usable programmer's model for x86 multiprocessors. Commun. ACM **53**(7), 89–97 (2010)

34. La Torre, S., Madhusudan, P., Parlato, G.: Reducing context-bounded concurrent reachability to sequential reachability. In: Bouajjani, A., Maler, O. (eds.) CAV 2009. LNCS, vol. 5643, pp. 477–492. Springer, Heidelberg (2009). https://doi.org/10.1007/978-3-642-02658-4_36

35. Torre, S.L., Madhusudan, P., Parlato, G.: Analyzing recursive programs using a fixed-point calculus. In: Hind, M., Diwan, A. (eds.) Proceedings of the 2009 ACM SIGPLAN Conference on Programming Language Design and Implementation, PLDI 2009, Dublin, Ireland, 15–21 June 2009, pp. 211–222. ACM (2009). https://doi.org/10.1145/1542476.1542500

A Summary and Personal Perspective on Recent Advances in Privacy Risk Assessment in Digital Pathology Through Formal Methods

Tomáš Brázdil[✉]

Masaryk University, 621 00 Brno, Czech Republic
xbrazdil@fi.muni.cz

Abstract. This paper summarizes a recently published approach to assessing privacy risks in sharing whole-slide images. The particular focus is on aspects related to the novel application of formal methods to evaluate possible privacy breaches due to the unrestricted sharing of microscopic tissue images. This paper also briefly describes the process of creating such a model and the obstacles a theoretical computer scientist must overcome to apply formal methods in medicine successfully.

Keywords: digital pathology · formal methods · whole-slide image

1 Introduction

Disclaimer: *This paper summarizes the most exciting aspects of the paper* [4] *from the perspective of formal methods. When citing the original results, please cite* [4] *directly.*

Histopathology is concerned with examining tissue samples in search of typically serious diseases. It is one of the crucial branches of medicine, especially in connection with oncology. A typical pathologist specializing in, say, prostate cancer would look at amounts of small cuts from prostates using a simple optical microscope and search for any malignancies. This work is highly specialized, and pathologists must be trained to notice and classify patterns in tissue images.

Nowadays, the examination process has become digital. There are sophisticated scanning microscopes that allow the transfer of microscopic images into a computer [5]. As the scanner usually scans the whole glass slide with samples, the result is called a whole-slide image (WSI, see Fig. 1). WSIs are usually huge images. The typical size of such an image is measured in gigabytes. WSIs are typically stored in databases linked to other data about patients (personal data, results of other examinations, etc.).

As usual, these days, whenever data is available, various types of processing are being applied. Thus, WSIs are scrutinized by multiple machine learning algorithms, shared in large public datasets, etc. It may easily happen that images of samples taken from the same patient appear in different datasets linked to different types of information.

S. Kiefer et al. (Eds.): *Taming the Infinities of Concurrency*, LNCS 14660, pp. 148–154, 2024.
https://doi.org/10.1007/978-3-031-56222-8_8

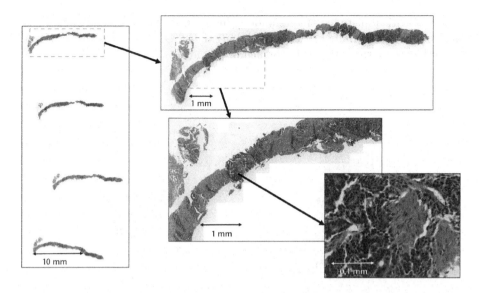

Fig. 1. An illustration of a WSI in various magnifications. The image has been taken from [4]

And here we come to the question of privacy in shared WSI data: Is it possible to link two different WSIs of the same patient? In other words, does WSI contain any identification of its origin as fingerprint or genetic information does?

Currently, WSIs are considered safe from this point of view. Pathologists happily share anonymized images of tissue, discuss the samples, and even share them online as fine art. Our paper [4] shows that this behavior is probably not as safe as it seems. We especially argue that in some specific cases, two WSIs of tissue from the same patient can be linked with a reasonable probability of success, potentially allowing the leakage of private information about the patient.

But now, where there are the formal methods? I will demonstrate how formal methods help to formulate the above privacy problem precisely.

1.1 How Is WSI Acquired

It is necessary to understand the formulation and results in more detail to understand the data acquisition process. First, the biological material is acquired from a patient, typically in a surgery or biopsy. Consequently, the material is cut into blocks, fixed in formalin, and paraffin-embedded. Such blocks are then cut into tiny slices (called cuts), mounted on glass, and stained (to give them colors highlighting essential features). The resulting glass slides are subsequently scanned using a high resolution, such as $0.250\mu m/px$, yielding the whole-slide image.

One may expect that spatially close cuts would be more similar to each other than the distant ones (see Fig. 2). Also, images of cuts from the same block should be more similar to cuts from different blocks of the same patient.

Is there a critical distance of cuts under which the WSIs are so similar that privacy could be potentially breached by linking them? Our answer is yes. However, the problem is formulating this "breach of privacy."

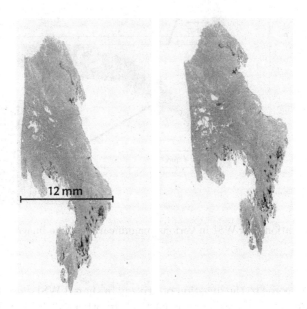

Fig. 2. Example of WSIs from consecutive cuts. The image has been taken from [4].

1.2 The Attacker Model

First, Let us define an attack and how to measure its success. Consider a set $\mathcal{H}$ of *patients*. Now, we want to model a situation in which an attacker possesses the WSI of a patient and wants to match it with the patient (possibly matching it with another patient's WSI). In our model, we abstract away the notion of WSI and talk about a *probe*, which is supposed to be mapped to a patient from $\mathcal{H}$. Denote the set of all probes by $\mathcal{G}$. To measure the efficiency of an attack, we need to have *probe ground truth* $G : \mathcal{H} \to 2^{\mathcal{G}}$ which maps patients to their probes (note that each patient may and typically does produce several WSIs, i.e., probes).

Now we model an *attack* as a function $f : \mathcal{G} \to \mathcal{H}$ which assigns each probe $p \in \mathcal{G}$ to a patient $f(p)$. How good is such an attack? The attacker aims to identify as many patients as possible. So, counting the number of patients who are targets of a successful mapping seems reasonable. We say that a patient h is f-vulnerable if there is a probe $p \in G(h)$ such that $h = f(p)$; that is, if at least one of the probes of the patient h is correctly assigned to h by the attack.

We define *worst-case probe attack success rate* by

$$R_s(f) = \frac{\text{number of } f\text{-vulnerable patients}}{|\mathcal{H}|} \tag{1}$$

i.e., the ratio of f-vulnerable patients to the total number of patients. This is equivalent to the standard definition of a success rate as defined in [6].

Observe that there is always a perfect attack f under which all patients are f-vulnerable: a perfect attack assigns a patient correctly to at least one of his/her probes. However, such an attack cannot be practically implemented as attackers typically have limited background knowledge. So, we consider families of possible attacks, an *attack domain*, based on the type of background knowledge and algorithms used for the probe-patient assignment.

In [4], we consider the attack domain, in which attack probes are WSIs mapped to the patient's background knowledge, which is another WSI based on similarity. In other words, the attacker compares the given probe WSI p with patients' WSIs and selects the most similar one.

Personal Comments. Let me comment on how the above model came into being. Some time ago, I got into a mixed group of pathologists and computer scientists (of mixed, mainly applied backgrounds). I attended lengthy meetings where they discussed for hours things called "privacy," "WSI," "security," etc. At the time, I only had a rough idea of digital pathology and knew nothing about privacy. I wanted to understand what they were talking about. Fortunately, the first author of [4] is my close colleague, so we arranged several long and intense face-to-face meetings where I could make him explain in simple terms what it's all supposed to be about. At first, the privacy problem looked impossibly complex, containing many levels of possible security issues, modes of sharing, etc. Ultimately, we obtained a very rough version of the model presented above. Then, of course, other co-authors came in, and together, we polished the model and built several hierarchies around it, set up experiments, derived guidelines for data sharing, etc.

It is perhaps interesting to mention how multidisciplinary research may restrict the creativity of individual participants. The original model allowed the attacker to randomize his attack. So, instead of deterministically pointing at concrete patients, a random distribution of patients was assigned to a probe, and then we measured the probability of a successful attack. However, another team member insisted on simplifying things by saying nobody would read such complex math in a medical computer science paper. However, in the end, one of the reviewers objected to deterministic attackers and demanded stochastic ones (which we have not provided and persuaded the reviewer that our model is rich enough).

1.3   The Attack Model Implementation

As indicated above, we assume that attack probes are WSIs mapped to the patient's background knowledge (another WSI) based on similarity. Our attacker takes both a WSI probe and a patient's WSI, feeds them into a deep learning model, obtains vectors of extracted features, and computes a distance between the two feature vectors. The patient with a background WSI closest to the given probe is attacked.

The following describes a particular attack implementation as presented in [4]. The attacker is given a WSI probe p and a background knowledge of WSI $b_1, \ldots, b_n \in \mathcal{B}$ associated with the patients $h_1, \ldots, h_n$, respectively. Then, the attacker proceeds as follows:

- Apply *feature extractor* to all WSIs, obtaining feature vectors $w[p], w[b_1], \ldots, w[b_n] \in \mathbf{R}^k$ corresponding to the WSIs, respectively. Here, k is the number of features extracted from each WSI, typically in the thousands. We use several standard neural networks for this extraction, such as VGG-16 [8], ResNet [3], etc.
- Apply *similarity measure* M to all pairs of vectors $w[p]$ and $w[b_i]$, obtaining $M(w[p], w[b_i])$ for all $1 \leq i \leq n$.
- Assign the WSI probe p to the patient with the WSI b_i with the maximum $M(w[p], w[b_j])$ among all $b_1, \ldots, b_n$, i.e., such that

$$i \in argmax_j \{M(w[p], w[b_j]) \mid j = 1, \ldots, n\} \tag{2}$$

In case *argmax* contains more than one index, we select the smallest one.

We used the cosine similarity and Euclidean distance as the similarity measure.

Only later we realized that our implementation of the attack model is related to the "prosecutor model" [1,2]—i.e., the attacker knowing or assuming that the patient is in the background.

1.4   Experimental Results

A quite extensive evaluation of our approach is presented in the later parts of [4]; strictly speaking, these parts are unrelated to the formal methods. Here comes dirty experimental computer science with a bag full of nasty tricks. However, let me present at least some highlights. We evaluated our attacker model using the R_s metric on 558 slides from 80 patients. The most interesting (hopefully) are the following observations:

- When the probe and the patient's WSI come from consecutive cuts (i.e., directly side by side), our attacker matches them with the worst-case probe attack success rate R_s close to one.
- When the probe and the patient's WSI come from cuts that are not consecutive, the average value of R_s drops with distance. However, even with the relatively large distance of approximately 3 - 5 mm, the R_s has been 0.56 on average (the experiment repeated 20 times, IQR of R_s equal to 0.055). This is an unacceptable vulnerability for patients. Considering that we used a rather primitive model that almost everybody can employ using off-the-shelf neural networks, high-school math, and basic Python reveals a rather severe insecurity in sharing WSIs.

– We considered both whole slides (where borders of the samples might have been used to recognize concrete cuts) but also a restricted view of the samples where boundaries were not visible (see Fig. 3), which means that the similarity has to be guessed just from the structure of the tissue. Surprisingly, the attacker was still quite good. With the best feature extractor neural network and slides with a 3 - 5 mm distance, the average R_s was 0.33 (IQR 0.06).

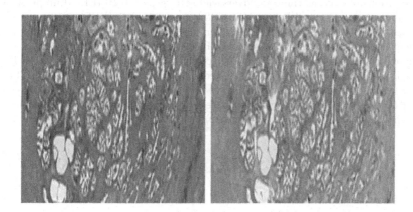

Fig. 3. Example of restricted areas of consecutive cuts. The image has been taken from [4].

2 Conclusion

This short text gives a basic idea behind formal methods to formulate a privacy problem precisely in digital pathology. It presents selected results of the subsequent experimental evaluation. The conclusion is that one has to be rather careful when sharing WSIs. They can be relatively successfully matched when they contain scans of spatially close cuts from the same block. The privacy problem is also relevant in the light of data provenance tracking [7,9]. See [4] for a more complete description of the problem, solution methods, and implications to the field of digital pathology. I conclude that formal methods are still a great (but painful) way to go when you want to formulate a practical problem precisely.

References

1. El Emam, K.: Risk-based de-identification of health data. IEEE Secur. Priv. **8**(3), 64–67 (2010)
2. El Emam, K.: Guide to the De-identification of Personal Health Information. CRC Press (2013)

3. He, K., Zhang, X., Ren, S., Sun, J.: Deep residual learning for image recognition. In: 2016 IEEE Conference on Computer Vision and Pattern Recognition (CVPR), pp. 770–778 (2015)
4. Holub, P., et al.: Privacy risks of whole-slide image sharing in digital pathology. Nat. Commun. **14**, 2577 (2023)
5. Holzinger, A., et al.: Machine learning and knowledge extraction in digital pathology needs an integrative approach. In: BIRS-IMLKE (2015)
6. Papernot, N., McDaniel, P., Jha, S., Fredrikson, M., Celik, Z.B., Swami, A.: The limitations of deep learning in adversarial settings. In: 2016 IEEE European Symposium on Security and Privacy (EuroS&P), pp. 372–387. IEEE (2016)
7. Plass, M., et al.: Provenance of specimen and data - a prerequisite for AI development in computational pathology. New Biotechnol. **78**, 22–28 (2023)
8. Simonyan, K., Zisserman, A.: Very deep convolutional networks for large-scale image recognition. In: Bengio, Y., LeCun, Y. (eds.) 3rd International Conference on Learning Representations, ICLR (2015)
9. Wittner, R., et al.: Lightweight distributed provenance model for complex real-world environments. Sci. Data **9**(1), 503 (2022)

A Uniform Framework for Language Inclusion Problems

Kyveli Doveri[1,2] , Pierre Ganty[1(✉)] , and Chana Weil-Kennedy[2]

[1] IMDEA Software Institute, Madrid, Spain
{kyveli.doveri,pierre.ganty}@imdea.org
[2] Universidad Politécnica de Madrid, Madrid, Spain
chana.weilkennedy@imdea.org

Abstract. We present a uniform approach for solving language inclusion problems. Our approach relies on a least fixpoint characterization and a quasiorder to compare words of the "smaller" language, reducing the inclusion check to a finite number of membership queries in the "larger" language. We present our approach in detail on the case of inclusion of a context-free language given by a grammar into a regular language. We then explore other inclusion problems and discuss how to apply our approach.

Keywords: Formal Languages · Inclusion · Containment · Algorithm · Quasiorders

1 Introduction

We are interested in the classical problem of language inclusion, which given two language acceptors, asks whether the language of one acceptor is contained into the language of the other one. This problem is traditionally solved by complementing the "larger" language, intersecting with the "smaller" language and checking for emptiness. Here, we avoid explicit complementation. We present a simple and uniform approach for deciding language inclusion problems based on the use of quasiorder relations on words. In this paper we are interested in the decidable cases of this problem, where the underlying alphabet of the language is a finite set of symbols. Even though we focus mainly on words of finite length our approach also applies to languages of infinite words. At its core, our approach relies on two notions: a *fixpoint characterization* of the "smaller" language and a *quasiorder* to compare words. Intuitively, the language inclusion algorithms we derive leverage the fixpoint characterization to compute increasingly many words of the "smaller" language. After a finite amount of time the computation is stopped. The algorithm then tests whether each of the computed words of the "smaller" language also belong to the "larger" one. If one word fails the test, the inclusion does not hold and we have a counterexample. Whether we can correctly conclude that inclusion holds depends on whether we have computed "enough" words. The rôle of the quasiorder is precisely that of detecting when "enough"

© The Author(s), under exclusive license to Springer Nature Switzerland AG 2024
S. Kiefer et al. (Eds.): *Taming the Infinities of Concurrency*, LNCS 14660, pp. 155–171, 2024.
https://doi.org/10.1007/978-3-031-56222-8_9

words have been computed. It must satisfy two properties: the first one ensures that it takes only a finite amount of time to compute "enough" words, and the second one ensures that if there exists a counterexample to inclusion, then it has been computed.

We present our approach in detail on the case of inclusion of a context-free language given by a grammar into a regular language, an EXPTIME-complete problem [20]. This case is simple yet non-trivial. After presenting our approach in Sect. 3, we give distinct quasiorders that can be used in the decision procedure in Sect. 4. Section 5 then dives into the algorithmic aspects related to using the so-called state-based quasiorders. The state-based quasiorders enable some modifications of the inclusion algorithm ultimately leading to the so-called antichains algorithms [6,17]. We also show how the saturation approach put forward by Esparza et al. [10] can be leveraged for the particular inclusion problem of a straight-line program[1] into a finite state automaton. In Sect. 6 we talk about the other language classes to which our framework can be applied. We revisit the case where the two languages are given by finite state automata. Next, we investigate the case asking whether the trace set of a finite process (which is a regular language) is contained into the trace set of a Petri net, a case that was first solved by Esparza et al. [19]. To demonstrate the generality of the approach, we survey how it can also be leveraged for the case of two languages of infinite words accepted by Büchi automata. We finish by briefly mentioning a few more cases that can be tackled using our approach.

This paper works as an overview of our previous work on the topic, providing a simplified explanation and pointers to the previous papers. In particular, the section presenting our approach greatly simplifies the framework put forward in [13].

2   Preliminaries

Well-Quasiorders, Complete Lattices and Kleene Iterates. A *quasiorder* (qo) on a set E, is a binary relation $\ltimes \subseteq E \times E$ that is reflexive and transitive. A quasiorder $\ltimes$ is a *partial order* when $\ltimes$ is antisymmetric ($x \ltimes y \wedge y \ltimes x \implies x = y$). A *complete lattice* is a set E and a partial order $\ltimes$ on E such that every subset $X \subseteq E$ has a least upper bound (the *supremum*) in E.

A sequence $\{s_n\}_{n \in \mathbb{N}} \in E^{\mathbb{N}}$ on quasiordered set $(E, \ltimes)$ is *increasing* if for every $n \in \mathbb{N}$ we have $s_n \ltimes s_{n+1}$. For a function $f \colon E \to E$ on a quasiordered set $(E, \ltimes)$ and for all $n \in \mathbb{N}$, we define the n-th iterate $f^n \colon E \to E$ of f inductively as follows: $f^0 \triangleq \lambda x. x$; $f^{n+1} \triangleq f \circ f^n$. The denumerable sequence of *Kleene iterates* of f starting from the bottom value $\bot \in E$ is given by $\{f^n(\bot)\}_{n \in \mathbb{N}}$. A *fixpoint* of f is x such that $f(x) = x$. The *least fixpoint* of f is the smallest fixpoint of f with respect to $\ltimes$, if f has at least one fixpoint; it is denoted lfp f. Recall that when $(E, \ltimes)$ is a complete lattice and $f \colon E \to E$ is an monotone function (i.e. $d \ltimes d' \implies f(d) \ltimes f(d')$) then it follows from the Knaster-Tarski theorem

---

[1] Straight-line program are context-free grammars where at most one word is derived from each grammar variable.

that f has a least fixpoint lfp f which, provided f is continuous[2], is given by the supremum of the increasing sequence of Kleene iterates of f.

Given a quasiorder $\ltimes$ on a set E, and $X \subseteq E$ a subset, let $\uparrow_\ltimes X$ denote the upward closure of X with respect to $\ltimes$ given by $\{y \in E \mid \exists x \in X.x \ltimes y\}$. A quasiorder $\ltimes$ on E is a *well-quasiorder* (wqo) if for every infinite sequence $\{S_n\}_{n \in \mathbb{N}} \in \wp(E)^{\mathbb{N}}$ such that $\uparrow_\ltimes S_1 \subseteq \uparrow_\ltimes S_2 \subseteq \cdots$ we have that there exists $i \in \mathbb{N}$ such that $\uparrow_\ltimes S_i \supseteq \uparrow_\ltimes S_{i+1}$, namely, $\ltimes$ is a wqo iff there is no infinite strictly increasing chain of upward closed subsets in E.

There are other equivalent definitions for wqo but the one using upward closed sets is the most convenient for our purpose. One property of wqo we will leverage throughout the paper is that the component wise lifting of a wqo remains a wqo, namely, given $n \in \mathbb{N}$, if $\ltimes$ is a wqo then so is $\ltimes^n$.

Finally, we introduce the lifting of the qo $\ltimes$ to sets by defining $\sqsubseteq_\ltimes \subseteq \wp(E) \times \wp(E)$ as follows:

$$X \sqsubseteq_\ltimes Y \overset{\triangle}{\Longleftrightarrow} \forall x \in X, \exists y \in Y, y \ltimes x \ .$$

It is routine to check that $\sqsubseteq_\ltimes$ is a quasiorder as well and also that $X \sqsubseteq_\ltimes Y$ iff $\uparrow_\ltimes X \subseteq \uparrow_\ltimes Y$. Given the previous equivalence, the rationale to introduce $\sqsubseteq_\ltimes$ is algorithmic since $\sqsubseteq_\ltimes$ is straightforward to implement for finite sets X, Y given a decision procedure for $\ltimes$; whereas $\uparrow_\ltimes X \subseteq \uparrow_\ltimes Y$ does not give a straightforward implementation even when X and Y are finite and $\ltimes$ is decidable.

Alphabets, Words and Languages. An *alphabet* is a nonempty finite set of symbols, generally denoted by Σ. A *word* is a sequence of symbols over the alphabet Σ. The set of finite words and the set of infinite words over Σ are denoted by Σ^* and Σ^ω respectively. We denote by ε the *empty word* and define $\Sigma^+ \triangleq \Sigma^* \setminus \{\varepsilon\}$. A *language of finite words* over Σ is a subset of Σ^*. A *language of infinite words* or *ω-language* over Σ is a subset of Σ^ω.

Finite Automata. A *finite automaton* (FA) on an alphabet Σ is a tuple $\mathcal{A} = (Q, \delta, q_I, F)$ where Q is a finite set of states including an initial state $q_I \in Q$, $\delta: Q \times \Sigma \to \wp(Q)$ is a transition function, and $F \subseteq Q$ is a subset of final states. Let $q \overset{a}{\to} q'$ denote a transition $q' \in \delta(q, a)$ that we lift to finite words by transitive and reflexive closure, thus writing $q \overset{u}{\to}{}^* q'$ with $u \in \Sigma^*$. The language of finite words accepted by $\mathcal{A}$ is $L^*(\mathcal{A}) \triangleq \{u \in \Sigma^* \mid \exists q \in F.q_I \overset{u}{\to}{}^* q\}$. An *accepting trace* of $\mathcal{A}$ on an infinite word $w = a_0 a_1 \cdots \in \Sigma^\omega$ is an infinite sequence $q_0 \overset{a_0}{\to} q_1 \overset{a_1}{\to} q_2 \cdots$ such that $q_0 = q_I$ and $q_j \in F$ for infinitely many j's. The ω-language accepted by $\mathcal{A}$ is $L^\omega(\mathcal{A}) \triangleq \{\xi \in \Sigma^\omega \mid$ there is an accepting trace of $\mathcal{A}$ on $\xi\}$. We call $\mathcal{A}$ a Büchi automaton (BA) when we consider it as an acceptor of infinite words. A language $L \subseteq \Sigma^\omega$ is *ω-regular* if $L = L^\omega(\mathcal{A})$ for some BA $\mathcal{A}$.

---

[2] f is continuous iff f preserves least upper bounds of nonempty increasing chains.

Context-Free Grammars. A *context-free grammar* (CFG) or simply *grammar* on Σ is a tuple $\mathcal{G} = (V, P)$ where $V = \{X_1, \ldots, X_n\}$ is the finite set of variables, and P is the finite set of production rules $X_i \to \beta$ where $\beta \in (V \cup \Sigma)^*$. Given $\alpha, \alpha' \in (V \cup \Sigma)^*$, we write $\alpha \Rightarrow \alpha'$ if there exists $\gamma, \delta \in (V \cup \Sigma)^*$ and $X_i \to \beta \in P$ such that $\alpha = \gamma X_i \delta$ and $\alpha' = \gamma \beta \delta$. The reflexive and transitive closure of $\Rightarrow$ is written $\Rightarrow^*$. For $i \in [1, n]$, let $L_i(\mathcal{G}) = \{w \in \Sigma^* \mid X_i \Rightarrow^* w\}$. When we omit the subscript i it is meant to be 1, hence we define the *language accepted* by $\mathcal{G}$ as $L(\mathcal{G})$, that is $L_1(\mathcal{G})$ given by $\{w \in \Sigma^* \mid X_1 \Rightarrow^* w\}$. A CFG is in Chomsky normal form (CNF) if all of its production rules are of the form $X_j \to X_k X_l$, $X_j \to a$, or $X_1 \to \varepsilon$ where $X_j, X_k, X_l \in V$ and $a \in \Sigma$.

Example 1. Let $\mathcal{G}' = (V', P')$ be the CFG on $\Sigma = \{a, b\}$ given by $V' = \{X_1\}$ and $P' = \{X_1 \to \varepsilon, X_1 \to a X_1 b\}$. Notice that this grammar is not in CNF. The language $L(\mathcal{G}')$ is $\{a^n b^n \mid n \geq 0\}$. We can define a grammar $\mathcal{G} = (V, P)$ in CNF such that $L(\mathcal{G}) = L(\mathcal{G}')$. Let $V = \{X_1, X_2, X_3, X_4\}$ and P be the rules

$$X_1 \to \varepsilon \qquad\qquad X_2 \to a \qquad\qquad X_1 \to X_2 X_3$$
$$X_4 \to b \qquad\qquad X_3 \to X_1 X_4 \ .$$

3   Algorithm

In this section we outline the quasiorder-based approach to solving the inclusion problem of a context-free language into a regular language, which reduces the problem to finitely many membership queries. A membership query is a check of whether a given word belongs to a given language. More precisely, we consider the inclusion problem $L(\mathcal{G}) \subseteq M$ where $\mathcal{G}$ is a CFG and M is a regular language. To solve the inclusion problem, we select a subset S of words of $L(\mathcal{G})$ such that (i) S is finite, (ii) S is effectively computable, and (iii) S contains a counterexample to $L(\mathcal{G}) \subseteq M$ if the inclusion does not hold. Upon computing such a set S the inclusion check $L(\mathcal{G})$ into M reduces to finitely many membership queries of the words of S into M.

More concretely, the computation of S will be guided by a quasiorder $\ltimes$ on words. The set S of words is such that, as per the quasiorder $\ltimes$, the following holds: $S \subseteq L(\mathcal{G})$ and $L(\mathcal{G}) \sqsubseteq_\ltimes S$.[3] In that setting, for S to satisfy (i), we will require (1) $\ltimes$ to be a well-quasi order. Moreover for S to comply with (ii), we will require (2) $\ltimes$ to be decidable but also "monotonic" (it will become clear what it means and why we need this condition later). Finally, for S to comply with (iii), we first formalize the requirement:

$$L(\mathcal{G}) \subseteq M \iff \forall u \in S, \ u \in M \ . \qquad\qquad (\star)$$

Intuitively, it means that whatever set S we select needs to be included in M if the inclusion $L(\mathcal{G}) \subseteq M$ holds and otherwise the set S needs to contain at least one counterexample to the inclusion. To achieve this, we will require (3) $\ltimes$ to be M-preserving: A quasiorder $\ltimes \subseteq \Sigma^* \times \Sigma^*$ is said to be *M-preserving* when for every $u, v \in \Sigma^*$ if $u \in M$ and $u \ltimes v$ then $v \in M$.[4] To see how $\ltimes$

---

[3] We can even relax the inclusion $S \subseteq L(\mathcal{G})$ to the weaker condition $S \sqsubseteq_\ltimes L(\mathcal{G})$.

[4] This is equivalent to saying that M is upward-closed w.r.t. the quasiorder $\ltimes$.

being M-preserving enforces $(\star)$ let us first assume that $L(\mathcal{G}) \subseteq M$ holds. Since $S \subseteq L(\mathcal{G})$ and $L(\mathcal{G}) \subseteq M$, the direction $\Rightarrow$ of Eq. $(\star)$ holds. This still holds if we have the weaker condition $S \sqsubseteq_{\ltimes} L(\mathcal{G})$. In this case, for every $s \in S$ there exists $u \in L(\mathcal{G})$ such that $u \ltimes s$, hence the assumption $L(\mathcal{G}) \subseteq M$ together with the M-preservation show that $s \in M$. Now assume that the right-hand side of $(\star)$ holds and let $u \in L(\mathcal{G})$. Since $L(\mathcal{G}) \sqsubseteq_{\ltimes} S$ there is $s \in S$ such that $s \ltimes u$. Since $s \in M$, $s \ltimes u$ and $\ltimes$ is M-preserving we have $u \in M$.

To compute S we leverage a fixpoint characterization of $L(\mathcal{G})$. Then we effectively compute the set S by computing finitely many Kleene iterates of the fixpoint characterization of $L(\mathcal{G})$ so as to obtain a set S such that $L(\mathcal{G}) \sqsubseteq_{\ltimes} S$. In order to decide we have computed enough Kleene iterates we rely on $\sqsubseteq_{\ltimes}$ (which is why we need $\ltimes$ to be decidable). We also need $\ltimes$ to satisfy a so-called monotonicity condition for otherwise we cannot guarantee that S satisfies $L(\mathcal{G}) \sqsubseteq_{\ltimes} S$.

Let us now turn to the characterization of $L(\mathcal{G})$ as the least fixpoint of a function. Fix a grammar $\mathcal{G}$ in CNF and M a regular language. Our algorithms also work when the grammar $\mathcal{G}$ is not given in CNF, we assume CNF for the simplicity of the presentation.

Least Fixpoint Characterization. To compute our finite set S we use a characterization of $L(\mathcal{G})$ as the least fixpoint of a function, and show that we can iteratively compute the function's Kleene iterates until we compute a set S such that $L(\mathcal{G}) \sqsubseteq_{\ltimes} S$.

Example 2. Take the grammar $\mathcal{G}$ of Example 1 such that $L(\mathcal{G}) = \{a^n b^n \mid n \geq 0\}$. We define the function $F_{\mathcal{G}} \colon \wp(\Sigma^*)^4 \to \wp(\Sigma^*)^4$ where $(L_1, L_2, L_3, L_4) \in \wp(\Sigma^*)^4$ is a vector of languages of finite words as follows:

$$F_{\mathcal{G}} \colon (L_1, L_2, L_3, L_4) \mapsto (L_2 L_3 \cup \{\varepsilon\}, \{a\}, L_1 L_4, \{b\}) \ .$$

If we apply $F_{\mathcal{G}}$ to the empty vector $(\emptyset, \emptyset, \emptyset, \emptyset) \in \wp(\Sigma^*)^4$, we get the vector of languages $(\{\varepsilon\}, \{a\}, \emptyset, \{b\})$ (recall that $L\emptyset = \emptyset$ and $\emptyset L = \emptyset$ for any language L). Applying $F_{\mathcal{G}}$ to this last vector we obtain $(\{\varepsilon\}, \{a\}, \{b\}, \{b\})$, i.e. $F_{\mathcal{G}}^2(\emptyset, \emptyset, \emptyset, \emptyset) = (\{\varepsilon\}, \{a\}, \{b\}, \{b\})$. We give a list of the first few repeated applications of $F_{\mathcal{G}}$ to the empty vector.

$$F_{\mathcal{G}}(\vec{\emptyset}) = (\{\varepsilon\}, \{a\}, \emptyset, \{b\})$$
$$F_{\mathcal{G}}^2(\vec{\emptyset}) = (\{\varepsilon\}, \{a\}, \{b\}, \{b\})$$
$$F_{\mathcal{G}}^3(\vec{\emptyset}) = (\{ab, \varepsilon\}, \{a\}, \{b\}, \{b\})$$
$$F_{\mathcal{G}}^4(\vec{\emptyset}) = (\{ab, \varepsilon\}, \{a\}, \{ab^2, b\}, \{b\})$$
$$F_{\mathcal{G}}^5(\vec{\emptyset}) = (\{a^2 b^2, ab, \varepsilon\}, \{a\}, \{ab^2, b\}, \{b\})$$
$$F_{\mathcal{G}}^6(\vec{\emptyset}) = (\{a^2 b^2, ab, \varepsilon\}, \{a\}, \{a^2 b^3, ab^2, b\}, \{b\})$$
$$F_{\mathcal{G}}^7(\vec{\emptyset}) = (\{a^3 b^3, a^2 b^2, ab, \varepsilon\}, \{a\}, \{a^2 b^3, ab^2, b\}, \{b\}) \ .$$

It is not hard to see that for all words $a^n b^n \in L(\mathcal{G})$, there exists an i such that $a^n b^n$ appears in the first component of $F_{\mathcal{G}}^i(\vec{\emptyset})$. In fact $i = 2n + 1$.

We now formally define the function $F_\mathcal{G}$ over $\wp(\Sigma^*)^n$, i.e. over n-vectors of languages of finite words over Σ, where n is the number of variables of our grammar $\mathcal{G}$. Let $\mathcal{L} = (L_1, \ldots, L_n) \in \wp(\Sigma^*)^n$ be an n-vector of languages $L_1, \ldots, L_n$. For each $j \in [1, n]$, the j-th component of $F_\mathcal{G}(\mathcal{L})$, denoted $F_\mathcal{G}(\mathcal{L})_j$, is defined as:

$$F_\mathcal{G}(\mathcal{L})_j \triangleq \bigcup_{X_j \to X_k X_{k'} \in P} L_k L_{k'} \cup \bigcup_{a \in \Sigma \cup \{\varepsilon\},\, X_j \to a \in P} \{a\} \ .$$

We have the following least fixpoint characterization for $\mathcal{G}$.

Proposition 3 (Least fixpoint characterization). *For all $i \in \{1, \ldots, n\}$ we have $L_i(\mathcal{G}) = (\mathrm{lfp}\, F_\mathcal{G})_i$.*

Proof. The function $F_\mathcal{G}$ is increasing and the supremum of the increasing sequence of its Kleene iterates starting at the bottom value $(\emptyset, \ldots, \emptyset) \in \wp(\Sigma^*)^n$ is the vector equal to $\{u \in \Sigma^* \mid X_j \Rightarrow^* u\}$ for each $j \in [1, n]$. Therefore, by the Knaster-Tarski theorem applied to the complete lattice $(\wp(\Sigma^*)^n, \subseteq^n)$ and $F_\mathcal{G}$, $\mathrm{lfp}\, F_\mathcal{G} = (\{u \in \Sigma^* \mid X_j \Rightarrow^* u\})_{j \in [1,n]}$. Thus, $(\mathrm{lfp}\, F_\mathcal{G})_i = L_i(\mathcal{G})$. □

Remark 4. The function definition uses the fact that $\mathcal{G}$ is given in CNF, notably that its rules are of the form $X_j \to X_k X_{k'}$. However a function $F'_\mathcal{G}$ can be defined for a grammar $\mathcal{G}$ in any form such that $(\mathrm{lfp}\, F'_\mathcal{G}) = (L_1(\mathcal{G}), \ldots, L_n(\mathcal{G}))$ and if $\mathcal{G}$ is in CNF then $F'_\mathcal{G}$ and $F_\mathcal{G}$ coincide, see [12, Definition 2.9.1 and Theorem 2.9.3].

The ordering $\sqsubseteq_{\ltimes^n}$ is used to compare the Kleene iterates of the function $F_\mathcal{G}$. For it to be apt to detect convergence, hence when the algorithm should stop, the quasiorder $\ltimes$ needs to be monotonic. A quasiorder is *monotonic* if it is right-monotonic and left-monotonic. A quasiorder $\ltimes$ on Σ^* is *right-monotonic* (respectively *left-monotonic*) if for all $u, v \in \Sigma^*$, for all $a \in \Sigma$, $u \ltimes v$ implies $ua \ltimes va$ (respectively $u \ltimes v$ implies $au \ltimes av$).

Proposition 5 ($\sqsubseteq_\ltimes$ monotonicity). *Let $\ltimes$ be a monotonic quasiorder on Σ^*. If $Y \sqsubseteq_{\ltimes^n} S$ then $F_\mathcal{G}(Y) \sqsubseteq_{\ltimes^n} F_\mathcal{G}(S)$.*

Proof. Fix $j \in [1, n]$. We want to show that for all $y \in F_\mathcal{G}(Y)_j$ there exists $s \in F_\mathcal{G}(S)_j$ such that $s \ltimes y$. Let $y \in F_\mathcal{G}(Y)_j$. If there is an $a \in \Sigma \cup \{\varepsilon\}$ such that $X_j \to a \in P$ and $y = a$, then y is also in $F_\mathcal{G}(S)_j$ by definition. Since $\ltimes$ is a quasiorder it is reflexive, so $y \ltimes y$. Otherwise, by definition of $F_\mathcal{G}(Y)_j$, there exist $y_k \in Y_k, y_{k'} \in Y_{k'}$ such that $X_j \to X_k X_{k'} \in P$ and $y = y_k y_{k'}$. Since $Y \sqsubseteq_{\ltimes^n} S$, there exist $s_k \in S_k, s_{k'} \in S_{k'}$ such that $s_k \ltimes y_k$ and $s_{k'} \ltimes y_{k'}$. Using $X_j \to X_k X_{k'} \in P$ and the definition of $F_\mathcal{G}(S)_j$, we have $s_k s_{k'} \in F_\mathcal{G}(S)_j$. By right-monotonicity of our quasiorder, $s_k s_{k'} \ltimes y_k s_{k'}$. By left-monotonicity, $y_k s_{k'} \ltimes y_k y_{k'}$. Since quasiorders are transitive, we obtain $s_k s_{k'} \ltimes y_k y_{k'}$. We thus conclude from the above that $F_\mathcal{G}(S)_j \sqsubseteq_\ltimes F_\mathcal{G}(Y)_j$, hence it is easy to see that $F_\mathcal{G}(S) \sqsubseteq_{\ltimes^n} F_\mathcal{G}(Y)$. □

Under the assumption of monotonicity on our M-preserving well-quasiorder we can iteratively compute a finite set S such that $L(\mathcal{G}) \sqsubseteq_\ltimes S$ using the function $F_\mathcal{G}$ as shown by the next proposition.

Proposition 6 (Stabilization). *Let $\ltimes$ be a wqo on Σ^*. There is an $m \geq 0$ such that $F_{\mathcal{G}}^{m+1}(\vec{\emptyset}) \sqsubseteq_{\ltimes^n} F_{\mathcal{G}}^m(\vec{\emptyset})$; and if $\ltimes$ is monotonic then $\mathrm{lfp}\, F_{\mathcal{G}} \sqsubseteq_{\ltimes^n} F_{\mathcal{G}}^m(\vec{\emptyset})$.*

Proof. For simplicity, we write this proof for the case where n, the number of variables in $\mathcal{G}$, is equal to 1. It holds also for $n > 1$ by reasoning component-wise. Since $\ltimes$ is a wqo on Σ^*, the set of upward closed sets of $\wp(\Sigma^*)$ ordered by inclusion has the ascending chain condition [5, Theorem 1.1], meaning there is no infinite strictly increasing sequence of upward closed sets. It is routine to check by induction using Proposition 5 that $F_{\mathcal{G}}^i(\emptyset) \sqsubseteq_\ltimes F_{\mathcal{G}}^{i+1}(\emptyset)$ for all $i \geq 0$. Therefore also $\uparrow_\ltimes F_{\mathcal{G}}^i(\emptyset) \subseteq \uparrow_\ltimes F_{\mathcal{G}}^{i+1}(\emptyset)$ for all $i \geq 0$. By the ascending chain condition, there exists a positive integer m such that $\uparrow_\ltimes F_{\mathcal{G}}^{m+1}(\emptyset) \subseteq \uparrow_\ltimes F_{\mathcal{G}}^m(\emptyset)$, which is equivalent to $F_{\mathcal{G}}^{m+1}(\emptyset) \sqsubseteq_\ltimes F_{\mathcal{G}}^m(\emptyset)$.

Assume that $\ltimes$ is monotonic. An induction using Proposition 5 and the above shows that for every $k \geq m$, $F_{\mathcal{G}}^{k+1}(\emptyset) \sqsubseteq_\ltimes F_{\mathcal{G}}^k(\emptyset)$. Hence, by transitivity of $\sqsubseteq_\ltimes$ we deduce that for every $k \geq m$, $F_{\mathcal{G}}^k(\emptyset) \sqsubseteq_\ltimes F_{\mathcal{G}}^m(\emptyset)$. Recall that $\mathrm{lfp}\, F_{\mathcal{G}}$ is the supremum of the sequence of Kleene iterates of $F_{\mathcal{G}}$, i.e. of $\{F_{\mathcal{G}}^n(\emptyset)\}_{n\in\mathbb{N}}$. In the complete lattice $(\wp(\Sigma^*)^n, \subseteq^n)$, the supremum of $\{F_{\mathcal{G}}^n(\emptyset)\}_{n\in\mathbb{N}}$ is equal to $\bigcup_{n\in\mathbb{N}} F_{\mathcal{G}}^n(\emptyset)$. Thus $\mathrm{lfp}\, F_{\mathcal{G}} \sqsubseteq_\ltimes F_{\mathcal{G}}^m(\emptyset)$. $\square$

Algorithm. Given a regular language $M \subseteq \Sigma^*$ we say that a quasiorder $\ltimes \subseteq \Sigma^* \times \Sigma^*$ is *M-suitable* if it is 1) a wqo, 2) M-preserving, 3) monotonic and 4) decidable i.e., given two words u and v we can decide whether $u \ltimes v$. Intuitively a quasiorder is M-suitable if it can be used in our quasiorder-based framework to decide the inclusion problem $L(\mathcal{G}) \subseteq M$.

Algorithm 1: Algorithm for deciding $L(\mathcal{G}) \subseteq M$

Data: $\mathcal{G} = (V, P)$ CFG with n variables.
Data: M-suitable quasiorder $\ltimes$.
Data: Procedure deciding $u \in M$ given u.

1   cur $:= \vec{\emptyset}$;
2   **repeat**
3   prev $:=$ cur;
4   cur $:= F_{\mathcal{G}}(\text{prev})$;
5   **until** cur $\sqsubseteq_{\ltimes^n}$ prev;
6   **foreach** $u \in (\text{prev})_1$ **do**
7   **if** $u \notin M$ **then return** false
8   **return** true;

Theorem 7. *Algorithm 1 decides the inclusion problem $L(\mathcal{G}) \subseteq M$.*

Proof. As established by Proposition 6, given a monotonic decidable wqo $\ltimes$, lines 2 to 5 of Algorithm 1 compute, in finite time, a finite set equal to $F_{\mathcal{G}}^m(\vec{\emptyset})$

for some m such that lfp $F_{\mathcal{G}} \sqsubseteq_{\ltimes^n} F_{\mathcal{G}}{}^m(\vec{\emptyset})$. Moreover, since $F_{\mathcal{G}}{}^m(\vec{\emptyset}) \subseteq$ lfp $F_{\mathcal{G}}$, we find that $F_{\mathcal{G}}{}^m(\vec{\emptyset}) \sqsubseteq_{\ltimes}$ lfp $F_{\mathcal{G}}$. Since $\ltimes$ is M-preserving, Equation $(\star)$ holds for $F_{\mathcal{G}}{}^m(\vec{\emptyset})_1$, i.e.

$$L(\mathcal{G}) \subseteq M \iff \forall u \in F_{\mathcal{G}}{}^m(\vec{\emptyset})_1, \ u \in M \ .$$

Thus the algorithm is correct, and it terminates because there are only finitely many membership checks $u \in M$ in the for-loop at lines 6 and 7. □

Remark 8. The loop at lines 2 to 5 of the algorithm iteratively computes a vector of sets of words cur, updating its value to $F_{\mathcal{G}}$(prev) at line 4. The algorithm remains correct if we remove some words from prev before each new update, as long as the resulting vector prev is included in cur with respect to $\sqsubseteq_{\ltimes}$ (intuitively this ensures we do not lose any counter-examples). That is, we can replace the assignment line 3 by prev := cur' for any cur' $\subseteq$ cur such that cur $\sqsubseteq_{\ltimes}$ cur'; the correctness follows from Proposition 5.

4   Quasiorder Instantiation

We instantiate the algorithm with a quasiorder and give an example run. We then discuss other quasiorders with which the algorithm can be instantiated.

4.1   A State-Based Quasiorder

We present an M-suitable quasiorder to instantiate Algorithm 1. The quasiorder is derived from a finite automaton with language M. Given an automaton $\mathcal{A} = (Q, q_I, \delta, F)$ with $L(\mathcal{A}) = M$ and a word $u \in \Sigma^*$, we define the *context set* of u

$$\mathrm{ctx}^{\mathcal{A}}(u) \triangleq \{(q, q') \in Q^2 \mid q \xrightarrow{u}^* q'\} \ .$$

We derive the following quasiorder on Σ^*:

$$u \leq^{\mathcal{A}}_{\mathrm{ctx}} v \xLeftrightarrow{\triangle} \mathrm{ctx}^{\mathcal{A}}(u) \subseteq \mathrm{ctx}^{\mathcal{A}}(v) \ .$$

Proposition 9. *The quasiorder $\leq^{\mathcal{A}}_{ctx}$ is M-suitable.*

Proof. The result [13, Lemma 7.8] shows that $\leq^{\mathcal{A}}_{\mathrm{ctx}}$ is a M-preserving, monotonic wqo. Since for every $u \in \Sigma^*$ we can compute the finite set $\mathrm{ctx}^{\mathcal{A}}(u)$, we deduce that given two words u and v we can decide $u \leq^{\mathcal{A}}_{\mathrm{ctx}} v$. Thus, $\leq^{\mathcal{A}}_{\mathrm{ctx}}$ is M-suitable. □

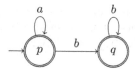

Fig. 1. Finite automaton $\mathcal{A}$ recognizing language a^*b^*.

Let M be the regular language a^*b^*. Consider the automaton $\mathcal{A}$ depicted in Fig. 1. It has two states p, q and accepts M, i.e. $L(\mathcal{A}) = M$. We give an execution of our algorithm instantiated with $\leq_{\mathrm{ctx}}^{\mathcal{A}}$ to decide $L \subseteq M$, where L is the language recognized by the grammar $\mathcal{G}$ of Example 1, that is $L = L(\mathcal{G}) = \{a^n b^n \mid n \geq 0\}$. We compute the contexts of the words appearing in the first iterations of $F_{\mathcal{G}}$, as computed in Example 2.

$$\mathrm{ctx}^{\mathcal{A}}(\varepsilon) = \{(p,p),(q,q)\} \qquad \mathrm{ctx}^{\mathcal{A}}(b) = \{(p,q),(q,q)\}$$
$$\mathrm{ctx}^{\mathcal{A}}(a) = \{(p,p)\} \qquad \mathrm{ctx}^{\mathcal{A}}(w) = \{(p,q)\}, \qquad \forall w \in a^+ b^+ \ .$$

The algorithm computes the first four iterations of $F_{\mathcal{G}}$ and then stops. We have $F_{\mathcal{G}}^5(\emptyset,\emptyset,\emptyset,\emptyset)_1 = \{a^2b^2, ab, \varepsilon\}$, $F_{\mathcal{G}}^4(\emptyset,\emptyset,\emptyset,\emptyset)_1 = \{ab, \varepsilon\}$, and the languages of the other component are the same. Since $ab \leq_{\mathrm{ctx}}^{\mathcal{A}} a^2b^2$, we have that $F_{\mathcal{G}}^5(\emptyset,\emptyset,\emptyset,\emptyset) \sqsubseteq_{(\leq_{\mathrm{ctx}}^{\mathcal{A}})^4} F_{\mathcal{G}}^4(\emptyset,\emptyset,\emptyset,\emptyset)$, hence lfp $F_{\mathcal{G}} \sqsubseteq_{(\leq_{\mathrm{ctx}}^{\mathcal{A}})^4} F_{\mathcal{G}}^4(\emptyset,\emptyset,\emptyset,\emptyset)$. For each $u \in F_{\mathcal{G}}^4(\emptyset,\emptyset,\emptyset,\emptyset)_1$ we check if $u \in a^*b^*$. This is the case, and the algorithm returns true.

4.2   Other Quasiorders

The first kind of quasiorder we presented was a *state-based* quasiorder derived from a finite automaton for the language M. Here we present a *syntactic* quasiorder based on the syntactic structure of the language M. Given a word $u \in \Sigma^*$, we define the set

$$\mathrm{ctx}^M(u) \triangleq \{(w,w') \in \Sigma^* \times \Sigma^* \mid wuw' \in M\} \ .$$

We derive the following quasiorder on Σ^*:

$$u \leq_{\mathrm{ctx}}^M v \overset{\triangle}{\Longleftrightarrow} \mathrm{ctx}^M(u) \subseteq \mathrm{ctx}^M(v) \ .$$

Following [5], we call this the Myhill order.

Proposition 10. *The quasiorder $\leq_{\mathrm{ctx}}^M$ is M-suitable. Moreover, it is the coarsest among the M-suitable quasiorders.*

Proof. Since M is a regular language, by Lemma 7.6 (a) in [13] $\leq_{\mathrm{ctx}}^{\mathcal{A}}$ is M-suitable. By Lemma 7.6 (b) if $\ltimes$ is a M-suitable quasiorder then for every $u \in \Sigma^*$ we have $\uparrow_{\ltimes}\{u\} \subseteq \uparrow_{\leq_{\mathrm{ctx}}^M}\{u\}$, in other words $u \ltimes v$ implies $u \leq_{\mathrm{ctx}}^M v$. Hence, $\leq_{\mathrm{ctx}}^M$ is coarser than any M-suitable quasiorder. $\qquad\qquad\square$

Notice that given two words u and v deciding $u \leq_{\text{ctx}}^{M} v$ reduces to an inclusion between two regular languages, it is therefore PSPACE-complete to decide it. On the other hand deciding $u \leq_{\text{ctx}}^{\mathcal{A}} v$ is PTIME.

5 Algorithmic Aspects

In Sect. 4.2 we considered the so-called state-based quasiorders for Algorithm 1. We can leverage state-based quasiorders even further and modify the algorithm to drop words entirely and replace them by their context. As we will see, contexts (that is sets of pairs of states) carry sufficient information to perform all the tasks required by the algorithm (namely comparison between words, updates via word concatenation and word membership tests).

5.1 A State-Based Variant

As a first step, consider a variant of Algorithm 1 where words are stored together with their context: instead of w we will store $(w, \text{ctx}^{\mathcal{A}}(w))$. This change preserves the logic of the algorithm, hence its correctness. Observe that because the contexts are readily available they can be used directly for comparisons: instead of computing contexts each time two words need to be compared, the algorithm compares the already-computed contexts. Furthermore, and this is key, contexts can be updated during computations because they can be characterized inductively. Indeed, given $\text{ctx}^{\mathcal{A}}(w)$ and $\text{ctx}^{\mathcal{A}}(w')$, $\text{ctx}^{\mathcal{A}}(ww')$ can be computed as follows:

$$\text{ctx}^{\mathcal{A}}(ww') = \{(p, q) \mid \exists p' : (p, p') \in \text{ctx}^{\mathcal{A}}(w) \land (p', q) \in \text{ctx}^{\mathcal{A}}(w')\} \ .$$

In addition, membership queries in $M = L(\mathcal{A})$ have an equivalent counterpart on contexts: $w \in M$ iff $\text{ctx}^{\mathcal{A}}(w) \cap (\{q_I\} \times F) \neq \emptyset$. As a consequence of the above, Algorithm 1 can drop words entirely and focus exclusively on contexts. We call this algorithm the antichains algorithm following a prolific history of such algorithms like [17] (for the CFG into REG case) and starting with [6] (for the REG into REG case).

Next, we will see a data-structure for contexts tailored to the case where $L(\mathcal{G})$ is a singleton. This data-structure, which leverages the automaton structure of regular languages, has been studied by Esparza, Rossmanith and Schwoon in a paper from 2000 [10]. Their paper list several potential use of the data-structure but not the one we are giving next.

5.2 A Data-Structure for the Case of Straight Line Programs

In 2000 Esparza, Rossmanith and Schwoon published a paper [10] in the EATCS bulletin where they give an algorithm which allows to solve a number of elementary problems on context-free grammar including identifying useless variables, and deciding emptiness or finiteness. The algorithm is a "saturation" algorithm that takes as input a finite state automaton $\mathcal{A} = (Q, \delta, q_I, F)$ and a context-free grammar $\mathcal{G} = (V, P)$ on an alphabet Σ. It adds transitions to $\mathcal{A}$ so that, upon saturation, its resulting language corresponds to the following set of words on alphabet $(V \cup \Sigma)$:

$$\{\alpha \in (V \cup \Sigma)^* \mid \exists w \in L(\mathcal{A}) \colon \alpha \Rightarrow^* w\} \ .$$

This set, which they denote as $\mathrm{pre}^*(L(\mathcal{A}))$, comprises the sentences of the grammar $\mathcal{G}$ which, upon application of zero or more production rules, becomes a word in $L(\mathcal{A})$. At the logical level, the algorithm consists of one saturation rule and nothing more which states that if $X \to \beta \in P$ and $q \xrightarrow{\beta}{}^* q'$ then add a transition $q \xrightarrow{X} q'$ to $\mathcal{A}$.

We show that this approach is relevant to our problem. Let us consider the inclusion problem CFG into REG where we have the restriction that for every $i \in [1, n]$ we have that $L(\mathcal{G})_i$ is either a singleton word or it is empty: $L(\mathcal{G})_i \neq \emptyset \implies L(\mathcal{G})_i \in \Sigma^*$. Such grammars are called straight line programs (SLP) in the literature. As we have shown in the past [14], the inclusion problem for straight line programs has direct applications in regular expression matching for text compressed using grammar-based techniques. Intuitively, the regular expression is translated into $L(\mathcal{A})$ and the compressed text is given by $L(\mathcal{G})$. Then we have that the regular expression has a match in the decompressed text iff $L(\mathcal{G}) \subseteq L(\mathcal{A})$.

In the context of our inclusion algorithm, the assumption that $\mathcal{G}$ is a straight line program ensures that, for every m, each entry in the vector $F_{\mathcal{G}}^m(\vec{\emptyset})$ is either the empty set or a singleton word. Now consider the state-based variant of Algorithm 1 discussed above where words are replaced by their contexts. Because of the SLP assumption we have that each entry of the cur and prev vectors in Algorithm 1 stores a set of pairs of states: each entry is given by a set $P \subseteq Q^2$ as opposed to $P \subseteq \wp(Q^2)$ when $\mathcal{G}$ need not be a SLP.

A possible data-structure to store such a set P is a graph where nodes are given by Q and whose edges coincides with the pairs of states of P. Add labels on edges and you can encode a vector of sets like P, namely an edge from q to q' with label m encodes that the pair (q, q') belongs to the mth component of the vector. Next, observe that the updates to be carried out on the vectors cur and prev via $F_{\mathcal{G}}$ as prescribed by Algorithm 1 can be implemented via the saturation rule described above. For instance, assume $F_{\mathcal{G}}$ requires to update the m-th entry of cur following the production rule $X_m \to X_k X_{k'}$. The corresponding update to the graph-based data structure adds an edge labelled m between states (q, q') if there exists a node q'' such that (q, q'') and (q'', q') are two edges respectively labelled by k and k'. It is worth pointing that this update rule coincides with the above saturation rule for the rule $X_m \to X_k X_{k'}$. Therefore the saturation rule together with the underlying graph data-structure leveraging the automaton $\mathcal{A}$ enable a state-based implementation of Algorithm 1 tailored to the case SLP into REG. It is worth pointing out that Esparza et al. [10] work out the precise time and space complexity of implementing the saturation rule. Ultimately, we obtain an algorithm in PTIME for the SLP into REG inclusion problem. A more detailed complexity analysis can be found in Valero's PhD thesis [22, Chapter 5].

6 Other Language Inclusion Problems

In this section we talk about the other language classes to which our framework can be applied.

6.1 REG ⊆ REG

We consider the case where $\mathcal{G}$ is a right regular grammar i.e. a grammar in which all production rules are of the form $X_j \rightarrow X_k\, a$, $X_j \rightarrow a$, or $X_j \rightarrow \varepsilon$ where X_j and X_k are variables and $a \in \Sigma$. The function $F_{\mathcal{G}}$ of the least fixpoint characterization of $L(\mathcal{G})$ is now defined as follows. Let $\mathcal{L} = (L_1, \ldots, L_n) \in \wp(\Sigma^*)^n$ define:

$$F_{\mathcal{G}}(\mathcal{L})_j \triangleq \bigcup_{X_j \rightarrow X_k\, a \in P} L_k\{a\} \cup \bigcup_{a \in \Sigma \cup \{\varepsilon\},\ X_j \rightarrow a \in P} \{a\} \ .$$

The same algorithm with this new $F_{\mathcal{G}}$ is also correct. Notice however that for Propositions 5 and 6 to be correct it is now sufficient for ⋉ to only be right-monotonic. This is because the new $F_{\mathcal{G}}$ only uses right-concatenations in its production rules. As a consequence of this, we can relax $\leq_{\text{ctx}}^{\mathcal{A}}$ into the coarser quasiorder $\leq_{\text{post}}^{\mathcal{A}}$ where, we just replace the context ctx of a word u by the set post containing all the states reachable with the word u from the initial state of $\mathcal{A}$, that is, $\{q \mid q_I \xrightarrow{u}{}^* q'\}$. Similarly, we can relax $\leq_{\text{ctx}}^{M}$ into the Nerode quasiorder of M. In the Nerode quasiorder, a word u subsumes v if, for every $w \in \Sigma^*$, $uw \in M$ implies $vw \in M$.

6.2 REG ⊆ Petri Net Traces

In 1999 Petr Jančar, Javier Esparza and Faron Moller [19] published a paper which solved several language inclusion problems including the problem asking whether the trace set of a finite-state labelled transition system is included in the trace set of a Petri net (which defines a labelled transition system with possibly infinitely many states). In this section we give a decision procedure following the framework we put in place in the previous sections. As we will see our decision procedure is very close yet slightly different from the one they proposed.

It is worth pointing that their exposition favors a process theory viewpoint rather than an automata theory viewpoint which is why they talk about trace sets and labelled transition systems (or processes) instead of languages and acceptors. With this view in mind, the notion of alphabet Σ becomes a set of *actions* in which they include a distinguished *silent* action τ. The τ resembles the ε symbol used in the automata theoretic setting. In their paper, they define and prove correct an algorithm to decide whether the trace set given by a finite-state labelled transition system is included into the trace set given by a Petri net.

Our first step is to extract from their paper an ordering on words that is M-suitable. In our setting, M is the trace set given by a Petri net. The ordering is a "state-based" ordering defined upon the underlying Petri net. The definition relies on the notion of ω-markings which, intuitively, are vectors with as many entries as there are places in the Petri net and such that each entry takes its value in $\mathbb{N} \cup \{\omega\}$. Let P be the set of places of the Petri net, then $\mathbb{N}_\omega^P$ denote the set of ω-markings thereof. Given two ω-markings $\hat{M}$ and $\hat{M}'$ they define (p. 481) an ordering $\leqslant$ between them such that $\hat{M} \leqslant \hat{M}'$ if $\hat{M}(p) \leqslant \hat{M}'(p)$ for all $p \in P$ such that ω is greater than every natural. They then lift the ordering $\leqslant$ to sets of ω-markings as follows. Given two sets $\mathcal{M}, \mathcal{M}' \subseteq \mathbb{N}_\omega^P$ define $\mathcal{M} \leqslant \mathcal{M}'$ iff for each $M \in \mathcal{M}$ there exists $M' \in \mathcal{M}'$ such that $M \leqslant M'$. This relation is a quasiorder on sets of ω-marking which becomes a well-quasiorder when restricted to the finite sets of ω-markings. That is $\leqslant$ is a wqo on $\wp_{\mathrm{fin}}(\mathbb{N}_\omega^P)$ (their Corollary 2.17).

We are now in position to define our ordering on words (what they call traces). Let $u, v \in (\Sigma \setminus \{\tau\})^*$ define

$$u \lessdot v \text{ iff } \max(\mathcal{C}(\overset{u}{\Rightarrow}(\{M_0\}))) \leqslant \max(\mathcal{C}(\overset{v}{\Rightarrow}(\{M_0\}))) \ .$$

Let us discuss this definition starting with the expressions $\max(\mathcal{C}(\overset{u}{\Rightarrow}(\{M_0\})))$ which denote finite sets of ω-markings (i.e. $\max(\mathcal{C}(\overset{u}{\Rightarrow}(\{M_0\}))) \in \wp_{\mathrm{fin}}(\mathbb{N}_\omega^P)$ so that the ordering $\leqslant$ is the well-quasiorder described above). The details of the definition $\max(\mathcal{C}(\overset{u}{\Rightarrow}(\{M_0\})))$ would take too much space to include here but intuitively the finite set of ω-markings is a finite description of the possibly infinitely many markings (which are ω-markings with no entry set to ω) the Petri net can reach guided by the sequence of actions in u from its initial marking M_0 (the $\mathcal{C}$ and the max operator turn a possibly infinite sets of markings into a finite set of ω-markings).

Let us now turn to the M-suitability of $\lessdot$. As we have already shown the ordering $\lessdot$ is a wqo. Second it is routine to check that monotonicity follows from their Lemma 2.5(a) and Lemma 2.9 [19]. Indeed Lemma 2.5(a) states that if $\mathcal{M} \leqslant \mathcal{M}'$ then $\overset{a}{\Rightarrow}(\mathcal{M}) \leqslant \overset{a}{\Rightarrow}(\mathcal{M}')$ for every $a \in \Sigma \setminus \{\tau\}$; while Lemma 2.9 states that $\mathcal{M} \leqslant \mathcal{M}'$ then $\max(\mathcal{C}(\mathcal{M})) \leqslant \max(\mathcal{C}(\mathcal{M}'))$.

Next we show that M-preservation holds by simply observing that w is a trace of the Petri net iff $\overset{w}{\Rightarrow}(\{M_0\}) \neq \emptyset$, hence that if $u \lessdot v$ and u is a trace then v is a trace by definition of $\lessdot$, their Lemma 2.7(a) showing $\mathcal{M} \subseteq \mathcal{C}(\mathcal{M})$, and the definition of max (p. 482).

It remains to show that $\lessdot$ is decidable which is easily established by first using the result of their Lemma 2.15 stating that we can effectively construct $\max(\mathcal{C}(\overset{a}{\Rightarrow}(\{\mathcal{M}\})))$ given a finite set $\mathcal{M}$ of ω-markings and an action $a \in \Sigma$; and second by using the result of their Lemma 2.14 to lift (inductively) their effectivity result from actions to finite sequences of actions. Notice that this effectivity result for finite sequences of actions also gives a decision procedure for the membership in the trace set of the Petri net.

With all the ingredients in place, we obtain an algorithm deciding whether the trace set of a finite-state labelled transition system is included into the trace set of a Petri net. It is worth pointing out that their algorithm [19, Theorem 3.2] performs less comparisons of finite sets of ω-markings than ours. A tree structure restricts the comparisons they do during the exploration to pairs of sets of ω-markings, provided one is the ancestor (w.r.t. tree structure) of the other. Since our algorithm does not have such a restriction, we claim that we are making at least as many comparisons as their algorithm. This potentially results in a shorter execution time and less membership checks in our algorithm.

6.3   Languages of Infinite Words

In this section we give the idea on how we extended the framework to the inclusion problem between languages of infinite words [9]. In particular we studied the inclusion between two ω-regular languages and the inclusion of an ω-context-free language into an ω-regular language.

Consider the inclusion problem $L^\omega(\mathcal{A}) \subseteq M$ where $\mathcal{A}$ is a BA and M is an ω-regular language. The first step is to reduce the inclusion check to the ultimately periodic words of the languages, as they suffice to decide the inclusion [3]. These are infinite words of the form uv^ω for $u \in \Sigma^*$ a finite prefix and $v \in \Sigma^+$ a finite period. We compare two ultimately periodic words using a pair of quasiorders $\bowtie_1$ and $\bowtie_2$ on finite words. The first quasiorder, $\bowtie_1$, compares the prefixes of ultimately periodic words, while the second quasiorder, $\bowtie_2$, compares their periods. As expected the quasiorders need to be M-preserving right-monotonic decidable wqos. In this setting M-preservation means that if $uv^\omega \in M$ and $(u,v) \bowtie_1 \times \bowtie_2 (u',v')$ then $u'v'^\omega \in M$. For example, by taking $\bowtie_1$ to be $\leq^{\mathcal{B}}_{post}$ and $\bowtie_2$ to be $\leq^{\mathcal{B}}_{ctx}$, where $\mathcal{B}$ is a BA such that $L^\omega(\mathcal{B}) = M$, we have an M-preserving pair of right-monotonic decidable wqos.

An M-preserving pair of wqos ensures the existence of a finite subset $S = S_1 \times S_2$ of ultimately periodic words that is sufficient to decide the inclusion. In order to compute such a subset S we establish a fixpoint characterization for the sets of prefixes and periods of L. Finally, we decide the inclusion by checking membership in M for every ultimately periodic word uv^ω such that $(u,v) \in S$.

In the case where $\mathcal{A}$ is a Büchi Pushdown (and therefore where $L^\omega(\mathcal{A})$ is an ω-context-free language), the only difference lies in the fixpoint functions which now use both right and left concatenations. Thus the pair of quasiorders in this case should be monotonic. For example we can take both orders to be $\leq^{\mathcal{B}}_{ctx}$.

6.4   Pointers to Other Cases

In our paper [7], the approach is adapted to the inclusion problem between Visibly Pushdown Languages (VPL) (of finite words) and ω-VPL (of infinite words), classes of languages defined in [1]. In these cases, defining monotonicity conditions is challenging.

In the work by Henzinger et al. [16], the authors adapt our framework to solve their inclusion problem between operator-precedence languages [11]. These languages fall within a class that is strictly contained in deterministic context-free languages and, in turn, strictly contains VPL [4].

In [8], we further extend the framework for solving the inclusion $L^\omega(\mathcal{A}) \subseteq M$, for $\mathcal{A}$ an BA and M an ω-regular language, using a family of quasiorders instead of a pair of quasiorders. A family of quasiorders allows more pruning when searching for a counterexample, thus lesser membership queries at the end.

As we show in [13] it is also possible to define an M-suitable quasiorder leveraging pre-computed simulation relations on the states of an automaton for M. This quasiorder might be coarser than the state-based one presented in Sect. 4.1.

Some directions for future work are the inclusion of a context-free language into a superdeterministic context-free language [15], and the inclusion between tree automata. It is worth noting that least fixpoint characterizations exist for a very large number of language classes [18]. Eventually, we want to explore whether our approach can be adapted to the emptiness problem of alternating automata for finite and infinite words. The PhD thesis of Nicolas Maquet [21] suggests it can be done. In [2], Bonchi and Pous compare antichains and bisimulation up-to techniques. We want to extend this comparison, given the novel insights of our approach.

Acknowledgments. Pierre visited Javier during his first year of PhD, a visit that turned out to be a milestone in Pierre's career and has had influence up to this day. This visit also got Pierre a new colleague, a mentor and, most importantly, a friend. Pierre wishes to thank Javier from the bottom of his heart for all the good memories throughout the years. Chana is grateful to have had Javier as a PhD advisor and as an academic role model. She learned a lot from him, and benefited from the kind and studious atmosphere that he has established in his Chair at the Technical University of Munich. We also are thankful to the reviewers for their valuable feedback. This publication is part of the grant PID2022-138072OB-I00, funded by MCIN, FEDER, UE and has been partially supported by PRODIGY Project (TED2021-132464B-I00) funded by MCIN and the European Union NextGeneration.

References

1. Alur, R., Madhusudan, P.: Visibly pushdown languages. In: Proceedings of the Thirty-Sixth Annual ACM Symposium on Theory of Computing, pp. 202–211. ACM (2004). https://doi.org/10.1145/1007352.1007390
2. Bonchi, F., Pous, D.: Checking NFA equivalence with bisimulations up to congruence. ACM SIGPLAN Not. **48**, 457–468 (2013). https://doi.org/10.1145/2429069.2429124
3. Calbrix, H., Nivat, M., Podelski, A.: Ultimately periodic words of rational ω-languages. In: Brookes, S., Main, M., Melton, A., Mislove, M., Schmidt, D. (eds.) MFPS 1993. LNCS, vol. 802, pp. 554–566. Springer, Heidelberg (1994). https://doi.org/10.1007/3-540-58027-1_27

4. Crespi Reghizzi, S., Mandrioli, D.: Operator precedence and the visibly pushdown property. J. Comput. Syst. Sci. **78**(6), 1837–1867 (2012). https://doi.org/10.1016/j.jcss.2011.12.006
5. de Luca, A., Varricchio, S.: Well quasi-orders and regular languages. Acta Informatica **31**(6), 539–557 (1994). https://doi.org/10.1007/BF01213206
6. De Wulf, M., Doyen, L., Henzinger, T.A., Raskin, J.-F.: Antichains: a new algorithm for checking universality of finite automata. In: Ball, T., Jones, R.B. (eds.) CAV 2006. LNCS, vol. 4144, pp. 17–30. Springer, Heidelberg (2006). https://doi.org/10.1007/11817963_5
7. Doveri, K., Ganty, P., Hadži-Đokić, L.: Antichains algorithms for the inclusion problem between ω-VPL. In: Sankaranarayanan, S., Sharygina, N. (eds.) Tools and Algorithms for the Construction and Analysis of Systems. TACAS 2023. Lecture Notes in Computer Science, vol. 13993. Springer, Cham (2023). https://doi.org/10.1007/978-3-031-30823-9_15
8. Doveri, K., Ganty, P., Mazzocchi, N.: FORQ-based language inclusion formal testing. In: Shoham, S., Vizel, Y. (eds.) Computer Aided Verification. CAV 2022. Lecture Notes in Computer Science, vol. 13372. Springer, Cham (2022). https://doi.org/10.1007/978-3-031-13188-2_6
9. Doveri, K., Ganty, P., Parolini, F., Ranzato, F.: Inclusion testing of büchi automata based on well-quasiorders. Leibniz Int. Proc. Inform. **203**, 1–22 (2021). https://doi.org/10.4230/LIPIcs.CONCUR.2021.3
10. Esparza, J., Rossmanith, P., Schwoon, S.: A uniform framework for problems on context-free grammars. Bull. Eur. Assoc. Theor. Comput. Sci. **72**, 169–177 (2000). https://archive.model.in.tum.de/um/bibdb/esparza/ufpcfg.pdf
11. Floyd, R.W.: Syntactic analysis and operator precedence. J. ACM **10**(3), 316–333 (1963). https://doi.org/10.1145/321172.321179
12. Gallier, J.: Languages, automata, theory of computation, preprint on webpage at https://www.cis.upenn.edu/~jean/gbooks/toc.pdf
13. Ganty, P., Ranzato, F., Valero, P.: Complete abstractions for checking language inclusion. ACM Trans. Comput. Logic **22**(4), 1–40 (2021). https://doi.org/10.1145/3462673
14. Ganty, P., Valero, P.: Regular expression search on compressed text. In: 2019 Data Compression Conference (DCC), pp. 528–537. IEEE (2019). https://doi.org/10.1109/DCC.2019.00061
15. Greibach, S.A., Friedman, E.P.: Superdeterministic PDAs: a subcase with a decidable inclusion problem. J. ACM **27**(4), 675–700 (1980). https://doi.org/10.1145/322217.322224
16. Henzinger, T.A., Kebis, P., Mazzocchi, N., Saraç, N.E.: Regular methods for operator precedence languages. arXiv:2305.03447 (2023). https://doi.org/10.4230/LIPIcs.ICALP.2023.129
17. Holík, L., Meyer, R.: Antichains for the verification of recursive programs. In: Bouajjani, A., Fauconnier, H. (eds.) NETYS 2015. LNCS, vol. 9466, pp. 322–336. Springer, Cham (2015). https://doi.org/10.1007/978-3-319-26850-7_22
18. Istrail, S.: Generalization of the ginsburg-rice schützenberger fixed-point theorem for context-sensitive and recursive-enumerable languages. Theor. Comput. Sci. **18**(3), 333–341 (1982)
19. Jančar, P., Esparza, J., Moller, F.: Petri nets and regular processes. J. Comput. Syst. Sci. **59**(3), 476–503 (1999). https://doi.org/10.1006/jcss.1999.1643
20. Kasai, T., Iwata, S.: Some problems in formal language theory known as decidable are proved EXPTIME complete (1992). https://www.kurims.kyoto-u.ac.jp/~kyodo/kokyuroku/contents/pdf/0796-02.pdf

21. Maquet, N.: New algorithms and data structures for the emptiness problem of alternating automata, Ph. D. thesis, Université Libre de Bruxelles, Belgium (2011). http://hdl.handle.net/2013/ULB-DIPOT:oai:dipot.ulb.ac.be:2013/209961
22. Valero Mejía, P.: On the use of quasiorders in formal language theory, Ph. D. thesis, Universidad Politecnica de Madrid - University Library (2020). https://doi.org/10.20868/upm.thesis.64477

On the Home-Space Problem for Petri Nets

Petr Jančar[1] and Jérôme Leroux[2(✉)]

[1] Department of Computer Science, Faculty of Science, Palacký University Olomouc, Olomouc, Czech Republic
petr.jancar@upol.cz
[2] LaBRI, CNRS, University Bordeaux, Bordeaux, France
jerome.leroux@labri.fr

Abstract. In a recent paper (at Concur 2023) we answered a former question by D. de Frutos Escrig and C. Johnen, by showing the decidability of the "semilinear home-space problem" for Petri nets (that asks if a given semilinear set H is a home-space for a given semilinear set X of markings of a Petri net). We used an approach constructing semilinear "non-reachability cores" for linear sets. This was sufficient for a decision algorithm, a detailed analysis of which even showed that the problem is Ackermann-complete, but it has remained unclear if such semilinear cores can be constructed for general semilinear sets. Here we give a positive answer to this question; this also yields a conceptually simpler decision algorithm for the mentioned home-space problem, though with no complexity bound.

Keywords: Petri net · home-space property · semilinear set

1 Introduction

On an abstract level, various practical systems and theoretical models can be viewed as instances of transition systems $(S, \rightarrow)$ where S is a (possibly infinite) set of configurations and $\rightarrow \subseteq S \times S$ is a relation capturing when one configuration can change into another by an atomic step; the reachability relation $\rightarrow^*$ is then the reflexive and transitive closure of $\rightarrow$.

Given a system $(S, \rightarrow)$ and two sets $X, H \subseteq S$, we say that H is a *home-space for* X if from every configuration reachable from (some configuration in) X we can reach (some configuration in) H. The *home-space problem* asks, given $(S, \rightarrow)$, X, H, whether H is a home-space for X. For instance, we can ask whether our system is always resettable.

The aim of this paper is to clarify some questions that were left open in our recent study [7] of the home-space problem for (transition systems generated by) Petri nets. A starting point of [7] was the work by David de Frutos Escrig and Colette Johnen from 1989 [4], who showed the decidability of the home-space problem in a special case, leaving open the decidability question for the general "semilinear home-space problem", in which the given sets X and H

S. Kiefer et al. (Eds.): *Taming the Infinities of Concurrency*, LNCS 14660, pp. 172–180, 2024.
https://doi.org/10.1007/978-3-031-56222-8_10

are semilinear (i.e., expressible in Presburger arithmetic). We recall that the reachability sets of Petri nets are more general than semilinear sets, and that the reachability problem for Petri nets has recently turned out to have an enormous computational complexity, being Ackermann-complete [2,10,11].

In [7] we answered the question from [4] positively, by showing the decidability of the semilinear home-space problem for Petri nets. Moreover, by a detailed analysis of our approach we have shown this problem to be Ackermann-complete as well. The main idea of our approach was to construct a "non-reachability core" C for H such that it is decidable if we can reach C from X, which is possible precisely in the cases when H is not a home-space for X. We managed to show that we can construct a semilinear core C for any linear set, and we used this for our decidability result, but it was not clear if such a semilinear core is possible to construct for any semilinear set (which is a finite union of linear sets). Here we show that it is possible, using the results from [8] that enable even to show that such a core is not only semilinear but also inductive (i.e., closed w.r.t. the one-step relation $\rightarrow$); this main addition to [7] is here captured by Theorem 2 in Sect. 3. That section is preceded by Sect. 2 describing our approach in the context of general transition systems, and is followed by Sect. 4 where we discuss the question of positive and negative witnesses corresponding to our home-space problem.

In [7] we also mentioned a related problem: Eike Best and Javier Esparza [1] considered the problem if there exists a home-configuration for a given initial configuration of a Petri net, and showed that this problem is decidable. A natural question is if this can be generalized to decide if there is a semilinear home-space included in the reachability set of a given Petri-net configuration; currently we have no answer to this question.

2   A General Approach to the Home-Space Problem

In this section we provide an overview of the way how the home-space problem can be solved via the so-called *non-reachability cores*, and in particular *inductive non-reachability cores*. Though we apply this approach to Petri nets, we start with presenting it for a general transition system given as a pair $(S, \rightarrow)$ where S is a (possibly infinite) set of *states* (or *configurations*) and $\rightarrow \subseteq S \times S$ is a *transition relation*. The *reachability relation* $\rightarrow^* \subseteq S \times S$ is then the reflexive and transitive closure of $\rightarrow$. For sets $X \subseteq S$, we introduce the following notions and notation:

- by $\overline{X}$ we denote the complement of X (hence $S \smallsetminus X$);
- $\mathrm{PRE}^*(X) = \{s \in S \mid \exists s' \in X : s \rightarrow^* s'\}$;
- $\mathrm{POST}^*(X) = \{s \in S \mid \exists s' \in X : s' \rightarrow^* s\}$;
- X is *inductive* (or *closed w.r.t.* $\rightarrow$) if $\mathrm{POST}^*(X) = X$;
- $H \subseteq S$ is a *home-space* for X if $\mathrm{POST}^*(X) \subseteq \mathrm{PRE}^*(H)$.

We might implicitly use simple observations like the facts $X \subseteq \mathrm{PRE}^*(X) = \mathrm{PRE}^*(\mathrm{PRE}^*(X))$ or $\mathrm{PRE}^*(X_1 \cup X_2) = \mathrm{PRE}^*(X_1) \cup \mathrm{PRE}^*(X_2)$, or the fact that

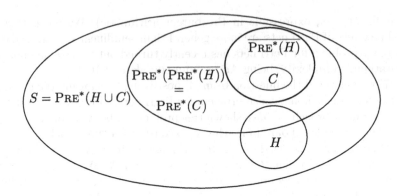

Fig. 1. C is a non-reachability core for H.

$X_1 \cap X_2$ is inductive when both X_1 and X_2 are inductive. We also observe that H is a home-space for X iff it is a home-space for every $s \in X$ (implicitly viewed as the singleton $\{s\}$).

Figure 1 depicts the set S of states of a system, and a subset $H \subseteq S$ as a potential "home-space" in which we are interested. The set $\overline{\text{PRE}^*(H)}$ consists of the states from which H is not reachable, which entails that $\overline{\text{PRE}^*(H)}$ is inductive (i.e., $\text{POST}^*(\overline{\text{PRE}^*(H)}) = \overline{\text{PRE}^*(H)}$). We observe that

$$\text{PRE}^*(\overline{\text{PRE}^*(H)}) = \{s \in S \mid H \text{ is not a home-space for } s\};$$

hence H is a home-space for X iff $X \cap \text{PRE}^*(\overline{\text{PRE}^*(H)}) = \emptyset$.

We also note that H and $\overline{\text{PRE}^*(H)}$ are disjoint, but $\text{PRE}^*(\overline{\text{PRE}^*(H)})$ might intersect H. Since $S = \text{PRE}^*(H) \cup \overline{\text{PRE}^*(H)}$, we have

$$S = \text{PRE}^*(H \cup \overline{\text{PRE}^*(H)}).$$

For some (infinite-state) systems it might be hard to construct (a description of) the set $\overline{\text{PRE}^*(H)}$ and/or to decide for $s \in S$ whether $s \in \text{PRE}^*(\overline{\text{PRE}^*(H)})$. Surely, for Turing-powerful systems such problems are not algorithmically solvable. But in the case of Petri nets it has turned out useful to introduce the notion of a *non-reachability core*, or just a *core, for* H: it is a set $C \subseteq S$ (also depicted in Fig. 1) such that

$$C \subseteq \overline{\text{PRE}^*(H)} \subseteq \text{PRE}^*(C),$$

which entails that $S = \text{PRE}^*(H \cup C)$ (since $S = \text{PRE}^*(H) \cup \overline{\text{PRE}^*(H)}$); in other words, C is a subset of the inductive set $\overline{\text{PRE}^*(H)}$ that is its home-space (i.e., C is a home-space for $\overline{\text{PRE}^*(H)}$). Hence if C is a core for H, then

$$\text{PRE}^*(\overline{\text{PRE}^*(H)}) = \text{PRE}^*(C);$$

therefore H is not a home-space for X iff some $s \in X$ can reach C.

Of course, such a notion can help us only if there are cores C for H that are somehow simpler than $\overline{\mathrm{PRE}^*}(H)$ itself. We have noted that $\overline{\mathrm{PRE}^*}(H)$ is inductive; the cores $C \subseteq \overline{\mathrm{PRE}^*}(H)$ do not need to be inductive, but inductive non-reachability cores will be of special interest for us.

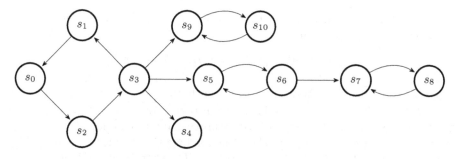

Fig. 2. Let $H = \{s_3, s_4\}$. We have $\mathrm{PRE}^*(H) = \{s_0, s_1, s_2, s_3, s_4\}$, and the bottom SCCs of $\overline{\mathrm{PRE}^*}(H)$ are $\{s_7, s_8\}$ and $\{s_9, s_{10}\}$. Hence $C = \{s_7, s_9\}$ is one non-reachability core for H, while $C' = \{s_7, s_8, s_9, s_{10}\}$ is the least inductive non-reachability core for H.

It is straightforward to characterize the non-reachability cores in finite-state systems, which are exemplified by the system in Fig. 2. We can partition $\overline{\mathrm{PRE}^*}(H)$ into the strongly connected components (SCCs), and observe that a set C is a core if, and only if, it is included in $\overline{\mathrm{PRE}^*}(H)$ and contains at least one state in each bottom SCC of $\overline{\mathrm{PRE}^*}(H)$ (from which no other SCC is reachable). The union of the bottom SCCs (in $\overline{\mathrm{PRE}^*}(H)$) is the least *inductive* non-reachability core for H. (This holds in *finite-state* systems, not in general.)

A "home-space" set $H \subseteq S$ can be sometimes naturally given as the union of smaller sets (in the case of Petri nets we are interested in semilinear home-space sets, which are defined as finite unions of linear sets). For instance, in Fig. 2 we have $H = H_1 \cup H_2$ where $H_1 = \{s_3\}$ and $H_2 = \{s_4\}$. We can consider $C_1 = \{s_9, s_7, s_4\}$ as a core for H_1 and $C_2 = \{s_{10}, s_8\}$ as a core for H_2; in this case C_1 and C_2 do not yield a core for H (none of the sets $C_1 \cap C_2$ and $C_1 \cup C_2$ is a core for H). Nevertheless, if we choose C_1 and C_2 that are inductive, then $C_1 \cap C_2$ is an inductive core for H; we now prove this useful fact generally. (The next lemma did not appear in [7], since it was of no use there.)

Lemma 1. *Given $(S, \rightarrow)$ and $H \subseteq S$, let $H = H_1 \cup H_2 \cdots \cup H_k$ for some $k \in \mathbb{N}_+$, and let $C_1, C_2, \ldots, C_k$ be inductive non-reachability cores for $H_1, H_2, \ldots, H_k$, respectively. Then $C_1 \cap C_2 \cdots \cap C_k$ is an inductive non-reachability core for H.*

Proof. By induction on k. The case $k = 1$ is trivial, so we now suppose $k = 2$, hence $H = H_1 \cup H_2$. Since C_1 and C_2 are inductive, the intersection $C = C_1 \cap C_2$ is inductive as well. Since $C_1 \subseteq \overline{\mathrm{PRE}^*}(H_1)$ and $C_2 \subseteq \overline{\mathrm{PRE}^*}(H_2)$, we have

$$C_1 \cap C_2 \subseteq \overline{\mathrm{PRE}^*}(H_1) \cap \overline{\mathrm{PRE}^*}(H_2) = \overline{\mathrm{PRE}^*(H_1) \cup \mathrm{PRE}^*(H_2)} = \overline{\mathrm{PRE}^*}(H_1 \cup H_2),$$

hence $C \subseteq \overline{\text{PRE}^*(H)}$.

Let us show that $\overline{\text{PRE}^*(H)} \subseteq \text{PRE}^*(C)$; we recall that $\overline{\text{PRE}^*(H)}$ is inductive. If $s \in \overline{\text{PRE}^*(H)}$, then

$$\text{POST}^*(\{s\}) \subseteq \overline{\text{PRE}^*(H)} = \overline{\text{PRE}^*(H_1 \cup H_2)} = \overline{\text{PRE}^*(H_1)} \cap \overline{\text{PRE}^*(H_2)}.$$

Since $s \in \overline{\text{PRE}^*(H_1)}$, there is $s_1 \in C_1$ such that $s \to^* s_1$. Using the fact that C_1 is inductive, we deduce that

$$\text{POST}^*(\{s_1\}) \subseteq C_1 \cap \overline{\text{PRE}^*(H_1)} \cap \overline{\text{PRE}^*(H_2)}.$$

Since $s_1 \in \overline{\text{PRE}^*(H_2)}$, there is $s_2 \in C_2$ such that $s_1 \to^* s_2$; we thus have $s_2 \in C_1 \cap C_2$. Since $s \to^* s_2$, we have shown that $\overline{\text{PRE}^*(H)} \subseteq \text{PRE}^*(C)$, which finishes the proof that $C = C_1 \cap C_2$ is a non-reachability core for $H = H_1 \cup H_2$.

The claim for $k \geq 3$ follows by the induction hypothesis, since $H_1 \cup H_2 \cdots \cup H_k$ can be viewed as $H_1 \cup H_2 \cdots \cup H_{k-2} \cup (H_{k-1} \cup H_k)$ where we consider $C_{k-1} \cap C_k$ as the inductive core for the set $(H_{k-1} \cup H_k)$. $\square$

3   Semilinear Inductive Cores for Semilinear Sets

We now turn our attention to transitions systems $(S, \to)$ generated by (unmarked place/transition) Petri nets. We start by recalling concise definitions.

By $\mathbb{N}$, $\mathbb{N}_+$, and $\mathbb{Z}$ we denote the sets of nonnegative, positive, and all integers, respectively. For $i, j \in \mathbb{N}$ we put $[i, j] = \{i, i+1, \ldots, j\}$ (which is empty for $i > j$).

For $d \in \mathbb{N}$, by a *d-dimensional Petri-net action* we mean a pair $a = (\mathbf{a}_-, \mathbf{a}_+) \in \mathbb{N}^d \times \mathbb{N}^d$. With $a = (\mathbf{a}_-, \mathbf{a}_+)$ we associate the binary relation $\xrightarrow{a}$ on the set $\mathbb{N}^d$ by putting $(\mathbf{x} + \mathbf{a}_-) \xrightarrow{a} (\mathbf{x} + \mathbf{a}_+)$ for all $\mathbf{x} \in \mathbb{N}^d$.

A *Petri net A of dimension d* (with d places in more traditional definitions) is a finite set of d-dimensional Petri-net actions (transitions). A d-dimensional Petri net A generates the transition system $\mathcal{S}_A = (\mathbb{N}^d, \to)$ where $\to = \bigcup_{a \in A} \xrightarrow{a}$. Hence we freely use the notation introduced for general transition systems $(S, \to)$; the states, or rather *configurations* (or markings), are now vectors from $\mathbb{N}^d$.

We recall that a *set* $\mathbf{L} \subseteq \mathbb{N}^d$ is *linear* if there are d-dimensional vectors $\mathbf{b}$, the *basis*, and $\mathbf{p}_1, \mathbf{p}_2, \ldots, \mathbf{p}_k$, the *periods* (for $k \in \mathbb{N}$), such that

$$\mathbf{L} = \{\mathbf{x} \in \mathbb{N}^d \mid \mathbf{x} = \mathbf{b} + \mathbf{u}(1) \cdot \mathbf{p}_1 + \mathbf{u}(2) \cdot \mathbf{p}_2 \cdots + \mathbf{u}(k) \cdot \mathbf{p}_k \text{ for some } \mathbf{u} \in \mathbb{N}^k\}.$$

(For $\mathbf{u} \in \mathbb{N}^k$ we use the notation $\mathbf{u} = (\mathbf{u}(1), \mathbf{u}(2), \ldots, \mathbf{u}(k))$.)

In this case, by a *presentation of* $\mathbf{L}$ we mean the tuple $(\mathbf{b}, \mathbf{p}_1, \mathbf{p}_2, \ldots, \mathbf{p}_k)$.

A *set* $\mathbf{S} \subseteq \mathbb{N}^d$ is *semilinear* if it is a finite union of linear sets, i.e.

$$\mathbf{S} = \mathbf{L}_1 \cup \mathbf{L}_2 \cdots \cup \mathbf{L}_m$$

where $\mathbf{L}_i$ are linear sets (for all $i \in [1, m]$). In this case, by a *presentation of* $\mathbf{S}$ we mean a sequence of presentations of $\mathbf{L}_1, \mathbf{L}_2, \ldots, \mathbf{L}_m$. When we say that a *semilinear set $\mathbf{S}$ is given*, we mean that we are given a presentation of $\mathbf{S}$; when we say that $\mathbf{S}$ is *effectively constructible* in some context, we mean that there is an algorithm computing its presentation (in the respective context).

We also recall that a set $\mathbf{S} \subseteq \mathbb{N}^d$ is semilinear iff it is expressible by a formula of Presburger arithmetic [5]; the respective transformations between presentations and formulas are effective. Hence if $\mathbf{S}_1, \mathbf{S}_2 \subseteq \mathbb{N}^d$ are semilinear, then also the complement $\overline{\mathbf{S}_1}$ and the intersection $\mathbf{S}_1 \cap \mathbf{S}_2$ are (effectively) semilinear.

In [7] we studied the *semilinear home-space problem*:

Instance: a triple $A, \mathbf{X}, \mathbf{H}$ where A is a Petri net, of dimension d, and $\mathbf{X}$, $\mathbf{H}$ are two (finitely presented) semilinear subsets of $\mathbb{N}^d$.
Question: is $\mathbf{H}$ a home-space for $\mathbf{X}$?

We showed that the problem is decidable, and Ackermann-complete, in fact; an important ingredient was the following lemma:

Lemma 2 (Lemma 8 in [7]). *Given a Petri net A of dimension d, and (a presentation of) a linear set $\mathbf{L} \subseteq \mathbb{N}^d$, there is an effectively constructible semilinear non-reachability core $\mathbf{C}$ for $\mathbf{L}$.*

The core $\mathbf{C}$ in the claim was not inductive in general; but we managed to show that it can be constructed in Ackermannian time, and this was sufficient for our (Ackermannian) algorithm solving the semilinear home-space problem. In [7] we left unclear if there is a semilinear non-reachability core for a general semilinear set. Here we clarify this issue positively, by Theorem 2, for which we use the following known result:

Theorem 1 ([8]). *Given a Petri net and two semilinear sets $\mathbf{X}, \mathbf{Y}$ of configurations, we have $\mathbf{X} \subseteq \overline{\mathrm{PRE}^*(\mathbf{Y})}$ if, and only if, there exists an effectively constructible inductive semilinear set $\mathbf{I}$ such that $\mathbf{X} \subseteq \mathbf{I} \subseteq \overline{\mathbf{Y}}$.*

Since $\mathbf{I}$ is inductive, $\mathbf{X} \subseteq \mathbf{I} \subseteq \overline{\mathbf{Y}}$ entails that $\mathrm{POST}^*(\mathbf{X}) \subseteq \mathbf{I} \subseteq \overline{\mathrm{PRE}^*(\mathbf{Y})}$ (by noting that $\mathrm{POST}^*(\mathbf{I}) = \mathbf{I}$, $\mathbf{I} \subseteq \overline{\mathbf{Y}}$ iff $\mathbf{Y} \subseteq \overline{\mathbf{I}}$, and $\mathrm{PRE}^*(\overline{\mathbf{I}}) = \overline{\mathbf{I}}$).

Theorem 2. *Given a Petri net A of dimension d, and (a presentation of) a semilinear set $\mathbf{H} \subseteq \mathbb{N}^d$, there is an effectively constructible semilinear inductive non-reachability core $\mathbf{C}$ for $\mathbf{H}$.*

Proof. If $\mathbf{H} = \emptyset$, then we can take $\mathbf{C} = \mathbb{N}^d$.

Now we assume that $\mathbf{H} = \mathbf{H}_1 \cup \mathbf{H}_2 \cdots \cup \mathbf{H}_k$ for some $k \in \mathbb{N}_+$, where $\mathbf{H}_i$ is a linear set for each $i \in [1, k]$. By Lemma 2 we can construct semilinear sets $\mathbf{C}_1, \mathbf{C}_2, \ldots, \mathbf{C}_k$ that are non-reachability cores for $\mathbf{H}_1, \mathbf{H}_2, \ldots, \mathbf{H}_k$, respectively (hence $\mathbf{C}_i \subseteq \overline{\mathrm{PRE}^*(\mathbf{H}_i)} \subseteq \mathrm{PRE}^*(\mathbf{C}_i)$).

For each $i \in [1, k]$, by Theorem 1 we can construct an inductive semilinear set $\mathbf{I}_i$ such that $\mathbf{C}_i \subseteq \mathbf{I}_i \subseteq \overline{\mathrm{PRE}^*(\mathbf{H}_i)}$, which also entails that $\overline{\mathrm{PRE}^*(\mathbf{H}_i)} \subseteq \mathrm{PRE}^*(\mathbf{I}_i)$; hence $\mathbf{I}_i$ is a semilinear *inductive* non-reachability core for $\mathbf{H}_i$.

By Lemma 1 we deduce that $\mathbf{I}_1 \cap \mathbf{I}_2 \cdots \cap \mathbf{I}_k$ is a semilinear inductive non-reachability core for $\mathbf{H}$ (using the fact that the intersection of semilinear sets is semilinear). $\qquad\square$

Remark 1. Theorem 2 yields the decidability of the semilinear home-space problem, since the problem if $\mathbf{X} \to^* \mathbf{C}$ (i.e., if $\mathbf{x} \to^* \mathbf{c}$ for some $\mathbf{x} \in \mathbf{X}$ and $\mathbf{c} \in \mathbf{C}$) for semilinear sets $\mathbf{X}, \mathbf{C}$ of configurations of a given Petri net is decidable. This "semilinear reachability problem" is easily reducible to the standard reachability problem, thus being also Ackermann-complete. Nevertheless, Theorem 1 from [8] gives us no complexity bound for constructing the inductive semilinear set I; hence we cannot derive an Ackermannian upper bound for the semilinear home-space problem in this way (and we had to use a more technical way in [7] to derive such a bound).

4   Home-Space Witnesses

We recall that the reachability problem for Petri nets is decidable but extremely hard, namely Ackermann-complete. Nevertheless there are positive witnesses of reachability that are easily verifiable: given a Petri net A and two configurations $\mathbf{x}, \mathbf{y}$, a witness of the fact $\mathbf{x} \to^* \mathbf{y}$ is simply a word $w \in A^*$ such that $\mathbf{x} \xrightarrow{w} \mathbf{y}$ (where $\xrightarrow{w}$ for $w = a_1 a_2 \cdots a_m$ denotes the composition $\xrightarrow{a_1} \circ \xrightarrow{a_2} \cdots \circ \xrightarrow{a_m}$). Verifying the validity of $\mathbf{x} \xrightarrow{w} \mathbf{y}$ is trivial; of course, the size of such a witness w is another issue. A negative witness, meaning a witness of the fact $\mathbf{x} \not\to^* \mathbf{y}$, is a more involved question; a solution is provided by Theorem 1: we have $\mathbf{x} \not\to^* \mathbf{y}$ iff there is an inductive semilinear $\mathbf{I}$ such that $\mathbf{x} \in \mathbf{I}$ and $\mathbf{y} \notin \mathbf{I}$. Verifying if a given semilinear set $\mathbf{I}$ is inductive and satisfies $\mathbf{x} \in \mathbf{I}$ and $\mathbf{y} \notin \mathbf{I}$ is much easier than solving the reachability problem (we can refer, e.g., to [6] for complexity details); again, the size of such a witness $\mathbf{I}$ is another issue.

When looking for similar witnesses in the case of the semilinear home-space problem, in the concluding remarks in [7] we formulated a conjecture whose stronger version is now proved by the following lemma.

Lemma 3. *Given a Petri net A of dimension d, and two semilinear sets $\mathbf{X}, \mathbf{H} \subseteq \mathbb{N}^d$, we have $\mathrm{POST}^*(\mathbf{X}) \subseteq \mathrm{PRE}^*(\mathbf{H})$ (i.e., $\mathbf{H}$ is a home-space for $\mathbf{X}$) iff there is an inductive semilinear set $\mathbf{I}$ such that $\mathrm{POST}^*(\mathbf{X}) \subseteq \mathbf{I} \subseteq \mathrm{PRE}^*(\mathbf{H})$.*

Proof. The "if" direction is trivial.

Now we show the "only if" direction. Let us assume that $\mathrm{POST}^*(\mathbf{X}) \subseteq \mathrm{PRE}^*(\mathbf{H})$, and let $\mathbf{C}$ be a semilinear non-reachability core for $\mathbf{H}$ guaranteed by Theorem 2. Since $\mathbf{C} \subseteq \overline{\mathrm{PRE}^*(\mathbf{H})}$, the assumption $\mathrm{POST}^*(\mathbf{X}) \subseteq \mathrm{PRE}^*(\mathbf{H})$ entails that $\mathbf{X} \cap \mathrm{PRE}^*(\mathbf{C}) = \emptyset$, i.e., $\mathbf{X} \subseteq \overline{\mathrm{PRE}^*(\mathbf{C})}$. Hence by Theorem 1 there is an inductive semilinear set $\mathbf{I}$ such that $\mathbf{X} \subseteq \mathbf{I} \subseteq \overline{\mathbf{C}}$. Since $\mathbf{I}$ is inductive, we get that $\mathrm{POST}^*(\mathbf{X}) \subseteq \mathbf{I}$ and $\mathbf{I} \subseteq \overline{\mathrm{PRE}^*(\mathbf{C})}$. Since $\mathbf{C}$ is a non-reachability core for $\mathbf{H}$, we also get that $\mathbf{I} \subseteq \mathrm{PRE}^*(\mathbf{H})$. $\qquad\square$

Let us look at the question of verifying the validity of a witness $\mathbf{I}$ suggested by Lemma 3. Given a Petri net A and two semilinear sets $\mathbf{X}, \mathbf{H}$ of its configurations, for a given semilinear $\mathbf{I}$ we can "easily" (see [6]) decide if $\mathbf{I}$ is inductive and subsumes $\mathbf{X}$ (which entails that $\mathrm{POST}^*(\mathbf{X}) \subseteq \mathbf{I}$). For deciding if $\mathbf{I} \subseteq \mathrm{PRE}^*(\mathbf{H})$

we also try to avoid solving the (semilinear) reachability problem; we achieve this by the following extension of (positive) witnesses **I**.

Given a d-dimensional Petri net A, a *positive home-space witness for a pair* $(\mathbf{X}, \mathbf{H})$ of semilinear subsets of $\mathbb{N}^d$ is a pair

$$(\mathbf{I}, (w_1, w_2, \ldots, w_k))$$

(for some $k \in \mathbb{N}$) where $\mathbf{I} \subseteq \mathbb{N}^d$ is an inductive semilinear set that contains $\mathbf{X}$, and $w_1, w_2, \ldots, w_k$ are words from A^+ satisfying the following formula:

$$(\forall \mathbf{y} \in \mathbf{I})(\exists n_1, n_2, \ldots, n_k \in \mathbb{N})(\exists \mathbf{h} \in \mathbf{H})\, \mathbf{y} \xrightarrow{w_1^{n_1} w_2^{n_2} \cdots w_k^{n_k}} \mathbf{h}. \tag{1}$$

From [9] we deduce that there exists a sequence $(w_1, w_2, \ldots, w_k)$ satisfying (1) precisely when $\mathbf{I} \subseteq \textsc{Pre}^*(\mathbf{H})$ (since $\mathbf{I}$ and $\mathbf{H}$ are semilinear).

Corollary 1. *Given a Petri net A and two semilinear sets $\mathbf{X}, \mathbf{H}$ of its configurations, then $\mathbf{H}$ is a home-space for $\mathbf{X}$ iff there is a positive home-space witness $(\mathbf{I}, (w_1, w_2, \ldots, w_k))$ for $(\mathbf{X}, \mathbf{H})$.*

We note that by compiling the relation $\mathbf{y} \xrightarrow{w_1^{n_1} w_2^{n_2} \cdots w_k^{n_k}} \mathbf{h}$ into a Presburger formula over the free variables $\mathbf{y}, n_1, \ldots, n_k, \mathbf{h}$ (see [3] for details), we deduce that formula (1) can be efficiently transformed into a Presburger formula. Since the complexity of Presburger arithmetic is at most 3-exponential [12], checking if a tuple $(\mathbf{I}, (w_1, w_2, \ldots, w_k))$ is a positive home-space witness for a pair $(\mathbf{X}, \mathbf{H})$ is elementary (while the general reachability problem is nonelementary, namely Ackermann-complete).

Remark 2. A negative home-space witness for a pair $(\mathbf{X}, \mathbf{H})$ of semilinear sets of configurations, which exists precisely when $\mathbf{H}$ is not a home space for $\mathbf{X}$, can be defined as a tuple $(\mathbf{x}, \mathbf{y})$ where $\mathbf{x} \in \mathbf{X}$, $\mathbf{x} \to^* \mathbf{y}$, and $\mathbf{y} \not\to^* \mathbf{H}$. To avoid requirements to solve instances of the reachability problem, we can define such a negative witness as a tuple $(\mathbf{Y}, \mathbf{x}, w, \mathbf{y})$ where $\mathbf{Y}$ is an inductive semilinear set disjoint from $\mathbf{H}$, and we have $\mathbf{x} \in \mathbf{X}$, $\mathbf{y} \in \mathbf{Y}$, and $\mathbf{x} \xrightarrow{w} \mathbf{y}$.

Hence deciding if $\mathbf{H}$ is a home-space for $\mathbf{X}$ can be performed by simultaneously searching for a positive or a negative witness. This yields the decidability of the semilinear home-space problem; nevertheless, for establishing the (Ackermannian) complexity, we have to refer to the more technical approach in [7].

Disclosure of Interests. The authors have no competing interests to declare that are relevant to the content of this article.

References

1. Best, E., Esparza, J.: Existence of home states in petri nets is decidable. Inf. Process. Lett. **116**(6), 423–427 (2016). https://doi.org/10.1016/j.ipl.2016.01.011

2. Czerwinski, W., Orlikowski, L.: Reachability in vector addition systems is Ackermann-complete. In: 62nd IEEE Annual Symposium on Foundations of Computer Science, FOCS 2021, Denver, CO, USA, February 7–10, 2022, pp. 1229–1240. IEEE (2021). https://doi.org/10.1109/FOCS52979.2021.00120

3. Fribourg, L., Olsén, H.: Proving safety properties of infinite state systems by compilation into Presburger arithmetic. In: Mazurkiewicz, A., Winkowski, J. (eds.) CONCUR 1997. LNCS, vol. 1243, pp. 213–227. Springer, Heidelberg (1997). https://doi.org/10.1007/3-540-63141-0_15

4. de Frutos Escrig, D., Johnen, C.: Decidability of home space property. Univ. de Paris-Sud, Centre d'Orsay, Laboratoire de Recherche en Informatique, LRI-503 (1989)

5. Ginsburg, S., Spanier, E.H.: Semigroups, Presburger formulas and languages. Pac. J. Math. **16**(2), 285–296 (1966). https://doi.org/10.2140/pjm.1966.16.285

6. Haase, C.: A survival guide to Presburger arithmetic. ACM SIGLOG News **5**(3), 67–82 (2018). https://doi.org/10.1145/3242953.3242964

7. Jančar, P., Leroux, J.: The semilinear home-space problem is Ackermann-complete for Petri nets. In: Pérez, G.A., Raskin, J. (eds.) 34th International Conference on Concurrency Theory, CONCUR 2023, September 18–23, 2023, Antwerp, Belgium. LIPIcs, vol. 279, pp. 36:1–36:17. Schloss Dagstuhl - Leibniz-Zentrum für Informatik (2023). https://doi.org/10.4230/LIPICS.CONCUR.2023.36

8. Leroux, J.: The general vector addition system reachability problem by Presburger inductive invariants. Log. Methods Comput. Sci. **6**(3), 1–25 (2010). https://doi.org/10.2168/LMCS-6(3:22)2010

9. Leroux, J.: Presburger vector addition systems. In: 28th Annual ACM/IEEE Symposium on Logic in Computer Science, LICS 2013, New Orleans, LA, USA, June 25–28, 2013, pp. 23–32. IEEE Computer Society (2013). https://doi.org/10.1109/LICS.2013.7

10. Leroux, J.: The reachability problem for Petri nets is not primitive recursive. In: 62nd IEEE Annual Symposium on Foundations of Computer Science, FOCS 2021, Denver, CO, USA, February 7–10, 2022, pp. 1241–1252. IEEE (2021). https://doi.org/10.1109/FOCS52979.2021.00121

11. Leroux, J., Schmitz, S.: Reachability in vector addition systems is primitive-recursive in fixed dimension. In: 34th Annual ACM/IEEE Symposium on Logic in Computer Science, LICS 2019, Vancouver, BC, Canada, June 24–27, 2019, pp. 1–13. IEEE (2019). https://doi.org/10.1109/LICS.2019.8785796

12. Oppen, D.C.: A $2^{2^{2^{pn}}}$ upper bound on the complexity of Presburger arithmetic. J. Comput. Syst. Sci. **16**(3), 323–332 (1978). https://doi.org/10.1016/0022-0000(78)90021-1

Newton's Method – There and Back Again

Michael Luttenberger[(✉)] and Maximilian Schlund

Technical University of Munich, Munich, Germany
luttenbe@in.tum.de

Abstract. We give an overview on the development of Newton's method for systems of polynomial fixed-point equations on semirings, retracing the work which eventually led to [EKL10b], and further present some extensions for noncommutative semirings.

1 Introduction

This article gives an *informal* overview on the development of Newton's method for context-free grammars originally started in [KLE07]. Instead of the original presentation [KLE07, EKL10b], the following is based on the definition of Newton's method as an unfolding or annotation of the context-free grammar resp. that of the associated system of fixed-point equations as originally presented in [LS13b]. The main goal is to convey the central ideas by small examples,[1] not mathematical rigor. For this reason we assume the reader to be familiar with the basic concepts of context-free grammars, and basic algebraic structures, specifically, *semirings*: in the following, a semiring is – if not explicitly stated otherwise – assumed to be ω-continuous with a noncommutative multiplication. Accordingly, we will write *commutative semiring* to refer to a ω-continuous semiring with a commutative multiplication; and, as it customary, if the addition of an ω-continuous semiring is idempotent, we will simply write *idempotent semiring*. For details on context-free grammars, semirings, and systems of polynomial fixed-point equations please refer to e.g. [CS63, SS78, DK09].

2 Motivation

The motivation for the study of Newton's method for context-free grammars originated in the work by Esparza et al. on the verification of recursive programs with only a finite amount of memory (see e.g. [Esp+00, EKS01, ES01, SSE05]): these programs can be naturally described by *pushdown automata* (PDA) or *context-free grammars* (CFG) where nondeterminism is used to describe unknown user input.

Example 1. *Consider the following Python program, based on the example of [EE04], with the corresponding rewrite rules of the CFG as comments. The program models a plotter, that outputs a word in $\{u, d, r\}^*$*

---

[1] Some of these examples are taken from [Lut20].

S. Kiefer et al. (Eds.): *Taming the Infinities of Concurrency*, LNCS 14660, pp. 181–205, 2024.
https://doi.org/10.1007/978-3-031-56222-8_11

```
def M():
    if input() != 'y':        # M₀ → ȳM₁ | yM₅
        S()                   # M₁ → S₀M₂
        print('r')            # M₂ → rM₃
        if input() == 'y':    # M₃ → yM₄ | ȳM₈
            M()               # M₄ → M₀M₈
    else:
        print('u')            # M₅ → uM₆
        M()                   # M₆ → M₀M₇
        print('d')            # M₇ → dM₈
    return                    # M₈ → ε


def S():
    if input() != 'y':        # S₀ → ȳS₁ | yS₂
        return                # S₁ → ε
    print('u')                # S₂ → uS₃
    M()                       # S₃ → M₀S₄
    print('d')                # S₄ → dS₅
    return                    # S₅ → ε
```

The indexed nonterminal X_l refers to the l-th line in procedure X. The terminals $u, d, r, y, \overline{y}$ represent the actual operations, the rewrite rules describe the control flow of the recursive program, and the nondeterminism underlying the rewrite process allows us to abstract from the a-priori unknown user input. The input is a string of $\{y, \overline{y}\}^*$, where $\overline{y}$ denotes that the input is not y. Note that in the grammar, there is no visible difference between reading and printing. We model the input via the terminals $y, \overline{y}$ and model the output using r, u, d. The result of one run can be seen in Fig. 1. Note that this plotter only plots a single "mountain", i.e. the output is a word in $\{u, r\}^* \{r, d\}^*$ with an equal number of u's and d's.

Fig. 1. Skyline plotted via the input $y\overline{y}y\overline{y}^3$ yielding the output $uurdrd$.

The context-free grammar represents the possible runs of the program: every run corresponds to a leftmost derivation and thus a derivation tree w.r.t. the grammar. For instance, a potential run resulting from a call of the procedure S is given by the following derivation tree where nodes are labeled by rewrite rules:

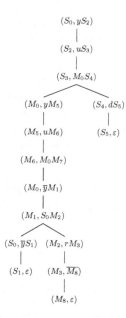

More generally, the rewrite rules of the context-free grammar give rise to a system of fixed-point equations

$$
\begin{array}{lll}
M_0 = \overline{y}M_1 + yM_5 & M_5 = uM_6 & S_1 = 1 \\
M_1 = S_0 M_2 & M_6 = M_0 M_7 & S_2 = uS_3 \\
M_2 = rM_3 & M_7 = dM_8 & S_3 = M_0 S_4 \\
M_3 = yM_4 + \overline{y}M_8 & M_8 = 1 & S_4 = dS_5 \\
M_4 = M_0 M_8 & S_0 = \overline{y}S_1 + yS_2 & S_5 = 1
\end{array}
$$

over some suitable semiring $(S, +, \cdot, 0, 1)$ where addition $(+)$ yields the "joint" effect of the given (partial) runs of the program, whereas multiplication $(\cdot)$ captures the effect of the concatenation of two consecutive partial runs. Note that in a semiring only addition, but not multiplication is assumed to be commutative.

E.g. we recover the context-free grammar by interpreting addition as union of sets, multiplication as concatenation of languages, 1 as the language $\{\varepsilon\}$ and 0 as $\emptyset$, respectively. The language generated by the grammar is then by its inductive definition the least solution of the equation system.

If we consider non-deterministic branching, we obtain the denotational semantics of the program as the least fixed point of the system: to this end, interpret the terminals as memory transformations instead, with the constants 1 and 0 representing the identity and the completely undefined memory transformation, respectively. Considering non-deterministic branching, we obtain the denotational semantics of the program as the least fixed point of the system. This least fixed point is not computable in general so techniques like widening or abstraction have to be used to safely approximate the semantics. For instance, we may weaken distributivity to sub-distributivity, i.e. one only requires $a(b + c) \leq ab + ac$ and $(b + c)a \leq ba + ca$, see e.g. [EKL10b]. Often, these abstractions can be viewed as *homomorphisms from the semiring of languages to some less expressive semiring where the least fixed point can be computed.*   □

In 2004 [EKM04] Esparza et al. considered the alternative approach to abstract from user input by means of probabilities resulting in analysis of *probabilistic pushdown automata* (pPDA). At the same time and independently, Etessami and Yannakakis (e.g. [EY05]) were working on the problem using the equivalent model of probabilistic recursive state machines which they called *recursive Markov chains* (RMC). Another equivalent model is that of *probabilistic context-free grammars*[2] (pCFG).

Example 2. *For instance, consider the program fragment (in Python) from above now with the user input replaced by a fair-coin toss:*

```python
import random

def M():
    if random.randrange(2) == 1:      # M_0 → ȳM_1 | yM_5
        S()                           # M_1 → S_0M_2
        print('r')                    # M_2 → rM_3
        if random.randrange(2) == 1:  # M_3 → yM_4 | ȳM_8
            M()                       # M_4 → M_0M_8
    else:
        print('u')                    # M_5 → uM_6
        M()                           # M_6 → M_0M_7
        print('d')                    # M_7 → dM_8
    return                            # M_8 → ε

def S():
    if random.randrange(2) == 1:       # S_0 → ȳS_1 | yS_2
        return                         # S_1 → ε
    print('u')                         # S_2 → uS_3
    M()                                # S_3 → M_0S_4
    print('d' )                        # S_4 → dS_5
    return                             # S_5 → ε
```

Now, the rules of the grammar are all implicitly weighted by probabilities, i.e. the program gives rise to a pCFG. If we are only interested in the probability to terminate eventually, we may instantiate the free parameters of the associated equations (i.e. the terminals of the context-free grammar) with the probabilities $y = \bar{y} = \frac{1}{2}$ and $d = r = u = 1$ (i.e., we ignore the output) and move to an algebraic system over the nonnegative reals (a commutative semiring):

---

[2] Also known as *stochastic context-free grammar*.

$$M_0 = \tfrac{1}{2}M_1 + \tfrac{1}{2}M_5 \qquad M_5 = M_6 \qquad\qquad S_1 = 1$$
$$M_1 = S_0 M_2 \qquad\qquad M_6 = M_0 M_7 \qquad\quad S_2 = S_3$$
$$M_2 = M_3 \qquad\qquad\quad M_7 = M_8 \qquad\qquad S_3 = M_0 S_4$$
$$M_3 = \tfrac{1}{2}M_4 + \tfrac{1}{2}M_8 \qquad M_8 = 1 \qquad\qquad\quad S_4 = S_5$$
$$M_4 = M_0 M_8 \qquad\qquad S_0 = \tfrac{1}{2}S_1 + \tfrac{1}{2}S_2 \qquad S_5 = 1$$

Simplifying the system by contracting chains of linear substitutions leads to:

$$M_0 = \tfrac{1}{2}S_0 M_3 + \tfrac{1}{2}M_0$$
$$M_3 = \tfrac{1}{2}M_0 + \tfrac{1}{2}$$
$$S_0 = \tfrac{1}{2} + \tfrac{1}{2}M_0$$

The probability of eventual termination of the procedure M is the least nonnegative solution of the equation

$$M_0 = \tfrac{1}{2}(\tfrac{1}{2} + \tfrac{1}{2}M_0)^2 + \tfrac{1}{2}M_0 = \tfrac{1}{8}M_0^2 + \tfrac{3}{4}M_0 + \tfrac{1}{8}$$

which turns out to be 1 in this case. □

As known from the translation of PDA into CFGs and vice versa, the central idea to analyze PDA is to compute summaries for each recursive call in order to directly jump to the result of the recursive call. In the case of pPDA resp. RMC these summaries are simply the termination probabilities of the respective calls; and they are the least solution of a system of polynomial fixed-point equations $X = f(X)$ describing the control flow of the program with $f = (f_1, \ldots, f_n)$ a vector of n polynomials in the variables $X_1, \ldots, X_n$ arranged into the vector X. In order to compute the termination probabilities, Esparza et al. used in [EKM04] essentially standard fixed-point iteration $0, f(0), f(f(0)), \ldots$ which is also known as Kleene iteration.[3] In contrast, Etessami et al. proposed to use Newton's method instead because of its higher speed of convergence.

3 Newton's Method: Iterated Linearization

As motivated in the previous subsection, the termination probabilities are the solution of a system $X = f(X)$ of fixed-point equations where the right-hand side f is given by polynomials. In other words, we are interested in a certain root of the nonlinear function $g(X) = f(X) - X$.

---

[3] Depending on the properties of the (semi)ring there are different ways of implementing Kleene iteration more efficiently: e.g. chaotic iteration, round-robin (Gauss-Seidel) iteration, recursively computing A^* for a matrix A, LDU-decomposition of said A, Floyd-Warshall (resp. Kleene's algorithm) or Bellman-Ford. We won't discuss these details here, see e.g. [Sch16] for a detailed discussion.

The central idea by Newton is to replace the nonlinear g by some linear function l that approximates f at least in the vicinity of some value x_0 and then solve the linear system $l(X) = 0$ to obtain an update of x_0 which is closer to a root of g.[4]

It is worthwhile to note that this idea itself does not depend on the concept of differentation: for instance, also *strategy iteration* (also: *policy iteration*) used for solving nonlinear systems built from min, max and e.g. linear, but also nonlinear polynomials can be understood as iterated linearization. See e.g. [FV97] for a discussion in the context of stochastic games, and e.g. [Esp+08] in case of min-max-polynomial systems.

For a differentiable function $g\colon \mathbb{R}^n \to \mathbb{R}^n$ its best (e.g. w.r.t. the standard Euclidean norm) linear approximation at $(x_0, g(x_0))$ is

$$l(X) = g(x_0) + g'(x_0)(X - x_0)$$

where $g'(x_0)$ is the derivative of g. If $g\colon \mathbb{R}^n \to \mathbb{R}^n$, then $g'(x_0)$ can be represented as a $n \times n$-matrix of the partial derivatives of components of g called the Jacobian. The root of $l(X)$ is then used as updated approximation x_1 of a root of $g(X)$ in the vicinity of x_0

$$x_1 = x_0 - g'(x_0)^{-1} g(x_0)$$

Of course, this requires $g(x_0)$ to be invertible in $\mathbb{R}^{n \times n}$. In our case, we have $g(X) = f(X) - X$ so that

$$x_1 = x_0 - (f'(x_0) - \mathsf{Id})^{-1}(f(x_0) - x_0) = x_0 + (\mathsf{Id} - f'(x_0))^{-1}(f(x_0) - x_0)$$

where Id denotes the $n \times n$-identity matrix.

Example 3. *The following table lists the first five approximations, starting at* $x_0 = 0$, *obtained via standard fixed-point iteration, also known as Kleene iteration, resp. Newton's method when applied to above equation*

$$X = f(X) := \tfrac{1}{8}X^2 + \tfrac{1}{2}X + \tfrac{1}{8}$$

for the probability of termination of the procedure M from the plotter example.[5]

i	$x_{i+1} = f(x_i)$	$x_{i+1} = x_i + \frac{f(x_i) - x_i}{1 - f'(x_i)}$
0	0	0
1	0.125	0.5
2	0.220703125	0.75
3	0.2966160774230957	0.875
4	0.35845969524055477	0.9375
5	0.40990644056941	0.96875

---

[4] For better distinction, we use upper-case letters like X to denote variables resp. nonterminals, and lower-case letters like x_0 for concrete values resp. terminals.

[5] Note that since we only have a single variable X here, we can only consider the (lockstep) Kleene iteration.

Actually, in this example, Newton's method starting at $x_0 = 0$ reduces to

$$x_{i+1} = \tfrac{1}{2}x_i + \tfrac{1}{2}$$

so that a straight-forward induction shows that $x_i = 1 - 2^{-i}$, i.e. with every additional iteration, Newton's method yields one additional bit of precision.   □

The value of the expression $(\mathsf{Id} - f'(x_0))^{-1}$ is given by the geometric series, if it converges, i.e.

$$(\mathsf{Id} - f'(x_0))^{-1} = \sum_{k=0}^{\infty} f'(x_0)^k =: (f'(x_0))^*.$$

We will use A^* as short hand for the geometric series $\sum_{k=0}^{\infty} A^k$ of a matrix $A \in \mathbb{R}^{n \times n}$ as it can be understood to compute the reflexive-transitive closure of a transient Markov chain given by $f'(0)$ and is thus a special case of the Kleene star.

As shown in [EKL10a] for fixed-point systems describing the termination properties, it is always the case that $(f'(x_0))^* = (\mathsf{Id} - f'(x_0))^{-1}$ as long as x_0 is a strict under-approximation of the termination probabilities. In [EKL10a] it is further shown that after some "ramp-up phase", a constant number of additional iterations of Newton's method will increase the precision of the approximation by at least one bit, similar as in the example above.[6]

4   Approximation by Unfolding

For the following, it will be useful to understand how the approximations computed via Kleene iteration and Newton's method are related to the concrete runs of a recursive program. Consider the following very simply program:

```
def X():
    z = input()       # assume z ∈ {a, b, c}
    if z == 'a':      # X → aXX
        X()
        X()
    elif z == 'b':    # X → bX
        X()
    else:             # X → c
        pass
    return
```

The corresponding fixed-point equation is then

$$X = f(X) := c + bX + aXX$$

---

[6] The "ramp-up phase" results e.g. from the longest simple path between two variables in the dependency graph given by the Jacobian of the system.

Applying standard fixed-point iteration to this particular f yields

i	$f^i(0)$
0	0
1	c
2	$c + bc + acc$
3	$c + b\,(c + bc + acc) + a\,(c + bc + acc)^2$
$\vdots$	$\vdots$

By the inductive definition of the language produced by a context-free grammar it immediately follows that the i-th approximation $f^i(0)$ coincides with the sum of the yields[7] of the derivation trees of height *less than* i, see e.g. [Boz99]. For our example, the derivation trees of height at most one are:

And the trees of height exactly two are:

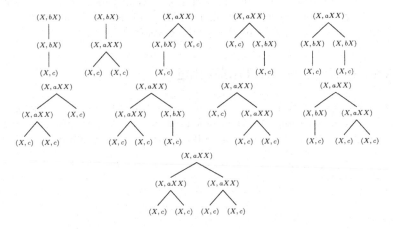

In the case of a recursive program, the associated derivation trees simply describe the recursive calls that led to a specific run of the program. By annotating the nonterminal X with the maximal height of a derivation it can produce, we can unfold the context-free grammar as follows

$$X^{(0)} \to c$$
$$X^{(1)} \to X^{(0)} \mid bX^{(0)} \mid aX^{(0)}X^{(0)}$$
$$\vdots$$
$$X^{(i+1)} \to X^{(i)} \mid bX^{(i)} \mid aX^{(i)}X^{(i)}$$

---

[7] The terminal word of the derivation represented by the tree.

so that $X^{(i)}$ generates only derivation trees of height *exactly* i. As simple induction shows that the derivation trees generated by $X^{(i)}$ are in bijection with the derivation trees generated by X of height *at most* i: informally, we only need to contract the chain rules $X^{(i+1)} \to X^{(i)}$ and forgetting the superscript. This unfolding corresponds to adding a parameter which limits the maximal depth of recursion:

```
def X(i: int):
    z = input()          # assume z ∈ {a,b,c}
    if i > 0:
        if z == 'a':      # X⁽ⁱ⁾ → aX⁽ⁱ⁻¹⁾X⁽ⁱ⁻¹⁾
            X(i-1)
            X(i-1)
        elif z == 'b':    # X⁽ⁱ⁾ → bX⁽ⁱ⁻¹⁾
            X(i-1)
        else:             # X⁽ⁱ⁾ → X⁽ⁱ⁻¹⁾
            X(i-1)
    else:                 # X⁽⁰⁾ → c
        pass
    return
```

Naturally, the question arises if Newton's method can also be related to certain runs resp. derivation trees of the context-free grammar describing the control-flow of the recursive program.

As shown in [KLE07] the runs resp. derivation trees evaluated by Newton's method are characterized by the *Strahler number*.[8]

Just as the height, the Strahler number is defined for any rooted or even ordered tree. For its formal definition we represent ordered trees as nested tuples, i.e. the tree of height 0 corresponds to the empty tuple $()$, any other tree is a tuple $(t_1, \ldots, t_r)$ of trees $t_1, \ldots, t_r$. The height of a tree t is inductively defined as

$$h((t_1, \ldots, t_r)) = \begin{cases} 0 & \text{if } r = 0 \\ 1 + \max\{h(t_i) \mid 1 \leq i \leq r\} & \text{otherwise} \end{cases}$$

and its Strahler number is

$$s((t_1, \ldots, t_r)) = \begin{cases} 0 & \text{if } r = 0 \\ \max_{1 \leq i \leq r} s(t_i) & \text{if } r > 0 \text{ and } |\arg\max_{1 \leq i \leq r} s(t_i)| = 1 \\ 1 + \max_{1 \leq i \leq r} s(t_i) & \text{if } r > 0 \text{ and } |\arg\max_{1 \leq i \leq r} s(t_i)| > 1 \end{cases}$$

While the definitions are stated in a bottom-up way, we may also read them top-down: the main difference is that when moving from $(t_1, \ldots, t_r)$ to any t_i the height must always decrease, whereas the Strahler number must only drop *for all except at most one* t_i. For instance, consider the following derivation trees

---

[8] In [KLE07] the concept of *tree dimension* was introduced to characterize Newton's method which was actually already known both as *Strahler number* and also *register number*, see [ELS14] for more details.

which only differ in how often the *linear* rule $X \to bX$ is iterated in the left-most branch:

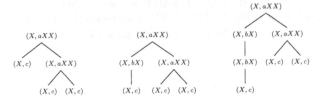

the first and second tree have height 2 and the right-most one has height 3, but all of them have only a Strahler number of 1. In particular, iterating the linear rule $X \to bX$ does not change the Strahler number, but eventually increases the height with each additional iteration. This exemplifies that in general there can be infinitely many derivation trees of a given Strahler number, but only finitely many of a given height.

Similar to the height, we can also unfold the original grammar, as shown in [LS13b], w.r.t. the Strahler number:

$$
\begin{aligned}
X^{(=0)} &\to c \mid bX^{(=0)} \\
X^{(=1)} &\to bX^{(=1)} \mid aX^{(=1)}X^{(=0)} \mid aX^{(=0)}X^{(=1)} \mid aX^{(=0)}X^{(=0)} \\
X^{(\leq 1)} &\to X^{(=0)} \mid X^{(=1)} \\
&\;\;\vdots \\
X^{(=i+1)} &\to bX^{(=i+1)} \mid aX^{(=i+1)}X^{(\leq i)} \mid aX^{(\leq i)}X^{(=i+1)} \mid aX^{(=i)}X^{(=i)} \\
X^{(\leq i+1)} &\to X^{(\leq i)} \mid X^{(=i+1)}
\end{aligned}
$$

In contrast to the unfolding w.r.t. the height, we need to distinguish whether the Strahler number stays the same (by means of $X^{(=i+1)}$) or whether it decreases by at least one (by means of $X^{(\leq i)}$). E.g. consider

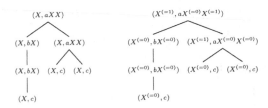

Formally, describing the unfolding w.r.t. the Strahler number becomes quite technical because of the combinatorial explosion that results from the case distinction w.r.t. the precise value of $|\arg\max_{1 \leq i \leq r} s(t_i)|$ which requires an enumeration of all possible subsets of size at least 2. By introducing auxiliary variables, as e.g. in the Kuroda normal form, we can always achieve that on the right-hand side of every rule at most two nonterminals occur: then the construction just discussed in the example immediately generalizes.

As already hinted at in the above discussion, every context-free grammar gives rise to a system of fixed-point equations whose right-hand sides are polynomials with the variables being the nonterminals of the grammar. Conversely, every system of polynomial equations is related to a context-free grammar via the Kleene iteration. This observation was first made by Chomsky and Schützenberger in [CS63].

In case of a system of polynomial, or *algebraic*, fixed-point equations

$$X_1 = f_1(X_1, \ldots, X_n) \wedge \ldots \wedge X_n = f(X_1, \ldots, X_n)$$

each f_i is a polynomial in the variables $X_1, \ldots, X_n$ over some suitable algebraic structure that defines addition $+$ and multiplication $\cdot$. By introducing auxiliary variables, we may assume that each f_i is at most quadratic and of the form

$$f_i = c^{(i)} + \sum_{1 \le k \le n} b_k^{(i)} X_k + \sum_{1 \le k, l \le n} a_{k,l}^{(i)} X_k X_l$$

with $a_{k,l}^{(i)}, b_k^{(i)}, c^{(i)}$ the coefficients. The unfolding w.r.t. height h is then

$$
\begin{aligned}
X_i^{(0)} &= c^{(i)} \\
X_i^{(1)} &= X_i^{(0)} + \sum_{1 \le k \le n} b_k^{(i)} X_k^{(0)} + \sum_{1 \le k, l \le n} a_{k,l}^{(i)} X_k^{(0)} X_l^{(0)} \\
&\vdots \\
X_i^{(h+1)} &= X_i^{(h)} + \sum_{1 \le k \le n} b_k^{(i)} X_k^{(h)} + \sum_{1 \le k, l \le n} a_{k,l}^{(i)} X_k^{(h)} X_l^{(h)}
\end{aligned}
$$

whereas the one w.r.t. the Strahler number s is

$$
\begin{aligned}
X_i^{(=0)} &= c^{(i)} + \sum_{1 \le k \le n} b_k^{(i)} X_k^{(=0)} \\
X_i^{(=1)} &= \sum_{1 \le k \le n} b_k^{(i)} X_k^{(=1)} \\
&\quad + \sum_{1 \le k, l \le n} a_{k,l}^{(i)} \left(X_k^{(=0)} X_l^{(=1)} + X_k^{(=1)} X_l^{(=0)} + X_k^{(=0)} X_l^{(=0)} \right) \\
X_i^{(\le 1)} &= X_i^{(=0)} + X_i^{(=1)} \\
&\vdots \\
X_i^{(=s+1)} &= \sum_{1 \le k \le n} b_k^{(i)} X_k^{(=s+1)} \\
&\quad + \sum_{1 \le k, l \le n} a_{k,l}^{(i)} \left(X_k^{(\le s)} X_l^{(=s+1)} + X_k^{(=s+1)} X_l^{(\le s)} + X_k^{(=s)} X_l^{(=s)} \right) \\
X_i^{(\le s+1)} &= X_i^{(\le s)} + X_i^{(=s+1)}
\end{aligned}
$$

This is just the direct generalization as for the case of the univariate grammar $X \to c \mid bX \mid aXX$ resp. the equation $X = c + bX + aXX$.

As shown in [LS13b], this unfolding when applied to the fixed-point systems describing the termination probabilities of a stochastic recursive program indeed specializes to Newton's method over the reals, more precisely the subsemiring of nonnegative real numbers.

Informally, this can be deduced from the representation of Newton's method using the geometric series discussed in the preceding section:

$$x_{i+1} = x_i + (f'(x_i))^*(f(x_i) - x_i)$$

The Jacobian $f'(x_i)$ substitutes in each monomial for each variable (except one) the corresponding value of the current approximation x_i, i.e. the Jacobian "flattens" the recursive program into a "linear" recursive program whose control flow can be described by a linear context-free grammar; the geometric series then simply computes the reflexive-transitive closure of the flattened program whose runs are the language of the linear context-free grammar.

Example 4. *Going back to our original example of the stochastic plotter, recall that the termination probabilities in the end were given by the equation*

$$x = f(x) := 0.125x^2 + 0.75x + 0.125$$

i.e. we have $c = 1/8$, $b = 3/4$ and $a = 1/8$. Substituting these values into the unfolding w.r.t. the Strahler number yields

$$
\begin{aligned}
X^{(=0)} &= \tfrac{1}{8} + \tfrac{3}{4}X^{(=0)} \\
X^{(=1)} &= \tfrac{3}{4}X^{(=1)} + \tfrac{1}{8}\left(X^{(=1)}X^{(=0)} + X^{(=0)}X^{(=1)} + X^{(=0)}X^{(=0)}\right) \\
X^{(\leq 1)} &= X^{(=0)} + X^{(=1)}
\end{aligned}
$$

$$\vdots$$

$$
\begin{aligned}
X^{(=s+1)} &= \tfrac{3}{4}X^{(=s+1)} + \tfrac{1}{8}\left(X^{(=s+1)}X^{(\leq s)} + X^{(\leq s)}X^{(=s+1)} + X^{(=s)}X^{(=s)}\right) \\
X^{(\leq s+1)} &= X^{(\leq s)} + X^{(=s+1)}
\end{aligned}
$$

Solving the system for $X^{(=0)}$, $X^{(=1)}$ and $X^{(\leq 1)}$ yields

$$
\begin{aligned}
X^{(=0)} &= \tfrac{1}{8} + \tfrac{3}{4}X^{(=0)} \\
&= \left(1 - \tfrac{3}{4}\right)^{-1}\tfrac{1}{8} = \tfrac{1}{2} \\
X^{(=1)} &= \tfrac{3}{4}X^{(=1)} + \tfrac{1}{8}\left(X^{(=1)}X^{(=0)} + X^{(=0)}X^{(=1)} + X^{(=0)}X^{(=0)}\right) \\
&= \left(1 - \tfrac{3}{4} - \tfrac{1}{8}\cdot\tfrac{1}{2} - \tfrac{1}{8}\cdot\tfrac{1}{2}\right)^{-1}\tfrac{1}{8}\cdot\tfrac{1}{2}\cdot\tfrac{1}{2} = \tfrac{1}{4} \\
X^{(\leq 1)} &= X^{(=0)} + X^{(=1)} \\
&= \tfrac{1}{2} + \tfrac{1}{4} = \tfrac{3}{4}
\end{aligned}
$$

which exactly coincides with the Newton approximations x_1, $x_2 - x_1$, and x_2. Induction then shows that solving for $X^{(=s)}$ yields exactly the value of $x_{s+1} - x_s$ s.t. the value of $X^{(\leq s)}$ equals the $s + 1$-st Newton approximation x_{s+1}. □

Representing Newton Approximations. An immediate consequence of the preceding discussion is that we can define Newton's method for any system of polynomial fixed-point equations without the need of subtraction (additively inverse elements).

In [EKL07,EKL10b] it is still required that a suitable difference $f(x_i) - x_i$ is computable: e.g. if addition is idempotent, then we have $x_i + f(x_i) = f(x_i)$ by monotonicity of Newton's method, and thus we can replace $f(x_i) - x_i$ by $f(x_i)$.

As already mentioned in [LS13a], the unfolding of the system or grammar w.r.t. the Strahler number allows us to represent each approximation using rational tree expressions. Informally, a tree series is a function from the terms over a ranked alphabet to some semiring, and a rational tree expression generalizes the concept of regular expressions in order to describe the construction of tree series using some notion of addition, multiplication, and linear iteration (expressed by the Kleene star). To avoid the technicalities, we use *contexts* [DKV09]: A pair (u, v) of words $u, v \in \Sigma^*$ is called a *context* where (u, ε) can be identified with the word u; addition of contexts is simply the "free" unevaluated addition, while multiplication of contexts simply corresponds to substitution "in-the-middle", i.e. $(u, v)(x, y) := (ux, yv)$ and $(u, v)w := uwv$ for $u, v, w, x, y \in \Sigma^*$. The Kleene star $(u, v)^*Y$ then denotes the least solution of $X = uXv + Y$. Inductively, we can extend this from contexts to expressions built from contexts. E.g. $((a, b)^*c, d)^*$ represents $\sum_{n, k \in \mathbb{N}_0} (a^k c b^k)^n d^n$. Hence, we may represent the language generated by linear context-free grammars in this way.

As in the unfolding w.r.t. the Strahler number, the variable $X^{(=s)}$ only depends linearly on itself, or on variables of strictly lower Strahler number, we can express the values of all variables $X^{(=s)}$ and $X^{(\leq s)}$ as "rational context expressions".[9] E.g. in case of

$$X = aXX + bX + c$$

we only need to consider

$$X^{(=s+1)} = bX^{(=s+1)} + aX^{(=s+1)}X^{(\leq s)} + aX^{(\leq s)}X^{(=s+1)} + aX^{(=s)}X^{(=s)}$$

We can either directly solve for $X^{(=s+1)}$ and obtain

$$X^{(=s+1)} = \left((b, \varepsilon) + (a, X^{(\leq s)}) + (aX^{(\leq s)}, \varepsilon)\right)^* aX^{(=s)}X^{(=s)}$$

or we may first use the Kleene star to remove $bX^{(=s+1)}$

$$X^{(=s+1)} = b^*aX^{(=s+1)}X^{(\leq s)} + b^*aX^{(\leq s)}X^{(=s+1)} + b^*aX^{(=s)}X^{(=s)}$$

and then in a second step obtain:

$$X^{(=s+1)} = \left((b^*a, X^{(\leq s)}) + b^*(aX^{(\leq s)}, \varepsilon)\right)^* b^*aX^{(=s)}X^{(=s)}$$

This corresponds to removing right-linear rules (in particular chain rules) in context-free grammars. We then have

$$
\begin{aligned}
X^{(=0)} \;&= (b, \varepsilon)^*c = b^*c \\
X^{(=1)} \;&= ((a, b^*c) + (ab^*c, \varepsilon) + (b, \varepsilon))^*a(b^*c)(b^*c) \\
&= ((b^*a, b^*c) + (b^*acb^*, \varepsilon))^* b^*a(b^*c)(b^*c) \\
X^{(\leq 1)} \;&= X^{(=0)} + X^{(=1)} \\
&\;\;\vdots \\
X^{(=s+1)} \;&= ((b^*a, X^{(\leq s)}) + (b^*aX^{(\leq s)}, \varepsilon))^* b^*aX^{(=s)}X^{(=s)} \\
X^{(\leq s+1)} \;&= X^{(\leq s)} + X^{(s+1)}
\end{aligned}
$$

---

[9] Usually, "regular expression" is used if addition is idempotent, but to represent Newton's method in general, we must keep track of multiplicities, hence the resulting expressions are called "rational".

If we allow the coefficients to commute, as it is the case of the termination probabilities, we have $(u, v) = (uv, \varepsilon) = uv$, so that conventional rational expressions in monomials suffice.

$$\begin{aligned}
X^{(=0)} &= (b, \varepsilon)^* c = b^* c \\
X^{(=1)} &= \left(2ab^* b^* c\right)^* ab^* b^* b^* c \\
X^{(\leq 1)} &= X^{(=0)} + X^{(=1)}
\end{aligned}$$

$$\vdots$$

$$\begin{aligned}
X^{(=s+1)} &= \left(2ab^* X^{(\leq s)}\right)^* ab^* X^{(=s)} X^{(=s)} \\
X^{(\leq s+1)} &= X^{(\leq s)} + X^{(s+1)}
\end{aligned}$$

Note that for *regular* expressions we would assume idempotence, so that

$$2ab^* X^{(\leq s)} = ab^* X^{(\leq s)}$$

holds; but for rational expressions we do not assume idempotence – then the additional natural numbers count the ambiguity of a word *modulo commutativity*.

Example 5. *Going back to the stochastic plotter, evaluating the expressions w.r.t. $a = c = 1/8$ and $b = 3/4$ gives rise to a homomorphism from the free semiring generated by a, b, c to the semiring of non-negative reals that maps b^* to the geometric series s.t.*

$$(x)^* \mapsto (1 - x)^{-1}$$

The above recurrence becomes

$$\begin{aligned}
X^{(=s+1)} &= \left(2\tfrac{1}{8}(\tfrac{3}{4})^* X^{(\leq s)}\right)^* \tfrac{1}{8} \left(\tfrac{3}{4}\right)^* \left(\tfrac{3}{4}\right)^* X^{(=s)} X^{(=s)} \\
&= \left(2\tfrac{1}{8} \cdot 4 X^{(\leq s)}\right)^* \tfrac{1}{8} \cdot 4^2 X^{(=s)} X^{(=s)} \\
&= \left(1 - X^{(\leq s)}\right)^{-1} 2 X^{(=s)} X^{(=s)} \\
X^{(\leq s+1)} &= X^{(\leq s)} + X^{(=s+1)}
\end{aligned}$$

which yields the already computed Newton approximations again:

$$\begin{aligned}
X^{(=0)} &= \left(\tfrac{3}{4}\right)^* \tfrac{1}{8} = \tfrac{1}{2} \\
X^{(=1)} &= \left(1 - \tfrac{1}{2}\right)^{-1}\left(2 \cdot \tfrac{1}{2} \cdot \tfrac{1}{2}\right) = \tfrac{1}{4} \\
X^{(\leq 1)} &= \tfrac{1}{2} + \tfrac{1}{4} = \tfrac{3}{4} \\
X^{(=2)} &= \left(1 - \tfrac{3}{4}\right)^{-1} 2 \cdot \tfrac{1}{4} \cdot \tfrac{1}{4} = \tfrac{1}{8} \\
X^{(\leq 2)} &= \tfrac{3}{4} + \tfrac{1}{8} = \tfrac{7}{8}
\end{aligned}$$

$$\vdots$$

Induction then shows that we indeed have $X^{(=s)} = 2^{-s-1}$ and $X^{(\leq s)} = 1 - 2^{-s-1}$ so that $X^{(\leq s)}$ is indeed the $(s+1)$-th Newton approximation. $\square$

Sharing of Common Subterms. Given the recursive structure of the unfolding, we can effectively solve the recursion using the Kleene star by treating $X^{(\leq s)}, X^{(=s)}$ as parameters. For simplicity, in the univariate case we have

$$X^{(=s+1)} = aX^{(\leq s)}X^{(=s+1)} + aX^{(=s+1)}X^{(\leq s)} + bX^{(=s+1)} + aX^{(=s)}X^{(=s)}$$
$$= \left(2ab^*X^{(\leq s)}\right)^* ab^*X^{(=s)}X^{(=s)}$$

This avoids the exponential blow-up that would result from substituting the expressions for $X^{(\leq s)}$ and $X^{(=s)}$ as we can share common subterms leading to a "circuit" built from addition, multiplication and the Kleene star as operators. Depending on the additional properties of the given semiring, we then may further simplify the expressions resulting in a more succinct representation of the Newton approximations, see e.g. [LS14].

Contexts and the Kronecker Product. Finally, we like to remark that in certain cases contexts can be represented as matrices using the *Kronecker product*. Let S be a *commutative* semiring. For matrices $A \in S^{m \times n}$, $B \in S^{p \times r}$ the map $h(X) := AXB$ which maps a matrix $X \in S^{n \times p}$ to a matrix in $S^{m \times r}$ is linear. It thus has to be representable as a matrix – at least if we serialize $X \in S^{n \times p}$ into a vector $v_X \in S^{np}$. The corresponding operation is called the *Kronecker product*, usually denoted by $\otimes$ as it also allows us to represent the product of tensors in general. It can be shown that matrix representing AXB is then given by $(B^{\top} \otimes A) \in S^{mr \times np}$, i.e. we then have

$$AXB = C \quad \text{if and only if} \quad (B^{\top} \otimes A)v_X = v_C$$

For instance, in case of the semiring of endorelations $R \subseteq \Omega \times \Omega$ with $|\Omega| = K$ finite, we may represent every semiring element as $K \times K$-adjacency matrix (over the boolean semiring), and thus a context (R, S) can be represented by the $K^2 \times K^2$ matrix $S^{\top} \otimes R$.

In general, the advantage of using this explicit representation over the general representation using rational context expressions is not obvious, as the latter can simply be evaluated to the $K \times K$-matrix and also works for noncommutative semirings. In particular, the rational expressions encode explicitly cycles in the recursive program and thus allow one to apply acceleration techniques like repeated squaring or general widening. For instance, Presburger definable relations can be represented as finite automata and libraries like *lash* offer functions for computing the Kleene star at least for certain relations [Boi03].

Example 6. *For a simple example consider the program*

```
def F(x: int):
    if x >= 0:      # F₁ → a
        pass
    else:           # F₁ → āF₂
        x = x + 1   # F₂ → bF₃
        F(x)        # F₃ → F₁F₄
        x = x - 1   # F₄ → b̄
    return
```

Here, the terminal a denotes the partial identity on $\mathbb{Z}$ with $a(x) = x$, if $x \geq 0$, and $a(x)$ undefined, if $x < 0$. Similarly, $\bar{a}$ denotes the complementary identity, b stands for the increment, and $\bar{b}$ decrement on $\mathbb{Z}$. Contracting the rules gives rise to the equation:

$$F_1 = a + \bar{a}bF_1\bar{b} = (\bar{a}b, \bar{b})^*a$$

From this expression, we still can deduce that the program terminates for all inputs (The expression describes all finite runs and we can reason that every behavior is covered by that: every initial argument $x \in \mathbb{Z}$ will eventually be incremented beyond 0 and then F terminates and restores x to its initial value).

For comparison, assume we want to represent these operations by (finite) matrices. For simplicity, assume that we "collapse" $\mathbb{Z}$ at 1 and -1, respectively, so that $-1 - 1 = -1$ and $1 + 1 = 1$. Then we may represent these functions as boolean matrices where the values $-1, 0, 1$ are represented by the canonical unit vector e_1, e_2, e_3, respectively: To represent the test a, note that for inputs 0 $(= e_2)$ and 1 $(= e_3)$ it reproduces those inputs and for -1 $(= e_1)$ it results in 0. Hence we have

$$M_a = \begin{pmatrix} 0 & 0 & 0 \\ 0 & 1 & 0 \\ 0 & 0 & 1 \end{pmatrix} \quad M_{\bar{a}} = \begin{pmatrix} 1 & 0 & 0 \\ 0 & 0 & 0 \\ 0 & 0 & 0 \end{pmatrix}$$

for the "test"-operation "$\texttt{if x>=0}$". Similarly we obtain the matrices representing the increment and decrement operations:

$$M_b = \begin{pmatrix} 0 & 1 & 0 \\ 0 & 0 & 1 \\ 0 & 0 & 1 \end{pmatrix} \quad M_{\bar{b}} = \begin{pmatrix} 1 & 0 & 0 \\ 1 & 0 & 0 \\ 0 & 1 & 0 \end{pmatrix}$$

We now may compute in the semiring of boolean matrices with addition given by disjunction or maximum, and multiplication by conjunction or minimum. Of course, the Kleene star becomes directly the reflexive-transitive closure of the relations represented by the matrices:

$$F_1 = M_a + M_{\bar{a}}M_bF_1M_{\bar{b}}$$

Using the Kronecker product this can be written

$$v_{F_1} = v_{M_a} + \left(M_{\bar{b}}^{\top} \otimes (M_{\bar{a}}M_b)\right) v_{F_1} = \left(M_{\bar{b}}^{\top} \otimes (M_{\bar{a}}M_b)\right)^* v_{M_a}$$

Given the evaluated matrix expression it becomes at least more difficult to deduce termination of the procedure.

Still, in certain cases the representation using the Kronecker product seems to have some advantages, see e.g. [RTP16], and also see also the discussion in [Sch16]. However, note that boolean matrices form a finite semiring where there is no need to use Newton's method – the real advantage would only be visible for matrices over an infinite (commutative) semiring!

5   Convergence via Combinatorics on Trees

One reason for studying Newton's method for context-free grammars and, more generally, algebraic systems over semirings was the question whether the convergence result for the nonnegative real numbers could be recovered using combinatorial and language-theoretical arguments. The question was motivated by the observation [EKL07] that a result by Hopkins and Kozen on a generalization of Parikh's theorem [HK99] can be understood as the proof that Newton's method converges within N iterations for every system of N fixed-point equations over commutative Kleene algebras. While their result is based on Kozen's axiomatization of Kleene algebras, by virtue of Redko's theorem [Con12] it suffices to consider the free commutative and idempotent semiring of languages generated by the coefficients resp. terminals [EKL07].

Example 7. *The basic idea is that given a derivation tree t we rewrite it into a derivation tree t' by relocating subtrees while reducing the dimension at the same time. In general, we need to type derivation trees w.r.t. the variables. We sketch the basic idea again for the univariate case by means of*

$$X = aXX + bX + c \qquad resp. \qquad X \to aXX \mid bX \mid c$$

As mentioned before, we may identify derivation trees with terms over the ranked alphabet $\{a, b, c\}$. I.e. we may identify

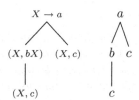

Then commutativity implies the following equivalences for all terms t, t', t'':

$$a(b(t), t') = a(t, b(t')) \qquad a(t, a(t', t'')) = a(a(t', t), t'') \qquad b(a(t, t')) = a(t, b(t'))$$

which allows us to relocate all bs into the right-most subtree, while relocating all as into the left-most subtree. This translates into the following rewrite rules

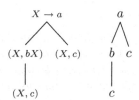

Hence, we can normalize any term resp. derivation tree s.t. it is of the form

$$(ac)^k b^m c$$

Modulo idempotence, the rational expression $(ac)^*b^*c$ *thus already describes all derivation trees which are all have Strahler number at most one and are thus already evaluated by* $X^{(\le 1)}$. □

More generally, it was shown in [LS13b] that Newton's method converges *modulo commutative multiplication* in general at least double exponentially in the following sense: *If the coefficient of a monomial in the* $N + k + 1$-*st Newton approximation has not converged, then it is at least* 2^{1+2^k}, *where* N *is the number of equations.* We examplify this result by means of the Catalan numbers:

Example 8. *For simplicity, we drop the linear part and only consider*

$$X = aXX + c \qquad resp. \qquad X \to aXX \mid c$$

Note that we did not specify a semiring on which to interpret $+, \cdot,$ *or what "0" is, but we can just consider the "most general semiring", i.e. the free semiring generated by the terminals. The least solution then becomes a formal power series. E.g. when applying Kleene iteration we obtain the following approximations:*

i	$f^i(0)$	$f^i(0) \mod (ac = ca)$
0	c	c
1	$c + acc$	$c + ac^2$
2	$c + acc + aaccc + acacc + aaccacc$	$c + ac^2 + 2a^2c^3 + a^3c^4$
⋮	⋮	⋮

The column in the middle shows the approximations in the noncommutative case, while the column on the right lists the approximations when we further assume that the terminals commute (so that words become monomials).

Treating a *and* c *again as operator symbols, every word corresponds to a binary tree, in other words, the grammar resp. equation generates all binary trees. As the grammar is unambiguous, every tree is generated exactly once, thus the least solution is simply the sum of over all words representing binary trees. Hence,* $f^i(0)$ *is the sum over all words representing binary trees of height less than* i.

If we assume multiplication to be commutative, all words containing the letter a *exactly* n *times (and thus the letter* c *exactly* $n+1$ *times) will become equivalent to the monomial* $a^n c^{n+1}$. *The least solution is thus the formal power series*

$$\sum_{n \in \mathbb{N}} C_n a^n c^{n+1} = 1c + 1ac^2 + 2a^2c^3 + 5a^3c^4 + 14a^4c^5 + 42a^5c^6 + 132a^6c^7 + 429a^7c^8 + \dots$$

with $C_n = \frac{1}{n+1}\binom{2n}{n}$ *the Catalan numbers. The first time that modulo commutativity* $f^i(0)$ *will evaluate* $a^n c^{n+1}$ *for a given* n *is for the minimal height of a tree with* $n+1$ *leaves, namely* $i = 1 + \lceil \log_2(n+1) \rceil$. *And the coefficient of* $a^n c^{n+1}$ *will have converged only for* $i \ge n$. *One way of measuring the speed of convergence is thus to count the monomials* $a^n c^{n+1}$ *whose coefficient in the approximation has already converged to* C_n.

Now consider the Newton approximations. Modulo commutativity, we obtain (see the preceding section for $b = 0$)

$$
\begin{aligned}
X^{(=0)} &= c \\
X^{(=1)} &= (2ac)^* ac \\
X^{(\leq 1)} &= X^{(=0)} + X^{(=1)}
\end{aligned}
$$

$$
\vdots
$$

$$
\begin{aligned}
X^{(=s+1)} &= \left(2aX^{(\leq s)}\right)^* aX^{(=s)}X^{(=s)} \\
X^{(\leq s+1)} &= X^{(\leq s)} + X^{(s+1)}
\end{aligned}
$$

For instance, we have

$$
\begin{aligned}
X^{(\leq 2)} &= (2a((2ac)^*ac^2 + c))^*a((2ac)^*ac^2)^2 \\
&= 1c + 1ac^2 + 2a^2c^3 + 5a^3c^4 + 14a^4c^5 + 42a^5c^6 + 132a^6c^7 + 428a^7c^8 + \ldots
\end{aligned}
$$

which has already converged in the coefficients of a^nc^{n+1} up to $n = 6$. Recall that $X^{(\leq k)}$ evaluates all derivation trees of Strahler number k and that k is also the maximal height of a perfect binary tree that is a minor of the given derivation tree. Hence, in $X^{(\leq k)}$ exactly the coefficients of the monomials a^nc^{n+1} with $\log_2(n+1) \leq k$ have converged which yields at least an exponential convergence rate w.r.t. the number of monomials whose coefficient have converged.[10] A more careful analysis shows that for the remaining a^nc^{n+1} with $\log_2(n+1) > k$ their coefficient in $X^{(\leq k)}$ is at least 2^{1+2^k} which is still a very conservative lower bound, at least in this example. For instance, expanding $X^{(\leq 2)}$ further yields

$$
\begin{aligned}
\ldots &+ 428a^7c^8 + 1416a^8c^9 + 4744a^9c^{10} + 16016a^{10}c^{11} + 54320a^{11}c^{12} \\
&+ 184736a^{12}c^{13} + 629280a^{13}c^{14} + 2145600a^{14}c^{15} + 7319744a^{15}c^{16} + \ldots
\end{aligned}
$$

Comparing the coefficients with the Catalan numbers

$$
\ldots, 429, 1430, 4862, 16796, 58786, 208012, 742900, 2674440, 9694845, \ldots
$$

we see that $2^{1+2^2} = 32$ is a very loose lower bound.   □

From the result in [LS13b], we may conclude that Newton's method converges over any commutative semiring that is *collapsed* at $m \in \mathbb{N}_0$, i.e. $m = m + 1$, within at most $N + \log_2 \log_2 m$ iterations for N the number of equations. (An idempotent semiring is collapsed at $m = 1$.) Unfortunately, this result is too conservative to recover the convergence results of the termination probabilities. Yet, the combinatorial study of the derivation trees resp. terms evaluated by Newton's method underlying its proof turned out to be useful. We give a short overview of some of its most interesting applications, for details we refer the reader to the respective original article.

Idempotent Semirings [LS13b]. Idempotent addition on its own cannot guarantee convergence as seen in the preceding example of the language of binary trees

---

[10] In [PSS12a] this is called *quadratic convergence*.

generated by $X = aXX + c$. In fact, the characterization of Newton's method by means of the Strahler number immediately yields that modulo idempotent addition Newton's method will converge in k steps if and only if every word of the generated language has a derivation tree of Strahler number at most k. Still this allows us to relate Newton's method to the notion of *nonexpansive grammars* and *bounded derivations* studied by Ginsburg and Spanier in [GS68]:

By always rewriting the nonterminal along which the Strahler number does not decrease, it follows that every derivation tree of Strahler number s corresponds to a derivation in which each sentential form contains at most $s + 1$ terminals. This was called a *bounded derivation* by Ginsburg and Spanier [GS68].[11] They also show that given a general phrase-structure grammar, the sublanguage L_s generated by only allowing $(s+1)$-bounded derivations is always context-free; in particular, there is a *nonexpansive* CFG that generates the same language L_{s+1}.[12]

One-Bounded Semirings [EKL11]. A semiring is *one-bounded* if $1 + x = x$ holds for all semiring elements x. Such a semiring is necessarily idempotent with 1 the greatest element w.r.t. the natural order. This is a slight generalization of e.g. boolean algebras with 0 the least and 1 the greatest element. But note that the semiring is not required to be commutative. In particular, we have thus $a^* = 1 + aa^* = 1$, i.e. any kind of iteration can be skipped, which implies that we only need to consider derivation trees of height less than N. Hence, the least solution is already given by $f^N(0)$.

Star-Distributive Semirings [EKL11]. A semiring is *star-distributive* if $(x+y)^* = x^* + y^*$. Informally, this means that instead of considering all possible ways of iterating between two cycles reduces to the iteration of each cycle on its own. If the semiring is further idempotent and commutative, this implies that instead of N Newton steps, we only need N Kleene steps followed by a single Newton step to compute the least solution. This can be seen as a generalization of the Bellman-Ford algorithm to pushdown systems.

Lossy Semirings [EKL11]. A semiring is *lossy* if $1 + x = x$ holds for all semiring elements x other than 0. A lossy semiring is thus necessarily idempotent, but it is not required to be commutative. The motivation for studying such semirings is a "lossy" channel where a message might lose some symbols [ABJ98], e.g. sending $abcacc$ might result in receiving only $acac$. In case of context-free grammar, this corresponds to the *downward closure* of the language w.r.t. the infix order. If the system of equations is strongly connected, i.e. every variable depends on every other one transitively, and the maximal degree of every monomial is two,[13] then it can be shown that again N Kleene steps followed by a single Newton step suffices to compute the least solution and thus a regular expression representing the context-free language modulo "lossiness". This allows us to rephrase a result by

---

[11] See also [Ers58] where the Strahler number is called register number.

[12] A CFG is nonexpansive if every nonterminal X can only be rewritten into a sentential forms containing X at most once.

[13] Essentially Chomsky normal form with chain rules.

Courcelle [Cou91] as convergence result based on the combination of linearization and standard fixed-point iteration.

K-closed Semirings [LS14]. A semiring is *K-closed* if $x^* = 1 + x + x^2 + \ldots + x^K$ holds for every semiring element. Note that we have $1^* = (K+1)1 = K+1$, so any *K*-closed semiring is collapsed at $K+1$. If addition is even idempotent in a *K*-closed semiring, then we have $x^* = (1+x)^K$. For instance, consider the semiring of all endorelations $R \subseteq \Omega \times \Omega$ over some universe Ω: if $|\Omega| = K+1$, then $R^* = \bigcup_{i=0}^{\infty} R^i = \bigcup_{i=0}^{K} R^i = (\mathsf{Id} \cup R)^K$ as it suffices to consider only simple paths of lenght at most K.

Another example is the so-called *why-provenance* [GKT07]: in provenance analysis the question is which facts of the external database (ground truth) contributed to the answer to a given query. In case of *Datalog*, the query is essentially a first-order Horn clause set, and w.r.t. the Herbrand structure the query can be translated into a context-free grammar resp. polynomial equation system whose least solution is the answer to the query, i.e. the unique minimal Herbrand model. The *why-provenance* amounts to the assumption that addition is idempotent, and multiplication is both commutative and idempotent, i.e. we have $x^2 = x$. From this it follows that $x^* = (1+x)^{|\Sigma|}$ with Σ the alphabet, i.e. the constant symbols of the Herbrand universe – the classic example is that of a boolean semiring where monomials correspond to min-terms and polynomials to formulas in disjunctive normal form.

As discussed above, solving the unfolding w.r.t. the Strahler number for $X^{(\leq N)}$ yields a regular expression – assuming idempotent addition and commutative multiplication – that represents the least solution. If the semiring is further *K*-closed, we may unfold the Kleene star and thus obtain a finite sum of finite words or monomials (essentially a multiset of min-terms). Instead of explicitly expanding the regular expression, we may read the unfolding $X^{(\leq N)}$ as a straight-line program and use subterm sharing to encode $x^* = (1+x)^K$ by means of iterated squaring. This might also be considered a "circuit" representation, see e.g. [Deu+14].

6   Conclusion

The main goal of this article was to retrace the research that eventually led to [EKL10b]: From the initial question how Newton's method can be related to the runs of a recursive program, over the characterization of these runs by means of the Strahler number (originally called *tree dimension*), and the representation of Newton's method as an unfolding of the equation system w.r.t. the Strahler number – without the need of commutative multiplication, idempotent addition, or invertible addition.

As already briefly mentioned, one motivation for the study of Newton's method on semirings was the question if the convergence on the nonnegative reals could be explained using combinatorial and language-theoretical arguments. While the result obtained in [LS13b] is an improvement over the result in [EKL07], the obtained bound is still too conservative. Most likely, an improved bound has to take into account the structure of the system of equations in a more detailed way. Still the combinatorial study of the derivations trees associated with Newton's method allows one to prove its convergence at least for particular semirings where addition is idempotent or, slightly more general, collapsed.

Another application of the characterization of Newton's method as an unfolding w.r.t. the Strahler number is that the latter can be can also be understood as a form of *annotation* in the sense of natural language processing (NLP). In NLP the nonterminals of a given context-free grammar are *annotated* with a restricted from of context, corresponding to state of a tree automaton, which can improve e.g. parsing accuracy: experiments indicate that combining the Strahler number with classic annotations used in NLP can further improve parsing accuracy [SLE14].

We also like to mention that besides the combinatorial study of Newton's method itself, it is also used in *analytic combinatorics* for efficient random sampling of combinatorial structures see e.g. [PSS12b] where the relation of Newton's method and the Strahler number was also rediscovered independently of [EKL07].

To close the circle, while originally, Esparza et al. used a saturation approach based on standard fixed-point iteration to analyze pushdown automata [BEM97, Esp+00, EKS01, ES01, SSE05], this obviously cannot terminate as soon as the underlying algebraic structure admits infinite strictly monotonically increasing sequences (ω-chains) and in general then only yields a very slow approximation method as seen in the case of the termination probabilities [EE04]. While also Newton's method cannot converge in these cases in a finite number of steps, the representation of the approximations via the unfolding encodes the iterated cyclic computations. This allows one to also obtain faster convergence speed or even converge to a safe over-approximation within a finite number of steps by means of techniques like widening. The latter has still to be studied in more detail: one potential candidate would be the combination of Newton's method with weights represented by number decision diagrams e.g. using *lash*.

References

[ABJ98] Abdulla, P.A., Bouajjani, A., Jonsson, B.: On-the-fly analysis of systems with unbounded, lossy FIFO channels. In: Hu, A.J., Vardi, M.Y. (eds.) CAV 1998. LNCS, vol. 1427, pp. 305–318. Springer, Heidelberg (1998). https://doi.org/10.1007/BFb0028754

[Boi03] Boigelot, B.: On iterating linear transformations over recognizable sets of integers. English. Theor. Comput. Sci. **309**, 1–3 (2003). ISSN: 0304–3975. https://doi.org/10.1016/S0304-3975(03)00314-1

[BEM97] Bouajjani, A., Esparza, J., Maler, O.: Reachability analysis of pushdown automata: application to model-checking. In: Mazurkiewicz, A.W., Winkowski, J. (eds.) CONCUR 1997: Concurrency Theory, 8th International Conference, Warsaw, Poland, 1–4 July 1997, Proceedings. LNCS, vol. 1243, pp. 135–150. Springer, Cham (1997). https://doi.org/10.1007/3-540-63141-0_10

[Boz99] Bozapalidis, S.: Equational elements in additive algebras. Theory Comput. Syst. **32**(1), 1–33 (1999). https://doi.org/10.1007/s002240000110

[CS63] Chomsky, N., Schützenberger, M.P.: The algebraic theory of context-free languages*. In: Braffort, P., Hirschberg, D. (eds.) Computer Programming and Formal Systems. Studies in Logic and the Foundations of Mathematics, vol. 35, pp. 118–161. Elsevier (1963). https://doi.org/10.1016/S0049-237X(08)72023-8

[Con12] Conway, J.H.: Regular Algebra and Finite Machines. Chapman and Hall Mathematics Series. Dover Publications, Incorporated, London (2012). ISBN: 9780486485836

[Cou91] Courcelle, B.: On constructing obstruction sets of words. Bull. EATCS **44**, 178–186 (1991)

[Deu+14] Deutch, D., et al.: Circuits for datalog provenance. In: Proceedings of 17th International Conference on Database Theory (ICDT), Athens, Greece, 24–28 March 2014, pp. 201–212 (2014). https://doi.org/10.5441/002/icdt.2014.22

[DK09] Droste, M., Kuich, W.: Handbook of Weighted Automata. In: Vogler, H., Droste, M., Kuich, W. (eds.) Chap. 1: Semirings and Formal Power Series, vol. 1, pp. 3–27. Springer, Cham (2009)

[DKV09] Droste, M., Kuich, W., Vogler, H.: Handbook of Weighted Automata, 1st edn. Springer, Cham (2009). ISBN: 3642014917, https://doi.org/10.1007/978-3-642-01492-5

[Ers58] Ershov, A.P.: On programming of arithmetic operations. Commun. ACM **1**(8), 3–9 (1958). https://doi.org/10.1145/368892.368907

[EE04] Esparza, J., Etessami, K.: Verifying probabilistic procedural programs. In: Lodaya, K., Mahajan, M. (eds.) FSTTCS 2004: Foundations of Software Technology and Theoretical Computer Science, 24th International Conference, Chennai, India, 16–18 December 2004, Proceedings. LNCS, vol. 3328, pp. 16–31. Springer, Cham (2004). https://doi.org/10.1007/978-3-540-30538-5_2

[EKL07] Esparza, J., Kiefer, S., Luttenberger, M.: An extension of Newton's method to Omega-continuous semirings. In: Harju, T., Karhumäki, J., Lepistö, A. (eds.) Developments in Language Theory, 11th International Conference, DLT 2007, Turku, Finland, 3–6 July 2007, Proceedings. LNCS, vol. 4588, pp. 157–168. Springer, Cham (2007). https://doi.org/10.1007/978-3-540-73208-2_17

[EKL10a] Esparza, J., Kiefer, S., Luttenberger, M.: Computing the least fixed point of positive polynomial systems. SIAM J. Comput. **39**(6), 2282–2335 (2010). https://doi.org/10.1137/090749591

[EKL10b] Esparza, J., Kiefer, S., Luttenberger, M.: Newtonian program analysis. J. ACM **57**(6), 33:1–33:47 (2010). https://doi.org/10.1145/1857914.1857917

[EKL11] Esparza, J., Kiefer, S., Luttenberger, M.: Derivation tree analysis for accelerated fixed-point computation. Theor. Comput. Sci. **412**(28), 3226–3241 (2011). https://doi.org/10.1016/j.tcs.2011.03.020

[EKM04] Esparza, J., Kucera, A., Mayr, R.: Model checking probabilistic pushdown automata. In: 19th IEEE Symposium on Logic in Computer Science (LICS 2004), 14–17 July 2004, Turku, Finland, Proceedings, pp. 12–21. IEEE Computer Society (2004). https://doi.org/10.1109/LICS.2004.1319596

[EKS01] Esparza, J., Kucera, A., Schwoon, S.: Model-checking LTL with regular valuations for pushdown systems. In: Kobayashi, N., Pierce, B.C. (eds.) Theoretical Aspects of Computer Software, 4th International Symposium, TACS 2001, Sendai, Japan, 29–31 October 2001, Proceedings. LNCS, vol. 2215, pp. 316–339. Springer, Cham (2001). https://doi.org/10.1007/3-540-45500-0_16

[ELS14] Esparza, J., Luttenberger, M., Schlund, M.: A brief history of Strahler numbers. In: Dediu, A.-H., et al. (eds.) Language and Automata Theory and Applications - 8th International Conference, LATA 2014, Madrid, Spain, 10–14 March 2014. Proceedings. LNCS, vol. 8370, pp. 1–13. Springer, Cham (2014). https://doi.org/10.1007/978-3-319-04921-2_1

[ES01] Esparza, J., Schwoon, S.: A BDD-based model checker for recursive programs. In: Berry, G., Comon, H., Finkel, A. (eds.) Computer Aided Verification, 13th International Conference, CAV 2001, Paris, France, 18–22 July 2001, Proceedings. LNCS, vol. 2102, pp. 324–336. Springer, Cham (2001). https://doi.org/10.1007/3-540-44585-4_30

[Esp+00] Esparza, J., et al.: Efficient algorithms for model checking pushdown systems. In: Emerson, E.A., Sistla, A.P. (eds.) Computer Aided Verification, 12th International Conference, CAV 2000, Chicago, IL, USA, 15–19 July 2000, Proceedings. LNCS, vol. 1855, pp. 232–247. Springer, Cham (2000). https://doi.org/10.1007/10722167_20

[Esp+08] Esparza, J., et al.: Approximative methods for monotone systems of min-max-polynomial equations. In: Aceto, L., et al. (eds.) Automata, Languages and Programming, 35th International Colloquium, ICALP 2008, Reykjavik, Iceland, 7–11 July 2008, Proceedings, Part I: Track A: Algorithms, Automata, Complexity, and Games. LNCS, vol. 5125, pp. 698–710. Springer, Cham (2008). https://doi.org/10.1007/978-3-540-70575-8_57

[EY05] Etessami, K., Yannakakis, M.: Recursive Markov chains, stochastic grammars, and monotone systems of nonlinear equations. In: Diekert, V., Durand, B. (eds.) STACS 2005, 22nd Annual Symposium on Theoretical Aspects of Computer Science, Stuttgart, Germany, 24–26 February 2005, Proceedings. LNCS, vol. 3404, pp. 340–352. Springer, Cham (2005). https://doi.org/10.1007/978-3-540-31856-9_28

[FV97] Filar, J., Vrieze, K.: Competitive Markov Decision Processes. Springer, New York (1997). https://doi.org/10.1007/978-1-4612-4054-9

[GS68] Ginsburg, S., Spanier, E.H.: Derivation-bounded languages. J. Comput. Syst. Sci. 2(3), 228–250 (1968). https://doi.org/10.1016/S0022-0000(68)80009-1

[GKT07] Green, T.J., Karvounarakis, G., Tannen, V.: Provenance semirings. In: PODS, pp. 31–40 (2007)

[HK99] Hopkins, M.W., Kozen, D.C.: Parikh's theorem in commutative Kleene algebra. In: Proceedings. 14th Symposium on Logic in Computer Science (Cat. No. PR00158), pp. 394–401 (1999). https://doi.org/10.1109/LICS.1999.782634

[KLE07] Kiefer, S., Luttenberger, M., Esparza, J.: On the convergence of Newton's method for monotone systems of polynomial equations. In: Johnson, D.S., Feige, U. (eds.) Proceedings of the 39th Annual ACM Symposium on Theory of Computing, San Diego, California, USA, 11–13 June 2007, pp. 217–226. ACM (2007). https://doi.org/10.1145/1250790.1250822

[Lut20] Luttenberger, M.: Algebraic Systems of Equations: Theory and Applications in Formal Languages and Game-Based Synthesis. Habilitation. Technische Universität München (2020)

[LS13a] Luttenberger, M., Schlund, M.: An extension of Parikh's theorem beyond idempotence (2013). arXiv:1112.2864 [cs.FL]

[LS13b] Luttenberger, M., Schlund, M.: Convergence of Newton's method over commutative semirings. In: Dediu, A.-H., Martín-Vide, C., Truthe, B. (eds.) Language and Automata Theory and Applications - 7th International Conference,

LATA 2013, Bilbao, Spain, 2–5 April 2013. Proceedings. LNCS, vol. 7810, pp. 407–418. Springer, Cham (2013). https://doi.org/10.1007/978-3-642-37064-9_36

[LS14]   Luttenberger, M., Schlund, M.: Regular expressions for provenance. In: Chapman, A., Ludäscher, B., Schreiber, A. (eds.) 6th Workshop on the Theory and Practice of Provenance, TaPP 2014, Cologne, Germany, 12–13 June 2014. USENIX Association (2014)

[PSS12a] Pivoteau, C., Salvy, B., Soria, M.: Algorithms for combinatorial structures: well-founded systems and Newton iterations. J. Comb. Theory, Ser. A **119**(8), 1711–1773 (2012). https://doi.org/10.1016/j.jcta.2012.05.007

[PSS12b] Pivoteau, C., Salvy, B., Soria, M.: Algorithms for combinatorial structures: well-founded systems and Newton iterations. J. Comb. Theory Ser. A **119**(8), 1711–1773 (2012). https://doi.org/10.1016/j.jcta.2012.05.007

[RTP16]   Reps, T.W., Turetsky, E., Prabhu, P.: Newtonian program analysis via tensor product. In: Proceedings of the 43rd Annual ACM SIGPLAN-SIGACT Symposium on Principles of Programming Languages, POPL 2016, St. Petersburg, FL, USA, 20–22 January 2016, pp. 663–677 (2016). https://doi.org/10.1145/2837614.2837659

[SS78]   Salomaa, A., Soittola, M.: Automata-Theoretic Aspects of Formal Power Series. Texts and Monographs in Computer Science. Springer, Cham (1978). ISBN: 978-0-387-90282-1. https://doi.org/10.1007/978-1-4612-6264-0

[Sch16]   Schlund, M.: Algebraic systems of fixpoint equations over semirings: theory and applications. Ph.D. thesis. Technical University Munich (2016)

[SLE14]   Schlund, M., Luttenberger, M., Esparza, J.: Fast and accurate unlexicalized parsing via structural annotations. In: Bouma, G., Parmentier, Y. (eds.) Proceedings of the 14th Conference of the European Chapter of the Association for Computational Linguistics, EACL 2014, 26–30 April 2014, Gothenburg, Sweden, pp. 164–168. The Association for Computer Linguistics (2014)

[SSE05]   Suwimonteerabuth, D., Schwoon, S., Esparza, J.: jMoped: a Java bytecode checker based on moped. In: Halbwachs, N., Zuck, L.D. (eds.) Tools and Algorithms for the Construction and Analysis of Systems, 11th International Conference, TACAS 2005, Held as Part of the Joint European Conferences on Theory and Practice of Software, ETAPS 2005, Edinburgh, UK, 4–8 April 2005, Proceedings. LNCS, vol. 3440, pp. 541–545. Springer, Cham (2005). https://doi.org/10.1007/978-3-540-31980-1_35

Template-Based Verification
of Array-Manipulating Programs

Viktor Malík[1]([✉])[iD], Peter Schrammel[2,3][iD], and Tomáš Vojnar[1][iD]

[1] Brno University of Technology, Faculty of Information Technology, Brno, Czech Republic
{imalik,vojnar}@fit.vutbr.cz
[2] Diffblue Ltd., Oxford, UK
peter.schrammel@diffblue.com
[3] University of Sussex, Brighton, UK

Abstract. This work deals with the 2LS program verification framework that combines several verification techniques—namely, abstract domains, templated invariants, k-induction, bounded model checking, and SAT/SMT solving. A distinguishing feature of the approach used by 2LS is that it allows for seamless combinations of various program abstractions. In this work, we introduce a novel abstract template domain allowing 2LS to reason about arrays, using an arbitrary abstract domain to describe values that are stored inside the arrays (including nested arrays and dynamic linked data structures), and with the arrays possibly nested inside other structures. The approach uses array index expressions to split each array into multiple contiguous, non-overlapping segments and computes a different invariant for each of them. We illustrate the approach on a program dealing with a list of arrays and subsequently present how the new domain allowed 2LS to improve in the international software verification competition SV-COMP.

Keywords: Formal software verification · Arrays · Abstract domains · Templates of invariants · k-Induction · Bounded model checking · SAT/SMT solving

1 Introduction

Arrays are arguably one of the most fundamental data structures in software engineering. A majority of programs use them in one way or the other. This means that verification of array-manipulating programs has many potential applications. On the other hand, it still faces a lot of challenges which often stem from the very essential features of arrays.

One of such problems is that arrays are by definition compound data structures which have an arbitrary underlying (element) data type, but at the same time their number of elements may be parametric and not bounded in advance. Moreover, the size of an array can also change at runtime using low-level operations such as `realloc`. Therefore, it is often not sufficient to directly use existing scalar value analyses, but it is

The work was supported by the Czech Science Foundation project GA23-06506S, the FIT BUT internal project FIT-S-23-8151, and the Horizon Europe Chess project.

S. Kiefer et al. (Eds.): *Taming the Infinities of Concurrency*, LNCS 14660, pp. 206–224, 2024.
https://doi.org/10.1007/978-3-031-56222-8_12

necessary to combine these with specialised techniques reflecting the way how arrays are structured.

In this work, we address this problem in a way which allows us to reuse as many existing program analyses as possible. To this end, we develop our approach within the framework of so-called *template-based verification* implemented in the 2LS tool [9,24,31]. One of the main ideas of this framework is that it uses abstract interpretation with domains that are all required to have the same form of parametrized, fixed, quantifier-free, first-order logic formulae. This allows 2LS to use an SMT solver to reason about program properties and at the same time enables a straightforward combination of abstract domains with delegating a lot of the complexity to the solver itself.

Our main contribution is a proposal of an abstract domain for reasoning about the contents of arrays in 2LS. Thanks to the fact that 2LS already contains a number of existing abstract domains (such as the template polyhedra domain or the heap shape domain), our domain can be easily combined with them and can be used to reason about arrays containing various kinds of elements as well as about complex data structures containing arrays. One of such structures are *unrolled linked lists*, which we describe in the running example introduced at the end of this section.

Since 2LS uses an original approach to implement its abstract interpretation, we present its most important concepts in Sect. 2. After that, we propose our new array abstract domain in Sect. 3 and show how the results of 2LS in the International Competition on Software Verification (SV-COMP) improved once we implemented the proposed domain (Sect. 4). Finally, Sect. 5 gives an overview of other existing approaches to verification of array-manipulating programs, some of which were a great inspiration for our method.

Running Example. In Fig. 1, we introduce an example program, which we will use to illustrate the mechanisms proposed in this paper. The program features initialization of a data structure called an *unrolled linked list* [32], which is a linked list whose nodes contain arrays of values (in our case, up to 1000 integer values with the number of cells really in use given by the field `size`). To check correctness of operations over such a data structure, the verification tool needs to be able to reason over linked heap structures as well as the integer contents of arrays at the same time. 2LS already contains abstract domains for analyzing integer values as well as the shape of the heap, and, in this paper, we complement these with a new abstract domain for analyzing arrays.

2   Template-Based Verification of Programs

In this section, we present the most important concepts of 2LS that our work builds upon—for more details, see [9,24,31]. In its main verification loop, 2LS gradually unfolds program loops. Let k be the applied number of unfolding steps. Each version of the program obtained this way is translated into a *static single assignment (SSA)* form while approximating the (partially unrolled) program loops as described below. The SSA form is then translated into a first-order logical formula, and an attempt to find a k-inductive program invariant is done. If the discovered invariant is sufficient to show safety of the program, the verification succeeds. Otherwise, bounded model checking

```
1  struct node {
2    int data[1000];
3    int size;
4    struct node *next;
5  };
6
7  int main() {
8    struct node *list = NULL;
9    while (nondet()) {
10     struct node *n = malloc(sizeof(*n));
11     for (int i = 0; i < 1000; i++)
12       n->data[i] = 0;
13     n->size = 0;
14     n->next = list;
15     list = n;
16   }
17   int x = nondet(0,1000); // 0 <= x < 1000
18   assert(!list || list->data[x] == 0);
19 }
```

Fig. 1. Running example

is used to see whether a real error can be reached in k steps. If so, the verification fails. Otherwise, k gets increased, and another iteration of the main verification loop follows.

Since the SSA form used in 2LS has several unusual features that cannot be found in other verification approaches and since their understanding is important for understanding the rest of this work, we present it in detail in Sect. 2.1. Likewise, in Sects. 2.2 and 2.3, we present in more details the algorithm for inference of inductive invariants, which is at the heart of the 2LS' approach to abstract interpretation. The most important one is that all abstract domains are required to have the same form of so-called *templates* (hence, we denote the approach as *template-based verification*).

Templates are fixed, parametrized, first-order logic formulae, which allows 2LS to use an SMT solver to reason about them. Additionally, the unified form of the templates makes it easy to combine multiple abstract domains together (in the simplest form by just taking a conjunction of their templates) since the heavy-lifting of abstract operation combinators can be left to the underlying solver. Thanks to this feature, our newly proposed domain for reasoning about array contents can be easily combined with other domains already present in 2LS, which will, e.g., allow us to verify the running example program from Fig. 1.

2.1 Internal Program Representation

The 2LS framework is built upon the CPROVER infrastructure [14] and therefore uses the same intermediate representation called *GOTO programs*. In this procedural language, any non-linear control flow, such as if or switch statements, loops, or jumps, is translated to equivalent *guarded goto* statements. These statements are branch instructions that include (optional) conditions. CPROVER generates one GOTO program per C function found in the parse tree. Furthermore, it adds a new main function that first calls an initialization function for global variables and then calls the original program entry function.

After obtaining a GOTO representation of the analyzed program from CPROVER, 2LS performs a light-weight static analysis to resolve function pointers to a case split over all candidate functions, resulting in a static call graph. Furthermore, assertions guarding against invalid pointer operations or memory leaks are inserted. In addition, 2LS uses a local constant propagation and expression simplification to increase efficiency.

After running the mentioned transformations, 2LS performs a static analysis to derive data flow equations for each function of the GOTO program. Struct types are decomposed into their members. The result is a static single assignment (SSA) form which we describe in detail in the following section.

The Static Single Assignment Form. Program verification in 2LS is based on generating program abstractions using a constraint solver. In order to simplify the generation of a formula representing the program semantics, 2LS uses the *static single assignment form* (SSA) to represent programs. SSA is a standard program representation used in many contexts including compilers as well as various program verifiers or analysers. We use common concepts of SSA—introducing a fresh copy (version) x_i of each variable x at program location i in case x is assigned to at i, using the last version of x whenever x is read, and introducing a *phi* variable x_i^{phi} at a program join point i in case different versions of x come from the joined program branches. For an acyclic program, SSA yields a formula that represents exactly the post condition of running the code.

In 2LS, the traditional SSA is extended by two new concepts: (1) an over-approximation of loops in order to make the SSA acyclic and (2) a special encoding of the control-flow [9]. These concepts allow a straightforward transformation of the SSA form into a formula that can be passed to an SMT solver. In addition, 2LS leverages *incremental SMT solving*, which means that it tries to reuse as large parts of the generated formulae as possible for successive solver invocations.

Over-Approximation of Loops. In order to be able to use a solver for reasoning about program abstractions, 2LS extends the SSA by *over-approximating* the effect of loops. As was said above, the value of a variable x is represented at the loop head by a phi variable x_i^{phi} joining the value of x from before the loop and from the end of the loop body (here, we assume that all paths in the loop join before its end, and the same holds for the paths before the loop). However, instead of using the version of x from the loop end, it is replaced by a *free "loop-back" variable* x_i^{lb}. This way, the SSA remains acyclic, and, since the value of x_i^{lb} is initially unconstrained, the effect of the loop is over-approximated. To improve the precision, the value of x_i^{lb} can be later constrained using a *loop invariant* that will be inferred during the analysis. A loop invariant is a property that holds at the end of the loop body after any iteration and can therefore be assumed to hold on the loop-back variable.

To illustrate, let us take the variable `list` from the example in Fig. 1. It is updated in the outer loop, and so the value at the loop head is a join of the corresponding SSA variables from before the loop (denoted $list_8$) and from the end of the loop (denoted $list_{15}$). In the loop head phi node $list_9^{phi}$, we, however, use an unconstrained loop-back variable $list_{16}^{lb}$ instead of $list_{15}$ and join it non-deterministically with the value from before the loop using a new free Boolean *loop-select* variable g_{16}^{ls}. Overall, the final phi node expression will have the form $list_9^{phi} = g_{16}^{ls} ? list_8 : list_{16}^{lb}$. 2LS will then constrain the value of $list_{16}^{lb}$ by inferring an invariant in an appropriate domain.

Encoding the Control-Flow. In 2LS, the program is represented by a single monolithic formula. It is thus required that the formula encodes control-flow information. This is achieved using so-called *guard* variables that track the reachability information for each program location. In particular, for each program location i, we introduce a Boolean variable g_i whose value encodes whether i is reachable.

Memory Model. As we have already indicated, an important property of the analysis in 2LS is that it leverages incremental solving. This is a great benefit to the verification performance, however, it comes with several drawbacks. The main one is related to the encoding of pointer dereferencing operations since on-demand concretization of heap objects is not possible (as the formula representing the program cannot change). To overcome this limitation, 2LS uses a special memory model and representation of memory-manipulating operations [29].

The model is object-based, and it distinguishes objects allocated *statically* (i.e., variables on the stack and global variables) and *dynamically* (i.e., on the heap). Whereas 2LS has a mode using summarization for handling procedures [2], we consider here non-recursive programs with all functions inlined and, therefore, it does not need to consider the stack. Hence, the set of static memory objects corresponds, in fact, to the set of all program variables.

To represent dynamic memory objects (i.e., those allocated using `malloc` or some of its variants), 2LS uses *abstract dynamic objects*. An abstract dynamic object represents a set of concrete dynamic objects allocated by the same `malloc` call. We refer to a `malloc` call at a program location i as to an *allocation site i*.

Generally, a single abstract dynamic object is not sufficient to reasonably precisely represent all concrete objects allocated by a single `malloc` call. This is due to the fact that the analyzed program may use several concrete objects allocated at the same allocation site at the same time. If such objects are, e.g., compared, the memory model must allow us to distinguish them. This can be done either by concretization on demand or by pre-materialization of a sufficient number of objects at the beginning of the analysis. We have opted for the latter possibility since it matches better with the use of incremental solving in 2LS[1].

The number of abstract dynamic objects pre-materialized for each allocation size is determined using a simple *may-alias analysis* followed by choosing a sufficient number for the particular site such that the analysis is guaranteed to remain sound. For details on the exact algorithm, cf. [29].

Once the numbers of sufficient abstract memory objects are computed, each `malloc` call (or any of its variants) is replaced by a non-deterministic choice among one of these objects. Afterwards, 2LS performs a static *may-points-to analysis* which over-approximates—for each program location i and for each pointer p—the set of memory objects that p may point to at i. A dereference of p at i is then represented by a choice among the pointed objects. This way, the memory manipulating operations are pre-materialized and the formula representing the program may remain static for the rest of the analysis.

2.2 Template-Based Predicate Inference

A key phase of the program verification in 2LS is the generation of *Inv*, an inductive invariant. Instead of using algorithms for solving the semantical fixed point equations [16, 17], e.g. as implemented in off-the-shelf abstract interpreters, 2LS implements an algorithm for inferring such an invariant that exploits the power of incremental SMT solving.

When directly using a solver, 2LS would need to handle (the existential fragment of) second-order logic. As such solvers with reasonable efficiency are not currently available, the problem is reduced to a problem that can be solved by iteratively applying a first-order solver. We restrict ourselves to finding *inductive* invariants *Inv* of the form $\mathcal{T}(\vec{x}, \vec{\delta})$ where $\mathcal{T}$ is a fixed expression, a so-called *template*, over program variables $\vec{x}$ and template parameters $\vec{\delta}$. Fixing a template reduces the second-order search for an invariant to a first-order search for template *parameters*:

$$\exists \vec{\delta}. \forall \vec{x}, \vec{x'}. \left(Init(\vec{x}) \wedge \Rightarrow \mathcal{T}(\vec{x}, \vec{\delta}) \right) \wedge \\ \left(\mathcal{T}(\vec{x}, \vec{\delta}) \wedge Trans(\vec{x}, \vec{x'}) \Rightarrow \mathcal{T}(\vec{x'}, \vec{\delta}) \right) \tag{1}$$

where *Trans* is the transition relation representing the semantics of the program, generated from the SSA form described in Sect. 2.1.

We resolve the $\exists \forall$ problem by an iterative solving of the negated formula, particularly of the second conjunct of (1), for different choices of constants $\vec{d}$ as the values of the parameter $\vec{\delta}$:

$$\exists \vec{x}, \vec{x'}. \neg \left(\mathcal{T}(\vec{x}, \vec{d}) \wedge Trans \Rightarrow \mathcal{T}(\vec{x'}, \vec{d}) \right). \tag{2}$$

---

[1] When the pre-materialization is used, all the variables needed to represent the semantics are known at the start of the analysis, and the representation of the semantics of the program stays constant. On the other hand, the approach used in 2LS would require new variables and a new representation of the program be generated every time an on-demand concretization was found necessary, making the solver to discard everything it discovered so far.

The reason why we concentrate on iteratively solving (2) instead of the entire (1) is the usage of incremental solving combined with the internal program representation of 2LS. Since the SSA of the program is pre-computed, *Init* and *Trans* are "learned" by the solver and hence do not need to be re-solved for every iteration of the invariant inference algorithm.

The formula (2) can be expressed in quantifier-free logics and efficiently solved by SMT solvers. Using this as a building block, one can decide the mentioned $\exists\forall$ problem for finite types (e.g. fixed-size bitvectors).

From the abstract interpretation point of view, $\vec{d}$ is an abstract value, i.e., it represents (*concretizes to*) the set of all program states $\vec{s}$ that satisfy the formula $T(\vec{s}, \vec{d})$ where a state is a vector of values of variables from $\vec{x}$. The choice of the template is hence analogous to choosing an abstract domain in abstract interpretation. The abstract values representing the infimum $\bot$ and supremum $\top$ of the abstract domain denote the empty set and the whole state space, respectively: $T(\vec{s}, \bot) \equiv \textit{false}$ and $T(\vec{s}, \top) \equiv \textit{true}$ [9].

Formally, the concretization function γ is:

$$\gamma(\vec{d}) = \{\vec{s} \mid T(\vec{s}, \vec{d}) \equiv \textit{true}\}. \tag{3}$$

In the abstraction function, to get the most precise abstract value representing the given concrete program state $\vec{s}$, we let

$$\alpha(\vec{s}) = \{\min(\vec{d}) \mid T(\vec{s}, \vec{d}) \equiv \textit{true}\}. \tag{4}$$

for templates that are monotonic in $\vec{d}$, for instance. If the abstract domain forms a complete lattice, existence of such a minimal value $\vec{d}$ is guaranteed.

The algorithm for the invariant inference takes an initial value of $\vec{d} = \bot$ and iteratively solves (2) using an SMT solver. If the formula is unsatisfiable, then an invariant has been found, otherwise a model of satisfiability $\vec{d'}$ is returned by the solver. The model represents a counterexample to the current instantiation of the template being an invariant. The value of the template parameter $\vec{d}$ is then updated by combining the current value with the obtained model of satisfiability using a domain-specific join operator [9].

For example, assume we have a program with a loop that counts from 0 to 10 in a variable x, and we have a template $x \leq d$. Let us assume that the current value of the parameter d is 3, and we get a new model $d' = 4$. Then we update the parameter to 4 by computing $d \sqcup d' = \max(d, d')$ because max is the join operator for the domain that tracks numerical upper bounds.

In 2LS, we use a single template to compute all invariants of the analyzed program. Therefore, typically, a template is composed of multiple parts, each part describing an invariant for a set of program variables. With respect to this, we expect a template $T(\vec{x}, \vec{\delta})$ to be composed of so-called *template rows* $T_r(\vec{x}_r, \delta_r)$, each row r describing an invariant for a subset $\vec{x}_r$ of variables $\vec{x}$ and having its own row parameter δ_r. The overall invariant is then a composition of individual template rows with computed values of the corresponding row parameters. The kind of the composition (it can be, e.g., a simple conjunction) is defined by each domain.

Guarded Templates. Since we use the SSA form rather than control flow graphs, we cannot use templates directly. Instead we use *guarded templates*. As described above, a template is composed of multiple template rows, each row describing an invariant for a subset of program variables. In a guarded template, each row r is of the form:

$$G_r(\vec{x}_r) \Rightarrow \widehat{T}_r(\vec{x}_r, \delta_r) \tag{5}$$

for the rth row $\widehat{T}_r$ of the base template domain (e.g., template polyhedra). G_r is the conjunction of the SSA guards g_r associated with the definition of variables $\vec{x}_r$ occurring in $\widehat{T}_r$. Since we intend to infer loop invariants, $G_r(\vec{x}_r)$ denotes the guard associated to variables $\vec{x}_r$ appearing at the loop head. Hence, template rows for different loops have different guards.

We illustrate the above on the variable i from the inner loop of the example program from Fig. 1. Let the phi node for i have the form $i_{11}^{phi} = g_{12}^{ls} ? i_{11} : i_{12}^{lb}$. We use a guarded interval template which has the form:

$$T(i_{12}^{lb}, (\delta_1, \delta_2)) = \begin{array}{l} g_{11} \wedge g_{12}^{ls} \Rightarrow i_{12}^{lb} \leq \delta_1 \wedge \\ g_{11} \wedge g_{12}^{ls} \Rightarrow -i_{12}^{lb} \leq \delta_2. \end{array} \tag{6}$$

Here, g_{11} is a boolean guard expressing the reachability of line 11 (i.e., the loop head), and g_{12}^{ls} is a non-deterministic guard expressing that i_{12}^{lb} is chosen as the value of i_{11}^{phi}. In this example, the inferred values of the template parameters would be $\delta_1 = 1000$ and $\delta_2 = -1$.

2.3 Abstract Domains in 2LS

Over the past years, several abstract domains were introduced in 2LS. All of these have the same form of templates as described in Sect. 2.2 and hence can be arbitrarily combined. The list of the most important simple domains contains the *template polyhedra domain* [9], the *heap shape domain* [29], and the *ranking domains* [13]. From more complex domains, we mention the *product domain* allowing to use multiple simple domains to analyze a single program and the *power templates domain* allowing to infer different invariants for different symbolic paths through the analyzed program [29].

In this work, we will combine our newly proposed array abstract domain with the *interval domain* (being the specialization of the template polyhedra domain) and with the *heap shape* domain. The former is used for invariants over numerical variables and the latter is used for pointer-typed variables (and numerical and pointer-typed fields of dynamic objects, respectively). As for the combination itself, it is done using a so-called *product domain* which allows to combine templates from multiple domains by taking a conjunction of the corresponding formulae.

3 Abstract Domain for Arrays

In this section, we introduce our abstract domain for analyzing the contents of arrays—we refer to it as *the array domain*.

Similarly to all other domains in 2LS, the array domain has the form of a template. An important property of arrays is that they may have an arbitrary element type. Therefore, using a simple domain is not sufficient and our array domain is a so-called *combination domain* where the domain itself describes only the form (the memory layout) of the array and it delegates reasoning about the actual array element values to another abstract domain, which we denote as the *inner domain*. Note that the inner domain may be any domain present in 2LS, including the array domain itself, which can be used to analyze arrays with multiple dimensions.

The domain is intended to be used to deal with variables from the set Arr of all array-typed variables of the given program. In particular, since we deal with loop invariants, we concentrate on arrays that are updated inside loops. In our SSA representation described in Sect. 2.1, such arrays are abstracted using so-called loop-back array variables. We denote Arr^{lb} the set of such variables, and our array domain is then limited to this set.

The primary idea of our array domain, inspired by [15], is that each array $a \in Arr^{lb}$ is split into several *segments*, and an invariant is computed for each segment in the appropriate inner domain (based on the element type of a). For each a, the set of segments is determined using so-called *segment borders* that we infer at the beginning of the analysis (using the set of index expressions that the analyzed program uses to write into a—cf. Sect. 3.2 for details). A segment border can be any valid SSA expression.

In the rest of this section, we describe different aspects of the array abstract domain and invariant inference using it. First, we show in Sect. 3.1 how, given a set of borders, an array is split into segments and how the array domain template looks like. Next, we introduce the way we determine array segment borders in Sect. 3.2. Last, in Sect. 3.3, we present how invariants are computed in the array domain and how they can be used to verify program properties. To facilitate understanding of the presented concepts, we illustrate all of them on our running example in Sect. 3.4.

In the rest of this chapter, let us assume that we compute a loop invariant for an array $a \in Arr^{lb}$ updated in a loop l. We use N_a to denote the size (number of elements) of a.

3.1   Array Domain Template

We now describe the form of our array domain template. As outlined before, each array is split into multiple segments, and an invariant for each segment is computed in the array inner domain. Hence, the form of the array template is given by *array segmentation*, i.e., the way that each array is split into segments.

Let us denote B_a the set of segment borders for the array a. Prior to creating the segments, we perform two pre-processing steps: (1) making the borders unique and (2) ordering the borders.

Making the Borders Unique. In order to decrease the number of segment borders and avoid empty segments, we first remove duplicate borders. This is done using an SMT solver—in particular, for each pair of segment borders $b_1, b_2 \in B_a$, we check whether the formula

$$b_1 \neq b_2 \wedge Trans \tag{7}$$

is satisfiable. In Eq. (7), *Trans* denotes the transition relation formula created from the SSA form of the analyzed program and representing the (over-approximated) program semantics. If Eq. (7) is unsatisfiable, then the values of the borders are always equal and hence one of them can be removed from B_a. By repeating this process for each pair of borders, we obtain the set of unique borders.

Ordering Borders. After making B_a contain unique indices only, we try to order them. Again, we query the SMT solver, this time using two formulae:

$$\neg(b_1 \leq b_2) \wedge Trans, \tag{8}$$
$$\neg(b_2 \leq b_1) \wedge Trans. \tag{9}$$

If exactly one of Eqs. (8) and (9) is unsatisfiable for each pair of $b_1, b_2 \in B_a$, then a total ordering over B_a can be found. Otherwise, B_a is left unordered.

Array Segmentation. Once the array segment borders are unique and possibly ordered, we create the array segmentation. We distinguish two situations:

1. B_a cannot be totally ordered. In such a case, we create multiple segmentations, one for each $b \in B_a$:

$$\{0\} \, S_1^b \, \{b\} \, S_2^b \, \{b+1\} \, S_3^b \, \{N_a\}. \tag{10}$$

   The idea here is that if $a[b]$ is written to in a loop with gradually incrementing b, then, for any iteration b of the loop, S_1^b will abstract all array elements that have already been traversed, S_2^b will be the element accessed in the current iteration, and S_3^b will abstract elements to be traversed in the following iterations.
2. B_a can be totally ordered s.t. $b_1 \leq \ldots \leq b_n$ for $B_a = \{b_1, \ldots, b_n\}$. In such a case, we create a single segmentation for the entire array a:

$$\{0\} \, S_1 \, \{b_1\} \, S_2 \, \{b_1 + 1\} \, \cdots \, \{b_n\} \, S_{2n} \, \{b_n + 1\} \, S_{2n+1} \, \{N_a\}. \tag{11}$$

Array Segments. A single array segment S denoted

$$\{b_l\} \, S \, \{b_u\} \tag{12}$$

is an expression abstracting the elements of a between the indices b_l (inclusive) and b_u (exclusive). We refer to b_l and b_u as to the *lower* and *upper segment bounds*, respectively. In addition, for each S, we define two special variables: (1) the *segment element variable* $elem^S$ being an abstraction of the array elements contained in S and (2) the *segment index variable* idx^S being an abstraction of the indices of the array elements contained in S.

Template Form. Having the set of loop-back arrays Arr^{lb} and a set of segments $\mathcal{S}^a$ for each $a \in Arr^{lb}$, we define the array domain template as:

$$T^A \equiv \bigwedge_{a \in Arr^{lb}} \bigwedge_{S \in \mathcal{S}^a} \left(G^S \Rightarrow T^{in}(elem^S) \right) \tag{13}$$

where T^{in} is the inner domain template and G^S is the conjunction of guards associated with the segment S.

The inner domain template abstracts the elements within a segment S. It is typically chosen based on the data type of $elem^S$ (e.g., we usually use the interval domain for numerical types and the shape domain for pointer types).

The purpose of G^S is to make sure that the inner invariant is limited to the elements of the given segment $\{b_l\}\ S\ \{b_u\}$. In particular, G^S is a conjunction of several guards:

$$b_l \leq idx^S < b_u \land \tag{14}$$

$$0 \leq idx^S < N_a \land \tag{15}$$

$$elem^S = a[idx^S] \tag{16}$$

where Eq. (14) makes sure that the segment index variable stays between the segment borders, Eq. (15) makes sure that the segment index variable stays between the array borders (since segment borders are generic expressions, they may lie outside of the array, hence Eq. (14) is not sufficient), and Eq. (16) binds the segment element variable with the segment index variable.

Using the above template, 2LS is able to compute a different invariant for each segment. For example, for a typical array iteration loop, this would allow to infer a different invariant for the part of the array that has already been traversed than for the part of the array that is still to be visited.

3.2   Computing Array Segment Borders

In the previous section, we assumed that we already have the set of segment borders for each array. In this section, we describe how this set is obtained. As we outlined earlier, the verification approach of 2LS requires the domain template to be a fixed, parametrized, first-order formula. To be able to fulfil the "fixed" property, we need to determine the set of segments at the beginning of the analysis so that we are able to create a finite set of array segments which will form the array domain template.

The main idea of our approach is that the segment borders should be closely related to the expressions that are used to access array elements in the analyzed program (we denote these as *array index expressions*). Therefore, we perform a static *array index analysis* which collects the set of all expressions occurring as array access indices (i.e., expressions that appear inside the square bracket operators). In addition, we distinguish between *read* accesses (occurring on the right-hand side of assignments and in conditions) and *write* accesses (occurring on the left-hand side of assignments).

Once the array index analysis is complete, for each loop-back array a, we determine the set of its segment borders by taking the set of all index expressions used to write into a in the corresponding loop. In addition, if some of those expressions contain a variable whose value is updated inside the same loop, we also take the pre-loop value of the expression as a segment border.

To illustrate the above, let us have a simple loop initializing the second half of an array:

```
1  for (int i = N / 2; i < N; i++)
2      a[i] = 0;
```

The set of index expressions used to write into the array is $\{i\}$, but we would also use $N/2$ (the initial value of i) as a segment border. Hence, the segmentation of a would be:

$$\{0\} \cdots \{N/2\} \cdots \{N/2 + 1\} \cdots \{i\} \cdots \{i + 1\} \cdots \{N\}. \qquad (17)$$

Thanks to this segmentation, 2LS is able to differentiate three important parts of the array: (1) the first half of the array (which is untouched in the loop), (2) the part between $N/2$ and i which in any iteration represents the already initialized part, and (3) the part from i to the array end which represents the part to be initialized in future iterations. In particular, 2LS would be able to infer an invariant stating that all elements in part (2) are equal to 0, which would mean that the entire second half of the array is set to 0 once the loop ends.

3.3 Array Domain Invariant Inference

Once the array domain template is created, the invariant inference algorithm of 2LS (see Sect. 2.2) is used to compute loop invariants for individual segments. As we already described, most of the work is delegated to the inner domain, and the array domain is mainly responsible for making sure that the segment element variables, for which the inner invariants are computed, are properly constrained.

Additionally, there is one more necessary step after the array invariants are computed. The problem is that the invariants describe properties of the segment element and index variables, however, these variables are not actually used inside the analyzed program. Therefore, in order for the invariant to properly constrain the program semantics, we *bind* the computed invariants with all index expressions used to read from the arrays. We do not need to constrain the array elements that are written by the program since their value gets overridden, hence binding with read elements is sufficient. The set of expressions to bind the invariant with is obtained using the array index analysis introduced in Sect. 3.2.

In particular, for each segment S of each loop-back array a, we create a binding between the segment element and index variables $elem^S$ and idx^S and each index expression i_r used to read from a as follows. We take the computed invariant for S and replace all occurrences of idx^S by i_r and all occurrences of $elem^S$ by $a[i_r]$. Then, the obtained formula is passed to the solver which constrains the values of a for the given access through i_r. This process is done for the final invariant as well as for each candidate invariant found during the analysis to allow the invariant inference algorithm to account for the already computed constraints.

3.4 Running Example

We now illustrate usage of the array domain on the running example from Fig. 1. The arrays in the program are contained within dynamically allocated objects. For simplicity, let us assume that all objects allocated by the malloc on line 10 are represented by a single abstract dynamic object ao_{10}[2]. We demonstrate inference of a loop invariant for the inner loop of the program, hence the SSA object that we work with is $ao_{10}.data_{12}^{lb}$.

First, 2LS runs the array index analysis to determine the set of indices used to access the array. In this case, there is a single index used for writing (i on line 12) and one index used for reading (x on line 18).

After the array index analysis is run, the analyzed array must be segmented. There is a single written index, hence there will be three segments in total. In addition, the index is updated inside the same loop, hence we will use its loop-back variant (i_{12}^{lb}) inside the segmentation

$$\{0\} \ S_1 \ \{i_{12}^{lb}\} \ S_2 \ \{i_{12}^{lb} + 1\} \ S_3 \ \{1000\}. \tag{18}$$

For each segment S_j, $j \in \{1, 2, 3\}$, we introduce a segment element variable $elem^j$ and a segment index variable idx^j.

Since the array is of integer type, we will use the interval abstract domain as the inner domain. The interval domain has two template rows for each variable, hence our template will contain 6 rows in total (two for each segment element variable). For the sake of legibility, we only give the two rows for $elem^1$:

$$g_{11} \wedge g_{12}^{ls} \ \wedge \ 0 \le idx^1 < i_{12}^{lb} \ \wedge \ 0 \le idx^1 < 1000 \ \wedge \ elem^1 = ao_{10}.data_{12}^{lb}[idx^1]$$
$$\Rightarrow elem^1 \le d_1 \ \wedge$$
$$g_{11} \wedge g_{12}^{ls} \ \wedge \ 0 \le idx^1 < i_{12}^{lb} \ \wedge \ 0 \le idx^1 < 1000 \ \wedge \ elem^1 = ao_{10}.data_{12}^{lb}[idx^1]$$
$$\Rightarrow -elem^1 \le d_2. \tag{19}$$

Both rows have the same guard (the implication antecedent) consisting of multiple parts:

- The first two conjuncts ($g_{11} \wedge g_{12}^{ls}$) are standard row guards used in other domains that guard the reachability of the loop and the definition of the loop-back variable.
- The second part ($0 \le idx^1 < i_{12}^{lb}$) guards that the segment index variable stays within the segment bounds.
- The third part ($0 \le idx^1 < 1000$) guards that the segment index variable stays within the array bounds.
- The last part ($elem^1 = ao_{10}.data_{12}^{lb}[idx^1]$) binds the segment element variable with the analyzed array object and the segment index variable.

The properties of interest to be computed (the implication consequences) are determined from the inner domain, in this case the interval abstract domain.

Using the above template in the invariant inference algorithm of 2LS, we will obtain values of $d_1 = d_2 = 0$ (i.e., values of all array elements in the segment S_1 are equal to 0). After the loop ends, the value of i_{12}^{lb} will be 1000 (thanks to the loop condition and the invariant computed for i_{12}^{lb} from the template given in (6)), which will effectively prove that all elements of the given array are equal to 0 at that moment.

The remaining part of the array domain usage is binding of the invariant onto indices used to read from it. Our example program features one array read at line 18

---

[2] In practice, we would need at least 2 abstract dynamic objects to distinguish between the current node pointed by n and the next node pointed by n->next.

(list->data[x]). At this point of the program, list may point to the dynamic object ao_{10}, hence an access to $ao_{10}.data$ is possible in this expression. Therefore, we bind the invariant computed from the template from Eq. (19) with the read index x_{17} as follows:

$$g_{11} \wedge g_{12}^{ls} \wedge 0 \le x_{17} < i_{12}^{lb} \wedge 0 \le x_{17} < 1000 \Rightarrow ao_{10}.data_{12}^{lb}[x_{17}] \le 0 \wedge$$
$$g_{11} \wedge g_{12}^{ls} \wedge 0 \le x_{17} < i_{12}^{lb} \wedge 0 \le x_{17} < 1000 \Rightarrow -ao_{10}.data_{12}^{lb}[x_{17}] \le 0. \tag{20}$$

The equation has been obtained from Eq. (19) by supplying the actual computed values of d_1 and d_2 and by replacing occurrences of idx^1 by x_{17} and the occurrences of $elem^1$ by $ao_{10}.data_{12}^{lb}[x_{17}]$. We removed the last part of each row guard as $elem^1$ is no longer used. Also, note that we bind the invariant to $ao_{10}.data_{12}^{lb}$ rather than to the SSA version of $ao_{10}.data$ valid on line 18 (which would be $ao_{10}.data_9^{phi}$) because we only want to constrain the value of the array coming from the loop that the invariant is computed for. In other words, Eq. (20) allows to leverage the computed array invariant during further program analysis.

As we already mentioned, the last step would be done after each round of the invariant inference algorithm, however, we omit that here for the sake of simplicity and give the binding for the final invariant only.

When combined with a heap invariant computed for the next field of ao_{10}, our array invariant will allow us to prove that all array elements of all the unrolled list nodes are equal to zero.

4   Experimental Evaluation

We have implemented our proposed array domain in the 2LS framework. In this chapter, we evaluate the impact of this implementation. Since 2LS regularly competes in the *International Competition on Software Verification (SV-COMP)*, we present results of 2LS from this competition. In particular, we check results in the *ReachSafety-Arrays* category which features verification tasks requiring reasoning about (mainly numerical) contents of arrays.

2LS has traditionally received negative score in this category (-28 in 2020–2022) which has only changed in 2023 with the introduction of our proposed domain into 2LS [30]. Using the new array domain, 2LS was able to successfully verify 17[3] and 16 error-free tasks from this category in 2023 and 2024, respectively (as opposed to 2 from the previous years). In 2024, this would place 2LS to the 9th place out of 18 tools participating in the *ReachSafety-Arrays* category (excluding the tools participating as "Hors Concours") in terms of the number of correctly verified error-free programs.

While these are not large numbers, they show that our new domain is a good first step towards better analysis of array contents in 2LS. In addition, due to the nature

---

[3] The given number for 2023 is different from the official results of 2LS in SV-COMP 2023. The reason is that a number of tasks was last-minute disqualified due to past-deadline changes which were often related to the tasks being added to new categories (e.g., *NoOverflows*) rather than real modifications of the tasks or their verdicts. Hence, we present results from the entire benchmark instead of the competition benchmark set as those results are more representative and can be better compared to the previous year results.

of program analysis in 2LS, the domain may leverage from combination with other abstract domains (e.g., the shape domain), however, SV-COMP benchmarks do not yet feature tasks requiring such a combination.

5   Related Work

There exists a vast body of works aimed at analysis of array contents and verification of programs manipulating arrays. We describe the most important works in this section. Many of the works are related and use a similar principle, hence we divide the overview into three categories.

5.1   Methods Based on Array Segmentation

One of the first works in the area [8] introduced two basic techniques for reasoning about the contents of arrays: (1) *array expansion* where each array element is represented using a single abstract value and (2) *array smashing* (also presented in [19]) where all elements of the array are abstracted using a single value. These approaches represent two extremes in approaching the arrays—while the first one often does not scale due to unbounded nature of the arrays, the second one abstracts away too much information that is often crucial for proving the required array properties.

An approach to overcome these problems, which we also take in our work, is to split arrays into multiple parts, usually called segments. This technique was first introduced in [20] where it was combined with simple numerical domains and was mainly able to reason about array initialization loops. This method was improved in [22] by extending it to handle relational abstract properties and consequently in [15] which proposed to use an arbitrary abstract domain for reasoning about array elements. Our approach is heavily based on the latter work, mainly due to the fact that it is compatible with the verification approach in 2LS. The proposed method uses automatic inference of segment bounds based on semantic pre-analysis of the array usage in the program.

Compared to all of these works, which are mainly aimed at analysis of numerical contents of arrays, we leverage other domains present in 2LS. In particular, the combination with our newly introduced shape domain allows us to expand program verification to analysis of structures combining arrays and linked structures on the heap. In addition, it was necessary to formulate our approach in the very specific 2LS framework, hence the introduced domain has several unique features that cannot be found in other approaches.

The segmentation-based approaches were further extended to non-contiguous and overlapping segments [10, 28] but these are much more difficult to be described using first-order logic formulae, and therefore we did not consider them for our approach.

5.2   Methods Based on Analysis of Array-Manipulating Loops

A completely different approach to the typical array verification problems is taken by the VERIABS verification tool [1]. Instead of trying to describe the contents of (potentially huge) arrays in an abstract way, the tool focuses on analysis of loops manipulating the arrays. In particular, VERIABS features two important techniques related to verification of array contents: (1) *loop shrinking* [25] and (2) *full-program induction* [11].

The first technique automatically analyzes loops that manipulate program arrays and for each loop it determines the so-called *shrink factor* k—the sufficient number of iterations that are necessary to prove the property being checked. After k is obtained, the processed array is reduced to the size k and filled with k non-deterministically chosen elements of the original array. The reduced program is then verified using state-of-the-art BMC tools.

In some cases, the shrink factor is not sufficiently low for BMC to scale and prove or refute program correctness. In such a case, VERIABS transforms the arrays to be of symbolic size N and performs so-called full-program induction. This technique, given a program P_N parametrized by the array size N and pre- and post-conditions denoted $\varphi(N)$ and $\psi(M)$, respectively, is able to very efficiently check validity of the Hoare triple $\{\varphi(N)\ P_N\ \psi(N)\}$ for all values of $N > 0$.

The above methods have proven very effective since VERIABS has been the most successful tool in the *ReachSafety-Arrays* sub-category of SV-COMP in the recent years [4–6]. On the other hand, VERIABS does not compete in memory safety, so the effectiveness of these methods on programs combining arrays and linked structures remains questionable. Still, we may consider implementing modified versions of the proposed techniques in future to improve efficiency of verification of array-manipulating programs in 2LS.

5.3 Predicate Abstraction and Non-automatic Methods

In the last group of works, we present those that use completely different verification approaches than 2LS does, and hence were not considered for our case.

First, there is a large group of works [26, 27] based on predicate abstraction [18], possibly improved by counterexample guided refinement [7] and Craig interpolants [23]. It is, however, not clear how to combine predicate abstraction efficiently with the computation loop of 2LS. Moreover, we note that methods based on predicate abstraction make use of the property to be proved while our approach allows one to also discover (previously unknown) existing properties.

Second, besides fully automated works, there exist approaches which require some user intervention. For instance, [21] also specifies abstract domains using templates, but their domains are universally quantified (as opposed to our quantifier-free templates). This naturally makes the domains much stronger, however, the verification approach requires all the abstract domains to be specified manually. In contrary, the verification approach of 2LS is fully automatic. Other techniques based on deductive methods [3, 12] suffer from a similar issue when they require users to provide loop invariants (which our method is able to infer automatically).

6 Conclusions and Future Work

We have presented a new abstract template domain for the 2LS verification framework. In particular, the domain allows 2LS to compute invariants of programs dealing with arrays that can be storing various types of data (including nested arrays and dynamic linked data structures) and that can be themselves nested in other structures. The domain is based on segmenting arrays according to array index expressions (computed statically) and on computing an invariant for each array segment independently. We have illustrated the approach on a program with linked lists whose cells contain arrays, and we have shown that the implementation of the approach within 2LS significantly improved its score on benchmark programs dealing with arrays.

Nevertheless, the array abstract template domain and the techniques for dealing with it that we have introduced are so far still rather simple. Further improvements are needed to handle an even wider spectrum of array-manipulating programs. For instance, our current approach would not be able to verify properties describing relationship between different array elements as that would require to combine our array domain with more advanced template polyhedra domains, such as *zones* or *octagons*. Also, in the future, it might be interesting to attempt to combine some of the techniques introduced in VERIABS [1] with those we proposed for 2LS in this work.

References

1. Afzal, M., et al.: VeriAbs: verification by abstraction and test generation. In: Proceedings of the 34th IEEE/ACM International Conference on Automated Software Engineering (ASE), pp. 1138–1141 (2019). https://doi.org/10.1109/ASE.2019.00121
2. Alur, R., Bouajjani, A., Esparza, J.: Model checking procedural programs. In: Clarke, E.M., Henzinger, T.A., Veith, H., Bloem, R. (eds.) Handbook of Model Checking, pp. 541–572. Springer (2018). https://doi.org/10.1007/978-3-319-10575-8_17
3. Barnett, M., Leino, K.R.M., Schulte, W.: The spec# programming system: an overview. In: Proceedings of the 2004 International Conference on Construction and Analysis of Safe, Secure, and Interoperable Smart Devices, pp. 49–69. CASSIS 2004, Springer-Verlag, Berlin, Heidelberg (2004). https://doi.org/10.1007/978-3-540-30569-9_3
4. Beyer, D.: Advances in automatic software verification: SV-COMP 2020. In: TACAS 2020. LNCS, vol. 12079, pp. 347–367. Springer, Cham (2020). https://doi.org/10.1007/978-3-030-45237-7_21
5. Beyer, D.: Software verification: 10th comparative evaluation (SV-COMP 2021). In: TACAS 2021. LNCS, vol. 12652, pp. 401–422. Springer, Cham (2021). https://doi.org/10.1007/978-3-030-72013-1_24
6. Beyer, D.: Progress on software verification: SV-COMP 2022. In: TACAS 2022. LNCS, vol. 13244, pp. 375–402. Springer, Cham (2022). https://doi.org/10.1007/978-3-030-99527-0_20
7. Beyer, D., Henzinger, T.A., Majumdar, R., Rybalchenko, A.: Path invariants. In: Proceedings of the 28th ACM SIGPLAN Conference on Programming Language Design and Implementation, pp. 300–309. PLDI 2007, Association for Computing Machinery, New York, NY, USA (2007). https://doi.org/10.1145/1250734.1250769
8. Blanchet, B., et al.: Design and implementation of a special-purpose static program analyzer for safety-critical real-time embedded software. In: Mogensen, T.Æ., Schmidt, D.A., Sudborough, I.H. (eds.) The Essence of Computation. LNCS, vol. 2566, pp. 85–108. Springer, Heidelberg (2002). https://doi.org/10.1007/3-540-36377-7_5
9. Brain, M., Joshi, S., Kroening, D., Schrammel, P.: Safety verification and refutation by k-invariants and k-induction. In: Blazy, S., Jensen, T. (eds.) SAS 2015. LNCS, vol. 9291, pp. 145–161. Springer, Heidelberg (2015). https://doi.org/10.1007/978-3-662-48288-9_9

10. Chakraborty, S., Gupta, A., Unadkat, D.: Verifying array manipulating programs by tiling. In: Proceedings of the 24th Static Analysis Symposium, pp. 428–449 (2017). https://doi.org/10.1007/978-3-319-66706-5_21
11. Chakraborty, S., Gupta, A., Unadkat, D.: Verifying array manipulating programs with full-program induction. In: TACAS 2020. LNCS, vol. 12078, pp. 22–39. Springer, Cham (2020). https://doi.org/10.1007/978-3-030-45190-5_2
12. Chalin, P., Kiniry, J.R., Leavens, G.T., Poll, E.: Beyond assertions: advanced specification and verification with JML and ESC/Java2. In: Proceedings of the 4th International Conference on Formal Methods for Components and Objects, pp. 342–363. FMCO 2005, Springer-Verlag, Berlin, Heidelberg (2005). https://doi.org/10.1007/11804192_16
13. Chen, H.Y., David, C., Kroening, D., Schrammel, P., Wachter, B.: Bit-precise procedure-modular termination proofs. ACM Trans. Prog. Lang. Syst. **40**, 1–38 (2017)
14. Clarke, E., Kroening, D., Lerda, F.: A tool for checking ANSI-C programs. In: Jensen, K., Podelski, A. (eds.) TACAS 2004. LNCS, vol. 2988, pp. 168–176. Springer, Heidelberg (2004). https://doi.org/10.1007/978-3-540-24730-2_15
15. Cousot, P., Cousot, R., Logozzo, F.: A parametric segmentation Functor for fully automatic and scalable array content analysis. In: Proceedings of the 38th ACM SIGPLAN-SIGACT Symposium on Principles of Programming Languages, pp. 105–118. POPL 2011, Association for Computing Machinery, New York (2011). https://doi.org/10.1145/1926385.1926399
16. Esparza, J., Kiefer, S., Luttenberger, M.: Newtonian program analysis. J. ACM **57**(6), 33:1-33:47 (2010). https://doi.org/10.1145/1857914.1857917
17. Esparza, J., Luttenberger, M., Schlund, M.: FPSOLVE: a generic solver for fixpoint equations over semirings. Int. J. Found. Comput. Sci. **26**(7), 805–826 (2015). https://doi.org/10.1142/S0129054115400018
18. Flanagan, C., Qadeer, S.: Predicate abstraction for software verification. In: Proceedings of the 29th ACM SIGPLAN-SIGACT Symposium on Principles of Programming Languages, pp. 191–202. POPL 2002, Association for Computing Machinery, New York (2002). https://doi.org/10.1145/503272.503291
19. Gopan, D., DiMaio, F., Dor, N., Reps, T., Sagiv, M.: Numeric domains with summarized dimensions. In: Jensen, K., Podelski, A. (eds.) TACAS 2004. LNCS, vol. 2988, pp. 512–529. Springer, Heidelberg (2004). https://doi.org/10.1007/978-3-540-24730-2_38
20. Gopan, D., Reps, T., Sagiv, M.: A framework for numeric analysis of array operations. In: Proceedings of the 32nd ACM SIGPLAN-SIGACT Symposium on Principles of Programming Languages, pp. 338–350. Association for Computing Machinery, New York (2005)
21. Gulwani, S., McCloskey, B., Tiwari, A.: Lifting abstract interpreters to quantified logical domains. In: Proceedings of the 35th ACM SIGPLAN-SIGACT Symposium on Principles of Programming Languages, pp. 235–246. POPL 2008, Association for Computing Machinery, New York (2008). https://doi.org/10.1145/1328438.1328468
22. Halbwachs, N., Péron, M.: Discovering properties about arrays in simple programs. In: Proceedings of the 29th ACM SIGPLAN Conference on Programming Language Design and Implementation, pp. 339–348. PLDI 2008, Association for Computing Machinery, New York (2008). https://doi.org/10.1145/1375581.1375623
23. Jhala, R., McMillan, K.L., Array abstractions from proofs: Array abstractions from proofs. In: Damm, W., Hermanns, H. (eds.) CAV 2007. LNCS, vol. 4590, pp. 193–206. Springer, Heidelberg (2007). https://doi.org/10.1007/978-3-540-73368-3_23
24. Kroening, D., Malík, V., Schrammel, P., Vojnar, T.: 2LS for Program Analysis. Tech. rep. (2023). https://doi.org/10.48550/arXiv.2302.02380
25. Kumar, S., Sanyal, A., Venkatesh, R., Shah, P.: Property checking array programs using loop shrinking. In: Beyer, D., Huisman, M. (eds.) TACAS 2018. LNCS, vol. 10805, pp. 213–231. Springer, Cham (2018). https://doi.org/10.1007/978-3-319-89960-2_12

26. Lahiri, S.K., Bryant, R.E.: Indexed predicate discovery for unbounded system verification. In: Alur, R., Peled, D.A. (eds.) CAV 2004. LNCS, vol. 3114, pp. 135–147. Springer, Heidelberg (2004). https://doi.org/10.1007/978-3-540-27813-9_11

27. Lahiri, S.K., Bryant, R.E., Cook, B.: A symbolic approach to predicate abstraction. In: Hunt, W.A., Somenzi, F. (eds.) CAV 2003. LNCS, vol. 2725, pp. 141–153. Springer, Heidelberg (2003). https://doi.org/10.1007/978-3-540-45069-6_15

28. Liu, J., Rival, X.: Abstraction of arrays based on non contiguous partitions. In: D'Souza, D., Lal, A., Larsen, K.G. (eds.) VMCAI 2015. LNCS, vol. 8931, pp. 282–299. Springer, Heidelberg (2015). https://doi.org/10.1007/978-3-662-46081-8_16

29. Malík, V., Hruška, M., Schrammel, P., Vojnar, T.: Template-based verification of heap-manipulating programs. In: Proceedings of the 2018 Formal Methods in Computer-Aided Design, pp. 103–111 (2018). https://doi.org/10.23919/FMCAD.2018.8603009

30. Malík, V., Nečas, F., Schrammel, P., Vojnar, T.: 2ls: Arrays and loop unwinding (competition contribution). In: Sankaranarayanan, S., Sharygina, N. (eds.) Tools and Algorithms for the Construction and Analysis of Systems. TACAS 2023. Lecture Notes in Computer Science, vol. 13994, pp. 529–534. Springer, Cham (2023). https://doi.org/10.1007/978-3-031-30820-8_31

31. Schrammel, P., Kroening, D.: 2LS for program analysis - (competition contribution). In: Chechik, M., Raskin, JF. (eds.) Tools and Algorithms for the Construction and Analysis of Systems. TACAS 2016. Lecture Notes in Computer Science, vol. 9636, pp. 905–907. Springer, Berlin (2016). https://doi.org/10.1007/978-3-662-49674-9_56

32. Shao, Z., Reppy, J.H., Appel, A.W.: Unrolling lists. In: Proceedings of the 1994 ACM Conference on LISP and Functional Programming, pp. 185–195. Association for Computing Machinery, New York (1994). https://doi.org/10.1145/182409.182453

Memoryless Strategies in Stochastic Reachability Games

Stefan Kiefer[1]([⊠]), Richard Mayr[2], Mahsa Shirmohammadi[3], and Patrick Totzke[4]

[1] University of Oxford, Oxford, UK
stekie@cs.ox.ac.uk
[2] University of Edinburgh, Edinburgh, UK
[3] IRIF & CNRS, Université Paris cité, Paris, France
[4] University of Liverpool, Liverpool, UK

Abstract. We study concurrent stochastic reachability games played on finite graphs. Two players, Max and Min, seek respectively to maximize and minimize the probability of reaching a set of target states. We prove that Max has a memoryless strategy that is optimal from all states that have an optimal strategy. Our construction provides an alternative proof of this result by Bordais, Bouyer and Le Roux [4], and strengthens it, as we allow Max's action sets to be countably infinite.

Keywords: Stochastic games · Reachability · Strategy Complexity

1 Introduction

Background. We study 2-player zero-sum stochastic games. First introduced by Shapley in his seminal 1953 work [22], they model dynamic interactions in which the environment responds randomly to players' actions. Shapley's games were generalized in [11,16] to allow infinite state and action sets and non-termination.

In *concurrent games*, the two players (Max and Min) jointly create an infinite path through a directed graph. In each round of the play, both independently choose an action. The next state is then determined according to a pre-defined distribution that depends on the current state and the chosen pair of actions. *Turn-based games* (also called switching-control games) are a subclass where each state is owned by some player and only this player gets to choose an action. These have received much attention by computer scientists, e.g., [2,5,6,12,14]. An even more special case of stochastic games are *Markov Decision Processes (MDPs)* where all states are owned by Max (i.e., Min is passive). MDPs are also called *games against nature*.

We consider *reachability objectives* which are defined w.r.t. a given subset of *target* states. A play is defined as winning for Max iff it visits a target state at least once. Thus Max aims to maximize the probability that the target set is reached. Dually, Min aims to minimize the probability of reaching the target. So Min pursues the dual *safety objective* of avoiding the target.

S. Kiefer et al. (Eds.): *Taming the Infinities of Concurrency*, LNCS 14660, pp. 225–242, 2024.
https://doi.org/10.1007/978-3-031-56222-8_13

Reachability is arguably the simplest objective in games on graphs. It can trivially be encoded into reward-based objectives; i.e., every play that reaches the target gets reward 1 and all other plays get reward 0.

In turn-based reachability games over finite state spaces, there always exist optimal Max strategies that are memoryless (choices only depend on the current state and not the history of the play; this is also called positional) and deterministic (always chose on action as opposed to randomising among several) [7], [17, Proposition 5.6.c, Proposition 5.7.c].

This does not carry over to finite concurrent reachability games. E.g., in the *snowball game* (aka *Hide-or-Run* game) [9, Example 1] [1,16] (also see Example 4 later in this paper), Max does not have an optimal strategy. However, by [21, Corollary 3.9], Max always has ε-optimal randomized memoryless strategies, and this holds even in countably infinite reachability games with finite action sets. (Deterministic strategies are generally useless in concurrent games, even in very simple games such as *Rock-Paper-Scissors*.)

Even though optimal Max strategies do not always exist, it is still interesting how much memory they need in those instances where they do exist. For finite concurrent reachability games with finite action sets, it was recently shown by Bordais, Bouyer and Le Roux [4] that optimal Max strategies, if they exist, can be chosen as randomized memoryless. The proof is constructive and iteratively builds the strategy on the finite state space. To show the correctness, one needs to argue about the performance of the constructed strategy. The proof in [4] heavily relies on the properties of induced finite MDPs, obtained by fixing one strategy in the game. In particular, it uses the existence of end components in these finite MDPs and their particular properties.

Our Contribution. We give an alternative proof of this result by Bordais, Bouyer and Le Roux [4]. While our proof is also constructive, it is simpler and works directly from first principles on games, without using properties of induced MDPs. Moreover, it uses a construction that we call "leaky games", by which we reduce the reachability objective to its dual safety objective. Finally, our result is slightly stronger, because it holds even if Max is allowed countably infinite action sets (while Min still has finite action sets).[1]

This result requires the state space to be finite. However, for other results in this paper we allow the state space and action sets to be countably infinite, unless explicitly stated otherwise.

2   Preliminaries

A *probability distribution* over a countable set S is a function $\alpha : S \to [0,1]$ with $\sum_{s \in S} \alpha(s) = 1$. The *support* of α is the set $\{s \in S \mid \alpha(s) > 0\}$. We write $\mathcal{D}(S)$ for the set of all probability distributions over S. For $\alpha \in \mathcal{D}(S)$ and a

---

[1] It may be possible to generalize the proof in [4] to countably infinite Max actions sets, but this would require (at least) a generalization of the fixpoint theorem [4, Theorem 12] to this setting.

function $v : S \to \mathbb{R}$ we write $\langle \alpha, v \rangle \overset{\text{def}}{=} \sum_{s \in S} \alpha(s)v(s)$ for the expectation of v with respect to α.

Stochastic Games

We study perfect information stochastic games between two players, Max(imizer) and Min(imizer). A *(concurrent) game* $\mathcal{G}$ is played on a countable set of states S. For each state $s \in S$ there are nonempty countable *action* sets $A(s)$ and $B(s)$ for Max and Min, respectively. A *mixed action* for Max (resp. Min) in state s is a distribution over $A(s)$ (resp. $B(s)$).

Let $Z \overset{\text{def}}{=} \{(s, a, b) \mid s \in S,\ a \in A(s),\ b \in B(s)\}$. For every triple $(s, a, b) \in Z$ there is a distribution $p(s, a, b) \in \mathcal{D}(S)$ over successor states. We call a state $s \in S$ a *sink* state if $p(s, a, b) = s$ for all $a \in A(s)$ and $b \in B(s)$. We extend the *transition function* p to mixed actions $\alpha \in \mathcal{D}(A(s))$ and $\beta \in \mathcal{D}(B(s))$ by letting

$$p(s, \alpha, \beta) \overset{\text{def}}{=} \sum_{a \in A(s)} \sum_{b \in B(s)} \alpha(a)\beta(b)p(s, a, b),$$

which is a distribution over S. A *play* from an initial state s_0 is an infinite sequence in Z^ω where the first triple contains s_0. Starting from s_0, the game is played in stages $\mathbb{N} = \{0, 1, 2, \dots\}$. At every stage $n \in \mathbb{N}$, the play is in some state s_n. Max chooses a mixed action $\alpha_n \in \mathcal{D}(A(s_n))$ and Min chooses a mixed action $\beta_n \in \mathcal{D}(B(s_n))$. The next state s_{n+1} is then chosen according to the distribution $p(s_n, a_n, b_n)$.

Strategies and Probability Measures

The set of *histories* at stage n, with $n \in \mathbb{N}$, is denoted by H_n. That is, $H_0 \overset{\text{def}}{=} S$ and $H_n \overset{\text{def}}{=} Z^n \times S$ for all $n > 0$. Let $H \overset{\text{def}}{=} \bigcup_{n \in \mathbb{N}} H_n$ be the set of all histories; note that H is countable. For each history $h = (s_0, a_0, b_0) \cdots (s_{n-1}, a_{n-1}, b_{n-1})s_n \in H_n$, let $s_h \overset{\text{def}}{=} s_n$ denote the final state in h.

A *strategy* for Max is a function σ that to each history $h \in H$ assigns a mixed action $\sigma(h) \in \mathcal{D}(A(s_h))$. Denote by Σ the set of strategies for Max. Analogously, a *strategy* for Min is a function π that to each history h assigns a mixed action $\pi(h) \in \mathcal{D}(B(s_h))$, and Π denotes the set of strategies for Min. A Max strategy is called *memoryless* if $\sigma(h)$ depends only on s_h; i.e., for all $h, h' \in H$ with $s_h = s_{h'}$ we have $\sigma(h) = \sigma(h')$. A memoryless strategy σ is fully determined by $(\sigma(s))_{s \in S}$. A *memory-based strategy* bases its decisions not only on the current state, but also on the current mode of its memory, and it can update its memory at every step, depending on the observed events in this step. Memory is called *public* if the content is also observable by the opposing player and *private* otherwise. Finite-memory strategies use a memory with only finitely many different possible modes. A step counter is a special case of infinite memory in the form of a discrete clock that gets incremented at every step, independently of the actions of the players. Strategies that use just a step counter are also called *Markov strategies*.

An initial state s_0 and a pair of strategies σ, π for Max and Min induce a probability measure on sets of plays. We write $\mathcal{P}_{\mathcal{G},s_0,\sigma,\pi}(E)$ for the probability of a measurable set of plays E starting from s_0. It is initially defined for the cylinder sets generated by the histories and then extended to the sigma-algebra by Carathéodory's unique extension theorem [3]. Given a random variable $V : Z^\omega \to \mathbb{R}$, we will write $\mathcal{E}_{\mathcal{G},s_0,\sigma,\pi}(V)$ for the expectation of V w.r.t. $\mathcal{P}_{\mathcal{G},s_0,\sigma,\pi}$. We may drop $\mathcal{G}$ from the subscript when it is understood.

Objectives

We consider reachability and safety objectives. Given a set $T \subseteq S$ of states, the *reachability* objective $\mathtt{Reach}(T)$ is the set of plays that visit T at least once, i.e., $s_h \in T$ holds for some history h that is a prefix of the play. The dual *safety* objective $\mathtt{Avoid}(T) \stackrel{\text{def}}{=} Z^\omega \setminus \mathtt{Reach}(T)$ consists of the plays that never visit T. We can and will assume that $T = \{\top\}$ holds for a sink state $\top \in S$ and write $\mathtt{Reach}(\top)$ for $\mathtt{Reach}(\{\top\})$. Similarly, we assume that there is another sink state $\bot \in S$, with $\bot \neq \top$, and write $\mathtt{Avoid}(\bot)$ for $\mathtt{Avoid}(\{\bot\})$. Max attempts to maximize the probability of achieving the given objective (usually $\mathtt{Reach}(\top)$ or $\mathtt{Avoid}(\top)$), whereas Min attempts to minimize it.

Value and Optimality

For a game $\mathcal{G}$, objective E and initial state s_0, the *lower value* and *upper value* of s_0 are respectively defined as

$$\mathtt{val}^{\downarrow}_{\mathcal{G},E}(s_0) \stackrel{\text{def}}{=} \sup_{\sigma \in \Sigma} \inf_{\pi \in \Pi} \mathcal{P}_{\mathcal{G},s_0,\sigma,\pi}(E) \quad \text{and} \quad \mathtt{val}^{\uparrow}_{\mathcal{G},E}(s_0) \stackrel{\text{def}}{=} \inf_{\pi \in \Pi} \sup_{\sigma \in \Sigma} \mathcal{P}_{\mathcal{G},s_0,\sigma,\pi}(E).$$

The inequality $\mathtt{val}^{\downarrow}_{\mathcal{G},E}(s_0) \leq \mathtt{val}^{\uparrow}_{\mathcal{G},E}(s_0)$ holds by definition. If $\mathtt{val}^{\downarrow}_{\mathcal{G},E}(s_0) = \mathtt{val}^{\uparrow}_{\mathcal{G},E}(s_0)$, then this quantity is called the *value*, denoted by $\mathtt{val}_{\mathcal{G},E}(s_0)$. For reachability objectives, like all Borel objectives, the value exists if all action sets are finite [18], and even if for all states s we have that $A(s)$ is finite or $B(s)$ is finite [10, Theorem 11]. We always assume the latter, so that $\mathtt{val}_{\mathcal{G},E}(s_0)$ exists. For $\varepsilon \geq 0$, a Max strategy σ is called ε-*optimal* from s_0 if for all Min strategies π we have $\mathcal{P}_{\mathcal{G},s_0,\sigma,\pi}(E) \geq \mathtt{val}_{\mathcal{G},E}(s_0) - \varepsilon$. A 0-optimal strategy is also called *optimal*. For $E = \mathtt{Reach}(\top)$ or $E = \mathtt{Avoid}(\bot)$ we have

$$\mathtt{val}_{\mathcal{G},E}(s_0) = \sup_{\alpha \in \mathcal{D}(A(s_0))} \inf_{\beta \in \mathcal{D}(B(s_0))} \langle p(s_0, \alpha, \beta), \mathtt{val}_{\mathcal{G},E} \rangle. \tag{1}$$

We note in passing that the equality in (1) also holds in the states $\top, \bot$, as these are sink states.

3 Martingales for Safety

For the remainder of the paper we fix a game $\mathcal{G}$ over a countable state space S. Whenever we make finiteness assumptions on S and the action sets, we state them explicitly. Several times we use the following lemma, a consequence of the optional-stopping theorem for submartingales.

Lemma 1. *Let σ and π be Max and Min strategies, respectively. Suppose v : $S \to [0,1]$ is a function with $v(\perp) = 0$ such that $\langle p(s_h, \sigma(h), \pi(h)), v\rangle \geq v(s_h)$ holds for all histories h. Then $\mathcal{P}_{s_0,\sigma,\pi}(\texttt{Avoid}(\perp)) \geq v(s_0)$ holds for all $s_0 \in S$.*

Proof. Let $s_0 \in S$. Define a sequence of random variables $V(0), V(1), \ldots$ with $V(i) : Z^\omega \to [0,1]$ by

$$V(i)((s_0, a_0, b_0)(s_1, a_1, b_1) \cdots) \overset{\text{def}}{=} v(s_i).$$

Similarly, denote by $H(i) : Z^\omega \to H_i$ the function that maps each random play to its unique prefix in H_i. Recall that we can create random variables via composition of functions. Consider the function $s : H \to S$ that maps each finite history h to its final state s_h; this function composed with $H(i)$ is the random variable $s_{H(i)} : Z^\omega \to S$. Moreover, the function v composed with $s_{H(i)}$ is the random variable $v(s_{H(i)})$. Note that $V(i) = v(s_{H(i)})$. For $i \geq 0$, let $\mathcal{F}_i$ be the sigma-algebra generated by the cylinder sets corresponding to the histories $h \in H_i$. Then $V(i)$ and $H(i)$ are $\mathcal{F}_i$-measurable. By the assumption on v we have

$$
\begin{aligned}
\mathcal{E}_{s_0,\sigma,\pi}(V(i+1) \mid \mathcal{F}_i) &= \mathcal{E}_{s_0,\sigma,\pi}(v(s_{H(i+1)}) \mid \mathcal{F}_i) \\
&= \sum_{s \in S} p(s_{H(i)}, \sigma(H(i)), \pi(H(i)))v(s) \\
&= \langle p(s_{H(i)}, \sigma(H(i)), \pi(H(i))), v\rangle \\
&\geq v(s_{H(i)}) = V(i).
\end{aligned}
$$

It follows that $V(0), V(1), \ldots$ is a submartingale with respect to the filtrations $\mathcal{F}_0, \mathcal{F}_1, \ldots$. Moreover $|V(i)| \leq 1$ holds for all i. This boundedness condition together with the optional-stopping theorem imply that, almost surely, $V(0), V(1), \ldots$ converges to a random variable $V(\infty)$ with

$$\mathcal{E}_{s_0,\sigma,\pi}(V(\infty)) \geq \mathcal{E}_{s_0,\sigma,\pi}(V(0)) = v(s_0).$$

On the other hand, since $\perp$ is a sink,

$$
\begin{aligned}
\mathcal{E}_{s_0,\sigma,\pi}(V(\infty)) &= \mathcal{P}_{s_0,\sigma,\pi}(\texttt{Avoid}(\perp)) \cdot \mathcal{E}_{s_0,\sigma,\pi}(V(\infty) \mid \texttt{Avoid}(\perp)) \\
&\quad + \mathcal{P}_{s_0,\sigma,\pi}(\texttt{Reach}(\perp)) \cdot \mathcal{E}_{s_0,\sigma,\pi}(V(\infty) \mid \texttt{Reach}(\perp)) \\
&\leq \mathcal{P}_{s_0,\sigma,\pi}(\texttt{Avoid}(\perp)) \cdot 1 + \mathcal{P}_{s_0,\sigma,\pi}(\texttt{Reach}(\perp)) \cdot 0 \\
&= \mathcal{P}_{s_0,\sigma,\pi}(\texttt{Avoid}(\perp)).
\end{aligned}
$$

$\square$

4   Optimal Safety

We will construct memoryless strategies for reachability from strategies for safety. The following proposition will be useful for this purpose and is of independent interest.

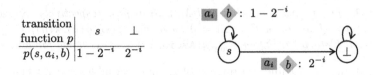

transition function p	s	$\perp$
$p(s, a_i, b)$	$1 - 2^{-i}$	2^{-i}

Fig. 1. A finite-state MDP where Max has no ε-optimal memoryless strategy for safety objective $\mathtt{Avoid}(\perp)$. The state $\perp$ is a sink state. The set $\{a_i \mid i \in \mathbb{N}\}$ of Max's actions at s is countable, while Min only has a single action b.

Proposition 2. *Suppose Max's action sets are finite. Then Max has a memoryless strategy σ that is optimal for $\mathtt{Avoid}(\perp)$ from every state. That is, for all $s \in S$ and all Min strategies π*

$$\mathcal{P}_{s,\sigma,\pi}(\mathtt{Avoid}(\perp)) \geq \mathtt{val}_{\mathtt{Avoid}(\perp)}(s).$$

Proof. Since Max has only finite action sets, the supremum in (1) is taken over a compact set of mixed actions. Therefore, it is a maximum; i.e., for every $s \in S$ there is a mixed action, say $\sigma(s) \in \mathcal{D}(A(s))$, such that for all mixed Min actions $\beta \in \mathcal{D}(B(s))$

$$\mathtt{val}_{\mathtt{Avoid}(\perp)}(s) \leq \langle p(s, \sigma(s), \beta), \mathtt{val}_{\mathtt{Avoid}(\perp)} \rangle. \tag{2}$$

Extend σ to a memoryless Max strategy in the natural way, and let π be an arbitrary Min strategy. Then the function $\mathtt{val}_{\mathtt{Avoid}(\perp)}$ satisfies the conditions of Lemma 1. Thus, $\mathcal{P}_{s,\sigma,\pi}(\mathtt{Avoid}(\perp)) \geq \mathtt{val}_{\mathtt{Avoid}(\perp)}(s)$ holds for all s. $\square$

Example 3. The assumption that Max has finite action sets cannot be dropped from Proposition 2. This assumption is required even for finite-state MDPs, i.e., when S is finite and Min has only one action per state. In fact, memoryless ε-optimal strategies do not always exist for safety objectives. As an example, consider the game depicted in Fig. 1, which was first discussed in [15]. The strategy that plays a_{i+k} at stage i is $\frac{1}{2^k}$-optimal for Max; indeed, the probability of reaching $\perp$ at stage i will be at most $2^{-(i+k+1)}$. Hence, the probability of $\mathtt{Avoid}(\perp)$ is at least $1 - \sum_{i \in \mathbb{N}} 2^{-(i+k+1)} = 1 - \frac{1}{2^k}$, as required. This implies that $\mathtt{val}_{\mathtt{Avoid}(\perp)}(s) = 1$.

Let σ be some arbitrary memoryless strategy for Max. The probability that state $\perp$ is not reached at stage i is $(1 - p(s, \sigma(s), b)(\perp))^i$. Clearly, the probability of the event $\mathtt{Avoid}(\perp)$ is 0. $\square$

5 ε-Optimal Reachability

Max does not always have optimal strategies for reachability, even when S and all action sets are finite.

Example 4. Consider the game depicted in Fig. 2, introduced in [16], also known as *snowball* or *hide-or-run* [8]. Following the intuition given in [8], Max initially

transition function p	s	$\top$	$\perp$
$p(s,h,w)$	1	0	0
$p(s,h,t)$	0	1	0
$p(s,r,w)$	0	1	0
$p(s,r,t)$	0	0	1

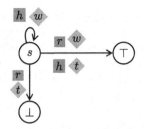

Fig. 2. The snowball game where Max has no optimal strategy for Reach($\top$). The states $\top$ and $\perp$ are sink states. Max's action set at s is $\{hide, run\}$, shown as h and r in the figure, while Min's action set is $\{wait, throw\}$, shown as w and t.

hides behind a bush (state s) and his goal is to reach home (state $\top$) without being hit by a snowball; Min is armed with a single snowball.

Below, in order to show that $\mathbf{val}_{\texttt{Reach}(\top)}(s) = 1$, for all ε, such that $0 < \varepsilon < 1$, we exhibit an ε-optimal strategy for Max. Given ε, consider the memoryless Max's strategy σ defined by $\sigma(s)(hide) = 1 - \varepsilon$ and $\sigma(s)(run) = \varepsilon$. After fixing σ in the game, by Proposition 2, Min has optimal memoryless strategies π for Avoid($\top$) in the new game. Let π be a memoryless strategy for Min, defined as

$$\pi(s)(throw) = x \qquad \text{and} \qquad \pi(s)(wait) = 1 - x.$$

for some $0 \le x \le 1$. Then

$$\mathcal{P}_{s,\sigma,\pi}(\texttt{Reach}(\top)) = \varepsilon(1-x) + (1-\varepsilon)x + (1-\varepsilon)(1-x)\mathcal{P}_{s,\sigma,\pi}(\texttt{Reach}(\top)).$$

Solving this for $\mathcal{P}_{s,\sigma,\pi}(\texttt{Reach}(\top))$ yields

$$\mathcal{P}_{s,\sigma,\pi}(\texttt{Reach}(\top)) = 1 - \frac{x\varepsilon}{\varepsilon + x(1-\varepsilon)} \ge 1 - \frac{x\varepsilon}{x\varepsilon + x(1-\varepsilon)} = 1 - \varepsilon,$$

implying that σ is an ε-optimal strategy for Max.

A straightforward argument shows that there is no optimal strategy for Max in this game. If Max always plays hide, Min can wait forever. If not, assume that at some stage Max plays run with probability $\varepsilon > 0$; then Min would throw to reach $\perp$ with a positive probability.

$\square$

In this section we prove the following proposition.

Proposition 5. *Suppose that Min's action sets are finite. Then for every $\varepsilon > 0$ and every finite subset of states $S_0 \subseteq S$ Max has a memoryless strategy σ that is ε-optimal for Reach($\top$) from all $s_0 \in S_0$ and for each $s \in S$ the support of $\sigma(s)$ is finite.*

Remark 6. The assumption that Min's action sets are finite can be replaced by the assumption that S is finite. The proof requires an extension of Lemma 1.

Proposition 5 does not carry over to countably infinite reachability games with infinite action sets for Min; see Sect. 7.

For the rest of the section we assume that Min's action sets are finite. Towards a proof of Proposition 5 we consider, for $n \geq 0$, the horizon-restricted reachability objective $\text{Reach}_n(\top) \subseteq \text{Reach}(\top)$ consisting of the plays that reach $\top$ within at most n steps. For $s \in S$ write $\text{val}_n(s)$ for $\text{val}_{\text{Reach}_n(\top)}(s)$. We have $\text{val}_0(\top) = 1$ and $\text{val}_0(s) = 0$ for all $s \neq \top$. For all $n \geq 0$, since $\text{Reach}_n(\top) \subseteq \text{Reach}_{n+1}(\top)$, we have for all $s \in S$

$$\text{val}_n(s) \leq \text{val}_{n+1}(s) = \sup_{\alpha \in \mathcal{D}(A(s))} \inf_{\beta \in \mathcal{D}(B(s))} \langle p(s, \alpha, \beta), \text{val}_n \rangle$$

$$= \sup_{\alpha \in \mathcal{D}(A(s))} \min_{b \in B(s)} \langle p(s, \alpha, b), \text{val}_n \rangle,$$

as Min's action sets are finite. For all $s \in S$, since $\text{val}_0(s) \leq \text{val}_1(s) \leq \ldots \leq 1$, there is a limit $\text{val}_\infty(s) \stackrel{\text{def}}{=} \lim_{n \to \infty} \text{val}_n(s)$.

Lemma 7. *Suppose that Min's action sets are finite. For all $s \in S$ we have*

$$\text{val}_\infty(s) = \sup_{\alpha \in \mathcal{D}(A(s))} \min_{b \in B(s)} \langle p(s, \alpha, b), \text{val}_\infty \rangle.$$

Proof. Let $s \in S$. Towards the "$\leq$" inequality, for any n we have

$$\text{val}_{n+1}(s) = \sup_{\alpha \in \mathcal{D}(A(s))} \min_{b \in B(s)} \langle p(s, \alpha, b), \text{val}_n \rangle$$

$$\leq \sup_{\alpha \in \mathcal{D}(A(s))} \min_{b \in B(s)} \langle p(s, \alpha, b), \text{val}_\infty \rangle.$$

Thus, $\text{val}_\infty(s) \leq \sup_{\alpha \in \mathcal{D}(A(s))} \min_{b \in B(s)} \langle p(s, \alpha, b), \text{val}_\infty \rangle$.

Towards the "$\geq$" inequality, for any fixed α and b the function $\langle p(s, \alpha, b), \cdot \rangle : \mathbb{R}^S \to \mathbb{R}$ is a linear map and, thus, continuous. Hence, for any α

$$\lim_{n \to \infty} \min_{b \in B(s)} \langle p(s, \alpha, b), \text{val}_n \rangle = \min_{b \in B(s)} \lim_{n \to \infty} \langle p(s, \alpha, b), \text{val}_n \rangle$$

$$= \min_{b \in B(s)} \langle p(s, \alpha, b), \text{val}_\infty \rangle.$$

It follows that

$$\text{val}_\infty(s) = \lim_{n \to \infty} \text{val}_{n+1}(s) = \lim_{n \to \infty} \sup_{\alpha \in \mathcal{D}(A(s))} \min_{b \in B(s)} \langle p(s, \alpha, b), \text{val}_n \rangle$$

$$\geq \sup_{\alpha \in \mathcal{D}(A(s))} \lim_{n \to \infty} \min_{b \in B(s)} \langle p(s, \alpha, b), \text{val}_n \rangle$$

$$= \sup_{\alpha \in \mathcal{D}(A(s))} \min_{b \in B(s)} \langle p(s, \alpha, b), \text{val}_\infty \rangle.$$

$\square$

Now the following lemma follows from Lemma 1.

Lemma 8. *Suppose that Min's action sets are finite. Then* $\mathtt{val}_{\mathtt{Reach}(\top)} = \mathtt{val}_\infty$.

Proof. Since $\mathtt{Reach}(\top) \supseteq \mathtt{Reach}_n(\top)$, we have $\mathtt{val}_{\mathtt{Reach}(\top)} \geq \mathtt{val}_n$. Towards the other inequality, define a function $v : S \to [0,1]$ by $v(s) \overset{\text{def}}{=} 1 - \mathtt{val}_\infty(s)$. We have $v(\top) = 1 - \mathtt{val}_\infty(\top) = 0$. Let σ be an arbitrary Max strategy. For every history h, let $b_h \in \arg\min_{b \in B(s_h)} \langle p(s_h, \sigma(h), b), \mathtt{val}_\infty \rangle$. Define a Min strategy π with $\pi(h)(b_h) = 1$ for all histories h. For all histories h we have

$$
\begin{aligned}
\langle p(s_h, \sigma(h), \pi(h)), v \rangle &= 1 - \langle p(s_h, \sigma(h), \pi(h)), \mathtt{val}_\infty \rangle && \text{from the definition of } v \\
&\geq 1 - \mathtt{val}_\infty(s_h) && \text{Lemma 7} \\
&= v(s_h) && \text{definition of } v.
\end{aligned}
$$

By Lemma 1, for all $s \in S$

$$
\mathcal{P}_{s,\sigma,\pi}(\mathtt{Reach}(\top)) = 1 - \mathcal{P}_{s,\sigma,\pi}(\mathtt{Avoid}(\top)) \leq 1 - v(s) = \mathtt{val}_\infty(s).
$$

Since σ was arbitrary, we conclude that $\mathtt{val}_{\mathtt{Reach}(\top)} \leq \mathtt{val}_\infty$. $\qquad\square$

Let us introduce an operation on games which makes transitions "leak" to $\bot$. The intention is to "reduce" reachability to safety, in the sense that in a leaky game, $\mathtt{Avoid}(\bot)$ is included in (and, hence, equal to) $\mathtt{Reach}(\top)$ up to a measure-zero set of plays. We set up the leaky game so that Max has an optimal strategy for $\mathtt{Avoid}(\bot)$, which, according to Proposition 2, can be chosen to be memoryless.

For technical reasons, which will manifest themselves later, we associate the leaks with Min actions. Concretely, for a state s, a Min action $b \in B(s)$, and some $\varepsilon > 0$, by *making b leak ε* we refer to obtaining from p another transition function $\breve{p}$ by setting, for all $a \in A(s)$ and $t \in S$,

$$
\breve{p}(s, a, b)(t) \overset{\text{def}}{=} \begin{cases} (1 - \varepsilon)p(s, a, b)(t) & \text{if } t \neq \bot \\ (1 - \varepsilon)p(s, a, b)(\bot) + \varepsilon & \text{if } t = \bot. \end{cases}
$$

Intuitively, a fraction of ε of the probability mass leaks to $\bot$ whenever b is taken. We use leaks to prove Proposition 5.

Proof. (of Proposition 5*).* Let $\varepsilon > 0$, and let $S_0 \subseteq S$ be finite. Choose $\varepsilon_1, \varepsilon_2, \varepsilon_3 > 0$ such that $\varepsilon_1 + \varepsilon_2 + \varepsilon_3 = \varepsilon$. For each $s \in S$ choose $a(s) \in A(s)$. By Lemma 8, since S_0 is finite, there is $n \geq 0$ such that $\mathtt{val}_n(s) \geq \mathtt{val}_{\mathtt{Reach}(\top)}(s) - \varepsilon_1$ holds for all $s \in S_0$. Inductively define (in general non-memoryless) Max strategies $\sigma_0, \ldots, \sigma_n$ as follows. For each history h, define $\sigma_0(h)(a(s_h)) \overset{\text{def}}{=} 1$. For $i \in \{0, \ldots, n-1\}$ and each state $s \in S$ we have $\sup_{\alpha \in \mathcal{D}(A(s))} \min_{b \in B(s)} \langle p(s, \alpha, b), \mathtt{val}_i \rangle = \mathtt{val}_{i+1}(s)$; thus we can define $\sigma_{i+1}(s)$ so that $\min_{b \in B(s)} \langle p(s, \sigma_{i+1}(s), b), \mathtt{val}_i \rangle \geq \mathtt{val}_{i+1}(s) - \frac{\varepsilon_2}{n}$. Since $\frac{\varepsilon_2}{n} > 0$, we can assume without loss of generality that the support of $\sigma_{i+1}(s)$ is finite. Finally, define $\sigma_{i+1}(zh) \overset{\text{def}}{=} \sigma_i(h)$ for all $z \in Z$ and $h \in H$.

We show inductively that for all $i \in \{1, \ldots, n\}$ and all $s \in S$

$$
\inf_{\pi \in \Pi} \mathcal{P}_{g,s,\sigma_i,\pi}(\mathtt{Reach}_i(\top)) \geq \mathtt{val}_i(s) - i \cdot \frac{\varepsilon_2}{n}. \tag{3}
$$

This is immediate for $i = 0$. For $i \in \{0, \ldots, n-1\}$ we have

$$\inf_{\pi \in \Pi} \mathcal{P}_{\mathcal{G}, s, \sigma_{i+1}, \pi}(\mathrm{Reach}_{i+1}(\top))$$

$$\geq \min_{b \in B(s)} \langle p(s, \sigma_{i+1}(s), b), \inf_{\pi \in \Pi} \mathcal{P}_{\mathcal{G}, \cdot, \sigma_i, \pi}(\mathrm{Reach}_i(\top)) \rangle$$

$$\geq \min_{b \in B(s)} \langle p(s, \sigma_{i+1}(s), b), \mathrm{val}_i \rangle - i \cdot \frac{\varepsilon_2}{n} \qquad \text{induction hypothesis}$$

$$\geq \mathrm{val}_{i+1}(s) - \frac{\varepsilon_2}{n} - i \cdot \frac{\varepsilon_2}{n} \qquad \text{definition of } \sigma_{i+1}(s),$$

proving (3).

Now in every state except $\top$, make each Min action leak $\frac{\varepsilon_3}{n}$. Further, remove any Max actions that σ_n never takes. Call the resulting game $\mathcal{G}^-$. Then Max's action sets in $\mathcal{G}^-$ are finite and we have for all $s_0 \in S$ and all Min strategies π

$$\mathcal{P}_{\mathcal{G}^-, s, \sigma_n, \pi}(\mathrm{Avoid}(\bot))$$

$$\geq \mathcal{P}_{\mathcal{G}^-, s, \sigma_n, \pi}(\mathrm{Reach}_n(\top)) \qquad \mathrm{Avoid}(\bot) \supseteq \mathrm{Reach}_n(\top)$$

$$\geq \mathcal{P}_{\mathcal{G}, s, \sigma_n, \pi}(\mathrm{Reach}_n(\top)) - \varepsilon_3 \qquad \text{at most } n \cdot \frac{\varepsilon_3}{n} \text{ leaks in } n \text{ steps}$$

$$\geq \mathrm{val}_n(s) - \varepsilon_2 - \varepsilon_3 \qquad \text{by (3)}$$

$$\geq \mathrm{val}_{\mathcal{G}, \mathrm{Reach}(\top)}(s) - \varepsilon_1 - \varepsilon_2 - \varepsilon_3 \qquad \text{choice of } n$$

$$= \mathrm{val}_{\mathcal{G}, \mathrm{Reach}(\top)}(s) - \varepsilon \qquad \text{choice of } \varepsilon_1, \varepsilon_2, \varepsilon_3.$$

Thus, for all $s \in S_0$

$$\mathrm{val}_{\mathcal{G}^-, \mathrm{Avoid}(\bot)}(s) \geq \mathrm{val}_{\mathcal{G}, \mathrm{Reach}(\top)}(s) - \varepsilon. \qquad (4)$$

Due to the leaks, in $\mathcal{G}^-$ the events $\mathrm{Reach}(\top)$ and $\mathrm{Avoid}(\bot)$ coincide up to measure zero for all Max and all Min strategies. Since Max's action sets in $\mathcal{G}^-$ are finite, by Proposition 2 Max has a memoryless strategy σ that is optimal for $\mathrm{Avoid}(\bot)$ from every state. Thus, for all $s \in S_0$ and all Min strategies π

$$\mathcal{P}_{\mathcal{G}, s, \sigma, \pi}(\mathrm{Reach}(\top)) \geq \mathcal{P}_{\mathcal{G}^-, s, \sigma, \pi}(\mathrm{Reach}(\top))$$

$$= \mathcal{P}_{\mathcal{G}^-, s, \sigma, \pi}(\mathrm{Avoid}(\bot)) \qquad \text{as argued above}$$

$$\geq \mathrm{val}_{\mathcal{G}^-, \mathrm{Avoid}(\bot)}(s) \qquad \sigma \text{ is optimal}$$

$$\geq \mathrm{val}_{\mathcal{G}, \mathrm{Reach}(\top)}(s) - \varepsilon \qquad \text{by (4)}.$$

That is, the memoryless strategy σ is ε-optimal from all $s \in S_0$, and for each $s \in S$ the support of $\sigma(s)$ is finite. $\qquad \square$

6   Optimal Reachability

In this section we show the following result, a generalization of Bordais et al. [4, Theorem 28], via a different proof.

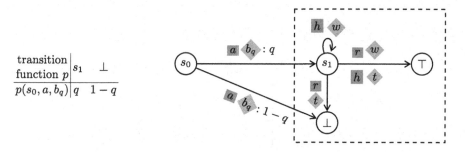

Fig. 3. A game where Max has no *memoryless* optimal strategy for Reach($\top$). The states $\top$ and $\bot$ are sink states. Min's action set at s_0 is $\{b_q \mid q \in (\frac{1}{2}, 1) \cap \mathbb{Q}\}$, while Max has a single action a at s_0. The game in dashed box is the snowball game from Fig. 2.

Theorem 9. *Suppose that S and Min's action sets are finite. Then for every $\varepsilon > 0$ Max has a memoryless strategy σ that is ε-optimal for Reach($\top$) from all states and optimal from all states from which Max has any optimal strategy.*

The assumption that Min's action sets are finite cannot be dropped, as the following example shows.

Example 10. Consider the game depicted in Fig. 3, wherein state s_1 is the start state of the snowball game from Example 4. Recall that $\mathtt{val}_{\mathtt{Reach}(\top)}(s_1) = 1$, but Max does not have an optimal strategy from s_1. By this, and the fact that Min can choose b_q for q arbitrary close to $\frac{1}{2}$, we deduce that $\mathtt{val}_{\mathtt{Reach}(\top)}(s_0) = \frac{1}{2}$. Observe that when taking action b_q at s_0, Min is increasing the value from $\frac{1}{2}$ to $q > \frac{1}{2}$. Indeed, we claim that Max has an optimal strategy from s_0. If Max observes which action b_q Min takes in s_0, and plays a $(q - \frac{1}{2})$-optimal strategy from s_1, the probability of reaching $\top$ will be at least $q \cdot (1 - (q - \frac{1}{2})) \geq q - (q - \frac{1}{2}) = \frac{1}{2}$. But Max has to "remember" Min's value increase in order to play sufficiently well in s_1. So Max does not have a memoryless optimal strategy from s_0. In fact, a step counter (discrete clock) would not help Max either, since the step counter value does not contain any information about q. □

The assumption that S is finite cannot be dropped either, not even for the subclass of turn-based games, as the following example shows.

Example 11. Consider the finitely-branching turn-based reachability game depicted in Fig. 4 (from [13, Sect. 9]). The initial state is u_1, states u_i are Min-controlled, states s_i are Max-controlled and t is the target state.

At every state u_i, Min can either go right (red transition) or go up. At every state s_i, Max can either go right (red transition) or go down. It is easy to show that $\mathtt{val}_{\mathcal{G}}(s_i) > \mathtt{val}_{\mathcal{G}}(u_i)$ for all i. Thus the only locally optimal Min move is to go right. Similarly, $\mathtt{val}_{\mathcal{G}}(s_i) > y_i$, and thus the only locally optimal Max move is to go right.

Max has an optimal strategy from u_1 (and also from every other state) as follows. First, always go right. If Min ever goes up at some u_i then go down at s_i.

Transition function p:

transition function p	s_1	$\bot$
$p(s_0, a, b_q)$	q	$1 - q$

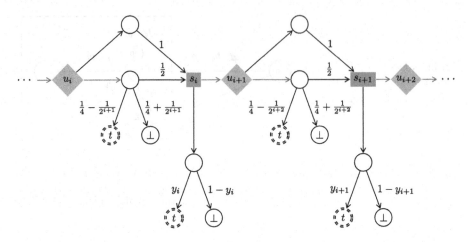

Fig. 4. A finitely-branching turn-based reachability game $\mathcal{G}$ with initial state u_1, where optimal Max strategies cannot be memoryless (and cannot even be Markov). For clarity, we have drawn several copies of the target state t. The number y_i is defined as $\frac{1}{2} - \frac{1}{2^{i+1}}$.

Intuitively, by going up, Min increases the value (i.e., gives a "gift" to Max). By going down at s_i, Max plays sub-optimally locally, but realizes most of the value of s_i, i.e., loses less than Min's previous gift.

However, no memoryless strategy (and not even any Markov strategy, i.e., any strategy that uses only a step counter) can be optimal for Max from u_1. First, a step counter gives no advantage to Max, since in this example the step counter is implicit in the current state anyway. For any memoryless Max strategy, there are to cases. Either this strategy never goes down with any positive probability at any state s_i. Then Min can avoid the target t completely by always playing up, and thus this Max strategy is not optimal. Otherwise, let s_j be first state where Max goes down with some positive probability. This Max strategy is not optimal either, since Min can always go right (locally optimal), and Max's choice at s_j is locally sub-optimal.

See [13, Sect. 9] for a formal proof of this example. It is also shown there that, in every countably infinite finitely-branching turn-based reachability game, optimal Max strategies (if they exist at all) can be chosen as deterministic and using a step counter plus 1 bit of public memory. So the example above is tight.   □

Now we prove Theorem 9. Let S and Min's action sets be finite. We partition the finite state space S into S_0, S_1 so that S_0 contains exactly the states from which Max has an optimal strategy for $\text{Reach}(\top)$, and S_1 contains exactly the states from which Max does not have an optimal strategy. Clearly, $\top, \bot \in S_0$.

By the finiteness of Min's action sets and (1), for every value-0 state s and every mixed Max action $\alpha \in \mathcal{D}(A(s))$ Min has an action b that keeps the game (surely) in a value-0 state. Therefore, an optimal Max strategy cannot rely on Min "gifts" in value-0 states. Hence, we can assume without loss of generality that $\perp$ is the only value-0 state. We write $S_0^+ \stackrel{\text{def}}{=} S_0 \setminus \{\perp\}$, so that all states in S_0^+ have a positive value.

The challenge is that the play can "cross over" between S_0 and S_1. Our approach is as follows. First we fix a memoryless strategy σ_0 on S_0 that is optimal for Max as long as Min responds optimally. Then, building on the idea of the previous section, we add "leaks" to the game so that

- in S_0 the leaks do not decrease the value and Max still has an optimal strategy;
- in S_1 the leaks decrease the value only by little.

After having fixed σ_0 on S_0 and introduced suitable leaks, an optimal safety strategy for $\texttt{Avoid}(\perp)$ will serve as the memoryless strategy σ claimed in Theorem 9. This strategy extends σ_0 to the whole state space and is optimal from S_0 (no matter what Min does).

Below, to avoid clutter whenever we write $\texttt{val}(s)$ we mean $\texttt{val}_{\mathcal{G},\texttt{Reach}(T)}(s)$ where $\mathcal{G}$ is the original game, even when other auxiliary games are discussed.

We start by defining a memoryless strategy, σ_0, only on S_0 so that σ_0 is optimal from S_0 as long as Min "does not increase the value".

For a state $s \in S_0$, call a mixed Max action $\alpha \in \mathcal{D}(A(s))$ *optimality-preserving* if for all Min actions $b \in B(s)$ we have $\langle p(s,\alpha,b), \texttt{val} \rangle \geq \texttt{val}(s)$ and if $\langle p(s,\alpha,b), \texttt{val} \rangle = \texttt{val}(s)$ then the support of $p(s,\alpha,b)$ is a subset of S_0. Note that every optimal Max strategy from S_0 is optimality-preserving at least in the first step. Therefore, every state in S_0 has an optimality-preserving mixed Max action.

For a state $s \in S_0$ and an optimality-preserving mixed action α, call a Min action $b \in B(s)$ *value-preserving* if $\langle p(s,\alpha,b), \texttt{val} \rangle = \texttt{val}(s)$ and *value-increasing* otherwise (i.e., $\langle p(s,\alpha,b), \texttt{val} \rangle > \texttt{val}(s)$).

We define inductively a non-decreasing sequence $R(0), R(1), R(2), \ldots$ of subsets of S_0. Define $R(0) \stackrel{\text{def}}{=} \{\top\}$. For every $n \geq 0$, define $R(n+1)$ as $R(n)$ union the set of those states $s \in S_0$ from which Max has an optimality-preserving mixed action, say α_s, and a number $\delta_s > 0$ such that for all value-preserving Min actions $b \in B(s)$ we have $p(s,\alpha_s,b)(R(n)) \geq \delta_s$. We note in passing that the existence of $\delta_s > 0$ is guaranteed due to finiteness of Min's action set. Informally speaking, $R(n+1)$ consists of those states that are already in $R(n)$ or have an optimality-preserving mixed action α_s so that in the next step $R(n)$ is entered with a positive probability unless Min takes a value-increasing action. Defining $R \stackrel{\text{def}}{=} R(|S|-1)$, since S is finite we have $R = R(|S|-1) = R(|S|) = R(|S|+1) = \ldots$. Moreover, we can define $\delta \stackrel{\text{def}}{=} \min_{s \in R} \delta_s > 0$.

Lemma 12. *We have $R = S_0^+$.*

Proof. By an easy induction, $\perp \notin R$. Hence $R \subseteq S_0^+$. Towards the reverse inclusion, suppose there is $s \in S_0 \setminus R$. It suffices to show that $s = \perp$. Let σ be an arbitrary optimal Max strategy starting from s. Note that $\sigma(s)$ is optimality-preserving. Since $s \notin R = R(|S|)$, there is a value-preserving Min action $b \in B(s)$ such that the support of $p(s,\sigma(s),b)$ does not overlap with $R(|S|-1) = R$. That is, the support of $p(s,\sigma(s),b)$ is a subset of $S_0 \setminus R$ and, thus, does not contain $\top$. Since σ is optimal, σ has to play optimally—and, thus, has to use optimality-preserving mixed actions—as long as Min has taken only value-preserving actions. Then it follows inductively that there is a deterministic Min strategy (playing b in the very first step) that keeps the play in $S_0 \setminus R$ forever. In particular, $\top$ is not reached. Since the optimal strategy σ was arbitrary, we have $\mathtt{val}(s) = 0$; i.e., $s = \bot$. □

Define σ_0 to be the memoryless Max strategy on S_0 with $\sigma_0(s) = \alpha_s$ for all $s \in S_0$, where α_s is from the definition of $R(n)$. For $s \in S_0$, call $b \in B(s)$ *value-preserving* (or *value-increasing*) if b is value-preserving (or value-increasing, respectively) for s and $\sigma_0(s)$.

Lemma 13. *For any Max strategy that plays σ_0 on S_0 and any Min strategy, almost all plays that eventually remain in S_0^+ and eventually contain only value-preserving Min actions reach $\top$.*

Proof. Let σ be a Max strategy that plays σ_0 on S_0, and let π be a Min strategy. Since the set of (finite) histories is countable, it suffices to consider the set of plays which always remain in S_0^+ and contain only value-preserving Min actions. Let $s \in S_0^+$. By Lemma 12, we have $s \in R$. Let $n \leq |S| - 1$ be the smallest n with $s \in R(n)$. We have $p(s, \sigma_0(s), b)(R(n-1)) \geq \delta$ for all value-preserving Min actions b. It follows that at any time the probability that in at most $|S| - 1$ steps $R(0) = \{\top\}$ is reached is at least $\delta^{|S|-1} > 0$. Thus, almost surely $\top$ is eventually reached. □

Since S_0 and Min's action sets are finite, we can choose an $\varepsilon > 0$ small enough so that for all $s \in S_0$ and all value-increasing Min actions b we have

$$\langle p(s, \sigma_0(s), b), \mathtt{val} \rangle \geq \mathtt{val}(s) + 2\varepsilon \tag{5}$$

So any value increase by a Min action is at least 2ε.

Define a game $\mathcal{G}_1$ with state space $S_1 \cup \{\top, \bot\}$. Its transition function p_1 is obtained from p by redirecting probability mass away from $S_0 \setminus \{\top, \bot\}$ as follows. Each transition to a state $s \in S_0 \setminus \{\top, \bot\}$ is redirected to $\top$ with probability $\mathtt{val}(s)$ and to $\bot$ with probability $1 - \mathtt{val}(s)$. Then the value of each state in $\mathcal{G}_1$ is equal to its value in $\mathcal{G}$.

As in the proof of Proposition 5 we obtain from $\mathcal{G}_1$ a "leaky" version, $\mathcal{G}_1^-$, with transition function p_1^-, such that Max's action sets are finite and, defining $v(s) \stackrel{\text{def}}{=} \mathtt{val}_{\mathcal{G}_1^-, \mathtt{Avoid}(\bot)}(s)$ for all $s \in S_1 \cup \{\top, \bot\}$, we have

$$v(s) \geq \mathtt{val}(s) - \varepsilon \qquad \text{for all } s \in S_1. \tag{6}$$

By Proposition 2 Max has a memoryless optimal (for safety) strategy σ_1 in $\mathcal{G}_1^-$. Thus, for all $s \in S_1$ and all $b \in B(s)$, as in Equation (2), we have

$$\langle p_1^-(s, \sigma_1(s), b), v \rangle \geq v(s).$$

Next we define a "leaky" version, $\mathcal{G}^-$, of the whole game $\mathcal{G}$ with the whole state space S and a transition function p^-. On S_1, function p^- is defined similarly to p_1^-, except that the probability mass that was directed away from $S_0 \setminus \{\top, \bot\}$ in the definition of $\mathcal{G}_1$ is now not directed away and instead enters S_0 as originally. However, the leaks in every transition from S_1 are also present in p^-. Extend the function v to the whole state space S by defining $v(s) \stackrel{\text{def}}{=} \mathtt{val}(s)$ for all $s \in S_0$. Then, for all $s \in S_1$ and all $b \in B(s)$

$$\langle p^-(s, \sigma_1(s), b), v \rangle = \langle p_1^-(s, \sigma_1(s), b), v \rangle \geq v(s).$$

On S_0, the transition function p^- is obtained from p by making value-increasing Min actions leak ε, in the sense defined in Sect. 5. For all $s \in S_0$ and all value-increasing Min actions $b \in B(s)$

$$\langle p^-(s, \sigma_0(s), b), v \rangle$$
$$\geq \langle p^-(s, \sigma_0(s), b), \mathtt{val} \rangle - \varepsilon \qquad \text{by (6) and the definition of } v \text{ on } S_0$$
$$\geq \langle p(s, \sigma_0(s), b), \mathtt{val} \rangle - \varepsilon - \varepsilon \qquad \text{from the definition of } p^-$$
$$\geq \mathtt{val}(s) + 2\varepsilon - \varepsilon - \varepsilon \qquad \text{by (5)}$$
$$= v(s) \qquad \text{definition of } v \text{ on } S_0.$$

For all $s \in S_0$ and all value-preserving Min actions $b \in B(s)$

$$\langle p^-(s, \sigma_0(s), b), v \rangle$$
$$= \langle p(s, \sigma_0(s), b), v \rangle \qquad \text{from the definition of } p^-$$
$$= \langle p(s, \sigma_0(s), b), \mathtt{val} \rangle \qquad \text{support of } p(s, \sigma_0(s), b) \text{ is a subset of } S_0$$
$$= \mathtt{val}(s) \qquad b \text{ is value-preserving}$$
$$= v(s) \qquad \text{definition of } v \text{ on } S_0.$$

Define the memoryless strategy σ by naturally combining σ_0 and σ_1. We have shown above that for all $s \in S$ and all $b \in B(s)$ we have $\langle p^-(s, \sigma(s), b), v \rangle \geq v(s)$. From applying Lemma 1 we conclude that for all $s \in S$ and all Min strategies π we have

$$\mathcal{P}_{\mathcal{G}^-, s, \sigma, \pi}(\mathtt{Avoid}(\bot)) \geq v(s).$$

In $\mathcal{G}^-$, due to the leaks, almost all $\bot$-avoiding plays eventually remain in S_0^+ and eventually have only value-preserving Min actions. But by Lemma 13, almost all of these plays reach $\top$. Thus, we have for all $s \in S$ and all Min strategies π

$$\mathcal{P}_{\mathcal{G}^-, s, \sigma, \pi}(\mathtt{Reach}(\top)) = \mathcal{P}_{\mathcal{G}^-, s, \sigma, \pi}(\mathtt{Avoid}(\bot)) \geq v(s),$$

which, by definition, equals $\mathtt{val}(s)$ if $s \in S_0$ and, by (6), is at least $\mathtt{val}(s) - \varepsilon$ if $s \in S_1$. Since $\mathcal{P}_{\mathcal{G}, s, \sigma, \pi}(\mathtt{Reach}(\top)) \geq \mathcal{P}_{\mathcal{G}^-, s, \sigma, \pi}(\mathtt{Reach}(\top))$, this completes the proof of Theorem 9.

7 Conclusion and Related Work

We have shown that, in finite reachability games with finite action sets for Min, optimal Max strategies, where they exist, can be chosen as memoryless randomized. However, this does not carry over to countably infinite reachability games.

Intuitively, the reason for this is that Min can play sub-optimally and give "gifts" to Max that increase the expected value of the current state, but delay progress towards the target. In countably infinite reachability games, Min might give infinitely many smaller and smaller gifts and delay progress indefinitely, unless Max uses memory to keep track of these gifts in order to react correctly.

Finite reachability games are simpler, because gifts from Min to Max are universally lower bounded in size, due to the finite state space and the finiteness of Min's action sets. Therefore, Min cannot give infinitely many gifts to Max, except in a nullset of the plays. Without such distracting gifts, Max can make steady progress towards the target. Moreover, if Min does give a gift once, then Max does not need to remember how large it was, since it is universally lower bounded.

The existence of optimal strategies is also affected by the size of the state space. While finite turn-based reachability games always admit optimal Max strategies [7], even in countably infinite MDPs, optimal Max strategies for reachability need not exist. However, it was shown by Ornstein [20, Thm. B] that ε-optimal Max strategies for reachability in countably infinite MDPs can be chosen as memoryless and deterministic. These strategies can even be made uniform, i.e., independent of the start state. Moreover, if an optimal strategy does exist for Max in a countable MDP, then there also exists one that is memoryless and deterministic [20, Prop. B].

These results on countable MDPs do not carry over to countable 2-player stochastic reachability games. While Max always has ε-optimal randomized memoryless strategies in countable concurrent reachability games with finite action sets [21, Corollary 3.9], these strategies depend on the start state and cannot be made uniform [19]. This non-uniformity even holds for the subclass of countable finitely branching turn-based reachability games [13]. However, uniformity can be regained with 1 bit of public memory, i.e., there exist uniformly ε-optimal Max strategies in countable concurrent reachability games with finite action sets that are deterministic and use just 1 bit of public memory [13]. Optimal Max strategies in countable turn-based finitely branching reachability games, where they exist, can be chosen to use just a step counter and 1 bit of public memory (but not just a step counter or just finite memory). On the other hand, in concurrent games with finite action sets, a step counter plus finite private memory does not suffice for optimal Max strategies in general [13].

If Min is allowed infinite action sets (resp. infinite branching) in countably infinite reachability games, then Max generally needs infinite memory for ε-optimal, optimal and almost surely winning strategies. There exists a turn-based countable reachability game with infinite Min branching (and finite Max branching), such that every state admits an almost surely winning strategy for Max, and yet every Max strategy that uses only a step counter plus finite private memory is still useless (in the sense that Min can make its attainment arbitrarily close to zero) [13].

References

1. de Alfaro, L., Henzinger, T.A., Kupferman, O.: Concurrent reachability games. In: Annual Symposium on Foundations of Computer Science (FOCS), pp. 564–575. IEEE Computer Society (1998). https://doi.org/10.1109/SFCS.1998.743507
2. Bertrand, N., Genest, B., Gimbert, H.: Qualitative determinacy and decidability of stochastic games with signals. J. ACM **64**(5), 33:1-33:48 (2017). https://doi.org/10.1145/3107926
3. Billingsley, P.: Probability and Measure, Third Edition. Wiley, New York (1995)
4. Bordais, B., Bouyer, P., Le Roux, S.: Optimal strategies in concurrent reachability games. In: Computer Science Logic (CSL). LIPIcs, vol. 216, pp. 7:1–7:17. Schloss Dagstuhl - Leibniz-Zentrum für Informatik (2022). https://doi.org/10.4230/LIPIcs.CSL.2022.7
5. Bouyer, P., Markey, N., Randour, M., Sangnier, A., Stan, D.: Reachability in networks of register protocols under stochastic schedulers. In: International Colloquium on Automata, Languages and Programming (ICALP), vol. 55, pp. 106:1–106:14. Schloss Dagstuhl-Leibniz-Zentrum fuer Informatik, Dagstuhl, Germany (2016). https://doi.org/10.4230/LIPIcs.ICALP.2016.106
6. Chen, T., Forejt, V., Kwiatkowska, M., Parker, D., Simaitis, A.: PRISM-games: a model checker for stochastic multi-player games. In: Piterman, N., Smolka, S.A. (eds.) TACAS 2013. LNCS, vol. 7795, pp. 185–191. Springer, Heidelberg (2013). https://doi.org/10.1007/978-3-642-36742-7_13
7. Condon, A.: The complexity of stochastic games. Inf. Comput. **96**(2), 203–224 (1992). https://doi.org/10.1016/0890-5401(92)90048-K
8. De Alfaro, L., Henzinger, T.A., Kupferman, O.: Concurrent reachability games. Theor. Comput. Sci. **386**(3), 188–217 (2007). https://doi.org/10.1016/j.tcs.2007.07.008
9. Everett, H.: Recursive games. In: Contributions to the Theory of Games, Volume III, Annals of Mathematics Studies, vol. 39, pp. 47–78. Princeton University Press, Princeton (1957). https://doi.org/10.1515/9781400882151-004
10. Flesch, J., Predtetchinski, A., Sudderth, W.: Positive zero-sum stochastic games with countable state and action spaces. Appl. Math. Optim. **82**, 499–516 (2020). https://doi.org/10.1007/s00245-018-9536-3
11. Gillette, D.: Stochastic games with zero stop probabilities. In: Contributions to the Theory of Games (AM-39), Volume III, pp. 179–188. Princeton University Press (1958). https://doi.org/10.1515/9781400882151-011
12. Gimbert, H., Horn, F.: Solving simple stochastic tail games. In: Annual ACM-SIAM Symposium on Discrete Algorithms, pp. 847–862 (2010). https://doi.org/10.1137/1.9781611973075
13. Kiefer, S., Mayr, R., Shirmohammadi, M., Totzke, P.: Strategy complexity of reachability in countable stochastic 2-player games. Dynamic Games and Applications. arXiv:2203.12024 (2023)
14. Kiefer, S., Mayr, R., Shirmohammadi, M., Wojtczak, D.: On strong determinacy of countable stochastic games. In: ACM/IEEE Symposium on Logic in Computer Science (LICS), pp. 1–12. IEEE Computer Society (2017). https://doi.org/10.1109/LICS.2017.8005134
15. Kiefer, S., Mayr, R., Shirmohammadi, M., Wojtczak, D.: Parity objectives in countable MDPs. In: ACM/IEEE Symposium on Logic in Computer Science (LICS) (2017). https://doi.org/10.1109/LICS.2017.8005100

16. Kumar, P.R., Shiau, T.H.: Existence of value and randomized strategies in zero-sum discrete-time stochastic dynamic games. SIAM J. Control. Optim. **19**(5), 617–634 (1981). https://doi.org/10.1137/0319039
17. Kučera, A.: Turn-based stochastic games. In: Apt, K.R., Grädel, E. (eds.) Lectures in Game Theory for Computer Scientists, pp. 146–184. Cambridge University Press (2011). https://doi.org/10.1017/CBO9780511973468.006
18. Maitra, A., Sudderth, W.: Finitely additive stochastic games with Borel measurable payoffs. Internat. J. Game Theory **27**(2), 257–267 (1998). https://doi.org/10.1007/s001820050071
19. Nowak, A., Raghavan, T.: Positive stochastic games and a theorem of Ornstein. In: Raghavan, T.E.S., Ferguson, T.S., Parthasarathy, T., Vrieze, O.J. (eds.) Stochastic Games And Related Topics. Theory and Decision Library, vol. 7. Springer, Dordrecht (1991). https://doi.org/10.1007/978-94-011-3760-7_11
20. Ornstein, D.: On the existence of stationary optimal strategies. Proc. Am. Math. Soc. **20**(2), 563–569 (1969). https://doi.org/10.2307/2035700
21. Secchi, P.: Stationary strategies for recursive games. Math. Oper. Res. **22**(2), 494–512 (1997). https://doi.org/10.1287/moor.22.2.494
22. Shapley, L.S.: Stochastic games. Proc. Natl. Acad. Sci. **39**(10), 1095–1100 (1953). https://doi.org/10.1073/pnas.39.10.1095

Region Quadtrees Verified

Tobias Nipkow[✉]

Technische Universität München, Munich, Germany
https://www.proof.cit.tum.de/~nipkow/

Abstract. This paper presents the formalization and verification (in the proof assistant Isabelle) of two variants of quadtrees: standard region quadtrees and quadtrees for matrix algebra.

1 Introduction

This paper presents the formalization and verification of different variants of quadtrees in the proof assistant Isabelle [8,9]. Quadtrees are a well-known data structure for the hierarchical representation of two-dimensional space in computer graphics, image processing, computational geometry, geographic information systems, and related areas [2,11,12]. There are many variants of quadtrees and we concentrate on **region quadtrees**. They are particularly well suited to the representation of two-dimensional images of pixels because of potential significant compression of the image. As all hierarchical data structures, they support parallel processing naturally. We consider the following two variants:

- Basic region quadtrees are formalized in Sect. 3.
- The representation of block matrices via region quadtrees is the subject of Sect. 4.

In each case we verify a small selection of representative operations. The Isabelle proofs are available online [7]. They are largely automatic—once one has found suitable notions and lemmas! Our formalization is executable and Isabelle can generate code in various functional languages.

2 Isabelle Notation

Isabelle types are built from type variables, e.g. $'a$, and (postfix) type constructors, e.g. $'a$ *list*; the function type arrow is $\Rightarrow$. The notation $t :: \tau$ means that term t has type τ. The notation $f \; ' \; A$ is the image of the function $f :: \tau \Rightarrow \tau'$ over the set $A :: \tau$ *set*.

Type $'a$ *list* are lists of elements of type $'a$. Concrete lists are written $[a_0, \ldots, a_n]$. Lists come with the following operations: $x \; \# \; xs$ (list constructor), $xs \; @ \; ys$ (append), *length*, *set xs* (the set of elements of list xs), *take n xs* (take the first n elements of xs), *drop n xs* (drop the first n elements of xs), $xs \; ! \; n$ (the n-th element of xs, starting at 0).

Types *nat* and *real* are the natural and real numbers. Logical equivalence is written $=$ instead of $\longleftrightarrow$.

Dedicated to Javier Esparza on the occasion of his 60th birthday.

© The Author(s), under exclusive license to Springer Nature Switzerland AG 2024
S. Kiefer et al. (Eds.): *Taming the Infinities of Concurrency*, LNCS 14660, pp. 243–254, 2024.
https://doi.org/10.1007/978-3-031-56222-8_14

3   Region Quadtrees

Region quadtrees are the best-known form of quadtrees. They represent two-dimensional images of **pixels** that can be black or white. The image is recursively subdivided into four quadrants until all pixels in a quadrant have the same value. Consequently the image must be of size $2^n \times 2^n$ pixels. The number n is called the **resolution** of the quadtree. The quadrants are numbered like this:

$$
\begin{array}{|c|c|}
\hline
1 & 3 \\
\hline
0 & 2 \\
\hline
\end{array}
\tag{1}
$$

An image and its quadtree representation is show in Fig. 1. The gray nodes in the tree represent subdivided squares.

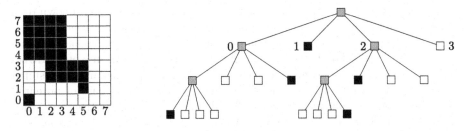

Fig. 1. Image and corresponding quadtree

The representation of quadtrees as a data type

datatype $'a$ $qtree = L\ 'a \mid Q\ ('a\ qtree)\ ('a\ qtree)\ ('a\ qtree)\ ('a\ qtree)$

supports leafs (constructor L) where all pixels have the same value of the parameter type $'a$. Black and white images as seen in Fig. 1 are represented by boolean quadtrees, i.e. where $'a = bool$.

The height of a quadtree is defined as usual:

$height :: 'a\ qtree \Rightarrow nat$

$height\ (L\ \_) = 0$

$height\ (Q\ t_0\ t_1\ t_2\ t_3) = Max\ \{height\ t_0,\ height\ t_1,\ height\ t_2,\ height\ t_3\} + 1$

A quadtree is *compressed* if no subtree could be replaced by a leaf:

$compressed :: 'a\ qtree \Rightarrow bool$

$compressed\ (L\ \_) = True$

$compressed\ (Q\ t_0\ t_1\ t_2\ t_3)$

$= ((compressed\ t_0 \wedge compressed\ t_1 \wedge compressed\ t_2 \wedge compressed\ t_3) \wedge$

$\quad (\nexists x.\ t_0 = L\ x \wedge t_1 = t_0 \wedge t_2 = t_0 \wedge t_3 = t_0))$

To keep our quadtrees compressed, we construct them with the compressing constructor Qc, which assumes that its arguments are already compressed:

Qc :: $'a$ qtree $\Rightarrow$ $'a$ qtree $\Rightarrow$ $'a$ qtree $\Rightarrow$ $'a$ qtree $\Rightarrow$ $'a$ qtree

Qc $(L\ x_0)$ $(L\ x_1)$ $(L\ x_2)$ $(L\ x_3)$
$=$ (if $x_0 = x_1 \wedge x_1 = x_2 \wedge x_2 = x_3$ then $L\ x_0$
    else Q $(L\ x_0)$ $(L\ x_1)$ $(L\ x_2)$ $(L\ x_3)$)
Qc t_0 t_1 t_2 t_3 $=$ Q t_0 t_1 t_2 t_3

The following property of Qc is a frequently used lemma:

compressed t_0 $\wedge$ compressed t_1 $\wedge$ compressed t_2 $\wedge$ compressed t_3 $\longrightarrow$
compressed $(Qc\ t_0\ t_1\ t_2\ t_3)$

A quadtree does not specify the resolution of the image it represents. For example, L *True* can represent a square of any size $2^n \times 2^n$. One can explicitly pair a quadtree with its resolution, or one can keep both separate, as we will do. Either way, the tree and the resolution have to match, i.e. *height* $t \le n$, which one can see as an invariant of the pair (t, n). Otherwise t cannot always represent an image of size $2^n \times 2^n$. For example, Q $(L$ *True*$)$ $(L$ *True*$)$ $(L$ *True*$)$ $(L$ *False*$)$ does not represent an image of size 1×1 but requires at least 2×2 pixels. Therefore functions on quadtrees often take the intended resolution n as an argument. Function *get* that we introduce now is an example.

3.1   Functions *get* and *put*

Trees of type $'a$ *qtree* can be viewed as representations of mappings from (i, j) coordinates to values of type $'a$. Thus the operation *get* for extracting a single pixel doubles as the abstraction function:

get :: $nat \Rightarrow$ $'a$ qtree $\Rightarrow$ $nat \Rightarrow$ $nat \Rightarrow$ $'a$

get _ $(L\ b)$ _ _ $= b$
get $(n + 1)$ $(Q\ t_0\ t_1\ t_2\ t_3)$ $i\ j$
$=$ $get\ n$ $(select\ (i < 2^n)\ (j < 2^n)\ t_0\ t_1\ t_2\ t_3)$ $(i\ mod\ 2^n)$ $(j\ mod\ 2^n)$

$select$ :: $bool \Rightarrow bool \Rightarrow$ $'a \Rightarrow$ $'a \Rightarrow$ $'a \Rightarrow$ $'a \Rightarrow$ $'a$

$select\ x\ y\ t_0\ t_1\ t_2\ t_3$
$=$ (if x then if y then t_0 else t_1 else if y then t_2 else t_3)

The call $get\ n\ t\ i\ j$ returns the pixel at coordinate (i, j) from the image of resolution n represented by tree t . Function *select* selects one of four quadrants addressed by two booleans. For an efficient implementation one should replace 2^n by something like a table lookup or work directly with machine words.

Note that $get\ n\ t\ i\ j$ is only defined if *height* $t \le n$. The reason for this was discussed above. Partiality is the norm for functions that take both a quadtree and its resolution. This is reflected in the functions' properties, which are conditional (e.g. the properties of *put* below).

Although *get* does not require $i, j < 2^n$—they are simply forced into that range via *mod*—this natural restriction is sometimes needed. The restriction is conveniently expressed as $(i, j) \in sq\ n$ where

$$sq\ n \equiv \{0..<2^n\} \times \{0..<2^n\}$$

and $\{m..<n\}$ is the set of natural numbers from m up to but excluding n and $\times$ is the Cartesian product.

The converse of *get* is *put* for setting a single pixel:

$$put :: nat \Rightarrow nat \Rightarrow\ 'a \Rightarrow nat \Rightarrow\ 'a\ qtree \Rightarrow\ 'a\ qtree$$

$put\ \_\ \_\ a\ 0\ (L\ \_) = L\ a$
$put\ i\ j\ a\ (n + 1)\ t$
$= modify\ (put\ (i\ mod\ 2^n)\ (j\ mod\ 2^n)\ a\ n)\ (i < 2^n)\ (j < 2^n)$
   (**case** t **of** $L\ b \Rightarrow (L\ b, L\ b, L\ b, L\ b)\ |\ Q\ t_0\ t_1\ t_2\ t_3 \Rightarrow (t_0, t_1, t_2, t_3))$

$modify ::$
   $('a\ qtree \Rightarrow\ 'a\ qtree)$
   $\Rightarrow bool \Rightarrow bool \Rightarrow\ 'a\ qtree \times\ 'a\ qtree \times\ 'a\ qtree \times\ 'a\ qtree \Rightarrow\ 'a\ qtree$

$modify\ f\ x\ y\ (t_0, t_1, t_2, t_3)$
$= ($**if** x **then if** y **then** $Qc\ (f\ t_0)\ t_1\ t_2\ t_3$ **else** $Qc\ t_0\ (f\ t_1)\ t_2\ t_3$
   else if y **then** $Qc\ t_0\ t_1\ (f\ t_2)\ t_3$ **else** $Qc\ t_0\ t_1\ t_2\ (f\ t_3))$

Note that when recombining quadrants on the way back up, Q is replaced by Qc to take care of possible compressions.

Correctness is expressed by a triple of properties: functional correctness, preservation of resolution and compression.

$height\ t \leq n \wedge (i, j) \in sq\ n \wedge (i', j') \in sq\ n \longrightarrow$
$get\ n\ (put\ i\ j\ a\ n\ t)\ i'\ j' = ($**if** $i' = i \wedge j' = j$ **then** a **else** $get\ n\ t\ i'\ j')$
$height\ t \leq n \longrightarrow height\ (put\ i\ j\ a\ n\ t) \leq n$
$height\ t \leq n \wedge compressed\ t \longrightarrow compressed\ (put\ i\ j\ a\ n\ t)$

Note that the special case of *bool qtree* can be viewed as a representation of a set of points: $\{(i, j)\ |\ (i, j) \in sq\ n \wedge get\ n\ t\ i\ j\}$. Function *get* is also the *isin*-test and *put* combines *insert* and *delete*.

There is a wide range of interesting functions on quadtrees. What follows should be considered a not quite random sample from a much larger space.

3.2   Boolean Operations

As remarked above, boolean quadtrees represent sets. It turns out that they support binary set operations like $\cup$, $\cap$ etc. even more naturally than manipulation of individual elements. They can be expressed as a simple simultaneous traversal of both trees and basic boolean operations on the leafs. As an example we consider intersection:

$$inter :: bool\ qtree \Rightarrow bool\ qtree \Rightarrow bool\ qtree$$

$inter\ (L\ b)\ t = ($**if** b **then** t **else** $L\ False)$
$inter\ t\ (L\ b) = ($**if** b **then** t **else** $L\ False)$
$inter\ (Q\ s_1\ s_2\ s_3\ s_4)\ (Q\ t_1\ t_2\ t_3\ t_4)$
$= Qc\ (inter\ s_1\ t_1)\ (inter\ s_2\ t_2)\ (inter\ s_3\ t_3)\ (inter\ s_4\ t_4)$

Other set operations (union, difference, xor) can be defined analogously, with different base cases.

The correctness theorems are easily stated and proved

$height\ t_1 \leq n \wedge height\ t_2 \leq n \longrightarrow$
$get\ n\ (inter\ t_1\ t_2)\ i\ j = (get\ n\ t_1\ i\ j \wedge get\ n\ t_2\ i\ j)$
$height\ (inter\ t_1\ t_2) \leq max\ (height\ t_1)\ (height\ t_2)$
$compressed\ t_1 \wedge compressed\ t_2 \longrightarrow compressed\ (inter\ t_1\ t_2)$

3.3   Extracting Subimages

As a an example of a graphics-oriented function consider the extraction of a subimage (a square of size $2^m \times 2^m$) in the form of a new quadtree. Figure 2 shows such a subimage with a red border.

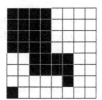

Fig. 2. Image and subimage

Below we define a function $get\_sq\ n\ t\ m\ i\ j$ that takes a quadtree t and its resolution n and extracts a quadtree of the subimage of resolution m with lower left corner at (i, j). It is a bit tricky because it can involve subimages of varying size from all four quadrants of a quadtree. Function get_sq recurses over t Below we define a function $get\_sq\ n\ t\ m\ i\ j$ that takes a quadtree t and its resolution n and extracts a quadtree of the subimag and m as follows. If the subimage is completely within one quadrant, get_sq descends into that quadrant (via *select*). Otherwise the subimage needs to be assembled from smaller subimages from multiple quadrants.

$get\_sq\ ::\ nat \Rightarrow\ 'a\ qtree \Rightarrow nat \Rightarrow nat \Rightarrow nat \Rightarrow\ 'a\ qtree$

$get\_sq\ \_\ (L\ b)\ \_\ \_\ \_\ = L\ b$
$get\_sq\ n\ t\ 0\ i\ j = L\ (get\ n\ t\ i\ j)$
$get\_sq\ (n + 1)\ (Q\ t_0\ t_1\ t_2\ t_3)\ (m + 1)\ i\ j$
$= (\textbf{if}\ i\ mod\ 2^n + 2^{m + 1} \leq 2^n \wedge j\ mod\ 2^n + 2^{m + 1} \leq 2^n$
$\quad\quad \textbf{then}\ get\_sq\ n\ (select\ (i < 2^n)\ (j < 2^n)\ t_0\ t_1\ t_2\ t_3)\ (m + 1)\ (i\ mod\ 2^n)$
$\quad\quad\quad\quad (j\ mod\ 2^n)$
$\quad\quad \textbf{else}\ qf\ Qc\ (get\_sq\ (n + 1)\ (Q\ t_0\ t_1\ t_2\ t_3)\ m)\ i\ j\ 2^m)$

$qf\ q\ f\ i\ j\ d \equiv q\ (f\ i\ j)\ (f\ i\ (j + d))\ (f\ (i + d)\ j)\ (f\ (i + d)\ (j + d))$

Note that in the **else** branch the four subimages do not necessarily come from all four quadrants: the recursive calls are still on the full tree $Q\ t_0\ t_1\ t_2\ t_3$ but reduce the size of the subimage until it fits into a single quadrant.

Although we have explained *get_sq* graphically, it works for any quadtree, not just boolean ones. Functional correctness is expressed like this: pixel (i', j') in the image extracted at (i, j) is the same as pixel $(i + i', j + j')$ in the original image.

$height\ t \leq n \wedge i + 2^m \leq 2^n \wedge j + 2^m \leq 2^n \wedge i' < 2^m \wedge j' < 2^m \longrightarrow$
$get\ m\ (get\_sq\ n\ t\ m\ i\ j)\ i'\ j' = get\ n\ t\ (i + i')\ (j + j')$
$height\ t \leq n \wedge compressed\ t \longrightarrow compressed\ (get\_sq\ n\ t\ m\ i\ j)$

The first correctness theorems requires that the extracted subimage must lie completely within the original image. In contrast, the compression property is simple enough that does not require this precondition.

3.4   From and to Matrix

Finally, we may also want to convert between quadtrees and some external format. An obvious candidate is a matrix represented by a list of lists:

type_synonym $'a\ mx = {}'a\ list\ list$

Function *mx_of* converts a quadtree into a matrix:

$mx\_of :: nat \Rightarrow {}'a\ qtree \Rightarrow {}'a\ mx$
$mx\_of\ n\ (L\ x) = replicate\ 2^n\ (replicate\ 2^n\ x)$
$mx\_of\ (n + 1)\ (Q\ t_0\ t_1\ t_2\ t_3)$
$= Qmx\ (mx\_of\ n\ t_0)\ (mx\_of\ n\ t_1)\ (mx\_of\ n\ t_2)\ (mx\_of\ n\ t_3)$

$Qmx :: {}'a\ mx \Rightarrow {}'a\ mx \Rightarrow {}'a\ mx \Rightarrow {}'a\ mx \Rightarrow {}'a\ mx$

$Qmx\ mx_0\ mx_1\ mx_2\ mx_3 = map2\ (@)\ mx_0\ mx_1\ @\ map2\ (@)\ mx_2\ mx_3$

$map2\ f\ [x_1,\ldots,x_m]\ [y_1,\ldots,y_n] = [f\ x_1\ y_1,\ \ldots,\ f\ x_k\ y_k]$ where $k = min\ m\ n$

For example, $mx\_of\ 1\ (Q\ (L\ 0)\ (L\ 1)\ (L\ 2)\ (L\ 3)) = [[0, 1], [2, 3]]$, which we can regard as a two dimensional image:

$$[\ [0, 1]\ ,$$
$$[2, 3]\ ]$$

This is a 90° rotation of (1) and Fig. 1 where (0,0) is the lower left corner, now it is the upper left one. This is necessary because we want to address a point (i,j) in some *mx* by $mx\ !\ i\ !\ j$. With the above definition of *mx_of* this works. For example, $[[0, 1], [2, 3]]\ !\ 0\ !\ 1 = 1$ and $[[0, 1], [2, 3]]\ !\ 1\ !\ 0 = 2$. In general we can prove that indexing the matrix yields the same value as function *get*:

$height\ t \leq n \wedge (i, j) \in sq\ n \longrightarrow mx\_of\ n\ t\ !\ i\ !\ j = get\ n\ t\ i\ j$

Conversely, we can also translate a matrix into a quadtree.

$qt\_of :: nat \Rightarrow \,'a \; mx \Rightarrow \,'a \; qtree$

$qt\_of \; (n + 1) \; mx$
$= (\textbf{let} \; (mx_0, \; mx_1, \; mx_2, \; mx_3) = decomp \; n \; mx$
$\quad \textbf{in} \; Qc \; (qt\_of \; n \; mx_0) \; (qt\_of \; n \; mx_1) \; (qt\_of \; n \; mx_2) \; (qt\_of \; n \; mx_3))$
$qt\_of \; 0 \; [[x]] = L \; x$

$decomp :: nat \Rightarrow \,'a \; mx \Rightarrow \,'a \; mx \times \,'a \; mx \times \,'a \; mx \times \,'a \; mx$

$decomp \; n \; mx$
$= (\textbf{let} \; mx_{01} = take \; 2^n \; mx; \; mx_{23} = drop \; 2^n \; mx$
$\quad \textbf{in} \; (map \; (take \; 2^n) \; mx_{01}, \; map \; (drop \; 2^n) \; mx_{01}, \; map \; (take \; 2^n) \; mx_{23},$
$\qquad map \; (drop \; 2^n) \; mx_{23}))$

This function is also correct w.r.t. *get* and yields a compressed tree:

$sq\_mx \; n \; mx \; \wedge \; (i, j) \in sq \; n \; \longrightarrow \; get \; n \; (qt\_of \; n \; mx) \; i \; j = mx \; ! \; i \; ! \; j$
$sq\_mx \; n \; mx \; \longrightarrow \; compressed \; (qt\_of \; n \; mx)$

where $sq\_mx \; n \; mx = (length \; mx = 2^n \wedge (\forall \, xs \in set \; mx. \; length \; xs = 2^n))$.

The matrix correctness proofs depend on the following auxiliary lemmas:

$height \; t \leq n \; \longrightarrow \; sq\_mx \; n \; (mx\_of \; n \; t)$
$sq\_mx \; n \; mx \; \longrightarrow \; height \; (qt\_of \; n \; mx) \leq n$
$height \; (Q \; t_0 \; t_1 \; t_2 \; t_3) \leq n \; \longrightarrow$
$get \; n \; (Qc \; t_0 \; t_1 \; t_2 \; t_3) \; i \; j = get \; n \; (Q \; t_0 \; t_1 \; t_2 \; t_3) \; i \; j$

4 Matrix Quadtrees

This section is not about quadtrees *per se* but about their usage. The application is the efficient (because easily parallelizable) implementation of matrix operations, which was discovered and elaborated by David Wise [13–15]: The recursive decomposition of a matrix into four submatrices can be represented by a quadtree. It is well-known that many operations on matrices can be expressed very succinctly on block matrices and we will show how a few of them can be implemented easily on quadtrees.

Our abstract type of (real) matrices is simply a function from indices to real numbers:

type_synonym $ma = nat \Rightarrow nat \Rightarrow real$

We have chosen a more abstract model of matrices than the one in Sect. 3.4 because the purpose is to state correctness properties and not to implement algorithms.

Functions are in general infinite objects, matrices are restricted to finite dimensions. We model this by requiring matrices to be 0 outside of their dimensions:

$sq\_ma \; n \; a \equiv \forall \, i \; j. \; 2^n \leq i \vee 2^n \leq j \longrightarrow a \; i \; j = 0$

The restriction is required for many nontrivial theorems about matrices, but luckily we get away without requiring it in what follows.

How to convert a quadtree into such a matrix is obvious, except that $L\ x$ has more than one reasonable interpretation. We follow [15] and interpret $L\ x$ as the diagonal matrix with x everywhere on the diagonal. Thus the abstraction function ma is defined like this:

$ma :: nat \Rightarrow real\ qtree \Rightarrow ma$
$ma\ n\ (L\ x) = D\ n\ x$
$ma\ (n+1)\ (Q\ t_0\ t_1\ t_2\ t_3) = Qma\ n\ (ma\ n\ t_0)\ (ma\ n\ t_1)\ (ma\ n\ t_2)\ (ma\ n\ t_3)$

$D :: nat \Rightarrow real \Rightarrow ma$
$D\ n\ x = mk\_sq\ n\ (\lambda i\ j.\ \textbf{if}\ i = j\ \textbf{then}\ x\ \textbf{else}\ 0)$

$mk\_sq :: nat \Rightarrow ma \Rightarrow ma$
$mk\_sq\ n\ a = (\lambda i\ j.\ \textbf{if}\ i < 2^n \wedge j < 2^n\ \textbf{then}\ a\ i\ j\ \textbf{else}\ 0)$

$Qma :: nat \Rightarrow ma \Rightarrow ma \Rightarrow ma \Rightarrow ma \Rightarrow ma$
$Qma\ n\ a\ b\ c\ d$
$= (\lambda i\ j.\ \textbf{if}\ i < 2^n\ \textbf{then if}\ j < 2^n\ \textbf{then}\ a\ i\ j\ \textbf{else}\ b\ i\ (j - 2^n)$
$\qquad\qquad \textbf{else if}\ j < 2^n\ \textbf{then}\ c\ (i - 2^n)\ j\ \textbf{else}\ d\ (i - 2^n)\ (j - 2^n))$

As before, we need to supply the resolution n to obtain a matrix of dimension $2^n \times 2^n$ and to restrict the diagonal matrix D to a square. Note that the correspondence of the four subquandrants of Q to the standard is not like in (1) but like this, assuming the standard notation for matrices, where the upper left corner is the element with index $(0, 0)$:

0	1
2	3

4.1   Addition and Multiplication of Matrices

First we define matrix addition and multiplication on abstract functional matrices, then we implement both operations on quadtrees and finally we show the correctness of the implementation via the abstraction function ma.

On the level of matrices, addition and multiplication are defined as in mathematics:

$(+) :: ma \Rightarrow ma \Rightarrow ma$
$a + b = (\lambda i\ j.\ a\ i\ j + b\ i\ j)$

$mult\_ma :: nat \Rightarrow ma \Rightarrow ma \Rightarrow ma$
$a *_n b = (\lambda i\ j.\ \sum k = 0..<2^n.\ a\ i\ k * b\ k\ j)$

The following lemma library is easily proved and is used implicitly below:

$$D \; n \; x + D \; n \; y = D \; n \; (x + y)$$
$$D \; n \; 0 + a = a$$
$$a + D \; n \; 0 = a$$
$$D \; n \; 0 *_n a = D \; n \; 0$$
$$a *_n D \; n \; 0 = D \; n \; 0$$
$$D \; n \; x *_n D \; n \; y = D \; n \; (x * y)$$

4.2 Addition and Multiplication of Quadtrees

Matrices are represented by quadtrees over real numbers. As before, we have Qc, a smart version of Q that is used when creating a quadtree. It compresses the four quadrants if they form a diagonal:

$Qc :: real \; qtree \Rightarrow real \; qtree \Rightarrow real \; qtree \Rightarrow real \; qtree \Rightarrow real \; qtree$

$Qc \; (L \; x_0) \; (L \; x_1) \; (L \; x_2) \; (L \; x_3)$
$= (\textbf{if} \; x_1 = 0 \land x_2 = 0 \land x_0 = x_3 \; \textbf{then} \; L \; x_0$
$\quad \textbf{else} \; Q \; (L \; x_0) \; (L \; x_1) \; (L \; x_2) \; (L \; x_3))$
$Qc \; t_0 \; t_1 \; t_2 \; t_3 = Q \; t_0 \; t_1 \; t_2 \; t_3$

A quadtree is compressed if it does not contain a compressible Q:

$compressed :: real \; qtree \Rightarrow bool$

$compressed \; (L \; \_) = True$
$compressed \; (Q \; (L \; x_0) \; (L \; x_1) \; (L \; x_2) \; (L \; x_3)) = (\neg \; (x_1 = 0 \land x_2 = 0 \land x_0 = x_3))$
$compressed \; (Q \; t_0 \; t_1 \; t_2 \; t_3)$
$= (compressed \; t_0 \land compressed \; t_1 \land compressed \; t_2 \land compressed \; t_3)$

Addition and multiplication on quadtrees is defined as follows:

$(\oplus) :: real \; qtree \Rightarrow real \; qtree \Rightarrow real \; qtree$

$Q \; s_0 \; s_1 \; s_2 \; s_3 \oplus Q \; t_0 \; t_1 \; t_2 \; t_3 = Qc \; (s_0 \oplus t_0) \; (s_1 \oplus t_1) \; (s_2 \oplus t_2) \; (s_3 \oplus t_3)$
$L \; x \oplus L \; y = L \; (x + y)$
$L \; x \oplus Q \; t_0 \; t_1 \; t_2 \; t_3 = Qc \; (L \; x \oplus t_0) \; t_1 \; t_2 \; (L \; x \oplus t_3)$
$Q \; t_0 \; t_1 \; t_2 \; t_3 \oplus L \; x = Qc \; (t_0 \oplus L \; x) \; t_1 \; t_2 \; (t_3 \oplus L \; x)$

$(\otimes) :: real \; qtree \Rightarrow real \; qtree \Rightarrow real \; qtree$

$Q \; s_0 \; s_1 \; s_2 \; s_3 \otimes Q \; t_0 \; t_1 \; t_2 \; t_3$
$= Qc \; (s_0 \otimes t_0 \oplus s_1 \otimes t_2) \; (s_0 \otimes t_1 \oplus s_1 \otimes t_3) \; (s_2 \otimes t_0 \oplus s_3 \otimes t_2)$
$\quad (s_2 \otimes t_1 \oplus s_3 \otimes t_3)$
$L \; x \otimes Q \; t_0 \; t_1 \; t_2 \; t_3 = Qc \; (L \; x \otimes t_0) \; (L \; x \otimes t_1) \; (L \; x \otimes t_2) \; (L \; x \otimes t_3)$
$Q \; t_0 \; t_1 \; t_2 \; t_3 \otimes L \; x = Qc \; (t_0 \otimes L \; x) \; (t_1 \otimes L \; x) \; (t_2 \otimes L \; x) \; (t_3 \otimes L \; x)$
$L \; x \otimes L \; y = L \; (x * y)$

The Q-Q and L-L cases follow the standard definition of how block matrices are added and multiplied. The Q-L and L-Q cases are dealt with by implicitly expanding L x to Q $(L$ $x)$ $(L$ $0)$ $(L$ $0)$ $(L$ $x)$ and following the Q-Q case while simplifying addition and multiplication with 0.

Correctness is expressed by showing that the quadtree operations correctly implement the abstract matrix operations via the abstraction function ma:

$$height\ s \leq n \wedge height\ t \leq n \longrightarrow ma\ n\ (s \oplus t) = ma\ n\ s + ma\ n\ t$$
$$height\ s \leq n \wedge height\ t \leq n \longrightarrow ma\ n\ (s \otimes t) = ma\ n\ s *_n ma\ n\ t$$

Moreover, both operations preserve compression:

$$compressed\ s \wedge compressed\ t \longrightarrow compressed\ (s \oplus t)$$
$$compressed\ s \wedge compressed\ t \longrightarrow compressed\ (s \otimes t)$$

The proofs employ the following lemmas:

$$ma\ (n+1)\ (Qc\ t_0\ t_1\ t_2\ t_3) = ma\ (n+1)\ (Q\ t_0\ t_1\ t_2\ t_3)$$

$$Qma\ n\ a\ b\ c\ d + Qma\ n\ a'\ b'\ c'\ d'$$
$$= Qma\ n\ (a+a')\ (b+b')\ (c+c')\ (d+d')$$

$$\boldsymbol{D}\ (n+1)\ x + Qma\ n\ a\ b\ c\ d = Qma\ n\ (\boldsymbol{D}\ n\ x + a)\ b\ c\ (\boldsymbol{D}\ n\ x + d)$$

$$compressed\ (Qc\ t_0\ t_1\ t_2\ t_3)$$
$$= (compressed\ t_0 \wedge compressed\ t_1 \wedge compressed\ t_2 \wedge compressed\ t_3)$$

$$Qma\ n\ a\ b\ c\ d *_{n+1} Qma\ n\ a'\ b'\ c'\ d'$$
$$= Qma\ n\ (a *_n a' + b *_n c')\ (a *_n b' + b *_n d')\ (c *_n a' + d *_n c')$$
$$\quad (c *_n b' + d *_n d')$$

$$\boldsymbol{D}\ (n+1)\ x = Qma\ n\ (\boldsymbol{D}\ n\ x)\ (\boldsymbol{D}\ n\ 0)\ (\boldsymbol{D}\ n\ 0)\ (\boldsymbol{D}\ n\ x)$$

$$height\ (Qc\ t_0\ t_1\ t_2\ t_3) \leq height\ (Q\ t_0\ t_1\ t_2\ t_3)$$
$$height\ (s \oplus t) \leq max\ (height\ s)\ (height\ t)$$
$$height\ (s \otimes t) \leq max\ (height\ s)\ (height\ t)$$

5   Related Formalization Work

Region quadtrees seem to have been formalized before only by Brouwer [4] who presents a formalization in the proof assistant Agda [1]. He describes a verified lense-based [6] quadtree library focussing on lens operations and manipulation of individiual pixels, covering some of the same ground as we do in Sect. 3.

6   Conclusion

Region quadtrees are a widely used data structure and a plethora of algorithms for them have been developed [2,11,12]. We could only scratch the surface of this rich area. In particular, we have completely ignored point quadtrees (but see the work of Rau [10]). However, we have already verified a k-dimensional generalization of region quadtrees [7] that we have not yet described in this paper.

An open research question is if quadtrees could be used to advantage in a model checker, in particular a verified one [5]. A possible application are the matrix computations in a probabilistic model checker [3].

In the context of matrix quadtrees we have investigated only the variant where leaves represent diagonal matrices. Wise [15] started with these but later moved to quadtrees where leaves are scalar values representing a 1×1 matrix [16]. Their formalization would be interesting as well.

References

1. Agda. https://github.com/agda/agda
2. Aluru, S.: Quadtrees and octrees. In: Mehta, D.P., Sahni, S. (eds.) Handbook of Data Structures and Applications, 2nd edn. Chapman and Hall/CRC, Boca Raton (2017). https://doi.org/10.1201/9781315119335
3. Baier, C., Katoen, J.: Principles of Model Checking. MIT Press, Cambridge (2008)
4. Brouwer, J.: Practical verification of quadtrees (2021). http://resolver.tudelft.nl/uuid:550c654e-0443-4f00-bab3-d24ed3afc879
5. Esparza, J., Lammich, P., Neumann, R., Nipkow, T., Schimpf, A., Smaus, J.-G.: A fully verified executable LTL model checker. In: Sharygina, N., Veith, H. (eds.) CAV 2013. LNCS, vol. 8044, pp. 463–478. Springer, Heidelberg (2013). https://doi.org/10.1007/978-3-642-39799-8_31
6. Foster, J.N., Greenwald, M.B., Moore, J.T., Pierce, B.C., Schmitt, A.: Combinators for bidirectional tree transformations: a linguistic approach to the view-update problem. ACM Trans. Program. Lang. Syst. **29**(3), 17 (2007). https://doi.org/10.1145/1232420.1232424
7. Nipkow, T.: Region quadtrees. Archive of Formal Proofs (2024). https://isa-afp.org/entries/Region_Quadtrees.html. Formal proof development
8. Nipkow, T., Klein, G.: Concrete Semantics with Isabelle/HOL. Springer, Heidelberg (2014). http://concrete-semantics.org
9. Nipkow, T., Wenzel, M., Paulson, L.C. (eds.): Isabelle/HOL—A Proof Assistant for Higher-Order Logic. LNCS, vol. 2283. Springer, Heidelberg (2002). https://doi.org/10.1007/3-540-45949-9
10. Rau, M.: Multidimensional binary search trees. Archive of Formal Proofs (2019). https://isa-afp.org/entries/KD_Tree.html. Formal proof development
11. Samet, H.: The quadtree and related hierarchical data structures. ACM Comput. Surv. **16**(2), 187–260 (1984). https://doi.org/10.1145/356924.356930
12. Samet, H.: The Design and Analysis of Spatial Data Structures. Addison-Wesley, Boston (1990)
13. Wise, D.S.: Representing matrices as quadtrees for parallel processors. Inf. Process. Lett. **20**(4), 195–199 (1985). https://doi.org/10.1016/0020-0190(85)90049-3
14. Wise, D.S.: Parallel decomposition of matrix inversion using quadtrees. In: International Conference on Parallel Processing, ICPP 1986, pp. 92–99. IEEE Computer Society Press (1986)

15. Wise, D.S.: Matrix algebra and applicative programming. In: Kahn, G. (ed.) FPCA 1987. LNCS, vol. 274, pp. 134–153. Springer, Heidelberg (1987). https://doi.org/10.1007/3-540-18317-5_9
16. Wise, D.S.: Matrix algorithms using quadtrees (invited talk). In: Hains, G., Mullin, L.M.R. (eds.) ATABLE-92, International Workshop on Arrays, Functional Languages and Parallel Systems (1992). https://legacy.cs.indiana.edu/ftp/techreports/TR357.pdf

Computing *pre** for General Context Free Grammars

Peter Rossmanith[✉] [iD]

RWTH Aachen University, 52064 Aachen, Germany
rossmani@cs.rwth-aachen.de
https://tcs.rwth-aachen.de

Abstract. A systematic approach for addressing various problems related to context-free grammars involves employing the *pre**-method. This method calculates, for a given regular language L (given as an NFA), the language of all strings α (represented by an NFA) for which there exists a $\beta \in L$ such that $\alpha \overset{*}{\Rightarrow} \beta$. The range of admissible problems encompasses, inter alia, the word problem, the emptiness problem, the finiteness problem, and the identification of useless symbols.

Efficient algorithms have been developed to compute $pre^*(L)$, but they assume that the grammar adheres to a restricted normal form. In this context, we introduce a novel algorithm that is both straightforward and efficient, while working with general context-free grammars.

In addition to the computation of *pre**, this algorithm proves valuable for the construction of parse trees. The running time is in general cubic, but quadratic for parsing unambiguous context-free languages. We provide some evidence suggesting the running times cannot be improved significantly with current techniques.

Keywords: Problems on context-free languages · parsing · formal languages

1 Introduction

Formal languages and automata theory play a pivotal role in computer science, having done so since its inception. Their significance extends across a spectrum of applications, from pattern matching to the parsing of programming languages, as highlighted by seminal works such as those by Hopcroft and Ullman (1979) and Aho and Ullman (1977) [3,28].

Beyond these applications, formal languages and automata theory serve as the solid bedrock for numerous software and hardware verification techniques. (See, e.g., [5–7,11,15,16,19–23], a list that concentrates on contributions in which Javier Esparza has played an important role). Their fundamental importance in these domains ensures that they consistently hold a prominent position in computer science education.

An introductory course on formal languages usually contains the theory of regular languages, finite automata, regular expressions, context-free grammars, and their properties. All these topics can be taught in an algorithm oriented way,

S. Kiefer et al. (Eds.): *Taming the Infinities of Concurrency*, LNCS 14660, pp. 255–280, 2024.
https://doi.org/10.1007/978-3-031-56222-8_15

including implementing and experimenting with the underlying mathematical concepts.

Javier Esparza has demonstrated a strong commitment to computer science education, striving to convey complex concepts in an easily understandable manner. A recent testament to this commitment is the publication of the book *Automata Theory: An Algorithmic Approach*, co-authored by Esparza and Michael Blondin [17]. This comprehensive resource adeptly navigates the intricacies of finite automata theory, featuring elegant illustrations and a plethora of illustrative examples.

Inspired by the clarity and approachability of Esparza's and Blondin's work, I aim to emulate their style in this paper to the best of my ability, in particular to follow their principle

> *"The shape of the book is also very influenced by two further design decisions. First, automata-theoretic constructions are best explained by means of examples, and examples are best presented with the help of pictures. Automata on words are blessed with a graphical representation of instantaneous appeal. We have invested much effort into finding illustrative, nontrivial examples whose graphical representation still fits in one page."* [17]

While their book is about finite automata only, Javier Esparza also pioneered teaching concepts for problems on context-free languages. Algorithmic problems in this domain encompass the questions of whether a given CFL is empty or infinite. Another crucial task to solve is the *word problem:* Given a context free grammar G and a word w, is $w \in L(G)$? Various such questions have been addressed in the form of specialized algorithms. For example, determining whether $L(G) = \emptyset$, can be accomplished by a depth-first search on the grammar and its starting symbol. Another noteworthy example is the Cocke–Kasami–Younger algorithm designed for the word problem [12,29,34].

Javier Esparza used the insight from a technique to compute images in monadic string rewriting systems by Book and Otto [9] to compute *pre-images* of regular languages. More specifically, if $G = (N, T, P, S)$ is a context-free grammar and L is a regular language (represented by an NFA) there is a polynomial time algorithm to compute an NFA that accepts

$$pre_G^*(L) = \{\, \alpha \in (N \cup T)^* \mid \alpha \overset{*}{\Rightarrow} \beta \text{ for some } \beta \in L \,\}.$$

In other words, we can compute all strings that can produce some string from a given regular language. While this principle turned out to be helpful in verification algorithms [18,24], it is also a technique that can be used to solve many problems on context-free languages in a uniform way [10,25,26]. For example, to answer whether a context-free language is empty, we can just check whether $S \in pre^*(T^*)$: This is the case iff there is a $w \in T^*$ with $S \overset{*}{\Rightarrow} w$. Similarly you can use pre^* to find unproductive or unreachable symbols in G. A symbol B is productive iff $B \in pre^*(T^*)$ and B is reachable iff $S \in pre^*(\Sigma^* B \Sigma^+ \cup \Sigma^+ B \Sigma^*)$ with $\Sigma = N \cup T$. Of course, you can also solve the word problem ($w \in L(G)$?) just by testing $S \in pre^*(\{w\})$. A fascinating more recent application of the pre^*-method has been found by Ganty and Valero [27]. Many dictionary based text compression algorithms, like Lempel–Ziv, basically use a context free grammar that generates a single word: $L(G) = \{w\}$. The uncompressed text is w and G is the compressed text. For example, the grammar $S \to ABABAA$, $A \to aaab$, $B \to ababa$ gives us the word $w = aaababababaaaababababaaaabaaab$. Gantry and Valero search for a regular expression R in w by looking at $pre^*(L(R))$, which contains S iff w matches R. They generalize this approach to find all lines in a text that match a regular expression without the need to uncompress the text.

It turned out that the *pre**-based algorithms by Boujjani et al. usually are competitive with their specialized counterparts with regard to their running times [10]. For example, solving the word problem matches the cubic running time of the Cocke–Kasami–Younger algorithm (although there is the slightly faster algorithm by Valiant that is based on fast matrix multiplication [32], see also [8]).

Esparza used the *pre**-technique in the teaching of introductory courses on formal languages and automata theory quite early. The first related homework assignment I could find was handed out on the 14th January, 1997. It presented the context-free grammar G with rules $S \to AB \mid \epsilon$, $A \to aASb \mid a$, $B \to bS$ and the DFA M on the left side of the following picture (Fig. 1). The question asked was "Does $L(G) \subseteq L(M)$ hold?" A reproduction of the original exercise sheet (in German) is shown on the right side.

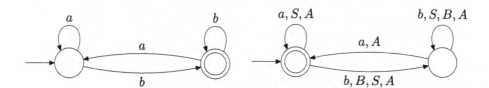

Fig. 1. Left: The deterministic finite automaton M. Right: The NFA for $pre^*(L(\overline{M}))$.

We can solve this exercise by computing the complement automaton $\overline{M}$ and then checking whether $S \in pre^*(L(\overline{M}))$. You can see the NFA for $pre^*(L(\overline{M}))$ on the right hand side of Fig. 1. The answer is $L(G) \not\subseteq L(M)$ because $S \in pre^*(L(\overline{M}))$, which means there is some w with $S \stackrel{*}{\Rightarrow} w$ and $w \notin L(M)$. (Actually, every word in $L(G)$ except ϵ ends with b, so $w = \epsilon$ is the only word with that property.) It is easy to see the answer without using this mechanism, so the exercise serves to reassure the students that the *pre** method works.

Algorithm 1. A simple, but slow algorithm to compute $pre^*(L)$ [10]. Just as $\widehat{\delta}$, we define $\widehat{rel}(q, \epsilon) = \{q\}$ and $\widehat{rel}(q, aw) = \bigcup_{q' \in rel(q,a)} \widehat{rel}(q', w)$ for $a \in \Sigma$ and $w \in \Sigma^*$.

Input: $G = (V, T, P, S)$, $M = (Q, \Sigma, \delta, q_0, F)$
Output: δ_{pre^*}

> $rel \leftarrow \delta$;
> **repeat**
>   **for** $q, q' \in Q$, $A \rightarrow \beta \in P$ **do**
>   **if** $q' \in \widehat{rel}(q, \beta)$ **then** $rel \leftarrow rel \cup \{(q, A, q')\}$ **fi**
>   **od**
> **until** rel does not change any more;
> **return** rel

To compute $pre^*(L(M))$ you can just look at all rules $A \rightarrow \beta$ and all pairs of states $q, q' \in Q$ and find out if the NFA can go from q to q' while reading β. If this is the case, we just add the transition (q, A, q') to M. We stop, when no transitions can be added any more, which gives us Algorithm 1 [10]. It is a good algorithm to be performed by hand or implemented easily for instructional purposes. Its running time is polynomial, but not very efficient. It might have to carry out a quadratic number of tests of the form $q' \in \widehat{rel}(q, \beta)$ if we provide a cache for $\widehat{rel}$ and $O(|Q|^5|G|)$ such tests if we do not. Each such test requires quadratic time itself by a standard NFA simulation.

Algorithm 2 [10] was suggested to overcome this issue. Its running time is $O(|G| \cdot |Q|^3)$, where $|Q|$ is the number of states in the NFA and $|G|$ is the length of a natural encoding of the grammar G, i.e., basically listing all its rules. A drawback of Algorithm 2 is that it assumes that all rules are of the forms $A \rightarrow \epsilon$, $A \rightarrow b$, $A \rightarrow B$, or $A \rightarrow BC$, which is similar to Chomsky normal form [28], but allows additional chain rules. Any grammar can be converted into this normal form with only a linear increase in its size [10]. From an educational viewpoint the need to convert the grammar first is a big disadvantage. Usually the symbols and rules of a grammar clearly reflect the intentions of the grammar's designer. This holds true for real world grammars, for example, grammars for programming or special domain languages, but also for toy grammars like $S \rightarrow aSa \mid bSb \mid a \mid b \mid \epsilon$. You can easily see that this grammar generates palindromes. Converting the grammar into Chomsky normal form leads to something like

$$S \rightarrow AX \mid BY \mid a \mid b \mid \epsilon, \ A \rightarrow a, \ B \rightarrow b, \ X \rightarrow SA, \ Y \rightarrow SB,$$

which is no longer user or student friendly. Lange and Leiß discuss the usage of normal forms in text books and point out that often the conversion is a problem. In particular, many text books glance over the issue that they use transformations that blow up the size of the grammar significantly (sometimes even exponentially) [30].

Nevertheless, this leaves us with two possibilities: A slow algorithm for general grammars or a fast one, but only for restricted grammars. It is the main purpose of this paper to design a third algorithm that is as fast as Algorithm 2, almost as simple as Algorithm 1, and can be used on unrestricted grammars.

Algorithm 2. A faster algorithm that requires a normal form for the grammar [10]. It uses tables *direct* and *impl* to speed up the computation. If $(q, A, q') \in direct(q, B, q')$, then you can directly add the transition (q, A, q') if you know that (q, B, q') is present without a long computation. This speeds up the processing of chain rules of the form $A \to B$. The table *impl* works similarly, but for rules of the form $A \to BC$. Line 12 has been slightly changed from the version in [10] and N is used instead of V.

Input: $G = (N, T, P, S)$, $M = (Q, T, \delta, q_0, F)$
Output: δ_{pre^*} such that $M' = (Q, T, \delta_{pre^*}, q_0, F)$ with $L(M') = pre^*(L)$

```
1    rel ← ∅; trans ← δ;
2    for every A → ε ∈ P, q ∈ Q
3        add (q, A, q) to trans;
4    for every A → a ∈ P, q, q' ∈ Q
5        if (q, a, q') ∈ δ then add (q, A, q') to trans;
6    for every q, q' ∈ Q, A ∈ N
7        direct(q, A, q') ← ∅; impl(q, A, q') ← ∅;
8    for every A → B ∈ P, q, q' ∈ Q
9        add (q, A, q') to direct(q, B, q')
10   for every A → BC ∈ P, q, q', q'' ∈ Q
11       add (q', C, q'') → (q, A, q'') to impl(q, B, q');
12       add (q, B, q') → (q, A, q'') to impl(q', C, q'')
13   while trans ≠ ∅
14       pop t from trans; add t to rel;
15       append direct(t) to trans;
16       while impl(t) ≠ ∅
17           pop t' → t'' from impl(t);
18           if t' ∈ rel then add t'' to trans
19           else add t'' to direct(t')
20   return rel
```

One way to design such an algorithm would be to combine Algorithm 2 with a transformation into the CNF-like normal form. While possible, this does not lead to a particularly simple algorithm, which is not a problem in a software tool, but is unsuited for an educational setting. Hence, we design a new algorithm, which will be based on two ideas:

First, instead of adding transitions to an NFA, we will use a more general automaton model in the intermediate steps. At the end, we still get a normal NFA for $pre^*(L(M))$. We call the generalized version an *extended NFA* and the only difference is that we allow transitions of the form (q, α, q') where $\alpha \in \Sigma^*$ can be a word instead of a single symbol. Such enhanced transitions are not used excessively. A transition (q, α, q') will only then be present, if there is a rule $A \to \alpha\beta$ in the grammar, i.e., if α is a prefix of some rule's body.

Second, both Algorithms 1 and 2 start with an NFA M and then transitions are added. Instead, the new algorithm starts with an empty NFA. Then we use an algorithm to add the original transitions, which will trigger recursive calls that add all other needed transitions. This new design makes the algorithm significantly simpler.

To summarize, in principle we use only the following very simple observation: If $(q, \alpha, p), (p, \beta, r) \in \delta$, then we can also add $(q, \alpha\beta, r)$ to δ and if $(q, \alpha, p) \in \delta$ and there is a rule $A \to \alpha$ we can add (q, A, p) to δ. The resulting Algorithm 3 runs in $O(|G| \cdot |Q|^3)$ time. A small change gives us Algorithm 4, which takes only quadratic time to solve the word problem for unambiguous grammars. We also address the question whether it is possible to compute pre^* for unambiguous grammars and arbitrary NFAs in quadratic time. It turns out that Algorithm 4 is not able to do this even for acyclic NFAs with a linear number of transitions. Moreover, it seems unlikely that pre^*-computations in the form of computing a saturated NFA (as is done by Algorithms 3 and 4) can be done in quadratic time, as we can solve the Boolean matrix multiplication problem with the help of such an algorithm in the same time.

A special case of pre^*-computations is the word problem. Usually we are not only interested in a *yes*- or *no*-answer, but require more information. If the answer to $w \in L(G)$ is *yes* we would like to have a parse tree for w. Constructing a parse tree is an important step in compiling a program or doing a static analysis (including the simple task of pretty-printing the program or reformatting it) [3]. It is easy to use Algorithms 3 and 4 to construct a parse tree.

If, on the other hand, $w \notin L(M)$, we usually like to know the reason why not. The obvious application is again compiling a computer program that contains a syntactic error. A very generic way is to spot the first symbol that causes the program to be incorrect. We can find this symbol with the pre^*-method, too, by solving the related *valid prefix* problem: Given a grammar $G = (N, T, P, S)$ and a word $u \in T^*$, does $uT^* \cap L(G) \neq \emptyset$ hold? The latter is true iff $S \in pre^*(uT^*)$. The longest valid prefix can then be found by, for example, binary search, which gives us the location of the symbol in w that causes the "syntax error."

In conclusion, I think that these techniques can enhance basic lectures on formal languages by giving students the possibility to implement and use nontrivial tools on almost realistic problems. The main advantage is the ability to process general grammars in a simple, yet efficient way. Experiments show that both the implementation workload is low enough, and the efficiency of the algorithms is high enough, to use real-world examples.

2   Preliminaries

We use the notations of [10], which are mostly from the classical book by Hopcroft and Ullman [28] for the standard notations for finite automata and context-free languages. In addition, [10] uses some notations for the newly introduced concepts. They are as follows:

An NFA $M = (Q, \Sigma, \delta, q_0, F)$ consists of its set of states Q, input alphabet Σ, the set of transitions $\delta \subseteq Q \times \Sigma \times Q$, the initial state $q_0 \in Q$, and the set of final states $F \subseteq Q$.

We define the *transition function* $\widehat{\delta} \colon (Q \times \Sigma^*) \to 2^Q$ by:

- $\widehat{\delta}(q, \epsilon) = \{q\}$,
- $\widehat{\delta}(q, a) = \{q' \mid (q, a, q') \in \delta\}$, and
- $\widehat{\delta}(q, wa) = \{p \mid p \in \widehat{\delta}(r, a) \text{ for some state } r \in \widehat{\delta}(q, w)\}$

We usually write $q \xrightarrow{\alpha} q'$ instead of $q' \in \widehat{\delta}(q, \alpha)$.

For a context-free grammar $G = (N, T, P, S)$, we denote $\Sigma = N \cup T$. The rules in P are of the form $A \to \alpha$ with $A \in N$ and $\alpha \in (N \cup T)^*$. We say that A is the *head* and α the *body* of the rule. There are the two relations $\Rightarrow$ and $\overset{*}{\Rightarrow}$ between words in Σ^*: If $A \to \beta$ is a rule of P and α, γ are words in Σ^*, then $\alpha A \gamma \Rightarrow \alpha \beta \gamma$. The relation $\overset{*}{\Rightarrow}$ is the reflexive and transitive closure of $\Rightarrow$. Given $L \subseteq \Sigma^*$, we define

$$pre^*(L) = \{\alpha \in \Sigma^* \mid \alpha \overset{*}{\Rightarrow} \beta \text{ for some } \beta \in L\}.$$

Here is a small example: Let $G = (N, T, P, S)$ with $N = \{S\}$, $T = \{a, b\}$, $P = \{S \to aSa \mid bSb \mid \epsilon\}$ and $L = (aa)^*$. Then $pre^*(L) = (S + aS^*a)^*$.

Usually, we call the symbols in T *terminals* or *terminal symbols* and the symbols in N *non-terminals* or *variables*. Finally, the symbols in Σ (usually $\Sigma = N \cup T$) are simply called *symbols*.

3 Computing *pre** for General Grammars

We have defined NFAs with the help of a transition relation $\delta \in Q \times \Sigma \times Q$. A single transition is of the form $(q, a, p) \in \delta$ with $a \in \Sigma$. In the following we will work with *extended NFAs* whose transitions are a subset of $Q \times \Sigma^* \times Q$ and a single transition is (q, α, p) with $\alpha \in \Sigma^*$.

For an extended NFA we define

$$\widehat{\delta}(q, w) = \begin{cases} \{p \in Q \mid q' \in \widehat{\delta}(q, u), (q', v, p) \in \delta \\ \qquad \text{for } q' \in Q, \ u \in \Sigma^*, \ v \in \Sigma^+ \text{ with } uv = w\} & \text{for } w \neq \epsilon \\ \{q\}, & \text{for } w = \epsilon, \end{cases}$$

which are the states reachable from q when reading w. As before we say $p \xrightarrow{w} q$ iff $q \in \widehat{\delta}(p, w)$. Moreover, we assume by convention that $(q, \epsilon, q) \in \delta$ for all $q \in Q$. Except for self-loops we do not allow ϵ-transitions in extended NFAs.

Please note, that $p \xrightarrow{w} q$ does not imply that we can get from p to q reading "one symbol at a time." In Fig. 2 there is an extended NFA M_1 with $q_1 \xrightarrow{aba} q_4$, but there is no way to reach q_4 from q_1 using transitions with only single symbols. The latter is possible in M_2.

We say an extended NFA has the *interpolation property*, if $p \xrightarrow{w_1 w_2 \ldots w_n} q$ with $w_i \in \Sigma$ implies the existence of states $q_1, \ldots, q_{n-1}$ such that

$$p \xrightarrow{w_1} q_1, \ q_1 \xrightarrow{w_2} q_2, \ q_2 \xrightarrow{w_3} q_3, \ldots, q_{n-2} \xrightarrow{w_{n-1}} q_{n-1}, \ q_{n-1} \xrightarrow{w_n} q.$$

In other words, if $w = uv$ then the interpolation property allows us to split $p \xrightarrow{w} q$ into $p \xrightarrow{u} r$ and $r \xrightarrow{v} q$ for some $r \in Q$.

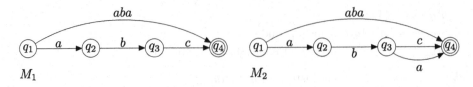

Fig. 2. Two extended NFAs. M_2 has the interpolation property, but M_1 does not.

If you remove all transitions (q, w, p) with $|w| > 1$ from an extended NFA M with the interpolation property, then you do not change its language, and each transition $q' \xrightarrow{u} q''$ remains possible.

Now we are ready to introduce the new Algorithm 3 for the computation of $pre_G^*(L(M))$ for general context-free grammars G and NFAs M. In contrast to Algorithms 1 and 2, Algorithm 3 does not compute an NFA for $pre^*(L(M))$ in one shot from M, but is designed to add a single transition at a time, while calling itself recursively to add all other necessary transitions. To use Algorithm 3 you have to start with an empty extended NFA M that has no transitions except (q, ϵ, q) for all states q.[1] Then we have to call $add(q, X, q')$ with $X \in \Sigma = (N \cup T)$ and $q, q' \in Q$ for every transition (q, X, q') that we want to be present and also call $add(q, A, q)$ for all $q \in Q$ and $A \to \epsilon \in P$. At the end M is turned into an extended NFA that recognizes exactly. $pre^*(L)$.

So if you have an NFA M and want to compute an NFA M' with $L(M') = pre^*(L(M))$ you start with an empty M' and add all transitions of M to M' by using add from Algorithm 3.

Algorithm 3

---

1    $add(p, \beta, q)$:
2   **if** $(p, \beta, q) \in \delta$ **then return**;
3        $\delta := \delta \cup \{(p, \beta, q)\}$;
4   **for every** $A \to \beta \in P$ **do** $add(p, A, q)$;
5   **for every** $(p, \beta, q) \to (p, \beta\gamma, r) \in impl$ **do** $add(p, \beta\gamma, r)$;
6   **for every** $A \to \alpha\beta\gamma \in P$, $q' \in Q$ **do**
7   **if** $(q', \alpha, p) \in \delta$ **then** $add(q', \alpha\beta, q)$
8   **else** $impl := impl \cup \{(q', \alpha, p) \to (q', \alpha\beta, q)\}$

Roughly speaking, Algorithm 3 proceeds as follows. If we add a new transition (p, β, q) and there is a rule $A \to \beta$, then the algorithm adds the transition (p, A, q), too. If there is already a transition (q', α, p) present and we add a new transition (p, β, q), then $(q', \alpha\beta, q)$ is added, but only if $\alpha\beta$ is a prefix of some rule's body. Without this restriction too many useless transitions would be added and the running time would suffer. Finally, if (q', α, p) is *not* present, we cannot

---

[1] The reason for the ϵ-self-loops becomes clear later. They are needed to preserve the invariant that the NFA is "saturated."

add the transition $(q', \alpha\beta, q)$, but we can remember that in the future, if (q', α, p) is added, then we can also add $(q', \alpha\beta, q)$. To remember this implication we have a table *impl* and we add $(q', \alpha, p) \rightarrow (q', \alpha\beta, q)$ to this table.

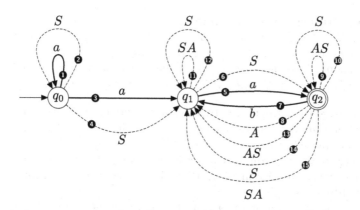

Fig. 3. An example how Algorithm 3 computes *pre**(L).

Here is an example, how the algorithm proceeds. Let us say we have a grammar with the rules

$$S \rightarrow AS \mid SA \mid a \text{ and } A \rightarrow b.$$

We would like to compute $pre^*(L(M))$ for the NFA M depicted in Fig. 3, where the transitions of M are the ones with solid lines. If we want to compute pre^* with the help of Algorithm 3, we simply add all transitions with solid lines to an empty NFA by calling $add(q_0, a, q_0)$, $add(q_0, a, q_1)$, $add(q_1, a, q_2)$, and $add(q_2, b, q_1)$ in this order. The dashed transitions are added by Algorithm 3 in addition to the manually added ones. A timeline of when each transition is added is shown by numbered labels attached to each transition, where ❶ is the first and ⓰ the last one. In detail, the following happens:

- We call $add(q_0, a, q_0)$ and the transition ❶ is added to δ in line 3. Then, in line 4, the matching rule $S \rightarrow a$ is found, leading to a call to $add(q_0, S, q_0)$ and ❷ is added.
- We call $add(q_0, a, q_1)$❸, which triggers $add(q_0, S, q_1)$❹.
- We call $add(q_1, a, q_2)$❺, which triggers $add(q_1, S, q_2)$❻ (and also adds – for later – $(q_2, A, q_1) \rightarrow (q_2, AS, q_2)$ to *impl*).
- Finally, we call $add(q_2, b, q_1)$❼, which triggers $add(q_2, A, q_1)$❽ because of $A \rightarrow b$.
  When ❽ is added, *impl* already contains $(q_2, A, q_1) \rightarrow (q_2, AS, q_2)$. Therefore $add(q_2, AS, q_2)$❾ is called in line 5. Then, because of $S \rightarrow AS$ a call to $add(q_2, S, q_2)$❿ is made. Moreover, ❽ also triggers $add(q_1, SA, q_1)$⓫ because $(q_1, S, q_2) \in \delta$ (line 7). This leads to $add(q_1, S, q_1)$⓬ because of $S \rightarrow SA$. Another event triggered by ❽ is $add(q_2, AS, q_1)$⓭ because $(q_2, A, q_1) \rightarrow$

$(q_2, AS, q_1) \in impl$. Then ⑭ is added because of $S \to AS$ and finally ⑮ appears because of ⑧ and ⑩. The addition of ⑩ is triggered by the addition of ⑧ quite late. The reason that many other transitions were added before ⑮ is the depth-first nature of the recursive calls.

Lemma 1 (Interpolation Lemma). Let $M = (\Sigma, Q, \delta, q_0, F)$ be an extended NFA and $G = (N, T, P, S)$ a context-free grammar with $\Sigma = N \cup T$, but $\delta = \{(q, \epsilon, q) \mid q \in Q\}$, i.e., M has no real transitions.

If we modify M by performing operations of the form $add(q', \gamma, q'')$ (in Algorithm 1) where $q', q'' \in Q$ and $\gamma \in \Sigma$, then M has the interpolation property.

Proof. We have to distinguish between *add*-operations that are applied directly and those that are done indirectly by recursive calls within Algorithm 3. Recursive calls are placed in lines 4, 5, and 7.

If $add(q', \gamma, q'')$ is a direct call or is done in line 4 of Algorithm 3, then $|\gamma| = 1$, i.e., γ is a single symbol. In that case the interpolation property cannot be violated by $q' \xrightarrow{\gamma} q''$.

Let us look at line 5 of Algorithm 3. It does an $add(p, \beta\gamma, r)$ and we know that at that point of time $(p, \beta, q) \to (p, \beta\gamma, r) \in impl$. Before this implication was placed into $impl$ (in line 8) the transition (q, γ, r) was added to δ (in line 3). Because this happened in the past we can assume by induction that the interpolation property held for (q, γ, r). The same holds for (p, β, q), which was also added to δ before $(p, \beta\gamma, r)$. Hence, when $(p, \beta\gamma, r)$ is added to δ the interpolation property holds for both $p \xrightarrow{\beta} q$ and $q \xrightarrow{\gamma} r$ and therefore also for $p \xrightarrow{\beta\gamma} r$.

The last possibility is line 7, where $add(q', \alpha\beta, q)$ is called. Here already $(q', \alpha, p), (p, \beta, q) \in \delta$, and we can assume that the interpolation property holds for both $q' \xrightarrow{\alpha} p$ and $p \xrightarrow{\beta} q$ and therefore also for $q' \xrightarrow{\alpha\beta} q$. □

Definition 1. We say that an extended NFA $M = (\Sigma, Q, \delta, q_0, F)$ is *saturated* (for a context-free grammar $G = (N, T, P, S)$, $\Sigma = N \cup T$), if the following conditions are met for every $p, q, r \in Q$, $A \in N$, $\alpha \in \Sigma^+$, $\beta \in \Sigma^*$.

1. If $p \xrightarrow{\alpha} q$ and $\beta \xRightarrow{*} \alpha$, then $p \xrightarrow{\beta} q$.
2. If $p \xrightarrow{\alpha} q$ and $A \to \alpha\beta \in P$, then $(p, \alpha, q) \in \delta$.

Remember that $p \xrightarrow{\alpha} q$ means that reading α can get M from p to q in one or in multiple steps, but $(p, \alpha, q) \in \delta$ implies that it is possible in a single step. More importantly, if we want to know whether $p \xrightarrow{\alpha} q$ and α is the prefix of some rule's body, then we can get the information *in constant time*.

Lemma 2 (Saturation Lemma). Let $M = (\Sigma, Q, \delta, q_0, F)$ be an extended NFA for a context-free grammar $G = (N, T, P, S)$ with $\Sigma = N \cup T$, but $\delta = \{(q, \epsilon, q) \mid q \in Q\}$, i.e., M has no real transitions.

If we modify M by performing operations of the form $add(q', \gamma, q'')$ where $q', q'' \in Q$ and $\gamma \in \Sigma$, then M stays saturated for G.

Proof. Let us assume we already have performed all operations. We have to prove that both conditions of Definition 1 are met for all possible $p, q \in Q$, $A \in N$, and $\alpha, \beta \in \Sigma^*$.

Let us look at the second condition and assume that indeed $p \xrightarrow{\alpha} q$ and $A \to \alpha\beta \in P$. We have to show that then $(p, \alpha, q) \in \delta$. We use induction on the length of α.

If $\alpha = \epsilon$, then $p = q$ because there are no ϵ-transitions and $(p, \epsilon, p) \in \delta$ by convention.

Otherwise, we can assume that $\alpha = \alpha'X$ and $p \xrightarrow{\alpha'} r \xrightarrow{X} q$ for some $X \in \Sigma$ and $r \in Q$. We can split $p \xrightarrow{\alpha} q$ in that way because M has the interpolation property guaranteed by Lemma 1.

In that case, $(p, \alpha', r) \in \delta$ (by induction hypothesis) and $(r, X, q) \in \delta$ (because $r \xrightarrow{X} q$ consists of a single step). At some point of time these two transitions were added to δ by two calls $add(p, \alpha', r)$ and $add(r, X, q)$. We do not know in which order those calls were performed.

If $add(p, \alpha', r)$ came first and then $add(r, X, q)$, the second call would also recursively do an $add(p, \alpha'X, q)$ in line 7 of Algorithm 3, which means that $(p, \alpha, q) \in \delta$ and we are done.

If $add(r, X, q)$ came first, it would add $(p, \alpha', r) \to (p, \alpha'X, q)$ to *impl* in line 8 of Algorithm 3 and then $add(p, \alpha', r)$ would call $add(p, \alpha'X, q)$ in line 5, which again puts (p, α, q) into δ.

It remains to check the validity of the first condition in Definition 1. Here we assume that $p \xrightarrow{\alpha} q$ and $\beta \overset{*}{\Rightarrow} \alpha$ hold and we have to show that then $p \xrightarrow{\beta} q$.

Let us look at a derivation

$$\beta = \beta_1 \Rightarrow \beta_2 \Rightarrow \cdots \Rightarrow \beta_k = \alpha.$$

We prove that

$$p \xrightarrow{\beta_i} q \text{ implies } p \xrightarrow{\beta_{i-1}} q \text{ for } i = 2, \ldots k. \tag{1}$$

Because of $\beta_{i-1} \Rightarrow \beta_i$ we can write $\beta_{i-1} = \beta'B\beta'''$ and $\beta_i = \beta'\beta''\beta'''$ for some $B \in N$ with $B \to \beta'' \in P$. Then $p \xrightarrow{\beta_i} q$ can be split into

$$p \xrightarrow{\beta'} p' \xrightarrow{\beta''} q' \xrightarrow{\beta'''} q$$

for some $p', q' \in Q$ because of the interpolation property. In particular, $p' \xrightarrow{\beta''} q'$ means that $add(p', \beta'', q')$ was called in the past. While $add(p', \beta'', q')$ was processed, another call to $add(p', B, q')$ was issued in line 4, which guarantees $p' \xrightarrow{B} q'$ and therefore both $p \xrightarrow{\beta'} p' \xrightarrow{B} q' \xrightarrow{\beta'''} q$ and $p \xrightarrow{\beta_{i-1}} q$ (because of $\beta_{i-1} = \beta'B\beta'''$). This concludes the proof of (1).

By repeatedly applying (1) to $p \xrightarrow{\alpha} q$ we get $p \xrightarrow{\beta} q$ and condition 1 is proven, too. $\qquad\qquad\qquad\qquad\qquad\qquad\qquad\qquad\qquad\qquad\qquad\qquad$ $\square$

We assume that a context-free grammar is encoded in the natural way: A list of all productions. If $G = (N, T, P, S)$ with $P = \{ A_i \to \beta_i \mid i = 1, \ldots k \}$, then the length of the encoding of G is $|G| = O\big(k + \sum_{i=1}^{k} |\beta_i|\big)$. We assume that the encoding length of a single symbol is constant, which corresponds to a constant cost measure that is commonly used in algorithm design and analysis. For example, a graph with n vertices and m edges has an encoding of size $O(n + m)$ and a depth-first search takes time $O(n + m)$. We assume that the algorithm is performed on a standard RAM with logarithmic word size. It is therefore natural to assume that a single symbol can be stored in a single memory cell and processed (e.g., copied or compared) in constant time.

If we take a context-free grammar G and convert it into a CNF-like normal form G' with rules of the form $A \to a$, $A \to \epsilon$, $A \to B$, and $A \to BC$, its size grows only by a constant factor (in contrast to full CNF without chain-rules). For example, if there is a single rule $A \to b_1 \ldots b_k$ with $b_i \in \{0, 1\}$, a conversion into the normal form yields rules $A \to A_1 B_1$, $B_1 \to A_2 B_2, \ldots A_{k-1} \to A_k B_k$, $A_k \to \epsilon$ and $B_i \to b_i$ for $i = 1, \ldots, k$. Although the number of symbols grows from constant to linear, the encoding size is still $|G'| = O(|G|)$. This almost lossless conversion was crucial for Algorithm 2, which works on grammars in this normal form, and is able to compute $pre^*(M)$ in $O(n^3|G|)$ time, where n is the number of states in the NFA M [10].

In order to analyze the running time of Algorithm 3 we have to be very careful because now the size of a single rule no longer has a constant size. After all, Algorithm 3's *raison d'être* is its ability to operate directly on general CFGs.

Please note that all operations that are performed on strings α and transitions (q, β, p) in Algorithm 3 take only *constant time*, if we encode the strings in a clever way. All strings are either single symbols or an infix of some rule's body. They can be encoded in constant space by providing the number of the rule and the offsets into its body. To ensure constant processing time of all basic operations some straightforward, precomputed lookup tables for the rules are sufficient.

Lemma 3 (Running time). *Let $G = (N, T, P, S)$ be a context-free grammar and $M = (N \cup T, Q, \delta, q_0, F)$ an NFA. We can use Algorithm 3 in such a way that it computes an extended NFA M' with $L(M') = pre^*_G(L(M))$ by starting with an empty extended NFA M' and then calling $add(q, a, p)$ for every $(q, a, p) \in \delta$, and $add(q, A, q)$ for every $q \in Q$ and $A \to \epsilon \in P$. Algorithm 3 can be implemented in such a way that computing M' takes $O(|Q|^3|G|)$ time.*

Proof. If we call $add(p, \beta, q)$ multiple times with the same arguments, all calls except the first one take only constant time. Lines 2 and 3 always take constant time. Line 4 takes time $O(|G| \cdot |Q|^2)$ *in total* because there are at most $|G| \cdot |Q|^2$ combinations of q, β, p for which $add(q, \beta, p)$ is called. Even if it is called multiple times with the same parameters, only the first invocation reaches line 4.

Let us look at line 5, which is a little harder to analyze. Because p, β, and q are fixed in one call to $add(p, \beta, q)$, there are $|Q|$ possibilities left for r and potentially $\Theta(|G|)$ possibilities for γ. This crude estimate gives us a running time of $O(|Q| \cdot |G|)$ for line 5. The total time spent in line 5 is then at most $O(|Q|^3|G|^2)$, which is not good enough.

If we look at the correctness proof for Algorithm 3 and the Saturation Lemma (Lemma 2) we notice that in line 5 it suffices to consider only γ's with $\gamma \in N \cup T$, i.e., $|\gamma| = 1$. If we modify the algorithm accordingly, there are only $O(|\Sigma|)$ possibilities for γ. To be even more precise we have to look at the total running time spent in line 5. There are now only $O(|G|)$ many possibilities for $\beta\gamma$ and the *total* running time for line 5 is bounded by $O(|Q|^3|G|)$.

A similar analysis can be done for lines 6–8. Looking at the proof of Lemma 2 reveals that it is only necessary to visit line 6 if $|\beta| = 1$. Therefore, there are only $O(|G|)$ many possibilities to choose $A \to \alpha\beta\gamma \in P$ and the total running time of lines 6–8 also becomes $O(|Q|^3|G|)$ because there are $|Q|^3$ possibilities to choose q, q', and p. $\square$

Now we have the most important ingredients to prove the correctness of Algorithm 3 and of an algorithm that uses Algorithm 3 to construct from M an M' such that $L(M') = pre^*(L(M))$. Indeed, we would like to prove a little more:

Theorem 1. *Let $M = (\Sigma, Q, \delta, q_0, F)$ be an NFA and $G = (N, T, P, S)$ be a context-free grammar with $\Sigma = N \cup T$. Let M' be the NFA resulting from an empty extended NFA M', on which $add(q, X, p)$ has been called for every $(q, X, p) \in \delta$ and every (q, A, q) with $A \in N$ and $A \to \epsilon \in P$.*

Then $q \xrightarrow[M']{\alpha} p$ iff $\alpha \xRightarrow{*} \beta$ and $q \xrightarrow[M]{\beta} p$. Moreover, M' is saturated and $L(M') = pre^*(L(M))$.

Proof. "$\Longleftarrow$" We start with $q \xrightarrow[M']{\alpha} p$ if $q \xrightarrow[M]{\beta} p$ and $\alpha \xRightarrow{*} \beta$:

Let us first assume that $\beta = \epsilon$. Then $p = q$ and $\alpha \xRightarrow{*} \epsilon$, which means that $\alpha = A_1 \ldots A_k$ with $A_i \in N$ and $A_i \xRightarrow{*} \epsilon$, which means that $A_i \xRightarrow{*} X_1 \ldots X_m$ with $X_j \in N$ and $X_i \to \epsilon \in P$ for all $1 \leq j \leq m$. We added the transitions (q, X_j, q) to M' and therefore $q \xrightarrow[M']{\alpha} p$.

Let now $\beta \neq \epsilon$. Please note that we started with an empty extended M'. It is easy to check that this M' is saturated.

The Saturation Lemma (Lemma 2) guarantees that M' stays saturated after each *add*-call. So, in the end, M' is still saturated. The first condition of Definition 1 guarantees that $q \xrightarrow[M']{\alpha} p$ if $q \xrightarrow[M']{\beta} p$ and $\alpha \xRightarrow{*} \beta$.

"$\Longrightarrow$": It is rather easy to see that Algorithm 3 never adds an "incorrect" transition to δ by recursive calls. In the following δ' is the (extended) transition relation of M' (which changes dynamically). The following correctness proof shows that if (q, α, p) is added to δ' then there is some β with $q \xrightarrow[M]{\beta} p$ and $\alpha \xRightarrow{*} \beta$.

If (q, A, p) was added by line 3, then $(q, \beta, p) \in \delta'$ and $A \to \beta$. Hence, $q \xrightarrow{\beta} p$ and $A = \alpha \xRightarrow{*} \beta$.

If $(q', \alpha\beta, p)$ was added to δ' by line 7, then there already was $(p, \beta, q) \in \delta'$ and $(q', \alpha, p) \in \delta'$. Hence, $q' \xrightarrow[M']{\alpha} p$, $p \xrightarrow[M']{\beta} q$ and therefore $q' \xrightarrow[M']{\alpha\beta} p$. Moreover, by induction hypothesis there are α', β' such that $q' \xrightarrow[M]{\alpha'} p$, $p \xrightarrow[M]{\beta'} q$ and $\alpha \xRightarrow{*} \alpha'$, $\beta \xRightarrow{*} \beta'$. Then also $q' \xrightarrow[M]{\alpha'\beta'} p$ and $\alpha\beta \xRightarrow{*} \alpha'\beta'$.

Finally, assume that $(p, \beta\gamma, r)$ was added to δ' because of line 5. Then some $(p, \beta, q) \to (p, \beta\gamma, r) \in impl$. This entry was added to *impl* in the past in line 8, which means that then $(p, \beta, q) \notin \delta'$. Before reaching line 8, Algorithm 3 added (q, γ, r) to δ' in line 3. By induction $q \xrightarrow{\gamma'}_{M'} r$ for some γ' with $\gamma \stackrel{*}{\Rightarrow} \gamma'$. In the current invocation of *add* before reaching line 5, in line 3 the algorithm added (p, β, q) and by induction hypothesis there is some β' with $p \xrightarrow{\beta'}_{M'} q$ and $\beta \stackrel{*}{\Rightarrow} \beta'$.

Combining both yields $p \xrightarrow{\beta'\gamma'}_{M'} r$ and $\beta\gamma \stackrel{*}{\Rightarrow} \beta'\gamma'$.

It is clear that M' is saturated, as stated above. Let us finally prove that indeed $L(M') = pre^*(L(M))$. By definition $\alpha \in pre^*(L(M))$ iff there is a β with $\alpha \stackrel{*}{\Rightarrow} \beta$ and $\beta \in L(M)$. The latter is true iff $q_0 \xrightarrow{\beta}_{M} q_f$ for some $q_f \in F$. This is again true iff $q_0 \xrightarrow{\alpha}_{M'} q_f$, as shown above. □

4   Unambiguous Grammars

A cubic running time, although polynomial, is not very fast. For the important special case that a context-free grammar is unambiguous it is well-known that both the word and parsing problems can be solved in quadratic time, for example by Earley's algorithm [13,14]. In this section we will address the more general pre^*-problem for unambiguous grammars. Can it be solved in quadratic time, too? The answer is a qualified yes. If the underlying NFA M consists of a single path, for example if $L(M) = \{w\}$ in order to solve the word problem, then the running time of the following Algorithm 4 is indeed quadratic in $|w|$. For general NFAs, even for acyclic ones, however, the running time of Algorithm 4 stays cubic.

Algorithm 4

---

1   $add(p, \beta, q)$:
2   **if** $(p, \beta, q) \in \delta$ **then return**;
3       $\delta := \delta \cup \{(p, \beta, q)\}$;
4   **for every** $A \to \beta \in P$ **do** $add(p, A, q)$;
5   **for every** $\gamma \in \Sigma$, $(*, \beta, q) \to (*, \beta\gamma, r) \in impl$ **do** $add(p, \beta\gamma, r)$;
6   **for every** $A \to \alpha\beta\gamma \in P$, $\beta \in \Sigma$ **do**
7   **for every** $(q', \alpha, p) \in \delta$ **do** $add(q', \alpha\beta, q)$
8           $impl := impl \cup \{(*, \alpha, p) \to (*, \alpha\beta, q)\}$

Algorithm 4 has three slight changes from Algorithm 3: Firstly, it uses only single symbols for γ and β in lines 5 and 6. Secondly, it does not iterate over all $q' \in Q$ (in line 7) but only over those, for which $(q', \alpha, p) \in \delta$. Finally, it does not add $(q', \alpha, p) \to (q', \alpha\beta, q)$ to *impl* for many $q' \in Q$, but adds $(*, \alpha, p) \to (*, \alpha\beta, q)$, where the star represents any state (but it is just a symbol).

Let us first look at an example with an unambiguous grammar G and an acyclic NFA M where Algorithm 4 suffers a cubic running time. The rules of G are $S \to aa$ and M looks as follows (see Fig. 4): The transitions are (q'_i, a, p_j) and (p_i, a, q_j) for all $1 \le i, j \le n$. We run Algorithm 4 on an empty NFA and first add all (q'_i, a, p_j). What happens if we then call $add(p_i, a, q_j)$? In line 7 the algorithm cycles through (q'_k, a, p_i) for all $q'_k \in Q$, which takes $\Omega(n)$ time and there are n^2 such calls. The time complexity is therefore $\Theta(n^3)$.

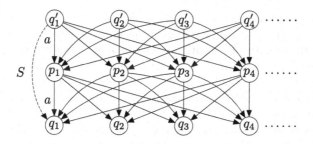

Fig. 4. An acyclic NFA M that enforces a cubic running time.

A drawback of this construction is that we already start with an NFA that has a quadratic number of transitions. Is it possible to be faster, if the initial number of transitions is lower? Unfortunately, no, as the following construction shows: We can create a bipartite completely connected transition graph using a grammar $A \rightarrow aa$, $B \rightarrow bb$, $S \rightarrow AB$ and an NFA with (among others) states $x_1, \ldots, x_n, z_1, \ldots, z_n, y$ and transitions (x_i, a, y) and (y, a, z_i) for $1 \leq i \leq n$. Algorithm 4 then adds all transitions (x_i, A, z_j), which can then be used as a starting point for the construction above. Altogether the NFA looks as follows (Fig. 5): The first level is completely connected to the second one by A-transitions and the second one to the third one by B-transitions. Adding each of the quadratically many S-transitions takes linear time *for each of them*.

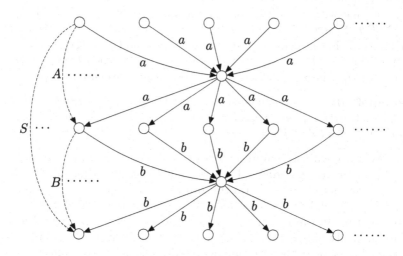

Fig. 5. A sparse acyclic NFA that enforces a cubic running time.

This construction gives us the following theorem:

Theorem 2. *There is an unambiguous grammar G with constant size and an acyclic NFA M with $O(n)$ states and transitions, such that Algorithm 4 takes $\Theta(n^3)$ time to compute the NFA for pre*($L(M)$).*

At this point of time we cannot rule out the existence of an algorithm that has a running time of $O(nm)$ for unambiguous grammars, where n is the number of states and m the number of transitions. We can, however, give some evidence that the existence of an algorithm with running time $O(n^2)$ is unlikely, if we allow arbitrarily dense NFAs. Boolean matrix multiplication is possible in subcubic time because it can be done by matrix multiplication over the integers. The so far fastest algorithm by Alman and Vassilevska Williams [4] takes $O(n^{2.37\cdots})$ time using algebraic method to compute the product of two matrices. The best "purely combinatorial" algorithms are still close to n^3 – only better by a polylog factor [35]. This means that it is at the moment hopeless to aim for an $O(n^2)$ running time and that improving over the cubic running time of Algorithm 4 probably requires advanced techniques.

Theorem 3. *Let G be an unambiguous grammar and M an acyclic NFA with n states. If we can compute a saturated NFA M' by adding only the necessary transitions to M in time $t(n)$, then we can solve the Boolean matrix multiplication problem in $O(t(n) + n^2)$ time.*

Proof. Let $Q, P \in \{0,1\}^{n \times n}$ be two quadratic Boolean matrices. We use the grammar $S \to aa$ and construct an NFA M with states x_i, y_i, z_i for $1 \leq 1 \leq n$. The transitions are (x_i, a, y_j) for $P_{ij} = 1$ and (y_i, a, z_j) for $Q_{ij} = 1$.

Now compute M' in $t(n)$ time. Let $R = PQ$. Due to $R_{ij} = 1$ iff M' contains the transition (x_i, S, z_j), we can compute R in time $O(t(n) + n^2)$.   □

The good news is, of course, that the word problem is indeed solvable in quadratic time with Algorithm 4. For the word problem we have a grammar $G = (N, T, P, S)$ and a word $w \in T^*$, $w = w_1 \ldots w_n$ with $w_i \in T$. We construct an NFA M_w with state set $q_0, \ldots, q_n$, initial state q_0 and q_n as the only final state. The transitions of M_w are (q_{i-1}, w_i, q_i) for $i = 1, \ldots, n$. Then $L(M_w) = \{w\}$ and $S \in pre^*(L(M_w))$ iff $S \Rightarrow w$ iff $w \in L(G)$. By $w[q_i, q_j]$ we denote $w_{i+1}w_{i+2} \ldots w_j$.

Theorem 4. *If G is an unambiguous context-free grammar without useless symbols, then Algorithm 4 can be used to compute $pre^*(L(M_w)) = pre^*(\{w\})$ in the form of an (extended) NFA M'_w with $pre^*(\{w\}) = L(M'_w)$ in time $O(|w|^2 \cdot |G|)$.*

Proof. We start with an empty extended NFA and then call $add(q_{i-1}, w_i, q_i)$ for $i = 1, \ldots, n$ (in this order). Then we call $add(q_i, A, q_i)$ for all $A \in N$ with $A \to \epsilon \in P$ and all $i = 0, \ldots, n$ (in this order).

In the proof of Lemma 3 we have already seen that line 4 takes at most $O(|Q|^2|G|)$ time in total even for the general case. We can disregard lines 1–3 because they take only constant time and, e.g., the *if*-instruction in line 2 cannot be executed more often then the number of *add*-calls in lines 5–7 plus the number of manual calls. The number of manual calls is clearly bounded by $|Q|^2|G|$.

Let us look at line 7 in Algorithm 4 and fix q', α, β, q. Then the number of iterations in line 7 is the number of $p \in Q$ such that $(q', \alpha, p) \in \delta$. We claim that this number of p's is at most one.

Assume otherwise and we have $(q', \alpha, p), (q', \alpha, p') \in \delta$ with $p \neq p'$. Then $\alpha \stackrel{*}{\Rightarrow} w[q', p]$, $\beta \stackrel{*}{\Rightarrow} w[p, q]$ and also $\alpha' \stackrel{*}{\Rightarrow} w[q', p']$, $\beta' \stackrel{*}{\Rightarrow} w[p', q]$ as the Saturation Lemma shows (Lemma 2).

Then there are two different parse trees for $\alpha\beta \overset{*}{\Rightarrow} w[q', p]$, which is impossible for an unambiguous grammar with no useless symbols: We know that $\alpha\beta$ is part of a rule $A \to \alpha\beta\gamma$. Therefore there is a subword of u'' of w with $A \overset{*}{\Rightarrow} u$ and there are two different parse trees with root A for u''. Finally, there must be words $u', u''' \in T^*$ such that $S \Rightarrow u'Au'''$. With the two parse trees for $A \overset{*}{\Rightarrow} u$ we can construct two parse trees for $S \overset{*}{\Rightarrow} u'u''u'''$. This is a contradiction to G being unambiguous.

Hence, the total number of (q', α, p)'s that are listed in line 7 over the total running time of the algorithm is bounded by $|G| \cdot |Q|^2$ (because $|\beta| = 1$ there are only $|G|$ many possibilities to choose $\alpha\beta$).

As for the total time spent in line 5 note that there are only $|w|^2|G|$ many ways to choose $(p, \beta\gamma, r)$. □

Finally a remark without proof. If we insert the initial transitions into the initially empty NFA in the order specified in the above proof, then we can leave out lines 5 and 8 in Algorithm 4 because the *impl*-table is not used at all. This yields a simpler algorithm that can be used for the word problem for all grammars, not only for unambiguous ones.

5   Applications to Parsing

Table 1 contains a grammar for the programming language PL/0 that was designed by Niklaus Wirth as a simple subset of Pascal for educational purposes [33]. Just like for Pascal itself it is easy to write a recursive descent parser for PL/0. We use the language as an example of applying the *pre**-technique to realistic examples, but keeping it simple enough for an introductory course on formal languages. The grammar has been changed slightly from the original by removing all ϵ-rules and replacing them by equivalent non-erasing ones. The disadvantage of avoiding ϵ-rules is that the grammar is slightly longer and harder to read. The advantage is that syntactic trees and NFAs for the *pre** of programs in PL/0 are a bit simpler and fit into a printed page for our upcoming not completely trivial example.

A very simple program in PL/0 looks at follows. It consists of exactly 17 tokens (:= is one token) and simply outputs the numbers 1 to 10, if you run it.

---

var k;
begin
  $k := 1$;
  while $k \le 10$ **do**
   $!k$
end.

Table 1. A grammar for PL/0 with no ϵ-rules.

BLOCK → CONSTBLOCK VARBLOCK PROCEDURES STATEMENT
  | VARBLOCK PROCEDURES STATEMENT | CONSTBLOCK PROCEDURES STATEMENT
  | PROCEDURES STATEMENT | CONSTBLOCK VARBLOCK STATEMENT
  | CONSTBLOCK STATEMENT | VARBLOCK STATEMENT | STATEMENT
CLIST → IDENT = NUMBER | IDENT = NUMBER , CLIST
CONDITION → odd EXPR | EXPR = EXPR | EXPR ≠ EXPR | EXPR < EXPR | EXPR > EXPR
  | EXPR ≤ EXPR | EXPR ≥ EXPR
CONSTBLOCK → const CLIST ;
EXPR → + TERMS | − TERMS | TERMS
FACTOR → IDENT | NUMBER | (EXPR)
FACTORS → FACTOR | FACTORS * FACTOR | FACTORS / FACTOR
PROCEDURE → procedure IDENT ; BLOCK ;
PROCEDURES → PROCEDURE | PROCEDURE PROCEDURES
PROGRAM → BLOCK .
STATEMENT → IDENT := EXPR | call IDENT | ? IDENT | ! EXPR
  | begin STATEMENTS end | if CONDITION then STATEMENT
  | while CONDITION do STATEMENT
STATEMENTS → STATEMENT | STATEMENT ; STATEMENTS
TERM → FACTORS
TERMS → TERM | TERMS + TERM | TERMS − TERM
VARBLOCK → var VLIST ;
VLIST → IDENT | IDENT , VLIST

If we add the tokens of the example program to an empty NFA from left to right by calling

$$add(0, \text{var}, 1); add(1, \text{k}, 2); add(2, ;, 3); \ldots add(15, \text{end}, 16); add(16, ., 17)$$

then Table 2 shows all transitions that are added to M. They include the 17 transitions $(0, \text{var}, 1)$, $(1, \text{k}, 2)^2, \ldots, (16, ., 17)$, which we added manually, but also the transitions that were added by recursive calls. The latter are marked by an additional letter. The letter P indicates that a transition (p, A, q) was added because a transition (p, β, q) was already present and there is a rule $A \rightarrow \beta$. For example, just after $(1, \text{IDENT}, 2)$, which is the second token we added manually, follows $P(1, \text{VLIST}, 2)$ because the grammar contains the rule VLIST → IDENT. Another example – it occurs much later – is $P(4, \text{STATEMENTS}, 15)$. It was added because there is a rule STATEMENTS → STATEMENT; STATEMENTS, and the transitions $(4, \text{STATEMENT}, 7)$, $(7, ;, 8)$, and $(8, \text{STATEMENTS}, 15)$ were already present. All transitions that are marked with a P are those added by a recursive call in line 4 of Algorithm 3.

---

[2] It is in fact the token $(1, \text{IDENT}, 2)$ and contains an "attribute" that the actual identifier is k. To construct the parse tree it is not important what the underlying name of the identifier is.

Table 2. Transitions of M when adding tokens from left to right.

$(0, \text{var}, 1)$ $(1, \text{IDENT}, 2)$ $P(1, \text{VLIST}, 2)$ $R(0, \text{var VLIST}, 2)$ $P(1, \text{FACTOR}, 2)$ $P(1, \text{FACTORS}, 2)$ $P(1, \text{TERM}, 2)$ $P(1, \text{TERMS}, 2)$ $P(1, \text{EXPR}, 2)$ $(2, ;, 3)$ $R(0, \text{var VLIST} ;, 3)$ $P(0, \text{VARBLOCK}, 3)$ $(3, \text{begin}, 4)$ $(4, \text{IDENT}, 5)$ $P(4, \text{VLIST}, 5)$ $P(4, \text{FACTOR}, 5)$ $P(4, \text{FACTORS}, 5)$ $P(4, \text{TERM}, 5)$ $P(4, \text{TERMS}, 5)$ $P(4, \text{EXPR}, 5)$ $(5, :=, 6)$ $R(4, \text{IDENT} :=, 6)$ $(6, \text{NUMBER}, 7)$ $P(6, \text{FACTOR}, 7)$ $P(6, \text{FACTORS}, 7)$ $P(6, \text{TERM}, 7)$ $P(6, \text{TERMS}, 7)$ $P(6, \text{EXPR}, 7)$ $R(4, \text{IDENT} := \text{EXPR}, 7)$ $P(4, \text{STATEMENT}, 7)$ $P(4, \text{BLOCK}, 7)$ $P(4, \text{STATEMENTS}, 7)$ $R(3, \text{begin STATEMENTS}, 7)$ $(7, ;, 8)$ $R(4, \text{STATEMENT} ;, 8)$ $(8, \text{while}, 9)$ $(9, \text{IDENT}, 10)$ $P(9, \text{VLIST}, 10)$ $P(9, \text{FACTOR}, 10)$ $P(9, \text{FACTORS}, 10)$ $P(9, \text{TERM}, 10)$ $P(9, \text{TERMS}, 10)$ $P(9, \text{EXPR}, 10)$ $(10, <=, 11)$ $R(9, \text{EXPR} <=, 11)$ $(11, \text{NUMBER}, 12)$ $P(11, \text{FACTOR}, 12)$ $P(11, \text{FACTORS}, 12)$ $P(11, \text{TERM}, 12)$ $P(11, \text{TERMS}, 12)$ $P(11, \text{EXPR}, 12)$ $R(9, \text{EXPR} <= \text{EXPR}, 12)$ $P(9, \text{CONDITION}, 12)$ $R(8, \text{while CONDITION}, 12)$ $(12, \text{do}, 13)$ $R(8, \text{while CONDITION do}, 13)$ $(13, !, 14)$ $(14, \text{IDENT}, 15)$ $P(14, \text{VLIST}, 15)$ $P(14, \text{FACTOR}, 15)$ $P(14, \text{FACTORS}, 15)$ $P(14, \text{TERM}, 15)$ $P(14, \text{TERMS}, 15)$ $P(14, \text{EXPR}, 15)$ $R(13, ! \text{EXPR}, 15)$ $P(13, \text{STATEMENT}, 15)$ $P(13, \text{BLOCK}, 15)$ $P(13, \text{STATEMENTS}, 15)$ $R(8, \text{while CONDITION do STATEMENT}, 15)$ $P(8, \text{STATEMENT}, 15)$ $P(8, \text{BLOCK}, 15)$ $P(8, \text{STATEMENTS}, 15)$ $R(4, \text{STATEMENT ; STATEMENTS}, 15)$ $P(4, \text{STATEMENTS}, 15)$ $R(3, \text{begin STATEMENTS}, 15)$ $(15, \text{end}, 16)$ $R(3, \text{begin STATEMENTS end}, 16)$ $P(3, \text{STATEMENT}, 16)$ $P(3, \text{BLOCK}, 16)$ $P(3, \text{STATEMENTS}, 16)$ $R(0, \text{VARBLOCK STATEMENT}, 16)$ $P(0, \text{BLOCK}, 16)$ $(16, ., 17)$ $R(3, \text{BLOCK} ., 17)$ $P(3, \text{PROGRAM}, 17)$ $R(0, \text{BLOCK} ., 17)$ $P(0, \text{PROGRAM}, 17)$

There are additional transitions marked with R. They are incorporated by a recursive call to *add* in line 7. The first such transition is $R(0, \text{var VLIST}, 2)$, introduced owing to the presence of both $(0, \text{var}, 1)$ and $(1, \text{VLIST}, 2)$, where var VLIST is a prefix of a rule's body in the grammar of PL/0. This rule is the following:

$$\text{VARBLOCK} \rightarrow \text{var VLIST} ;$$

Subsequently, the transition $R(0, \text{var VLIST} ;, 3)$ is also added. This addition is triggered by the existence of two transitions: $R(0, \text{var VLIST}, 2)$ and $(2, ;, 3)$. Another noteworthy case is the final transition, denoted as $P(3, \text{PROGRAM}, 17)$. This transition shows that tokens $3, \ldots, 17$ collectively constitute a syntactically correct PL/0 program. This program excludes the first line "**var** k;" represented by tokens $0, 1, 2$. Of course, the whole program (tokens $0, \ldots, 17$) is also a PROGRAM, i.e., a syntactically correct PL/0 program, which is indicated by the transition $(0, \text{PROGRAM}, 17)$.

You might notice that no transitions are added by using the *impl*-table. That is not a coincidence, but due to the insertion order of tokens from left to right. What happens if we use a different insertion order? Then *impl* is used, of course (but we get the same set of transitions).

An interesting observation is what happens if we insert tokens from right to left. It turns out that then no R-additions take place at all, but there are of course additions due to the *impl*-table. Analogous to Table 2 we show in Table 3 what happens if we insert the tokes from right to left. All transitions that are added because of the *impl*-table are marked with an I.

Table 3. Transitions of M when adding tokens from right to left.

(16, ., 17) (15, end, 16) (14, IDENT, 15) $P(14, \text{VLIST}, 15)$ $P(14, \text{FACTOR}, 15)$ $P(14,$
$\text{FACTORS}, 15)$ $P(14, \text{TERM}, 15)$ $P(14, \text{TERMS}, 15)$ $P(14, \text{EXPR}, 15)$ $(13, !, 14)$ $I(13, ! \text{ EXPR}, 15)$
$P(13, \text{STATEMENT}, 15)$ $P(13, \text{BLOCK}, 15)$ $P(13, \text{STATEMENTS}, 15)$ $(12, \text{do}, 13)$ $(11, \text{NUMBER}, 12)$
$P(11, \text{FACTOR}, 12)$ $P(11, \text{FACTORS}, 12)$ $P(11, \text{TERM}, 12)$ $P(11, \text{TERMS}, 12)$ $P(11, \text{EXPR}, 12)$
$(10, \texttt{<=}, 11)$ $(9, \text{IDENT}, 10)$ $P(9, \text{VLIST}, 10)$ $P(9, \text{FACTOR}, 10)$ $P(9, \text{FACTORS}, 10)$ $P(9, \text{TERM}, 10)$
$P(9, \text{TERMS}, 10)$ $P(9, \text{EXPR}, 10)$ $I(9, \text{EXPR} \texttt{<=}, 11)$ $I(9, \text{EXPR} \texttt{<=} \text{EXPR}, 12)$ $P(9, \text{CONDITION}, 12)$
$(8, \text{while}, 9)$ $I(8, \text{while CONDITION}, 12)$ $I(8, \text{while CONDITION do}, 13)$ $I(8, \text{while CONDITION}$
$\text{do STATEMENT}, 15)$ $P(8, \text{STATEMENT}, 15)$ $P(8, \text{BLOCK}, 15)$ $P(8, \text{STATEMENTS}, 15)$ $(7, ;, 8)$
$(6, \text{NUMBER}, 7)$ $P(6, \text{FACTOR}, 7)$ $P(6, \text{FACTORS}, 7)$ $P(6, \text{TERM}, 7)$ $P(6, \text{TERMS}, 7)$ $P(6, \text{EXPR}, 7)$
$(5, \texttt{:=}, 6)$ $(4, \text{IDENT}, 5)$ $P(4, \text{VLIST}, 5)$ $P(4, \text{FACTOR}, 5)$ $P(4, \text{FACTORS}, 5)$ $P(4, \text{TERM}, 5)$
$P(4, \text{TERMS}, 5)$ $P(4, \text{EXPR}, 5)$ $I(4, \text{IDENT} \texttt{:=}, 6)$ $I(4, \text{IDENT} \texttt{:=} \text{EXPR}, 7)$ $P(4, \text{STATEMENT}, 7)$
$P(4, \text{BLOCK}, 7)$ $P(4, \text{STATEMENTS}, 7)$ $I(4, \text{STATEMENT} ;, 8)$ $I(4, \text{STATEMENT} ; \text{STATEMENTS}, 15)$
$P(4, \text{STATEMENTS}, 15)$ $(3, \text{begin}, 4)$ $I(3, \text{begin STATEMENTS}, 7)$ $I(3, \text{begin STATEMENTS}, 15)$
$I(3, \text{begin STATEMENTS end}, 16)$ $P(3, \text{STATEMENT}, 16)$ $P(3, \text{BLOCK}, 16)$ $I(3, \text{BLOCK} ., 17)$
$P(3, \text{PROGRAM}, 17)$ $P(3, \text{STATEMENTS}, 16)$ $(2, ;, 3)$ $(1, \text{IDENT}, 2)$ $P(1, \text{VLIST}, 2)$ $P(1, \text{FACTOR}, 2)$
$P(1, \text{FACTORS}, 2)$ $P(1, \text{TERM}, 2)$ $P(1, \text{TERMS}, 2)$ $P(1, \text{EXPR}, 2)$ $(0, \text{var}, 1)$ $I(0, \text{var VLIST}, 2)$
$I(0, \text{var VLIST} ;, 3)$ $P(0, \text{VARBLOCK}, 3)$ $I(0, \text{VARBLOCK STATEMENT}, 16)$ $P(0, \text{BLOCK}, 16)$
$I(0, \text{BLOCK} ., 17)$ $P(0, \text{PROGRAM}, 17)$

Let us take a closer look at Table 3. The first entry is, of course, $(16, ., 17)$ because it is the last token and was manually added as the first transition. This insertion did not trigger any recursive calls to *add* because there is no rule with '.' as its body. The next two entries are also added manually, but then a cascade of recursive *add*'s is triggered because of the chain rules

$$\text{EXPR} \to \text{TERMS} \to \text{TERM} \to \text{FACTORS} \to \text{FACTOR} \to \text{IDENT}.$$

Then $(13, !, 14)$ is added which triggers the first recursive addition based on the *impl*-table. When $(14, \text{EXPR}, 15)$ was added, also $(13, !, 14) \to (13, ! \text{ EXPR}, 15)$ was put into *impl*. This entry in *impl* together with $(13, !, 14)$ creates a call to $add(13, ! \text{ EXPR}, 15)$.

If you look at Tables 2 and 3 you might wonder whether they contain the same set of transitions. Yes, they do. In fact, the extended NFA computed by Algorithms 3 and 4 is always the same – regardless of implementation details, for example the order of the **for every**-loops, and independent on the order we insert initial transitions. The *order* in which the other transitions are inserted into δ can be different, though, as demonstrated by Tables 2 and 3.

Solving the word problem is fine, but if we want more we can enhance Algorithm 4 in order to compute more useful information rather than just δ. The resulting NFA for this example is shown in Fig. 6. It is the NFA that we get when taking δ from the extended NFA computed by Algorithm 4 and then discarding all "extended" transitions. In other words, we preserve those transitions $(p, \alpha, q) \in \delta$ where $|\alpha| = 1$. Often we would like to compute a syntactic tree for the derivation $S \overset{*}{\Rightarrow} w$. It is not easy to do that with just the information from δ, although Fig. 6 suggests on first glance that we can just read off the parse tree from that picture.

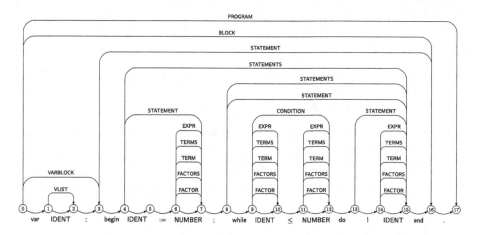

Fig. 6. The resulting NFA without extended transitions. Only those transitions are shown that are needed to find $(0, \text{PROGRAM}, 17)$ and only they are needed to construct the corresponding parse tree. For example, the transition $(3, \text{PROGRAM}, 17)$ is not shown.

Unfortunately that is not true for at least two reasons. Firstly, the NFA shown in Fig. 6 is not drawn in a random fashion. The "height" of a transition t that was added because of a transition t' is bigger than the "height" of t'. If you look at the transition $(4, \text{STATEMENT}, 7)$ then it corresponds to a node STATEMENT in the parse tree with children IDENT, :=, and EXPR. In order to facilitate the construction of a parse tree we can store additional information with each transition telling us *why* this transition has been added.

For example $(6, \text{TERM}, 7)$ has been added because of $(6, \text{FACTORS}, 7)$ and the rule TERM $\rightarrow$ FACTORS. The transition $(8, \text{STATEMENT}, 15)$ has been added because of the transition $(8, \text{while CONDITION do STATEMENT}, 15)$, which is not shown in Fig. 6 because it is an "extended" transition. It is, however, present in the extended NFA computed by Algorithm 4.

But why is $(8, \text{while CONDITION do STATEMENT}, 15) \in \delta$? The reason is as follows:

$(8, \text{while CONDITION do STATEMENT}, 15)$
   because of $(8, \text{while CONDITION do}, 13)$ and $(13, \text{STATEMENT}, 15)$

$(8, \text{while CONDITION do}, 13)$
   because of $(8, \text{while CONDITION}, 12)$ and $(12, \text{do}, 13)$

$(8, \text{while CONDITION}, 12)$
   because of $(8, \text{while}, 9)$ and $(9, \text{CONDITION}, 12)$

We just have to "unroll" these reasons one by one in order to see that the node $(8, \text{STATEMENT}, 15)$ tree has the children $(8, \text{while}, 9)$, $(9, \text{CONDITION}, 12)$,

(12, do, 13), (13, STATEMENT, 15) in the parse tree. In that way it is easy to construct a parse tree provided that the additional information has been generated. Computing and storing it does not change the asymptotic running time of Algorithm 4 and the actual construction of the parse tree can be carried out in linear time. A tree generated automatically by this method is shown in Fig. 7.

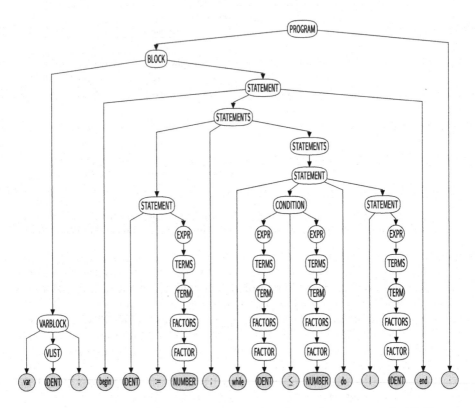

Fig. 7. An automatically generated parse tree for a short program in PL/0.

6   Some More Applications

Let us look at some examples motivated by the will to generate good error messages when parsing a program source. An important step is to find the first symbol that renders the input syntactically incorrect. Formally, we have a grammar $G = (N, T, P, S)$ and a word $w \in T^*$ and look for the longest prefix u of w such that $uv \in L(G)$ for some $v \in T^*$. This problem has been addressed for the typical parsers applied in compiler construction, e.g. LL(k), LR(k), operator precedence, and recursive descent parsers [2] and also for Earley parsers, which means that there is a polynomial algorithm that works for general grammars.

We can solve this problem also within the *pre**-framework. To check whether a prefix u of w is good (i.e., if there is a $v \in T^*$ such that $uv \in L(G)$) we just have to find out whether $S \in pre^*(uT^*)$. The language uT^* can be represented by an NFA with $|u| + 1$ states. Using binary search we can find the longest u with $O(\log |w|)$ many *pre**-computations. There is also a way to find the longest such u while computing only one saturated automaton starting with the NFA in Fig. 8.

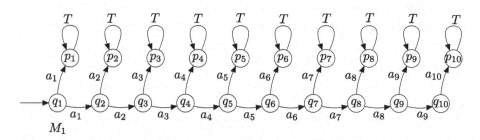

Fig. 8. An NFA for finding the longest prefix u of $w = a_1 \ldots a_n$ such that u is a prefix of a word in $L(G)$.

If we compute the saturated NFA the Saturation Lemma guarantees that there is a transition (q_0, S, p_i) iff $S \overset{*}{\Rightarrow} a_1 \ldots a_i T^*$. Finding the longest good prefix is then easy.

Aho and Peterson investigated the following problem: Given a CFG G and a word w, what is the closest word $w' \in L(G)$ with regard to the edit distance between w and w'? The motivation is obvious: If a program has syntax errors, we can find the closest correct program. The running time of their algorithm is cubic in $|w|$ (and quadratic in the size of the grammar) [1].

With a small modification in Algorithm 4 we can solve this problem, too. An informal overview how to proceed is the following. Some details are left out.

For simplicity we assume that the grammar $G = (N, T, P, S)$ is in a normal form where rules' bodies consist of ϵ, a single terminal symbol, or a string of non-terminal symbols; so $A \to \alpha$ only if $\alpha \in T \cup N^*$.

We augment the grammar with additional rules. If there is a rule $A \to a$, we introduce new "heavy" rules $A \longrightarrow \epsilon$ (if $A \to \epsilon \notin P$) and $A \longrightarrow b$ for all terminal symbols b for which there is no rule $A \to b \in P$.

If there is a derivation $S \overset{*}{\Rightarrow} \alpha a \beta$, then, with the help of new rules, there are derivations $S \overset{*}{\Rightarrow} \alpha b \beta$ and $S \overset{*}{\Rightarrow} \alpha \beta$. In other words, we can now derive a string that has a symbol erased or replaced.

Second, for every variable A we also create new rules $A \longrightarrow Ab$ and $A \longrightarrow bA$ for every $b \in T$. With these rules we can derive a string that has a symbol inserted. The new heavy rules with the longer arrow have a *weight* of 1, while the original rules have a weight of 0.

The *weight of a derivation* is the total weight of all rules used in the derivation. For example, take the grammar $S \to ASA \mid BSB \mid \epsilon$, $A \to a$, $B \to b$. The derivation $S \Rightarrow ASA \Rightarrow aSA \Rightarrow aA \Rightarrow aa$ has cost zero. Any string with edit distance k to aa can be derived with a weight at most k. For example, aab has edit distance one and a weight 1 derivation is

$$S \Rightarrow ASA \Rightarrow aSA \Rightarrow aA \Rightarrow aAb \Rightarrow aab.$$

The only step with weight 1 is $aA \Rightarrow aAb$.

We can modify Algorithm 4 such that each transition tracks the weight of deriving the substring for which it is responsible. (The transition (q_{i-1}, α, q_j) is responsible for the substring $w_i \ldots w_j$.)

If a transition is added because of two older transitions, its weight becomes the sum of their weights. If a transition (q, A, p) is added because of the rule $A \to \alpha$ or $A \longrightarrow \alpha$ and a transition $(q, \alpha, p) \in \delta$, it inherits its weight in the case of $A \to \alpha$ or adds one in case of $A \longrightarrow \alpha$.

When transitions are added multiple times, then the weight becomes the minimum. In that way we can solve the minimum edit distance problem quite easily. For a given word w we also find the closest w' with $w' \in L(G)$ and construct a parse tree with weight k for w' if k is the edit distance between w and w'.

7   Conclusion

The pre^*-method cannot be used to solve every problem on context free languages. For example, there is a polynomial algorithm to find the longest common prefix of all words in a context-free language [31], but there seems no way to apply the pre^*-method for that problem. Nevertheless, the pre^*-method's applications are numerous and it can be a valuable contribution in the teaching of formal languages, making pre^* a star in teaching methodology.

I hope that Javier will include it in a future book that introduces us to context-free languages in an algorithm oriented way, just as *Automata Theory: An Algorithmic Approach* pioneers the same task for regular languages.

Acknowledgments. I like to thank Daniel Mock for suggesting changes in the implementation of the new pre^*-program that improved the running time. I also like to thank anonymous referees for numerous suggestions to improve the writeup of this paper. In particular, one referee found a typo in Algorithm 2 that was already present in [10]. Another referee pointed me to the recent interesting application of pre^* by Ganty and Valero [27], which has not been known to me. Most of all I like to thank Javier Esparza for the pleasure and privilege to work for and with him in Munich during several years. His great way to do science and his open and cheerful personality have been a great influence on my life.

Disclosure of Interests. I have no competing interests.

References

1. Aho, A.V., Peterson, T.G.: A minimum distance error-correcting parser for context-free languages. SIAM J. Comput. **1**(4), 305–312 (1972). https://doi.org/10.1137/0201022

2. Aho, A.V., Sethi, R., Ullman, J.D.: Compilers: Principles, Techniques, and Tools. Addison-Wesley Series in Computer Science. World Student Series Edition. Addison-Wesley (1986). https://www.worldcat.org/oclc/12285707

3. Aho, A.V., Ullman, J.D.: Principles of Compiler Design. Pearson, London (1977)

4. Alman, J., Vassilevska Williams, V.: A refined laser method and faster matrix multiplication. In: Marx, D. (ed.) Proceedings of the 2021 ACM-SIAM Symposium on Discrete Algorithms, SODA, pp. 522–539. SIAM (2021). https://doi.org/10.1137/1.9781611976465.32

5. Alur, R., Bouajjani, A., Esparza, J.: Model checking procedural programs. In: Clarke, E., Henzinger, T., Veith, H., Bloem, R. (eds.) Handbook of Model Checking, pp. 541–572. Springer, Cham (2018). https://doi.org/10.1007/978-3-319-10575-8_17

6. Baier, C., Katoen, J.: Principles of Model Checking. MIT Press, Cambridge (2008)

7. Balasubramanian, A.R., Esparza, J., Lazić, M.: Complexity of verification and synthesis of threshold automata. In: Hung, D.V., Sokolsky, O. (eds.) ATVA 2020. LNCS, vol. 12302, pp. 144–160. Springer, Cham (2020). https://doi.org/10.1007/978-3-030-59152-6_8

8. Bernardy, J., Claessen, K.: Efficient divide-and-conquer parsing of practical context-free languages. In: Morrisett, G., Uustalu, T. (eds.) ACM SIGPLAN International Conference on Functional Programming, pp. 111–122. ACM (2013). https://doi.org/10.1145/2500365.2500576

9. Book, R.V., Otto, F.: String-Rewriting Systems. Texts and Monographs in Computer Science. Springer, Heidelberg (1993). https://doi.org/10.1007/978-1-4613-9771-7

10. Bouajjani, A., et al.: An efficient automata approach to some problems on context-free grammars. Inf. Process. Lett. **74**(5–6), 221–227 (2000). https://doi.org/10.1016/S0020-0190(00)00055-7

11. Brázdil, T., Esparza, J., Kiefer, S., Kučera, A.: Analyzing probabilistic pushdown automata. Formal Methods Syst. Des. **43**(2), 124–163 (2013). https://doi.org/10.1007/S10703-012-0166-0

12. Cocke, J.: Global common subexpression elimination. In: Northcote, R.S. (ed.) Proceedings of a Symposium on Compiler Optimization, Urbana-Champaign, Illinois, USA, pp. 20–24. ACM (1970). https://doi.org/10.1145/800028.808480

13. Earley, J.: R68-46 use of transition matrices in compiling. IEEE Trans. Comput. **17**(11), 1098 (1968). https://doi.org/10.1109/TC.1968.226868

14. Earley, J.: An efficient context-free parsing algorithm. Commun. ACM **13**(2), 94–102 (1970). https://doi.org/10.1145/362007.362035

15. Esparza, J.: An automata-theoretic approach to software verification. In: Ésik, Z., Fülöp, Z. (eds.) DLT 2003. LNCS, vol. 2710, p. 21. Springer, Heidelberg (2003). https://doi.org/10.1007/3-540-45007-6_2

16. Esparza, J.: Back to the future: a fresh look at linear temporal logic. In: Maneth, S. (ed.) CIAA 2021. LNCS, vol. 12803, pp. 3–13. Springer, Cham (2021). https://doi.org/10.1007/978-3-030-79121-6_1

17. Esparza, J., Blondin, M.: Automata Theory: An Algorithmic Approach. The MIT Press, Cambridge (2023)

18. Esparza, J., Hansel, D., Rossmanith, P., Schwoon, S.: Efficient algorithms for model checking pushdown systems. In: Emerson, E.A., Sistla, A.P. (eds.) CAV 2000. LNCS, vol. 1855, pp. 232–247. Springer, Heidelberg (2000). https://doi.org/10.1007/10722167_20

19. Esparza, J., Kupferman, O., Vardi, M.Y.: Verification. In: Pin, J. (ed.) Handbook of Automata Theory, pp. 1415–1456. European Mathematical Society Publishing House, Zürich (2021). https://doi.org/10.4171/AUTOMATA-2/16
20. Esparza, J., Kučera, A., Schwoon, S.: Model checking LTL with regular valuations for pushdown systems. Inf. Comput. **186**(2), 355–376 (2003). https://doi.org/10.1016/S0890-5401(03)00139-1
21. Esparza, J., Křetínský, J., Raskin, J.-F., Sickert, S.: From LTL and limit-deterministic Büchi automata to deterministic parity automata. In: Legay, A., Margaria, T. (eds.) TACAS 2017. LNCS, vol. 10205, pp. 426–442. Springer, Heidelberg (2017). https://doi.org/10.1007/978-3-662-54577-5_25
22. Esparza, J., Křetínský, J., Sickert, S.: One theorem to rule them all: a unified translation of LTL into ω-automata. In: Dawar, A., Grädel, E. (eds.) Proceedings of the 33rd Annual ACM/IEEE Symposium on Logic in Computer Science, LICS, pp. 384–393. ACM (2018). https://doi.org/10.1145/3209108.3209161
23. Esparza, J., Lammich, P., Neumann, R., Nipkow, T., Schimpf, A., Smaus, J.: A fully verified executable LTL model checker. Arch. Formal Proofs **2014** (2014). https://www.isa-afp.org/entries/CAVA_LTL_Modelchecker.shtml
24. Esparza, J., Podelski, A.: Efficient algorithms for pre* and post* on interprocedural parallel flow graphs. In: Wegman, M.N., Reps, T.W. (eds.) Proceedings of the 27th ACM SIGPLAN-SIGACT Symposium on Principles of Programming Languages, POPL 2000, pp. 1–11. ACM (2000). https://doi.org/10.1145/325694.325697
25. Esparza, J., Rossmanith, P.: An automata approach to some problems on context-free grammars. In: Freksa, C., Jantzen, M., Valk, R. (eds.) Foundations of Computer Science. LNCS, vol. 1337, pp. 143–152. Springer, Heidelberg (1997). https://doi.org/10.1007/BFb0052083
26. Esparza, J., Rossmanith, P., Schwoon, S.: A uniform framework for problems on context-free grammars. Bull. EATCS **72**, 169–177 (2000)
27. Ganty, P., Valero, P.: Regular expression search on compressed text. In: Bilgin, A., Marcellin, M.W., Serra-Sagristà, J., Storer, J.A. (eds.) Data Compression Conference, DCC, pp. 528–537. IEEE (2019). https://doi.org/10.1109/DCC.2019.00061
28. Hopcroft, J.E., Ullman, J.D.: Introduction to Automata Theory, Languages and Computation. Addison-Wesley, Boston (1979)
29. Kasami, T.: An efficient recognition and syntax-analysis algorithm for context-free languages. Technical report, R-257, University of Illinois-Urbana, March 1966
30. Lange, M., Leiß, H.: To CNF or not to CNF? An efficient yet presentable version of the CYK algorithm. Informatica Didact. **8** (2009). http://www.informatica-didactica.de/cmsmadesimple/index.php?page=LangeLeiss2009
31. Luttenberger, M., Palenta, R., Seidl, H.: Computing the longest common prefix of a context-free language in polynomial time. In: Niedermeier, R., Vallée, B. (eds.) 35th Symposium on Theoretical Aspects of Computer Science, STACS. LIPIcs, vol. 96, pp. 48:1–48:13. Schloss Dagstuhl - Leibniz-Zentrum für Informatik (2018). https://doi.org/10.4230/LIPICS.STACS.2018.48
32. Valiant, L.G.: General context-free recognition in less than cubic time. J. Comput. Syst. Sci. **10**(2), 308–315 (1975). https://doi.org/10.1016/S0022-0000(75)80046-8
33. Wirth, N.: Algorithms + Data Structures = Programs. Prentice-Hall (1975)
34. Younger, D.H.: Recognition and parsing of context-free languages in time n^3. Inf. Control **10**(2), 189–208 (1967). https://doi.org/10.1016/S0019-9958(67)80007-X
35. Yu, H.: An improved combinatorial algorithm for Boolean matrix multiplication. Inf. Comput. **261**, 240–247 (2018). https://doi.org/10.1016/J.IC.2018.02.006

2-Pointer Logic

Helmut Seidl[1]([⊠]), Julian Erhard[1,2], Michael Schwarz[1], and Sarah Tilscher[1,2]

[1] Technische Universität München, Garching, Germany
{helmut.seidl,julian.erhard,m.schwarz,sarah.tilscher}@tum.de
[2] Ludwig-Maximilians-Universität München, Munich, Germany

Abstract. For reasoning about properties of pointers, we consider conjunctions of equalities and dis-equalities between terms built up from address constants by addition of offsets and dereferencing. We call the resulting class of formulas 2-pointer logic. We introduce a quantitative version of congruence closure to provide polynomial time algorithms for deciding satisfiability as well as implication between formulas. By generalizing quantitative congruence closure to quantitative finite automata, we succeed in constructing canonical normal forms so that checking of equivalence between conjunctions reduces to syntactic equality.

We apply our techniques to realize abstract transformers for dedicated forms of assignments via pointers, in particular, *indefinite*, *definite* and *locally invertible* assignments. Quantitative finite automata here allow us to restrict formulas to properties expressible by some subterm-closed subset of terms only.

Keywords: 2-pointer logic · quantitative equalities and dis-equalities · quantitative congruence closure · polynomial normal form · abstract transformers for assignments

1 Introduction

In this paper, we continue the investigation [24] of relational domains that only track properties of variables and relationships between pairs of variables. Such domains have been called *weakly* relational and are promising candidates for a reasonable compromise between expressiveness and efficiency. The most prominent example are *Octagons* whose elements are conjunctions such as

$$(-x \leq -5) \wedge (x \leq 6) \wedge (x + y \leq 20)$$

that allow tracking upper bounds for variables, negated variables, or sums of two possibly negated variables [11,13]. In previous work [24], further *non-numerical* weakly relational domains have been studied, namely, 2-disjunctive constants to express properties such as

$$(x = \mathsf{foo} \wedge f = \&h) \vee (x = \mathsf{bar} \wedge f = \&g)$$

or conjunctions of ordering constraints for lattices or partial orders. For sets, one may for example state that

S. Kiefer et al. (Eds.): *Taming the Infinities of Concurrency*, LNCS 14660, pp. 281–307, 2024.
https://doi.org/10.1007/978-3-031-56222-8_16

$$({\{a, b\}} \subseteq x) \land (y \subseteq x) \land (y \subseteq {\{a, b, c\}})$$

holds. Properties like that allow to reason, e.g., about the sets of characters occurring in strings [1].

Instead, we here study a fragment of *pointer logic* as introduced by Kroening and Strichman [9]. The expressiveness of this fragment goes way beyond what has been considered, e.g., in [16] where constant differences between plain variables are tracked. Here, we enhance the latter domain by adding dereferencing.

Example 1. Consider the following slightly stylized C program.

```
struct s {                    . . .
   mutex m;                   lock(&(x-> m));
   int *addr;                 x->addr = &y;
} *x;                         . . .
int y;                        unlock(&(x->m));
```

Assume that we want to verify that *the same* mutex is unlocked which was locked before, and also that &y is written into the memory next to the mutex. If the offsets of m and addr inside the struct are 0 and 2, respectively, the addresses a of the locked mutex and b of the written memory cell can be represented by the terms *x and 2+*x, respectively, i.e., a static analysis may record

$$(a = *x) \land (b = 2 + *x)$$

This conjunction implies the equality $b = 2 + a$, an invariant which might hold throughout the program when accessing structs of type s.

In many cases, tracking the values of local variables is sufficient to prove that the same mutex is unlocked that has been locked before entering the critical section – even when an accompanying heap analysis has assigned the heap allocated struct a *non-unique* heap address.   □

In presence of dereferences, however, tracking conjunctions of equalities between pointer expressions alone, is too imprecise to deal with assignments via pointers. Therefore, we also take known dis-equalities between pointer expressions into account. Consider, e.g., the pre-condition

$$\Psi \equiv (\&x = *(3 + \&y)) \land (\&z = *(2 + \&z))$$

before the assignment $*(1 + \&y) := 1 + \&z$. We are certain that the address $3 + \&y$ is distinct from the address of the memory cell receiving a new value. Assuming that Ψ holds before the assignment, we conclude that the first equality of Ψ will also hold after the assignment. The case is not so clear-cut for the second equality. Only if the precondition before the assignment guarantees that $1 + \&y \neq 2 + \&z$ or, equivalently, $\&y \neq 1 + \&z$, the second equality will survive the assignment as well. In detail, the contributions of this paper are the following:

- To handle the dereferencing operator, we consider $*$ as a unary uninterpreted function symbol, and extend the notion of congruence closure to *quantitative* congruence closure in order to take into account not only $*$, but also numerical offsets between terms;

- We provide precise characterizations of equalities and dis-equalities implied by a conjunction;
- We introduce *quantitative* finite automata (qfa) for providing *syntactic* normal forms that allow us to reduce equivalence between formulas to equality of their respective normal forms;
- We provide abstract transformers which construct, from given pre-conditions before an assignment between pointer expressions, valid post-conditions; these constructions again rely on qfas for restricting a formula to properties expressible by certain subsets of terms only.

2   Quantitative Equalities

Subsequently, we present *2-Pointer Logic*. This logic consists of finite conjunctions of equalities between *terms* built up from *auxiliaries* and address *constants* by means of addition of constant offsets and dereferencing. Later, we will extend this logic with dis-equalities. Auxiliaries in formulas can be considered as program variables whose address is never taken. They may reside, e.g., in registers so that their location cannot be reached via address arithmetic or dereferencing. This is different for address constants or any other location represented by pointer terms: all these are assumed to live within one linear address space. Here, address constants take the form $\&x$ for variable names x.

Let $\mathcal{X}, \mathcal{A}$ denote disjoint finite sets of variable names and auxiliaries, respectively. Terms t and propositions p are constructed according to the following grammar:

$$t ::= A \mid \&x \mid *(z + t)$$
$$p ::= t_1 = z + t_2$$

where $x \in \mathcal{X}$ is a variable with address $\&x$, $z \in \mathbb{Z}$ is an integer, and $A \in \mathcal{A}$ is an auxiliary (e.g., a register) distinct from any memory cell. Terms $\&x$ or A will also be called *atoms*. As in C, $*$ denotes the dereferencing operator. To increase readability, we use $*t$ as an abbreviation for $*(0 + t)$, and x as an abbreviation for $*(0 + \&x)$. Also, in equalities, we may abbreviate $0 + t$ with t.

Example 2. A formula Ψ such as

$$(y = 1 + x) \wedge (*y = x)$$

may imply further equalities, in this case, e.g., the equality $*(1 + x) = x$. A possible class of memory layouts and assignments satisfying Ψ is shown below with the memory cell corresponding to the implied equality highlighted in red.

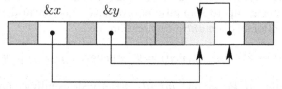

The conjunction Ψ does not state how $\&x$, $\&y$, and the other cells are laid out relative to each other in memory. The figure shows the layout when $\&x$ occurs to the left of $\&y$, and the pointer targets are to the right of $\&y$.

Still, conjunctions of formulas can also be used to specify *exact memory layouts*, namely the relative addresses of variables. The conjunction

$$(\&y = 1 + \&x) \wedge (\&z = 3 + \&y)$$

specifies that the address of variable x is immediately followed in memory by the address of variable y, while the address of variable z follows only three memory cells past $\&y$:

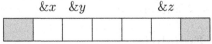

$\square$

A similar logic has also been considered by Miné [12] or Kroening and Strichman [9] for reasoning about memory. Our logic can be considered as a restriction of these logics to terms that refer to one address or auxiliary each.

Semantics. Conjunctions Ψ are interpreted over one linear address space $\mathbb{Z}$, relative to mappings $\rho : \mathcal{X} \to \mathbb{Z}$, $\nu : \mathcal{A} \to \mathbb{Z}$ assigning addresses to variables and values to auxiliaries, respectively, and a map $\mu : \mathbb{Z} \to \mathbb{Z}$ providing a value for each address. Each term t then is interpreted as the value $[\![t]\!](\rho, \nu, \mu)$ defined by

$$
\begin{aligned}
[\![\&x]\!] (\rho, \nu, \mu) &= \rho\, x \\
[\![A]\!] (\rho, \nu, \mu) &= \nu\, A \\
[\![*(z + t)]\!] (\rho, \nu, \mu) &= \mu\, (z + [\![t]\!] (\rho, \nu, \mu))
\end{aligned}
$$

Given the values of terms, the validity of equalities is obtained as

$$(\rho, \nu, \mu) \models t_1 = z + t_2 \quad \text{iff } [\![t_1]\!] (\rho, \nu, \mu) = z + [\![t_2]\!] (\rho, \nu, \mu)$$

If $(\rho, \nu, \mu) \models e$ for each equality e occurring in Ψ, we say that $(\rho, \nu, \mu) \models \Psi$. We remark that, according to our assumption of one linear address space,

$$t \neq z + t \tag{1}$$

holds in all models for all terms t and $z \neq 0$. If $(\rho, \nu, \mu) \models \Psi$, then also $(\rho + n, \nu + n, \mu + n) \models \Psi$ for every $n \geq 0$ where we define $(\rho + n)\, x = (\rho\, x) + n$, $(\nu + n)\, A = (\nu\, A) + n$, and $(\mu + n)\, a = (\mu\, (a - n)) + n$.

The domain of 2-Pointer Logic $\mathcal{P}_2[=]$ then consists of all finite conjunctions of equalities of terms up to semantic equivalence. The natural partial ordering between conjunctions is *semantic implication*, i.e.,

$$\Psi \to \Psi' \quad \text{iff} \quad (\rho, \nu, \mu) \models \Psi' \text{ whenever } (\rho, \nu, \mu) \models \Psi \tag{2}$$

The partial order on $\mathcal{P}_2[=]$ has *infinite* strictly descending chains, as well as *infinite* strictly ascending chains.

Example 3. Consider the sequence of conjunctions

$$\Phi_n \equiv \bigwedge_{i=1}^{n} (\&y = *(i + \&x)) \qquad (n \geq 0)$$

Then $\Phi_{n+1} \implies \Phi_n$ for all $n \geq 0$ and all are inequivalent. Thus, the $\Phi_n, n \geq 0$, constitute an infinite strictly descending chain in $\mathcal{P}_2[=]$.
Now for each $n \geq 0$, consider the equality

$$\Psi_n \equiv (*^{2^n} \&x = \&x)$$

where $*^m$ denotes m-fold deference, i.e., technically m-fold application of the function $\lambda.x : *(0 + x)$. Then we have for each $n \geq 0$, $\Psi_n \implies \Psi_{n+1}$ while the reverse does not hold. Accordingly, the $\Psi_n, n \geq 0$, represent an infinite strictly ascending chain in $\mathcal{P}_2[=]$. □

Conjunctions Ψ can be considered as quantifier-free formulas from LIN+U, the theory of linear arithmetic extended with uninterpreted function symbols, here with the single unary function symbol $*$. To the quantifier-free fragment of this logic, the techniques of Nelson-Oppen for the combination of theories can be applied to obtain a decision procedure [17,18]. Further algorithmic improvements have been developed, e.g., by Shostak [26] and Rueß and Shankar [22]. Recent advances of techniques for this logic with quantifiers can be found in [8].

The arithmetic part of 2-pointer logic, though, is more in the spirit of [16] where just constant values and constant *differences* of variables are expressible – but neither dereferencing, nor any form of dis-equalities.

Quantitative Congruence Closure. For some term t, we define its set of *subterms* $\mathsf{sub}(t)$ inductively by

$$\begin{aligned}
\mathsf{sub}(a) &= \{a\} & &\text{if } a \text{ is an atom} \\
\mathsf{sub}(*(z + t')) &= \{*(z + t')\} \cup \mathsf{sub}(t') & &\text{otherwise}
\end{aligned}$$

To efficiently reason about 2-pointer logic properties, we rely on *canonical normal forms* of equalities. For that, we assume that we are given a linear order $<$ on the atoms possibly occurring in our formulas. This linear order is extended to a linear order of arbitrary terms by

- $a < *(z + t)$ for all atoms a, $z \in \mathbb{Z}$ and terms t;
- $*(z_1 + t_1) < *(z_2 + t_2)$ whenever $t_1 < t_2$ or $t_1 = t_2$ holds (according to the linear ordering) together with $z_1 < z_2$.

Assuming an order on atoms that orders auxiliaries before addresses of variables, we thus have, e.g.,

$$A < x < *(1 + \&x) < *(1 + *x)$$

To efficiently compute canonical normal forms, we generalize the concept of *congruence closure* to *quantitative* congruence closure by additionally taking constant offsets between terms into account. Let $\overline{\mathcal{T}}$ denote the set of *all* terms with variable names from $\mathcal{X}$ and auxiliaries from $\mathcal{A}$. Let $\mathcal{T}_\Psi \subseteq \overline{\mathcal{T}}$ denote the set of all subterms of terms occurring in Ψ. For every subset $\mathcal{T} \subseteq \overline{\mathcal{T}}$ with $\mathcal{T}_\Psi \subseteq \mathcal{T}$ which is closed by subterms, the formula Ψ induces a set of *quantitative equalities* of the form $t_1 \equiv z + t_2$ for terms $t_1, t_2 \in \mathcal{T}$ and $z \in \mathbb{Z}$. This set or unsatisfiability of the conjunction Ψ, is determined as the least set $\equiv$ of quantitative equalities on $\mathcal{T}$ satisfying the following rules:

[E0] $t_1 \equiv z + t_2$ for all equalities $t_1 = z + t_2$ contained in Ψ;
[E1] If $t_1 \equiv z + t_2$ holds then also $t_2 \equiv -z + t_1$.
  If $t_3 \equiv z_2 + t_2$ and $t_1 \equiv z_1 + t_3$ holds then also $t_1 \equiv z + t_2$ for $z = z_1 + z_2$.
  If $t_1 \equiv z_1 + t_2$ and $t_1 \equiv z_2 + t_2$ for some $z_1 \neq z_2$, then Ψ is unsat.
[E2] If $*(z_i + t_i) \in \mathcal{T}$ for $i = 1, 2$ and $t_1 \equiv (z_2 - z_1) + t_2$, then $*(z_1 + t_1) \equiv *(z_2 + t_2)$ holds.

Let us call the quantitative equivalence relation the *quantitative congruence closure* of the conjunction Ψ for $\mathcal{T}$ and denote it by $\equiv_{\Psi,\mathcal{T}}$. In case $\mathcal{T}$ is equal to $\mathcal{T}_\Psi$, we skip the second index and just write $\equiv_\Psi$.

Quantitative Union-Find. The quantitative equivalence relation $\equiv_{\Psi,\mathcal{T}}$ can be represented by a *quantitative partition* (Π, τ, ω) on the set $\mathcal{T}$ which consists of a partition Π of $\mathcal{T}$, a mapping $\tau : \Pi \to \mathcal{T}$ assigning a *representative* $\tau Q \in Q$ to every equivalence class of Π, together with a mapping $\omega : \mathcal{T} \to \mathbb{Z}$ assigning to each $t \in \mathcal{T}$ its *offset* from the representative τQ of the equivalence class of t, thus representing the equality $t \equiv_{\Psi,\mathcal{T}} (\omega t) + (\tau Q)$. In particular, $\omega (\tau Q) = 0$ for all $Q \in \Pi$. The quantitative partition corresponding to $\equiv_{\Psi,\mathcal{T}}$ can be determined by means of a *quantitative union-find* data-structure. Such a data-structure can be realized along the lines of an ordinary *union-find* data-structure – only that for each element in an equivalence class Q, the offset to the representative of Q must be maintained. Let $\langle \Pi, \tau, \omega \rangle$ denote such a data-structure. The operation find $\langle \Pi, \tau, \omega \rangle t$ for a term $t \in \mathcal{T}$ should return the pair $(\omega t, \tau Q)$ where $Q \in \Pi$ is the component with $t \in Q$ and ωt the offset so that $t \equiv_{\Psi,\mathcal{T}} (\omega t) + (\tau Q)$ holds. The operation union $\langle \Pi, \tau, \omega \rangle t_1 t_2 z$ for terms t_1, t_2 from components Q_1, Q_2 merges Q_1, Q_2 with offset z – or *fails* if this is not possible. Assume that find $\langle \Pi, \tau, \omega \rangle t_i = (z_i, t'_i)$ where $\tau Q_i = t'_i$ holds. Then union $\langle \Pi, \tau, \omega \rangle t_1 t_2 z = \langle \Pi', \tau', \omega' \rangle$ is defined as follows.

- If $t'_1 = t'_2$ and $z_1 = z + z_2$, then $\Pi' = \Pi$, $\tau' = \tau$ and $\omega' = \omega$. If $t'_1 = t'_2$ and $z_1 \neq z + z_2$, then the union operation *fails*.
- If $t'_1 \neq t'_2$, then $\Pi' = \Pi \setminus \{Q_1, Q_2\} \cup \{Q_1 \cup Q_2\}$, where $\tau' Q' = \tau Q'$ for all $Q' \notin \{Q_1, Q_2\}$, and $\tau' (Q_1 \cup Q_2)$ either equals t'_1 or t'_2 depending, e.g., on whether $|Q_1| > |Q_2|$ or not. Likewise, $\omega' t = \omega t$ for all $t \notin Q_1 \cup Q_2$. If $\tau (Q_1 \cup Q_2) = t'_1$, then $\omega' t = \omega t$ for all $t \in Q_1$, and $\omega' t = (\omega t) + (\omega t_1) - z - (\omega t_2)$ for $t \in Q_2$. Conversely, if $\tau' (Q_1 \cup Q_2) = t'_2$, $\omega' t = \omega t$ for all $t \in Q_2$, and $\omega' t = (\omega t) - (\omega t_1) + z + (\omega t_2)$.

To construct $\langle \Pi, \tau, \omega \rangle$ from Ψ, we first set $\Pi = \{\{t\} \mid t \in \mathcal{T}\}$, $\tau = \{\{t\} \mapsto t \mid t \in \mathcal{T}\}$, and $\omega = \{t \mapsto 0 \mid t \in \mathcal{T}\}$, i.e., every term t is put into its own component with offset 0. Then the following rules are applied:

– If Ψ has the equality $t_1 = z + t_2$ then union is called for t_1, t_2 and z; i.e.,

$$\textbf{forall} \, (t_1 = z + t_2 \in \Psi)$$
$$\langle \Pi, \tau, \omega \rangle = \text{union} \, \langle \Pi, \tau, \omega \rangle \, t_1 \, t_2 \, z;$$

– If terms t_1, t_2 are in the same component, i.e., $(z_i', t') = \text{find} \, \langle \Pi, \tau, \omega \rangle \, t_i$, and there are terms $*(z_1 + t_1), *(z_2 + t_2) \in \mathcal{T}$ so that $z_1 + z_1' = z_2 + z_2'$, then their components are combined with offset 0, i.e.,

$$\textbf{forall} \, (*(z_1 + t_1), *(z_2 + t_2) \in \mathcal{T}) \, \{$$
$$(z_1', t_1') = \text{find} \, \langle \Pi, \tau, \omega \rangle \, t_1;$$
$$(z_2', t_2') = \text{find} \, \langle \Pi, \tau, \omega \rangle \, t_2;$$
$$\textbf{if} \, ((t_1' \equiv t_2') \wedge (z_1' + z_1 = z_2' + z_2))$$
$$\langle \Pi, \tau, \omega \rangle = \text{union} \, \langle \Pi, \tau, \omega \rangle \, (*(z_1 + t_1)) \, (*(z_2 + t_2)) \, 0;$$
$$\}$$

Since the operation union may merge distinct components at most once, we obtain an effective algorithm – which runs in time polynomial in the size of the formula Ψ and the cardinality of the set $\mathcal{T}$ (which, in case of $\mathcal{T} = \mathcal{T}_\Psi$, is also proportional to the size of Ψ). According to this algorithm, the offset ωt of every term t is bounded by Z where Z is the sum of absolute values $|z|$ of offsets z occurring in equalities in Ψ. Let $(\Pi_{\Psi, \mathcal{T}}, \tau_{\Psi, \mathcal{T}}, \omega_{\Psi, \mathcal{T}})$ denote the quantitative partition represented by the resulting data-structure.

Example 4. Consider the conjunction Ψ consisting of the equalities

$$(y = 1 + x) \wedge (z = -1 + x)$$

Then

$$\mathcal{T}_\Psi = \{\&x, \&y, \&z, x, y, z\}$$

and the corresponding quantitative partition (Π, τ, ω) consists of

$$\Pi = \{\{\&x\}, \{\&y\}, \{\&z\}, \{x, y, z\}\}$$
$$\tau = \{\{\&x\} \mapsto \&x, \{\&y\} \mapsto \&y, \{\&z\} \mapsto \&z, \{x, y, z\} \mapsto x\}$$
$$\omega = \{\&x \mapsto 0, \&y \mapsto 0, \&z \mapsto 0, x \mapsto 0, y \mapsto 1, z \mapsto -1\}$$

The set $\overline{\mathcal{T}}$, on the other hand, is infinite. The last component $Q' = \{x, y, z\}$ gives, e.g., rise to the component

$$\{(*^k x), (*^k(1 + y)), (*^k(-1 + z))\}$$

for each $k > 0$. In general, the equivalence classes of $\Pi_{\Psi, \overline{\mathcal{T}}}$ may also be infinite. For the formula

$$\Psi \equiv (x = -1 + \&x)$$

the equivalence class of $* \, \&x$ (i.e., x) is given by

$$\{\&x, \, x, \, *(1 + x), \, *(1 + *(1 + x)), \, \ldots\}$$

with offsets $\omega = \{\&x \mapsto 0, x \mapsto -1, *(1 + x) \mapsto -1, \ldots\}$. For visualization, a possible graphical representation of this formula is given by

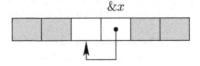

$$\&x$$

□

Quantitative Finite Automata. In general, the representation of the conjunction Ψ by a triple (Π, τ, ω), is not *canonical*: it obviously depends on the set T of terms as well as the choice of the representatives. To deal with that, we introduce *quantitative* finite automata to capture *all* non-trivial quantitative equivalences between terms and select among these, *minimal* representatives.

A *quantitative finite automaton* (qfa) M is a triple (S, η, δ) where

- S is a finite set of states
- $\eta : (\mathcal{A} \cup \{\&x \mid x \in X\}) \to \mathbb{Z} \times S$ is a partial mapping which provides initial offsets and states for atoms; and
- $\delta : \mathbb{Z} \to S \to \mathbb{Z} \times S$ is the partial transition function.

The mappings η, δ of M can be extended to a partial mapping $M : \overline{T} \to \mathbb{Z} \times S$ by $M[a] = \eta\, a$ for atoms a; and $M[*(z + t_1)] = \delta\,(z + z_1)\, s$ for terms t_1 if $M[t_1] = \langle z_1, s \rangle$. Let $\mathcal{L}(M)$ denote the set of terms t so that $M[t]$ is defined. We call a pair $\langle z, s \rangle \in \mathbb{Z} \times S$ *inhabited* if $M[t] = \langle z, s \rangle$ for some term t. A state s is inhabited if $\langle 0, s \rangle$ is inhabited. W.l.o.g., we may assume that s is inhabited if and only if $\langle z, s \rangle$ is inhabited for some $z \in \mathbb{Z}$. For later use, we also define an action $(+) : \mathbb{Z} \to (\mathbb{Z} \times S) \to (\mathbb{Z} \times S)$ by

$$z_1 + \langle z_2, s \rangle = \langle z_1 + z_2, s \rangle$$

The quantitative partition (Π, τ, ω) for Ψ and T gives rise to a qfa $M[\Psi, T] = (S, \eta, \delta)$ where $S = \Pi$, $\eta\, a = \langle \omega\, a, Q \rangle$ if $a \in Q$ for some $Q \in \Pi$, and $\delta\, z\, Q = \langle z', Q' \rangle$ if there is a $t' \in Q'$ with $\omega\, t' = z'$ such that $t' = *(z_1 + t_1)$ with $t_1 \in Q$ and $z = z_1 + (\omega\, t_1)$.

Indeed, the value $\delta\, z\, Q$ is well defined. Assume that there were another term $*(z_2 + t_2) \in T$ with $t_2 \in Q$ so that $z = z_2 + (\omega\, t_2)$. Since $t_i \equiv (\omega\, t_i) + (\tau\, Q)$ for $i = 1, 2$, it follows that $t_1 \equiv (z_2 - z_1) + t_2$, and therefore also $t' \equiv *(z_2 + t_2)$, i.e., $*(z_2 + t_2) \in Q'$ with offset $\omega\,(*(z_2 + t_2)) = z'$. Altogether, the qfa $M[\Psi, T]$ is well defined. We call it the *canonical* qfa for Ψ and T. According to this definition, $T \subseteq \mathcal{L}(M[\Psi, T])$.

Proposition 1. *Assume that the set of terms T is closed by subterms and contains all terms from Ψ. Assume that the quantitative partition (Π, τ, ω) for Ψ and T is defined, and let $M = M[\Psi, T]$ denote the canonical qfa for Ψ and T. Then for every $t \in \mathcal{L}(M)$, the following statements are equivalent:*

1. $M[t] = \langle z, Q \rangle$;
2. $t \equiv z + (\tau\, Q)$ *follows by means of [E0], [E1], [E2].*   □

From Proposition 1, we conclude for terms $t_1, t_2 \in \mathcal{L}(M)$ with $M[t_i] = \langle z_i, Q_i \rangle$, that $Q_1 = Q_2$ iff the equivalence $t_1 \equiv (z_1 - z_2) + t_2$ follows by means of [E0], [E1], [E2].

Example 5. Consider the conjunction Ψ given by

$$(*y = 1 + x) \wedge (*z = 2 + a) \wedge (z = \&y) \wedge (*(5 + x) = 3 + \&z)$$

The set $\mathcal{T} = \mathcal{T}_\Psi$ of terms and subterms occurring in Ψ equals

$$\mathcal{T} = \{\&a, \&x, \&y, \&z, a, x, y, z, *y, *z, *(5 + x)\}$$

while the quantitative partition for Ψ on $\mathcal{T}$ consists of the elements

	0	1	2	3
Q_1	$\&a$			
Q_2	$\&x$			
Q_3	$\&z$			$*(5 + x)$
Q_4	$\&y, z$			
Q_5	a		$y, *z$	
Q_6	x	$*y$		

where each row enumerates the occurring offsets within the respective component, and each element with offset 0 may serve as a representative. The set of inhabited pairs is

$$R = \{\langle 0, Q_1 \rangle, \langle 0, Q_2 \rangle, \langle 0, Q_3 \rangle, \langle 3, Q_3 \rangle, \langle 0, Q_4 \rangle, \langle 0, Q_5 \rangle, \langle 2, Q_5 \rangle, \langle 0, Q_6 \rangle, \langle 1, Q_6 \rangle\}$$

and the initial states and transition function of $M_{\Psi, \mathcal{T}}$ are given by

$\&a$	$\langle 0, Q_1 \rangle$
$\&x$	$\langle 0, Q_2 \rangle$
$\&z$	$\langle 0, Q_3 \rangle$
$\&y$	$\langle 0, Q_4 \rangle$

	0	2	5
Q_1	$0, Q_5$		
Q_2	$0, Q_6$		
Q_3	$0, Q_4$		
Q_4	$2, Q_5$		
Q_5		$1, Q_6$	
Q_6			$3, Q_3$

A visualization of the partial function is given in Fig. 1. For offsets j without terms, the corresponding entry of a block is shaded grey. Since the resulting graph contains cycles, the language for the given formula is infinite.   □

Subsequently, we refer to the notion of *contexts*. A context c is constructed according to the grammar

$$c ::= \bullet \mid *(z + c) \qquad (z \in \mathbb{Z})$$

where $\bullet$ is a dedicated symbol. For a context c and a term t, $c[t]$ denotes the term obtained from c by replacing $\bullet$ with t. We state our first main theorem.

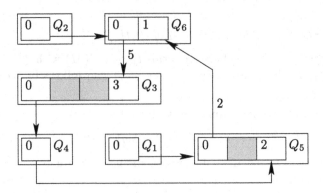

Fig. 1. The transitions between equivalence classes.

Theorem 1. *Assume that Ψ is a conjunction of equalities, let $\mathcal{T}$ be some subterm-closed set of terms which contains all terms and subterms occurring in Ψ. Then:*

1. *Ψ is satisfiable iff $\equiv_{\Psi,\mathcal{T}}$ is defined.*
2. *Assume that $\equiv_{\Psi,\mathcal{T}}$ is defined with corresponding quantitative partition (Π, τ, ω), and canonical qfa $M = (\Pi, \eta, \delta)$.*
   (a) For every $t \in \mathcal{L}(M)$, $M[t] = \langle z, Q \rangle$ iff $\Psi \implies (t = z + (\tau Q))$. In particular, for terms $t_1, t_2 \in \mathcal{L}(M)$, it holds that $\Psi \implies (t_1 = z + t_2)$ iff $M[t_1] = z + M[t_2]$.
   (b) For $t \notin \mathcal{L}(M)$, $\Psi \implies (t = z+t')$ iff z is 0 and either t, t' are syntactically equal or the terms t, t' are of the form $t = c[*(z_1+v)], t' = c[*(z_1'+v')]$ for the same context c with $v, v' \in \mathcal{L}(M)$ so that for $M[v] = (z_1' - z_1) + M[v']$.

Proof. For statement (1), first assume that $(\rho, \nu, \mu) \models \Psi$. Then by induction of the definition of the congruence closure for Ψ and $\mathcal{T}$, we find that $[\![t_1]\!](\rho, \nu, \mu) = z + [\![t_2]\!](\rho, \nu, \mu)$ whenever an equality $t_1 \equiv z + t_2$ is added to $\equiv_{\Psi,\mathcal{T}}$. In particular, never equalities $t_1 \equiv z_i + t_2$, $i = 1, 2$ are encountered with $z_1 \neq z_2$.

Conversely, assume that the quantified congruence closure for Ψ and $\mathcal{T}$ is defined and equals $\equiv_{\Psi,\mathcal{T}}$. Then we construct an interpretation (ρ, ν, μ) as follows. Let (Π, τ, ω) denote the corresponding quantitative partition where $Q_0, \ldots, Q_{m-1}$ is an enumeration of the equivalence classes in Π. W.l.o.g., we may assume that generally, $\omega\, t \geq 0$ for all $t \in \mathcal{T}$. In particular, every value $\omega\, t$ is bounded by the sum Z of absolute values of offsets z occurring in equalities in Ψ. Let $\Delta \geq 0$ denote some sufficiently large *slack* value which we use to separate the blocks of addresses corresponding to the components Q_i. For now, it suffices to consider any $\Delta \geq Z + 1$ which also exceeds the maximal absolute value of z occurring in some $*(z + t') \in \mathcal{T}$. The interval $[(3i + 1)\Delta, (3i + 2) \cdot \Delta]$ then will be reserved for values of terms in Q_i. More specificly, we construct a model of Ψ so that $[\![t]\!](\rho, \nu, \mu) = (3i + 1)\Delta + z$ whenever $t \in Q_i$ and $\omega\, t = z$, i.e., whenever $M[t] = \langle z, Q_i \rangle$ holds. Since the intervals of values for the components Q_i are separated by 2Δ, we conclude from Proposition 1 that

[S1] For $t_1, t_2 \in \mathcal{T}$, $[\![t_1]\!](\rho, \nu, \mu) = z + [\![t_2]\!](\rho, \nu, \mu)$ holds iff $t_1 \equiv z + t_2$ is an equality in $\equiv_{\Psi, \mathcal{T}}$;

[S2] For every pair of terms $*(z_1 + t_1), *(z_2 + t_2) \in \mathcal{T}$, it holds that $z_1 + [\![t_1]\!](\rho, \nu, \mu) = z_2 + [\![t_2]\!](\rho, \nu, \mu)$ iff $t_1 \equiv (z_2 - z_1) + t_2$ holds in $\equiv_{\Psi, \mathcal{T}}$.

For the construction, we proceed by induction on terms t' in $\mathcal{T}$. Let (ρ, ν, μ) partial mappings. Initially, all three mappings are empty. Now assume that term $t \in \mathcal{T}$.

- If $t \equiv \&x$ for some $x \in \mathcal{X}$, and $\&x \in Q_i$ with $\omega(\&x) = z$, we set $\rho x := (3i + 1)\Delta + z$.
- If $t \equiv A$ for some $A \in \mathcal{A}$, and $A \in Q_i$ with $\omega A = z$, we set $\nu A := (3i+1)\Delta + z$.
- Now assume that $t \equiv *(z_1 + t_1)$ and $[\![t_1]\!](\rho, \nu, \mu)$ is already defined. Let $z' = z_1 + [\![t_1]\!](\rho, \nu, \mu)$. If $\mu z'$ is not yet defined, we set $\mu z' = (3i+1)\Delta + z$ whenever $t \in Q_i$ and $\omega t = z$.

  If on the other hand, $\mu z'$ is already defined, then by induction hypothesis for t_1 with $M[t_1] = \langle z_1', Q_{i_1} \rangle$, and every term $*(z_2 + t_2) \in \mathcal{T}$ already encountered with $M[t_2] = \langle z_2', Q_{i_2} \rangle$ so that $z' = z_2 + [\![t_2]\!](\rho, \nu, \mu)$, it holds that $i_1 = i_2$, and $z_1 + z_1' = z_2 + z_2'$. But then $M[t] = M[*(z_2 + t_2)]$ holds, and the claim follows also for t.

This completes the proof of statement (1). For later use, let us call a model (ρ, ν, μ) obtained from the partial mappings constructed for the proof, by completing the partial mappings to complete mappings a *standard* model for Ψ with slack Δ.

We now turn to statement (2). First, assume that $t \in \mathcal{L}(M)$ with $M[t] = \langle z, Q \rangle$. By Proposition 1, the equality $t \equiv z + (\tau Q)$ follows from the equalities in Ψ by means of the closure rules [E1], [E2]. Since the closure rules [E1] and [E2] hold in every model of Ψ, it follows that for every model (ρ, ν, μ) with $(\rho, \nu, \mu) \models \Psi$ that $(\rho, \nu, \mu) \models (t' = (\omega t') + (\tau Q))$, and one direction of the statement (2.a) follows.

In order to prove the reverse implication, we consider a standard model $(\bar{\rho}, \bar{\nu}, \bar{\mu})$ of Ψ with the same slack Δ as in the proof of statement (1). Define a mapping $H : \mathbb{Z} \to \mathbb{Z} \times \Pi$ by $H z = \langle z', Q_i \rangle$ if $i = z/(3\Delta)$ and $z' = z\%((3i+1)\Delta)$ ("/" integer division, and "%" the remainder). From $\bar{\rho}, \bar{\nu}$, we define a mapping η' by $\eta' A = H(\nu A)$ for $A \in \mathcal{A}$, and $\eta(\&x) = H(\rho x)$. From the mapping $\bar{\mu}$, we then construct a partial mapping $\delta' : \mathbb{Z} \to \Pi \to \mathbb{Z} \times \Pi$ by $\delta' z Q_i = H(\mu((3i+1)\Delta + z)$. Then η' and δ' coincide with the mappings η, δ. Now assume that the equality $t_1 = z + t_Q$ is implied by Ψ where $t_Q = \tau Q \in Q$ for some $Q \in \Pi$. In particular, $(\bar{\rho}, \bar{\nu}, \bar{\mu}) \models (t_1 = z + t_Q)$. Consequently, $M[t_1] = \langle z, Q \rangle$. But then, due to Proposition 1, the reverse direction follows.

It remains to consider the statement (2.b). Again, one direction is easy, namely, when t, t' are of the form $t = c[*(z + v)]$ and $t' = c[*(z' + v')]$ for some context c and terms $v, v' \in \mathcal{L}(M)$ with $M[v] = \langle v_1, Q \rangle$, $M[v'] = \langle v_1', Q \rangle$ so that $z + z_1 = z' + z_1'$, then Ψ implies the equality $v = (z' - z) + v'$, and therefore (by induction on the structure of c) also the equality $t = 0 + t'$.

For the reverse implication of the second claim, assume that t, t' are distinct where $t = z + t'$ is implied by Ψ. Assume that $t = c[v]$ and $t' = c'[v']$ where v, v' are minimal subterms of t, t', respectively, which are not in $\mathcal{L}(M)$.

We claim that then

1. Ψ implies that $v = v'$ holds;
2. c and c' are the same.

In order to prove the claim, we consider standard models with appropriately large slack Δ exceeding the absolute value of z as well as of the offsets occurring in t, t'. First assume (for a contradiction) that Ψ does *not* imply $v = v'$. Then the standard model can be selected so that $[\![v]\!](\rho, \nu, \mu)$ is distinct from $[\![v']\!](\rho, \nu, \mu)$ and both are more than Δ larger than any bound of any block of addresses for the components Q_i. Likewise, by always introducing fresh address values, $[\![c_1[v]]\!](\rho, \nu, \mu)$ can be made distinct from $[\![c_1'[v']]\!](\rho, \nu, \mu)$ for all proper subterms $c_1[v], c_1'[v']$ of t, t', respectively, so that in the end also $[\![t]\!](\rho, \nu, \mu)$ is distinct from $z + [\![t']\!](\rho, \nu, \mu)$. In the selected model, the equality $t = z + t'$ does not hold – implying that Ψ cannot imply $t = z + t'$.

Now assume that Ψ implies $v = v'$, but (for a contradiction) that the second claim fails, i.e., c and c' are distinct. Let c_0 denote the maximal common prefix of c, c' so that $c = c_1[c_0]$ and $c' = c_1'[c_0]$ for appropriate non-trivial contexts c_1, c_1'. Then we select a standard model in such a way that for all non-trivial proper prefixes c_2, c_2' of c_1, c_1', the values for $c_2[c_0[v]]$ differ from $c_2'[c_0[v]]$. Ultimately, the model can be equipped with values for $t \equiv c_1[c_0[v]]$ and $t' \equiv c_1'[c_0[v']]$ such that their difference does not equal z – again a contradiction. We conclude that c and c' must coincide.

Finally, consider the minimal subterms v, v' of t, t' not in $\mathcal{L}(M)$. We claim that they are of the form $*(z_1 + u)$ and $*(z_1' + u')$ for $u, u' \in \mathcal{L}(M)$, respectively. For a contradiction, assume that this were not the case. Then either v or v' is an atom not in $\mathcal{L}(M)$. As we can select a standard model which assigns *any* value to a, this means that both v, v' must be identical to a. As, due to the second statement, also the contexts c, c' are equal, t and t' then are identical. Altogether this completes the proof of the theorem. □

Every qfa $M = (S, \eta, \delta)$ itself gives rise to a quantitative equivalence relation $\equiv_M$ on $\mathcal{L}(M)$ by

$$t_1 \equiv_M z + t_2 \quad \text{whenever} \quad M[t_1] = z + M[t_2] \tag{3}$$

which can be extended to *all terms* by defining

$$*(z + t_1) \equiv_M *(z + t_2) \quad \text{whenever} \quad t_1 \equiv_M t_2 \tag{4}$$

For each inhabited $s \in S$, there is a *minimal* term m_s together with a corresponding offset z_s so that $M[m_s] = \langle z_s, s \rangle$ holds.

Proposition 2. *W.l.o.g., assume that all states of M are inhabited. Then the collection $(m_s, z_s), s \in S$, can be computed in polynomial time.*

Proof. We use a variant of Dijkstra's shortest path algorithm for a directed graph $G = (V, E)$ where $V = S$ is the set of states of M, and there is an edge from s to s' with edge label z if $\delta\, z\, s = \langle z', s' \rangle$ holds for some z'. For each $s \in S$, we compute the pair (m_s, z_s) consisting of the minimal representative m_s and its offset z_s by the following algorithm. Initially, all pairs are undefined, which we indicate by $\top$.

A FIFO queue P is used to maintain all $s \in S$ which have already received a pair (m_s, z_s) but whose outgoing edges have not yet been processed.

We proceed in two rounds. First, we process all atoms a where $\eta\, a$ is defined in ascending order. For each a we do:

> **let** $\langle z, s \rangle = \eta\, a$;
> **if** $((m_s, z_s) = \top)$ {
> $\qquad (m_s, z_s) := (a, z)$;
> $\qquad$ **add** $P\, s$;
> }

Second, repeatedly, the *first* element from P, i.e., the element with least representative is extracted until P is empty. For each extracted element s, the outgoing edges are processed in order of ascending edge labels. For each outgoing edge (s, z, s'), with $\delta\, z\, s = \langle z', s' \rangle$ we do:

> **if** $((m_{s'}, z_{s'}) = \top)$ {
> $\qquad (m_{s'}, z_{s'}) := (*((z - z_s) + m_s), z')$;
> $\qquad$ **add** $P\, s'$;
> }

For the correctness of the algorithm, we note that *longer* paths always result in larger representatives than shorter paths. Thus, pairs once computed, never need to be updated to smaller pairs. Altogether, the algorithm runs in polynomial time. $\qquad\qquad\square$

Example 6. Consider the canonical qfa A for the conjunction

$$(A = 1 + x) \wedge (*y = 7 + *(2 + x))$$

with a set $\mathcal{T} = \{A, \&x, \&y, x, *(2 + x)\}$. Assume that quantitative congruence closure has provided us with the quantitative partition (Π, τ, ω) where

$$\Pi = \{\{\&x\}, \{\&y\}, \{A, x\}, \{y\}, \{*y, *(2 + x)\}\}$$
$$\tau = \{\{\&x\} \mapsto \&x, \{\&y\} \mapsto \&y, \{A, x\} \mapsto x, \{y\} \mapsto y, \{*y, *(2 + x)\} \mapsto *(2 + x)\}$$
$$\omega = \{A \mapsto 1, \&x \mapsto 0, \&y \mapsto 0, x \mapsto 0, y \mapsto 0, *y \mapsto 7, *(2 + x) \mapsto 0\}$$

Assuming that $A < \&x < \&y$, the minimal representatives and corresponding offsets are given by

$$
\begin{array}{llll}
m_{\{\&x\}} & = \&x & z_{\{\&x\}} & = 0 \\
m_{\{\&y\}} & = \&y & z_{\{\&y\}} & = 0 \\
m_{\{A,x\}} & = A & z_{\{A,x\}} & = -1 \\
m_{\{y\}} & = y & z_{\{y\}} & = 0 \\
m_{\{*y,*(2+x)\}} & = *(1 + A) & z_{\{*y,*(2+x)\}} & = 0
\end{array}
$$

In particular, the new representatives need no longer be contained in $\mathcal{T}$. $\square$

Each qfa $M = (S, \eta, \delta)$ with minimal representatives and offsets $(m_s, z_s), s \in S$, gives rise to the conjunction $\mathsf{eq}[M]$ by the conjunction

$$\bigwedge_{\eta\, a = \langle z, s\rangle} (a = (z - z_s) + m_s) \wedge \\ \bigwedge_{\delta\, z\, s = \langle z', s'\rangle} (*((z - z_s) + m_s) = (z' - z_{s'}) + m_{s'}) \tag{5}$$

where all repeated equalities as well as all trivial equalities of the form $t = 0 + t$ have been removed. The *canonical normal form* $\mathsf{nf}[\Psi, \mathcal{T}]$ of Ψ (for $\mathcal{T}$) is defined as the conjunction $\mathsf{eq}[M[\Psi, \mathcal{T}]]$ corresponding to the canonical qfa $M[\Psi, \mathcal{T}]$ for Ψ and $\mathcal{T}$. Subsequently, we show that the canonical normal form is *independent* of the choice of $\mathcal{T}$.

Example 7. Consider the conjunction Ψ from Example 6. The canonical normal form then is given by the conjunction

$$(x = -1 + A) \wedge (*y = *(1 + A))$$

From $\eta\, A = \langle 1, \{A, x\}\rangle$, $\eta\, (\&x) = \langle 0, \{\&x\}\rangle$, $\eta\, (\&y) = \langle 0, \{\&y\}\rangle$ only the trivial equalities $A = A$, $\&x = \&x$, and $\&y = \&y = \&y$ originate. The transition $\delta\, 0\, \{\&x\} = \langle 0, \{A, x\}\rangle$, on the other hand, gives rise to the first equality, while the transition $\delta\, 0\, \{y\} = \langle 7, \{*y, *(2+x)\}\rangle$ gives rise to the second. The transition $\delta\, 2\, \{x, A\} = \langle 0, \{*y, *(2 + x)\}\rangle$ again gives rise only to a trivial equality, namely, $*(1 + A) = *(1 + A)$. $\square$

We call state s of a qfa $M = (S, \eta, \delta)$ *unreachable* if s neither occurs in a return value of η, nor of δ. Unreachable states never occur as values for terms and therefore can be abandoned. There is a second class of states that can be abandoned since they do not contribute to non-trivial equalities. We call a reachable state s *trivial*, if

1. s occurs at most once in the image of η or δ; and
2. for every transition $\delta\, z\, s = \langle z', s'\rangle$, s' is again trivial.

Proposition 3. *Assume that $M = (S, \eta, \delta)$ and $M' = (S', \eta', \delta')$ are qfas where*

- $S \subseteq S'$, *where each state in $S' \setminus S$ is trivial;*
- $\eta'\, a$ *is defined whenever $\eta\, a$ is defined where $\eta'\, a = \eta\, a$ or $\eta'\, a$ is trivial; and*
- $\delta'\, z\, s$ *is defined whenever $\delta\, z\, s$ is defined where $\delta'\, z\, s = \delta\, z\, s$, and otherwise $\delta'\, z\, s$ is trivial.*

Then the following holds:

1. $\mathcal{L}(M) \subseteq \mathcal{L}(M')$ *where $M[t] = M'[t]$ for all $t \in \mathcal{L}(M)$, and $M'[t]$ is trivial for all $t \in \mathcal{L}(M') \setminus \mathcal{L}(M)$;*
2. $\mathsf{eq}[M]$ *and $\mathsf{eq}[M']$ are equal.* $\square$

In essence, Proposition 3 follows since the only equalities to be extracted for trivial states are themselves trivial and therefore can be abandoned.

Equivalence Between qfas. It still remains to be proven that Ψ and the normal form of Ψ are indeed equivalent. To see this, we consider for qfas $M = (S, \eta, \delta), M' = (S', \eta', \delta')$ mappings $H : S \to \mathbb{Z} \times S'$. H is called *homomorphism* if the following properties are satisfied:

1. If for atom a, $\eta a = \langle z, s \rangle$ then $\eta' a = z + (H s)$;
2. If for some $z \in \mathbb{Z}$, $\delta z s = \langle z', s' \rangle$ and $H s = \langle z_1, s_1 \rangle$, then $\delta' (z + z_1) s_1 = z' + (H s')$.

The homomorphism is an *isomorphism* if there is an inverse homomorphism $H' : S' \to \mathbb{Z} \times S$ from M' to M such that for all $s \in S, s' \in S'$, $H s = \langle z, s' \rangle$ iff $H' s' = \langle -z, s \rangle$ holds. We have:

Proposition 4. *Assume that M, M' are isomorphic qfas. Then $\mathcal{L}(M) = \mathcal{L}(M')$ holds where for all $t_1, t_2 \in \mathcal{L}(M)$, $t_1 \equiv_M z + t_2$ iff $t_1 \equiv_{M'} z + t_2$ holds.* □

This means that isomorphic qfas imply the same set of quantitative equivalences.

Proposition 5. *Assume that T is some subterm-closed superset of T_Ψ, that (Π, τ, ω) and (Π', τ', ω') are corresponding quantitative congruence closures, and $M = (\Pi, \eta, \delta)$ and $M' = (\Pi', \eta', \delta')$ the canonical qfas of Ψ for T_Ψ and T, respectively. Let $\Pi_1 = \{Q' \in \Pi \mid Q' \cap T_\Psi \neq \emptyset\}$ and $M_1 = (\Pi_1, \eta_1, \delta_1)$ the restriction of M_1 to Π_1, i.e., $\eta_1 a = \eta' a$ whenever $\eta' a \in \mathbb{Z} \times \Pi_1$, and $\delta_1 z Q_1 = \delta' z Q_1$ whenever $Q_1 \in \Pi_1$ and also $\delta' z Q_1 \in \mathbb{Z} \times \Pi_1$. Then the following holds:*

1. *Every $Q' \in \Pi' \backslash \Pi_1$ is trivial; in particular, M_1 and M' satisfy the assumptions of Proposition 3*
2. *M and M_1 are isomorphic. More precisely, the mapping $H : \Pi \to \mathbb{Z} \times \Pi_1$ defined by*

$$H Q = \langle \omega' (\tau Q), Q_1 \rangle$$

for $Q \in \Pi$ and $Q_1 \in \Pi_1$ with $Q \subseteq Q_1$ is a homomorphism with inverse

$$H_1 Q_1 = \langle \omega (\tau' Q_1), Q_1 \cap T_\Psi \rangle$$

□

As a corollary, we therefore obtain:

Corollary 1. *The normal form nf$[\Psi, T]$ is independent of the set T used for its construction.* □

Due to Corollary 1, we henceforth write nf$[\Psi]$ instead of nf$[\Psi, T]$. Furthermore, we observe:

Corollary 2. *Let Ψ denote a satisfiable conjunction with canonical qfa M where M has no trivial states. Then the following holds:*

- *M is isomorphic to $M[eq[M]]$;*
- *For all $t_1, t_2 \in \mathcal{L}(M)$, $t_1 \equiv_\Psi z + t_2$ iff $t_1 \equiv_{nf[\Psi]} z + t_2$.*

– Ψ and $\mathsf{nf}[\Psi]$ are logically equivalent.   □

Altogether, we summarize our findings in our second theorem:

Theorem 2. Assume that Ψ is a satisfiable conjunction from $\mathcal{P}_2[=]$.

1. The normal form $\mathsf{nf}[\Psi]$ is independent of the choice of the set $\mathcal{T}$ and can be computed in polynomial time.
2. For conjunctions Ψ_1, Ψ_2, it holds that Ψ_1 and Ψ_2 are equivalent iff both are unsat or sat and their normal forms $\mathsf{nf}[\Psi_1]$ and $\mathsf{nf}[\Psi_2]$ are conjunctions over the same set of equalities.   □

Restriction. Quantitative automata allow specifying certain *subterm-closed* subsets of terms. Examples of such subsets are

– The set of all terms using a specific address $\&x$;
– The set of all terms which do *not* have subterms from some set F of forbidden terms.

Assume that we are given some qfa $M_0 = (S_0, \eta_0, \delta_0)$ which we would like to use to *restrict* to equalities which can be expressed by referring to terms in $\mathcal{L}(M_0)$ only. Let (Π, τ, ω) denote the congruence closure of the satisfiable conjunction Ψ and $M = (\Pi, \eta, \delta)$ the corresponding canonical automaton for Ψ and $\mathcal{T}$. We call M_0 a *refinement* of M if there is a homomorphism $H : S_0 \to (\mathbb{Z} \times \Pi)$ between M_0 and M which is *injective* in the second component, i.e., $H\, s_i = \langle z_i, Q_i \rangle$ for $i = 1, 2$ with $s_1 \neq s_2$ implies that $Q_1 \neq Q_2$ holds. It follows that for all $t_1, t_2 \in \mathcal{L}(M_0)$, $M_0[t_1] = z + M_0[t_2]$ holds iff $M[t_1] = z + M[t_2]$ holds. In particular, this means that $\equiv_{M_0} \subseteq \equiv_M$. In this case, we define the restriction of Ψ to M_0 as the normal form

$$\Psi|_{M_0} \equiv \mathsf{eq}[M_0] \tag{6}$$

In particular, the restriction can be computed in polynomial time in the size of the qfa M_0.

Theorem 3. Let Ψ denote a conjunction, $\mathcal{T}_\Psi \subseteq \mathcal{T}$ some subterm-closed set of terms and M_0 a refinement of the canonical qfa M for Ψ and $\mathcal{T}$. Then for all $t_1, t_2 \in \mathcal{L}(M_0)$, the following statements are equivalent:

1. $M_0[t_1] = z + M_0[t_2]$;
2. $(t_1 = z + t_2)$ is implied by Ψ;
3. $(t_1 = z + t_2)$ is implied by $\mathsf{eq}[M_0]$.   □

3   Adding Dis-Equalities

Consider an assignment $*(1 + x) := ?$ through a pointer and assume that some equality $y = 3 + \&z$ holds before the assignment. For that equality to survive the given assignment, we must be sure that the address value $\&y$ is definitely different from the address value $1 + x$ where the unknown value is going to be stored. So far, dis-equality could only be inferred for terms for which a constant offset different from 0 is known. If, e.g., the equality $\&y = 2 + x$ is known before the assignment, then $\&y$ is definitely different from $1 + x$, implying that the equality $y = 3 + \&z$ still holds after the assignment.

Constant offsets between terms, however, may not always be known. Still, dis-equality information in a program may be extracted from guard expressions corresponding to, e.g., conditional branching or asserted invariants provided by the programmer. To account for that, we extend the 2-pointer logic $\mathcal{P}[=]$ with *quantitative dis-equalities*, i.e., propositions of the form

$$t_1 \neq z + t_2$$

where t_1, t_2 are terms and $z \in \mathbb{Z}$ is an offset. We also write $t_1 \neq t_2$ when $z = 0$. The semantics of a quantitative dis-equality is defined as

$$(\rho, \nu, \mu) \models (t_1 \neq z + t_2) \quad \text{whenever} \quad [\![t_1]\!]\,(\rho, \nu, \mu) \neq z + [\![t_2]\!]\,(\rho, \nu, \mu)$$

Let us denote the resulting class of conjunctions (modulo semantic equivalence) $\mathcal{P}[=, \neq]$.

Closure Rules. Assume now that Ψ is a finite conjunction of quantitative equalities and dis-equalities different from $\bot$. The dis-equalities derivable from Ψ are the least binary relation $\not\equiv$ relative to a quantitative equivalence relation $\equiv$ by means of the following rules:

[D0] If $t_1 \neq z + t_2$ occurs in Ψ, then $t_1 \not\equiv z + t_2$;
[D1] Assume that $t_1 \not\equiv z + t_2$. Then
- $t_2 \not\equiv -z + t_1$;
- $t_1' \not\equiv (z_1 + z) + t_2$ whenever $t_1' = z_1 + t_1$ is implied by Ψ.
- If $t_1 \equiv z + t_2$ holds, the construction *fails*.
[D2] If $*(z_1 + t_1) \not\equiv *(z_2 + t_2)$ then also $t_1 \not\equiv (z_2 - z_1) + t_2$.
[D3] If $t_1 \equiv z' + t_2$, then $t_1 \not\equiv z + t_2$ for all $z \neq z'$.

Here, [D2] indicates how dis-equalities are propagated backward through dereferences, while the dis-equalities [D3] are immediate consequences of the equalities provided by $\equiv$. The latter set of dis-equalities can be infinite. These dis-equalities, however, *implicitly* follow $\equiv$. Therefore, we do not represent them explicitly by dis-equalities. Furthermore, we note that, while dis-equalities may be derived from equalities, no equalities are implied by dis-equalities.

Based on the given set of rules, we provide a *normal* representation of the equalities occurring in Ψ. Assume that $\Psi \equiv \Psi_= \wedge \Psi_{\neq}$ where $\Psi_=$, $\Psi_{\neq}$ are the conjunctions of quantitative equalities and dis-equalities, respectively, occurring in Ψ. W.l.o.g., assume that $\Psi_=$ is already in normal form. Let $\mathcal{T}$ denote the set of all subterms of term occurring in Ψ. This set may be a strict superset of the set of terms occurring in $\Psi_=$ alone. Let (Π, τ, ω) denote the quantitative partition for $\Psi_=$ and $\mathcal{T}$, and M denote the corresponding canonical qfa. In particular, we assume that for every $Q \in \Pi$, τQ is the smallest term t such that $M[t] = \langle z, Q \rangle$ for some $z \in \mathbb{Z}$.

Normal Form. In order to obtain a unique representation, we record explicit dis-equalities only between *minimal representatives* of components $Q \in \Pi$. For this, we construct the least set of explicit dis-equalities $m_{Q_1} \neq z + m_{Q_2}$ which follow by means of the rules [D0], [D1], [D2], [D3] or report *unsat*. This set is *finite* since each quantitative dis-equality from Ψ gives rise to at most one quantitative dis-equality on distinct representatives, while for the same representative, obviously, infinitely many dis-equalities can be spelled out – but are omitted. The closure rules [D3] together with [D2] may add further dis-equalities between representatives – but repeated application of this rule for the same pair of terms will always result in the same dis-equality. Since no new terms are constructed, only a polynomial number of (explicit) dis-equalities can be derived.

Let $\mathsf{nf}[\Psi_{\neq}]$ denote the resulting conjunction (after removal of trivial dis-equalities such as $t \neq z + t$). The normal form of Ψ then is defined by

$$\mathsf{nf}[\Psi] \equiv \mathsf{nf}[\Psi_{=}] \wedge \mathsf{nf}[\Psi_{\neq}] \tag{7}$$

Theorem 4. *For a formula* $\Psi \equiv \Psi_{=} \wedge \Psi_{\neq}$ *consisting of finite conjunctions* $\Psi_{=}, \Psi_{\neq}$ *of equalities and dis-equalities, respectively, the following statements hold:*

1. Ψ *is satisfiable iff the constructions of* $\mathsf{nf}[\Psi_{=}]$ *and* $\mathsf{nf}[\Psi_{\neq}]$ *succeed.*
2. *If* Ψ *is satisfiable, then* Ψ *and* $\mathsf{nf}[\Psi]$ *are equivalent.*
3. *Two satisfiable conjunctions* Ψ_1, Ψ_2 *are equivalent iff their normal forms agree in the sets of equalities and dis-equalities.*

□

Proof. Assume that Ψ is satisfiable. Then in particular, $\Psi_{=}$ is satisfiable. Therefore, the corresponding normal form $\mathsf{nf}[\Psi_{=}]$ can be constructed and is equivalent to $\Psi_{=}$. Likewise, the construction of the normal form $\mathsf{nf}[\Psi_{\neq}]$ does not fail, since every closure rule is semantically sound, i.e., adds only dis-equalities which are implied by Ψ. For the reverse implication, assume that the construction of the normal forms of $\Psi_{=}$ and $\Psi_{\neq}$ has succeeded. Since $\mathsf{nf}[\Psi_{=}]$ has succeeded, a standard model for $\mathsf{nf}[\Psi_{=}]$ can be constructed along the lines of the proof of Theorem 1. By including sufficiently large *slack* between the blocks of addresses for the respective equivalence classes, it can be ensured that all dis-equalities between their representatives as provided by $\mathsf{nf}[\Psi_{\neq}]$ are satisfied as well. Hence, the conjunction $\mathsf{nf}[\Psi_{=}] \wedge \mathsf{nf}[\Psi_{\neq}]$ is satisfiable. Moreover, in presence of the equalities in $\mathsf{nf}[\Psi_{=}]$, the dis-equalities in $\Psi_{\neq}$ can be deduced from the dis-equalities in $\mathsf{nf}[\Psi_{\neq}]$. Thus, due to the equivalence between $\Psi_{=}$ and $\mathsf{nf}[\Psi_{=}]$, it follows that $\Psi_{=} \wedge \Psi_{\neq}$ is satisfiable, and, moreover, is implied by $\mathsf{nf}[\Psi_{=}] \wedge \mathsf{nf}[\Psi_{\neq}]$. Thus, the first two statements of the theorem follow. For the third statement, we note that, if the normal forms agree, then also the conjunctions are equivalent. For the reverse implication, consider conjunctions $\Psi_{=}, \Psi_{\neq}$ of equalities and dis-equalities, respectively, where $\Psi \equiv \Psi_{=} \wedge \Psi_{\neq}$ is in normal form. Consider one more dis-equality $m_Q \neq z + m_{Q'}$ for distinct minimal representatives $m_Q, m_{Q'}$ which is not contained in $\Psi_{\neq}$. Assume that after addition of the new dis-equality (together with its finitely many transitively implied dis-equalities on representatives, if any), the formula still remains satisfiable. Now consider, on the other hand, the conjunction $\Psi' \equiv \Psi \wedge (m_Q = z + m_{Q'})$. Let (Π, τ, ω) denote the quantitative partition for $\Psi_=$. Then (Π', τ', ω') is obtained from (Π, τ, ω) by means of as sequence of quantitative union operations starting with the quantitative equality $(m_Q = z + m_{Q'})$. Since $Q \neq Q'$, this operation will always succeed. Further transitive union operations may conflict with previous quantitative equalities or dis-equalities. Due to closure of Ψ via rules [D2], however, this would imply that the dis-equality $m_Q \neq z + m_{Q'}$ already occurs in $\Psi_{\neq}$ – which is not the case. Consequently, the construction of (Π', τ', ω') succeeds without contradicting any dis-equality in $\Psi_{\neq}$. It follows that Ψ' is satisfiable. We conclude that the dis-equality $m_Q \neq z + m_{Q'}$ cannot be implied by Ψ. $\qquad\square$

Assume that $\Psi \equiv \Psi_= \wedge \Psi_{\neq}$ is in normal form where $\Psi_=$ and $\Psi_{\neq}$ are the conjunctions of the equalities and dis-equalities occurring in Ψ. Let $\mathcal{T}$ denote some subterm-closed set of terms containing all terms occurring in Ψ. Assume that (Π, τ, ω) is the congruence closure of $\Psi_=$ for $\mathcal{T}$, and M the canonical qfa for $\Psi_=$ and $\mathcal{T}$. Assume that $M_0 = (S, \eta, \delta)$ is a refinement of M with injective homomorphism $H : S \to \mathbb{Z} \times \Pi$. Then we define the *restriction* of Ψ to M_0 as the conjunction

$$\Psi|_{M_0} \equiv \Psi_=|_{M_0} \wedge \Psi'$$

where the conjunction Ψ' consists of all dis-equalities $m'_s \neq \bar{z} + m'_{s'}$, for the new minimal representatives $m'_s, m'_{s'}$ for states $s, s' \in S$ where for $M[m'_s] = H\,s = \langle z_s, Q_s \rangle$, $M[m'_{s'}] = H\,s' = \langle z_{s'}, Q_{s'} \rangle$, it holds that $t \neq z_1 + t'$ in $\Psi_{\neq}$ with and $M[t] = \langle z, Q_s \rangle$, $M[t'] = \langle z', Q_{s'} \rangle$, $\bar{z} = z_1 + (z' - z) + (z_s - z_{s'})$.

Theorem 5. *For $t_1, t_2 \in \mathcal{L}(M_0)$, a dis-equality $t_1 \neq z + t_2$ is implied by $\Psi|_{M_0}$ iff it is implied by Ψ.* $\qquad\square$

4   Assignments

We consider assignments ass of the form $s_1 := s_2$. The left-hand side s_1 either equals an auxiliary $B \in \mathcal{A}$ or a pointer term of the form $*(z + t)$, while the right-hand side s_2 either equals the symbol ? (in which case an unknown value is assigned) or is of the form $z_1 + s$ for some term s – in which case the value of $z_1 + s$ is assigned.

For a set H of models (ρ, ν, μ), we define the concrete semantics of the assignment ass as the transformation $[\![\mathsf{ass}]\!]\, H$ where

$$
\begin{aligned}
[\![B := ?]\!]\, H &= \{(\rho, \nu \oplus \{B \mapsto z'\}, \mu) \mid (\rho, \nu, \mu) \in H, z' \in \mathbb{Z}\} \\
[\![*(z + t) := ?]\!]\, H &= \{(\rho, \nu, \mu \oplus \{(z + [\![t]\!]\,(\rho, \nu, \mu)) \mapsto z'\}) \mid (\rho, \nu, \mu) \in H, z' \in \mathbb{Z}\} \\
[\![B := z_1 + s]\!]\, H &= \{(\rho, \nu \oplus \{B \mapsto z_1 + [\![s]\!]\,(\rho, \nu, \mu)\}, \mu) \mid (\rho, \nu, \mu) \in H\} \\
[\![*(z + t) := z_1 + s]\!]\, H &= \\
&\{(\rho, \nu, \mu \oplus \{(z + [\![t]\!]\,(\rho, \nu, \mu)) \mapsto z_1 + [\![s]\!]\,(\rho, \nu, \mu))\} \mid (\rho, \nu, \mu) \in H\}
\end{aligned}
$$

Here, $f \oplus \{m \mapsto z\}$ is the mapping obtained from f by setting the value of f for m to z.

The *abstract* semantics $[\![\mathsf{ass}]\!]^\sharp$ of the assignment ass, on the other hand, does not operate on concrete models, but on formulas where the conjunction Ψ represents the set $\gamma\Psi$ consisting of all (ρ, ν, μ) with $(\rho, \nu, \mu) \models \Psi$. In particular, $\gamma\top$ equals the set of *all* models, while $\gamma\bot = \emptyset$. Thus, we define $[\![\mathsf{ass}]\!]^\sharp \bot = \bot$.

Subsequently, let $\Psi \neq \bot$ denote a precondition of ass.

Indefinite Assignments. Let us first consider an assignment ass of the form $s_1 := ?$, i.e., the value of the right-hand side is unknown. This means that the value of s_1 after the assignment is no longer (known to be) quantitatively equal to any other term. In case that the left-hand side s_1 is the auxiliary B, we define

$$[\![B := ?]\!]^\sharp \Psi \equiv \Psi|_{M_{\neg B}} \tag{8}$$

where $M_{\neg B}$ is the refinement of the canonical qfa $M = (\Pi, \eta, \delta)$ for the quantitative equalities in Ψ which rules out terms containing B, i.e., $M_{\neg B} = (\Pi, \eta_{\neg B}, \delta)$ with $\eta_{\neg B}$ being the restriction of η to atoms different from B.

In case that the left-hand side $s_1 \equiv *(z + t)$ is a pointer term $*(z + t)$, any term t' of the form $c[*(z' + v)]$ where $z' + v$ is *possibly* equal to $z + t$, now may have an unknown value and thus, is no longer known to be quantitatively equal to or different from any term besides itself. This means that only those quantitative equalities or dis-equalities between terms t_1, t_2 from the precondition Ψ survive where for every subterm of t_1 or t_2 of the form $*(z' + v)$, Ψ implies that $t \neq (z' - z) + v$ holds. Assume that the precondition $\Psi \neq \bot$ is in canonical normal form. Let $\Psi_=$ denote the conjunction of equalities occurring in Ψ, (Π, τ, ω) denote the congruence closure of $\Psi_=$ for $\mathcal{T} = \mathcal{T}_\Psi \cup \mathsf{sub}(t)$, and $\Psi_{\neq}$ the normalized conjunction of dis-equalities for Ψ. Furthermore, let M denote the canonical qfa for $\Psi_=$ and $\mathcal{T}$. From M, we construct the refinement qfa $M_{z,t}$ for the subterm-closed subset $\mathcal{T}_{z,t} \subseteq \mathcal{T}$ consisting of all terms t' where for each subterm $*(z' + v)$ one of the following properties holds:

- $M[v] = z_1 + M[t]$, with $z \neq z' + z_1$; or
- $M[v] = \langle z_1', Q' \rangle$ and $M[t] = \langle z_1, Q \rangle$ that there is a dis-equality $(\tau Q) \neq z_2 + (\tau Q')$ in $\Psi_{\neq}$ with $z_2 = (z' - z) + (z_1 - z_1')$.

Let $M[t] = \langle z_2, Q_2 \rangle$. Then $M_{z,t}$ is defined by $(\Pi, \eta_{z,t}, \delta_{z,t})$ by $\eta_{z,t} = \eta$, and $\delta_{z,t} z' Q = \delta z' Q$ whenever one of the following two properties are satisfied:

- $Q = Q_2$ and $z' \neq z + z_2$;
- $Q \neq Q_2$, and Ψ has a dis-equality $\tau Q \neq (z - z') + z_2 + (\tau Q_2)$.

The qfa $M_{z,t}$ is indeed a refinement of M with $\mathcal{L}(M_{z,t}) = \mathcal{L}(M) \cap \mathcal{T}_{z,t}$. Then we set

$$[\![*(z + t) := ?]\!]^\sharp \Psi \equiv \Psi|_{M_{z,t}} \tag{9}$$

This definition provides us with a sound abstract transformer for indefinite assignments. We have:

Proposition 6. *For left-hand side s_1 and conjunction Ψ,*

$$[\![s_1 := ?]\!] (\gamma\Psi) \subseteq \gamma ([\![s_1 := ?]\!]^\sharp \Psi)$$

Proof. We only consider the case where s_1 equals the expression $*(z + t)$. Let M denote the canonical qfa for the equalities in Ψ and the set $T_\Psi \cup \text{sub}(t)$, and $M_{z,t}$ the refinement of M. Now let $(\rho, \nu, \mu) \in \gamma\Psi$, i.e., $(\rho, \nu, \mu) \models \Psi$, $[\![t']\!](\rho, \nu, \mu)$, and $(\rho', \nu', \mu') \in [\![*(z + t) := ?]\!](\gamma\Psi)$ originating from (ρ, ν, μ), i.e., with $\rho' = \rho, \nu' = \nu$ and $\mu' = \mu \oplus \{z + [\![t]\!](\rho, \mu) \mapsto z'\}$ for some $z' \in \mathbb{Z}$. By induction on the structure of $t' \in \mathcal{L}(M_{z,t})$, we find that $[\![t']\!](\rho, \nu, \mu) = [\![t']\!](\rho', \nu', \mu')$ holds. We conclude therefore that for every proposition d with terms $t_1, t_2 \in \mathcal{L}(M_{z,t})$, that $(\rho, \nu, \mu) \models d$ iff $(\rho', \nu', \mu') \models d$ holds. The equalities and dis-equalities on terms from $\mathcal{L}(M_{z,t})$, however, are exactly the equalities and dis-equalities on these terms implied by $\Psi|_{M_{z,t}}$. This completes the proof.   □

Definite Assignments. Let us now consider the case where the right-hand side of the assignment ass is of the form $z_1 + s$ for $z_1 \in \mathbb{Z}$ and some term s. For an auxiliary B which neither occurs in s nor in the precondition Ψ, we define

$$[\![B := z_1 + s]\!]^\sharp \Psi \equiv (B = z_1 + s) \wedge \Psi \tag{10}$$

If on the other hand, B occurs either in s or in Ψ, we introduce a fresh auxiliary A and simulate the assignment $B := z_1 + s$ by the sequence of assignments

$$A := z_1 + s; \; B := ?; \; B := A; \; A := ?; \tag{11}$$

Altogether this sequence results in

$$[\![B := z_1 + s]\!]^\sharp \Psi \equiv ((B = A) \wedge ((A = z_1 + s) \wedge \Psi)|_{M_{\neg B}})|_{M_{\neg A}}$$

For a definite assignment ass with left-hand side s_1 of the form $*(z + t)$, we proceed analogously. Let A denote an auxiliary which neither occurs in ass nor in the precondition Ψ. Then we define

$$[\![\text{ass}]\!]^\sharp \Psi \equiv ((*(z + t) = A) \wedge ((A = z_1 + s) \wedge \Psi)|_{M_{z,t}})\Big|_{M_{\neg A}} \tag{12}$$

This means that the value of the right-hand side $z_1 + s$ of ass is first stored into the auxiliary variable A; then the contents of the memory cell with address $z + t$, is set to an arbitrary value; then $*(z + t)$ is equated with the value of A while finally, A is removed via the restriction to terms without occurrences of A.

Example 8. Consider the assignment $z := *(1 + z)$ with precondition

$$\Psi \equiv (z = -1 + \&x) \wedge (\&z \neq \&x)$$

Then

$$\begin{aligned}
[\![z := *(1 + z)]\!]^\sharp \Psi &\equiv ((z = A) \wedge ((A = *(1 + z)) \wedge \Psi)|_{M_{0,\&z}})\Big|_{\neg A} \\
&\equiv ((z = A) \wedge (A = x) \wedge (\&z \neq \&x))|_{\neg A} \\
&\equiv (z = x) \wedge (\&z \neq \&x)
\end{aligned}$$

□

Example 9. Consider the assignment $*z := 1 + x$ for the precondition

$$\Psi \equiv (z = \&x) \wedge (y = -1 + x) \wedge (z \neq \&y) \wedge (z \neq \&z)$$

Then

$$(\Psi \wedge (A = 1 + x))|_{M_{0,z}} \equiv (z = \&x) \wedge (z \neq \&y) \wedge (z \neq \&z)$$

and hence,

$$[\![*z := 1 + x]\!]^{\sharp} \Psi \equiv ((*z = A) \wedge (\&x = z) \wedge (\&x \neq \&z))|_{\neg A} \wedge (z \neq \&z)$$
$$\equiv (\&x = z) \wedge (\&x \neq \&z) \wedge (z \neq \&z)$$

This means that the equality $y = -1 + x$ is lost. Before the assignment, however, the equality $*z = x$ holds. We conclude, therefore, that the *old* value of x can be retrieved from the new one by subtracting 1. The equality $y = -1 + x$ *before* the assignment thus gives rise to the equality $y = -2 + x$ *after* the assignment. In the next paragraph, we will make this idea precise.   □

According to Example 9, we cannot hope for the general abstract transformer for $*(z + t) := z_1 + s$ to provide for every possible precondition Ψ the best possible post-condition. Still we have:

Proposition 7. *For every conjunction Ψ and an assignment* ass *taking the form* $s_1 := z_1 + s$,

$$[\![\text{ass}]\!] \, (\gamma \, \Psi) \subseteq \gamma \, ([\![\text{ass}]\!]^{\sharp} \, \Psi)$$

                                                                        □

Invertible Assignments. Next, we consider assignments ass where the original value of the left-hand side can be recovered from the new value. Such assignments, we consider as *invertible*. In general, though, invertability may depend on the precondition Ψ. We call the assignment ass of the form $s_1 := z_1 + s$ *locally invertible relative to* Ψ whenever Ψ implies the equality $(s = z_2 + s_1)$ for some $z_2 \in \mathbb{Z}$. If $z_1 + z_2 = 0$, i.e., $\Psi \implies (s = -z_1 + s_1)$, then ass is a *local identity*, and we set $[\![\text{ass}]\!]^{\sharp} \Psi = \Psi$.

So, assume now that $z_1 + z_2 \neq 0$. As a warm-up, assume that the left-hand side equals an auxiliary B where Ψ implies $s = z_2 + B$. Then we obtain the post-condition $[\![\text{ass}]\!]^{\sharp} \Psi$ by replacing each occurrence of B in Ψ with $-(z_1 + z_2) + B$, i.e., we define

$$[B := z_1 + s]^{\sharp} \equiv \Psi[(-(z_1 + z_2) + B)/B] \qquad (13)$$

In case that B occurs as left term in an equality or dis-equality of Ψ, we subsequently add $(z_1 + z_2)$ to both sides in order to meet our syntactical format for propositions.

When the left-hand side s_1 is a term $*(z + t)$, we proceed analogously. Before the substitution, however, we must make sure that for each occurring subterm $*(z' + v)$ it holds that either $z' + v$ denotes the same address as $z + t$ or is definitely different.

Accordingly, we define $[\![ass]\!]^\sharp \Psi$ as follows. Assume that $M = (\Pi, \eta, \delta)$ is the canonical qfa for the equalities in Ψ for a set of terms $T = T_\Psi \cup \mathrm{sub}(*(z+t)) \cup \mathrm{sub}(s)$. We consider the set $T_{z,t}^\pm$ of terms t' where for every subterm $*(z'+v)$, it holds that v is either definitely different from $(z - z') + t$ or definitely equal to $(z - z') + t$. Let $M[t] = \langle z_3, Q_3 \rangle$. Then we define a qfa $M_{z,t}^\pm = (\Pi, \eta, \delta_{z,t}^\pm)$ by defining $\delta_{z,t}^\pm z' Q = \delta z' Q$ whenever one of the following two properties are satisfied:

- $Q = Q_3$; or
- $Q \neq Q_3$, and Ψ has a dis-equality $\tau Q \neq (z - z' + z_3) + (\tau Q_2)$.

Then $M_{z,t}^\pm$ is a refinement of M with $\mathcal{L}(M_{z,t}) = \mathcal{L}(M) \cap T_{z,t}^\pm$. Let $\Psi' = \Psi|_{M_{z,t}^\pm}$ denote the restriction of Ψ to $M_{z,t}^\pm$. Then we define $[\![ass]\!]^\sharp \Psi$ as the conjunction of all equalities and dis-equalities in Ψ' where each occurrence of a subterm $*(z'+v)$ with $\Psi \implies (v = (z - z') + t)$, is, in outside-in order, replaced with $-(z_1 + z_2) + *(z' + v)$. In case that the rewritten term $*(z' + v)$ occurs on top-level on the *left-hand side* of an equality or dis-equality, again the constant $z_1 + z_2$ is added to both sides in order to re-establish the given format of propositions.

Example 10. Consider the assignment $*z := 1 + x$ for the precondition

$$\Psi \equiv (z = \&x) \wedge (y = -1 + x) \wedge (z \neq \&y) \wedge (z \neq \&z)$$

as in Example 9. Since the first equality implies that $*z = x$, we have that $\Psi \equiv \Psi|_{M_{0,z}^\pm}$ holds. Accordingly,

$$[\![*z := 1 + x]\!]^\sharp \Psi \equiv (z = \&x) \wedge (y = -1 + (-1 + x)) \wedge (z \neq \&y) \wedge (z \neq \&z)$$
$$\equiv (z = \&x) \wedge (y = -2 + x) \wedge (z \neq \&y) \wedge (z \neq \&z)$$

$\square$

Again we have:

Proposition 8. *For every conjunction Ψ and locally invertible assignment* ass,

$$[\![ass]\!] (\gamma \Psi) \subseteq \gamma ([\![ass]\!]^\sharp \Psi)$$

$\square$

Proof. Assume that the assignment is of the form $*(z + t) := z_1 + s$ where Ψ implies that $s = z_2 + *(z + t)$ holds. The proof follows the same lines as the proof of Proposition 6. We show that for every $t' \in \mathcal{L}(M_{z,t}^\pm)$, and model (ρ, ν, μ) of Ψ that $[\![t']\!](\rho, \nu, \mu) = [\![\mathrm{tr}(t')]\!](\rho', \nu', \mu')$ where

- $\mathrm{tr}(t')$ is the expression $z + t$ obtained from t' by replacing, outside-in, every subterm $*(z' + v)$ with $-(z_1 + z_2) + *(z' + v)$ whenever $v = (z - z') + t$ holds;
- (ρ', ν', μ') is the model derived from (ρ, ν, μ) via ass, i.e., $\rho' = \rho, \nu' = \nu$ and $\mu' = \mu \oplus \{u \mapsto z_1 + z_2 + (\mu u)\}$ for $u = z + [\![t]\!](\rho, \nu, \mu)$.

$\square$

5   Related Work

Disclaimer. The logic considered here may not serve as a full-fledged heap analysis as in [19,20] or [2,4,5,7,21,23], as our logic is able to exactly track a fixed set of pointers, but is unsuited for expressing *reachability* inside the heap or representing particular *shapes* of data-structures. As we only allow at most two addresses per proposition and also lack auxiliary predicates or quantification over variables, we obviously fail to express more intricate heap properties of the pointer logic in [9].

The *strength* of our design, however, is its simplicity. 2-pointer logic represents a combination of differences between variables with the theory of a single unary uninterpreted function to provide polynomial time algorithms for basic computational tasks concerning pointer arithmetic and dereferencing. In particular, a normal form is provided so that equivalence can be reduced to *syntactic* comparison of formulas.

Work on the combination of theories goes back to Nelson and Oppen [17], where congruence closure was introduced to deal with uninterpreted functions [18]. More efficient algorithms are discussed by Rueß and Shankar [22,26]. Application to static analysis in particular of Herbrand equalities between program expressions has been one motivation for Gulwani et al. [6] where *join* algorithms for conjunctions of equalities with uninterpreted functions are discussed. They provide a remarkable counter example to prove that the least upper bound of two congruences need no longer be representable by a finite conjunction of equalities. In the first place, this result refers to systems with multiple uninterpreted functions but can be carried over to conjunctions of quantitative equalities with the single unary function symbol $*$.

Example 11. Consider

$$\Psi_1 \equiv (a = b)$$
$$\Psi_2 \equiv (*a = a) \wedge (*b = b) \wedge (*(1 + a) = *(1 + b))$$

Then for each $n \geq 0$, the quantitative equality

$$*(1 + *^n a) = *(1 + *^n b)$$

is implied both by Ψ_1 and Ψ_2. Using an analogous proof argument as in [6] for theorem 3, one may deduce that the set of all quantitative equalities implied both by Ψ_1 and Ψ_2, cannot be represented by a finite conjunction.   □

Efficient algorithms, on the other hand, for tracking arbitrary affine equalities, are provided in Müller-Olm and Seidl [14,15]. The two-variable equalities of [16] can be considered as a simplification of affine equalities in the same spirit as difference-bound matrices [10] are simplified polyhedra [3,27]. Seidl et al. [25] present a smooth combination of Herbrand and affine equalities to deal with must-alias relationships within the same C memory block. However, none of these works consider any combination with the dereferencing operator.

6   Conclusion

In this paper, we have considered conjunctions of equalities and dis-equalities between pointer terms built up by addition of constants combined with dereferencing, and provided unique normal forms. These normal forms allow reducing equivalence to syntactic equality of formulas. The construction of normal forms relies on a quantitative version of a *union-find* data-structure to compute a quantitative congruence closure. Based on that data-structure we constructed quantitative finite automata and used a version of Dijkstra's algorithm to determine *minimal* representatives for quantitative equivalence classes. Moreover, we introduced the notion of a *refinement* of canonical qfas to restrict conjunctions to terms avoiding certain subterms, e.g., a particular auxiliary. Based on refinements, we provided abstract transformers for assignments to auxiliaries as well as through pointers. As one particular case, we provided a more precise, dedicated construction for *locally invertible* assignments.

So far, it remained open how a practically useful *join* operator can be constructed. According to [6], we cannot hope for an exact least upper bound operator – even if only equalities between terms are considered. Nonetheless, there is a series of *practical* candidates for *join* operators. It remains open which of them provide reasonable compromises between efficiency and precision.

The results presented here are just the starting point for the construction of further, more expressive, yet practical pointer logics. A minor extension is adding a constant **null**, making it possible to represent the constant integer value $z \in \mathbb{Z}$ of some term t by the quantitative equality $t = z + \textbf{null}$. Another exciting further extension would be to add *may*-equalities such as

$$x \in \{2, 3\} + y$$

to indicate that either $x = 2 + y$ or $x = 3 + y$ holds (but $x \neq z + y$ for all $z \notin \{2, 3\}$). Such an extension may retain more information at *join* points in a program – while still not resorting to full disjunctions in formulas and thus avoiding the corresponding blow-up.

Acknowledgements. This work was supported in part by the Shota Rustaveli National Science Foundation of Georgia under the project FR-21-7973 and Deutsche Forschungsgemeinschaft (DFG) - 378803395/2428 CoNVeY 2.

References

1. Arceri, V., Olliaro, M., Cortesi, A., Ferrara, P.: Relational string abstract domains. In: Finkbeiner, B., Wies, T. (eds.) VMCAI 2022. LNCS, vol. 13182, pp. 20–42. Springer, Cham (2022). https://doi.org/10.1007/978-3-030-94583-1_2

2. Chang, B.E., Rival, X.: Modular construction of shape-numeric analyzers. In: Banerjee, A., Danvy, O., Doh, K., Hatcliff, J. (eds.) Semantics, Abstract Interpretation, and Reasoning about Programs: Essays Dedicated to David A. Schmidt on the Occasion of his Sixtieth Birthday, Manhattan, Kansas, USA, 19–20th September 2013, EPTCS, vol. 129, pp. 161–185 (2013). https://doi.org/10.4204/EPTCS.129.11

3. Cousot, P., Halbwachs, N.: Automatic discovery of linear restraints among variables of a program. In: Aho, A.V., Zilles, S.N., Szymanski, T.G. (eds.) Conference Record of the Fifth Annual ACM Symposium on Principles of Programming Languages, Tucson, Arizona, USA, January 1978, pp. 84–96. ACM Press (1978). https://doi.org/10.1145/512760.512770

4. Giet, J., Ridoux, F., Rival, X.: A product of shape and sequence abstractions. In: Hermenegildo, M.V., Morales, J.F. (eds.) SAS 2023. LNCS, vol. 14284, pp. 310–342. Springer, Cham (2023). https://doi.org/10.1007/978-3-031-44245-2_15

5. Gotsman, A., Berdine, J., Cook, B., Sagiv, M.: Thread-modular shape analysis. In: PLDI 2007, pp. 266–277. ACM (2007). https://doi.org/10.1145/1250734.1250765

6. Gulwani, S., Tiwari, A., Necula, G.C.: Join algorithms for the theory of uninterpreted functions. In: Lodaya, K., Mahajan, M. (eds.) FSTTCS 2004. LNCS, vol. 3328, pp. 311–323. Springer, Heidelberg (2004). https://doi.org/10.1007/978-3-540-30538-5_26

7. Illous, H., Lemerre, M., Rival, X.: A relational shape abstract domain. Formal Methods Syst. Des. **57**(3), 343–400 (2021). https://doi.org/10.1007/S10703-021-00366-4

8. Korovin, K., Kovács, L., Reger, G., Schoisswohl, J., Voronkov, A.: ALASCA: reasoning in quantified linear arithmetic. In: Sankaranarayanan, S., Sharygina, N. (eds.) TACAS 2023. LNCS, vol. 13993, pp. 647–665. Springer, Cham (2023). https://doi.org/10.1007/978-3-031-30823-9_33

9. Kroening, D., Strichman, O.: Decision Procedures - An Algorithmic Point of View. Texts in Theoretical Computer Science. An EATCS Series. Springer, Heidelberg (2008). https://doi.org/10.1007/978-3-540-74105-3. ISBN 978-3-540-74104-6

10. Miné, A.: A new numerical abstract domain based on difference-bound matrices. In: Danvy, O., Filinski, A. (eds.) PADO 2001. LNCS, vol. 2053, pp. 155–172. Springer, Heidelberg (2001). https://doi.org/10.1007/3-540-44978-7_10

11. Miné, A.: The octagon abstract domain. In: WCRE 2001, p. 310. IEEE Computer Society (2001). https://doi.org/10.1109/WCRE.2001.957836

12. Miné, A.: Field-sensitive value analysis of embedded C programs with union types and pointer arithmetics. In: Irwin, M.J., Bosschere, K.D. (eds.) Proceedings of the 2006 ACM SIGPLAN/SIGBED Conference on Languages, Compilers, and Tools for Embedded Systems (LCTES 2006), Ottawa, Ontario, Canada, 14–16 June 2006, pp. 54–63. ACM (2006). https://doi.org/10.1145/1134650.1134659

13. Miné, A.: The octagon abstract domain. Higher Order Symbol. Comput. **19**(1), 31–100 (2006). https://doi.org/10.1007/s10990-006-8609-1. ISSN 1388-3690

14. Müller-Olm, M., Seidl, H.: A note on Karr's algorithm. In: Díaz, J., Karhumäki, J., Lepistö, A., Sannella, D. (eds.) ICALP 2004. LNCS, vol. 3142, pp. 1016–1028. Springer, Heidelberg (2004). https://doi.org/10.1007/978-3-540-27836-8_85

15. Müller-Olm, M., Seidl, H.: Precise interprocedural analysis through linear algebra. In: Jones, N.D., Leroy, X. (eds.) Proceedings of the 31st ACM SIGPLAN-SIGACT Symposium on Principles of Programming Languages, POPL 2004, Venice, Italy, 14–16 January 2004, pp. 330–341. ACM (2004). https://doi.org/10.1145/964001.964029

16. Müller-Olm, M., Seidl, H.: Upper adjoints for fast inter-procedural variable equalities. In: Drossopoulou, S. (ed.) ESOP 2008. LNCS, vol. 4960, pp. 178–192. Springer, Heidelberg (2008). https://doi.org/10.1007/978-3-540-78739-6_15

17. Nelson, G., Oppen, D.C.: Simplification by cooperating decision procedures. ACM Trans. Program. Lang. Syst. **1**(2), 245–257 (1979). https://doi.org/10.1145/357073.357079. ISSN 0164-0925

18. Nelson, G., Oppen, D.C.: Fast decision procedures based on congruence closure. J. ACM **27**(2), 356–364 (1980). https://doi.org/10.1145/322186.322198. ISSN 0004-5411

19. O'Hearn, P.W.: Resources, concurrency, and local reasoning. Theoret. Comput. Sci. **375**(1), 271–307 (2007). https://doi.org/10.1016/j.tcs.2006.12.035

20. O'Hearn, P.W.: Separation logic. Commun. ACM **62**(2), 86–95 (2019). https://doi.org/10.1145/3211968

21. Reps, T.W., Sagiv, M., Wilhelm, R.: Shape analysis and applications. In: Srikant, Y.N., Shankar, P. (eds.) The Compiler Design Handbook: Optimizations and Machine Code Generation, 2nd edn, p. 12. CRC Press (2007)

22. Rueß, H., Shankar, N.: Deconstructing Shostak. In: Proceedings of the 16th Annual IEEE Symposium on Logic in Computer Science, Boston, Massachusetts, USA, 16–19 June 2001, pp. 19–28. IEEE Computer Society (2001). https://doi.org/10.1109/LICS.2001.932479

23. Sagiv, S., Reps, T.W., Wilhelm, R.: Parametric shape analysis via 3-valued logic. ACM Trans. Program. Lang. Syst. **24**(3), 217–298 (2002). https://doi.org/10.1145/514188.514190

24. Seidl, H., Erhard, J., Tilscher, S., Schwarz, M.: Non-numerical weakly relational domains (2024). https://doi.org/10.48550/ARXIV.2401.05165

25. Seidl, H., Vojdani, V., Vene, V.: A smooth combination of linear and Herbrand equalities for polynomial time must-alias analysis. In: Cavalcanti, A., Dams, D.R. (eds.) FM 2009. LNCS, vol. 5850, pp. 644–659. Springer, Heidelberg (2009). https://doi.org/10.1007/978-3-642-05089-3_41

26. Shostak, R.E.: Deciding combinations of theories. J. ACM **31**(1), 1–12 (1984). https://doi.org/10.1145/2422.322411

27. Singh, G., Püschel, M., Vechev, M.: Fast polyhedra abstract domain. In: Proceedings of the 44th ACM SIGPLAN Symposium on Principles of Programming Languages, POPL 2017, New York, NY, USA, pp. 46–59. Association for Computing Machinery (2017). https://doi.org/10.1145/3009837.3009885. ISBN 9781450346603

Author Index

A
Abdulla, Parosh Aziz 1
Alon, Ravid 22
Atig, Mohamed Faouzi 1

B
Balachander, Mrudula 51
Beier, Simon 72
Bernemann, Rebecca 101
Best, Eike 122
Bouajjani, Ahmed 133
Brázdil, Tomáš 148

D
Devillers, Raymond 122
Doveri, Kyveli 155

E
Erhard, Julian 281

F
Filiot, Emmanuel 51

G
Ganty, Pierre 155
Godbole, Adwait 1

H
Holzer, Markus 72

J
Jančar, Petr 172

K
Kiefer, Stefan 225
König, Barbara 101
Kupferman, Orna 22

L
Leroux, Jérôme 172
Luttenberger, Michael 181

M
Malík, Viktor 206
Mayr, Richard 225

N
Nipkow, Tobias 243

R
Raskin, Jean-François 51
Rossmanith, Peter 255

S
Schaffeld, Matthias 101
Schlund, Maximilian 181
Schrammel, Peter 206
Schwarz, Michael 281
Seidl, Helmut 281
Shankaranarayanan, Krishna 1
Shirmohammadi, Mahsa 225

T
Tilscher, Sarah 281
Totzke, Patrick 225

V
Vahanwala, Mihir 1
Vojnar, Tomáš 206

W
Weil-Kennedy, Chana 155
Weis, Torben 101

S. Kiefer et al. (Eds.): *Taming the Infinities of Concurrency*, LNCS 14660, p. 309, 2024.
https://doi.org/10.1007/978-3-031-56222-8

Printed in the United States
by Baker & Taylor Publisher Services